AND STATE

ESSAYS ON
CHURCH AND STATE

by

LORD ACTON

Introduction by

DOUGLAS WOODRUFF

Thomas Y. Crowell Company

ESTABLISHED 1834

NEW YORK

Apollo Edition, 1968

CONTENTS

NOTE TO THE NEW AMERICAN EDITION

The essays in this volume are reprinted from the periodicals in which they originally appeared just over a hundred years ago. Advantage has been taken of this new edition to correct a number of copyist's errors and omissions, occurring chiefly in the first essay on Ultramontanism, to which reviewers of the English edition of 1952 drew attention.

The article on Bossuet has been very much abbreviated, and is only about half the original length of what was a book review as well as an article, in which Acton examined the work in question in great detail. I think this abbreviated version reflects the sense of the full article, but close students of Acton or Bossuet are referred to the full text.

D. W.

INTRODUCTION

THE EARLY WRITINGS OF LORD ACTON

By Douglas Woodruff

I

WHEN Lord Acton died in 1902 the tributes to him all commented on the disparity between so much massive erudition and the absence of any large sustained work which would remain as a monument to his powers. This was the first feeling of contemporaries who were writing about him as a Regius Professor and as the chief architect of the collective Cambridge Modern History. When his executors began to collect his lectures and other writings, they were quickly found to be sufficient to make four large volumes, two of them university lecture courses on modern history and the French Revolution, while two others, of greater depth and interest, *The History of Freedom* and *Historical Essays and Studies*, were mainly drawn from periodicals which had had a short life in the 1860s. Acton's Cambridge executors recorded, not without a note of surprise, that from the files of these periodicals they believed two other volumes of Acton's writings could have been culled. That this was a slight over-estimate, the papers here collected show. But with this volume, I believe that all the considerable articles which he wrote in his early period will have been reprinted. But at the end are some specimens of the shorter writings, the topical notes, and book notices, of which he did a great deal, that still remain in the files of the publications for which they were written.

Acton's intellectual life fell into two divisions. Where with most men, especially men who follow an academic routine, the output commonly describes a parabola, begins slowly, grows in volume in the middle years, and then declines again, Acton's activity shows a period of great industry extending over some twelve years but ending when he was thirty-six in 1870. There followed more than twenty years with but little to show, though these twenty years were never quite barren, the lectures on the

history of freedom, for example, belong to them. Then came a
final rich period, as professor at Cambridge for the last seven
years of his life.

It was significant of him that his early work is in no sense im-
mature. The eleventh essay in this volume, prompted by the outbreak of the American Civil War, attracted Mr Gladstone's
attention to the young scholar who was little by little to become
one of his closest friends and advisers. These articles represent
Acton as he first appeared in the intellectual life of Victorian
England, armed *cap-à-pie* from the armoury of the new German
scientific history.

This German education came about very naturally. Acton belonged to an old Shropshire family, but his grandfather had
made his career in the service of the King of Naples, whose
Prime Minister he was through the stormy years of the French
Revolution and Napoleon; and it was at Naples that Acton
himself was born in 1834. His father had died when he was an
infant, and his mother was a German, the daughter and heiress
of the Duke of Dalberg. Her father had made the transition from
the service of the Holy Roman Empire to the service of Napoleon,
had been rewarded with the dukedom, and had sat as a peer
of France as Talleyrand's colleague to represent France at the
Congress of Vienna. In this policy he was following his uncle, the
Archbishop Elector of Mainz, who had become President of
Napoleon's Confederation of the Rhine. But the family's roots
had long been in that southern, Catholic Germany of the
empire where Munich was second only to Vienna. They held the
town of Ratisbon, one of the scenes of the Imperial coronations,
where their leading position was marked by a ritual right to be
knighted before any other family at Imperial Coronations,
the herald demanding: "*Ist kein Dalberg da?*" before proceeding
with other candidates. It was a Bavarian kinsman through the
Dalbergs, Count Arco Valley, who was in due time to become
Acton's father-in-law, who arranged that Acton should live in
the house of Dr Döllinger, who would guide his reading.
Döllinger, then just turned fifty, was a leading light in the University, and one of the makers of the new school of German
scientific history. Döllinger had been born in 1799 in the Bavaria
of the Wittelsbachs still living in the tradition of the Vienna of the

Habsburgs, in that tightened form of State control which the Emperor Joseph II had caused to be termed, from his day to ours, "Josephism".

But the life of the Church under Pius VII, when Napoleon was his enemy and there was no other protecting or controlling power, had shown the possibility of a very different state of affairs; and this was the beginning of a new Ultramontanism as a movement to rescue the true and essential independence of the Church from civil control. Ultramontanism was the converse of Gallicanism. It was so that d'Alembert used the word in his account of the destruction of the Jesuits in France, published in 1764. It was a movement which, in emphasizing the high prerogatives of the Holy See, also attracted those who wanted for the Church, thus emancipated, a greater intellectual freedom. The British Isles, where the Catholic Church was neither established nor persecuted, looked a particularly interesting and hopeful field, while the Irish gave an example, so decisive in the intellectual history of Montalembert, of a Catholic life and culture which owed nothing to the government and was all the more robust on that account. England was a home of free discussion where the Catholic faith seemed to be making rapid headway on its merits in a free atmosphere. Acton was, in all, seven years in biblical apprenticeship as Döllinger's pupil, reading prodigiously in theology, and ecclesiastical and political history. It was reading diversified by travel. He visited Russia, where he was attached to the British Embassy, the U.S.A., and Rome, on a journey in the company of Döllinger which gave both the older and the younger man a lowered estimate of the curia of Pius IX, where they found little intellect and no wide views of the world outside Rome. At the end of this period of study, Acton came to England meaning to write and work in a place where journalism was uninhibited by censorship. His mother had married in 1840 Lord Granville, the future Liberal Foreign Secretary, and this connection with the centre of English Whiggery had decisive consequences for Acton's future. When he came back at the age of twenty-three, it was to a country which was his first country, although he had been born, and had spent so much time abroad.

He already knew the men whose attitude was to be so important for his work. The first Cardinal Archbishop of Westminster had been the President of Oscott, which he had founded, when the young Acton went there as a pupil in 1842. It was not his first school. His mother, who had the famous French bishop, Dupanloup, for her confessor, had placed her son for two years at a school which Dupanloup, like Newman a few years later, had founded. Acton was at Oscott for six years, and it was from Oscott that he wrote at the age of ten to his mother:

> I am a perfect linguist, knowing perfectly—that is, so as to be able to speak them—English, French, German, and can almost speak Latin. I can speak a few words of Chinese, Greek, Italian, Spanish, and Irish. I also know Chemistry, Astronomy, Mechanics, and many other sciences, but do not know botany. I am very happy here, and perfectly reconciled to the thought of stopping here seven more years. I am in a hurry, therefore good-bye.

In 1848 he went to Edinburgh to improve his Greek while living with Dr Logan, a former Vice-President of Oscott, and it was at this time that unsuccessful application was made to three Cambridge colleges to accept him. Even Magdalene, which had accepted his father and his uncle, Cardinal Acton, in 1822, as students, although they could not, of course, proceed to a university degree because the religious barrier had not been lifted, refused Acton. The refusal shows perhaps some of the greater nervousness which, in both universities, the conversions of so many Fellows and students in the 'forties had caused. That he should not have been accepted as a learner at the established homes of learning in England no doubt sharpened his resolve to show educated England the seriousness of the Catholic scholarship in which he had immersed himself in Munich.

When he arrived in England in his early twenties, in 1857, he had been for the previous seven years living, not only in the library of Dr Döllinger in Munich, but travelling and even spending a short time at the St Petersburg Embassy. In 1856 he had visited the United States with his stepfather, Lord Granville, and he had already seen Rome. The intense reading of theology, ecclesiastical and political history, which had preoccupied him in Munich, had all the time been balanced by these immediate personal experiences of the world. But the decision to send him to Germany, and his continuance there, largely because of the difficulties for a Catholic going to Oxford or Cambridge, determined his development as a scholar of the German mould. It made him an unwilling young member of Parliament from his twenty-fourth to his thirtieth year, but an enthusiastic conductor of serious periodicals. He formed a close connection successively with *The Rambler, The Home and Foreign Review, The Chronicle,* and *The North British Review,* all attempts, on the part of English Catholics, in the first generation of the Oxford Movement converts, to establish a serious Catholic periodical literature.

Acton was unique among the editors connected with these journals. His English colleagues were, without exception, convert clergymen. They were men who had broken with the loose discipline of the Church of England and its episcopate. But they remained men whose main interest was a theological one, who found themselves precluded by marriage from becoming priests, and when they threw themselves into the conduct of Catholic periodicals it was with a missionary purpose, to reach their fellow-countrymen and convince them that the Catholic religion had, intellectually, much weightier credentials than the Protestant world wished to admit. While they fully accepted the authority of the Church, and had taken the big step of conversion because they were convinced that there was a valid claim to their obedience, they were much less certain about the actual degree of authority that belonged to the newly-restored bishops in England. The elements of friction were present, and the friction soon emerged, though with different personalities it need never have become as serious as it did.

The story of the young Acton's great ambitions starts with his belief that he could show the educated world of England that Catholic scholars were, and delighted to be, in the very forefront of the new scientific history, which only sought the truth and had for the first time both the raw materials of the newly-opened archives of governments and the technique in the new canons of scientific scholarship. *The Rambler* and *The Home and Foreign Review* in his time made a great impression on the educated Englishmen of the 'sixties, who had not expected anything of such quality from the small Catholic body.

But it is not as an exponent of scientific history that Acton has continued to be read, and to be read with increasing attention, in

Europe and America half a century after his lifetime. His rele-
vance for the twentieth century comes from his prophetic preoccupation with the very questions with which the twentieth century has found itself preoccupied. The great objects of his studies
in history were the moral ends of government, the relation of politics to morality, and these are the questions which bitter experience has forced our age to think about more urgently than the
Victorians needed to do.

Reading Acton's well-known categorical and unqualified condemnations, his refusal to make allowances for time and place
and the spirit of the age, we can feel to-day that these very lofty
standards were in fact the judgments of a man who was singularly
fortunate in the period in which he lived; that to be born in 1834
and to die in 1902 was to know only through historical reading the
worst in human nature. But even the men who were Acton's contemporaries voluntarily limited themselves, lived inside inherited
canons and conventions, religious, moral, or social, from which
their twentieth-century successors were speedily and triumphantly to emancipate themselves altogether. The violence of the
twentieth century, and its wars, takes us nearer to the sixteenth
than to the nineteenth century. We have had forced upon us wider
definitions of warfare and of the rights of combatants than the last
century ever envisaged.

II

At the time of Acton's death, a generation had passed since he
had abandoned his first career in Catholic letters. Cambridge
had gladly and proudly claimed him and presented him to the
world as he appeared in those last fruitful years of his life. The
first book to appear about him, in 1904, was the edition of
Letters of Lord Acton to Mary Gladstone, letters of the 'eighties and
'nineties, with an introduction by Mr Herbert Paul, who wrote
as a liberal appreciating a fellow liberal, a Gladstonian doing the
honours for a fellow Gladstonian. To him Acton's religion was a
mystery of which he could give no intelligible account, and
although he wrote as a gentleman, anxious to use no language
that would wound Catholics, what he wrote did so little justice to Acton's religion that Abbot Gasquet's *Lord Acton and his
Circle* was brought out to redress the balance and give another
picture.

The Introduction to this volume has provided up to now the main account of Acton's editorial activities. The bulk of the volume consists of a series of letters written by Acton to his friend and close collaborator in *The Rambler* and *The Home and Foreign Review*, Richard Simpson. These letters were given to Gasquet by Simpson's brother, but Gasquet only used and printed about half of them, while he apparently made no effort to obtain from Acton's son the other half of the correspondence, Simpson's answers. The letters he did use he edited, from kindly motives, softening expressions about Father Faber which would have wounded Oratorians then living, who had known and revered their founder, or about men whose children would have been hurt. But he seldom indicated what he had removed. For his long Introduction he had at his elbow Mr Wetherell, the last survivor of the three or four men who had done the actual editorial work in the 'sixties. Wetherell was more interested in the story of the journals themselves than in Acton's part in them; so that Acton is central only in Gasquet's concluding five pages. Mr Herbert Paul had not known—it was natural that he should not have known—this chapter of Catholic history, and almost everything about *The Rambler* in his Introduction is inaccurate, and the volume which Gasquet sponsored was necessary and useful. It was the only volume which presented from the side of the lay editors an unhappy story which kept cropping up as the standard lives of Wiseman and Manning, and then of Newman and Ullathorne, appeared. For it was a story of the lay apostolate cut short, a parallel chapter to that of Newman's efforts to bring Catholics to Oxford thirty years before they began to go there.

Following out the story, we can see how very unfortunate Acton and his associates were in setting out on a new kind of apologetic in the very years when Pope Pius IX and his advisers were entering on the last desperate decade of the temporal power. That was the fundamental explanation why the times were so unpropitious, but there were also local circumstances in England, and two in particular; that there was a new Hierarchy, at once more nervous and more authoritarian than it was to be after it had matured as an institution, and, secondly, the emergence of the narrow, masterful ecclesiastic who succeeded Wiseman and became Cardinal Manning. In Wiseman's last troubled years, these very years of Acton's journalism, Manning was close at the Cardinal's elbow and deep in his counsels, and clear in his own mind that any advantages that might have come from a better educated laity would be bought at too high a price.

In the Rome of Pius IX Manning triumphed and until his death in 1892 the new fresh wind that blew from the Rome of Leo XIII did not penetrate into England. But in the 'fifties serious journalism was in the air of England. Wiseman himself had taken a leading part in founding *The Dublin Review* in 1836, two years after Acton's birth. Four years later a convert from the Quakers, but with little of their pacific qualities, Frederick Lucas, had founded *The Tablet*. As the converts from Oxford came into the Church in the 'forties they found the pulpit closed to them but they had the possibilities of the press. One such convert, Henry Wilberforce, had *The Weekly Register*, another, Frederick Capes, founded *The Rambler*. A fourth convert clergyman, Richard Simpson, came in to help Capes in 1856 and a fifth, Thomas Wetherell, to help Newman, when in 1859 Newman edited two issues of *The Rambler*.

Simpson was to become Acton's intimate friend until his death in 1876. He was fourteen years older, a serious and thorough scholar who wrote what has remained the standard life of Edmund Campion. He was a man of substantial private means, and when at the age of twenty-four he ceased to be Vicar of Mitcham and became a Catholic he could and did continue to be a student at leisure. He was a man of great independence of mind, with a certain Puckish spirit, and it was difficult for him and for Capes to understand either Rome or the restored Hierarchy. It was because they had been rebels inside the Church of England that they found themselves in the Catholic Church, no longer able to preach or minister since they were married (both Simpson and his wife were descendants of Cranmer's brother), and inclined to think that in the less august medium of journalism they were free to write very much what they fancied; and as their interests were theological they were constantly indulging in theological speculation, often rash, and often written in a way sure to irritate. This was exceedingly unfortunate, for it meant that they imported into Catholic life something which alienated the sympathies of the great majority of their new co-religionists. This was equally true whether those co-religionists were old Catholics rejoicing in the new-found freedoms and larger air, uncritical and only conscious that after enduring so much misrepresentation from the Protestant tradition for so long, the days of silence or defensive apology were ending, or whether they were the Irish, coming in increasing numbers, and for the most part quite uninterested in thought or literature, but if they did hear of it, quickly impatient with converts of a critical turn of mind and habit of outspoken speech.

Into this world Sir John Acton came when he was twenty-three, in 1857, and his early work in journalism dates from that year and appeared in *The Weekly Register*.[1] In the following year he became joint editor of *The Rambler*[2] together with Richard Simpson, who had already in his two years with the paper done as much or more than his editor Capes to cause episcopal doubts and misgivings about *The Rambler*'s influence.

Acton came with very different and much wider ideas than he found. He was a European man, born at Naples and to die at Tegernsee in Bavaria, with as much German and Italian as English blood, and he had been more on the Continent than in England ever since he was sixteen. He knew German journalism and all its difficulties with civil and religious authority at least as well as he knew English, and so he had acquired in his formative years in Munich with Döllinger strong ideas about religious journalism.

At that time Döllinger was a man of fifty. He had been ordained in the closing years of the Pontificate of Pius VII and he had caught a sight in the utterances of that long dispossessed Pope of the Church as she could be, standing on her own and not held in the suffocating embrace of any state, however Catholic. We have mentioned how he had himself been born in the heavy time of "Josephism", of the régime named after Maria

[1] As early as 1855 Henry Wilberforce was in correspondence with him.

[2] The circulations of these journals were all small even by nineteenth-century standards, from 500 to 3,000 copies, and their finances always difficult. Editors who had not private means suffered from severe poverty, and the later years of both Capes and Wetherell were so burdened. There was always difficulty in paying contributors; although printing was at that time cheap, there was no advertising revenue. It is rather surprising that men with considerable incomes derived from land or capital investment, like Acton and Simpson, were so exceedingly cautious about using their money in establishing these journals properly, while the old Catholics, who at that time counted numerous wealthy landed families, many of them very zealous to spread the faith, were living in a world in which the press was undervalued and its finance a mystery.

Theresa's son, by which the Church was a branch of the public service, the Bishops higher-grade and the priests lower-grade civil servants. It was not natural to the Church, nor essential, nor useful. It was as accidental as the more dignified régime of the Middle Ages, when the Church had exercised, for lack of any one else to exercise them, all sorts of powers which were no necessary part of her divine mission and prerogatives. To subjects living after 1815, under Habsburgs and Wittelsbachs who still regarded the eighteenth-century order as normal and right, who expected to appoint the Bishops and order the clergy through them, and to supervise the intellectual life in their dominions, ultramontanism was a gospel of liberation and the promise of a freer and more fruitful day.

Döllinger had done his own foundational reading in Italian sources before there were either German texts or German historians; he was in touch with a tradition of Italian scholarship whose glory had been Benedict XIV. His life was contemporary with the prodigious development of the German history school, of the search for original authorities and devotion to them; and he believed, and Acton with him, that the Church had everything to gain from the fullest acceptance of the new scientific history, that in proportion as the truth could be unearthed and recovered, and the past really known, while individuals and whole generations might have to be more stringently condemned on this score or on that, the nature of human life and the divine character and mission of the Church would be increasingly clear. But the essential thing was to show the scientific spirit, to sit down before fact like a little child, especially before the facts of history, the medium in which the Revelation was present and manifest.

For this it seemed that Catholic journalism in England could be carried on under quite exceptionally favourable conditions. Like Montalembert, for whom the Church in Ireland was so great an inspiration precisely because it was not established by nor bound up with the civil government, Döllinger saw the Catholics in England as peculiarly happily placed to strike this new note. No one then thought of the British Isles as other than one political community, and to any one looking at the English and Irish as one society, the Catholics although the minority were a considerable minority, one in five or six in a population of twenty-five million. It was a country of free inquiry, limited by massive Protestant prejudice, and a prejudice nourished and in a measure justified by the features of the Church which had been most in evidence in the Catholic Monarchies in the last centuries in which the Church had been organized as a subordinate part of the structure of absolutism. Acton's ambition was to produce periodicals which would be read by educated Englishmen and would show them that Catholic scholarship was quite as thorough and candid and fair as any of their own, and that often, indeed, it was better because freer from insular limitations. The educated Englishmen came away from Oxford and Cambridge much more closely versed in the history of the Mediterranean world before than after Christ. The English Universities were so little interested in the largest and greatest events on the mainland since the Incarnation that the whole subject of the Holy Roman Empire could, without any sense of incongruity, be set as a curious bypath, suitable as a subject for a Prize Essay, at Oxford in 1863, and the winning essay by James Bryce would then have the field to itself, for lack of interest, for another generation. The Catholic Professors in Munich had been preoccupied with their opponents, German Protestants and German Rationalists, and Acton brought this preoccupation with the non-Catholic world to his associates in England who had a smaller horizon and thought too much of the different groups among their co-religionists.

III

Acton himself was not at all indifferent to what he called the political education of Catholics. At the outset of their association he wrote his ideas to Simpson, considering himself as particularly in charge of the political side of the paper, and quite clear what he wanted to do:

> I think there is a philosophy of politics to be derived from Catholicism on the one hand and from the principles of our constitution on the other—a system as remote from the absolutism of one set of Catholics as from the doctrinaire constitutionalism of another set (*Le Correspondant*, etc.). I conceive it possible to appeal at once to the example and interest of the Church and to the true notion of the English constitution.

What these were, he came back to again and again, that the division and multiplicity of bodies was the secret of good government, believing that in proportion as this came to be understood, the existence and vitality of the Church would be valued instead of feared. He planned articles on Burke as a teacher for Catholics, the later Burke after 1792, and he proposed to explain to them that they owed emancipation neither to the Irish Catholics nor to the Whigs, and that "we need no longer humiliate ourselves or eat dirt to obtain the support of the Liberal or Radical party." He began with the intention of avoiding contention as far as might be, knowing that much he had to say would be new and unwelcome; but he was so little filled with either superiority or faction that at the outset he proposed a council for *The Rambler* on which every one distinguished for position and talent who could be reckoned a friend should be invited to sit; and he specially named Manning as, with Hope, one of two with whom he felt he would on most occasions agree.

He brought very high standards from Munich. Explaining why he did not take Father Faber seriously, he wrote to Simpson:

> Now I went through a three-year course of this kind of study of theology—i.e. of the sources, genesis and growth of the doctrines of the Church—so that although I did not exhaust any subject and am therefore no authority on any question, yet I know very well the method on which it is necessary to proceed, and can at once detect a writer who even with immense reading of theologians is but a dilettante in theology. That's why I said that Newman's essay on St Cyril, which on a minute point was original and progressive, was a bit of theology, which all the works of Faber, Morris, Ward, and Dalgairns will never be. It is the absence of scientific method and original learning in nearly all even of our best writers that makes it impossible for me to be interested in their writings.

So it was not really very surprising if before many months he was full of doubts about his suitability for the work and was telling Simpson that Simpson must be saying periodical writing was inconsistent with the kind of studies Acton had pursued and with "my slow and pacific habits of thought". "I once imagined it would help to overcome my natural aversion to rapid and spiderlike production. As to the use I might otherwise be to you I deceived myself from my ignorance of the real character of our public."

This was just before he went back to Munich for three months at the beginning of the critical year 1859, and wrote to Simpson in terms which showed that whatever reservations he had made about his own gifts he had as keen a sense as ever of the importance of the work.

The task of raising the level of thought and learning among us is arduous enough to employ us all our lives. It is one in which approbation and popularity are no test of success and in which success is necessarily slow; it is one too in which it is worthwhile to lose nothing by one's own fault. You are the only English Catholic possessing the positive qualifications for conducting such a review as *The Rambler* strives to be. You only want a couple of dull fellows to take my place as advocate of the devil and to carp at everything you write. As to politics, I leave you as my legacy the request that you will read Burke's speeches from 1790 to 1795. They are the law and the prophets.

(This was the Burke of whom he had written earlier that in those last years all that was Protestant or partial or revolutionary of 1688 in his political views had disappeared and what remained was a purely Catholic view of political principles and of history.)

For the next three years Acton passed his time between Aldenham, his Shropshire home, London when Parliament was sitting, and Munich. His mother died in 1860 and he found himself better off and embarked on great extensions of his library.

Mr Gladstone, having read and been impressed by his article on American politics which is included in this volume, began to take a growing interest in him. From Acton's side the admiration for Gladstone grew slowly. In 1860 he wrote of the Budget speech as "a tame, straightforward affair": "I rejoice at the confirmation it contains of my view that he is not inclined to democracy or class legislation, but tries to carry out true principles of economy," and he was pre-eminently the political commentator on the situation at the moment at home and abroad, with personal contacts denied to Simpson. But his main interest, to which he returns with relish and relief, is scientific ecclesiastical history. He annotated Simpson's *Campion* chapter by chapter.

This historical work was often more easily undertaken in Munich than in England. To the end of his life this was true of him: the list of the hundred best books he drew up in his later years had more titles in German than in any other one language. His two chief German teachers were Dr Döllinger and Professor

Lasaulx. Dr Döllinger died outside the Church, and Professor Lasaulx, Rector of the Munich University, had all his books placed on the Index in 1859. He made his submission before he died two years later. These were the years before Sadowa and the Hohenzollern Empire, years in which the struggle for more freedom of speculation in Germany was intimately linked with the struggle for more political constitutionalism.

In the essay on Ultramontanism, here reproduced, Acton describes this new spirit from beyond the mountains as intended to enlarge and liberate the energies of the Church.

He had been in Rome in 1857, and knew well how nervous and preoccupied the Government of Pius IX was in the presence of the advancing ambitions of the House of Savoy, with the England of Russell and Palmerston behind Cavour. It is easy in retrospect to blame the men who in Papal Rome fought so long and stubborn a rearguard action to save the temporal power. But they were men who in their boyhood had seen two Popes as prisoners of the French. They had no confidence at all in the moderation of the forces seeking possession of Rome, and the sequel was, in fact, to show that there was plenty of substance in their fears. There was no precedent in European history for the idea that the Pope could fulfil his spiritual office just as well dwelling in an enclave inside a secular kingdom; the historical picture was of all sovereigns, Catholic as well as Protestant, controlling religion very closely in their dominions, appointing the Bishops, and deciding how far the voice of the Holy See should be heard. It was not difficult to imagine the pressure that would be brought by such Governments on whatever civil Government ruled in Rome in order to hinder the effective action of the Pope. Even with full possession of the States of the Church, the Papacy in the eighteenth century had found itself increasingly subject to the pressure of the Catholic States. The great part played by the French Ambassador, Cardinal Bernis, in the election of Pius VI, in 1775, the success of the Catholic kings in securing the suppression of the Society of Jesus two years before, the habitual assumption at Versailles, even under a devoutly believing King like Louis XVI, that the King and not Rome was the proper source from which ecclesiastical promotions, even promotions to the Sacred College, should and did emanate; all this made the men around Pius IX cling to the States of the Church.

But behind kings and constitutional rulers they saw also the Jacobin shadow. Pius IX had been frightened out of his first tentative liberalism by the events of 1848, and the Roman Republic of 1849. The House of Savoy might claim Rome as the predestined capital of united Italy, Cavour might talk reasonably, but what security could there be that they, too, would not be swept away? It follows that throughout the 'fifties and 'sixties the preservation of the Pope's ruling position in Rome and the Campagna was deemed in Rome to be essential to that liberty, let alone that exaltation, of the Church, for which all Catholics have, since Leo XIII, prayed at the end of Mass. Everything tended to be looked at in the light of this preoccupation.

In the 'forties a patch of bright sky had emerged with the news that, after so long leading Protestant Europe, the English seemed to be returning to the faith, that an Italian Passionist, a son of that St Paul of the Cross who had besought and prayed so much about England, had met with strange and great answers to those prayers, and that both among the learned and among the nobility there was this marked movement of return. Perhaps the Catholic influence in England would grow in time to counterbalance the strong support the Italian enemies of the Holy See found in high places, as well as more generally in England. In these political expectations of what a new Catholic influence in English politics could do, the Roman authorities were soon disappointed.

The year 1858, that saw the beginning of Acton's connection with *The Rambler*, saw also the short-lived triumph of the Tories over the Whigs in Parliament, and Disraeli's hopes of bringing the Catholic M.P.s out of their long-established tendency to support the emancipating Whigs. The year that saw the final end of Acton's main period of Catholic writing, 1864, was also the year of the Syllabus of Errors and of Garibaldi's visit to England. In Rome they expected the Catholics in the Lords and Commons, men sitting for Irish Catholic seats, like Sir John Acton as member for Carlow, to be in opposition to the anti-Catholic Whig Government, and they were puzzled and indignant to find them supporting such a Government.

IV

If such was the Rome of those decades, the English Hierarchy also had its particular reasons for nervousness. These were its first years as a hierarchy, and its members had a difficult task to keep unity among a body of faithful of as highly different antecedents as could be imagined. They knew that for a long time the influential voice of Cardinal Acton in Rome had argued against any restoration of the English Hierarchy on the ground that it would delay instead of helping the spread of the faith. Cardinal Acton had said that the great powers of a Bishop would have to be entrusted to men who would, indeed, be good men, but who would be unequal to their responsibilities, would shelter nervously behind their prerogatives, and so would prove a drag on the growth of the Church in England. Wiseman, with Manning at his elbow, had to convince Rome that the English Hierarchy could be trusted to rise to its tasks.

Cardinal Wiseman was not by predisposition or character unfriendly to John Acton's aims. He was a man of wide intellectual interests and he had had the immense satisfaction of knowing that an article of his in *The Dublin Review* on the Donatists had been responsible for a very important step forward in the intellectual process of Newman's conversion. He was fully alive to the danger to religion from the new scientific theories and had, with his marked virtuosity, himself given lectures on the relations between science and scripture. But he derived from Ireland and Spain before he came from Rome, and had grown up in the Mediterranean world where there was little conception of a free press, least of all a free religious press. At the beginning he thought it quite within his province to issue a direction that no Catholic journals were to treat of any subject calculated to divide Catholics.

These years, 1858 to 1864, were the last period of Wiseman's life. From 1860 his health declined rapidly, with attacks of angina. His worries and his health interacted. He was in continual conflict with his coadjutor, Dr Errington, who tried to diminish the growing dependence of the Cardinal upon Manning; and Errington was, in the event, after lengthy investigations in Rome, removed.

Already, in 1856, when Simpson joined it, after eight years of publication, *The Rambler* was a source of anxiety to the Bishops, and among Catholics its tone was very generally disliked as un-Catholic: they felt it was the work of converts instructing, rather pontifically, their co-religionists, including ecclesiastical authorities, in a tone never suitable, but doubly out of place from men writing so soon after entering the Church. The atmosphere was already full of suspicion and recrimination when Acton appeared on the scene, bringing his own particular kind of superiority, the superiority of the more closely informed. He was as keenly interested in ecclesiastical history as in any other branch of learning; it was religious ideas and institutions, not only Catholic, that had been the great subject matter of Lasaulx and Döllinger, and the displacement of scholastic theology their great ambition.

The ideas of the frontier between free and reserved topics with which Acton approached journalism are shown in the letters to Newman which begin when Acton is no more than twenty-four, in 1858. Newman, from Dublin, wanted Acton to enter his name for his Catholic University, which Acton agreed to do. Very soon, however, he is asking Newman to edit a review to be written by his Dublin Professors, and writes, December 10th, 1858:

> The professors of Canon Law, of political science, of speculative philosophy are surely in every respect as much fitted to publish their opinions and their researches as the professors of mathematics and chemistry, and they are justified in instructing the public through the press ... I do not believe there is less certainty in those sciences than in others, and I am sure they are the most important. I should imagine, too, that the scientific treatment of these matters without party vehemence would be of great weight and value ... we have been long afflicted with the *Dublin Review* and it has accustomed a large portion of our numbers to that intellectual lethargy which is displayed. On the other hand many are carried away by a superficial brilliancy to errors of thought and feeling which are still more dangerous. *The Rambler* would not be so outspoken and so ill-humoured if those things were not felt as disasters by most of those who read it. But a monthly, especially with such traditions, can do no more than excite discontent and a wish for something better ... a large portion of Anglicans are very attentive to Catholic writings and there is a great deal to be done here and few Catholics know the importance of it.

Ten days later he writes again to Newman:

> My wish and object was simply to obtain for the Catholic

body the advantage of having its chief organ, and the chief director of its opinions, under your immediate influence ... I have no difficulty in agreeing with that part of your letter which I construe into advice for myself. I shall never obtain in *The Rambler* any sort of real influence and the hurry and haste of writing monthly articles harasses and disgusts me. The things that I have accumulated in the course of my studies can find no place in it and whatever I write in a review of such a popular character seems pedantic.

To this Newman replied, on December 31st:

I certainly think *The Rambler* is in a false position and I have long thought so. If I recollect rightly it began as a literary work and with the hope of raising the tone of Catholic literature. At one time it called itself a Journal of the Fine Arts. It generally had a tale in progress. It was properly a magazine. I think it has been a mistake to take up theology at all—and a double mistake to treat it after the fashion of a magazine—and a third mistake that laymen have done this. Then there is mistake the fourth, that *The Rambler* has attacked ecclesiastical authorities:

and Newman goes on to explain that where the Holy See has supported laymen against diocesans—Veuillot, Brownson—the laymen had gone all the way in support of the rights and claims of the Holy See. He concluded: "It is quite clear to me that if *The Rambler* goes on in its present course, there will be some way or other found of bringing it to an end": and in a sentence which recalls the enthusiasm with which Newman had read Wellington's dispatches which had made him burn to be a soldier, he goes on:

The Rambler should drop theology, should adopt the policy of Wellington in the Lines of Torres Vedras, become literary, attack the Protestants from time to time. The *Christian Remembrancer* and *Guardian* have gone on with much éclat without any principles at all. How have they gone on? Simply by attacking their opponents.

To this idea of dropping theology, not only Acton but Simpson agreed. The proposal for a quarterly under Newman did not advance, although Acton offered twenty pounds a year for three years towards it. In January 1859 he described himself as flattered and rather overwhelmed at the suggestion Newman made that they should collaborate, and wrote: "I am too conscious of the questionable character of the reputation I have unfortunately acquired to allow my name to be publicly connected just now with anything in which I am deeply interested," and professed himself anxious to disappear temporarily from the scene, only appearing occasionally in print.

At the same time, at the beginning of 1859, Newman was writing to Simpson that the Bishops had met about *The Rambler*.

> My own notion is that they had instructions from Rome to do so. It pains me exceedingly to entertain the very idea of *The Rambler*, which has done so much for us, and which is so influential, being censured from an authority—and the scandal would be considerable. I don't know what the Bishops could do, if they exerted their power to the utmost, but I suppose they could forbid their clergy to read it. That they will not be satisfied without doing a great deal, and that at once, is quite clear.

On the day Newman wrote that, February 16th, Bishop Ullathorne wrote to Newman that he had met Wiseman, Grant (Bishop of Southwark), Errington and

> after our business, we talked about *The Rambler*, and were unanimous that something must be done. The point is to act with as much quietness and considerateness as the case admits of. I mentioned my conversation with you and your kind offer to write to the Editor, Sir John Acton. Cardinal Wiseman said it was like you, and that everybody was always safe with you. It is our opinion that nothing short of Mr Simpson's retiring from the editorship will satisfy, as he plainly cannot judge what is and what is not sound in language.

It was made very plain that *The Rambler* would have to be mentioned in Pastoral Letters if Simpson did not retire at once.

Simpson went at once to see Newman, and said the March *Rambler* was printed all but six pages, and added: "I yield to their threats, but only provisionally and on condition of my being able to find another editor and the proprietors being able to carry on the magazine in the same or different form." The Bishops did not consider themselves bound by these stipulations between Newman and Simpson, and Newman felt aggrieved, "had not the experience of many years made me tire of indignation and complaint". Negotiation was at an end between Simpson and the Hierarchy, but the proprietors offered the editorship to Newman, and both Acton and Simpson said they would work for him as heartily as for themselves. For a moment it looked as though Newman might combine *The Rambler* with his Dublin quarterly *Atlantis*, and Simpson thought exultantly that this combination would give *The Dublin* the *coup de grâce*: "*The Dublin* is a gone coon." He saw the hand of the rival editor of *The Dublin* behind all the difficulties made for *The Rambler*, and wrote to Newman on March 7th: "I cannot help feeling a satisfaction that this struggle, which has been all along one of rival editors, should end not in changing *The Rambler* alone, but in multiplying the difficulties of its rival also."

This last sentiment did not elicit any response from Newman, who wrote back: "That I entertain the idea at all arises, first, from my gratitude to you for the confidence you have placed in me, and, secondly, from a real sense of the value of *The Rambler* as a periodical, as I have said to you already." But he added pointedly that he had no wish to "rival or embarrass *The Dublin*".

Newman's editorship was warmly welcomed in the other camp. W. G. Ward wrote, also on March 7th, that no one wrote for *The Dublin* except with the greatest distaste and sacrificed themselves out of detestation of *Rambler* principles. Now these were ended, every one would prefer to write for Newman. Ward, for all his extreme views on authority, was very anxious to keep Cardinal Wiseman out of *The Rambler*. He had at that time no idea of himself editing anything. "I am occupied with matters which interest me extremely; and for my own part would not care to walk across the room, if by merely doing so I could turn out a first-rate Quarterly."

But what made others happy alarmed Wiseman, who had a double affection for *The Dublin*, as both his child and his property, for not only had he started it, he still controlled it as proprietor. He wrote to Newman to express his dismay, since a *Rambler* edited by Newman "would leave no chance for a second periodical".

Newman took over *The Rambler* in March 1859, as the only way to preserve it as a property. To keep faith with the Bishops he had to relegate Simpson and Acton to the far background. He brought in Wetherell as sub-editor, after a first attempt to secure another convert, Thompson (the father of Alice Meynell and Elizabeth Butler).

Newman's editorship, however, was brief and unhappy. By May, after seeing his first number, the Bishops were asking him to give it up. He wrote to Simpson on May 25th: "The Bishop of Birmingham called on me to-day and said that he wished me to give up the editorship of *The Rambler* after July. I have promised to do so ... I believe the Bishops' wish is solely founded on the contents of the May number."

V

What the Bishops disliked in Newman's first issue came in the section Home Affairs, on the Bishops' attitude towards the Royal Commission then sitting on the poor-law schools. The episcopal attitude was that here was a subject obviously in their jurisdiction, and any criticism was considered interference. Newman replied that he had assumed that the Bishops would desire to know the opinion of the laity on subjects in which, like education, the laity were particularly concerned. Then he wrote the fateful sentence:

> If even in the preparation of a dogmatic definition the faithful are consulted, as lately in the instance of the Immaculate Conception, it is at least as natural to anticipate such an act of kind feeling and sympathy in the great practical questions, out of the condescension which belongs to those who are "forma facti gregis ex animo". If our words or tone were disrespectful, we deeply grieve and apologize for such a fault; but surely we are not disrespectful in thinking and having thought that the Bishops would like to know the sentiments of an influential portion of the laity before they took any step which perhaps they could not recall,

and went on to say, "We are too fully convinced of the misery of any division between the rulers of the Church and the educated laity" to do anything to bring about "so dire a calamity". This failed to mollify, and the precipitate and unfortunate decision was taken by the Bishops thus to terminate Newman's editorship, but he accepted it without protest—

> It is impossible with the principles and feelings on which I have acted all through life, that I could have acted otherwise. I never have resisted and never can resist the voice of a lawful superior, speaking in his own province.

Simpson wrote back suggesting that Acton should be editor and should make it primarily political—

> The thing now becomes a persecution and I am resolved to take the strongest measures for the preservation of my property and my rights, whatever may be the consequences. Will you allow me to tell Ward of the steps taken by the Bishops with the same reservation of secrecy as you have made with Thompson?

But Newman replied that Ward was a "prodigious blab".

In July, after producing his second and last number, which contained "On Consulting the Faithful in Matters of Doctrine", Newman wrote to Wetherell, "I am not editor in any sense", for he had very soon found he could not do it, and was extremely glad that Acton was prepared to take it over.

When Wetherell asked for more guidance, Newman wrote back, in August, "You will be able to give your confidence to Sir John Acton, the editor. I am sure he wishes to keep clear of what is likely to give offence to Catholics and has no wish to make *The Rambler* the organ of a party." Newman said afterwards that his own editorship, brief as it was, had secured Simpson and Acton three years more, and that by keeping Simpson from being editor again he had kept faith with the Bishops.

Acton thus emerged, with Simpson at his side, and in effect the interposition of Newman had had the effect of leaving the position at the end of 1859 very much what it had been at the beginning, except that Newman's name was a little less shining in the eyes of the Bishops and at Rome. "Consulting the Faithful in Matters of Doctrine" brought energetic remonstrance from Cardinal Barnato of Propaganda Fide to the English Hierarchy.

Newman wrote to Acton (June 20th, 1860) saying:[1]

My dear Sir John,
  It has always been a great perplexity to me who is to be the editor of *The Rambler*. I have thought of it again and again without any success. For myself the Bishop has hindered it and that is an end of it. If I said, on relinquishing the editorship, that I would still give my name to it, it was only under certain conditions, conditions made necessary by my arrangements with the Bishop. The principal of these was that I should only be one of several whose names would be more authoritative than my own—such as Father de Buck, F. Gratry, or l'Abbé

[1] Printed as in appendix to Ward's *Newman*, Vol. ii, p. 636.

Marat and Dr Döllinger. Considering both my responsibilities at the Oratory, and the circumstance of my being a convert, I could not act otherwise. As it was I had got into trouble by taking on myself *The Rambler as I found it*, without retracting anything that it had said. I took up and defended as my own its cause in the education question. I wrote an article on the right of the laity to be consulted, and as you know I thereby incurred a good deal of odium. It was this defence of the rights of the laity even in my May No. which was the chief cause of my Bishop's dissatisfaction with me. So much did my July No. increase this feeling that when I saw you about February last I told you that quite independent of anything in the recent Nos. of *The Rambler* I feared I should not be able to contribute anything more. And the chief condition was that there should be a responsible editor, which it was quite plain *you* could not be. I have the greatest opinion of Simpson as an able and honest man, and sincere gratitude for the way in which he has ever spoken of myself, but I deliberately thought him unfitted for the office of conductor of a work which was necessarily exposed to such jealous criticism.

Newman then explained that he withdrew altogether because he became convinced that Simpson was in fact the editor rather than Acton. Simpson was always in England, while Acton was as likely to be on the continent as not.

Acton felt this withdrawal very much; it had come as a great and unanticipated shock, and he had nearly denied it. He visited Newman to ask whether he too should give up, or should go on. He wrote in June 1860:

I beg of you, remembering the difficulties you encountered, to consider my position, in the midst of a hostile and illiterate episcopate, an ignorant clergy, a prejudiced and divided laity, with the cliques at Brompton, York Place, Ushaw, always on the watch, obliged to sit in judgment on the theology of the men you selected to be our patrons, deserted by the assistant whom you obtained for me, with no auxiliary or adviser but Simpson. And this after you had left us, with the opposition of *The Dublin Review*, of *The Tablet* in politics, and with the time-serving criticisms even of the paper which has owed me the greatest services[1]—at a time when the greatest and most difficult questions agitate the country and the Church.

[1] Presumably the *Weekly Register*.

He had a variety of reasons for not wanting to go on. He was expanding his library, and he wrote, June 9th, 1861, to Newman:

> My old master Lasaulx, one of the greatest German scholars, died the other day after expressing a wish that his library should not be sold by auction, but offered first of all to me, and I have bought it, both for his sake and for the excellent books. It will greatly add to the value and to the confusion of my library which I continue to hope will some day tempt you over to Aldenham . . . My books have an irresistible attraction for me which makes me miserable in London. In the House I find I am isolated and without hopes of obtaining any influence for my principles. I am sure I can do better in another sphere.

But he was really very anxious to go on.

An important letter to Newman, July 2nd, 1861, shows how he was unprepared for Newman's relative strictness of interpretation of the importance of ecclesiastical decrees.

> I am so much startled by your letter that you must not consider this an answer to it. There is something in your view of the importance belonging to decrees of authority for which I was not at all prepared, and which I must take time to consider. My own notion *was* that having excluded theology from *The Rambler*, nothing remained over which the ecclesiastical power possessed jurisdiction. In political life we should not be deterred, I suppose, by the threat or even the fear of excommunication from doing what we should have deemed our duty if no such consideration had presented itself, and I do not see how I am in a different position as editor and as M.P. I put aside, of course, the material point of view that it is very probable we should lose nearly all subscribers and contributors. I do not think I have been in the habit of exaggerating the merits or the value of *The Rambler*. I do not like the office of Editor, and I do not see that it has been doing much good. Father St John who discussed the question with me last year can bear witness that this was my opinion then. But if we do no great good by our views, we do some, I think, and especially now, by the spectacle of our independence. Perhaps it is because I am in the midst of Protestant society that I feel more strongly how bad the effect would be on them, if it should appear that the only organ among English Catholics of opinions with which it is possible for reasonable Protestants to sympathize was silenced by authority. Nor does it seem to me to the advantage of the

rulers of the Church that, having imposed silence, they should call it submission and agreement.

On this letter Newman noted:

I wrote a very strong answer to this—said I only differed with him on the fact. I thought *The Rambler* had trespassed on ground under the direct jurisdiction of the ecclesiastical authority.
(1) In the controversy about seminaries which had annoyed me very much.
(2) In flinging out, without natural course of the argument or necessity, against S. Pius V.
(3) In flinging out against the Sacred Congregation as impeding them in a review of Ward's philosophy.
That I thought Simpson incorrigible, that I 'despaired' of him. That a good sum of the public would be with the ecclesiastical authority if it came down upon *The Rambler*. I said that no good could come of a publication with which Simpson was connected.

Acton answered this mildly on July 8th. But about Pius V he asked:

Has the Church a right to censure me because I say of a canonized saint that on some occasion he committed an error of judgment, or even a mortal sin? Their biographies are full of such things—at least all the older lives. Sanctity really does not mean perfection, nor absolute wisdom; and in this case not the holiness but the wisdom of the saint was impugned.

He went on:

I have never been very zealous for particular views, but I care above almost everything for one or two principles or general opinions. I cannot bear that Protestants should say the Church cannot be reconciled with the truths or precepts of science, or that Catholics should fear the legitimate and natural progress of the scientific spirit. These two errors seem to me almost identical and if one is more dangerous than the other, I think it is the last, and that it comes more naturally to me to be zealous against the Catholic mistake than against the Protestant. But the weapon against both is the same, the encouragement of the true scientific spirit and disinterested love of truth. I have nowhere seen this principle sincerely adopted on the continent by any Catholic periodical, or by any group of

Catholics, and I really think it a merit of *The Rambler*, not that it does this successfully, but that it sees it and attempts to practise it. Yet I cannot conceive how such a cause can be pursued without collision with Rome, or how it can avoid being beset with difficulties in such a society as ours. I am sure I can conscientiously say I have not striven to give offence, or to insult what is venerable, but I believe I cannot always avoid the appearance of it. Do not these principles suffice to explain our position and attitude without the hypothesis of errors and failure in the pursuit of them? I always feel that I am deliberately and systematically further removed from the prevailing sentiments of good and serious Catholics than Simpson is with all his 'impudence'.

This letter ended with a comment on the irony in the contrast between Newman's real and supposed attitude:

Your imputed solidarity with *The Rambler* is very distressing when I consider how much my mind has been troubled with the idea of your disagreement and disapprobation. Would it were otherwise.

At the same time Manning, speaking for Cardinal Wiseman, visited Acton, to say a letter had come from Cardinal Antonelli, Secretary of State, with the Pope's knowledge, connecting the support given to the Government by Catholic members with things that had appeared in *The Rambler*. Acton wrote after this interview, telling Newman:

The upshot was that a censure was impending from Rome, that he was anxious I should disengage myself from *The Rambler* in time to escape it and should give him a promise that whatever the wish of the Holy Father might be should also be mine. Then he said *The Rambler* had appeared to him of late less Catholic in spirit and tendency, and was doing harm and that it was highly desirable to put an end to it altogether. The points of difference were numerous enough, both as to history and metaphysics, but, from his own statements as to my article on the Roman question not being up to the mark and Anglican in tone, and from the connection I perceived in the minds of people in Rome between *The Rambler* and support given to ministers in Parliament, it is obvious that the present political question is the decisive cause.

The rescript duly came from Rome and the Bishop of Shrews-

bury told Acton about it "as a very solemn thing". So it was for
a combination of reasons that in 1861 the two-monthly *Rambler*
gave place to a new quarterly, called *The Home and Foreign
Review* (published at 6s. by Williams and Norgate). In April 1862
Acton wrote to Newman:

> The violence of feeling in the Curia seems to have reached
> a height. You would be greatly shocked to hear of the mode in
> which—I greatly fear with the concurrence of Manning—they
> have lately attempted to do me a private injury, for the purpose
> of serving their public ends.

Wiseman was hostile to any continuation, and Newman
warned Acton in October that the two *Letters to the Clergy* on *The
Rambler* published by Bishop Ullathorne represented the attitude
of more than three quarters of the Hierarchy, and that Propaganda would confirm it. He added: "It does seem to me to be the
voice of the Church." Acton answered (October 31st, 1862) that
he "would never dream of receiving a canonical decision by a
Bishop with anything but the most entire respect, and if I could
have any temptation or inclination to protest and to answer, or
to defend myself, it would be sentenced by your example, even if
I had not received your advice." Newman advised Acton to give
twenty years to the production of a great work.

But Acton was determined to go on, and Newman's advice in
this case was that the editors should do some hard work for the
Church and earn the right to be heard. The man who was so soon
to write his own Apologia continued:

> There is no position, there are no circumstances in which
> there is not *the right* thing to do, if we have the skill to find it out.
> There is no move on the part of others towards us, but leaves
> room for a true counter-move on our part against them. There
> is no such thing as a cheque-mate [*sic*] except through our own
> fault. I allow it is difficult to find it, and perhaps when we see
> it at length, it is too late to avail ourselves of it. I can fancy a
> contra-statement to the Cardinal, which for its naturalness
> and straight-forwardness would win all candid minds. It is a
> great opportunity for a simple, manly, eloquent avowal of
> what you aim at.

He was not very well satisfied with the Reply which Wetherell
wrote and sent to him in October, and wished it had "more defi-

niteness and more warmth: definiteness to satisfy and warmth to win".

And in that same October he was very much put out by Acton's article on Döllinger's historical work, and wrote to Monsell that he could not talk of the other articles. "I have a lifelong disgust at speculations, as opposed to carefully argued theories or doctrines."

At this time Newman's continuing connection with *The Rambler* and its editors caused rumours that his newly founded Oratory School would be suppressed because the Oratorians were behind *The Home and Foreign Review*. Those who spread such rumours were out of date. Wiseman, as Newman noted twenty years later, "thought I had recanted" and wanted to seal the matter by a reconciliation with W. G. Ward, editing *The Dublin*, for which Newman should write. Ward himself wrote to Newman saying, "Your present view of *The Home and Foreign Review* is to me the happiest tidings I have had for many a long day." And Newman, while declining to write in *The Dublin*, said he was glad that Ward no longer entertained the "vague deep suspicions" he had harboured for eight years.

Newman's friend Monsell was writing (November 7th, 1862):

> I am afraid if Acton does not change, not his principles but his tone, he will be set aside by Catholics, and the resuscitated *Dublin*, which under Ward will be, I presume, a sort of echo of the *Univers*, will be the only acknowledged Catholic organ. I wrote to Acton to suggest a Council of Direction, such as the *Correspondant* is managed by, and the appointment of a theologian to revise articles on subjects such as Reason and Faith. He is so sensitive that I could not say what I wished to him about the affectation of superiority and the lecturing, as if from an eminence, of Bishops and priests. He does not see his way to any change. I look on the success of a Review on his principles as a matter of the deepest interest to us all. I have been much among the English Catholics in the last month, and they are so furious against the *Home and Foreign* that it is useless to argue with them about it . . . Perhaps my knowledge of the terrible evil caused by the *Univers* in France makes me realize more than most Englishmen can do the terrible evils that will follow from an ultra review being recognized as our only organ. Yet this must follow the repudiation by the Catholic body, priests, laymen of the *Home and Foreign*.

The letters which Bishop Ullathorne printed and circulated, under the names a *First, and a Second, Letter to his clergy*, set out some of the objectionable propositions he found in the *Review*, as, for example, that "in the natural point of view Adam is simply the highest link in the animal series; he was not a civilized man. The supernatural gift ruled this chaos of passions," and when he fell, "he was allowed to lapse into the animal condition," and, said Ullathorne, "words like religion, faith, morals, ethics, phenomena, forces, are used in a strange sense, drawn from the vocabularies of the philosophers and pantheist writers of Germany." In another field, he quoted:

> Political science can place the liberty of the Church on principles so certain and unfailing that intelligent and disinterested Protestants will accept them; and in every branch of learning with which religion is in any way connected the progressive discovery of truth will strengthen faith by promoting knowledge and correcting opinion, while it destroys prejudices and superstitions by dissipating the errors on which they are founded.

Although Simpson wrote an answer to the first letter invoking the authority of Cardinal Perrone for his account of Original Sin, between the two letters Dr Fröhschammer's excommunication took place. The critical year was, however, 1863, and the decisive event the Munich Congress. This was convened by Döllinger, the Church historian Alzog, and Abbot Kunsburg, and met at the end of September; its purpose was the better intellectual defence of the Church against the spreading rationalism, and the promotion of unity and concord among Catholic thinkers. It was a distinguished gathering of nearly a hundred Professors and Divines, mainly German and Austrian, and to them Döllinger as President delivered an address on the importance of breaking away from the cramping discipline of Scholastic theology. In its general sense the address was a demand for a much more drastic break with the intellectual past, a conception of development which distinguished sharply between the little that was dogma and all the elaboration and encrustation that had accompanied dogma. It was an address which called for exact interpretation, for it could be interpreted in a perfectly orthodox way or used as a justification and starting-point for modernism. It was almost immediately corrected by a Brief from Rome in December, excluding the more extreme interpretation by reminding the faithful that ecclesiastical discipline and authority and tradition all have their rights as well as scientific inquiry. This Brief was a great disappointment to Acton, as to Döllinger, and decided Acton to stop *The Home and Foreign Review* early in 1864, in view of the unpropitious atmosphere in the Church.

Acton told the story to Newman in March.

I have to give you the important news of the suppression of *The Home and Foreign Review*. The Pope has issued a Rescript to the Archbishop of Munich on the late conference in which he virtually approves the tone and purpose, but adds several propositions on the submission due to the Congregation (by which the Index is meant) of the authority belonging to received opinions in the schools, and to the Vetus Schola which are directly and flagrantly opposed to the principles of the Review ... I have determined not to risk a censure, but to take the significant warning of the document and put an end to the Review after the appearance of the next number. In an article on Frohschammer I shall find means of giving a full and intelligible explanation of my motives, which will be as satisfactory as it can be made without in any way renouncing any of our principles. I shall sign this paper in order to make the act and the declaration entirely my own.

Under the heading "Conflicts with Rome" he wrote a general survey which remains a guide to his own thought and an explanation of how he could combine trenchant condemnation, not merely of individuals in history, but whole movements like the Ultramontanism of his own time. He wrote:

There are few faults or errors imputed to Catholicism which individual Catholics have not committed or held, and the instances on which these particular accusations have been founded have sometimes been supplied by the axe of authority itself. Dishonest controversy loves to confound the personal with the spiritual element in the Church, to ignore the distinction between the sinful agents and the divine institution, and this confusion makes it easy to deny what would otherwise be too easy to question, that knowledge has a freedom in the Catholic Church which you will find in no other religion, though there, as elsewhere, freedom degenerates unless it has to struggle in its own defence.

He went on to trace the tragedy of Lamennais, "whose exaggeration of the infallibility of the Pope proved fatal to his religious faith". He went on to argue that the true interest of the Church was to be served by cherishing both political and intellectual liberty.

> Public law may make it imperative to overthrow a Catholic monarch like James II, or to uphold a Protestant monarch like the King of Prussia. The demonstrations of science may oblige us to believe that the earth revolves round the sun, or that the donation of Constantine is spurious. The apparent interests of religion have much to say against all this, but religion itself prevents those considerations from prevailing,

and then he continued the argument that the interests of the Church are not necessarily identical with those of the ecclesiastical Government, and that all Governments like to leave the extent of their powers vague and indefinite while their subjects want them to be precise. He wrote of the Index, that it would have been immediately inadequate as a way of keeping the knowledge of ecclesiastical history from the faithful if all history had not been regarded as the ammunition of controversy, until the introduction of the scientific spirit into history began in the German universities, where Catholics, Lutherans, and Rationalists all found a common interest in subordinating their passions to scientific objectivity.

This led him to discuss the case of Doctor Frohschammer, who incurred excommunication for writings on theories of pre-existence and against the doctrine that each soul is created directly by Almighty God, a personal history which threw into relief all the conflict between the two traditions of the German universities and the Roman Curia. Acton considered that a man like Dr Frohschammer when censured

> could in the first place yield an external submission either for the sake of discipline or because his conviction is too weak to support him against the weight of authority, but if the question at issue is more important than the preservation of peace, and if his conviction is strong, he inquires whether the authority that condemns him utters the voice of the Church. If he finds that it does he yields to it or ceases to profess the faith of Catholics; if he finds that it does not, that it is only the voice of authority, he owes it to his conscience and to the supreme

claims of truth to remain constant to that which he believes in spite of opposition. No authority has power to impose error, and if it resists the truth, the truth must be upheld until it is admitted.

This is not very conciliatory either in thought or language, even though it was followed by a full account of the extensive errors into which Dr Frohschammer fell in his attempts to justify himself. Acton condemned Dr Frohschammer, saying:

> When he found himself censured unjustly as he thought by the Holy See, it should have been enough for him to believe in his conscience that he was in agreement with the true faith of the Church. He would not then have proceeded to consider the whole Church affected with the liability to err from which her rulers are not exempt, or to degrade the fundamental truths of Christianity to the level of mere school opinions.

Frohschammer's attitude had been a main reason for the brief of Pius IX to the Archbishop of Munich, laying down that it is wrong, though not heretical, to reject the theological opinions or decisions of Roman Congregations. This document could be reconciled with the habitual language of *The Home and Foreign Review*, which Acton said

> has always maintained in common with all Catholics that if the one Church has an organ it is through that organ that she must speak, that her knowledge is not limited to the precise sphere of her infallibility, and that opinions which she has long tolerated or approved and has for centuries found compatible with the secular as well as the religious knowledge of the age cannot be lightly supplanted by new hypotheses of scientific men which have not yet had time to prove their consistency with dogmatic truth.

But having said so much, he rejected any such plausible accommodation and concluded that "it is therefore, not only more respectful to the Holy See, but more serviceable to the principles of the review itself, and more in accordance with the spirit in which it has been conducted, to interpret the words of the Pope as they were really meant."

He faced the divergence, seeing on the one hand scientific progress as beneficial to the Church, while it must inevitably be opposed by the guardians of traditional opinion, to whom as such no share in it belongs, and who by their own acts and those of their predecessors are committed to views which it menaces or destroys. A distinction between dogma and opinion, which *The Home and Foreign Review* existed to develop and emphasize, was being diminished intentionally by the Holy See, and the review would therefore find itself faced with the alternative of giving continual and reiterated offence to authority or of abandoning the essential purpose, and even if it were successful it would do no good, since the Holy See is the organ, the mouth, the head of the Church, and its strength consists in its agreement with the general convictions of the faithful.

The ecclesiastical Government based on the public opinion of the Church and acting through it cannot separate itself from the mass of the faithful and keep pace with the progress of the instructed minority. It follows slowly and warily and sometimes begins by resisting and denouncing what in the end it thoroughly adopts. Hence a direct controversy with Rome holds out the prospect of great evils, and at the best a barren and unprofitable victory.

He relied upon books, upon graver scientific literature, to be the agent of change. He concluded that the Review would cease, "since it could not deny its principles nor flout authority. The principles have not ceased to be true, nor the authority to be legitimate, because the two are in contradiction;" and he concluded:

I will sacrifice the existence of the Review to the defence of its principles, in order that I may combine the obedience that is due to legitimate ecclesiastical authority with an equally conscientious maintenance of the rightful and necessary liberty of thought.

And he took leave of his readers with the thought that

from the beginning of the Church it has been the law of her nature that the truths which prove themselves the legitimate fruits of her doctrine have had to make their slow way upwards through a phalanx of hostile habits and traditions, and to be rescued not only from open enemies but also from friendly hands that are not worthy to defend them,

and on that humble note he closed, looking to a development of Catholic learning too powerful to be arrested or repressed, and relegating *The Home and Foreign Review* to history as but a partial and temporary embodiment of an imperishable idea.

So closed the experiment of six years, a period long enough to produce writings, many of which have been found to retain interest and importance a century later, and long enough to show what a great work might have been done in England if the time had been more propitious, the preoccupations, traditions, and temper dominant at Rome different, and the spirit and temper of Newman, rather than of Manning, uppermost in the councils of the English Bishops. The sudden appearance in their midst of a young man so phenomenally gifted, so ardent and by nature so little provocative, was something the English Catholic body could not have anticipated, and unhappily could not use. A Review was produced which compelled the respect of the intellect of the country, so that Matthew Arnold, for example, paid a remarkable tribute, "that perhaps in no organ of criticism in this country was there so much knowledge, so much play of mind."

VII

The year 1864 was not quite the end. Three years later the *Chronicle* was launched. It was not a Catholic journal, although Mr Wetherell was the editor and wrote that "of course it would have a religion as the *Saturday Review* has and its religion will be Catholic. We are not founding a representative Catholic organ; we are not trying to propagate Catholicism, though we may have our own convictions as to the ultimate consequences of following a scientific method." The capital for this new venture was provided by Sir Roland Blennerhassett. It never began to pay its way and it lasted just a year, but during that year Acton contributed a good deal from Rome.

The last effort of all came two years later, when a Free Kirk journal, the *North British Review*, came into the market. Once again Mr Wetherell was the editor, until his health broke down at the beginning of 1871 and no one else was found to carry it on. The future Cardinal Vaughan had acquired *The Tablet* in 1868, and *The Dublin*, although edited by W. G. Ward, belonged to the Archbishop of Westminster; and Acton and Simpson continued to think there was no useful work for them to do in Catholic periodicals. Simpson devoted himself increasingly to musical and

Shakespearean studies. (Some of his material was published by
H. S. Bowden, of the Oratory, under the title *The Religion of
Shakespeare*, in 1903.) His health grew worse in the 'seventies and
he died at the age of fifty-six in 1876. Two years before his death,
and fortunately not leaving it until too late, the undemonstrative
Acton wrote to him:

> If the apprehensions of last September had been unfortu-
> nately realized I should not only have had to bear the grief of
> all your friends but especially my own, for having never ex-
> pressed, nor I fear shown, how great a part of the good things
> of many years of my life had come to me from your true and
> generous friendship, or how much reason I had to thank God
> for it.

Simpson's death may be taken as marking the end of this first
phase of Acton's life. He had a fruitful quarter of a century before
him, but it was in other fields than in higher Catholic periodical
journalism. The friendship with Mandell Creighton and the
English Historical Review in the 'eighties, the Cambridge Pro-
fessorship and the planning of the *Cambridge Modern History*, came
to make the setting for Acton as the public were to know him and
to think of him. The friendship with Mr Gladstone developed
year by year, and was not disturbed when Acton supported
Newman against Gladstone in the controversy in 1874 over the
bearing of the Vatican decrees on the civil allegiance of Catholics.
Acton never received from Gladstone in power any office except
that of Lord-in-Waiting to the Queen, where his knowledge of
things German made him a success, so that he earned the high
compliment that she wished Prince Albert could have known
him. But he had the satisfaction of knowing that he had an influence with Gladstone, all the greater because he was not looking for place; and in one of his later letters he records, after a
conversation with John Morley, who disclaimed having led
Gladstone to espouse Home Rule, "This leaves me the sole and
undisputed author of the policy." When all the correspondence
of these years is published Acton's share in the Liberal party
policy will be found considerable. But that it should have been
so, that he should have found congenial and welcoming society
more and more in the worlds of English liberal politics and the
Cambridge historical school, was also the measure of those

earlier disappointments he had both encountered and given in the Catholic Church. To the end of his life a devout Catholic, he had concluded that there was little for him to do for the Church in his own unpropitious time, when so much that he disliked and disapproved was in the ascendant. He had appeared in the 'fifties, when the older generation in authority in the Church still lived under the shadow of the French Revolution. Pius IX was born in 1795, and even Leo XIII as early as 1810. Acton was a generation too soon, and by the time his life ended there were few to recall, and fewer still to understand and sympathize with, the work which as a young man he had set out with such high hopes to do.

I

ULTRAMONTANISM[1]

KNOWLEDGE is treated by the Christian Church not merely
as a means, but much more as an end, because it is the
only atmosphere in which her progress is unwavering
and subject to no relapse. When in successive ages she defines or
surveys anew the system it is her mission to teach, she has
always to record some advance upon the past. Though amongst
the units of mankind the boundary of her dominion may waver
or recede, yet, in the order of truth, she works out a law of inevitable and invariable advance. She must teach all nations; but
she has no special promise that any one will listen to her. She
must watch over those within her fold, but she knows not
whether her vigilance will avail. No divine protection insures
her against losses by persecution, dogged unbelief, neglect of
her law, or apostasy from her creed; and there is no assurance
that the means of grace which she dispenses will effect by degrees
the moral improvement of our race, or that sanctity will gain
in intensity or in extent as time goes on. There may be diminution in the area of Christendom, and decline in the virtue of
Christians. But there must be some exception to the possibility
of retrogression, or Christianity would be inferior to Judaism;
nay, if stagnation could paralyse every function of the Church
of Christ, His works would be less perfect than the works of
men. The divine nature of the institution which He founded
must therefore be manifest in some element which is secured
against loss or deterioration by the assurance of a constant
growth. To refuse to the Church this character of progress is to
deny the divinity of her Founder; and if we seek it anywhere
else than in that order of truth which is subject to the immediate
guidance of the Holy Ghost, we are contradicted alike by the
holiness of the early ages, and by the most memorable lessons
of later religious history.

In this growth the Church does not yield to the action of

[1] *Home and Foreign Review*, July 1863, p. 162.

eternal forces, or simply consent to a change which she cannot impede. Progress is a necessity of her existence, and a law of her nature. She does not passively suffer it, but actively imposes it upon society. Whilst she continually and continuously develops her doctrines, and evolves truth from the inexhaustible tradition of the teaching of our Lord, her action is the ever-present impulse, pattern and guide of society in the formation of law, and in the advancement of learning.

How great is the influence thus exercised by the example of the Church on civil government, and how close is the parallel between her method and the principles of political science, we do not here inquire. Her more direct and necessary action is on human knowledge. For the full exposition of truth is the great object for which the existence of mankind is prolonged on earth. It may be that individual goodness is not greater, or the proportion of the saved larger, than in earlier times; but Almighty God is more fully known, the articles of faith are multiplied, and the certainty of knowledge is increased. This growth in knowledge is not by new revelations or by a continuance of inspiration, but it is a conquest of the Christian mind in its conflict with the phases of untruth. It is earned by exertion; it is not simply given by faith itself. The development of doctrine is essential to the preservation of its purity; hence its preservation implies its development; and the intellectual act which accompanies belief is the agent of the progress of the Church in religious knowledge. In the course of this process she lays under contribution all human learning, which she exacts and sanctifies by using it. As she does not possess at once the fulness of all knowledge, and as her authority leaves many things uncertain, she must rely on other resources for that which is not hers by inheritance; and her demand must necessarily promote the supply of that on which she so much depends. Therefore, by the side of the progressive study of revealed truth a vast intellectual labour continues incessantly, carried on in the presence of authority, on the basis of faith, and within the sphere of unity and charity, in order that all science may become tributary to religion, and that God may be worshipped in the harmony of His words, His works, and His ways.

This duty has been discharged in all ages, except the intervals of corruption and decline, with a zeal commensurate with its importance; and the bitter anxiety which has accompanied each rising doubt and division has equalled that excited by assaults on the faith itself. For in disputes with a hostile religion there is the certainty of belief to guide, and confidence in authority to sustain the combatant. He confesses himself inferior to the cause; he dares not degrade it by the introduction of personal motives or emotions, or allow it to be desecrated by the conditions of human controversy; and he is not tempted to do so, for neither fear nor doubt mingles with his feelings. But in discussions confined within the sphere of religious unity, which do not directly involve fundamental truths, and where private judgement occupies the place of faith and obedience, the antagonism is necessarily more personal, there is more selfishness in opinion and less assurance of victory, and the purest motives may become tainted by ignorance, interest or pride. Disputes which authority cannot decide are an excitement to those for whom its restraint is irksome, and an indulgence for those who are weary of acquiescing in silent unity. The lines of separation are most distinctly marked because the chasm is less wide.

Hence arise two phenomena which vex the Catholic and perplex the Protestant—the number of parties within the Church, and the heat of their dissensions. It is not always easy for a stranger to reconcile these things with the notion of unity, or for a friend to be sure that they involve no breach of charity; and it is very hard for either to discover, when orthodoxy is disputed and authority necessarily silent, the true exponent of the Catholic idea. As the rise of heresies furnished the text which defined Catholicism to be the most perfect expression of Christianity, so the growth of internal controversy requires some further test to ascertain the purest form of thought on open questions within the Church. For the control of religion extends further than its dogmas; and a view which contradicts no prescribed doctrine may be a more serious symptom of estrangement from the spirit of the Church than some unconscious doctrinal errors. There are certain questions to which the test of orthodoxy does not apply, which yet are more significant than some of those which it decides. The liberty which prevails on doubtful points does not justify a resignation that acquiesces in doubt, and deprecates the efforts by which it may be dispelled. In the absence of the degrees of authority, such points may be settled by scientific inquiry, and an opinion which can never be enforced may claim to be received. Yet, though Catholics may be ready to adopt a criterion which excludes some of those who are in communion with them, they dread what may repel those who are not; and they naturally conceal in the presence of strangers a weapon which they use among themselves. It is impossible that varying parties which cannot agree in a common definition should accept a common term.

Protestant observers have adopted a designation to indicate the esoteric spirit of Catholicism, the real essence of the system they oppose. That designation is Ultramontanism. Unquestionably the significance attached to it has a certain reality and truth which ought to overcome the reluctance to admit the term. Ultramontanism stands in the same relation to Catholicism in matters of opinion as Catholicism to Christianity in matters of faith. It signifies a habit of intellect carrying forward the inquiries and supplementing the work of authority. It implies the legitimate union of religion with science, and the conscious intelligible harmony of Catholicism with the system of secular truth. Its basis is authority, but its domain is liberty, and it reconciles the one with the other. A Catholic may be utterly deficient in human learning, or he may possess it in such a measure as presents no difficulties to his faith, or he may find a ready and universal solution for all such difficulties in an unhesitating sacrifice either of faith or of reason. In no one of these cases, whether he be a good or a bad Catholic, has he any pretensions to the name of Ultramontane. His religion derives no strength or resources from his knowledge, nor does his knowledge find a principle of unity or a guide in his religion. If neither of them has lost anything of its integrity and truth, neither has gained anything from the other. If there is no struggle in his mind, there has also been no combination—no generation of something previously non-existent which neither science alone nor religion alone could have produced. His conscience has obtained no security against the necessity of sacrificing faith to truth or truth to faith, and no impulse to that reflection which recognizes the ultimate unity.

It is plain that Ultramontanism, in this acceptation of the word, can only be a fruit of mature civilization and of a very advanced stage of scientific investigation. Natural science before it was purified by the methods of observation, and historical science before it was regenerated by criticism, consorted better with superstition and error than with religion. But a change took place in their nature at the beginning of this century. There is an interval, as it were, of centuries which divides Cuvier from Buffon, Niebuhr from Gibbon, with a distinctness almost as great as that which separates chemistry from alchemy, astronomy from astrology, history from legend. A similar change ensued in the political system, and established in almost every country the theory and the desire of freedom. In one of the contests arising from this altered condition of society, about a quarter of a century ago, the term Ultramontane began to be applied to those who advocated the rights and principles of the Catholic Church. In one sense the designation was just: in another it was a strange inversion of the meaning which had been hitherto attached to the word.

During the period between the Reformation and the Revolution, Ultramontanism, like Gallicanism, was used as a party term. It designated the strict Roman system as developed by the antagonism of the Gallican theories of the fifteenth century. In comparison with the practice of the Middle Ages, it was a jealousy of liberties, stimulated by an equal jealousy of authority. Such a controversy, raising a false issue on the law and constitution of the Church, could only engage the masters of ecclesiastical learning during an age when history, the touchstone and solvent of extreme systems, was very imperfectly known. At a time when it raged, little had yet been done to illustrate the mediaeval Church, and men were still without the means of solving such historical problems as that of the Donation of Constantine, the spurious Decretals, the story of Pope Joan, and all the various fables which furnished the bases of the rival claims for an almost absolute national independence, and for an arbitrary and universal power. In those days Gallicans and Ultramontanes contended for narrow, extreme, subordinate, we might almost say, uneducated views. The conflict between them was an abatement of the true Catholic spirit, and was lamented by the saints as a disaster for the Church. "Je hais", says St Francis of Sales, "par inclination naturelle, et, je pense, par inspiration céleste, toutes les contentions et disputes qui se font entre Catholiques, et dont la fin est inutile; encore plus celles dont les effets ne peuvent être que dissensions et différends, surtout en ce temps plein d'esprits disposés aux controverses, aux médisances, aux censures et à la ruine de la charité. Je n'ai pas même trouvé à mon goût certains écrits d'un saint et très-excellent prélat, dans lequels il a touché du pouvoir indirect du Pape sur les princes; non que j'ai jugé s'il a tort ou raison, mais parce qu'en cet age où nous avons tant d'ennemis en dehors, nous de devons rien émouvoir au dedans du corps de l'Église." St Francis also says: "Il est malaisé de dire choses qui n'offensent ceux qui, faisant les bons valets, soit du Pape, soit des princes, ne veulent pas que jamais on s'arrête hors des extremités."[1]

Intellectual indolence conspired with the ignorance of the age to promote these theories. Men were glad to find a formula which saved them the trouble of thinking, and a view which enabled them to shut their eyes. For the defence of a thesis is far easier than the discovery of truth. There is something alarming in the labour of distinguishing and comparing times and places, and of making due allowance for qualifying circumstances and conditions. The followers of a system dreaded lest the knowledge of facts should interfere with the certainty of their opinions, and lest the resistless stream of history should be let in upon their settled and compact conclusions.

The political condition of those times is an important element in the history of the controversy. Gallicanism and Ultramontanism both professed to represent liberty; but they both belonged to an age of absolute power. One system was the instrument by which absolute monarchs extended their power over the Church, whilst by the other the same principle of absolutism was introduced into the Church herself. Both were expedients by which ecclesiastical liberty was curtailed, and authority made superior to law. The source of their vitality and the reason of their existence disappeared when the Revolution put an end to the old society which tolerated, and even approved, the system of arbitrary government. At a later period, under the Restoration, the reverence for law, and the religious aversion for absolute power, which resisted the encroachment of civil government on the liberties of the Church, caused her to maintain, in her own internal system, the authority of law and tradition over the temporary will of her rulers. Instead of Church and State being

[1] Œuvres, xi, 406, 401.

rivals in absolutism, it came to be understood that both ought to obey their own legislation; while the horror of the lawless epochs they had lately traversed, in the Revolution and the Empire, came to be the predominant influence in the minds of men.

Early in the present century, while Chateaubriand was explaining the charm of religious emotions, and when in Germany the distinction of creeds was all but obliterated by the powerful current of Romanticism, it cannot be said that there were any distinguishable groups of Catholic opinions. Ecclesiastical literature was at a low ebb, and controversy was almost extinct. There was neither learning, nor leisure, nor definiteness enough to awaken the old discussions. They appeared again when peace and freedom were restored to religion, and literary activity revived, after 1814. In those days the memory of the revolutionary period and its unbelief was very vivid, and the ideas of the Holy Alliance found much favour with thinking Catholics. They dreamed of a league between Church and State, of a renovated loyalty identified with a revived religion, and of a combination between men of goodwill for the restoration of the great interests which had fallen before the common foe. It was hoped that religion might enable the State to protect society against the recurrence of such a catastrophe. There were many who relied for the realization of this scheme (half religious and half political) as much on the Czar as on the Pope. The strong practical purpose by which it was animated is one leading characteristic of the literary movement which followed. Another is, that its writers were chiefly laymen; for the problems of the day were rather social than ecclesiastical, and even theology was treated with a view to the State. Long before the French Revolution the schools of theology had generally declined, and then, for five and twenty years, ecclesiastical studies were almost everywhere suspended. No successors had sprung up to the great scholars who had lived far into the pontificate of Pius VI; and many of the most cultivated priests on the Continent were deeply marked with Rationalism. At the Restoration the clergy, as a body, were not in a condition to take an active part in literature. Their place in the van was supplied by laymen—often recent converts, seldom trained scholars, and all rather inspired by the lessons of recent history than versed in the older details of theological discussion.

The foremost of these men was the Comte de Maistre. During

the evil days he had made himself a name by two political pamphlets, written with the power, the eloquence and depth of Burke,
with more metaphysical ability than Burke possessed, but without his instinct for political truth, or his anxious attention to the
voice of history. In these pamphlets he had laid down some of the
most important principles of civil government, and had explained with special success the necessity of aristocracy for the
establishment of freedom. His writings had displayed extensive
knowledge, earnest faith, a pointed wit, and an almost unexampled union of common sense with love of paradox and passion
for extremes. After his return from St Petersburg, in the first
years of the Restoration, he published several works in rapid
succession, which have earned for him perhaps the highest place
next to Pascal among laymen who have defended religion without the advantage of a theological education.

Society, said M. de Maistre, has been ruined by the want of
faith, or by its equivalent in the civil order, the weakness of
authority. It is necessary that mankind should be taught the
duty of unconditional obedience, the merit of suffering, the sin-
fulness of self-assertion, the peril of liberty, and the evil of securities against the abuse of power.[1] Tyranny, poverty and slavery
are not the faults of society, but the penalties of sin. Monarchy
is the only legitimate form of government, because monarchy
alone gives the nations a master, and places the sovereign under
the restraint of conscience. It is his duty to promote as well as to
preserve religion, to suppress error and sinlike crime, and to
defend the faith by prescribing knowledge[2] and encouraging
superstition.[3]

[1] "Il est vrai au fond que les peuples ont des droits, mais non celui de les faire
valoir ou d'en punir la violation par la force" (*Correspondance Diplomatique*, ii, 36).
"Le dogme catholique, comme tout le monde sait, proscrit tout espèce de révolte
sans distinction; et pour défendre ce dogme nos docteurs disent d'assez bonne
raisons, philosophiques même, et politiques" (*Du Pape*, p. 161).

[2] "Les inconvénients inévitables de la science, dans tous les pays et dans tous les
lieux, sont de rendre l'homme inhabile à la vie active, qui est la vraie vocation de
l'homme; de le rendre souverainement orgueilleux, enivré de lui-même, et de ses
propres idées, ennemi de toute subordination, frondeur de toute loi et de toute
institution, et partisan-né de toute innovation. Elle tend donc nécessairement à
tuer l'esprit public et à nuire à la société" (*Quatre Chapitres inédits sur la Russie*, 1859,
p. 38). "Restreindre de même la science, de plusieurs manières, savoir . . . en
supprimant tout enseignement public des connaissances qui peuvent être livrée au
goût et au moyens de chaque particulier; comme l'histoire, la géographie, la

In these writings de Maistre unquestionably relinquished or modified some of his earlier opinions. There was no longer that love of freedom which he had opposed to the violence of the Revolution, or that admiration for England with which he had been inspired by her long resistance to Napoleon.[1] His ideal state had become more centralized, his sovereign more absolute, his nobility less independent, his people less free. The dread of revolutionary despotism had given place to a horror of constitutionalism. This was the current of the hour. But it inspired de Maistre with the theory which is the chief cause of his celebrity, a theory new to the Catholic thinkers of his time. Catholicism, he maintained, inculcates the absolute authority of the sovereign, and forbids resistance even to the gravest wrong.[2] This unity

---

métaphysique, la morale, la politique, le commerce" (ibid., p. 147). "Il y a dans la science, si elle n'est pas entièrement subordonnée aux dogmes nationaux, quelque chose de caché qui tend à ravaler l'homme, et à le rendre surtout inutile ou mauvais citoyen . . . Il faut subordonner toutes nos connaissances à la religion, croire fermement qu'on étudie en priant; et surtout lorsque nous nous occupons de philosophie rationnelle, ne jamais oublier que toute proposition de métaphysique, qui ne sort pas comme d'elle-même d'un dogme chrétien, n'est et ne peut pas être qu'un coupable extravagance" (*Soirées de St Petersburg*, ii, 221, 223).

[3] "Je crois que la superstition est un ouvrage avancé de la religion qu'il ne faut pas détruire, car il n'est pas bon qu'on puisse venir sans obstacle jusqu'au pied du mur, en mesurer la hauteur et planter les échelles . . . Croyez-vous que les abus d'une chose divine n'aient pas dans la chose même certaines limites naturelles, et que les inconvénients de ces abus puissent jamais égaler le danger d'ébranler la croyance?" (*Soirées de St Petersburg*, ii, 234).

[1] "On a bien dit: 'Il faut des lois fondamentales, il faut une constitution'. Mais qui les établira, ces lois fondamentales, et qui les fera exécuter? Le corps ou l'individu qui en aurait la force serait souverain . . . L'Angleterre seule a pu faire quelque chose dans ce genre; mais sa constitution n'a point encore subi l'épreuve du temps . . . Qu'arrivera-t-il? Je l'ignore; mais quand les choses tourneraient comme je le désire, un example isolé de l'histoire prouverait peu en faveur des monarchies constitutionelles, d'autant que l'expérience universelle est contraire à cet example unique" (*Du Pape*, pp. 159, 160). Ten years earlier he had said: "La constitution est l'ouvrage des circonstances . . . l'unité la plus compliquée et le plus bel équilibre des forces politiques qu'on ait jamais vu dans le monde" (*Essai sur le Principe Générateur des Constitutions Politiques*, p. 16).

[2] "Si l'on veut s'exprimer exactement, il n'y a point de souveraineté limitée; toutes sont absolues et infaillibles, puisque nulle part il n'est permis de dire qu'elles se sont trompées . . . Elle est toujours et partout absolue, sans que personne ait le droit de lui dire qu'elle est injuste ou trompée" (*Du Pape*, p. 165). "Il faudroit que les souverains protestants eussent perdu le sens pour ne pas apercevoir l'insigne folie qu'ils font, de soutenir une religion qui pose en maxime le jugement particulier

and absolutism of authority spring from the very nature of religion, and are not only necessary for the State, but essential to the Church. Civil society cannot subsist without the maxim that the king can do no wrong. The Church requires the same privilege for the Pope. Absolute infallibility in the one is a corollary of despotism in the other.[1] It is also its remedy. Denying to the people any part in the vindication of right, de Maistre transferred to the Pope alone the whole duty of moderating kings. Thus the argument for the Papal power flowed into two streams from one source—the theory of civil absolutism. Reasoning by analogy, the Pope ought to be an arbitrary ruler within the Church; while, by contrast, his power was extended over States, and the security of civil rights was to be sought in the completeness of hierarchical despotism.

Whoever studies the writings of de Maistre will find far more than the memorable theory by which he became the founder of a new school of Ultramontanism. He will find some of the best and wisest things ever written on religion and society—a generous one, an admirable style of discussion, and the Catholic system presented often in the noblest manner. These qualities have exercised a powerful and salutary influence on all the succeeding schools of Catholic thought; and some who differ most widely from de Maistre on the questions which he made more particularly his own owe much to his writings. But it was only in the course of years, as the publication of eight posthumous volumes defined more clearly and more amply the character of his mind, that men learned to separate the man from his peculiar theory. At first, all the merits of his system and his style served but to give attractiveness and splendour to the theory of the Papal power, which became the symbol of a party, and gave the impulse to an important movement. No distinct view had yet

---

et la souveraineté du peuple, contre une autre religion qui soutient que contre notre légitime souverain, fût-il même un Neron, nous n'avons d'autre droit que celui de nous laisser couper la tête en lui disant respectueusement la vérité" (*Correspondance Diplomatique*, ii, 132).

[1] "Il ne peut y avoir de société humaine sans gouvernement, ni de gouvernement sans souveraineté, sans infallibilité; et ce dernier privilège est si absolument nécessaire, qu'on est forcé de supposer l'infaillibilité, même dans les souverainetés temporelles (où elle n'est pas), sous peine de voir l'association se dissoudre. L'église ne demande rien de plus que les autres souverainetés" (*Du Pape*, p. 147).

been put forward so positively or so brilliantly; and its influence
on contemporaries was extraordinary. It appeared to a large
class of persons as the only perfect form of Catholicism. Everything that fell short of it seemed to them treason or surrender. To
limit the Holy See in Church or State was to attack religion, and
open the door to Jansenism, Protestantism, and infidelity. Inasmuch as authority was especially odious to irreligious Catholics, it became the part of good Catholics to vindicate it with at
least a corresponding zeal. All qualification was taken to be
opposition, and was deemed to imply a secret aversion.

Since the question raised by de Maistre was one of fact, and
not of speculation, its solution was to be found not in theory but
in history. For, as the standing object of his school was to establish a prejudice favourable to the supreme authority of the
Church in every period, their labour would be in vain if it could
be shown that the pontifical power had manifested itself in
various degrees in various times, or that there had been serious
vicissitudes in its spirit. Here an entrance was found for a personal element new to ecclesiastical literature, which caused the
discussion of character to become more prominent than the discussion of principle. Those who defended a particular view of
canon law, history, or politics with orthodoxy obliged themselves
to treat all objections to this view as blasphemies against religious
truth; whatever was inconsistent with the theory was regarded
as really equivalent to a denial of the continuity of tradition.[1]
Large tracts of history which had formally involved no theological interest became the arena of controversy; and their adverse and telling facts were only in the brief to be explained
away and amplified respectively. De Maistre had given the
example of discussing these questions with the arts of advocacy.
His rhetorical dexterity enabled him to put wit in the place of
argument, to disconcert adversaries by spirited retaliation, or
baffle them by ingenuously dissembling or boldly denying whatever might serve their purpose. Many followed him in good faith,

[1] On February 5, 1820, Lamennais wrote to de Maistre on the publication of
his book, *Du Pape*: "En défendant l'autorité du saint-siège, vous défendez celle de
l'église, et l'autorité même des souverains, et toute vérité et tout ordre. Vous devez
donc compter sur de nombreuses contradictions; mais il est beau de les supporter
pour une telle cause. L'opposition des méchants console le cœur de l'homme de
bien, il se sent plus séparé d'eux, et des lors plus près de celui à qui le jugement
appartient et à qui restera la victoire."

fully persuaded that nothing opposed to the theory could be true; but he had other followers who were not in good faith.

The long opposition of science and philosophy to religion had brought their methods into a discredit which the practice of the writers of that time by no means tended to dissipate. Men doubted whether scientific method could be really reconciled to religious truth; and it was felt that so ambiguous a weapon was least unsafe when least used. Men suspected that it was altogether inadequate to give certain demonstration of the truths with which it is conversant,[1] and without the aid of external authority. On this idea a theory was founded which seemed at first to support de Maistre's argument for the Papal authority, though it ended in decided contradiction of it. Lamennais, the author of this new philosophy, taught that no evidence amounts to certain demonstration unless confirmed by the universal consent of the general testimony; and that the organ of this universal reason is the Holy See. This principle, laid down in the second volume of the *Essai sur l'Indifférence*, led necessarily to the rejection of that theory of the absolute authority of the civil power which had furnished de Maistre with the analogy he used with such effect. If the infallibility of universal opinion is the origin of certainty, it is the source of authority; and the Holy See is therefore exalted over princes as much as over philosophers and thinkers. When, therefore, the French monarchy became odious to the people, and, at the same time, hostile to the Church, Lamennais denied its right, and appealed against it to the people as the source of power, and to the Pope as their organ. This was the spirit of the *Avenir*,[2] and it still largely tinges the political Catholicism of France. The doctrine of the impotence of reason was wrought into a system by Father Ventura, and was adopted by the Traditionalists, who, on the plea of Rationalism, anathematized all the writers who did most honour to the clergy of France. During many years Traditionalism preserved an organ in the journal of the indefatigable M. Bonnetty, until it was con-

---

[1] "Je n'irai point tenter follement d'escaler l'enceinte salutaire dont la sagesse divine nous a environnés; je suis sûr d'être de ce côté sur les terres de la vérité: qui m'assure qu'au delà (pour ne point faire de supposition plus triste) je ne me trouverai pas sur les domaines de la superstition?" (*Soirées de St Petersburg*, ii, 227).

[2] The Abbé Gerbet wrote in the number of February 21, 1831: "L'ordre légal peut cesser de la même manière qu'il a été établi, c'est-à-dire par voie de consentement."

demned, and the claims of reason vindicated both by Pope and Council.[1]

This theory of the vanity of science applied to history made it as uninteresting as an old almanac, and at the same time as arbitrary, unreal and unreliable as the annual prophecy of a new one. It made the teaching of the Church the sole foundation and test of certain knowledge, a criterion alike of the records of history and of the arguments of unbelief. It recognized no means of ascertaining the truth of facts, or the authenticity of documents, sufficiently trustworthy to interfere with theological opinions. It supposed the part of malice and ignorance to be so large, and the powers of unaided reason so minute, that ecclesiastical authority could be the only guide, even in matters foreign to its immediate domain—the next place given to the presumptive authority of the more probable opinion. Otherwise, it was thought, the constant fluctuations of profane science would oblige theology to obey all its movements, and religion would ape the mobility which passion, ignorance, and error impart to literature. Hence it was held impossible to verify the facts of religious history, or to argue from the monuments of tradition. Catholics had no basis of criticism in common with others. Every Protestant was *principia negans*. In all likelihood quite as strong a case might be made out against the Catholic view of the past as in its favour, and no appeal to history was expected to confound adversaries or to confirm belief. The immediate consequence was to set aside historical study as useless or dangerous;

[1] The decree of the Council of Amiens, quoted by Father Gratry, explains better than any description the extremes to which the school had come: "Dum rationalismum impugnant, caveant etiam, ne rationis humanæ infirmitatem quasi ad impotentiam reducant. Hominem, rationis exercitio fruentem, hujus facultatis applicatione posse percipere aut etiam demonstrare plures veritates metaphysicas et morales . . . constanti scholarum catholicarum doctrina compertum est. Falsum est, rationem solvendis istis quæstionibus esse omnino impotentem, argumenta quæ proponit nihil certe exhibere et argumentis oppositis ejusdem valoris destrui. Falsum est, hominem has veritates naturaliter admittere non posse, quin prius per actum fidei supernaturalis revelationi divinæ credat." The *Congregatio Indici* defined the doctrine of the Church against the Traditionalists in four sentences, of which this is the second: "Ratiocinatio Dei existentiam, animæ spiritualitatem, hominis libertatem cum certitudine probare potest. Fides posterior est revelatione, proindeque ad probandam Dei existentiam contra atheum, ad probandam animæ rationalis spiritualitatem ac libertatem contra naturalismi ac fatalismi sectatorem allegari convenienter nequit."

and that courageous logician, M. Veuillot, affirmed ignorance to be quite as serviceable as knowledge for the vindication of truth, and urged that no time should be wasted in exchanging the one for the other.

A particular suspicion rested on history, because, as the study of facts, it was less amenable to authority and less controllable by interest than philosophical speculation. In consequence partly of the denial of historical certainty, and partly of the fear of it, the historical study of Dogma in its original sources was abandoned, and the dialectical systematic treatment preferred. Theology became almost entirely scholastic. It was regarded as complete, not susceptible of development, looking backwards and not forwards, more interested in the vindication of authoritative names than in the cultivation of those original studies which are needed for its advance. This movement, which for a time had its centre at Rome, found its most brilliant expression in Father Kleutgen's work on the theology of the old times.

The principle of de Maistre's philosophy which is common to works so discordant in spirit and so dissimilar in execution as the *Essai sur l'Indifférence*, Ventura's *Traditionalism*, and the *Theologie der Vorzeit* of the accomplished Roman Jesuit, has displayed itself in politics as vividly as in theology. The same dread of an outward independent criterion, which causes divines to reject the facts of history, leads canonists, in disputes involving civil questions, to turn from the State to the sole and supreme authority of the Church. Building upon the weakness of human reason and the malice of the outer world, the men of this school arrived at the opinion that, as civil interests are subservient to those of religion, the civil law is necessarily subject to that of the Church. At the same time they could not admit that the interests of the Church might be sacrificed to the letter of her own law. They concluded that no merely political institution, no legislation which is so indirectly connected with the moral law that it can assume various forms in various Christian states, could be permitted to stand in the way of considerations of religious advantage. In canon law, they said, the Holy See can dispense from any obligation which is not of divine right. Why should civil law be more sacred? If the Pope can permit a brother and sister to marry for the sake of expediency, how can any opinion of political right and wrong be allowed to supersede that highest argument? They held, therefore, that no spiritual advantage could be surrendered in obedience to the variable legislation of any local power. Hence arose a system very remote from the servile loyalty of the Gallican Church, a system which assumed on many occasions a liberal and sometimes a revolutionary appearance. But if no civil authority was sacred beyond the limit of religious expediency, no civil rights could enjoy a higher immunity. The Church could make no distinction between political freedom and wrong, but must unite with that cause whose alliance promised most profit. The standard of political duty was held to exist for those only who recognized no higher law; those who did so felt no difficulty in bestowing an equal and consistent admiration for Gregory XVI, rebuking the Archbishop of Paris for his legitimist sympathies, and for Pius IX, supporting the Neapolitan Bourbons. Thus it was made to appear that Catholics are not guided in public life by sentiments which constitute the honour of other men, and that they absolutely repudiate political principle. A feeling of distrust and of contempt was thereby engendered in the minds of governments and nations. The religion which suffered by this conduct was appealed to by one party, and condemned by the other, as countenancing it. Catholic parties did duty for the Church, and eagerly transferred to her the obloquy which they themselves had incurred.

This theory, which has so much affected both theology and politics, has exercised a still deeper influence on the treatment of history; and in this field it has passed more gradually through the successive steps which have led to its complete display. First, it was held, the interests of religion, which are opposed to the study of history, require that precautions should be taken to make it innocuous where it cannot be quite suppressed. If it is lawful to conceal facts or statements, it is equally right to take out their sting when they must be brought forward. It is not truth, but error, which is suppressed by this process, the object of which is to prevent a false impression being made on the minds of men. For the effects of these facts or statements is to prejudice men against the Church, and to lead them to false conclusions concerning her nature. Whatever tends to weaken this adverse impression contributes really to baffle a falsehood and sustain the cause of truth. The statement, however true in its own subordinate place, will only serve to mislead in a higher order of truth, where the consequences may be fatal to the conscience and happiness of those who hear it without any qualification. Words, moreover, often convey to the uninstructed mind ideas contrary to their real significance, and the interpretation of facts is yet more delusive. Put the case of a Protestant sincerely seeking to be instructed, and earnestly inquiring into the spirit and practices of the Church, who perhaps on the very threshold of conversion, when the dogmatic difficulties are over and the longing for the sacraments is awakened, asks if it be true that the spiritual rulers of the Church have been sometimes men of scandalous lives, or whether Catholicism has encouraged or ordained persecution. If he finds the inquiry answered affirmatively in Catholic books, it is probable that he may be disappointed, or even disgusted, and that a few idle sentences of an indiscreet and superficial writer may undo the work of his conversion, and bring ruin to his soul. What end could that writer have in view that would bear comparison with the evil of such a consummation? Nothing obliged him to write at all, still less to write on so delicate a topic, and to handle it without reserve. If his words were true, they still deceived the reader who found in them the evidence of great defects in the Catholic system. The real duty of Catholics is not to gratify an idle curiosity or mere literary vanity, but to bring souls to Christ. The next step is to annul the effect of what has been said and what cannot be unsaid. This may be done in several ways. Reprisals are often successful; for in choosing between rival systems it is natural to compare them. But there are cases in which this argument does not apply, and minds on which it is without effect. Here there may be room for the simple contradiction—a favourite weapon with de Maistre. There have been many forgeries in the world, and it is natural to suspect that they proceed from enemies of truth. If documents on which the Church long relied are proved to be the works of fraud, it may reasonably be assumed that some of those on which her adversaries depend will ultimately meet with the same fate. And if the document is genuine, the writer may have been inspired with bad motives, or his text interpolated, or his information unauthentic. A great deal may be done in this way; and where there is really no room for doubt, it is still unnecessary to say so. For the object is not the discovery of objective truth, but the production of a right belief in a mind. When all is in vain—when the argument by reprisals, and the argument by denial, and the argument by insinuation of motives, or imputation of fraud, and last of all the argument by diversion, have failed, there is the last resource of admitting the fact and defending its righteousness. This may be done in two ways. The most common is to say that the only blame falls on those who shrink from heroic deeds, and judge them by the paltry cowardly standard of a selfish morality.[1] The other is to attribute acts which are hard to justify to the superior insight of those who committed them in the higher interests of religion, and their superiority to the conventional regulations which guide ordinary men. The examples of the Old Testament, the wisdom of the saints, the special illumination which God vouchsafes to those who rule His Church, may be appealed to in support of this argument. It is the duty of the son to cover the shame of his father; and the Catholic owes it to the Church to defend her against every adverse fact as he would defend the honour of his mother. He will not coldly examine the value of testimony, or concede any point because it is hard to meet, or assist with unbiased mind in the discovery of truth before he knows what its bearing may be. Assured that nothing injurious to the Church can be true, he will combat whatever bears an unfavourable semblance with every attainable artifice and weapon. Mindful of the guilt of those who scandalize the weak, or interpose between the waverer and the Church, and fully conscious that a lie may in some cases be the nearest approach to truth, he will allow no adverse statement to pass without contradiction, or without at least an antidote which may remove its danger. For there is but one thing needful; and all facts and all opinions are worthless except to minister to the salvation of men and the promotion of religion.

Those who traversed unconsciously the course which marks the genesis of these views, and arrived at the extreme we have indicated, were generally sincere at least in the belief that they

[1] M. de Falloux has shown, in his essay "Le Parti Catholique" (*Le Correspondant*, N.S. ii, 192), how this temper carried a party among the Catholics of France to defend the massacre of St Bartholomew and the revocation of the Edict of Nantes. He quotes the following characteristic passage from the *Univers*: "Aujourd'hui, avec les ridicules idées de liberté et de respect des opinions, avec l'opprobre public jeté sur l'inquisition et la crainte de la faire revivre, avec l'absence enfin de foi et de règle dans les consciences, peut-on supposer que les maires soupçonneront qu'ils ont en ce point quelque devoir à remplir."

were defending the cause of religion, and not merely their own interests or opinions; and they succeeded in communicating their belief to Protestants. The enemies of the Church supposed from their example that she could only be defended on the principle that the means are justified by the end; and this identification of her methods with those of a party within her led them to think that in exposing the latter they were tearing down a real outwork of Catholicism. They showed themselves expert in this, without discovering that they were really serving the Church which her own defenders were betraying. But those defenders were not conscious traitors, and honestly thought their own cause that of the Church. Hence they shrank from exposure and danger of scandal, and insisted that Catholics should not show them up, or renounce complicity with their arms, lest the world should lose all confidence in Catholic controversy, and come to believe that a cause so defended cannot be good. And when indignant men vindicated the Church from the suspicion which this conduct had brought upon her, they were accused of introducing discord into the sanctuary, of firing on their own troops, of exhibiting to adversaries the repulsive spectacle of internal discord in a Church whose mark is unity, of bringing sacred things before the incompetent judgement of the outer world. This consideration, and the fear of injuring influences that might be powerful for good, have restrained many from repudiating practices from which their hearts revolted.

The extracts which we are about to give in illustration of this spirit are taken chiefly from books of a popular kind, which have very little authority to lose. We might begin with Damberger's voluminous *History of the Middle Ages*. It would be hard to find in the whole range of Protestant literature since the Centuriators a more monstrous production. But the character of the work is so notorious that, in spite of the real erudition of the author, it has fallen into an obscurity which it is better not to disturb. A far cleverer writer, Wilhelm von Schütz, whose works were much read and admired twenty years ago, will supply us with an example of German aberrations in this direction. In the year 1845 he wrote a tract on the massacre of St Bartholomew, with a view to vindicate the Catholic cause from that long-standing imputation. He explains the case as follows: the massacre was planned for the purpose of ruining the Catholics, not the Huguenots;

and its author was not the Catholic royal family, but the Protestant leader, Henry of Navarre, whose marriage to Margaret of
Valois was part of a scheme to betray the Catholic Church and
introduce a reactionary policy in favour of the Protestants. His
accomplices were pseudo-Catholics acting in the Huguenot
interest. The mistake is to suppose that the massacre was a
blow aimed at the Huguenots, a conspiracy against them; it was
a conspiracy in their favour ... The court had sold Catholicism
to Protestantism ... Attention was to be diverted from the mixed
marriage. Therefore the spectacle of a pretended Protestant
massacre was instituted in order to deceive the Catholics.[1] In
short, it was a got-up thing, perfectly understood by the so-called
victims, and a shameful deception on the unfortunate Catholics.

Whilst Schütz in Germany attributes the massacre to the
Protestant interest, Rohrbacher in France shows that it proceeded from Protestant principles. His way of defending the
Catholics is to lay the blame on Protestant doctrines. Judged by
the Reformers' standard, "the massacre was a divine act, which
deserves our respect and admiration"; and "Charles IX had a
right to do what he did, not only as king but as private individual;
and any one may go and do likewise, whenever he has the power
and inclination."[2]

[1] "Darin berught das Missverstehen der Geschichte, dass man sich einbildet
die sogenannte Blutchochz eit sei ein Schlag gegen die Hugenotten, eine Verschwörung gegen sie gewesen: es war eine Verschwörung für die Hugenotten. Der Hof
hatte den Katholizismus an den Protestantismus verkauft und gab dafür den betro-
genen Katholiken ein Feuerwerk, das scheinen sollte einen Schlag gegen die
Hugenotten, statt mit Raketen, mit Blut zu feiern. Das Wesentliche lag in dem
Kathlisch-Protestantischen Beilager. Dies sollte niemand sehen: von ihm wollte
man die Blicke abwenden. Deshalb ward das Feuerwerk eines Protestantische
sein sollenden Blutbades abgebrannt, dessen Prasseln die Katholiken zu täuschen
die Bestimmung hatte. Die sogenannte Bluthochzeit war eine Anstiftung von
Pseudo-Katholiken zu Gunsten einer Katholisch-Hugenottischen Reaktion. Dies
geschah nur um die Katholiken zu täuschen und sie glauben zu machen, das, was
in hugenottischem Interesse geschahen war, sei zugunsten der Katholiken verübt
worden" (*Die aufgehellte Bartholomäusnacht*, pp. 11, 25, 31, 34).

[2] "D'après la croyance des huguenots et de leurs patriarches Luther et Calvin,
que Dieu opère en nous le mal comme le bien, c'est une opération divine qui
mérite nos respects et notre admiration. D'après le principe fondamental du protestantisme, que chacun n'a d'autre règle ni d'autre juge que soi-même, Charles
IX avait droit de faire ce qu'il a fait, non seulement comme roi, mais encore
comme particulier; et à chacun il est permit d'en faire autant, dès qu'il en a l'envie
et la puissance" (*Histoire Universelle de L'Église*, xxiv, 640).

The sixteenth century offers many tempting opportunities for manipulations of this kind. Rohrbacher's tone and manner may be gathered from what he says of Queen Elizabeth. Speaking of her refusal to marry, he says: "L'histoire remarque en effet qu'elle n'a pas eu un mari, mais plus d'un: Lingard en nomme jusqu'à huit."[1] The heading of the paragraph where this occurs, in which the author follows a notorious calumny of Cobbett, runs thus: "La papesse Elizabeth, avec ses maris et ses bâtards, ses emportements et sa tyrannie". Rohrbacher is still more unscrupulous in dealing with the death of Henry III. He was stabbed by a Dominican, and fell crying that he had been murdered by "ce méchant moine". For fear of scandal the historian says not a word of all this. Jacques Clément had only been "educated in a Dominican monastery"; he was carried away by Protestant principles, which justify his act, and Rohrbacher insinuates that he defied the authority of the Pope, and was at heart a Huguenot. So that the reader would never learn that the regicide was a Dominican, but might be led to suppose that he was in fact a crypto-Calvinist.[2]

In comparison with the systematic deceitfulness of Rohrbacher, the arts of Audin appear innocent. He is partial, unjust, and very often ill-informed or misguided, but he is rarely guilty of wilful mendacity. No man is honest who refuses to censure vice in persons of exalted station; but there is after all only a qualified dishonesty in such passages as that on the election of Alexander VI: "In these difficult times a man of the character of Alexander might well be regarded as an instrument of Providence. There is nothing, therefore, but what is quite natural in his election." Audin's irresolute wavering between straightforwardness and falsehood is fairly illustrated by his critical remark

---

[1] *Histoire Universelle de L'Église*, xxiv, 583.

[2] "Il fut tué la veille par Jacques Clément, né au village de Sorbonne, près de Sense, élevé au couvent des Dominicains de cette ville, et âgé alors de vingt-deux ans. Les assistants le mirent en pièces sur l'heure même. Il s'était porté a ce crime par de prétendue révélations. D'après le principe fondamental du Protestantisme, que chacun n'a de règle et de juge pour sa conscience que soi-même, Clément avait droit de faire ce qu'il a fait. D'après cet autre principe de Calvin et de Luther, que Dieu opère en nous le mal comme le bien, le régicide de Jaques Clément était une action divine. Il est criminel comme Catholique d'avoir agi en Huguenot, pour mettre la main, lui particulier, sur un roi, sur le chef d'une nation, sans le jugement ni l'ordre d'aucun tribunal supérieur à ce roi et à cette nation" (ibid., xxiv, 655).

on the authority of Burchard: "Nous voudrions bien savoir comment on doit s'en rapporter aveuglément au Protestant, qui s'est chargé de déchiffrer ce journal."[1] He knew perfectly well that MSS. of the Journal abound—there are at least half a dozen at Paris alone—and they have often been consulted by historians; but he preferred to take advantage of the badness of the published text to excuse his refusal to avail himself of the authority of the journalist.

M. Nicolas, one of the most popular Catholic writers in France, in a volume written for the purpose of repudiating the co-operation proposed by M. Guizot for the defence of society against the principles of the Revolution, has been obliged to speak of the moral and social influence of the Protestant religion. Wishing to show that Luther encouraged polygamy, he quotes the Reformer's well-known answer to Brück, which, though sufficiently discreditable, is not enough so for M. Nicolas: "Luther lui répondit par cet oracle vraiment delphien: 'Il m'est impossible, en vertu de l'Ecriture Sainte, de défendre à qui ce soit de prendre plusieurs femmes en même temps; mais je ne voudrais pas être le premier à introduire cette louable coutume chez les chrétiens'."[2] Here every word is omitted by which Luther expresses his real sentiment on the matter; another is coolly introduced which converts an expression of dislike and disapproval into a positive recommendation, and the words "nollem primo introduci" are insidiously misinterpreted. Although the passage is well known, we must quote it for the purpose of comparison: "Ego sane fateor, me non posse prohibere, si quis plures vult uxores ducere, nec repugnat Sacris literis; verum tamen apud Christianos id exempli nollem primo introduci, apud quos decet etiam ea intermittere, quæ licita sunt, pro vitando scandalo, et pro honestate vitæ."[3]

It is recorded that when Papabroch, at the beginning of his long career as a Bollandist, visited Rome, and explained to the Pope the scheme of that great undertaking, Alexander VII expressed delight at hearing that there were methods by which the authentic Lives of the Saints might be distinguished from spurious fabrications. The art of criticism was then just begin-

[1] *Leon X*, i, 157, 304.
[2] *Du Protestantisme et de toutes les Hérésies dans leur Rapport avec la Socialisme*, p. 560.
[3] *Luther's Briefe*, ed. de Wette, ii, 459.

ning; it soon made progress in the hands of Mabillon, Ruinart, and Tillemont; and, in the perfection it has now attained, it is one of the surest defences of the Catholic system. But to writers of the school we have described its control is naturally unwelcome; for it prevents the arbitrary selection of facts and authorities, interferes with the perfect freedom of speech, and establishes something different from convenience as a test of truth. They therefore reject its laws, not only on principle, but in detail and in practice, and deliberately return to the traditions of a period when the means of distinguishing truth from falsehood in ecclesiastical literature did not exist. Dom Guéranger, the learned Abbot of Solesmes, is the most outspoken of these systematic adversaries of modern knowledge. The critical spirit of the close of the seventeenth century, in which the members of the orders took the lead, and in which they were followed by the most learned men among the Jesuits as well as the Jansenists, sprang, he says, from a spirit of party, and belongs legitimately to the infidel Germans. If we would avoid scepticism, we must revise the canons of critical science, and we shall recover much contested literature.[1] On these principles, Dom Guéranger proceeds to rehabilitate many rejected documents and to revive exploded legends, such as the baptism of Constantine by Pope Sylvester. Before long we shall probably hear of writers who defend the authenticity of the Donation of Constantine, and the works of the Areopagite, and who will compensate for their credulity by an equally wilful rejection of authentic works; for the opposite exaggeration of literary scepticism and literary credulity are manifestations of the same reckless spirit.

Dom Guéranger's denial of the principles of science has necessarily conducted him to a position of hostility to all those who understand the manner in which learning serves religion. In particular, he has attacked the most accomplished layman

[1] "On commence à se douter déjà que l'entrainement et l'esprit de parti ont été pour quelque chose dans la rénovation pour ainsi dire complète qui s'opéra, vers la fin du XVIIe siècle, dans la science de l'antiquité ecclésiastique. Les principes critique qui prévalurent alors, et que les écoles incroyantes de l'Allemagne appliquent de si bon cœur aux évangiles même, ont l'inconvénient de conduire logiquement au pyrrhonisme historique; les esprits sensés se trouvent donc réduits à les soumettre à l'examen; et l'on ne peut nier qu'il n'y ait là un profit tout clair pour la science, en même temps qu'un secours pour la religion et la société, qui ne sauraient s'accommoder du scepticisme (*Essai sur le Naturalisme Contemporain*, i, 227).

among the French Catholics and the most eminent divine of the
French clergy; and he has elicited replies from both. We will
quote a passage from that of the Prince de Broglie, because it
describes so accurately the method of the school of which Dom
Guéranger is perhaps the most learned representative. He had
assailed the *History of the Fourth Century* in three articles in the
Univers, which were the beginning of those *Essays on Naturalism*
from which we have already quoted. M. de Broglie says: "In
the first and second articles I am a timorous Christian, who, to
please the philosophers, attenuates dogmas, dissembles and
tones down miracles, loves to give to the facts of the Gospel and
Church history a natural character and a rational interpretation. In the third, on the contrary, I am transformed into a blind
enemy of reason, who denies it even the power of demonstrating
the existence of God, and thus falls under the liberal decisions of
the Church, so clearly confirmed by a recent document. By
turns, I have passed so severe a judgement on the ancient nations
as to cast doubts on the goodness of God, and on the other hand,
have carried indulgence so far as completely to excuse idolatry.
Either I am guilty of the most contrary things, or everything
will serve to accuse me."[1]

While the Prince de Broglie treats his assailant with great consideration, the reply of Monseigneur Maret to the attack on his
work on the Dignity of Human Reason and the Necessity of
Divine Revelation strikes more vigorously home. Dom Guéranger had accused him of asserting the absolute necessity of revelation, and the impotence of the human reason. He was reminded
that M. Maret teaches only the moral necessity of revelation,
and that these words are in the heading of the chapter which he
criticized. To this he replied that he had, indeed, seen the words
in the summary, but that he had not paid regard to them, because they were contradicted—not by the text, but—by the title
of the book.[2] Monseigneur Maret adds some touches to the

[1] "Réponse aux Attaques du R. P. Guéranger", *Questions de Religion et d'Histoire*,
ii, 221.

[2] "Quand mon honorable ami M. l'Abbé Hugonin, s'étonnant d'une accusation
que rien ne justifie, rappelle à D. Guéranger que je soutiens uniquement la nécessité morale de la révélation, et qu'il a pu lire ces mots dans le sommaire même
du chapitre qu'il critique, que répond M. l'Abbé de Solesme? Il a vu en effet, dit-
il, ces mots dans le sommaire; mais il n'en a pas tenu compte, parce qu'ils sont
contredits par le titre du livre, qui porte, sans correctif, *Nécessité de la Révélation*.

description of the methods given by the Prince de Broglie: "I have shown that, in order to avenge some imaginary concessions to a separatist philosophy, and perhaps also unconsciously gratifying the jealousies of party spirit, Dom Guéranger consents to misrepresent, mutilate, and suppress my texts. He makes me say exactly the contrary of what I say; and if his quotation had been entirely faithful, he could not have made himself the accuser of my book. Carried away by controversy, he goes so far as to affirm absolute propositions which, if so stated, would deserve severe censure, and would be reached by pontifical condemnations."[1]

Nothing is more characteristic of the spirit of Dom Guéranger's writing than his repudiation of the liberty of conscience, and his denial of the inclination of the Church to freedom. M. de Broglie had written: "C'est donc avec la liberté et non avec le pouvoir qu'est l'alliance fructueuse et naturelle de l'Église. Elle a été autrefois le plus éclairé des pouvoirs, elle doit être aujourd'hui la plus pure et la plus regulière des libertés." Perhaps this may not be a very philosophical or exact statement; but to Dom Guéranger it appears as an insult to the Church: "De quel droit osez-vous ainsi dégrader celle qui n'a été élevée a la dignité d'Epouse d'un Dieu que pour régner avec lui?"[2] And in asserting the rights of the Church he is careful to assert his enmity to freedom: "Est-ce que par hasard l'Église serait exclue de la liberté, par la raison que l'erreur n'y a pas droit?"[3]

In this matter of the freedom of conscience Father Perrone, the last writer whom we shall cite among the representatives of the unscrupulous school, speaks with much greater judgement. But as a historical question he treats it with as little reverence for the moral obligations of literature as an Orangeman could have shown. Whilst the State punishes open non-conformity, but is compelled to respect concealed dissent, the peculiarity of the

---

Est il permis à un homme grave, à un religieux, à un prêtre, lorsqu'il s'agit de l'honneur d'un autre prêtre, de recourir à de pareilles échappatoires? Dans presque tous les traités de la religion, ne trouvons-nous pas un chapitre intitulé 'De necessitate revelationis', sans autre explication?" (Lettre de M. l'Abbé Maret, Doyen de la Faculté de Théologie de Paris à Nos Seigneurs les Evêques de France sur les attaques dirigées contre son livre: *Dignité de la Raison Humaine et Nécessité de la Révélation Divine*, par le R. P. D. Guéranger, 1858, p. 15).

[1] ibid., p. 23.   [2] *Essais*, Preface, p. xxxv.   [3] ibid., p. xvii.

penalties imposed by the Church consists in their being directed against the sin of the individual, not against the danger to society; hence they may be incurred by thought as well as by word or deed. The object of the Church is always the conversion of the sinner, whilst that of the State is simply his exclusion or suppression. Therefore it has always been deemed unnatural that capital punishment for heresy should be inflicted by the priesthood; and those who, like de Maistre[1] or Balmez, have defended the Inquisition as a political tribunal in Spain, have denied that persecution ever raged in Rome. Father Perrone boldly denies that the Church proceeded against private opinions, and says that executions for heresy were rare or unknown in Rome.[2]

In his catechism of the Protestant religions he used arguments of the most calumnious kind in order to turn the mind of the people away from it—that the Reformers were men whose private lives were infamous; that Calvin died of a shameful disease, blaspheming and invoking the devil; and that the reform of morals and discipline commonly attributed to the Council of Trent, was proceeding prosperously, and the Church improving daily, when the Reformation interrupted the reform.[3] Such language, if it was not intended to mislead uneducated persons, would read like a satire on the Council of the Lateran.

It would have been easy to quote from the writings of Monseigneur Gaume against the classics passages more striking than

---

[1] "Jamais le prêtre n'éleva d'échafaud; il y monte seulement comme martyr ou consolateur: il ne prêche que miséricorde et clémence; et sur tous les points du globe, il n'a versé d'autre sang que le sien. Voulez vous de plus connaître, par l'expérience, le véritable esprit sacerdotal sur ce point essentiel? Etudiez-le dans le pays où le prêtre a tenue le sceptre ou le tient encore ... Assurément, c'est dans le gouvernement des pontifes que le véritable esprit du sacerdoce doit se montrer de la manière le moins équivoque" (*Lettres sur l'Inquisition Espagnole*, pp. 18, 21, 22).

[2] "La chiesa non ha mai proceduto contro le opinione finche questa rimaneano nella conscienza or nel cervello balzano di chi le aveva. In Roma poi o non v'e o appena v'e qualche rarissimo esempio di alcuno messo a molte per sola eresia" (*Catechismo intorno alla Chiesa Cattolica ad uso del Popolo*, pp. 93, 94).

[3] "Gia parecchi di essi ai tempi di Lutero reano tolti, ed altri scemati, e la riforma dei costumi e della disciplina si perfezionava oggidi, allorche risorsero quegli uomini ribelli contro la chiesa.—Tali sono i corifei del protestantismo, uomini cioe, che a detta di un protestante, erano tutti per la loro malvagita degni del capestro.—Calvino per ultimo mori disperato bestemmiando e invocando il diavolo, di una malattia la piu vergognosa, roso dai vermi" (*Catechismo intorno al Protestantismo ad uso del Popolo*, pp. 11, 23).

these; but his writings belong to a different movement, and the object of his attack is not knowledge in itself, but profane learning. "It is the devil", says Gregory the Great, "who takes away from certain persons the desire of mastering secular sciences, because he knows how much they serve us in religious questions." The *Vex Rongeur* was the prelude to a general attack on the pursuit of all learning that is not purely religious; but writers like Father Ventura and others whom we have quoted went beyond this, and thought that even the things of the Church cannot be the objects of scientific knowledge. There is but one step from the denial of certainty to the denial of truth; and the theory of the applicability of falsehood followed immediately on the theory of the utility of ignorance. By a similar process calumny was grafted on mendacity.

There are two things which it specially behoves every Catholic engaged in controversy to observe in his treatment of adversaries: that the discussion ought to be a means of converting them from error, instead of repelling them from truth by the fault of its defenders; and that no bitterness or personality should scandalize them by occasions of sin. The course enjoined by the Church is to win over opponents by considerate, gentle, generous, and affectionate treatment, joined to the most uncompromising and relentless exposure of their errors. If gentleness is a duty in the case of those errors against faith which are sinful in themselves, it is even more imperative where the error is a defect of knowledge, which, though indeed it may be a consequence of sin, can hardly be traced to its origin in the will. All Christians must in some measure feel and acknowledge this duty: but Catholics especially can judge of its importance by the horror with which the Church regards the giving of scandal, combined with her doctrine of exclusive salvation. It has been often disregarded in former disputes; but in our time a regular theory has been devised which inverts the law and renounces the Catholic spirit. Two paths appear to have led to this transition. One is the transfer of ecclesiastical language to another sphere. Those who have the sacramental power to bind and to loose, and who administer the ecclesiastical discipline, speak, by virtue of their office, in language of severity and commination even to individuals. It may fall within their province to utter the most solemn maledictions, and they may judge it probable that vehement denunciations will move to repentance those who are not utterly deaf to a voice that unites all the kinds of authority that belong to the father, the judge, and the king. Naturally, and almost imperceptibly, in an age when laymen exerted through the press an influence not less deep, and an authority often more extended, than the bishops themselves, they usurped the same weapons, spoke in the same tone, and affected to deal blows of equal weight. When the most illustrious prelates themselves, like the Bishops of Orleans and Mentz, mingled in the fray and placed themselves on equal terms with adversaries, it very easily happened that some of their privileges were forgotten by those who fought beside as well as against them, and that the thunder was sometimes imitated by those who could not wield the lightning.

Another course was more consciously followed with the same result. Catholics continually see things stated against the Church by educated and even learned men which, they are persuaded, cannot be sincerely believed. They are aware of the malignity of some, and are unable to credit the ignorance in which others persist with regard to Catholic matters. When, therefore, the inventions of men whose trade is lying are repeated by men whose profession is controversy, it is almost impossible to understand that ignorance can assume so closely the guise of wilful calumny. The plea of ignorance may be allowed in the case of Dr Cumming or Mr Whalley, but how can it be urged for Baron Bunsen, or M. Michelet, or Mr Buckle? It is scarcely possible for Catholics to avoid feeling aversion and contempt for men whom they conceive to be wilfully distorting truth; and therefore, instead of confining themselves to the refutation of falsehood, which they are persuaded their opponent does not desire, they endeavour to expose his iniquity. This temper of mind was gradually transferred from controversy with aliens to discussions among Catholics, where there was the new element of insubordination, to which the origins of errors might be attributed. A Catholic might reasonably be supposed to know the religion he had been taught from childhood, and in which he ought to have been more and more confirmed by the practices of piety. If he erred, there was at once a suspicion that he had neglected those practices; or that he was moved by the dislike of obedience to hold what was not held by his teachers; or that he had culpably turned away from the proper guides to hearken to the flattering seduc-

tions of hostile parties. In every such dispute a question of morality was directly at issue. Both antagonists could not be equally
in harmony with the sentiment of authorities which both acknowledged. In casting off this blame from himself, each necessarily fixed it on the other as a prejudice against his virtue. But
where a writer is persuaded that his adversary is persisting in his
error insincerely, or from wrong motives, the triumph he seeks
is not to convince but to convict him. He desires to produce an
effect, not upon him, but upon the audience, which may be
impressed by the exposure of the man, while he will be insensible
to the confutation of his views. Therefore he strives less for truth
than for effect, and abandons the argument in order to pursue
the man. He tries to gain every advantage over him; and the
best chance he has is to disturb his presence of mind by making
him lose his temper. That which will irritate him most is most
likely to make him expose himself and give an opening to reply.
It would be too long to inquire how many things contributed to
promote this habit: in some places, the want of that forbearance
which public assemblies often engender between men subject in
common to a local special disciplinary system; in others, the
terror which anticipated or the temper which followed great
social convulsions; in others, the extreme fierceness or perfidy
of an infidel press. It was soon justified by theory; and in practice
it seems becoming more general and more vehement.

To these combined causes it is due that a strong and vitupera-
tive opposition has been uniformly offered to the progress of
Catholic thought. With scarcely one exception, all those who
were most eminent in religious science have been denounced, by
men not less zealous and devout than themselves, as the cor-
rupters of doctrine and enemies of the Church; and the distance
between the two parties was such as to justify a doubt as to their
agreement in the same faith or in the same morality. This persecution of those who really advanced religious knowledge is, on
the one hand, a natural and direct consequence of that common
spirit which manifests itself in different ways in the philosophy
of Ventura, the scholasticism of Kleutgen and Clemens, the
politics of Donoso Cortés, the polemics of Veuillot, the educational theories of Gaume, and the historical method of Rohrbacher and Guéranger, and, on the other, the most characteristic
symptom of the present condition of the Catholic Church. It

assailed alike the two greatest thinkers among the Italian clergy, Rosmini and Gioberti, and in a less degree the best of their ecclesiastical historians, whom their knowledge of the Middle Ages prevents from becoming the supporters of things as they are—the Benedictine Tosti, the Oratorian Capecelatro, and the Dominican Marchese. In France it fell on the theoretical defenders of profane learning, like the Bishop of Orleans, and on the first Catholic authorities on theology and metaphysics, Monseigneur Maret and Father Gratry. The two foremost living divines in Germany, Döllinger and Kuhn, were accused in like manner—the one for his treatment of Church history, the other for a dogmatic method which seems heretical to the advocates of the scholastic theology; both alike for their theory of development. The few laymen out of Germany who occupy a rank in Catholic literature approaching that of the ecclesiastical leaders fared scarcely better. The Baron d'Eckstein was held a dreamer and an innovator, indifferent to the Dogma of the Church, for reasons such as in earlier times procured Gerbert and Bacon the reputation of wizards. The Prince de Broglie, while he was attacked by Donoso Cortés with the courteous arms of chivalry for preferring liberty to feudalism, incurred the ruder censures of Dom Guéranger because he recognized in history, besides the action of Providence, the operation of natural and secondary causes. Beyond the Atlantic the spirit is the same. When Dr Brownson, urged forward by his powerful and independent mind, emancipated himself from the narrow and intolerant school which in the first moments of his conversion he had been taught to consider the legitimate form of Catholic thought, his great services did not protect him from denunciations as violent as those which, in the immaturity of his Catholic ideas, he had heaped on Dr Newman. These, however, are difficulties in the way of improvement, which eminent men are able to overcome; and it is well that they should confront the obstacles which they alone can ultimately remove.

That which one class of Catholics sought by a sacrifice of truth on behalf of religion, others aimed at by making some scientific opinion the arbiter of doctrine. If there was a deliberate denial of the moral law, there was on the other hand an unconscious surrender of dogmatic truths. The philosophies of Hermes and Günther, Frohschammer's theory of the independence of speculation, and the extreme proposals of ecclesiastical reform made by Hirscher, before he became the adviser and defender of the Archbishop of Freiburg, are instances of such a failure resulting rather from confidence in human reason than from timid solicitude for the safety of God's Church. But the errors of these men proceed from no common principle, and in no wise agree together. The real antithesis to the spurious Ultramontanism that ramified from de Maistre into so many branches is to be found, not in the opposite errors, but in the true course which deflects on neither side.

The rise of the school we have considered depended, first, on the low ebb of scientific knowledge, and on its open hostility to religion, and, secondly, on the absence of any literary co-operation of Catholics with Protestants. Among its leaders there were men of great virtues and talents, and at least one man of genius; but there is not one to whom secular learning is really indebted. As they renounced more and more the results and spirit of modern science, they repelled Protestants, and ended by presenting religion in an aspect which did not entirely attract converts. The want of contact with men who believed in other religions left them in ignorance of real difficulties and of their true solution. To the opposite circumstance of familiarity with non-Catholic science we trace the formation of that Ultramontanism which we have described as the highest intellectual development of the Catholic system.

The prostration of religion on the Continent at the close of the last century was shared by the Protestants in an equal measure. But it was followed by a revived literary activity among them to which there is no parallel in modern history except the Revival of the fifteenth century, to which it bears a real resemblance. For, first, the intellectual movement which proceeded from Weimar to Jena, and Halle, and Heidelberg, and then to other German universities, like that of the Medicean age, obeyed no religious impulse, but was indifferent to doctrine. The Churches were not then either feared for their power or envied for their wealth; and Rationalism ignored, as it had no inducement to assail, them. Secondly, the mental exertion of the period of Goethe, like that of Erasmus, had no definite practical end to attain, no reward to earn but that of literary enjoyment, no mission to fulfil but that of satisfying the thirst for knowledge.

Thirdly, the Revival of the nineteenth century, like that of the fifteenth, was distinguished principally by the recovery from oblivion of a forgotten age. But here the analogy is exhausted; for the effect of reviving antiquity was exactly contrary to that of the mediaeval restoration. The learning of the Renaissance was antiquarian. It overleapt a vast interval which it consigned to a complete neglect, in order to resuscitate an extinct society. It set up a remote ideal in all the arts of life, and bent its own civilization to fit the model it had disinterred. Therefore it predominated more in art than in science, because of its luxurious and idle temper, and it was also artificial, unnatural, imitative, and, like all imitators, arbitrary, and in theories of government absolute, and often revolutionary.

The character of the mediaeval Revival which is the distinctive achievement of the age in which we live was not antiquarian but historical. Its study was not of death, but of life—not of a world of ruins, but of that which is our own. Therefore its lesson was a lesson of continuity, not of sudden restoration of servile copying. It taught respect for the past, encouraged patriotic sentiments, and awakened the memory of hereditary rights. The study of national history, literature, and art was one of its most important results. This impulse was strongest in the north of Germany. There the feelings of men towards the Catholic Church were free from bitterness. She had been their companion in misfortune, had suffered under the same tyranny, and had been delivered by the same victories, and nowhere seemed to them formidable or oppressive. As the patriotic feeling carried back these thoughts to the preponderance of their country, the Reformation ceased to be the supreme glory of their nation, and the boundary of their retrospect. They recognized in its system one of the chief elements in their history, one of the most powerful influences over their ideas; but they also recalled a happier period of national greatness, when the princes of the Church were the best and the most beloved rulers of Germany. It was remembered that among the emperors who continued the long struggle with Rome there were many who could not be remembered by Germans with unmixed pride—that Henry IV and Henry VI were men of evil lives, Frederick I a tyrant, and Frederick II an alien; whilst the most devoted protectors of the Church—Charlemagne, St Henry, Otto the Great, Henry III, and Rudolph of Habsburg—were the greatest of the rulers of the Empire.

Men approached these studies with minds that had been trained in pursuits free from the temptations of party spirit, and from the influence of religious opinions. They came from the study of antiquity, which from the time of Heyne had its home in the schools of Germany; and they applied to the investigation of the mediaeval records the tone and method of classical philology. Other causes contributed to this indifferent rather than impartial temper. The union of the Prussian Protestants had expressed the ruling disregard of dogmatic definitions; and the vague theology which it established could not so heartily oppose Catholicism as a more consistent system. Something must also be attributed to the influence of the Hegelian philosophy on the Rationalists. The pantheism of that school, regarding all things alike as manifestations of the same universal nature, substituted the test of success, and even the order of succession, for the distinction of right and wrong. It was held that all religion is a form of truth, good of its kind; but that the law of life is progress, and the earlier is less perfect than the later. Therefore the advance constituted by Catholicism over the religions of antiquity was explained with the same curious interest as the progress, effected by the Reformation upon the mediaeval Church, or by the Philosophy of the Absolute on dogmatic Protestantism. The question of truth resolved itself into one of fact. Events were studied in their nature rather than in their character; and mankind was allowed to exhibit properties rather than qualities. The action of divine or human will was alike excluded; and accident was denied as well as morality. The Hegelians asserted the unbroken continuity of cause and effect, and held that all the phenomena of history are reasonable and intelligible. There ensued a kind of optimism very conducive to a dispassionate treatment of the past. Then out of the Hegelian philosophy arose the school of infidel and almost atheistic criticism, which ignored the dogmatic differences, and reserved its hardest blows for the foundations of Protestantism.

These causes did not indeed dissipate ignorance and prejudice, but they promoted a critical study of details, and prevented the interference of passion, or interest, or zeal. A school of historians arose who made it their business to write on the Middle Ages as they wrote on the Persian War; who spoke of the Church as they spoke of the Areopagus, and applied to the most obscure moments of her history those tests of credibility and authenticity which had been lavished on Herodotus and Livy. They had nothing of the spirit of panegyrists or accusers; but with all their learning, acuteness, and equity, most of these men were destitute of that faculty or experience which would have enabled them to understand the significance of religion. They understood, better than any Catholic writers before them, the outward action of the ecclesiastical organism, the moral, intellectual, and social influence of the Church; but they knew nothing of her religious character. They betrayed the same incapacity in the study of paganism; and their interpretation of the Hellenic theology was often as superficial as their explanation of Catholic doctrine. The most universal of all modern scholars believed that sacrifice originated in the idea that the gods required food; and the most learned of all writers on mythology explained its rise and power by the artifices of the priesthood.

Catholics were astonished to find that men who wrote with fairness, and often with admiration, of the Church, who made themselves the champions of her maligned or forgotten heroes, who threw a new splendour over the lives of saints, and gave meaning and reality to much that had seemed simply marvellous, cared nothing for the doctrines of the institution they laboriously defended, and repudiated with indignation the proposal to submit to its authority. Subsequently, under the influence of the rising Catholic literature, there were many conversions among the historians, such as Philipps, and Hurter, and Gfrörer; but the great schools of historians who wrote, like Luden and Menzel, under the influence of the War of Independence, the disciples of Eichhorn, who sought after legal antiquities, the pantheistic followers of Hegel, and the disciples of Ranke, who were the critics and commentators of the mediaeval texts, were generally as far as possible from the faith of the Church. But the method they pursued in the investigation of truth prevailed against all hostile inclinations; and the scientific spirit which arose out of the decomposition of Protestantism became in the hands of Catholics the safeguard of religious truth, and the most efficient weapon of controversy.

It is little more than thirty years since a class of writers arose

so completely masters of the science of the age that they required
to apply no other tests but its methods in order to judge of its
results. The name of Ultramontane was given in consequence
of their advocacy of the freedom of the Church against the civil
power; but the characteristic of their advocacy was, that they
spoke not specially for the interests of religion, but on behalf of
a general principle which, while it asserted freedom for the
Church, extended it likewise to other communities and institutions. Convinced of the efficacy and right of the fundamental
precepts of politics, they knew that the Church desires nothing
incompatible with them, and can no more require the suspension of political law than of the moral order from which it springs.
Pursuing the strict analogy between science and polity, they
carried out the same principle in the investigation of philosophy
and history. In history, they sought to obtain for the ecclesiastical authority no immunity but that which it would enjoy from
the promotion of political rights; and in philosophy, they provided no protection for religious doctrines but in the advancement of scientific truth.

The causes which in Germany gave rise to this school of
Catholic apologists did not exist in Italy, and were but partially
present in France. The overwhelming authority of de Maistre,
and the subtle influence of the theories of Lamennais, were serious
obstacles. The want of a severe scientific training was felt by
many very accomplished men whose natural place would have
been among the defenders of those higher principles. Yet if we
compare the tone of the writings of Eckstein and Lenormant,
Ozanam, Maret, and de Broglie, with the histories of the Counts
Montalembert and Falloux, or with the works of Father Lacordaire, and Monseigneur Dupanloup, the difference between the
more scientific and the more brilliant portion of the liberal party
among French Catholics is very apparent. But it is due to the
general spirit of this school of writers, rather than to the special
character of its deeper scholars, that so large a portion of the
higher intellects of France, formerly more or less separated from
the Church, have during the last few years gradually approached
her.[1] The strength of this school was necessarily confined to
Germany, where its most eminent representatives were the divines Mohler, Döllinger, and Kuhn, the metaphysicians Baader

[1] Cousin, Villemain, Augustin Thierry, Barrante, and even Guizot.

and Molitor, the political writers Görres and Radowitz, and historians such as Movers and Gfrörer. On all the questions on the authority of science and its agreement with religion; of the influence of the Church on the state of intellectual and political liberty; of the propriety of concealment for fear of scandal; the example and the precepts of this Ultramontane school are diametrically opposite to those of the Catholics whose language we have quoted.

The first Catholic theologian who commenced the protest on behalf of Christian science against obscurantism was Gügler of Lucerne, a man not surpassed in knowledge of Scripture and originality of mind by any of those whom we shall have to name. The intensity of the antagonism reveals itself very clearly in the energy of his language, which the present state of literature would not justify. In a lecture against the opponents of a scientific and critical study of Holy Writ, he expresses himself in the following terms: "Timidity is a child of darkness . . . Wherefore do you complain of us that we investigate the sacred writings? Because, indeed, we are in danger of falling away from the truth; as if truth resided only in unreason, as if the sun's light shone only for the blind! You may be led to unbelieving thoughts quite as easily by merely reading the Scriptures as by a deeper study of them; much more easily, indeed, for error floats upon the surface, while truth lies deep below. If you would be faithful to your cause, you must close these books, and conscientiously abstain from reading them; and this, in fact, is what you really do, and so are secure not only from evil thoughts but from all ideas whatever. At least the lofty freedom of the Christian spirit is far from you, and you labour zealously to reach an opposite extreme. We are to believe the voice of the Church, you say, without seeking to understand; but where do we hear that voice? Not in your mouths certainly, or with the ears of the body; it must be sought for in history and in the written records of the Church . . . We must examine each document historically, in order to know whether it is the authentic expression of the mind of the Church, without interpolation; only then does faith begin . . . You endeavour to lull to sleep the spirit of inquiry, to suppress it when it is wakened, to check it in its growth; and by what means? Is it by a great intellectual preponderance and authority which enable you to assume the guardianship of the rest of the world? Far from it; but by ignorance, and by blindly casting suspicion on that which you do not understand. These are your arts, these are your only weapons; and thus you resemble madmen who would extinguish a conflagration, not by work, but by outcry . . . The universal scorn under which you have fallen is of your own making; for as you will not listen to anything, and understand nothing, men deem that your cause is at an end, and you will seldom find any like ourselves who will honour you with a single word . . . By your resistance you cast a hideous shadow on Christianity. When the ignorant, who are carried along by the current of the hour, look on you who profess to be true Christians, must they not believe that Christianity is taking darkness under its protection, and making it essential to its own existence? Will they not suppose that Christianity must dread all inquiry, and dare not approach the light? You have betrayed the sanctuary; you are the cause of the decline of faith, because its purity was long ago dimmed in yourselves . . . Faith is not your motive, for it has no object but truth . . . Embrace reason and science, become what you ought to be, and your kingdom will rise again from the dead. Give us a protection not only against unbelief, but one equally potent against superstition. It can only be truth, which lies hidden in the depths. To depart but a hair-breadth from it is as bad as to be a hundred miles away . . . Your disposition is very remote from that love of truth which always asks, True or not true? Your question is, Shall we have it so or not? He that loves the truth has divested himself of all particular inclinations and preferences. He views everything with love or aversion as he finds it true or false. You, on the contrary, care only for externals, and, if the thing were not true, you still would not abandon it. This is the disposition that nailed Christ upon the cross, and made the Jews blind to the dazzling light."[1]

In 1826 the Baron d'Eckstein founded a review, *Le Catholique*, for the purpose of promoting these ideas in France. He pointed out the backwardness of the clergy in learning, and the necessity of a great improvement. The freedom of the press was requisite in order to restore to Catholicism its proper influence. Left without official protection, it would be obliged to look for support in all the sciences, and to furnish itself with new armour. But

[1] Gügler, *Rede gegen die Feinde wissenschaftlicher, besonders historisch-kritischer Untersuchung der heiligen Schrift, Nachgelassene Schriften*, i, 75-86.

if the Church of France should make no effort to recover the
supremacy of learning, and to master religion intellectually as
she practised it in life, she could not resist science and impiety.[1]

About the same time, Baader was expounding at Munich, in
an obscure, unsystematic, and aphoristic style, the most profound
philosophy yet attained by Catholic speculation. The understanding requires to be satisfied just as much as the religious feelings of men; we cannot therefore rest contented with faith alone.
Faith is the basis of true knowledge, and knowledge the comple-
ment of faith; for uninstructed faith is liable to be shaken, but
he who has proceeded from faith to knowledge is sure of his
belief. Therefore he insisted on the necessary progress of science
as the safeguard of religion against unbelief, the only conciliation
of authority and liberty, and the only means of protecting the
faithful from the burden of a merely external authority which,
when it imposes itself on the processes of the understanding instead of confining itself to its own sphere in the will and the
reason, becomes as arbitrary as the system of unbelievers.[2]
Molitor, the only rival of Baader among the Catholic philosophers of his day, dwells more particularly on the union of faith
and knowledge. Science, which seeks to clear up what our consciousness dimly and uncertainly perceives, is the guide through
the labyrinth of the feelings, and therefore harmonizes necessarily with faith. Human nature strives after unity with itself; and
the union of faith and reason, things equally necessary and im-

---

[1] *Le Catholique*, i, 100; iii, 202; vi, 536; vii, 326. "Nous insistons fortement sur
ces points, parce que l'Église est plus que jamais appelée au combat, et que si elle
néglige le soin d'unir le savoir aux croyances, toutes les connaissances, toutes les
découvertes des hommes tourneraient au profit du mauvais esprit et non celui de la
vérité. A l'avenir rien de ce qui constitue la science ne doit rester étranger à ses
principaux défenseurs. Avec la simplicité de la foi on opère la conversion des bar-
bares, et des sauvages; mais c'est avec la science unie a cette divine simplicité, que
l'on peut conquérir les peuples vieillis au sein d'une longue civilization. Il ne faut
pas craindre les véritables lumières, et redouter de s'en servir, si l'on veut anéantir
les fausses" (iii, 204).

[2] Hofmann, *Vorhalle zur spekulativen Lehre F. Baader's*, pp. 20, 31. "Es muss erkann
werden, dass jede neugewonnene Wahrheit keine frühere aufhebt, sodern vielmehr
bestätigt, indem sie dieselbe bestimmter entfaltet, und in der Aufzeichnung neue
Beziehungen bereichert . . . Sie müssen zur Erkenntnis kommen, dass eine neue
Wahrheit möglich ist, wenn sie nicht in der schon gewonnenen ihre Wurzel hat,
dass somit jede neue Wahrheit die alte voraussetzt, und derselben ihr offenbar
gewordenes sein zu verdanken hat" (p. 35).

portant, must be practically attainable at least to a certain extent.[1] "Knowledge", says Dr Döllinger, "is one of the forms, and a necessary portion of morality; and as without an enlightened understanding there can be no real and perfect morality, so also a true and comprehensive knowledge can subsist only in a mind disciplined by morality ... It is true that this love of wisdom, often as it is paraded and proclaimed, is as rare as it is precious; for he alone can claim to possess it who is willing and able to dedicate himself to Truth with an absolute and unreserved devotion, and to make even the most painful sacrifice in its behalf. This resolute determination ever to seek the truth, the whole truth, and nothing but the truth, is a most difficult and unusual thing; and a man of whom this may be fairly said is not more easy to find than a man who is really determined to fulfil God's will alone." He says more particularly in another passage: "The understanding of ethical matters, or of matters approaching the domain of ethics, cannot be acquired by the operation of the reason alone. Otherwise the clever and the educated would be infinitely superior to the poor and uninstructed even in the knowledge of good and evil. But it is not so, and by an equally wise and equitable law man cannot master with his head what he does not at the same time receive into his heart; and if he hardens his will, he hardens at the same time his understanding against the truth."[2]

Nothing is more striking in the contrasts which the opposite schools present in their treatment of religious opponents than the manner in which they speak of the Reformation. The difference cannot be explained by the national prejudices; for there are many Germans whose language is as sweeping as that of Audin or Perrone. The tone of the greater German writers is very different. Görres speaks as follows: "In truth, it was a great and noble movement in the German people that brought about the Reformation. The Latin nations may condemn it altogether, but we cannot, for it sprang from the inmost spirit of our race,

---

[1] *Über die Tradition*, ii, 215, 216.

[2] *Irrthum, Zweifel und Wahrheit*, pp. 25, 33, 37. "The real seat of certainty is in the conscience alone ... Do not expect that in return, as it were, for your supposed good intentions, a mere superficial acquaintance and dilettante occupation with science and its results will really lead you to truth and supply you with firm convictions."

and extended nearly to the same limits. It was the spirit of a lofty moral disgust at every outrage on what is holy, wherever it may appear; of that indignation that is roused by every abuse; of that indestructible love of freedom which is sure always to cast off every yoke that perfidious violence would impose; in a word, the whole mass of salutary qualities which God bestowed on this nation, in order, when need should be, to ward off the corruption to which the warm South so easily inclines."[1]

Möhler says in his *Symbolik:* "Protestantism arose from the opposition to much that was undeniably evil and defective in the Church, and this is its merit—a merit not indeed peculiarly its own, since those evils were incessantly attacked, both before and after, on Catholic principles. It sprang partly from hostility to certain scientific representations of dogma, and certain forms of ecclesiastical life, which we may designate by the common term mediaeval, although these, again, had been the object of transforming endeavours, on behalf of the true system of the Church, from the end of the fourteenth century ... The Lutheran system will appear more excusable, as it will be shown to have proceeded really from a true Christian zeal, which indeed was, as in most other cases, injudiciously directed."[2] "At the beginning of the sixteenth century", says Döllinger, "a profound disgust at the Papacy of those days, and a not undeserved indignation at the abuses in the Church and the moral depravity of a too wealthy and too numerous clergy, had spread widely over Germany."[3]

It belongs to the nature of this school of divines that their theology is not scholastic. The systematic discussion of doctrines occupies a subordinate place in their method, as it is but one of several modes of ascertaining the teaching of the Church. The historic method, which considers less the convenience of imparting than the means of advancing the knowledge of religious truth, and which proceeds directly to the study of its sources and original records, alone suited their scientific spirit and the necessities of their position; whilst they renounced and condemned the other as barren and obsolete. In his letter to Bautain, Möhler thus describes it: "You have repeatedly and vehemently assailed the scholastic method, which still prevails in the schools of France, as incapable of embracing the boundless substance of

---

[1] *Der Katholik,* xv, 279. [2] *Symbolik,* pp. 11, 113.
[3] *Kirche und Kirchen,* p. 10.

the Christian religion, and bringing it to its full development ...
You attack a form of theological science whose special characteristic I would describe as a love for external demonstration, with a
theology that supplies a quantity of proofs, but does not help us
to know the thing itself which is to be proved; a theology that
never gets through the mass of arguments to the truth itself, and
understands better how to hang Christianity round about a man
than how to convert him into a Christian ... This appears to me
your most signal merit."[1] Professor Kuhn expresses himself still
more strongly in reference to Kleutgen: "If we believe the
modern restorers of Scholasticism, the older divines taught with
one voice exactly the same doctrine on all the chief points of
science which they now proclaim as perfect wisdom and genuine
Catholic science ... From this wholly unhistorical view of the
theology of former days they draw conclusions for the pursuit of
theology in our day, which must inevitably injure it; besides
which the partisans of this view, by investing their own knowledge and opinions with the authority of the Catholic schools,
make their own intellectual work much too easy, and that of
others unnecessarily difficult."[2]

The principles of civil and intellectual freedom are maintained
by the Ultramontane writers as the necessary condition of that
harmony between religion and political as well as moral science
which it is their object to obtain. Eckstein deplores, in the first
number of his review, that the fear of revolution should have
given to the writings of apologists a reactionary taint which was
neither requisite nor useful for the maintenance of sound doctrine.[3] He thundered against that monstrous combination of
politics and religion which was sought by the intervention of a
religious police; and he warned the Royalists that a terrible ex-
plosion might be the fruit of such mean and secret efforts, and of
an impotent oppression exercised by men who, unable to obtain

---

[1] *Sendschreiben an Bautain, Gesammelte Schriften* ii, 142. Not long before, Eckstein
had sketched the state of scholastic theology in France: "Mère céleste des sciences,
la théologie n'est enseignée comme une scholastique stérile dans l'école cartésienne.
Dans celle de M. Lamennais, elle dégénère en une vaine ostentation de polémique
sur l'autorité. Nos aïeux, que nous appelons grossiers, étaient plus avancés que
nous dans la science catholique: aujourd'hui un certain parti semble croire que
tout a été dit, qu'il n'est plus besoin de penser, d'aimer de méditer, mais de croire
et de s'endormir" (*Le Catholique*, viii, 650).

[2] *Katholische Dogmatik*, i, 916.   [3] *Le Catholique*, i, 9.

a triumph by open combat, sought it by artifices.[1] A quarter of a century later, Döllinger appealed to the French clergy with a similar warning in favour of liberty: "The Church of France cannot expect that she will be allowed to constitute permanently an exceptional domain of freedom in a state which is not free . . . She will obtain her just share of the general freedom and will find it more satisfactory and more secure than if she only forms an exception to the general rule."[2] The Bishop of Mentz speaks with the same frankness of the political claims of the Church: "It is perfectly untrue that the Church now claims for her external position all that in former times may have been laid down by a Pontiff when all Christendom revered him as a father . . . The altered circumstances necessarily require a completely new arrangement of the relations between Church and State. This is what our age is struggling to effect. From the Reformation to the present day it has never been possible to realize it. The recollection of the old Catholic unity survived in men's minds, and they attempted to settle matters in accordance with these recollections in all the lesser states, without reflecting that the old conditions had departed. Thence arose a truly absurd imitation of mediaeval institutions; and that which had been great and legitimate, considered from the point of view of Catholic unity, became, in different circumstances, unnatural and intolerable. Let the world manage its relations with the Church after the manner of the Middle Ages, when by God's mercy it has returned to the unity of religious belief; till then another basis is needed, which I can discover nowhere but in an honest recognition of the freedom of all Christian communities admitted by the State."[3]

The defence of intellectual freedom is founded not on the rights of reason so much as on the duty and on the interests of the

[1] *Avant-propos*, pp. 85, 99: "La liberté eût conservé à la religion tout le terrain que les inquisitions lui on fait perdre."

[2] *Betrachtungen über die Kaiserkrönung*, 1853, p. 40. "It is the first principle of the constitutional system that the sovereignty resides, not in the person of the monarch alone, but in the monarch and the people in inseparable unity" (*Debates of the Bavarian Chamber of Deputies*, 1849, i, 432).

[3] Ketteler: *Soll die Kirche allein rechtlos sein?* p. 30. In the National Parliament of 1848 he spoke in the same way for the freedom of instruction: "I desire that the unbeliever shall be allowed to bring up his children in unbelief; but it must be lawful for the strictest Catholic to give his children a Catholic education" (*Frankfort Debates*, p. 2183).

Church. The danger to the priest, wrote Eckstein, is less in a momentary oppression than in exaggerated triumph. By every act that does violence to intellect he deludes himself, and the motive is either passionate anger or pure idleness.[1] Neither academies nor universities, but the Church alone can reconcile the unrestricted progress of science with human welfare; the Church, not by acting as she did in the Middle Ages, or by striving, as she strove through the Jesuits, to control the education of European society—for we are neither in the Middle Ages, nor in the sixteenth century—but by employing all the knowledge and reflection of mankind, without putting any impediment in its way.[2] With Görres this was also a favourite theme: "Where will this freedom of speech and writing end? Will not the eternal pillars of religion, law, virtue, and society at last be undermined and washed away? Fools! to believe that God has made the enduring order of the universe to depend on your vigilance, and has planted the foundations of the moral world in the blind wit of man! . . The mind tolerates no tyrants. You can measure off the fields, they bear your limits patiently; but draw your boundary round the flood, divide the air into compartments and districts, contain the fire—how shall you, with your rude instruments shut up ideas and arrest the beams of thought? All that you will gain is, that, by the indignation with which men will be animated at the sight of your violence, the spark that goes forth still and harmless will be transformed into a thunderbolt, and that which would have passed away in a mild electric glow will gather into a destroying tempest."[3]

In an address to King Lewis of Bavaria on his accession which he places in the mouth of the greatest prince of his line, Görres takes care to exhort him faithfully to protect the freedom of thought against the interference of the clergy: "Pride has ever been the rock on which the priesthood has most easily been

---

[1] *Historisch-politische Blätter*, xi, 578.   [2] ibid., p. 581.

[3] *Politische Schriften*, v, 166, 135. "Resist the advance of learning, and behold, the genius strikes with his staff, the waters are parted asunder, and the waves stand up like walls on either side; pursue with your hosts, with your warriors and chariots and horses, and the waters shall close over you, and Pharaoh shall be drowned with all his army . . . Go rather and cultivate the new land in the sweat of your brow, and learn to adapt yourself to the altered times. Learn that, in order to govern, wisdom, understanding, ability, and virtue are henceforth required, and make your peace with the coming generation."

wrecked. As they are always busy with exalted things . . . and are instituted by God Himself, it may but too easily happen that they will confound His spirit with their own, identify themselves with the sanctity of their vocation, and, instead of obeying the command to govern only by voluntary self-abasement, and to seek their pride in humility, will glory in their office, and extend its functions over a sphere from which by nature it is excluded."[1] The peculiar autonomy of science is accurately defined by Möhler. Science, he says, resting on a law of internal necessity which is identical with truth, can arrive at a conscious knowledge of it only by freedom. External bonds produce in literature miserable, superficial, sophistical results. He that has penetrated, by means of original research, to the inmost sanctuary of science, knows how solemn is the reception she gives to her followers—what self-denial, what sacrifice of their own will, and what renunciation of all personal interest she demands—and how she exacts that they shall give themselves up to her own laws.[2]

These extracts must suffice towards the solution of the doubt whether the Church desires the establishment of freedom as the highest phase of civil society, independently of her own interest in it, and of the question of her attitude towards the promotion of learning. But it is necessary to notice briefly an opinion held by some who are either ignorant of the Catholic system or especially hostile to it, that an arbitrary authority exists in the Church

---

[1] *Maximilian der Erste an den König Ludwig von Baiern, Politische Schriften,* v, 256, 241. "While faith, which is internally free and inevitably tends to freedom, is externally bound within the Church . . . knowledge, on the contrary, inasmuch as it acts through conviction, and compels minds by internal force, must be outwardly free, and the interchange of ideas in its special sphere must be arrested and controlled by no unnatural restriction . . . Be ye, therefore, a Christian prince, at once a pillar of faith and protector of the freedom of the intellect; and let your example put to silence the zealots of both kinds who hold the two things to be incompatible . . . As deep as thought can penetrate into the nature of things, as high as it can breathe on the summits of the intellectual world, everywhere let its course be kept free by you; and be not frightened if in the ardour of its progress it quits the established paths."

[2] *Gesammelte Schriften,* i, 280. "The union of reason and faith must be produced by no external coalition; for nothing is more contrary to reason than the introduction of a foreign authority into its sphere, which is the case where faith is assumed as a postulate; namely, when speculation, unable to proceed farther in its one-sided course, despairing in the power of reason, throws itself violently into the arms of faith" (Molitor, *Über die Tradition,* ii, 215).

which may deny what has been hitherto believed, and may suddenly impose upon the faithful, against their will, doctrines which, while there is no warrant for them in the past, may be in contradiction with the existing and received conclusions of ecclesiastical, or even profane, science. The Ultramontane divines, having regard to this impression, have stated with special care the limited nature of the limits of the Papal authority. Möhler affirms that it was at one time greater than it has since come to be in consequence of the general progress of civilization and knowledge, which rendered its leading-strings insupportable. Rude times, he says, required a strong concentration of power to reform them; and the violence of internal forces called into existence a strong external control. In this way a dictatorship was given to the Pope. But it had no sooner done the work for which it was created than the absolute power was again restricted by the influence of such men as St Bernard. It is a proof of the efficiency with which the Popes used their power that men grew tired of it so soon. In proportion as intellectual and moral culture improved under it, the temporary form of the Roman supremacy necessarily became intolerable.[1]

Such as it now canonically exists, this authority is described by Döllinger in several places. "You must allow me", he said in the Frankfort Parliament, "to put aside once for all, as entirely groundless, the assertion that the Pope is an absolute ruler in the Catholic Church . . . No authority is more hampered than his by divers established limitations, and by a legislation descending to the most minute details, which the Pope cannot set aside, and which binds him as much as every other Catholic. If you imagine that there is any room in the Catholic Church for a purely arbitrary power of Pope or bishop, you are greatly mistaken."[2] "There is no society in the world whose constitution is more carefully organized, or more exactly regulated, than the Catholic Church. In that Church it is provided that the means of oppression, the tyrannical abuse of entrusted power, shall enjoy the smallest possible scope that is possible among men. Like a vast encompassing net, our ecclesiastical law extends over the whole Church; and none can break through it without abandoning her communion . . . Blind obedience is neither exacted of the Christian nor conceded by him; and he must reject it as soon as

[1] *Gesammelte Schriften*, ii, 27.   [2] *Debates*, p. 1674.

he discerns, or believes that he discerns, something sinful in it. At the same time, he knows that nothing can be proposed to him that is not founded on the immutable order and the laws of the Church."[1]

It is sufficient to appeal to the example of Möhler,[2] Döllinger,[3] and the other principal authors of the school, as a token of their opinion on the propriety of concealing truth for fear of scandal. "Everything must be told", says Gügler, "openly, clearly and without reserve, lest the deceit and suspicion that already surround all the relations of life should penetrate into the temple of science. Here no accommodation, no inherited custom, can be tolerated; whatever checks the free and genuine exhibition of character must be laid aside."[4] Some friends remonstrated with Görres on the manner in which he had spoken of the Popes in his Introduction to Cardinal Diepenbrook's *Suso*. In one of his letters he replies: "They are wrong in wishing truth to be disguised; that is always the worst possible policy, and now most of all. It is dangerous because it is dishonest, and quite unavailing besides. I vote everywhere fearlessly for the pure freshness of truth."[5] This was the maxim with which Möhler inaugurated his lectures on ecclesiastical history: "It is obvious that the student of history must not pervert facts; and one may suppose that Christianity expressly prohibits falsehood. From the Christian point of

[1] *Die Freiheit der Kirche*, pp. 18, 19.

[2] *Symbolik*, p. 353; *Neue Untersuchungen*, p. 382.

[3] *Lehrbuch der Kirchengeschichte*, ii, 229, 231, 234.

[4] *Nachgelassene Schriften*, i, 88. "La vérité est dans l'Église; elle possède donc les lumières; elle ne cessera jamais de dominer par la religion et la science; . . . on répétera ce vieux mot de Fontenelle, que toutes les vérités ne sont pas bonnes à dire. C'est une erreur. Il faut les proclamer toutes, si l'on ne veut que l'imposture se serve de la vérité partielle contre la vérité générale, et de la vérité générale contre elle-même" (Eckstein, *Le Catholique*, vii, 326).

[5] *Gesammelte Briefe*, i, 314. The following are the passages alluded to: "The Popes had become enslaved to their passions; . . . and that very French policy which they had invoked in the House of Anjou, to protect them against the violence of the Germans, was the appointed instrument to heap shame upon their heads, and to forge the fetters, to escape from which they, distrusting God and his divine order, and their own right, had played a senseless game, and had connected themselves with degraded things. The thirst for treasure was soon accompanied by the thirst for power, and the internal government of the Church sank more and more into the principles of the absolute dominion of the spiritual head: . . . a scandal on the side of the spiritual authority that raged irreconcilably, without measure, without dignity, without charity" (*Einleitung*, pp. xxvii, xxix).

view most of all, therefore, we are forbidden to be partial, to alter facts, to omit one thing, to be silent on another, or to add any thing which we have not found."[1]

The Catholic is subject to the correction of the Church when he is in contradiction with her truth, not when he stands in the way of her interests. For there is nothing arbitrary or extemporaneous in the authority which she wields; the laws of her government are of general application, ancient, public, and distinctly defined. There is a certain number of ideas which the Christian irrefragably believes, with such a faith as no scientific man thinks of reposing in any of the progressive realizations of inductive science. And he feels that such ideas as the existence of God, the immortality of the soul, and the punishment of sin, can neither be destroyed by knowledge nor impede its acquisition. Not that he thinks these great religious ideas ought to remain in sterile isolation. Like other general principles, each of them is capable of being made the basis of a vast superstructure of doctrine, proceeding from it with logical necessity. The work of this development has been performed by the organic action of the Church, which in the course of centuries has worked out a consistent system of doctrine, altogether free from accidental or arbitrary elements, the inevitable result of the principles of faith reacting upon the strict laws of thought and historical growth. Every part of this system is equally certain, and, if not equally necessary to be known, yet equally incapable of being denied. No part of it can be destroyed by the progress of knowledge, the last defined dogma no more than the first, no more than the existence of God, or the immortality of the thinking being.

But there is an outward shell of variable opinions constantly forming round this inward core of irreversible dogma, by its contact with human science or philosophy, as a coating of oxide forms round a mass of metal where it comes in contact with the shifting atmosphere. The Church must always put herself in harmony with existing ideas, and speak to each age and nation in its own language. A kind of amalgam between the eternal faith and temporal opinion is thus in constant process of generation, and by it Christians explain to themselves the bearings of their religion, so far as their knowledge allows. No wonder if, morally, this amalgam should be valued by its eternal rather than by its

[1] *Gesammelte Schriften*, ii, 284.

temporary element, and that its ideas should come to be regarded as almost equally sacred with the dogmas on which they are partly built. For they have the prestige of possession in their favour; they have come to be mixed up with social institutions and with philosophical speculation; and they form the outside line of defence in the controversial stronghold of Christendom.

But as opinion changes, as principles become developed, and as habits alter, one element of the amalgam is constantly losing its vitality, and the true dogma is left in an unnatural union with exploded opinion. From time to time a very extensive revision is required, hateful to conservative habits and feelings; a crisis occurs, and a new alliance has to be formed between religion and knowledge, between the Church and society. Every victory thus gained, though in its personal aspect it is a victory of innovators over those who seem to stand in the old paths, and to defend the interests of the unchangeable, is in reality a victory of truth over error, of science over opinion. It is a change not to be deplored but to be accepted with joy. It is a process which, though it has its crises, must be always progressing. There is always some mass or other in the temporary element of the amalgam which is becoming rusty and worn out, and fit only to be thrown aside. And as this purging process is one that involves opinions and feelings nearly conjoined with faith, there will always be an apparent danger, which, however, will at once disappear before the vigour of Catholics who will break the bonds of human tradition, and associate themselves with the progress of their times. The danger is only for those who fail to distinguish the essential from the accidental, and who cling to their religion, not for its substance, but for its appendages. Such men fall away altogether if their own way of explaining dogmas to themselves, and reconciling them with opinions, is cut from them. And even those who see clearly the difference between substance and accident must feel how important it is that their love and allegiance to the Church should be exhibited in those outer spheres where attachment takes the place of faith.

The fear of giving scandal, and the unwillingness to question too closely the limits of authority, are therefore the two motives which make the best-informed Catholics very circumspect in destroying opinions which have become amalgamated with faith. But these motives are misplaced in an age when Catholics can no longer shut themselves out from contact with the world, nor shelter themselves in ignorance. When all opinions are perpetually canvassed in a literature over which no authority and no consideration for others has any control, Catholics cannot help attempting to solve the problems which all the world is discussing. The point is, that while they solve them religiously, they should likewise solve them scientifically; that they should so comprehend them as to satisfy both conscience and reason—conscience, by a solution consistent with the infallible criterion of faith, and reason, by one defensible on grounds quite external to religion.

When a man has really performed this double task—when he has worked out the problem of science or politics, on purely scientific and political principles, and then controlled this process by the doctrine of the Church, and found its results to coincide with that doctrine, then he is an Ultramontane in the real meaning of the term—a Catholic in the highest sense of Catholicism. The Ultramontane is therefore one who makes no parade of his religion; who meets his adversaries on grounds which they understand and acknowledge; who appeals to no extrinsic considerations—benevolence, or force, or interest, or artifice—in order to establish his point; who discusses each topic on its intrinsic merits—answering the critic by a severer criticism, the metaphysician by closer reasoning, the historian by deeper learning, the politician by sounder politics and indifference itself by a purer impartiality. In all these subjects the Ultramontane discovers a point pre-eminently Catholic, but also preeminently intellectual and true. He finds that there is a system of metaphysics, and of ethics, singularly agreeable to Catholicism, but entirely independent of it. Not that his labour is an easy one, or one capable of being brought to a close. Each generation has to carry it forward. None can complete it; for there will always be some progress to be made, some new discoveries to adopt and assimilate, some discord to harmonize, some half-truth which has become an error to lop away. It is a process never to be terminated, till God has finished the work of educating the human race to know Him and to love Him.

But it is a work which no Catholic can deem either impracticable or unnecessary. It is not an idle enterprise: if we seek, we shall find. Religion can be made intelligible if we take the pains to make it so; its proofs may be found, its laws ascertained, and the conscience and reason constrained to acknowledge them. And Catholics are the only persons who can enter on this field of labour with perfect freedom; for they alone have a religion perfectly defined, clearly marked off from all other spheres of thought; they alone therefore can enter these spheres free from all suspicion of doubt, and from all fear of discord between faith and knowledge. If this clear distinction has ever been forgotten by Catholics, defeat was sure to follow, and that defeat was the victory of truth. Authority may put itself in opposition to its own code; but the code is vindicated by the defeat of authority. Thus it was in politics during the drama of the Sicilian Vespers, and in physical science during the opposition to Galileo. Those experiments have taught authority its own bounds, and subjects the limits of obedience; and they have destroyed the last conceivable obstacle to the freedom with which a Catholic can move in the sphere of inductive truth.

II

THE STATES OF THE CHURCH[1]

THE Catholic Church, while she is militant on earth, is compelled to wage an incessant conflict, both for the preservation of the purity of her doctrines and for her own liberty in proclaiming them. The political disputes are a part and a consequence of the dogmatic controversy, and the mission of the Church resides in both alike. All modern history is filled with this double contest; on the one hand with her successive victories over new forms of error, and on the other with her gradual emancipation from every earthly influence. The latter aspect of ecclesiastical history is chiefly exhibited in the vicissitudes of the Papacy as a temporal power—in the growth and settlement of the Roman States. The conservation of the independence of the Holy See through the integrity of its territory has been an object of such importance as frequently to engage nearly the whole of Europe in the contests it has occasioned. Empires have risen and fallen in its behalf, and it has been the paramount interest and motive in most of the greatest changes in the political arrangement of Europe.

It was a glorious spectacle for mankind, that, through all the shocks and changes of our history, through barbarous and civilized ages, in spite of the temptations of ambition and of the instigation of religious hatred, during centuries of boundless covetousness and violence, the Church, whilst surrounded by heretical and infidel powers, should have continued in possession of her dominions, recovering them whenever they were attacked, and gradually increasing them for nearly a thousand years, although guarded by nothing but the awe of an unseen protector, and the dread of the mysterious avenger who watched over her. Now that this feeling has been discarded as a superstition, now that it has been discovered that the dreaded power is a phantom, that shame is childish and honour absurd, and that conscience is nothing but the unreasonable voice of habit—now that the spell which was on

[1] *The Rambler*, vol. ii, March 1860, pp. 291–323.

mankind is broken, and the safeguard of the Church removed, it may be interesting to consider how the head of the Church came to be a temporal governor, and how his government grew into the condition in which it has been overtaken by the storm that now rages. We will endeavour to explain the rise of the temporal power, and some of the changes it underwent during the Revolution.

Every record older than the thirteenth century which could be quoted as an authority for the full territorial rights of the Holy See is almost certainly spurious, whilst all those documents by which those rights were actually created have been lost. We possess neither the agreement which was made between Pepin and Stephen II at Quercy, previous to the first expedition to Italy and the first Frankish donation, nor the Act of Restitution of 755, nor the documents by which Charlemagne confirmed the gifts of his father in 773 and 787, nor the deed by which Henry III conceded Beneventum to the Pope in 1051. Even the act by which the Countess Matilda left her possessions to the Church of Rome, in the year 1077, was lost, and required to be renewed in the year 1102. But if the oldest authentic document describing in full the dominions of the Holy See is the Act of Otho IV in 1201, the historical monuments which are preserved amply make up for what has been lost,[1] and we are able to trace with something like completeness the formation and the changes of the patrimony of St Peter.

The origin of the patrimony belongs to the very earliest ages. Even under the pagan emperors, when the Church, not being recognized by law, was not legally entitled to hold property, she was not generally molested in the acquisition and enjoyment of it. About the middle of the second century it was usual for even distant churches to obtain relief and support from Rome. In a letter of that date, in which Dionysius, Bishop of Corinth, sends his thanks to the Pope for the assistance he has received, he speaks

---

[1] "Non opus foret divinam ipsam, et omni laude superexcellentissimam Romanam primam sedem, se his ambiguis juvare argumentis quae ex illis epistolis extracta, decreto Gratiani inserta inveniuntur. Sufficienter quidem et multo elegantius, veritas ipsa ex usitatis certis, et approbatis sacris scripturis, et doctorum scriptis, absque hæsitatione haberetur . . . quia etiam illis omnibus scripturis e medio sublatis sanctam Romanam Ecclesiam primam, summæ potestatis excellentiæ, inter cunctas sedes quisque Catholicus fateretur" (Nicholaus Cusanus, *Concordantia Catholica*, iii, 2).

of such gifts already as an ancient custom.¹ This however may refer only to money collected among the faithful; but early in the third century, the Christians enclosed a piece of land in Rome (not, therefore, the property of any private individual among them) for the purpose of building a church, and their right being disputed, the Emperor Alexander Severus decided in their favour.² The great cemetery which bears the name of St Callistus was placed under his direction by Pope Zephyrinus about the same time, and in the middle of the third century the Church of Rome was rich enough to support 1,580 Christian poor (Eusebius, *Hist. Eccl.*, vii 43). During the persecutions of Decius and Valerian, her property, consisting chiefly of churches and cemeteries, was confiscated; but Gallienus, in the edict by which Christianity was first made a *religio licita* (Eus., vii 13), orders the restitution to the Christians of the burying-places and other lands and houses of which they had been deprived. It appears, therefore, that the first occasion on which the law was enforced on an extensive scale led to its repeal.

At the last and greatest effort to extirpate Christianity under Diocletian, a vast amount of property was doubtless seized; and in the first edicts of toleration, lands and houses are expressly specified as belonging to the churches and their restitution is enjoined both by Constantine and Maximin.³ Finally, in the year 321, Constantine issued a decree permitting the Church of Rome to receive bequests, and he gave the example of generosity himself by munificently endowing the basilicas.⁴ This edict was

---

¹ Ἐξ ἀρχῆς γὰρ ὑμῖν ἔθος ἐστι τοῦτο πάντας μὲν ἀδελφοὺς ποικίλως εὐεργετεῖν, ἐκκλησίαις τε πολλαῖς ταῖς κατὰ πᾶσαν πόλιν ἐφόδια πεμπειν . . . ὃ οὐ μόνον διατετήρηκεν ὁ μακάριος ὑμῶν ἐπίσκοπος Σωτήρ, ἀλλὰ καὶ ἐπηύξηκεν (Routh, *Reliquiae Sacrae*, i, 167).

² "Quum Christiani quendam locum qui publicus fuerat occupassent, contra popinarii dicerent, sibi eum deberi, rescripsit (Imperator) melius esse ut quomodocumque illic Deus colatur quam popinariis dedatur" (Lampridius in *Alexandro Severo, Scriptores Hist. Aug.*, i, 1003, ed. 1671).

³ Eusebius mentions this in many places. He gives the decree of Maximin, as follows: Ἵνα μέντοι καὶ μείζων γένηται ἡ ἡμετέρα δωρεά, καὶ τοῦτο νομοθετῆσαι κατηξιώσαμεν, ἵν' εἴ τινες οἰκίαι καὶ χωρία τοῦ δικαίου τῶν Χριστιανῶν πρὸ τούτου ἐτύγχανον ὄντα, ἐκ τῆς κελεύσεως τῶν γονέων τῶν ἡμετέρων εἰς τὸ δίκαιον μετέπεσε τοῦ φίσκου, ἢ ὑπό τινος κατελήφθη πόλεως, εἴτε διάπρασις τούτων γεγένηται εἴτε εἰς χάρισμα δέδοταί τινι. ταῦτα πάντα εἰς τὸ ἀρχαῖον δίκαιον τῶν Χριστιανῶν ἀνακληθῆναι ἐκελεύσαμεν (*Hist. Eccl.*, x, 10). Constantine writes to Anulius (ibid., x, 5): Εἴτε κῆποι εἴτε οἰκίαι, εἴθ' ὁτιονδήποτε τῷ δικαίῳ τῶν αὐτῶν ἐκκλησιῶν διέφερον σύμπαντα αὐταῖς ἀποκατασταθῆναι ὡς τάχιστα.

⁴ "Habeat unusquisque licentiam sanctissimo Catholico venerabilique concilio decedens bonorum quod optaverit relinquere" (*Cod. Theodos.*, xiv, 2, 4).

not the beginning of the wealth of the Church, but it led to its rapid and secure increase.[1] The biographer of Pope Sylvester, whilst he gives an accurate account of all the gifts of Constantine, also distinctly enumerates donations both of land and of precious metals, which were made by the Pope himself, and which must have come from the Christians of Rome.[2] With the acquisition of wealth grew the thirst for it among the clergy, and serious abuses ensued. Valentinian I, in the year 370, issued a decree restricting the right of accepting testamentary bequests; and the necessity of this restriction was acknowledged at the time.[3] This law was, however, no permanent impediment to the accumulation of Church property, and it was afterwards revoked.

In the course of the fifth century we find the Popes attending to secular affairs, and exercising great authority, by virtue both of their spiritual character and of the claims which their wealth gave to the people, though without actually interfering in the government of the city. They had, however, already overstepped the bounds which at Constantinople a Bishop was expected to observe. For whereas the Popes had generally sought the assistance of orthodox emperors against the heretics, in the year 420, Celestine I, of his own authority, expelled the Novatians from the

---

[1] "Notandum est edictum hoc ad populum Romanum missum, et in urbe Roma propositum, et sic ad Ecclesiam urbis Romæ speciatim pertinere. Inde igitur postea proculdubio Ecclesiæ Romanæ opes in immensum auctæ" (Gothofredus, in *Cod. Theol.*, vol. vi, p. 27).

[2] Anastasius in *Vita Silvestri* (vol. i, cap. 3, p. 78, ed. Vignoli, 1724): "Hic fecit in urbe Roma ecclesiam in prædio cujusdam presbyteri sui . . . ubi et hæc dona contulit. Patenam argenteam pensantem lib. xx. ex dono Constantini Augusti. Donavit autem scyphos argenteos . . . calicem aureum . . . fundum Valerianum, etc."

[3] St Jerome writes in the year 394: "Pudet dicere, sacerdotes idolorum, mimi, et aurigæ, et scortæ, hæreditates capiunt: solis clericis et monachis hoc lege prohibetur; et prohibetur non a persecutoribus, sed a principibus Christianis. Nec de lege conqueror; sed doleo cur meruerimus hanc legem . . . Cauterium bonum est, sed quo mihi vulnus, ut indigeam cauterio? Provida severaque legis cautio, et tamen nec sic refrenatur avaritia. Per fidei commissa legibus illudimus . . . Audio præterea in senes, et anus absque liberis, quorumdam turpe servitium. Ipsi apponunt matulam, obsident lectum, purulentiam stomachi, et phlegmata pulmonis, manu propria suscipiunt. Pavent ad introitum medici trementibusque labiis, an commodius habeant, sciscitantur; et si paululum senex vegetior fuerit, periclitantur: simulataque lætitia, mens intrisecus avara torquetur" (*Ep.* 52, *ad Nepotianum*, i, 260, 261). St Augustine says: "Nobis etiam private successionis emolumenta recentibus legibus denegantur, et nemo conqueritur" (*Ep.* 18, *ad Valentinianum*, c. 14).

churches which they held. In the East, this was considered an alarming stretch of power;[1] but the history of the patriarchs of Constantinople is a perpetual justification of the policy of the Popes. In the year 449, Leo the Great writes to the Emperor Theodosius that he cannot be present at a synod in the East, because of the pressure of temporal affairs, "cum nec aliqua ex hoc ante exempla praecesserint, et temporalis necessitas me non patiatur deserere civitatem" (*Opp.* i, 887). That these temporal concerns were due in great measure to the obligations which the wealth of the Roman Church imposed upon the Bishops is evident from the use which they are recorded to have made of it for the support of the Roman people.[2]

As the strength and prosperity of the empire declined, the property of the Church increased. The estates of many patrician families residing in the capital, who had been owners of great part of the land of the Western Empire both in Italy and in the provinces, were added to her patrimony. The motives which induced the Romans of that day to make the Church their heir were the same which have been active at all times; but in an age of ruins and decay they had an extraordinary power. The population was dwindling away, and the aristocracy in particular declined with the decline of the State. Many great families became extinct, and in passing away without heirs, it was a natural thought to leave their earthly possessions to the only institution which seemed not to change and not to die. It was generally believed that the end of all things was at hand; and this belief was shared by many of the Fathers at a time when the vitality, the fidelity, and the genius of the barbarians were undistinguishable amid the havoc by which they were chiefly known.[3] Four cen-

---

[1] Τῆς Ῥωμαίων ἐπισκοπῆς ὁμοίως τῇ Ἀλεξανδρέων πέρα τῆς ἱεροσύνης ἐπὶ δυναστείαν ἤδη πάλαι προελούσης . . . οὐ μὴν οἱ ἐν Κωνσταντίνου πόλει πεπόνθασιν (Socrates, *H.E.*, vii, 11, p. 347, ed. Valesius).

[2] We read, for instance, of Gelasius, at the end of the fifth century: "Hic fuit amator pauperum, et clerum ampliavit. Hic liberavit a periculo famis civitatem Romam" (Anastasius, i, 167).

[3] Even Gregory the Great seems to have had this belief; for he wrote to the emperor: "Plus de venientis Jesu misericordia quam de vestræ pietatis justitia præsumo" (*Ep.* v, 40). And he frequently speaks of the approaching end of the world: "Futurum sæculum ipsa jam quasi propinquitate tangitur" (*Dial.* iv, 41). "Ecce enim mundum hunc quam vicinus finis urget aspicitis" (*Ep.* iv, 25). "Hoc jam ut videmus mundi hujus termino appropinquante" (*Ep.* ix, 68). "Appropinquante fine mundi" (*Ep.* ix, 123) etc. etc.

turies later, during another period of tribulation and despondency, the same belief once more prevailed, and it was supposed that the year 1000 would be the last. The consequence was, that numerous legacies were left to the Church; many foundations made at that time, and deeds with the preamble *appropinquante mundi termino*, attest the common expectation. The clergy, and especially the monks, generally opposed the delusion.[1] In the order of Cluny, in which the elements of regeneration were kept alive, holy men already looked forward to the great reform of which, half a century later, the brethren of Cluny were the foremost champions. A memorial of that time, and of the opposition of the Benedictines to the prevalent opinion, survives in the feast of All Souls.

There is no record of similar donations at the period of which we are speaking,[2] but there is no reason to doubt that in the sixth century, as in the tenth, the same cause operated in the same way; and at the close of the sixth century we find the Popes the richest landowners in Italy. From the letters of Gregory the Great and from the lives of the Popes, we know that their estates lay in Italy, Gaul, Africa, and especially in Calabria and Sicily, which produced alone a revenue of three talents and a half a year.[3] These vast estates were the foundation of the temporal power of the Popes. A recent Jewish historian, whose history of the Roman states has obtained a prize from the University of Göttingen, has rendered it unnecessary for us to cite on this point any of the

[1] "De fine mundi coram populo sermonem in ecclesia Parisiorum adolescentulus audivi, quod statim finito mille annorum numero Anti-christus adveniret, et non longo post tempore universale judicium succederet: cui prædicationi ex evangeliis ac apocalypsi et libro Danielis, qua potui virtute, restiti. Denique et errorem qui de fine mundi inolevit abbas meus beatæ memoriæ Richardus sagaci animo propulit . . . nam fama pæne totum mundum impleverat, quod quando annuntiatio dominica in Parasceve contigisset absque ullo scrupulo finis sæculi esset" (Abbo of Fleury, *Apol. ad Reges Francorum*, p. 471).

[2] Theodorus Lector says, indeed (writing at the beginning of the sixth century), that the Roman Church did not keep the property it acquired in land. Ἔθος τῇ ἐκκλησίᾳ τῆς Ῥώμης ἀκίνητα μὴ κρατεῖν δίκαια. Bingham observes: "If this was the custom of the Church of Rome, it was a very singular one" (*Antiquities*, ii, 63, ed. 1843). It is one which would prove, at least, that it was with no view to temporal aggrandisement that the property was acquired.

[3] Τάδε λεγόμενα πατριμόνια τῶν ἁγίων καὶ κορυφαίων Ἀποστόλων τῶν ἐν τῇ πρεσβυτέρᾳ Ῥώμῃ τιμωμένων ταῖς ἐκκλησίαις ἔκπαλαι τιμώμενα χρυσίου τάλαντα τρία ἥμισυ τῷ δημοσίῳ λόγῳ τελεῖσθαι προσέταξεν (Theophanes, *Chronogr.*, 273, ed. Venice).

numerous Catholic writers—such as Orsi, Fontanini, Cenni, Borgia—who in the last century wrote upon the subject. He expresses himself as follows: "It is not to be denied, that in this early possession of such extensive domains the germ of the temporal sovereignty of the Bishop already existed, and that at the close of the sixth century it laid the foundation of their subsequent dominion over the Eternal City. And it cannot be disputed that some of the Popes even then enjoyed a sort of temporal authority, and exercised various prerogatives of sovereignty over parts of the patrimony of St Peter."[1]

The times were particularly propitious to the development of the influence which was founded on the spiritual authority and on the possessions of the Holy See. It was the period of the great migration, when many a Bishop appeared, in virtue of his office, and in fulfilment of the trust and expectation of the people, as their guardian, while the imperial officers were unable to protect them. The position to which they were thus naturally elevated, through the helplessness of the civil authorities in the presence of the formidable invaders, was confirmed by the Emperor Justinian. In the pragmatic sanction of 554 he took advantage of the influence which they already *de facto* possessed, to establish by their means a control over the whole administration of the provinces. They were required to superintend the conduct of the governors, to report on their wrong-doings, and to act as defenders and advocates of the people. This was at once a portion of the extensive reform by which Justinian restored self-government to the towns and provinces and at the same time an attempt to save the crumbling system of the imperial government, by committing it in great measure to the care of the Church. The result was, to give to the clergy of the West a very extensive influence in matters of state; but it increased in far greater proportion the political power of the Pope, who could direct and command that of all the other Bishops.[2] Against Rome the efforts of the barbarians were especially directed. It was threatened alike by the Goths and the

---

[1] Sugenheim, *Entstehung und Ausbildung des Kirchenstaates*, 1864, p. 4.

[2] Thus Gregory the Great writes to Januarius, Bishop of Caralis in Sardinia: "Necesse est ut fraternitas vestra, dum licet, civitatem suam vel alia loca fortius muniri provideat, atque immineat ut abundanter in eis condita procurentur, quatenus dum hostis illuc Deo sibi irato accesserit, non inveniat quod lædat, sed confusus abscedat" (*Ep.* ix, 6).

Huns, Vandals and Lombards, Saracens and Normans. But as the danger was greatest in the capital, so was the influence of the Bishop who repeatedly saved it, and enabled it, by his generous assistance, to support the devastations which he could not prevent. In an old poem, published in Bunsen's *Description of Rome*, i 243, we find it declared that the Papacy had saved the city:

Nam nisi te Petri meritum Pauliquefoveret,
Tempore jam longo Roma misella foret.

In a petition addressed by the Romans to the exarch during the Lombard wars, they speak of the Pope as their sole defence against the ferocity of the invaders, whom he sometimes persuaded, sometimes bribed to spare them.[1] The position which they in this way acquired is thus described by a Protestant divine, whose works are well known in England: "The Popes were landowners like any others, but more wealthy than any, and exempt from taxation. But this wealth enabled them, during the troubles which beset Italy from the fifth century on all sides, to diminish the sufferings of the inhabitants, to save them from famine, to redeem captives, to conciliate the barbarians by their gifts. In this way the See of St Peter became, without any rights of sovereignty, the national centre of Italy, to which the people had recourse for help and relief even in temporal adversity."[2]

Whilst all these circumstances were uniting to raise the Bishop of the Western capital to a high political position, the emperors were absent from Rome, and from the time of Narses their authority in Italy was diminished and insecure. It was in their interest to promote an influence which could not rival and threaten their own, and could serve to support it against the senate and nobles of Rome. The popularity of the Pope, and his power with the barbarians rendered his assistance indispensable to preserve the city from the enemy and the people in their allegiance. Every political motive existed, therefore, to conciliate and

---

[1] "Propinquantium inimicorum ferocitas, quam nisi sola Dei virtus atque apostolorum principis per suum vicarium, hoc est Romanum Pontificem, ut omnibus notum est, aliquando monitis comprimit, aliquando vero flectit ac moderat hortatu, singulari interventu indiget, cum hujus solius pontificalibus monitis, ob reverentiam apostolorum principis, parentiam offerant voluntariam: et quos non virtus armorum humiliat, pontificalis increpatio cum obsecratione inclinat" (*Liber Diurnus Romanorum Pontificem*, ii, 4).

[2] Kurz, *History of the Church*, ii, 194 (1856).

strengthen the Pope; and it was only in consequence of religious misunderstandings that the fidelity of the Romans was at last shaken. For they were more attached to their Bishop and pastor, upon whose resources and benevolence they depended for those distributions of food and alms to which they had become accustomed in the better days of Rome, than to the Emperor, whom they never saw, who did nothing for them, and whose power made itself felt only by the money he demanded and the spoils he had carried away. Indeed the Pope was their advocate, to mitigate not only the violence of the Lombards, but the rapacity of the Byzantine officials.

The letters of Gregory the Great explain very distinctly the position of the Papacy in his time. The imperial power was sinking before the progress of the Lombards, and only the towns on the coast which were accessible to the Greek fleet remained constantly under the exarch, who held his court at Ravenna. In the other cities the emperor was represented by dukes and counts; but as they could do little for the people, their power was generally small in comparison with the preponderating influence of the Bishops. Pope Pelagius had been assured by the exarch that he could send him no assistance against the Lombards, and that he must defend himself as he could. Under these circumstances, on the death of Pelagius, Gregory was taken from his retirement and elected Pope. Bede says that he was distinguished from his predecessors by a higher notion of his office. What that notion was he tells us when he says he is ready to die, rather than that the Church should degenerate in his time: "Paratior sum mori, quam beati Petri apostoli ecclesiam meis diebus degenerare" (*Ep.* iv, 47). Instead of devoting his attention, like many of those who came before him, to the decoration of the churches of the city, he soon found himself plunged into affairs of state. "I have been recalled into the world," he complains, "under the appearance of being made a Bishop, and am more occupied with temporal concerns than when I was a layman."[1] He says that he discharged the office of the emperor's paymaster in Rome; that he was virtually the Bishop not so much of the Romans as of the Lombards, because they occupied all his attention, and carried away

---

[1] "Sub colore episcopatus ad sæculum sum reductus . . . tantis terræ curis inversio quantis me in vita laica nequaquam deservisse reminiscor" (*Ep.* 1, 5).

great part of his resources.[1] As he received no aid from the exarch, he made peace with the Lombards on his own authority; and as he could not obtain his assistance, he did not wait for his sanction.[2] The Lombards treated with him as an independent power.

It is probable that from this time forward it would have been possible for the Popes to throw off the yoke of the empire. In many respects it was a source of annoyance and oppression; and the necessity of awaiting the permission of government at each election caused a very troublesome delay. The people, too, were with the Pope; and the exarch, who could not protect them against the Lombards, would have been unable to subdue them by force of arms. Nevertheless this anomaly was tolerated, with all its injurious consequences, for a century and a half after the death of Gregory; so much did his successors dread the duties and responsibilities of sovereignty, and so great was their respect and forbearance for the imperial authority. But from this time the change was prepared in the minds of the people; they became familiarized with the idea of transferring their government from the hands of the distant, useless and generally unpopular emperor, to the Bishop, who was everything to them—who was ever solicitous and active for the interests of their city and their country—who already exercised the authority which was slipping from a grasp unable to hold it, and in whom Rome saw herself rising once more to the supremacy which it was believed that she would never lose.

> *His ego nec metas rerum nec tempora pono,*
> *Imperium sine fine dedi.*

They became attached to him by gratitude and interest, love and pride. All that was required was a breach between the emperor and the Pope, to afford them an opportunity of showing on which side their allegiance lay.

[1] Every Bishop, he considered, had in those days to attend to more than the purely spiritual welfare of his flock: "Nostis quia talis hoc tempore in regiminis debeat arce constitui, qui non solum de salute animarum, verum etiam de extrinseca subjectorum utilitate et cautela sciat esse sollicitus" (*Ep.* x, 62).

[2] He writes to Ravenna that the Lombards offer a separate peace: "Nobiscum quidem specialem pacem facere repromittit, sed scimus quia et diversæ insulæ et loca sunt alia proculdubio peritura" (*Ep.* iv, 29).

This opportunity at last came. In the year 692, the Emperor Justinian II required that the Pope should adopt the decrees of the Trullan Council, and Sergius refused, "eligens ante mori", says his contemporary biographer, "quam novitatum erroribus consentire." An officer was sent to bring him a prisoner to Constantinople; but the army of the exarchate marched to Rome to protect the Pontiff who was the pillar of Italian freedom, and the imperial emissary only saved his life by taking refuge under the bed of the Pope. The deposition of Justinian, by one of the frequent revolutions at Constantinople, put an end to the mutiny. But the jealousy of freedom was awakened in Italy; disturbances became frequent; several exarchs were murdered at Ravenna. The people were left to defend themselves against the Lombards, and acquired self-reliance and consciousness of their strength.[1] Under the Roman Empire the love and the appreciation of freedom were absorbed by the respect for law; and at the time of the Teutonic invasions, the latter alone survived. Even the turbulence and passion in which the Romans had found relief during the worst periods of tyranny had given way to a tame submission; and the people, who had so often, and so wantonly, changed their rulers, silently acquiesced in changes that were independent of their will. The long antagonism of the Greeks and the Lombards gave birth to new ideas; the notion arose that a balance of authorities is a security for the subject. They sought a protection for their own weakness in the weakness of their governors; and that practice then commenced of seeking always to have two masters, which has ever been the secret, the limit, and the bane of Italian freedom. "The freedom of the tyrant", says a great historian, "is the end at which the Italian aims." It is of this that the renowned history of the Italian Republics consists. Their notions of freedom are neither those of the ancient Romans, which survived in Venice, nor those of the Teutonic race, which sometimes animated the municipalities of Northern Italy. When the ablest of their patriots drew up a scheme of independence it resulted in a

[1] An excellent Italian historian speaks as follows of this period:

"Fino a quest'epoca quasi tutte le città romagnuole sfuggirono la signoria longobarda; mentre certo è che l'escara non avrebbe potuto conservarle all'impero, se i cittadini stessi non si forsero armati a difesa; e i cittadini si amarono non per affetto alla greca autorita, cui egualmente aborrivano che quella a de Longobardi, ma per un sentimento non conosciuto e negli umani animi innato di un viver più libero e independente" (Vesi, *Storia di Romagna*, i, 275).

code of the most unbounded tyranny; and, as Macchiavelli in the sixteenth century conceived a free Italy only by means of the despotism of a prince, so their patriots in our day can imagine liberty only in the form of the absolutism of the State. These ideas took their rise in the age of which we are speaking.

The events of the year 692 were repeated in 712, when the Emperor Philippicus, a Monothelite, was placed on the throne. The Romans refused to receive his image, his orders or his coins; his name was not pronounced in the Mass, his officer was not admitted into the city. He tried to force his way; and several lives had been lost, when the Pope sent the priests to stop the combat. Almost immediately after this, the heretical emperor was dethroned in his capital, and the excitement subsided. The decisive moment for the dominion of the Greeks in Italy, and for the formation of the Roman state, was brought on a few years later (in 728) by the Iconoclastic Controversy. Leo the Isaurian had sent emissaries to put the Pope to death, because he resisted the levying of a new tax. This was prevented by the people, and brought them more closely on the side of the Pope in the dispute which immediately followed. When the decree for the destruction of the images arrived, the Pope prepared for a severe conflict—"contra imperatorem quasi contra hostem se armavit." Leo ordered him to be put to death, and immediately seized all the patrimonies of St Peter in Calabria, Sicily, and the East. All the Italians of Venice and the Exarchate took the side of the Pope. The imperial officers were expelled, new governors were elected in their place; and the people would have elected another emperor, but the Pope prevented it.[1] Throughout this dispute, the Pope alone restrained the Italians from throwing off their allegiance to the emperor. He wrote to the Venetians to bring back the people of Ravenna to the empire. The Lombard king

[1] "Permoti omnes Pentapolenses atque Venetiarum exercitus contra imperatoris jussionem restiterunt, dicentes nunquam se in ejusdem pontificis condescendere necem, sed pro ejus magis defensione viriliter decertare . . . omnes ubique in Italia duces elegerunt, atque sic de pontificis deque sua immunitate cuncti studebant . . . omnis Italia consilium iniit ut sibi eligerent imperatorem, et Constantinopolim ducerent. Sed compescuit tale consilium pontifex, sperans conversionem principis" (Anast., *Vita Gregorii II*, cap. 6). "Omnis quoque Ravennæ exercitus, vel Venetiarum, talibus jussis uno animo restiterunt, et nisi eos prohibuisset pontifex imperatorem super se constituere aggressi sunt" (*Hist. Miscell. Additament.*— Muratori, *Scriptores*, i, 185).

Luitprand had seized the opportunity to conquer the Romagna. He was expelled by the Venetians: but Ravenna continued to fight for its independence; and in the year 733, the Greeks were defeated in a great battle, in which the slaughter was so enormous, that for six years the people would not eat the fish of that arm of the the Po on whose banks it was fought. In Rome, the position of the imperial dux had become untenable, and the office was henceforth completely dependent on the Pope. Gregory II is the first who governed the city without even the phantom of imperial authority beside him.[1]

This year 728, however, marks not only the commencement of actual independence in Rome, but of the pontifical sovereignty over other territories. The Greeks had endeavoured in vain to draw Luitprand to their side against the Pope. But the Lombards were now orthodox Catholics, and even at the time when they were Arians they had never persecuted religion.[2] Their hostility was directed against the Greeks only, whom they wished to expel from Italy. When, therefore, Luitprand took the town of Sutri, on the road to Rome, he was easily persuaded to cede it to the Holy See. No mention was made of the rights of the emperor; and this is the first territorial donation from which the States of the Church took their origin. It was considered that the claims of the empire did not survive the conquest by the Lombards, and that the parts of Italy which had so long remained in the hands of the Greeks became, by right of conquest, as much the property of the Lombard kings as those territories which they occupied from the time of their first invasion. When, therefore, the Lombards consented to restore any portion of their conquests, they restored it not to the Greeks but to the Pope. They had the same right to dispose of their new acquisitions as of their old possessions. Nor had the Pope any motive to intercede for the restoration of imperial property. He could only urge the rights of the Holy See as proprietor of its patrimonies, not the rights of the empire to the sovereignty of Italy. The Lombards were a colon-

[1] "Il ducato Romano spontaneamente per dedizione de'popoli si assoggetto a Romano Pontefice verso l'anno 730, ond'ebbe principio il temporale dominio della chiesa Romana" (Moroni, *Dizionario Storioco Ecclesiastico*, xxxiv, 117).

[2] "Super indignos nos divinæ misericordiæ dispensationem miror, qui Langobardorum sævitiam ita moderatur, ut eorum sacerdotes sacrilegos, qui esse fidelium quasi victores videntur, orthodoxorum fidem persequi minime permittat" (Gregorius Magnus, *Dial.*, iii, 28).

izing race, and the country which they conquered was considered
to belong, not only to the king as sovereign, but to his fellows as
their property. Of the original owners, some were slain; others
fled for safety, and this flight peopled Venice with patrician
families. None of the old Roman families were suffered to remain
on the land, except in the position of tenants.[1] The patrimonies
of the Holy See formed an exception to this. They were continually restored after each expedition of Luitprand, and at last the
Pope was probably the only landowner independent of the
Lombards. This independent possession under the Lombards
amounted to a virtual sovereignty, and one sort of claims came
to be identified with the other. As the restitution of the Lombards
went to form the States of the Church, a similar claim of sovereignty was advanced over those domains which had been confiscated by Leo the Isaurian. Whatever had belonged to the patrimonium S. Petri as property, was understood to belong by rights
to the same patrimony when it had become a sovereign state.
That these lost domains were numerous and extensive we know,
but we cannot determine their limits. We have, in anything like
completeness, only the letters of one Pope of that age. If we had
more, it is possible that we should find other places mentioned as
belonging to the Holy See besides those spoken of by St Gregory.
In this way, we conceive, the fiction of the Donation of Constantine very naturally arose. We know from St Gregory that the
deeds were frequently lost, that it was not always easy to determine the limits of the domains of the Church. But many authentic deeds of gift of Constantine were preserved. It was easy,
therefore, to attribute to him the origin of possessions which
came from forgotten sources; and when the property of the Holy
See began to develop itself into sovereignty, it was not unnatural
to attribute to Constantine the origin of both. We find the germ
of this idea in a letter of Hadrian to Charlemagne in the year
777.[2] Scarcely half a century later, the Donation of Constantine sprang into existence.

[1] "Multi nobilissimi Romanorum ob cupiditatem interfecti sunt, reliqui vero per
hostes divisi, ut tertiam partem suarum frugum Langobardis persolverent, tribu-
tarii efficiuntur" (Paulus Diaconus, *Hist. Langob.*, ii, 32—in Muratori, i, 436).

[2] "Sicut temporibus beati Sylvestri, Romani pontificis, a sanctæ recordationis
piissimo Constantino magno imperatore, per ejus largitatem sancta Dei catholica
et apostolica Romana Ecclesia elevata atque exaltata est, et potestatem in his
Hesperiæ partibus largiri dignatus est, ita et in his vestris felicissimis temporibus

The next considerable accession of territory was in the year 742. The Lombards had obtained great successes against the Greeks. The intercession of the Pope was invoked by the people of the exarchate, and he proceeded to Pavia to obtain peace for them. Luitprand consented to make peace, and to liberate all his prisoners. By this time the Pope is acknowledged by the exarchate, as well as by the duchy of Rome, as the only authority who could protect and save it. Luitprand also restored to the Pope all the *patrimonia* which he had occupied during the war, adding to them the four towns of Ameria, Orta, Bomarzo, and Bleda.[1] The growth of the temporal power was therefore simultaneous with the practical recognition of the Holy See as the real protector of Italy. The celebrated John Müller[2] says of the period of Gregory II, Gregory III, Zachary, and Stephen II: "Jamais la chaire de S. Pierre n'a été remplie par une suite aussi longue d'excellents princes et de vertueux Pontifes." Of Gregory II another Protestant divine writes: "Not the Church, but the government, was weak in Italy. The Pope could have declared himself supreme; but he disdained it."[3] But this could not continue; and his successors were obliged to accept a position which the Popes had long endeavoured to avoid. The whole condition of State and Church in Italy made it impossible for them longer to resist the general current of the age.

In the other great towns which had escaped the domination of

---

atque nostris, sancta Dei Ecclesia, id est beati Petri apostoli, germinet atque exultet . . . quia ecce Divus Christianissimus Dei Constantinus imperator his temporibus surrexit, per quem omnia Deus sanctæ suæ Ecclesiæ beati Ap. principis Petri largiri dignatus est, sed et cuncta alia quæ per diversos imperatores, patricios etiam et alios Deum timentes pro eorum animæ mercede et venia delictorum in partibus Tusciæ, Spoleto seu Benevento, atque Corsica, simul et Savinensi patrimonio beato Petro Ap. . . . concessa sunt, et per nefandam gentem Langobardorum per annorum spatia abstracta atque ablata sunt, vestris temporibus restituantur" (*Codex Carolinus*, 350).

[1] "Pacem cum ducatu Romano ipse Rex in viginti confirmavit annos" (Anast., *Vita Zachariae*, cap. 5).

[2] *Works*, viii, 335.

[3] Hasse, *Uber die Vereinigung der geistlichen und weltlichen Gewalt*, Haarlem, 1852, p. 28. This partial performance obtained the prize offered by the Academy at Haarlem for the best book on the subject. It is more unfair and superficial, but not so frivolous, as the similar work of Sugenheim, to which we have already referred. Both are weakest in the earlier parts, where the strength of the older Italian historians lies.

the Lombards, a process was going on at the same time strikingly analogous to what occurred in Rome; which, though modified and varied in a very characteristic way by local circumstances, proved how general and how natural was the change which made the Pope a temporal sovereign. Next to Rome, the chief of these towns were Ravenna, Venice, and Naples. In all these places a sort of independence was acquired at this time, under the pressure of the necessity of self-defence in the absence of aid from Constantinople; and in all the episcopal authority already rivalled that of the imperial vicar.

Naples was accessible to the Greeks by sea; and for this reason, and because of its remoteness, it was never taken by the Lombards, and an attempt, in the seventh century, to cast off the Greek yoke was at once suppressed. The growth of independence was therefore later and more gradual than elsewhere. At the general rising of Italy under Gregory II, Naples was the stronghold of the Iconoclastic party; and an expedition went forth from its walls against the Pope, in which the Neapolitan Dux Exhilaratus lost his life. But when the exarchate had fallen, and Rome and Venice had become really independent, the secular and ecclesiastical authorities united to obtain the independence of Naples. The Archbishop was very powerful, and it was found necessary, for the maintenance of order, to unite his authority with that of the civil and military governor. In the year 768, when the see was vacant, the dux or consul Stephen, a layman, was elected his successor; and the Pope confirmed his election, in consideration of his good administration as secular governor.[1] The same thing occurred once more a century later; but it is unnecessary for us to pursue the history of Naples beyond the period when it affords so striking a synchronistic parallel with what was going on in Rome.

The position of Venice secured it alike from the arms of the Lombards and from the fleets of the emperor, and its connection with Ravenna was for a long time very slight. The Venetians were particularly devoted to the Pope. They rose in arms to defend him against the emperor; they restored at his bidding the imperial authority in Ravenna; they separated themselves in the tricapitular controversy from the Patriarch of Aquileia, and ob-

[1] "Nam Parthenopensem ducatum laudabili quiete duodecim rexit annos" (Johannes Diaconus, *Chron. Episc. S. Neap. Eccl.*, cap. 41—in Muratori, i, 310).

tained a patriarch of their own in the Bishop of Grado. The authority of the Bishop was great, as in all Western cities; but he was without those advantages of wealth and ecclesiastical jurisdiction which made the Pope the monarch of Rome. When Venice became independent, he was the chief author of the change; but his supremacy did not long survive. The islands were governed severally by tribunes; but the decline of the power of the exarch made the people feel the want of a central authority, and the patriarch, who was the only bond and symbol of their union, caused the election of a doge (*dux*) in the year 697. This officer was elsewhere appointed by the emperor; but as there was none at Venice, the election was considered to indicate the union of the islands, not the establishment of independence, and the doges continued on good terms with the emperor. But the imperial authority was as completely gone as in Rome, and the year 697 is as important an epoch in the Venetian annals as the year 728 in the history of the Roman state. For a time there was a rivalry between the patriarch and the doge, and the former attempted to establish the same ecclesiastical authority over the state with which the Popes had been invested. But it was quite consistent with the purely Roman character of the place and people, and with the weakness of the hierarchical element, that the secular authority should prevail. The Bishop had not, like the Pope, the recommendation of being a national representative; for that distinction belonged to the Pope alone among the Italian Bishops, and at Venice the doge was the people's choice.

Whilst both at Venice and at Naples the Bishop was instrumental in the establishment of independence, and balanced for a time the power of the duke, at Ravenna, when the exarch disappeared, the Archbishop naturally and without opposition succeeded to his place; and it was so much in the order of things that the Bishop of every great community should rule it after the overthrow of the Greeks, that it was some time before the Archbishop of Ravenna would submit to the temporal authority of the Pope. A rivalry of honour had long subsisted between the Bishop of the new capital of Italy and the Bishop of the old. When, therefore, the exarchate was given to the Pope, the Archbishop Sergius resisted, and claimed in his own province the same temporal rights which the Pope enjoyed in Rome.[1] His successor Leo pursued

---

[1] "Judicavit iste a finibus Perticæ totam Pentapolim, et usque ad Tusciam, et

the same course; and in the year 774 Pope Hadrian complains to Charlemagne that the Archbishop claimed the whole of the exarchate.[1] Thus in every great town whose history at that time is sufficiently known, the same scene occurs on a smaller scale which in Rome was the origin of the temporal power.

We have seen how the position of the Holy See in the declining empire of the Greeks gradually led to the complete independence, and to the complete detachment of its territory and dependencies from that empire, although the forms of submission continued to be used, and although the Pope acknowledged the Eastern emperor as his sovereign until the revival of the empire in the West. We have seen that it was no sudden or single act, that it was part of a general analogous movement throughout Italy, and a result not of design, but of necessity; that it was a physiological process rather than a political act. The scene now passes from the Greeks to that of the Franks, in which the situation of the Pope is greatly altered; in which his temporal power receives a vast increase, but in which he is surrounded with the perils and difficulties of a new system, and commences a new contest for the freedom which his temporal sovereignty seemed rather to have imperilled than assured.

The almost total disappearance of the imperial armies from the West, in consequence of the war with the Saracens, left the Lombards free to conquer the whole of Italy, without meeting any independent power capable of resistance but the Pope. Luitprand, the most successful of their kings, died in 743. During his reign, the Pope had been obliged to appeal to Charles Martel for aid, which no longer came from his own sovereign; but that aid was not given, and at his death Luitprand was reconciled with the Pope.[2] But in the year 753, the Lombards under Aistolphus

---

usque ad mensam Uvulani, veluti exarchus, sic omnia disponebat, ut soliti sunt modo Romani facere" (Agnellus, *Liber Pontificalis, Vita Sergii*, 4).

[1] "Asserit . . . in ea potestate sibi exarchatum Ravennatium quam Sergius archiepiscopus habuit tribui" (*Cod. Carol.*, 52).

[2] The late Frankish chronicles represent this appeal as an offer to transfer the Roman territory from the Greek to the Frankish dominion: "Epistolam quoque decreto Romanorum principum sibi predictus præsul Gregorius miserat, quod sese populus Romanus, relicta imperatoris dominatione, ad suam defensionem et invictam clementiam convertere voluisset" (*Annal. Mettenses ad ann.* 741—in Pertz, *Monumenta*, i, 326).

conquered the exarchate, and the Greek domination in Central Italy came to an end. Aistolphus demanded the submission of the Pope. Stephen II applied first for help to the heretical emperor Constantine, before he took a step which must be fatal to the imperial rights over the exarchate. Constantine could send no expedition to Italy, and directed the Pope to negotiate with the Lombard king the restoration of his territory. Stephen proceeded to Pavia, where he obtained nothing, and then to France, where the new king Pepin, who had just been crowned by St Boniface, had already given him a secret promise of assistance. Pepin invaded Italy in two successive years, and formally gave the exarchate, which he wrested from the Lombards, back to the Pope. By this transaction, his position in Italy was not greatly altered. His authority was established over a territory in which his influence had already been paramount, and in which the imperial authority, long scarcely more than nominal, had expired altogether. Two or three years before, Pepin, then mayor of the palace in France, considering that the Merovingian dynasty had for several generations been merely a phantom on the throne, had sent to ask Pope Zachary whether it was necessary that, although without the royal power, they should continue to bear the title; and the Pope had answered that he that really possessed the power ought to have the name of king.[1] Pepin acted upon the same principle in restoring to the Pope that authority over the exarchate which the emperors were no longer able to exercise, and which he alone could effectually possess. At the same time, the Pope thus obtained compensation for the domains which the Greeks had confiscated.

It was only by slow degrees that they obtained possession of what had been conceded to them. The exarchate did not come completely into their hands for twenty years after the expedition of Pepin. In 774, Charlemagne overthrew the Lombard kingdom, and made new concessions to the Holy See. Some were in fulfilment of his father's engagements; some in satisfaction of old claims advanced by the Popes, which always required to be thoroughly substantiated. A complete account of all these con-

---

[1] "Missi fuerunt ad Zach. P. interrogando de regibus in Francia, qui illis temporibus non habentes regalem potestatem, an bene fuisset, an non. Et Z. P. mandabit Pippino, ut melius esset illum regem vocari, qui potestatem haberet, quam illum, qui sine regali potestate manebat" (*Annal. Laurissenses*—Pertz, i, 136).

cessions is to be found in the Lives of the Popes, and in their letters in the *Codex Carolinus*. In the *Monumenta Germaniae Historica* (IV, p. ii, 8) the celebrated Pertz of Berlin enumerates, as follows, the possessions of the Holy See at the death of Charlemagne:

I. Of their own right (*ex antiquo jure*) the Popes held: the city and duchy of Rome, that is, the Campagna and Maritima, as far south as Ceperano and Terracina; Tuscia Romanorum, with the towns of Portus, Centumcellae, Ceres, Bleda, Marturianum, Sutria, Nepes, Castellum, Gallisium, Ortum, Polimartium, Amezia, Tuda, Perusia *cum insulis tribus*, Narnia, Utriculum. All these possessions were, *de jure* or *de facto*, anterior to the French donation.

II. By the gift of Pepin and Charlemagne: the exarchate and Pentapolis, comprising the towns named by Anastasius in the life of Stephen II—"Tradidit . . . Ravennam, Ariminum, Pisaurum atque Fanum, Cesenas, Senogallias, Esium, Forum Pompilii, Forum Livii, cum castro Sussubio, Montemferetri, Acerragio, Montem Lucari, Serram, castellum Sancti Mariani, Bobrum, Urbinum, Callium, Luculos, Eugubium seu Comiaclum. Nec non et civitatem Narniensem." From the letters of Pope Hadrian we know of many other places, partly conceded by Pepin, partly by Charles after the defeat of Desiderius. The great critic we are quoting says: "Sed et faventiam, ducatum Ferrariae, nec non Imolam, Bononiam, et Gabellum simul traditas fuisse, ex subsequentibus patet . . . Annis duo-de-viginti post, Desiderio primum fuso, Spoletini, Reatini, incolae ducatus Firmani, Auximani, Anconitani, et habitatores castelli Felicitatis ad Hadrianam papam se contulerunt."

III. By virtue of the first agreement between Pepin and Stephen, and of old claims made good to Charlemagne (*ex pacto Carisiacensi et jure Karolo Regi probato*), the territorium Sarinense, the towns in Tuscia Langobarda, and certain rights in Beneventum.

This is the authentic and definite extent of the Roman States under the Carolingian empire. Some writers have wished to represent the temporal dominion as far older than the eighth century, and as far more extensive than this. The latter opinion is founded partly upon the vague traditions and fictitious documents of the Middle Ages, partly upon claims raised by the

Popes themselves at various times. These claims were themselves in part founded on those documents; and such as were not founded on them, and yet are not included in the above list—Corsica, for instance, which was claimed in vain by Leo III, and by Leo IX in the year 1054—were never satisfied; what was afterwards added was acquired in a different way. The notion of the greater antiquity of the actual sovereignty of the Popes originated partly also in the fancies of uncritical times, but in great part in the difficulty of believing that in ages of great violence and adversity the spiritual authority could be preserved without the support of a wide material basis. But that which the Holy See required was, in the first instance, not riches or power, but freedom. Temporal sovereignty was for a century within their reach; but they absolutely refused it, and at all times amply acknowledged and respected, under Catholic and heretical as well as under heathen emperors, the authority of the empire which was the cradle of the Church. In the fixed system of the old society, their mission was more exclusively spiritual than among the barbarous races who destroyed it. They had less contact with the world. Their independence was sufficiently secured by the general absence of the emperor and of the Teutonic kings from Rome. Sovereignty, when it came, was forced upon them; they regarded it as an evil and had for ages reason to doubt whether it was the less of two evils.

It is more easy to ascertain the extent of the dominions than the extent of the authority which they received from the Franks. Charlemagne introduced into Italy the political system which he had established in the rest of his monarchy. In that system he had given the Church a great part.[1] Many of her canons obtained force of law in the state, and her ministers were invested with great civil authority. The influence thus given to them in the

---

[1] "Volumus atque præcipimus ut omnes suis sacerdotibus tam majoris ordinis quam inferioris, a minimo usque ad maximum, ut summo Deo, cujus vice in Ecclesia legatione funguntur, obedientes existant. Nam nullo pacto agnoscere possumus qualiter nobis fideles existere possunt, qui Deo infideles et suis sacerdotibus apparuerint, aut qualiter nobis obedientes nostrique ministris ac legatis obtemperantes erunt, qui illis in Dei causis et Ecclesiarum utilitatibus non obtemperant . . . qui autem in his, quod absit, aut negligentes eisque inobedientes fuerint inventi, sciant se nec in nostro imperio honores retinere, licet etiam filii nostri fuerint . . . sed magis sub magna districtione et ariditate pœnas luere" (*Capitulare de honore Episcoporum*—Baluzius, *Capitularia*, i, 437).

scheme of Charlemagne was secured and increased by the property they acquired. The distribution of property determined, in the Frankish monarchy, the position, the power, and the rights of each individual and of every class. It was necessary and easy for the clergy to take their place in that hierarchy of landed proprietors. In order that they might not thus become subject, like all other classes of society, to the laws and to the will of the sovereign, they obtained for their domains and those who resided on them an immunity from the civil jurisdiction; and the domains themselves were called Immunities (*Immunitates*). These rights and privileges, and the most extensive participation in affairs of state, continued to be respected and even increased by the emperors; so that out of this position of the clergy in the state a territorial independence afterwards developed itself, and ecclesiastical states arose, almost identical in origin and character with that of the Popes. It was entirely in the interest of the sovereign that the clergy should be powerful; but it was in his interest that they should be subservient. The greater the influence of prelates in the state, the greater was the inducement to appoint only such as were most agreeable to the government. Hence the vital importance of the dispute which necessarily arose on the freedom of investiture.

The position of the Pope in the Carolingian empire already resembled in many respects that of other Bishops. His states were, in one aspect, the greatest Immunity of the empire. The limits of his jurisdiction cannot be ascertained in detail;[1] but the

---

[1] The most instructive document in this respect is the Constitution of the Emperor Lothar, in 824, and the oath which he exacted from the Romans:

"Volumus ut in electione Pontificis nullus præsumat venire, neque liber neque servus, qui aliquod impedimentum faciat, illis solummodo Romanis, quibus antiquitus fuit consuetudo concessa per constitutionem sanctorum patrum eligendi pontificem . . .

"Volumus ut missi constituantur de parte domni apostolici et nostra, qui annuatim nobis renuntiare valeant, qualiter singuli duces et judices justitiam populo faciant, et quomodo nostram constitutionem observent. Qui missi, decernimus, ut primum cunctos clamores qui per negligentiam ducum aut judicum fuerint inventi ad notitiam domni apostolici deferant, et ipse unum et duobus eligat, ut aut statim per eosdem missos fiant ipsæ necessitates emendatæ, aut si non, per nostrum missum fiat nobis notum, ut per nostros missos a nobis directos iterum emendentur.

"Volumus ut cunctus populus Romanus interrogetur, qua lege vult vivere, ut tali qua se professi fuerint vivere velle, vivant."

Sacramentum Romanorum, consequent on this decree:

great test of independence, the freedom of election, was as completely wanting under the Carolingian as under the Greek emperors. Until the elevation of Gregory III, the confirmation of each election had to be obtained from Constantinople or Ravenna before the Pope could be consecrated, and the delay which ensued from this practice is often complained of by the Popes. The Franks were supposed to have succeeded the Greeks in all the rights of their supremacy.[1] Accordingly, from the time of Charlemagne, the Popes sent to France for their confirmation. Stephen went himself to Rheims to obtain it. Paschal I was consecrated without the emperor's consent, and sent at once to excuse himself. Of most of his successors it is recorded that they awaited the imperial sanction.[2] With friendly emperors, there were no evil consequences from this arrangement; but at last the election came entirely into their hands.[3]

"Promitto . . . quod ab hac die in futuram fidelis ero domnis nostris imperatoribus . . . diebus vitæ meæ . . . salva fide quam repromisi domno apostolico; et quod non consentiam ut aliter in hac sede Romana fiat electio pontificis nisi canonice et juste . . . et ille qui electus fuerit me consentiente consecratus pontifex non fiat, prius quam tale sacramentum faciat in præsentia missi domni imperatoris et populi" (Pertz, *Monumenta*, iii, 240).

[1] "In supplemento historiæ Pauli Diaconi, quod extat in Corpore Francicæ historiæ veteris et sinceræ, ad hunc annum legitur: Lotharius Imperator primo ad Italiam venit, et diem sanctum Paschæ Romæ fecit. Paschalis quoque apostolicus potestatem, quam prisci imperatores habuere, ei super populum Romanum concessit" (Pagi, *Critica in Baronium*, iii, 510). "Statutum est juxta antiquum morem ut ex latere imperatoris mitterentur, qui judiciariam exercentes potestatem, justitiam omni populo . . . penderent" (*Vita Ludovici*, Pii—in Bouquet, *Receuil des Historiens de France*, vi, 106).

[2] "Eodem anno (816) Leo Papa Romanus obiit et Stephanus post eum successit, qui statim postquam pontificatum suscepit, jussit omnem populum Romanum fidelitatem cum juramento promittere Hludowico" (Thaganus, *Vita Ludovici Imp.*—Pertz, *Monumenta*, ii, 593).

"Paschalis successor electus, post completam solemniter ordinationem suam et munera et excusatoriam imperatori misit epistolam . . . missa tamen alia legatione, pactum quod cum præcessoribus suis factum erat, etiam secum fieri et firmari rogavit" (Einhardi, *Annales*—Pertz, i, 203).

"Gregorius . . . electus, sed non prius ordinatus est, quam legatus imperatoris Romani venit, et electionem populi, qualis esset, examinavit" (Ibid., 216).

[3] "Nicolaus præsentia magis ac favore Hindovici regi et procerum ejus quam cleri electione substituitur" (*Annales Vertrinani, ad ann.* 850).

"Romani, Pontificis sui morte comperta, Stephanum in locum ejus constituerunt. Unde imperator iratus quod eo inconsulto ullum ordinare præsumpserant, misit Liutwartum et quosdam Romanæ sedis episcopos, qui eum deponerent" (*Annales Fuldenses, ad ann.* 885—Pertz, i, 402).

When the Carolingian empire fell to pieces, the Holy See came under the dependence of factions and families in Rome, whom there was no power to restrain, and who were supreme during every vacancy. From these it was rescued for a time by Otho at the revival of the empire, who assumed once more the right of confirmation, and even the right of appointing and deposing Popes. In Germany, where the Bishops were a formidable power in the State, the freedom of election had been abolished, and the nominee of the emperor always succeeded. Otho attempted the same thing with the Papacy. In reality, he would have reduced the Pope nearly to the position of the Patriarch of Constantinople; but the oppression which the Holy See had suffered was so intolerable, that his rude violence appeared as a deliverance; and Pope John XIII soon after declared that Rome and the Church had been brought near to destruction by wicked men, but had been saved and restored to their ancient splendour by the emperor.[1] The Holy See was not delivered from this alternate dependence on the emperor and the nobles of Rome until the law of Nicholas II in 1059. Gregory VII, in his efforts to secure the freedom of the prelates throughout the Church, established also, for all future ages, the freedom of the Papal election. The full temporal sovereignty over the Roman States was first secured by the same act which established, on a foundation which has never since been permanently shaken, the independence of the head of the Church.[2]

The territorial losses of the Holy See during this period were as great as the Popes' political weakness and insecurity would lead us to expect. In the course of the ninth century, the Popes surrendered a great part of their possessions to the barons on feudal tenure. There was no other way of obtaining military service, and the feudal system was already quite in the spirit of the times. There were so many claimants for these concessions, and they were so often convenient for the purpose of conciliating dangerous or ambitious men, that the Popes were obliged to de-

---

[1] Roma caput totius mundi, et ecclesia universalis ab iniquis pene pessumdata, a Domino Ottone augusto imperatore, a Deo coronato Cæsare, et magno et ter benedicto ... erecta est, et in pristinum honorem omni reverentia redacta" (Mansi, *Consilia*, xviii, 509). Mansi questions the authenticity of this and other letters of John XIII (ibid., 506), but it is admitted by modern Catholic critics (Floss, *Privilegium Leonis VII*, 1858, p. 38).

[2] Council of Ravenna, 877; Jaffe, *Regesta Pontif.*, 269.

clare a portion of the *patrimonium* their own private domain, and inalienable *beneficialiter vel alio quolibet modo*. In the States of the Church, as in all other feudal states, this system soon overgrew the supreme power. Here, as elsewhere, the feudatories sought to make their fiefs hereditary; and often, from the weakness of the sovereign, they so far succeeded as to make the *dominium directum* of the Holy See little more than a name. For a long time it seemed probable that, as in Germany, the territories would make themselves permanently independent; and it was not until after a struggle of more than five centuries, that in Rome, as in France, and about the same time as in France, the temporal power triumphed over the feudal barons. Sacrifices of rights and territory were not, however, confined to the nobles. In the year 997, for instance, Gregory V surrendered to Gerbert, afterwards Sylvester II, the Archbishop of Ravenna, almost all his rights over the city and its territory.[1] In the time of Gregory VI, says William of Malmesbury, the Papal dominions were so much diminished, that the Pope had scarcely wherewithal to maintain himself.[2] In the same year in which Nicholas II settled the mode of the Papal election by the Cardinals, he concluded a treaty with Robert Guiscard the Norman, who undertook to recover all the lost rights and possessions of the Holy See; and thus, as we have already said, the temporal rights and the ecclesiastical independence were fixed at the same time. The Countess Matilda left her states to the Pope early in the following century, and this vast accession of territory was, after a long struggle with the emperors, finally recognized and confirmed under Innocent III. Before the dispute was concluded, the Popes had been exiled more than once, imprisoned, and deprived of nearly all their dominions; but in the act of Otho IV of the year 1201, repeated in 1209, the independence of the Roman States is definitely settled and acknow-

---

[1] "Districtum Ravennatis urbis, ripam integram, monetam teloneum, merceatum, muros et omnes portas civitatis" (Jaffe, 342).

The Archbishop of Ravenna continued to extend the dominion even till Gregory VII's time. He writes in the year 1073: "Quidam Imolenses . . . nobis indicavere quod confrater noster Guibertus archiepiscopus Ravennas eos contra honorem S. Petri, cui fidelitatem juravere, suæ omnino ditioni subigere, et ad juranda sibi fidelitatis attentet sacramenta compellere" (*Epis.* i, 10).

[2] "Ita apostolatus Romani statum per incuriam antecessorum diminutum invenit, ut præter pauca oppida urbi vicina et oblationes fidelium pene nihil haberet quo se sustentaret" (*De Gestis Regum Angl.*—Pertz, xii, 469).

ledged.[1] This document has been called, not unjustly, the Magna Charta of the papal dominions; and it was repeatedly cited and confirmed by later sovereigns.

During the three following centuries, the limits of the possessions of the Holy See were, if we except the acquisition of Venaissin and Avignon, not greatly changed, but the extent of their authority constantly varied. They triumphed at last over captivity and the schism; over the emperors, the barons and the republics. It would far exceed our limits to relate in what manner, and after what vicissitudes and revolutions, the unity of their states was completed by force of arms, first by Albornoz, and at last by Caesar Borgia and Julius II. During the pontificate of the latter, the Roman States formed for the first time a real monarchy, extending from Piacenza to Terracina. A few territories subsequently lapsed: Ancona, 1532; Camerino, 1539; Ferrara and Comacchio, 1598; Urbino, 1626; Castro, 1649. It was not, therefore, till the middle of the seventeenth century that the Papal dominions reached their highest point of increase. For more than a century the temporal authority of the Popes remained unchallenged and unaltered, and they enjoyed a period of repose such as they had never known in more Catholic times. Then, at the end of the eighteenth century, came a period of disaster and decline, of which we have not seen the end nor, we fear, the worst.

The external changes which have since occurred in the temporal condition of the Church were preceded and prepared by changes which had taken place within. She had resisted the outward assault of the Protestant Revolution to be sapped by the Revolution which had its seat in Catholic countries, and extensively prevailed in the Church herself. The spirit of opposition to the Holy See grew in energy, and the opposition to its system and ideas spread still more widely. In many respects, the Jansenists were the chief partisans of these opinions. The suppression of the Jesuits was their work; they had great part in the revolutionary reforms of such princes as Joseph II; and when the French

---

[1] "Ad has pertinet tota terra quæ est a Radicofocano usque Ceperanum; exarchatus Ravennæ, Pentapolis, Marchiae, ducatus Spoletanus, terra comitissæ Mathildis, comitatus Brittenorii, cum aliis adjacentibus terris expressis in multis privilegis imperatorum a tempore Lodovici" (*Ottonis juramentum Papae*—Pertz, iv, 205).

Revolution broke out, they supported the confiscation of the property of the Church. The assemblies of Ems and Pistoja prove how far subversive notions of Church government had extended among the higher prelates. It is to the prevalence of false political theories—or rather, perhaps, to the absence of a sound political system among Catholics—that the success of the Revolution against the Church, and the feebleness of the resistance, are to be ascribed.

The danger with which feudalism menaced the freedom of the Church was so great, that the two things were thought incompatible. Whilst, on the one hand, a simoniacal and wedded clergy was considered necessary to the well-being of the feudal state, it was deemed, on the other hand, that independence required exclusion; and one of the Popes proposed to cut the knot by surrendering all the feudal property held by ecclesiastics. The struggle between the Church and the world resolved itself into a contest between the Church and the State, the priesthood and the empire; and whilst neither thought it could secure its rights and respect those of the other, each conceived that it was safe only if it was predominant. The notion of the superiority of the ecclesiastical power ripened into the notion of the worthlessness of the civil power, and of the derivation of its authority from the Church.[1] No better speculative basis than this was found for the conflict with the state in those days. This anti-political theory was defended on Scriptural grounds, with that facility of quotation and respect for all written authority which is so characteristic of the Middle Ages. It was much assisted by that view of the antagonism of the two cities, of Church and State, which had been made popular by St Augustine. It was especially confirmed and promoted by the influence of ancient heathen literature, which gave to the theocratic doctrine a democratic basis. The heathen notion of tyrannicide became an auxiliary in the development of that view of the secondary and derivative nature of all civil authority on which the deposing power was often de-

---

[1] "Cui aperiendi claudendique cœli data potestas est, de terra judicare non licet? Absit . . . Quis nesciat, reges et duces ab iis habuisse principium, qui Deum ignorantes, superbia, rapinis, perfidia, homicidiis, postremo universis pæne sceleribus, mundi principe diabolo videlicet agitante, super pares scilicet homines, dominari cæca cupiditate et intolerabili præsumtione affectaverunt?" (Gregory VII, *Epist.* viii, 21).

fended. That the notion of the rightfulness of destroying tyrants came into Catholic theology from heathen sources, and is not a product of Christian ethics, is proved by its presence, in the most offensive form, in the works of a man who was more deeply imbued than almost any of his contemporaries with ancient learning, and who wrote before such questions were discussed in the schools, before what is called scholastic theology began to be known.[1] This combination of Jewish and Grecian notions was a welcome weapon in the hands of the Reformers against Catholic princes,[2] and was abundantly used by the Catholics in the days of absolute monarchy against Protestant sovereigns, such as Henry IV and James I. For the protection of their Catholic subjects, many of the divines of that day had recourse to the theory of the sovereignty of the people, and of the indirect derivation of all civil authority from God, not through the Church, as had been held before, but through the people. From this system, of which the most complete exposition is to be found in Suarez, and which has been revived in our own day chiefly by Ventura,[3] but which was at no time generally received, to the pure revolutionary theory of Rousseau—from the notion that power comes

---

[1] "Aliter cum amico, aliter vivendum est cum tyranno. Amico utique adulari non licet, sed auris tyranni mulcere licitum est. Ei namque licet adulari, quem licet occidere. Porro tyrannum occidere non modo licitum est, sed aequum et justum. Qui enim gladium accipit, gladio dignus est interire . . . Certe hostem publicum nemo ulciscitur, et quisquis eum non persequitur, in seipsum et in totum reipublicæ mundanæ corpus delinquit" (John of Salisbury, *Polycraticus*, iii, 15; vol. iii, p. 217, ed. Giles). And St Thomas, in defining the right of tyrannicide, rests it upon heathen authorities, and is careful to vindicate even Cicero from the reproach of false morality:

"Tullius loquitur in casu illo quando aliquis dominium sibi per violentiam surripit, nolentibus subditis, vel etiam ad consensum coactis, et quando non est cursus ad superiorem, per quem judicium de invasore possit fieri: tunc enim qui ad liberationem patriæ tyrannum occidit, laudatur et præmium accipit" (*Com. in ii Sent.*, dist. 44, art. 2, ad quintum).

[2] "Pacem civilem perturbat dogma illud Reformatos se dicentium, licita esse pro religione subditorum in regna arma . . . Intelligimus quid significat Reformatos se dicentium confessio, cum dicit tributa et obsequia deberi regibus, dummodo summum Dei imperium salvum maneat. Per summum enim Dei imperium intelligunt religionis suæ libertatem, qualem ipsi aliis, ubi invaluere, non concedunt" (Grotius, *Rivetiani Apologetici discussio*—Opera Theolog., iv, 701, 702).

[3] Memoria pel riconoscimento della Sicilia come stato sovrano ed indipendente, 1848: "La sovranità è trasmessa dalla communità civile a chi, e dentro i limiti e le condizioni che le è piaciuto di adottare" (p. 14).

from the nation, to the opinion that the nation may control, modify, or resume the power it has conferred—there is but one inevitable step.

At the period of the French Revolution, these ideas were not extinct among Catholic divines, and an adaptation of religious ideas to the popular system of the day was attempted by Speda-lieri, who is better known by his refutation of Gibbon, in his work on the rights of man (*I Diritti dell' Uomo*, 1791), which is said to have received the corrections of Pius VI and Gerdil, and was dedicated to Cardinal Ruffo. The author received a benefice in St Peter's, and the congratulations of the Universities of Padua and Pavia. He endeavoured to show the harmony subsisting between the teaching of the Gospel and the newly-proclaimed rights of man. The state is founded on the original contract, which is the work of the people alone, and of which God can only be called the author in so far as He is the First Cause of all things. By this contract, the people have the right of judging and cashier-ing their sovereigns; and every man may use force, whenever it is necessary for his defence or for the assertion of his rights.

These ideas met with great opposition; but they were shared by men of high station; and it is evident that the Revolution was required to bring back a safer and truer political system. When the French invaded the Legations, and established the Cispad-ane Republic, Cardinal Chiaramonti, Bishop of Imola, issued a Christmas pastoral, recommending the people to submit quietly to the invaders, and declaring that the French principles of government were not opposed to the maxims of the Gospel. He was denounced as Jacobin by the people of his diocese. Artaud de Montor, who has translated the pastoral, attributes the most questionable passages to the advisers of the cardinal. That it was not completely approved of in Rome, appears from the manner in which the Roman biographer of Pius VII, Pistoleri, deals with it. He says that it was directed against French principles, and brought its author into trouble with the French authorities.[1] The misfortune was, that this conciliatory tendency assisted the spread of revolutionary principles, by meeting half-way a fav-ourite argument of their supporters. For while Catholics who did

---

[1] *Vita di Pio VII*, i, 4. The same mistake is repeated in the article on Pius VII, in the dictionaries of Feller and Moroni. Probably until the publication of Artaud's Life, the pastoral was very rare.

not understand the revolutionary theory thought they could agree with it, the Revolutionists, who did not understand Christianity, often proclaimed themselves its real apostles.[1]

The danger of the Revolution, its real character and tendency, were not at first understood. In an allocution of March 29, 1790, Pius VI says, that at first it had seemed as if nothing was intended but arrangements of political economy; and that as these were designed for the alleviation of the imposts on the people, it appeared that they would concern nothing in his apostolic ministry.[2] It was not until Religion herself was attacked that the danger was recognized.[3] In a brief of August 17, the same year, Pius VI excuses himself with the French king that he had not from the first more openly declared his hostility to the revolutionary opinions;[4] and he says nearly the same thing in a letter to the French Bishops of March 10, 1791.[5]

In fact, there was a revolutionary element in the centralizing tendency of the age from which the government of the Roman States was not exempt. Thus at the Restoration, Consalvi not only takes advantage of the French reforms, but rejoices that they facilitate the execution of the projects of centralization, which he describes as essential to a well-governed state;[6] and a Bolognese

---

[1] We need hardly recall the answer of Camille Desmoulins before the revolutionary tribunal, when he was asked his age, which was 33.

[2] Artaud, *Histoire des Papes*, viii, 214.

[3] Even Artaud says of the Pope's letter to Louis XVI, "Ici Pie VI étend un peu trop la faculté qu'un roi de France a de renoncer aux droits de la couronne" (219).

[4] ibid., 221.   [5] ibid., 239.

[6] "Noi riflettemmo in primo luogo, che la unità ed uniformità debbono esser le basi di ogni politica istituzione, senza delle quale difficilmente si può assicurare la solidità di governi, e la felicità de'popoli; e che un governo tanto più può riguardarsi come perfetto, quanto più si avvicina a quel sistema di unità stabilito da Dio tanto nell' ordine della natura, quanto nel sublime edificio della religione. Questa certezza c'indusse a procurare perquanto fosse possibile la uniformità del sistema in tutto lo stato appartenente alla Santa Sede" (*Motu proprio*, 6 July 1816. *Bullarii Magni continuatio*, xiv, 47).

"Mancava ancora al nostro stato quella uniformità, che è cosi utile ai publici e privati interessi, perchè formato colla sucessiva riunione di dominii differenti, presentava un aggregato di usi, di leggi, di privilegij fra loro naturalmente difformi, cosicchè rendevano una provincia bene spesso straniera all altra, e talvolta disgiungeva nella provincia medesima l'uno dall' altro pæse.

"Penetrati i sommi pontefici nostri predecessori della verità delle massime sopra enunciate, profittarono di ogni opportunità per richiamare ai principii uniformi i diversi rami di publica amministrazione, e noi medesimi nel cominciamento del

historian, otherwise full of admiration for Pius VI, speaks of the invasion as having delivered the provinces from an oppressive and almost tyrannical system which was on the point of being introduced.[1] In reality, this unpopular process had not made much progress, and was impeded by the great privileges of the barons and the liberties of the towns. The most independent of these was Bologna. That town, in capitulating to Julius II, after many centuries of alternate submission and resistance, had stipulated for the maintenance of its rights as the condition of its fidelity. All civil causes were judged by a code called the Statute of Bologna. The taxes were imposed by the senate, which was composed of forty hereditary senators, belonging to the old nobility of the province, who conducted the whole financial administration, and superintended all internal interests. Bologna was represented in Rome by an ambassador, and the Pope sent a legate to represent him at Bologna. The whole province only paid 35,328 scudi a year to the Pontifical treasury, whilst the revenue from Ancona amounted to 363,599 scudi, and the whole revenue from the states to 2,278,923 scudi.[2]

The taxation was very low; for vast sums continued to be sent from other countries, and there were no longer the same demands on the Papal treasury which at the time of the Turkish wars, and of the wars of religion, were a constant and terrible drain. The annual revenue which the Pope derived from the whole Church,

---

nostro pontificato procurammo di servire in parte a queste vedute medesime. La collisione pero dei diversi interessi, l'attaccamento alle antiche abitudini, gli ostacoli che sogliono moltiplicarsi, ove si tratti di correggiare stabilimenti esistenti, ed usi inveterati, non permisero fin qui condurre al compimento quell'opera ...

"Ma la sempre ammicabile provvidenza divina, la quale sapientemente dispone le umane cose in modo, che talvolta d'onde sovrastano maggiori calamità, indi sà trarre anche copiosi vantaggi, sembra che abbia disposto, che le stesse disgrazie de' trascorsi tempi, e l'interrompimento medesimo dell' esercizio della nostra temporale sovranità aprissero la strada ad una tale operazione, allorchè pacificate le cose si dasse luogo alla ripristinazione delle legitime potestà. Noi dunque credemmo di dover cogliere questo momento per compite l'opera incominciata" (ibid., p. 48).

[1] "Desioso d'un autorità assoluta ed imperiosa, non poteva riguardare con occhio d'amico nemmeno quei vestigi di libertà, che davano a Bologna da gran tempo il primato sull'altre terre ecclesiastiche. Fù sconvolto l'ordine delle cose, si manomisero i diritti antiche; e il senato fù costretto colle minacce al silenzio ... E già pareva deciso che i redditi della provincia subirebbero l'amministrazione infedele dei ministri di chiesa" (Muzzi, Annali di Bologna, viii, 556).

[2] Lalande, Voyage en Italie, v, 281. Annali di Bologna dall'anno 1797 ai nostri giorni, dal Dottor L. A. 6.

independently of the income from his states, was estimated in the year 1595 at 700,000 scudi,[1] whilst the temporal sources did not produce more than 300,000. In the eighteenth century, the revenue from some countries was diminished. It is estimated by the traveller we have just quoted at 509,512 scudi. From Germany alone the annual income was 410,297 florins. A recent writer, who is often well-informed, computes the revenue from spiritual sources alone at 3,500,000 francs before the Revolution, and 1,500,000 in 1847.[2] The existence of this productive source of revenue was a great alleviation to the inhabitants of the Roman States. Since the Revolution, it has in great part ceased.[3] The domains of the Church, exceeding £8,000,000, were lost. The contributions levied by the French under Pius VI alone amounted to £9,000,000 sterling on a population of less than 2,000,000; and the revenue has increased from 2,300,000 scudi (£460,000) to 14,600,000 scudi, or nearly £3,000,000 in 1857. This is one great result of the Revolution; it rendered the Church dependent on the State, and the efforts made to meet the new expenses led to great social and constitutional changes.

By an edict for the restoration of the finances, November 28, 1797, Pius VI ordered the sale of the property of the towns (*communità*) and of a fifth of the property of the Church. The exile of the Pope followed soon after; and his successor, on his arrival in Rome, proclaimed at once the restoration of the old forms of administration.[4] But a few months later, it was decreed that the government should take upon itself the debts of the *communes*, and should assume for that purpose the administration of their estates, "i quali corsi, è a tutti abbastanza noto, sono di gran lunga in-

---

[1] Bozio, *De Signis Ecclesiæ*, lib. x, sign. 42, cap. 12.

[2] Neigebaur, *Der Pabst und sein Reich*, 106.

[3] This was Consalvi's argument for the restoration of the Papal States in his note to the Powers, dated London, June 23, 1814: "Ayant perdu presque entièrement les autres moyens pour pouvoir les supporter (les grandes dépenses pour le bien de la religion), le Saint Père, encore pour cet objet, ne saurait être privé des ressources qu'il pourrait trouver au moins en conservant la totalité de ses propriétés."

[4] *Reformatio curiae Romanae*, October 30, 1800. *Bullar. Cont.*, xi, 49: *Post Diuturnas*. "Cessare volumus illud temporarium regimen quo provideri publicis rebus necessitate cogente debuit, ac suam vim restituimus antiquis regiminis formis ...

"Maxime enim nobis in animo est ut esse debet, formas et regendi rationes a nostris praedecessoribus sapientissime stabilitas, et longo usu et multorum saeculorum experientia comprobatas, quantum fieri potest, retinere et conservare."

feriori all'immenza mole dei debiti che l'opprimono."[1] Thus the basis of the self-government of the country was lost.

During the French occupation, it was not restored; yet their administration was not felt as oppressive. It was particularly popular with those classes of the laity which have since been most discontented. For though the nobles did not recover their baronial rights, a great career was opened to them in the state which was closed before. But this compensation they afterwards lost, without recovering their old feudal authority.

At the restoration, Pius VII was preceded on his return to Rome by Rivarola as apostolic delegate. He issued a manifesto, May 15, 1814, announcing that the people would be relieved from the oppressions of the French administration, and that the whole of the earlier legislation and system of government should be restored.[2] At that time Consalvi was negotiating the restora-

[1] ibid., 132. *Motu Proprio*, March 19, 1801. In two allocutions of 1808, March 16 and July 11, Pius VII expresses himself as follows on the temporal authority of the Holy See, its obligations, and the incompatible proposal of the French Emperor that he should accept the Code Napoléon:

"Hoc nostro, nobis a Deo dato, temporalis principis munere nihil aggredi possumus, quod officiis apostolici ministerii, nobis item a Deo praecipueque commissi, adversetur.

"Itaque pro discrimine quod inter nos, aliosque interest principes, qui non iisdem obligantur vinculis, quibus ipsi obligati sumus, nobis non semper licet in ratione politicarum rerum iisdem atque illi principiis uti.

"Vim huic summo sedis apostolicæ imperio afferre, temporalem ipsius potestatem a spirituali discerpere, pastoris et principis munera dissociare, divellere, exscindere, nihil aliud est, nisi Opus Dei pessumdare, ac perdere velle, nihil nisi dare operam, ut religio maximum detrimentum capiat, nihil nisi eam efficacissimo spoliare praesidio" (xiii, 261, 263).

"Primum Romani, tum plures Italiæ civitates spontanea deditione Romanae ecclesiæ potestati se subjecerunt, cujus praeterea auctoritas mirum in modum amplificata est ex suavi et leni Summorum Pontificum imperio.

"Stephanus III adiit Pipinum Caroli magni patrem, ut Aistulphi insolentiam totam pene Italiam depopulantis compesceret, eumque ad reddendas eas urbes ac provincias astringeret, quas uti ad Romanum jam Pontificem spectantes Pontifex repetebat . . .

"Imo, si quis cujuscumque familiam tam longevo possessionis jure munitam a privato fundo exturbare auderet, neque a judice audiretur, et nonnisi per vim et calumniam id fieri posse unusquisque censeret . . .

"Postremo, codicem promulgari urgerique, in quo ut multa, sed leges praesertim, quæ de impedimentis matrimonii, divortiisque disponunt, divinis et ecclesiasticis institutis contrarias complorare cogimur" (ibid., 294, 296, 297).

[2] "Sua Santità crede dover sollevare i suoi sudditi dall'oppressione che hanno sofferta con tante pazienza e coraggio . . . Il codice di Napoleone e quello del com-

tion of the Legations at Vienna. At the second restoration, in 1815, the government was in his hands, and he proceeded on a different system. The point of contact between the French system and the tendency of the Roman government before the Revolution was the inclination towards unity and the increase of the central power. Whatever contributed to this end, in the French institutions, was preserved. The feudal rights were so greatly restricted,[1] that Prince Colonna and other nobles resigned them altogether. All municipal laws, all statutes and decrees, under whatever title and authority, and in whatever portion of the state they might be, whether given for a whole province or in a particular district, were abolished, excepting such as related to agriculture, pasturage, or watercourses. The revolution was so complete, that in a pamphlet written by a partisan of Consalvi during the conclave of 1823, it was defended on the plea, that Pius VII had treated his states, and justly treated them, as a conquered territory, "riconquisto colle arme altrui."[2] In the same year, the opposition to his reforms avenged itself upon him in the epigram

Il ciel ci salvi
D'un nom despotico qual è Consalvi.

On his way to Italy from his prison at Bézières, in April 1814, Cardinal Consalvi one day found himself delayed, as the post-horses were required for the emperor, who was passing on the road to Elba. Consalvi stood by the roadside to let the emperor's carriage pass. Napoleon recognized him, and pointed him out to the Austrian officer who accompanied him, saying, "C'est un

---

mercio, il codice penale e quello di procedura, resta da questo istante abolito in perpetuo in tutti i dominii di Sua Santità . . . L'antica legislazione civile e militare, tale ch'esisteva all'epoca della cessazione del governo pontificio, è rimessa da questo istante in vigore" (Pistolesi, iii, 191).

[1] "In tutte le popolazioni è communità dello stato, ove esistono i baroni sono e s'intendono fin da ora soppressi ed aboliti tutti i diritti tendenti ad obbligare i vassalli alla prestazione di qualunque servigio personale; tutti quelli di successione ereditaria riservata ai medisimi baroni . . . esenzioni . . . privative . . . e regalie feodali . . . senza che si possa dai baroni pretendere alcun compenso per tali abolizioni. 184. Sono parimente soppresse ed abolite tutte le riserve di caccia, e di pesca, eni fondi non proprii; e lo sono pure nei fondi proprii che non hanno recinti" (*Motu proprio*, 6 July 1816, par. 183).

[2] *Considerazioni sui Motu proprio del S. P. Pio VII, dei 6 Luglio,* 1816.

homme qui ne veut pas avoir l'air d'être prêtre, mais qui l'est plus que tous les autres." In his political notions Consalvi belonged to his age and country. He did not understand what we should call conservatism; like all counter-revolutionists, he had something of the revolutionist in his politics, and the words of de Maistre, "Nous ne voulons pas la contre révolution, mais le contraire de la Révolution," could not be applied to him. He upheld the principle of legitimacy only so far as the Church was interested in it; he treated the secret societies as dangerous, not to the State, but to the Church—as heretical, not as revolutionary; and he never would countenance the Holy Alliance. But although the State was centralized and secularized, although all other ecclesiastical governments had disappeared, and that of the Pope stood alone, he yet gave to the priesthood an unprecedented influence in it. In the town councils it was decreed that the clergy should preponderate,[1] and the great offices were given to them. This was, in fact, the greatest change of all. Before the Revolution, the administration was in the hands of the local authorities, of nobles and burgesses in their several spheres. The central authority had so little to do, that nobody complained of its being in clerical hands. There was no opposition or rivalry between the nobility and the clergy, because the higher grades of the *prelatura* were filled by the sons of noble families, who regarded it as their natural career. The Church was so rich, that it was worth the while of men of rank to belong to her, and the nobles were rich enough to support younger sons in the first and less profitable period of their ecclesiastical course. After the Revolution, this good understanding ceased. Both were impoverished; the nobility surrendered much of its authority into clerical hands, and ceased to form a considerable part of the body who now possessed it. The revolutionary movement was directed against the Church, and its institutions were generally calculated to diminish or control her influence. Yet these institutions were now preserved, and the clergy itself was to administer them, whilst the foundations of its power were destroyed. Thenceforward there was an unceasing and incurable antagonism between the clergy and the laity, who were excluded from the higher offices, and a still

[1] Besides sitting as deputies of the clergy, "ogni ecclesiastico inoltre potrà essere consigliere se avrà eletto", and "gli ecclesiastici sederanno in consiglio al di sopra dei laici" (*Motu proprio* of 1816, cap. 158).

more pernicious antagonism between the ecclesiastical body and the system by which they had to govern. This difficulty has made itself keenly felt ever since; and the efforts of three reforming Popes—of Leo XII, Gregory XVI, and Pius IX—have not succeeded in overcoming it, or in casting off the fatal legacy of the Revolution.

It does not come within the scope of this retrospect to discuss the crisis which has at last arrived. Decentralization is not a process which our age appears capable of achieving, and no State can escape from its own past, or swim twice down the same stream. The secularization of the Roman system is simply contrary to the notion of a State which exists as the property and for the benefit of the whole Catholic Church.[1] No scheme has been hitherto devised which could secure to her ruler the advantages, without the drawbacks, of temporal dominion, either by the old system of domains, by contributions of the faithful, by engagements of the powers, or by any combination of the three. Pius II has recorded[2] words, which were spoken in an age of equal tribulation which are not inapplicable to our own: "These are not times in which virtue is regarded. It is of all importance whether it resides in the strong or in the weak. A helpless virtue

[1] We may quote on this point the two most eminent Protestant canonists now living:

"It must not be forgotten that the Roman State has always been considered as a part of the property of the Church; that its revenues are intended to cover the expenses of the ecclesiastical government; and that when viewed in this light, its clerical administration is fully explained" (Richter's *Canon Law*, 247, 5th ed.).

"The States of the Church must be considered essentially the property of the Church. For in the guarantees of 1815, as well as in the donation of Pipin, the chief motive undoubtedly was to supply the great centre of administration with possessions whose revenues should contribute to maintain it in independence; . . . and the appointment of prelates to the high offices of state, which was usual also in the ecclesiastical states of Germany, follows from the nature of the state, and can hardly be blamed in principle" (Mejer, *Zeitschrift für Recht und Politik der Kirche*, 1847, i, 67).

"If we admit," says Ranke, "that the Catholic Church requires the Pope, that the Pope requires Cardinals, who elect him, and the Cardinals the prelature out of which they proceed; and if we acknowledge that the Pope, in order to be independent, must be a temporal sovereign;—it seems impossible to exclude those who are of the same nature and character as himself, and by whom his existence is determined, from the government of his dominions" (*Historich-politische Zeitschrift*, i, 772; 1832).

[2] *De Concilio Basil.*, pp. 107 sq.

is despised by the princes. I have often felt inclined to agree with those who think that the temporal power ought to be separated from the spiritual; for I thought that the priests would be better enabled to perform their functions, and that the princes would be more obedient to them. But now I have learned that virtue without power is scorned, and that the Pope without the patrimony of the Church is but a servant of kings."

The most powerful and prosperous of all the successors of St Peter has said, that what he relied on was not his own power, but the prayers of the whole Church—"Non de nostra virtute confidimus, sed de universalis Ecclesiae prece speramus."[1]

[1] Innocent III, *Epist.*, 1, 176.

III

THE POLITICAL SYSTEM OF THE POPES[1]

IT affords a melancholy comfort, in the midst of the dangers
which encompass the Holy See, and of the conspiracy which
is seeking to blot it out from the political world, to carry back
our thoughts to those ages of religious and political faith when
the temporal authority of the Pope was acknowledged by a great
portion of the European states. No writer has attempted to give
a complete account of the successive steps by which this authority
extended itself in opposition to the Empire; nor are the grounds
of its establishment generally understood. A short description of
what then occurred must, we conceive, interest alike the student
of history and the sincere Roman Catholic.

It is admitted by most, if not all historians, that in the Middle
Ages but two great systems of Christian states were known—the
East Roman, or Byzantine, and the West Roman, or German;
and, as Koch shows in his *Tableaux* of the revolutions of the
European states, a new system was inaugurated, only at the
threshold of modern times, by the expedition of Charles VIII to
Italy. Both mediaeval systems together comprised what is called
the *respublica Christiana*. To the first, the schismatical, belonged,
besides the Byzantine Empire in Europe and Asia, its Slavonic
and Rumanic dependencies; and, under Manuel Comnenus, it
tried to draw Hungary within its sphere, while to a certain degree
also the Russian countries might be given to it. Separation from
ancient Rome; spiritual connection with the Patriarch of Constantinople; the use of the Greek language in the liturgy and
administration; the acknowledgement of the Byzantine ruler
as temporal head; the absence of the characteristic signs of the
West, of parliamentary assemblies, of the independence of the
clergy, of the development of feudalism, of the freedom both of
peasants and towns; bureaucratic obstinacy; the use of mercenaries instead of national troops—these form the peculiar character of the Byzantine Empire, and of its influence in so far as it

[1] *The Rambler*, Jan. 1860, May 1860, Jan. 1861.

123

obtained complete authority. Add to this an intense and fatal hatred of the West, and of Rome in particular, together with a certain formal civilization, which made Byzantium the China of the Christian Middle Ages. Geographically the Byzantine system spread over the greater part of the Greek (Illyrian) peninsula; but when the Hungarian domination extended over Dalmatia and Croatia, it was expelled from the north-eastern coasts of the Adriatic and from the middle Danube; whilst on the lower Danube the boundaries were uncertain, as the Bulgarian Empire threw itself sometimes into the arms of Rome, sometimes of Byzantium.

Later than the Byzantine Empire, the imperial system of the Teutonic states arose. Together with the German empire, divided into seven duchies, it comprised from the time of Otho I the Italian Empire, from the time of Conrad II the kingdom of Arles, and from 962 the imperial dignity, which was considered as "Translatio imperii a Francis ad Germanos", as in the days of Charlemagne it had been conceived as "translatio imperii a Graecis ad Frances". An old book of the Gospels of the time of the Emperor Henry II describes how "Roma, Gallia, Germania, et Slavonia" render homage to the West Roman Emperor of the German nation. For "Gallia, Germania, et Italia" there were separate chancellors of the empire, in the Archbishops of Trèves, Mentz, and Cologne. The emperor, at the height of his power, considered the kings of the other countries as his provincial dependents, "reges provinciales"; which he could the more fairly do, since Poland, Bohemia, Denmark, and Hungary had attached themselves to the empire, either for a time or permanently. Thus one large empire, extending on both sides of the Alps from the centre of Europe as far north as south, included the principal nations of Europe—Germans, Romans, and Slavonians—and constituted the West as distinct from the East. The ancients, whose states either consisted of but one nation, which regarded and treated everything that was not Greek as barbarous, or else, where several nations were united in one empire, deprived them of right and liberty, could not show anything similar. Only dying and decaying nations belonged to the empire of the East; the new Roman Empire embraced the most vigorous and flourishing nations on earth, united them by one faith and one empire, and gave them the most free national development in political forms, in literature, art, commerce, and science. But the empire, in exhibiting its outward strength under the Franconian and Swabian emperors, occasioned the formation of the *Papal system*, which had originated in the opposition of the Catholic countries to the schismatical empire of Byzantium.

Long after the piety of the Anglo-Saxon kings induced them to offer at the shrine of the Prince of the apostles the Peter's pence in token of veneration and gratitude for the conversion of the Anglo-Saxon realm, Boris, king of the Bulgarians, sent his long hair to St Nicholas I (866) as a sign of submission, and called himself a servant of God, of St Peter and his successor. He demanded an explanation of 106 questions, and the grant of a special patriarch of Bulgaria. The Bulgarian prince had conceived the idea of an ecclesiastical independence of Constantinople, of the establishment of a special patriarchate for Bulgaria, and the attainment of Papal protection for the foundation of a new Catholic empire in Eastern Europe. The barbarian had commenced by the destruction of all the nobles who opposed him, together with their wives and children; then he applied to Rome, where the matter was taken in hand with great precaution, and where the sanguinary basis of negotiations was no more liked than the strange demands. In 870, Byzantine priests succeeded in winning Boris again for Constantinople. The hair remained at Rome, but the king sought his fortune at Constantinople; from whence, not quite 150 years after, under Basilius, the Bulgarian butcher, followed the almost entire destruction of his tribe.

The first transition from the act of veneration into an act of submission was thus made by the spontaneous act of the prince concerned, but it had no further effect; so that the centre which might in this manner have been formed for the Slavonic people who dwelt on the Danube was crushed in its germ. This people fell into the hands partly of the Byzantines, partly of the barbarous Magyars, and partly into those of the Germans. The last made Bohemia a tributary duchy; but Poland is said to have been raised to a kingdom by the Emperor Otho III through the coronation of the Duke Boleslaus Chrobvi, and to have been thus drawn into the German system of states. At all events, "Otho", as Thietmar of Merseburg writes, "made Ale king of Poland, who till then had been a tributary, a sovereign; and raised him so high, that he soon tried to bring those who were not set over him under his dominion and to make them slaves." The union with Germany, which brought only dependence, was soon dissolved by Boleslaus, and the preliminaries were laid of a similar connection with the Roman See; for to be subject to the Germans, to receive justice at their hands, was considered disgraceful for a Slavonian, as we see from the old Bohemian poem entitled "Libassa's Court". But it was no disgrace to pay tribute to St Peter; and it was considered a particular honour to receive from his successor a crown which, being sanctified by the papal protection, could not be withdrawn. Certain it is that Boleslaus sought for it in Rome; and it is hardly to be doubted that it was granted. Since that time Poland appears among the tributary Roman countries, and withdraws from the German Empire in order to join the Papal system of states.

This had already been the case with Hungary. When Stephen, the son of the Hungarian prince Geysa, tried to establish in Hungary a Christian Empire, he received baptism according to the Roman rite; it was only through the right estimation of its situation, between the Byzantine and German Empires, the two great political centres, as Pope Gregory writes, that Stephen committed his realm to the Pope, and received a Papal crown from Sylvester II. It became the real apostolic crown—a title applicable to no other. But this was not a mere title; it permanently secured the important borderland of Latin Christendom against the Greeks on one side, and against the supremacy of the German emperors on the other.

When the Emperor Henry III wished to appoint a German vassal in Hungary, even the German Pope Leo IX tried to preserve the original state of right against the emperor. In all other confederacies of states, each of them lost something of their independence, and the princes of their sovereignty, to the supreme power; that which we are describing conferred a guarantee of independence for the states and of sovereignty for the princes.

But time, which does not respect generalities, and which tended to constitute legislative rules in the place of vague and indefinite forms, and to create obligations accurately defined, had already found in vassalage the most natural expression for subordination, till, in the age of William the Conqueror, no other could be imagined than feudalism. By this the limits of both factors were most accurately and simply determined; the Church herself was obliged to submit to the feudal system, and, as we know, it cost more than fifty years' war (the war of Investitures) between the Pope and Emperor before this affair was arranged in the German Empire, and before the feudal system could be confined to the supreme dominion of the temporal power. But when, in the Concordat of Worms, in 1122, the dispute of Investitures had been brought to an end, the combat broke out anew, and with greater violence, in England, under Henry II, on account of the Constitutions of Clarendon. Thomas à Becket lost his life in the cause; and England, under John Lackland, almost lost her independence, and quite lost for a long time her power and authority.

The middle of the eleventh century, the age of Gregory VII, witnessed the rise, out of the elements already mentioned, of a political system which encircled the West Roman Empire of Germany, and from which even Germany and France could not entirely escape.

After the example of Poland, Bohemia also sought a nearer connection with Rome. The Duke Spitignew had voluntarily promised an annual tribute of a hundred pounds of silver to the Holy See, in acknowledgement of which he obtained in 1059 the right of wearing a cap. But the influence of the Emperor Henry IV in Bohemia soon supplanted the influence of the Pope. The Duke Wratislaus received from the German King the royal chain.[1]

It is evident that this was intended to preserve the imperial authority over Bohemia, as in later times when Wladislaus, the second King of Bohemia, received the royal crown from the hands of Frederick Barbarossa.[2] Neither, however, was acknowledged by the Roman See as a legitimate king; and it was not till 1204 that Prumysl Ottocar obtained from Innocent III the recognition of a dignity which had hitherto been a German and Ghibelline gift. The abandonment of the Bohemians of the course which they had adopted under Spitignew decided the future fate of the Western Slavs. They became, in contradistinction to Poland, a

[1] Cæsar (Henricus) ducem Bohemorum Wratislaum tam Bohemiæ quam Poloniæ præfecit imponens capiti ejus manu sua regalem circulum" (*Cosmas Pragensis*, 1086).

[2] "Imperator Wladislaum ducem Bohemiae regis inornat diademate de duce regem constitutum" (*Cosmae continuat*, 1159).

German province of the empire, remained so notwithstanding their Slavonic nationality, and quietly suffered the Slavs of the Elbe to be germanized. To the political divisions of the Slavonic tribes was added another fact of importance. In the year 1076, Demetrius (Swinomir), who had been unanimously elected king by the Croatian and Dalmatian people, received from the hands of the legate of Pope Gregory VII a banner, sword, sceptre, and crown, in return for the solemn promise of fidelity and obedience to the Holy See. At the beginning of the century the Croats had joined the Byzantine Empire; now their accession to the Latin ecclesiastical system was settled, and their independence secured. It was only when they were not able to maintain the latter against the Hungarians that their submission to the apostolic realm was made; not long before, Pope Gregory had written to the Hungarian king, Geysa: "We think that it is known to you that the kingdom of Hungary, as well as other very excellent kingdoms, must remain in the enjoyment of its own liberty." Substantially nothing was altered in Hungary through the annexation of the Croats; since, indeed, the Hungarian kingdom likewise belonged to the Papal system. But long after the Croats had become Hungarian through their own quarrels, when Biach, the favourite residence of the Dukes and Kings of Dalmatia and Croatia (at the Riviera della Castella) had been destroyed, when the Arpadian dynasty possessed the crown of Swinomir, and the Venetians the coast, the inhabitants of Castel Vecchio used to assemble at the annual change of the zupans, to celebrate the king's festival for eight days. The new zupan was clothed in the finest national dress; his sandals were adorned with gold thread, and he was hailed as king. He lived for eight days in the common hall, had guards around him, granted pardon and administered justice; and disappeared then like a meteor, as did the kingdom itself, and the history of this indolent and idle tribe.

While the Slavonic West was thus divided between Germany and Hungary, between the apostolic and imperial dominion, Poland, though divided in various ways, maintained its independence; and, moreover, in the year 1295 the Roman See agreed to an arrangement for its preservation. Przwislaus Duke of Kalisch was crowned and anointed in the name of Boniface VIII, and Poland obtained its renovation as a kingdom. Thus, by the establishment of the Papal system, was a formula devised by which different nations found a common centre, and by which their national unity and independence were as much as possible secured.

We turn now from the Eastern states to the south and the west of Europe.

Southern Italy had become a disagreeable boundary for the West Roman, or German power. Otho II had lost the battle of Rossano; and under Otho III the influence of the Greeks was still so great that they expelled the German Pope, Gregory V, with the aid of the Romans, and appointed a Pope of their own in 997. When the German emperors failed to form a state out of the Greeks, Longobards, Italians, and Saracens of Lower Italy, which from its situation beyond the Roman state could not but be of exceeding importance to maintain the imperial sway in Italy, it was undertaken by Norman adventurers. Conrad the Salian thought he had done his duty when he invested Ranulf the Norman with Aversa, conquered by Ranulf in 1028. But now a new centre was being formed in the important Melfi in Apulia, under the sons of the Norman Sire de Hauteville. As yet the threatening storm could be obviated by a union of the Byzantine and German Emperors with Pope Leo IX; but the Emperor Henry III abandoned the Pope; and the Pope, after the manner of the German Bishops, who used to go to war themselves, collected an army of Swabian and Longobard knights, and took the field against the Normans; but was defeated by them, and taken prisoner.

The defeat of Pope Leo IX at Civitata, on the 16th of June, 1053, settled the condition of Southern Italy for the rest of the Middle Ages. The Normans remained in the country as vassals of the Roman See. Some years later, Robert Guiscard was acknowledged by Nicholas II as Duke of Apulia and of both Calabrias, and as the future master of Sicily; and all this "by the grace of God and the Holy See". The new duke defended Pope Gregory VII against Henry IV; and the son of Henry III overthrew the Greek and Longobard dominions in Lower Italy, and threatened even the Byzantine Empire. Before Jerusalem was conquered, Sicily was taken from the Saracens by the Norman duke Roger, and the Italian sea freed from the power of the Moslem; but it was not before the twelfth century that the different Norman dominions were united under the descendants of Roger the conqueror of Sicily, and that the different Norman possessions in Italy still feudally dependent on the Roman See were raised to a kingdom, which was subject to the Church, September 27, 1130.

The new kingdom originated in the schism between Pope Anacletus and Innocent II and was acknowledged by the latter on July 27, 1139. It was in vain that the Emperor Lothar III had made the greatest efforts to destroy the new realm, and to extend the imperial dominion over the whole peninsula. The Emperor's departure for Germany, and early death; the death of Count Rainulf of Avellino, who had been raised by Lothar to the dignity of Duke of Apulia; and the death of Anacletus, 1137 or 1138—caused this change, which decided the fate of Italy for centuries. The Norman kingdom remained a Papal fief, and the same was afterwards the case with the kingdom of the Hohenstauffen. The French kingdom of the House of Anjou became so likewise; and many as were the lords Naples afterwards obeyed, by all of them the white palfrey was, up to the end of the eighteenth century, sent to Rome, even by the Bourbons, in token of dependence, which, indeed, in latter times scarcely existed more than in name. But as long as real vassalage existed, the greatest complications of the history of the world were caused by it. The fall of the House of Hohenstauffen stood in close connection with the feudal tenure of the Sicilian crown from the Holy See with that of the emperor; as also did the change in the states of Western Europe, which proceeded from the Sicilian Vespers, and became the cause of the greatest conflicts in Europe—the termination of the Crusades, and the decline of the Germanic Empire, as well as the accession of the royal house of France to the thrones of Naples and Hungary, which led to a complete change of European politics.

In the same years when the Roman See obtained in Lower Italy a powerful protector in the person of an oppressor who had borne arms against it, Bertrand, by the grace of God Count of Provence, surrendered to the Pope and his successors. He promised to be faithful to Pope Gregory VII, paid him all due honour, and left in 1081 all the churches he possessed to the Pope and his successors. Already some years earlier, Evalus, Count of Rocair in Spain, had committed to the Roman See his conquests over the Saracens. Alexander II accepted the donation. Gregory

VII[1] urged on this occasion the restoration of the old privileges which were due to the Roman See from the Visigoths in Spain, and were partly deduced from the supposed Donation of Constantine. And when, now some years after the defeat of the Christians by the Marobeths at Salaksa, the latter resumed the offensive, Berengarius Count of Barcelona (1091) gave, with the same expression as the Count of Provence, his whole honour, as it was due to him, together with the city of Tarragona, conquered in the year 1090, to St Peter; receiving it back as a Papal fief, for which he promised an annual tribute of five pounds of silver. Alfonso VI, King of Castile, had given up to the Count Henry, of the Burgundian house, the country between the Minho and Douro (Portugal) as a Castilian fief, in order to be better able to carry on the war with the Marobeths. When Alfonso, Henry's son, marched against the Saracens, previously to the great victory of Ourique, he placed himself and his kingdom under the protection of St Peter, and paid as victor the annual tribute of four ounces of gold to the Roman See. After he had taken Santarem and Evora, Lisbon and Alemtejo, Alexander III, the great adversary of Frederick I (Barbarossa), raised him to the dignity of an hereditary king; but he bound himself in 1179 to pay to the Roman Church a hundred byzantines (since 1212—two marks of gold). "The little annual tribute", says Spittler[2] "was the safest guarantee against all feudal pretentions of Castile." It has been erroneously inferred from the motto of the Portuguese kings, "Gratia Dei sum id quod sum," that the entrance of the kingdom of Portugal into the Papal System took place in a more independent manner.[3] But the princes of the Middle Ages did not perceive any loss of dignity in this proceeding, but rather increase of strength; since the independence of their realms from the Roman See, the supreme spiritual and judicial tribunal, was secured, and the protection of the new system was undertaken by the Popes. Twenty-five years later, Aragon followed the example of Portugal; and from the commencement

---

[1] "Non latere vos credimus," wrote the Pope in 1073, "regnum Hispaniæ ab antiquo proprii juris Petri fuisse; et adhuc licet diu a paganis sit occupantum, lege tamen justitiæ non evacuata, nulli mortalium sed soli apostolicæ sedi ex æquo pertinere" (1073, 34, 35).

[2] History of the European States, i, p. 126.

[3] Grammont, Hist. Galliae, lib. i, p. 126.

of the thirteenth century, the Iberian peninsula was bounded on the east and west by kingdoms which had voluntarily submitted to the Roman See. Whilst in the heart of Europe, by the pertinacious conflicts between the German Emperors, Henry IV, Henry V, and Frederick I (Barbarossa), and the Popes, the whole political system of the Middle Ages threatened to fall asunder, a new combination began to be formed in the east, south and west; and it is easy to understand the intrinsic right with which Pope Gregory VII could imagine, after Henry's deposition, that the new King of the Germans should solemnly bind himself to the Roman See—to become the *miles* of the Pope, not, as Henry had done, to fight against him.

The north of Europe received the faith under totally different circumstances from the Roman Empire. In the latter the emperors and their subordinates in authority embraced Christianity quite late, and indeed, only when all the means of resistance were exhausted. In the Germanic, and later in the Roman countries, it took root because *king* and *people* resolved to embrace it voluntarily and simultaneously. This may account for the eagerness of the neophytes not only, as was common, to place their crowns under the protection of St Peter, but like Ina King of the West Saxons, Offa King of Mercia, and at last Ethelwulf as King of all the Saxon tribes, to engage to pay tribute to St Peter. It was not that the Roman See obliged England to pay tribute to St Peter (the Peter's pence), but that the pence, collected from house to house, were a voluntary donation of the people; of which, moreover, only one half came into the hands of the Pope, while the other was given to the school of the Angles at Rome, and to the English hospital which was connected with it.

Under a banner which Nicholas II ordered to be presented to William the Conqueror, the latter had achieved the conquest of the Anglo-Saxon kingdom. The Pope had acknowledged him as the legitimate heir instead of Harold, and the battle of Hastings (1066) assumed the character of an ordeal. William, on his part, sent the banner, the usual sign of feudal dependence, as an oblation to Rome; refused the requisition of Pope Gregory to pay homage to him and his successor ("fidelitatem facere nolui nec volo, quia nec ego promisi nec antecessores meos antecessoribus tuis fecisse comperio"), but promised to pay the St Peter's pence. Nevertheless the Pope treated him as a trusted and well-beloved son of St Peter ("fidelis S. Petri et noster"),[1] and required of him to allow Norman and Anglo-Saxon bishops to go freely to Rome (1079).

After the dynasty of William the Conqueror had become extinct beneath the weight of its crimes, Henry II tried to subject the Church in England to the feudal system. The founder of the royal house of Plantagenet, however, being at war with his own sons, saw himself forced to do what William I had scouted; he acknowledged England's feudal dependence upon the Roman See.[2] England had become a patrimony of St Peter. Henry received for it the protection of the Pope; and the rebellious sons were excommunicated. Before this time, as early as 1155, Henry had notified to Pope Adrian his intention to invade Ireland, in order to subject the people to laws, of which they were considered to be destitute, and to extirpate at the same time the vices of which they were accused. When the Pope wrote thereupon that Ireland, and all islands which the Sun of Justice, Christ, shines upon, belonged to the rights of St Peter and the Roman Church, Henry promised to pay for each house in Ireland a denarius per annum to St Peter, and to guard the rights of the Church there. Upon this Pope Adrian allowed the English king to undertake the expedition to Ireland, which established the sovereign authority of the Anglo-Saxons and Normans over the Celts. The Anglo-Saxons did not object to the proceeding of the Pope concerning Ireland; though for England herself it became the commencement of a great change, and led to her entrance into the political system of Rome. It is, however, certain, that the proud and impetuous King Henry was not of opinion that England had by this drawn a humiliation upon herself: the extension of his power over Ireland, and the restoration of peace in the country were important advantages. If the powerful ruler whom the West of France obeyed did not sink in the eyes of his contemporaries because he was in one of his possessions a vassal of France—to become a vassal of the Pope offered, at all events,

---

[1] Baronius, 1080, 59.

[2] See Henry's letter to Pope Alexander III: "Vestrae jurisdictionis est regnum Angliae, et quantum ad feudatorii juris obligationem vobis duntaxat obnoxius teneor et obstringor. Experiatur Anglia quid possit Romanus Pontifex, et quia materialibus armis non utitur, patrimonium B. Petri spirituali gladio tueatur" (Baronius 1173, 9).

less danger and far greater advantages for the kingdom itself, than to be a feudatory of the French king. Henry had already made Ireland a tributary country, when he decided to make England a patrimony of the Roman See. He certainly knew what he was doing in 1155 and 1173, and that the step which he took in 1173 was a sure forerunner of the submission of England to the Roman See, as a complete feudal fief, although it is no less certain that this last change of affairs could have taken place only under such a miserable and contemptible prince as was John Lackland, whom the English felt called upon to resist, not only by themselves rebelling against him, but also by inviting Pope Innocent III to vindicate the rights of the Church. The submission of John, however, saved England from becoming a French province. The king transferred "spontaneously, and upon the council of his nobles, the two kingdoms of England and Ireland to the Roman See", in order to obtain them again from it as a vassal; promised to take the oath of a vassal (*homagium ligium*), which he also really did; so that he became a vassal to God, to St Peter, to the Roman Church, to his master Pope Innocent III and his legitimate successors, in 1213. He paid for England 700, for Ireland 300 marks of silver; but the Pope made him understand that he now possessed the two countries in a much more solemn and creditable manner, and that that which belonged to the priest belonged now to the kingdom, and *vice versa*, just as we read in Moses and St Peter.[1]

The Pope's words were about the royal priesthood of the Jews, but in deed he delayed the expedition of Philip Augustus to England; he protected King John against the English barons, who wished to deprive him of his crown, and against the Dauphin Louis, who had already come over to England; and when, amid these confusions, King John died, without so much as belonging to himself ("nec se ipsum possidere"), as Matthew Paris, says, Henry III, vassal of the Roman Church, maintained himself only through her protection against the enemies of the house of Plantagenet.

In a similar manner Pope Innocent had, at a general desertion of the followers of his father King Henry VI, protected the boy

---

[1] "Ecce sublimius et solidius nunc obtines illa regna quam hactenus obtinueris, cum jam sacerdotale sit regnum et sacerdotium sit regale sicut in epistola Petrus et Moses in lege testantur" (Raynaldus, 1213, 83).

Frederick II, feudatory King of Sicily, in the possession of his maternal inheritance, when the Norman hereditary kingdom in Lower Italy had, through Constance, come to Henry VI, the Hohenstauffen.

Three years after the death of King John, Reginald King of the Isle of Man, to whom the Hebrides and Orkneys also belonged, submitted his kingdom to the Roman See. As usual also, Reginald changed his hereditary possessions into a Papal fief, which he received back again as such, and for which he paid the annual tribute of twelve marks. There were then only a very few states that kept aloof from a system which, resting on a voluntary submission, promised to give the West of Europe quite a different centre than that which the German Emperor, the successor of Augustus, intended to establish by the force of arms. In the midst of the most violent struggles of the Emperors with the Popes, when the latter often did not possess a foot of land as quiet property, the Papal league formed itself as if off-hand, and had at last, up to the beginning of the thirteenth century, increased so vastly that it overshadowed the imperial league. Only the French crown, which still lived upon the memory of the Merovingian and Carolingian greatness, and which already Pope Gregory called the first empire of the West, kept entirely aloof from it; though the king had already become *rex Christianissimus*, an expression which is repeatedly used by John of Salisbury concerning the French king, when he was affording protection to Pope Alexander III against "the tyrant of Europe", Frederick I of Hohenstauffen.

So far we have intentionally omitted all mention of the States of the Church, because they not only formed no part of the European system of states which the popes wished to found, but, as the patrimony of St Peter, stood quite apart from the other states, like a stranger whose mission it seemed to be to present a contrast to the uniformity of the rest, and to be a centre of peace and quietness, while the others made war and rapine their business. While all other states naturally result from the migrations of nations, the patrimony of St Peter rests on essentially different bases. Rome is its nucleus; and though the city was sometimes overwhelmed with the overflow of the barbarians, and though portions of its territory were more than once absorbed by them, the migratory races never maintained a permanent settlement there. This kernel of the Papal power was not, as the superficial historians of France would have it, the gift of Pepin and Charlemagne; with whom the modern Emperors of the French have about as much in common as the wolf and the fox with the lion. They only extended the already existing ecclesiastical dominion to territories rescued from Lombard usurpation, or from the Church-enslaving chicanery of the Byzantine Empire.

The history of the States of the Church is quite independent of that of the Papal system of Europe, but runs parallel with that of the growth of the German Empire, which found Rome the great obstacle to the attainment of a universal sovereignty. Before the German kings could receive the imperial crown, they were obliged to acknowledge the independence of the States of the Church; and when "the new Pilate", as Dante calls Philip the Fair, prevailed upon Clement V to exchange Rome for Avignon, not only Rome, but the whole Church fell into trouble and confusion, through the preponderance of France; for after the removal of the Roman chair, the French cardinals plunged the world into a schism that lasted nearly forty years, during which the States of the Church fell into a state of decomposition, from which it required the unremitting exertions of the Popes during the fifteenth century to rescue them.

These endless fluctuations induced the Popes to adopt the policy of endeavouring to exclude foreign influence from Italy, and of checking the preponderance of one power by the opposition of another. Protestant England is now charmed with the Italian policy of self-deliverance and self-emancipation, though introduced under the suspicious patronage of the despot of France. But the great Popes of the fifteenth and sixteenth century had no other intention than to make Italy a free country. If they failed, they had to thank Charles VIII of France, who invaded Italy, overthrew the national governments of Milan, Florence and the rest, and, in union with Spain, founded a hierarchy of powers which has not been improved by the expulsion of the Austrians. It was not German interference that produced the misfortunes of Italy. The Germans, for the most part, prevented the petty and destructive wars, and smothered the violent antipathies which always were smouldering between the different territories and towns. They pacified Italy. Her misfortunes for centuries have been due to the interference of the French, who were continually blowing the embers of discord, and, though incapable of rearing any lasting political edifice, or of maintaining themselves in the possession of the country, were always on the watch for opportunities of fermenting divisions among the unfortunate people. Over and over again they marched their armies across the Alps when Italy had risen to a flourishing and prosperous condition, only to leave it an impoverished and desolate ruin. But we will not anticipate.

The Crusades added new motives to those which had already induced nations and princes to recognize in the Pope not only their spiritual, but also their temporal chief. The holy war was undertaken under the direct protection and guidance of Rome. It brought the Catholics of the West and the centre into contact with the schismatical nations of Eastern Europe; and while it raised the renown of the Latin world, it did no service to the Byzantine Empire, whose decay had been daily becoming more glaring since the time of Manuel Comnenus. The Emperor Frederick Barbarossa's conduct of his crusade induced the Servians to offer him their crown; but the Hohenstauffen refused to erect another Germano-Slavonic state (he had already set up Bohemia in 1158) behind the Magyars. Upon this, Pope Innocent III undertook to organize the southern Slavonians, and resolved to change Stephen the Servian Zupan into the apostolic king of the new state, and to withdraw Servia from the Byzantine system and to unite it with the Latin world. This design, so rich in its promises for Eastern Europe, was foiled by the jealousy of the Magyars. King Emerich of Hungary expelled the king-elect, to whom the Pope had already sent the insignia of royalty, and demanded that the Wulk whom he had appointed in Servia should be crowned instead. Upon this the Pope commissioned the Archbishop of Coloczk to perform the ceremony; but it was never done. The Hungarians treated Servia as they had treated Croatia. They wished to make their own country the centre of a circle of states in eastern Europe. They therefore saw with disgust the rise of a new Latin power between their empire and that of Constantinople; for Kalojohannes, the ruler of the new Bulgarian kingdom, had revived the plan of Boris, the Bulgarian prince of the ninth century, to separate from Byzantium, and to unite with the Western Empire, and had gone so far as to write to Innocent III that he wished to become a servant (*servus*) of St

Peter and His Holiness. The Pope sent him a crown and ordered him to prepare the Bulgarians to submit to the Latin Church. Emerich attempted also to foil this design, although the Pope, in order to secure the succession of his family to the Hungarian crown, had directed the Bishops to swear allegiance to his young son Ladislaus. Yet it was only a short time before Emerich's death, in August 1204, that the Pope's ambassador was permitted to pass through Hungary to Bulgaria. On the other hand, the Byzantines had vainly endeavoured to induce the Bulgarian prince to repair to their capital to be crowned, and had promised him a special (schismatic) patriarch for his new kingdom, which, they said, could not subsist without one. But the Bulgarians seemed at last to have opened their eyes to the fact that no good was to be expected from Constantinople. It happened, however, that as soon as the Bulgarians had joined the Papal system, the Greek schismatic empire became Latin and Catholic through the Crusade of 1204, and so the motive which had induced Kalojohannes to join the Western Empire ceased to exist. Nevertheless, the Bulgarians bestowed on their new neighbours, the Latins of Constantinople, the same enmity which they had formerly shown to the Greeks.

The overthrow of the Greek government at Constantinople had only tormented the Popes with fresh cares, without improving the condition of the Holy Land. The Latin West had to defend the Latin Empire of the East, as well as the Christian government of Asia; its action, already divided, was further paralysed by the renewal of the wars between the Hohenstauffen and the Popes, when the sudden invasion of the Tartars obliged it to concentrate itself within its own boundaries. This was the Bulgarians' opportunity; now or never they might crush the Latin Empire at Constantinople, and make themselves masters of the Byzantine world. They captured Baldwin I, the first Latin emperor of Constantinople, cut off his arms and legs, and threw him into a hole, where he was devoured by unclean birds; at the same time, the Emperor Frederick II, who owed so much to the protection given him, while King of Sicily, by Innocent III, and to the favour shown him in his rivalry as German king with Otho IV, made an alliance with Vatazes the Greek, the chief enemy of the Latins at Constantinople.

Thus failed the high promise of 1204 to form in Bulgaria and

Wallachia[1] a counterpart of the apostolic kingdom of Hungary, through the overthrow of the Greek Empire and the spread of the Latin Church in the Eastern peninsula of southern Europe. In 1261, eight hundred Greeks penetrated through subterraneous passages into Constantinople, and overthrew the Latin Empire, "to the everlasting reproach of the Latin name". And now the Bulgarians invited the Mogul Tartars to help them against the restored Romaic dominion, as they had formerly fought the Latins with the aid of the Romaic Greeks. Against this danger the Byzantines sought the aid of the Ottomans, while the Bulgarians looked as far as Egypt for friends in the Mamelukes, but to no purpose; they had at last to submit to Amurath, and have ever since repented at leisure their insincerity and fickleness in the matter of their annexation to the West.

The new system of States perished for want of a leader. The Popes, whether remaining in Rome, or at least in Italy, or whether seeking refuge in France from the German emperors, could not act like generals or victorious monarchs. From the first their system had borne the stamp of a voluntary submission. The consequences were disastrous. Thus in Poland, the Peter's pence were paid when the coinage, which was changed three times every year, had become most depreciated. Innocent III was obliged to censure this proceeding as early as 1207. In 1246, the Russian prince Daniel of Halicz, whose rule extended from the mouth of the Danube to beyond the Dnieper, placed himself under the protection of the Holy See, and was made king by the authority of Innocent IV. But in three years better times came and Daniel did not hesitate to fall away. Again, in 1256, the Lithuanian prince Mendaz (Mendanus, Mindane) applied to the Holy See, and Innocent IV received him under his protection, and ordered the Bishop of Kulm to crown him King of Lithuania. Soon afterwards Mendaz became a formidable patron of paganism, and thus the extension of the Christian system of Lithuania and Galicia was strangled in its birth. This was just a case in which a temporal head of the system of States might have called on the secular powers that owed him fealty to support his authority. But the Pope was obliged to think first

[1] Kalojohannes wrote to the Pope: "Et ita habeat imperium meum justitias Bulgariae et Vlachie, quod rex Ungariae habet justitias Ungariae" (Raynaldus, 1204, 31).

of the conversion of these people, and could not defend his temporal authority by means which would have frustrated its principal object. Thus, towards the end of the thirteenth century, the east of Europe was nearly in the same position as it had been at the beginning, before the Servians and the Bulgarians had entered into negotiations with Rome. In the middle of the century, the Mongols invaded Russia, and disabled her, and thus saved the Catholic Slavonians from Russian intrusion; but they also broke the power of Poland, and turned Hungary into a desert. From this time, the history of these two nations begins almost anew; both needed a fresh population. Poland received numbers of German colonists, and the Pope was obliged to erect it into a kingdom to defend it against Wenceslaus II of Bohemia, and to protect Hungary from an invasion of the Germans under Rudolph of Habsburg. At this time, the above-mentioned Daniel of Halicz had submitted to the Holy See, and there was a prospect of uniting Bosnia by stronger ties to the Latin political system. But the breaking out of the last great struggle between the Popes and the Hohenstauffen dashed all these hopes. Bosnia became the seat of the Patarenes, a widespread and pernicious sect, which carried on a deadly war against the Catholic Church in the towns of Italy. Pope John XXIII vainly invoked the aid of Frederick Duke of Austria, King John of Bohemia, King Wladislaus Lokietek of Poland, and King Charles Robert of Hungary against the Servians, who at times made as though they desired union with Rome, while they prevented the Byzantine Empire from recovering its strength, and at last assisted the Ottomans to consummate the fall of Constantinople.

While the Slavonians of Eastern Europe, after failing to secure a common centre in the empire, like the Germans, seemed to be seeking the same end by union with Rome, a similar attempt was being made in Western Europe.

The kingdom of Aragon had become a model of chivalry. It was governed by its high nobility (*riccos hombres*) more than by the king. The reigning monarch received knighthood on his marriage, or on his attaining the age of twenty years; this was all the coronation he received. In the hierarchy of the State, he was only first among his equals. This order of things was innovated upon by Don Pedro I, who went to Rome in 1204, and was anointed by the Cardinal-Archbishop of Porto, and afterwards crowned by Innocent III in S. Pancrazio. After his coronation, the king proceeded to St Peter's, where he laid his sceptre and crown on the altar of the Apostle, received his knight's sword from the Pope's hand, and in return gave to St Peter his kingdom as a tributary State in perpetuity, in confident hope that Innocent and his successors would ever defend it by their apostolic authority. The Pope ordered that the coronation of all future Kings of Aragon should be performed at Saragossa, by the Archbishop of Taragon.

The step of Don Pedro is sufficiently accounted for by the danger which menaced Christian Spain from the quarter of the Al-Mohades, and by his wish to emancipate the crown from the influence of the grandees. The step was successful; for when Mohammed Ben Nasser, Emir al Mumenim, was preparing the formidable expedition of 1212, which was to crush Christian Europe, Pope Innocent summoned the Provençals, the French, the Germans, and the Italians to defend Spain. One hundred and eighty-five thousand Saracenic knights, and countless infantry, marched into Africa. On July 16, 1212, the battle of Nares de Tolosa was fought, and decided the fate of Europe and Africa. Spain was completely victorious, and Africa was depopulated. The victory was celebrated in Aragon as a triumph of the cross. Valencia, Cordova, and Seville threw off the yoke of the Al-Mohades, and rendered the victory of the Christians more easy. Their superiority was decided for ever. But the next year brought evil days to Aragon; Don Pedro led an expedition to Toulouse to aid Count Raymond against Simon de Montfort, the conqueror of the Albigenses. The Spanish king was defeated and slain at Mures; his son, Don Jayme, after being educated by Simon at Carcassonne, took possession of the throne of Aragon, and received homage as early as 1214.

The first care of Honorius IV for his young vassâl was to prevent him declaring war on Simon de Montfort to avenge his father's death; the second step was to summon the Spanish princes to assist Don Jayme in his struggles with the Moors. This step carved out the course for the heroic *Conquistador*, and made him one of the most significant figures of the Middle Ages. As early as 1225 he had forced the King of Valencia and Murcia to become tributary. In 1229 he conquered Majorca, upon which Minorca submitted, and Iviza was overcome. Then came the great blow against Valencia, and the annexation of that rich and flourishing kingdom to the crown of Aragon. Don Jayme, the Pope's vassal, wrested Eastern Spain from the Moors, while Ferdinand of Castile drove back the infidels of the interior as far as Granada.

The early part of the thirteenth century, which witnessed these important events in the east and west of Europe, displayed equally stirring scenes in Southern Italy. The Sicilian crown of the Hohenstauffen would have been lost after Henry's death, if Innocent III, as feudal lord, had not protected the rights, as well as the person, of the boy Frederick, not only against the German princes, whom Henry VI had invested with Italian fiefs, but also against Walter Count of Brienne, who was about to become the husband of the eldest sister of the Norman king Henry III, and against Frederick's uncle Philip of Swabia and his adversary, Otho the Guelph, whom, however, Innocent crowned emperor. This great Pope's policy was always to keep the German crown, the highest political power of Christendom, apart from the Sicilian crown, the fief of the Holy See. He bestowed the first on Otho the Guelph, and the second on Frederick the Ghibelline; the first was recognized by restoring the suffrage of the German princes, and renewing the emperor's power in Central Italy; the second by securing the succession of the crown, limiting the ecclesiastical privileges that had been granted by Adrian to King William, fixing the annual feudal tribute, and establishing the canonical election of Bishops, thereby, as Innocent hoped, cutting off all occasions of future ecclesiastical disputes between the Pope as feudal lord and the king as his vassal.

And now the conquest of Constantinople by the Latins had, it was hoped, slain and buried the schismatical system of states for ever and ever. This event induced Otho to reverse, as far as he could, all the regulations of Innocent III. He violated his oath, a feat that drew upon him the excommunication of Innocent, and so caused the Hohenstauffen faction in Germany to raise the young King of Sicily, who had before been German king, to the imperial throne of his father.

In this crisis, the Holy See, as suzerain, still adhered to the policy of keeping distinct the imperial from the Papal circle of states; though with respect to Armenia an apparent exception is to be found in the fact that the Pope ordered Leo to be crowned

king of that country in 1199, by the Archbishop of Mayence, in
the joint names of the Pope and emperor.

When Frederick II became German king, he promised to
emancipate his eldest son Henry, and to make him king of Sicily.
If he had fulfilled his promise when he became emperor, the
House of Hohenstauffen might have been saved from its conflicts with the Church, and its two lines in Germany and Sicily
might have risen to vast importance. But the emperor was faith-
less to his promise; he brought his son from Sicily into Germany,
where he caused him to be clandestinely crowned German king,
while he himself usurped the government of Sicily. In order to
succeed in this political trick, he was obliged to involve himself
in engagements to Germany as well as to Rome, which weakened
the empire and at last put him in the unpleasant dilemma of
either appearing a manifest perjurer, or else of leading a crusade
to the East. The first effect was a rupture with the Pope (Gregory
IX); and when this was composed, another arose with his own
son, who was no more at ease on German ground than his father
could be. This dispute ended in the emperor's deposing his
eldest son, abolishing the rights of primogeniture, and thus de-
priving his grandsons by Henry of the succession, and raising his
second son Conrad to the German throne.

Then came the establishment of absolutism in Italy, which
had to be effected by violence and by strongholds filled with
Saracenic guards. This led to new ruptures with the Popes, who
could not but condemn Frederick's doings in Sicily, which he
ransacked and ruined, and deprived of its privileges, while he
imprisoned its prelates and nobles. Sicily was impoverished by
his tyranny, and Central and Upper Italy were split into the
two factions of Guelphs and Ghibellines, who fought for life or
death. There can be no doubt that Frederick, the vassal King of
Sicily, by his continual efforts, in spite of all his oaths, to undo
the relations of his kingdom with the Holy See, ruined Frederick
the Emperor and the whole imperial House of Hohenstauffen.
His impatience of the state of vassalage was the parent of an
insincerity which soon degenerated into utter faithlessness. He
rejected all offers of reconciliation; and the result was, that the
council which he had himself convoked to decide between him
and Gregory IX, but which he afterwards forcibly prevented
from meeting, pronounced him to be guilty of perjury, and of

violating the allegiance of a vassal, in 1245. He had begun as a
priest's king, and he was ending as a persecutor of the Church!
But his ruin might have been still delayed, if he had not obstinately adhered to the unnatural union of Sicily with Germany, and
if he had not bequeathed to his son Conrad, in 1245, a system
which had proved his own ruin. Innocent IV summoned Sicily
to vindicate her liberty, and his call has been echoing and re-
echoing there ever since. In its best days, the House of Hohenstauffen was divided against itself, and these intestine broils were
only aggravated in the days of its decay. Conrad IV's death was
mysteriously sudden, as were the deaths of Frederick's other sons
and grandsons. Men began to whisper about treason and assassination. The Emperor Manfred excluded Conrad II (Conradin)
from his inheritance of the crown of Sicily, which he usurped
for himself by spreading a false report of his nephew's death,
just as the Emperor Philip Hohenstauffen had served his nephew
Frederick. Manfred's unfortunate sons, the last of the Hohenstauffen, perished in the dungeons of Charles of Anjou early in
the fourteenth century. Peter of Aragon, the husband of their
sister Constance, was too knowing to demand their liberty, and
so to bar his wife's claims to Sicily. It was the unexpected vacancy
of the Sicilian crown, through the deposition of Frederick II,
the death of Conrad IV, the defeat of Manfred by Charles of
Anjou and his death, and the defeat and execution of Conradin,
that influenced the other States of the Papal system in a way that
at last led to the dissolution of the system itself. The influence
showed itself first of all in England.

In the latter part of the twelfth century, the royal house of
England was esteemed the principal support of the Guelphs.
Duke Henry the Lion, son-in-law of the Emperor Henry II,
found there his support against Frederick Barbarossa. Richard
Cœur-de-Lion made a most moving petition to Innocent III on
behalf of his nephew Otho, and promised in his name to maintain
the right of the Roman Church, and to observe the fealty that
had been sworn to her ("debitam et juratam fidelitatem"). But
when Otho IV had succeeded to the royal and imperial crowns,
and had proved false to his fealty, Frederick, his successor, withdrew the English support from the descendants of the Guelphs
by marrying Isabel Plantagenet, the daughter of King John, and
thus becoming brother-in-law of King Henry III, and of Rich-

ard, Earl of Cornwall, afterwards German king. In his disputes with the Popes, Frederick endeavoured to gain the support of England, but could only win over the barons to his side. There was at this time marvellous discontent in England against Rome, because of the numerous Italians who obtained English benefices while the States of the Church were in the hand of Frederick. The English ambassadors at the Council of Lyons, in 1245, represented to Innocent IV that Italians were receiving over 600,000 marks a year, a sum that exceeded the income of the king ("qui est tutor ecclesiæ, et regni gubernaculo moderator"). Not receiving an answer to their mind, the ambassadors withdrew, with the threat that England would no longer pay the Roman tribute. But in spite of the barons, the English Bishops declared in favour of the tax, and put their seal to the deed whereby King John surrendered his crown to Innocent III. The Parliament, however, in 1246, limited all further grants of English benefices to foreigners; and though Innocent's energetic measures prevented further resolutions to the same effect, he was unable to allay the national discontent against Rome, or to calm the tempest to which it gave rise.

In English history two antagonistic principles may always be found, not, as Thierry thought, the Anglo-Saxon and the Norman elements, or the partisans of elective against hereditary monarchy, or the party that supported the claims of the house of Montfort, the collateral line of the house of the Plantagenets through Eleanor, daughter of King John and wife of Simon of Leicester, in opposition to the party that supported the male and principal line. The dualism of English policy lay deeper than this, and consisted in the antagonistic principles of *common life*, peculiarly, almost exclusively expressed by the Church, and of *nationality*. Unless England was gradually to be brought to a state of complete isolation, which threatened to unchristianize her nationality, it was necessary for her to be bound with strong ties to the common centre of Christendom. It is said that, before King John became a vassal of Rome, he had been coquetting with the faith of the Koran; and the ferocious sensuality of his character disposes one to believe the report. We think that this nationality characterized the Anglo-Saxon period of English history.

A little later, Innocent IV had to spend one half of the Church revenues on the great contest which was called "negotium ecclesiasticæ libertatis", and the other on the defence of the Holy Land, for which he had to depend on the English and French, ever since Frederick II, King of Jerusalem, had allied himself with the Saracens against the Pope. The origin of the miserable state of Palestine may be traced to the hasty retreat of Richard I with his Englishmen, who for the last fifty years of the Christian power in the east were the chief cause that Saladin's favourite idea of transplanting the war of invasion into Europe could not be carried into effect in the thirteenth century.

In the days of Henry II, the Popes had to watch that the feudalism of the Normans did not use the Constitutions of Clarendon to crush all liberty. In like manner, Alexander IV had to write to Henry III with an earnest admonition to him to maintain the ecclesiastical rights, liberties, and immunities which were contained in the general charters that he had granted, and which had been sanctioned by the excommunication of all offenders. But whilst in Germany the lay opposition found its expression in the emperor, throughout the west of England it was concentrated in the nobility. The articles which the English Bishops declared themselves ready to prove in 1257 show how little the prosperity of England would have gained by a victory of the narrow-minded national party over the defenders of the common cause.[1] Prince Henry, the son of Isabella, was at first, as Matthew Paris pretends to know, destined by his father Frederick II to inherit the crown of Sicily; and some Apulians, Sicilians and Calabrians had already rendered him homage. But the Emperor on his deathbed declared in favour of keeping the whole monarchy undivided, and fixed the sum to be paid by the Emperor Conrad to Henry as his indemnity, unless he chose to give him the kingdom of Arles or of Jerusalem. But in 1255, after the premature death of Henry, Alexander IV offered the Sicilian throne to Edmund, second son of Henry III of England. Both Edmund and his elder brother Edward I thus seemed destined to become vassals of the Holy See; and their father was delighted with the thought that, by gaining Sicily for the House of Plan-

---

[1] "Imprimis quod vacantibus ecclesiis cathedralibus seu conventualibus, conventus talliantur, terrae relinquuntur incultae, vastantur nemora, parci, et vivaria, corruunt aedificia, diripiuntur bona, depauperantur villani et male tractantur, ita quod mendicare cogantur" (Matth. Paris, p. 129, ed. Paris, 1644).

tagenet, the French kingdom would be surrounded, and ground, as it were, between two millstones. Thus the annexation to the Papal system of states opened to England a splendid prospect not only of recovering the continental possessions which had been lost to Philip Augustus, but also of confining France to the right bank of the Loire. If this had taken place, there would have been no Babylonish captivity of Avignon in the Church's annals. In 1257, Prince Edmund had already received the Papal investiture by the ring; his father had recognized him as king, and had shown him to the English barons in an Apulian dress. But whilst Henry III was hesitating to advance the large sums required for the expedition to Naples, Manfred was strengthening himself in Lower Italy. Edmund preferred a crusade in the East to the doubtful chances of conquest in Sicily; and the Holy See, which was forced to find a vassal that could protect it, offered the crown that he slighted to the French Prince Charles of Anjou. Thus were all Henry's hopes for England dashed to the ground; and he had the further mortification of seeing the Count of Provence and new King of Sicily procure the apostolic crown of Hungary for his descendants, and threaten even the Byzantine Empire. The hesitation of the English gave the French the preponderance in the west, south, and east of Europe. But both in England and in Aragon the union with the Papal system of states tended to increase considerably the national power and greatness.

The nature of this political system is further elucidated by the relations of the Holy See with Don Pedro I of Aragon. Honorius III, the successor of Innocent III, demanded from Don Jayme I a tribute for Barcelona, in 1218; it was paid, and Jayme and his companion in arms, Theobald King of Navarre, were taken under the particular protection of the Holy See. The great King of Aragon wished to be crowned at Rome in 1229, but was prevented by the breaking out of the dispute of Frederick II with the Pope. When the last possessions of the Christians in the Holy Land were attacked by the Mamelukes, the conqueror of Valencia took the cross. His conquests had already freed the Spanish and Italian seas, and he prepared a great fleet to carry him and his army to Ptolemais. He had embarked, when a storm separated him from the rest of his fleet; and he was persuaded, it is said, by his beloved Berengaria to relinquish the crusade. This left Charles of Anjou, the King of Sicily, who had already wrested Provence from the Catalonian princes, at full liberty to give the expedition the more convenient turn of an attack on Tunis; but it was unsuccessful, on account of the death of King Louis IX of France in 1270.

We see, then, that the dependence of Aragon upon Rome did not hinder its greatest monarch from any important undertaking. Nor did it prevent the marriage of his successor, Don Pedro, with Constanza, daughter of Manfred, the great enemy of the Popes. This union was the cause of many political changes. Jayme—the hero, legislator, historian, and king, a combination rarely found in the mediaeval princes—died, and his kingdom was divided. His younger son Jayme received the Balearic Isles, together with Roussillon, Conflans and Montpellier, but in 1279 he was obliged to swear an oath of allegiance to his elder brother Don Pedro, who had inherited his father's principal possessions in the east of Spain, as Catalonia, Aragon and Valencia. For nearly a century past, the fate of Apulia and Sicily, the feudal kingdom of the Popes, had given rise to complications, which, after shaking Italy and the empire, were now about to draw France and Spain into their eddies.

The Papal system of states gradually extended itself, till in the thirteenth century it reached its culminating point, when its great semicircle encompassed the States of the German Emperors. The Slavs and Magyars of the East had joined the Latin nations of the West, and the Sicilian Empire of the South was the connecting link between them. But after the thirteenth century the East began to detach itself. After the intimate alliance of King Prumysl Ottocar with Otho IV, the Pope recognized Bohemia as an independent principality, no longer subject to the Roman See; and the union of the Servians and Bulgarians with Rome only served to manifest their inconstancy and political imbecility. The East was in progress of disintegration, in spite of the efforts of Hungary under the Arpades, and of the Anjous under Louis the Great, to become the centres of an Eastern Empire. A like effort had been also made by Prumysl Ottocar II, the celebrated adversary of Rudolph of Habsburg; but he scorned to accept the German crown, and refused to lean upon Rome, and was in consequence destroyed by the Germans. Afterwards the Habsburgs in Austria, the Anjous in Hungary, and the Luxembourgs in Bohemia endeavoured to set up a great Eastern Empire, in which the Habsburgs were at last successful. This house owed its power chiefly to the Popes, and its influence over the election of the German kings to the divisions of the Germans; and though the Bull of Charles IV abolished this interference in law, it still continued in fact.

The kingdom of Sicily continued to be the most important member, not only of the ecclesiastical system, but of all the political systems of Europe. From it the imperial system received its heaviest blow, and from it also the Papal system received that concussion which at length threw it out of gear, as we will relate as briefly as we can.

The Norman kingdom in Sicily was a prey to disputes more deadly than those which racked the English kingdom of William the Conqueror. William I of Sicily, who had beheld three of his sons go to the grave before him, and had grown prematurely old through the dissipations of his youth, attempted to throw off the vassalage due to the Pope, and thus caused Pope Adrian to form a coalition with the Byzantine and German Emperors against him, which reduced the Norman crown to its original condition. During the consequent disturbances William slew his own son, and was then succeeded by William II, his younger son. Under him the Normans once more endeavoured, but in vain, to subdue the Byzantine Empire. On this Henry the Hohenstauffen, son of Frederick Barbarossa, married Constanza, daughter of King Roger (1154), and the succession of the Norman kingdom was secured to their children (1185). But after the death of William II the Normans altered the succession in favour of Count Tancred, the grandson of King Roger I, whom that monarch had inherited out of hatred to his own son, Roger, in favour of Tancred's uncle, William I. In 1189, the Sicilian Parliament recognized Tancred as king, and he was instituted by the Pope in 1190, and crowned at Palermo. In consequence the war of succession broke out, and was conducted with the utmost vehemence and perfidy by Henry VI, who had succeeded his father in the empire in 1190. But Henry's lineage and the whole house of Hohenstauffen were afterwards destroyed by the Germans, at least as tragically as they had destroyed the Norman line. We have a contemporary anticipation of the future of Sicily in the pages of Hugo Falcandus, the Norman historian. He had not much hope of it. The different nations settled there—Longobards, Greeks, Normans, Saracens, and Italians—had as yet found no common centre. The love of the Apulians for change, and their cowardice in the field, the quarrels of the Normans with the Saracens, and the fears of a Saracen insurrection, made the prospect gloomy. But the historian was dead before his fears were accomplished.

After Tancred had been acknowledged in Sicily and Apulia, Roger, Count of Adria, called in King Henry. But the first expedition of the Germans was unsuccessful, and the Count of Adria was defeated at Ascoli. And when Henry, after he had become Emperor, put in his wife's claims, he found Naples too strong for him and was obliged to retreat. Constanza herself fell into Tancred's hands, but was left free to rejoin her husband; and the Germans, overcome both by generosity and by arms, were forced to evacuate the kingdom. And now the Italian policy of the Popes came clearly to light. The prospect of the union of the crown of Lower Italy with the power that ruled the central and upper provinces, and that wore the crowns of Lombardy, Germany, and Arles, necessarily caused great uneasiness for the fate of Italy, and particularly of Rome, and for the liberty of the Church; and the actual accomplishment of this union under Henry VI led to the enunciation of the fixed principle that the union of the imperial crown with the vassal crown of Sicily was unlawful, and that every effort must be made to prevent the prolongation of such a state of things. Frederick Barbarossa was meditating the conquest of Sicily in 1162, and made large promises to the Genoese in case of its success. In 1164 he sold to the Genoese the crown of Sardinia for 40,000 silver marks, and also sold it to Pisa for 13,000 golden lire. When the expedition against Sicily was really put in hand, an imperial patent from Gelnhausen secured to Pisa one half of the harbours and territories of Palermo, Messina, Salerno, and Naples. Luckily for Henry, Tancred died, February 20, 1194, a short time after his eldest son Roger, and both were buried in one grave. Tancred's younger son, William, who succeeded him, was under the regency of his mother, Sibylla. The kingdom was split by dissenting factions, and just at this moment Henry obtained the sinews of war by the ransom paid by the English for the liberation of King Richard of the Lion-Heart. Henry proceeded in person to Genoa, and purchased the assistance of the republic by promising to it Syra-

cuse and the Val di Noto, and declaring that when he had the
island he would only keep the honour and the title, and leave all
the profits to the Genoese: "As for me, I cannot remain there
with my Germans, but you and your successors will reside there,
and the kingdom will belong more to you than to me."

But after Messina had fallen, he put off fulfilling his promises
till he should also have Palermo; and after Palermo had surrendered, he could not do so till the Genoese ambassadors had
received full powers; and when this also was done: "Know ye",
he said, "that I shall give you nothing in the kingdom of Sicily,
nor shall you share its ownership with me, so you need not take
any trouble about the possession of it. But if you will undertake
an expedition against the King of Aragon" (Alphonso II, whose
daughter Constantia was afterwards the first wife of King Frederick II), "I will transfer his dominion to you, and it shall be
wholly yours." This gives us a clue to the resolution of Alphonso
III to place the crown of Aragon under the protection of the
Pope. The Genoese aided in the conquest of Naples, Salerno, and
Messina. Tancred's son, with his son and his widow, fell into the
power of the Hohenstauffen. Tancred's noble conduct towards
Constanza had merited a similar treatment for his own family;
but the Emperor put them on trial, for life or death, December
25-30, 1194. King William was blinded, and otherwise mutilated,
and imprisoned at Kohenems, near Bregenz, where he died,
probably in 1198. His mother and sister were incarcerated in
Alsace; the bodies of his father and brother were torn from their
grave and beheaded; the Norman grandees were mutilated,
buried or burnt alive; the kingdom given up to the Germans;
and then proclamation was made that, by the endeavours of the
Emperor, Sicily was brought into a better state. After this Henry
returned to Germany, to change the elective monarchy into an
hereditary one. The electors had already vested the succession in
the imperial house, when an insurrection broke out in Sicily.
The Pope excommunicated the haughty prince who respected
neither right nor breeding. Henry hastened to Italy, and his path
was deluged with blood; Constanza herself rose against him, and
was thrown into prison. At last the tyrant caught a fever at the
siege of Castro Giovanni, and died at Messina, September 1197,
aged thirty-two. His only son, Frederick II, heir of Sicily in right
of his mother, had been recognized as king by the German

princes in 1196, but he was now to lose both crowns. Duke Mark-wald, Henry's most faithful follower, was ready to swear that Frederick was not his son. The boy's own uncle, Philip, became a candidate, first for the German, and then for the Italian crown. It was entirely to the Pope that Frederick owed his life, his liberty, and the kingdom of Sicily. We have already related how he and his family perished.

After the fall of the Hohenstauffen the Empire sank lower than ever, while the French power was continually developing in Italy. And now, quite unexpectedly, a blow was struck in Sicily which convulsed all the south of Christendom, and gave its policy an entirely new turn. March 30, 1282, witnessed the Sicil-ian Vespers, and the revolt of the kingdom from Charles of Anjou. When all the Sicilians had followed the example of Palermo, and had murdered all the French in the island, the chiefs of the rebel-lion unfurled the banner of St Peter; and it was when the Roman Peter refused to help them that they turned to the more mundane Peter of Aragon. Pope Martin IV declared in favour of the King of Naples, the vassal of the Roman See, and against the tributary King of Aragon, Peter III, whom he deposed in 1284, giving Aragon, Valentia, and Catalonia to that pretender of so many crowns, Charles of Valois, second son of Philip III, King of France. The three crowns were to remain for ever separated from France, Castile, and England, and to remain with Charles and his descendants, who were required to swear fealty to the Pope, and to pay him annually 500l. as quit-rent. Sicily was to be re-conquered by Charles of Anjou, as well as Aragon, against which the Christian world was invited to aid the French arms by a cru-sade. But both undertakings failed; so that from the Sicilian Vespers dates the beginning of the dissolution of the political system of the Popes, as well as the cessation of the Crusades to the East. All the maritime states in the Spanish and Italian basin of the Mediterranean were overwhelmed with the Sicilian flood. The strife was bloody; but Naples failed to overcome Sicily, and France to overcome Aragon. King Peter died in the midst of the struggle, and his successor, Alphonso III, took possession of the crown of Aragon at Saragossa, with the words: "I accept the crown, neither from the Church, nor against her." But when the Papal institution of the sovereign was left out, the Cortes united against him, and compelled him to recognize the privileges of the Parliament, and to swear not to violate the constitution. Thus, Alphonso, in ceasing to be subject to the Pope, in 1288, became subject to the Cortes.

All efforts to isolate the Sicilians, or to gain them over to Naples, had hitherto been frustrated. But Pope Boniface VIII was not discouraged. At a large congress of Princes at Rome, he instituted the former King of Sicily, James, brother and successor of Alphonso III, as King of Corsica and Sardinia, paying an annual tribute of 3,000 silver marks; James became Gonfaloniere of the Roman See; but after the extinction of his legitimate heirs, he engaged in 1297 to subject to the crown of Naples the island of Sicily, which had recognized first Don Pedro, then himself, and then his brother Frederick, as king. All this was bargained for on the assumption that the Sicilians and their King Frederick of Aragon would submit to the arrangement. This was far from being the case; a fearful struggle ensued, till, by the treaty of Caltabilotta, in 1303, Frederick of Aragon was acknowledged as King of "Trinacria" for life. He married Eleanora, granddaughter of Anjou, and promised to take the oath of allegiance to Rome, and to pay quit-rent. The full title of King of Sicily was to remain with the House of Anjou, and the Roman treaty regarding Corsica and Sardinia was to be maintained. And now for the first time the East had discovered the great importance of Sicily. The war had lasted twenty years; four great sea-fights, two great battles by land, and many minor engagements, had been won by the Sicilians; three invading armies had been driven out of the island, Syracuse and Messina had successfully resisted the besieging armies, and two great naval battles had been lost. The tithes of almost all Europe, the treasure of the Popes and of the House of Anjou, the contributions of the Italian Guelphs, and 300,000 ounces of gold, which the Roman See had borrowed, had been spent, and yet the island remained unconquered. The Christian East had been lost, the power of the Palæologi at Constantinople had been confirmed, the Aragonese had gained a footing on the coast of Sicily, the wearisome war between England and France had broken out, and a still greater calamity was impending—the removal of the Papal See from Rome to Avignon.

In the beginning of the thirteenth century Frederick II had styled himself "German King, by the grace of God and of the

Roman See". Towards the end of it King Albert I acknowledged to Boniface VIII that both the temporal and spiritual swords belonged to the Pope, who also laid claim to the supreme power (*summum imperium*) over Hungary; whilst in the West Edward I of England and Philip IV of France refused to accept the mediation of the Pope in their quarrels, except in his private capacity. To the Popes the greatness of the French kings was chiefly due; and in return the House of Anjou reduced Rome, Central Italy, and even the College of Cardinals to dependence; the Roman chair had already been removed to Aquila and Naples when Boniface VIII liberated it from the "Neapolitan captivity". When the same Pope tried to break the pride of the French, they suddenly attacked him at Anagni, took him prisoner, and liberated him only a few weeks before his death in Rome. After the short Pontificate of Benedict IX, King Philip procured the election of a French Pope, Clement V, who removed the Papal residence to Avignon. During the whole of the fourteenth century the government of the Church remained in the hands of the French; and when the chair was restored to Rome, the French Cardinals commenced the schism of 1378, which for forty years produced such lamentable confusion within the Church.

France had kept herself out of both the imperial and the Papal systems of States, and now she came out in mediaeval history as a great power, rounded off her frontiers on the south and east, annexed Navarre, Toulouse, the Lyonnaise, etc., and entangled the Church, which had given her the means for winning all this, in an iron net, whose meshes became ever narrower and more rigid. The same weakness which showed itself in the general affairs of the Church became apparent also in the Mediterranean States. Benedict XI confirmed the donation of his predecessor to James III of Aragon. But then James emancipated his son Don Pedro, as Frederick II had done to his son Henry, perhaps not without an eye to the German crown, which could never, according to the treaty, be united with that of the Aragonese island. Hence the claims of Sardinia could not be vindicated before 1232, when the Infanta Alphonso took from Pisa the greater part of the island. But the Genoese would not cede their portion, and in reprisal took Corsica from the Aragonese in 1347, who in return united the Balearic Isles to their crown, which had in 1319 been aggrandized by the union of the Cortes of Aragon,

Catalonia and Valencia. In 1328 Alphonso IV was forced to swear not to alienate the crown lands on any pretence; and when he did so, his son Don Pedro IV rose against him, and Alphonso died in the contest, 1336. At his coronation Don Pedro seized the crown from the hands of the Archbishop of Saragossa, and put it on his own head, with the words: "On no account will I be a vassal of the Roman See." This was in 1336; but in 1365 Pope Urban V compelled him to render homage, at least for Sardinia and Corsica.

Meanwhile Charles II of Anjou was succeeded on the throne of Naples and Sicily by his third son, Robert, Duke of Catalonia, who was crowned King of Sicily at Avignon, by Pope Clement V, August 26, 1309. At the same time Frederick, King of "Trinacria", was soliciting for the title of King of Jerusalem, James of Aragon for the county of Pisa and the Isle of Elba, Charles of Valois for the Byzantine Empire, and Charles Robert, of the House of Anjou, for Hungary. To counteract this preponderance of the Romanic race, King Henry VII of Germany, and after him King Lewis of Bavaria, attempted to set up the German Empire again; but Frederick of Trinacria took the opportunity of King Henry's Roman expedition to attack King Robert of Sicily; he assumed the title of King of Sicily, and caused his son Don Pedro to be crowned, to whom he secured the succession in spite of all the censures of the Pope; while for his younger son John he obtained the principalities of Athens and Neopatra. But the dispute for the succession continued during the life of Pedro (1343), and of his son Lewis (1355), and up to the time of Frederick III, Lewis's brother, who declared himself and his successor vassals of Queen Joan of Naples (the granddaughter of King Robert), and appealed to King Gregory XI to grant them the kingdom of Trinacria. The Pope, who now maintained his rights to both kingdoms, that of Naples (the continental Sicily), and that of Trinacria (the island), fixed the formula of the oath of allegiance for Frederick, entailed the kingdom of Trinacria, defined the contigencies on which the crown would revert to the Roman See, enacted the liberty of the Church, the perpetual severance of Trinacria from Lombardy, Tuscia and Germany, and the mode and duration of the dependence of Trinacria upon the crown of Naples. This was in 1372; two years later Frederick took the prescribed oath at the hands of the legate, and was thereupon crowned king in 1375. On his death in 1377, his daughter Mary was protected by Gregory XI against her cousin, the mighty King Pedro IV of Aragon. But when this protection failed through the schism, she was forced to marry Prince Martin of Aragon. The second prince of this house, Alphonso V, was adopted by Queen Joan II of Sicily (Naples), and so obtained the crown of that country. He united Sicily and Sardinia to Aragon; while, with the Pope's consent, he bequeathed Naples to his natural son, Ferdinand I, and his successors, from 1458 to 1551, after which time Naples was united to the Spanish crown by Ferdinand the Catholic, through whom it descended to the House of Habsburg. Of the old feudal system there was not much more left than the remittance of the white bill. The House of Bourbon, which everywhere promoted this revolution, discontinued even this expression of homage.

Whilst thus the political system of the Popes continued to exist in the South quite up to the modern period, divested, however, of its old power and privileges, and only surviving in forms which were abandoned in the eighteenth century, it expired much earlier in the north-west. Yet it is noticeable that the union of Scotland and England attempted by Edward I met with decided opposition from Pope Nicholas IV, "because Scotland also belonged to the Roman See from old times". King Edward would not mount his father's throne as a vassal of the Roman See, and allowed eight years to elapse before he would pay the Roman tribute; he soon left it off, however, so that in 1316 the arrears amounted to 24,000 marks sterling. Edward's continual wars furnished the pretext for this neglect. The weak Edward II paid it again, and applied to Pope John XXII for a second coronation, which he hoped would help him to the Empire of the East. He had been told of a kind of oil which came from the Blessed Virgin, who had given it to the Apostle St Thomas, which had that special privilege, and with that he wished to be anointed. But with all his weak wishes for the Eastern Empire, he lost the crown of England. Urban V, who endeavoured with all his might to re-establish the political system of the Popes, asked Edward III to pay the English tribute, which had been dormant since 1333. But the wars with France emancipated England from its former dependence. Moreover, the rival Popes during the schism were reduced to a state of dependence on the

princes who embraced their respective parties; yet in the fourteenth century the Papal system seemed still on the increase.
Thus, Henry Duke of Halicz, Glogau, and Posna, and heir of
Poland, declared himself the immediate subject of the Roman
See, and also expressed a hope that if any German Emperor
tried to exercise any jurisdiction over him, the Pope would defend him against it. In the same year, Wladislaus, King of Poland,
acknowledged that Ruthenia ("de qua annua tributa consuever-
unt Papæ percipere") and Poland were both tributary to Rome.
King Robert of Scotland demanded the authority of the Pope
for his coronation, in order to secure Scotland against Edward
III. Pope John granted it in favour of Robert and his successors,
and delegated the performance of the ceremony to the Archbishop of St Andrews, or, in default, to the Archbishop of Glas-
gow. In 1331 the Dukes of Pomerania transferred their principality to the Roman See as a fief, like Sardinia, Corsica, and
Sicily. We find vestiges of the extension of the Papal system even
to Norway.

In 1340 Africa again invaded Spain; the Moors came over
with wives and children, bag and baggage, to establish themselves in the peninsula. This was the fifth and last invasion of
Spain, and was victoriously repulsed in the great battle of
Tarifa. Spain might now, if she could keep free from internal
dissensions, assume the offensive, and meditate the conquest of
Africa. In consequence of this victory a new principality, subject
to the Roman See, was formed by Pope Clement VI in 1344,
under the title of "the happy islands, situated in the sea Oceanus,
between the south and the west". The Pope gave it to the Castilian prince, Lavis, of the family of Ferdinand de la Cerda, son
of King Alphonso X and of the daughter of Lewis IX, who with
his descendants had been excluded from the crown of Castile.
The prince accepted the fief at an annual tribute of 400 florins
of good and pure gold, and was crowned and took the oath of
allegiance, November 28, 1344. But the new principality, whose
inhabitants—if it had any—were Mussulmans, was to be established by force. But before this could be done Alphonso, King
of Portugal, complained that these islands, which belonged to
Portugal, and for the conquest of which he had equipped a
squadron before the Moorish invasion took place, had been
given to a Castilian prince. The Pope in reply called upon the

Kings of France, Sicily, Aragon, Castile—the King of Portugal refused—the Genoese, and the Dauphin of Vienne, to aid in conquering the new principality. But the "five kings' battle" at Crécy, August 26, 1346, where the Kings of France, Navarre, Bohemia, and Majorca were conquered by the King of England, put a stop both to the diversion which the French and Bohemians were to make in Syria against the Ottomans, who were sweeping down upon Europe, and to the erection of the new principality on the coast of West Africa. It remained a mere diplomatic creation. Afterwards a Norman knight, John of Betancour, received these islands from Henry III of Castile, who now called himself king.

The little that remained of the Papal system was more and more eclipsed in the fifteenth century. In the apostolical kingdom of Hungary, Matthias, King of the Magyars, would not leave to Pope Sixtus IV even the patronage of prebendal stalls—such a change had come over Europe since the great schism of 1378. "Your holiness may rest assured", he wrote, "that the Hungarian nation will sooner change the double cross, which is the banner of our kingdom, into the triple cross, than allow the prebends and prelacies, which belong to the rights of the crown, to be bestowed by the Apostolic See."

The Hungarian double cross of Rome was not changed for the triple one of Byzantium, but the crescent soon triumphed there after the Magyar had ceased to regard any thing as higher than the interests of his own kingdom. So England also, when she secluded herself more and more from foreign connection, fell into that ecclesiastical Anglicanism which is foolish enough to call a national establishment in contradiction with itself by the grand name of Universal and Catholic.

IV

THE MUNICH CONGRESS[1]

THE authorized Report[2] of the Congress of Catholic divines and men of letters which was held at Munich three months ago has just been published. Combined with the testimony of several eye-witnesses, it gives us a clear idea of an event beyond measure interesting and suggestive in its details, and destined probably to exercise an almost incalculable influence in the Church. The inaugural address of the president, if it stood alone, would be a work of rare significance; but, in conjunction with the circumstances under which it was delivered, it forms an epoch in the ecclesiastical history of Germany which ought not to be overlooked or undervalued by Catholics in other lands. The circumstances, indeed, from which the Munich conference derives its character present no close analogy with the particular conditions of religion in the rest of Europe. We cannot, by altering the names, apply the narrative or point the allusions to ourselves. The idea would, in that case, have had no practical significance, and the means of realizing it could not have been found out of Germany. But its importance extends beyond national boundaries; and the tree that was planted in the chapter-house of St Boniface, if in time to come it bears fruit at all, will bear it for the whole of the Catholic world.

The outline of the facts is sufficiently familiar to the public. In the beginning of August a circular was put forth by Dr Döllinger and two of his friends, inviting the Catholic divines and scholars of Germany to a literary conference, to be opened on the 28th of September. Nearly a hundred professors, authors, and doctors of divinity assembled in the Benedictine monastery at Munich on the appointed day. Some of them were deputed by their bishops; and the assembly contained about a dozen laymen. During four successive days seven meetings were held, which lasted about

[1] *Home and Foreign Review*, No. 7, Jan. 1864, pp. 209-44.

[2] *Verhandlungen der Versammlung katholischer Gelehrten in München vom 28 September bis 1 October* 1863. Regensburg: Manz.

three hours each. Several of the speeches were ordered to be printed in the protocol; and two propositions affirming the rights of authority in matters of opinion were adopted after a short discussion. An address of fidelity to the Holy See was unanimously voted: and it was resolved that the meeting should be annually repeated. The proceedings terminated with a dinner in the refectory of the Benedictines, at which the Archbishop of Bamberg and the Bishop of Augsburg gave toasts; and the Pope, by a telegraphic message, bestowed his blessing on the Congress and on the work it had begun. What was the nature of the Congress, and of the work it had begun, we shall endeavour to explain.

In former times theologians were generally held together, as they still are in several countries, by the influence of a uniform system of education, and by fidelity to the traditions of the schools. But no such bond now unites the divines of Germany. Reared in universities which are governed by opposite opinions, and exposed to very different influences according as their lot may be cast in Austria or in Prussia, in Catholic Bavaria or amid the mixed population on the Rhine—sometimes familiar from early youth with the strength and the weakness of Protestant and Rationalist literature, and sometimes brought up in the elaborate seclusion of the seminary or the religious house—they often, according to the curriculum prescribed in certain states, combine a sound knowledge of classics, history, or philosophy, with the special studies of the priesthood, and often, on the other hand, are trained almost exclusively in the theological course. There are instances among the older priests that testify to the success with which, either from religious animosity or from political jealousy, governments have frequently tried to tinge the teaching of the school with uncatholic sentiments; and there are others who bear witness to an extreme reaction against these encroachments. Varying in national character and in mode of speech, disciples of masters whose contending systems have distracted the peace of the Church, they represent different modes of teaching and different schools of thought, the Catholicism of different countries and of different generations. There is no centre of learning in Germany, and no theological headquarters. They have nothing like the Sorbonne, or even like Maynooth; and there is no master among them whose works are the common text-books, or whose name altogether overshadows that of every rival. They have not yet fought out, with their own resources and on their own behalf, the great controversies of modern theology. Whilst some have benefited largely by the results of Protestant science, and others have been influenced by Protestant opinion, many have tried to intrench themselves against both influences behind the systems prevailing in Italy or France. Nearly all the great divisions, therefore, that subsist among the Catholics of other countries have been adopted and naturalized in Germany, in addition to the powerful but discordant action of Protestant learning; and the divines are almost as far as possible from harmony in their tone of thought and in the tendency of their theological views.

The first broad and fundamental distinction among them is one which ramifies into many others, and derives its importance from causes peculiar to the literary character of the German people. This is the distinction between writers of the practical and those of the scientific class. It is the habit of some men to think chiefly of the immediate interests of religion, and to be guided by them in the formation of opinions and the use of knowledge; whilst others consider principally the advancement of learning, with a general assumption that it must contribute to the glory of God. Men of the latter school never shrink from making an admission or concession to Protestants or unbelievers, nor from censuring Catholics, or abandoning and reversing received opinions, if they judge that such a course is demanded by scientific reasons, though they are conscious that the case may be used, and perhaps forcibly used, to prejudice people against the Church. They labour to add to the store of known truths without reference either to the shock which each discovery inflicts on those whose views it contradicts, or to the fear lest the new discovery should be misapplied; and they discard entirely the management and economy of knowledge. This very disregard, however, presupposes the existence of another class of men, whose work it is to adapt and explain the results of science to unprepared minds which would otherwise be puzzled or misled by them, to convert them into instruments of controversy, and to prevent them from being misinterpreted or abused.

Those who are charged with the duty of watching over the purity of the faith are naturally more alive to the importance of this latter function than to the benefit which accrues to religion from the progress of ecclesiastical science. The writers to whom they look for aid in their pastoral office labour not so much to instruct the learned as the ignorant, the prejudiced, and the young—to restore discipline, to defend authority, to refute calumny, and to prevent scandal. The spirit that animates the purely scientific divines, and the principle that guides their researches, often become almost unintelligible to men absorbed in this avocation. It appears to them that there can hardly be anything necessary or profitable to the Church in a kind of literature of which the results are frequently unwelcome, the professors deficient in sympathy with their wants and difficulties, and the immediate effects in some cases demonstrably pernicious. Hence very naturally proceeds jealousy, not only of particular views and certain definite propositions, but of the principle and tenour of a scientific theology. When the test applied to the spirit of a writer is the efficacy of his aid in the defence of religion, in meeting hostile arguments, and in augmenting the polemical resources of Catholics, the most profound theologian is very likely to be found wanting. For the growth of knowledge does not necessarily assist these objects; but it is perpetually bringing to light, or establishing, or repeating conclusions which strew the path of the controversialist with difficulties, or cut two ways, or compel a revision of opinions. A Catholic scholar will often be the first to ascertain a fact unknown to Protestants, and hostile to some view adopted among Catholics; he will disprove some cherished claim or assertion, weaken the force of some popular or conventional argument, and multiply problems as fast as he advances knowledge. The spirit which enables him to do this is widely different from that of the more purely practical and official functions of the priesthood; and it is abhorrent to many persons, even when manifested in questions touching which there is no dispute. An estrangement subsists even without any obvious or material cause of antagonism; and the opposition thus engendered, even when it expresses itself in a vague animosity against the tone and spirit of a school, is not the less profound and real.

There is naturally a close alliance between the episcopate and the divines of the second or practical class—those who, in order to shelter faith, seek to dispense and qualify the truth to the faithful. It generally happens that these men, while they uphold the liberties of the Church, together with the authority of the Holy See, which are essentially inseparable, proceed, with an inconsistency more apparent than real, and not peculiar to the advocates of their cause, to depress intellectual freedom as much as they sustain the rights of the Church. For it is in the learned literature of their country that they see the worst adversary of religion and morality; and therefore even Catholics who help to promote it are obnoxious to them. The obvious way to make it harmless, they conceive, is to bring it as much as possible under the control of ecclesiastical authority. Confident that the Church already possesses scientific systems and conclusions free from danger and error, and equal to any emergencies that may arise, they desire to arrest the uncertain movement of human thought. For this reason the common designation for the school is the Scholastic or the Roman. If the intellectual activity of Catholic Germany is to be brought under subjection to the Roman congregations, it must settle into those systems with which the Roman divines are conversant, and for which, therefore, a direct theological as well as dogmatic influence must be vindicated. The prodigious defects of many German writers, and the violent hostility to Rome which in many shapes survived amongst them until lately, have powerfully contributed to recommend these designs. Their most definite form is a demand that the fixed traditions of theology, as taught by the Jesuits in Rome, shall be made binding on the German Catholics, in order that Rome may not lose all control over their literature. The outward expression of these ideas is a demonstrative zeal for the spiritual and temporal claims of the Holy See, an unqualified reliance on the efficacy of the Index, and a predilection for scholastic theology.

A combination of circumstances has made the city of Mentz the stronghold of these opinions. The Bishop, von Ketteler, one of the most imposing characters in the Catholic episcopate, was raised to the see fifteen years ago, after the nominee of the Chapter had been refused by the Pope. This event, occurring in the midst of the troubles of 1848, violently agitated the public mind in Central Germany; and the University of Giessen, where the rival of the new Bishop was professor of theology, became a hotbed of the sentiments which he was resolved to put down. He accordingly removed the faculty of theology from that university, and reconstructed it under his own eye, and in his own spirit, in the seminary of Mentz. More recently came the obstinate assaults of the Hessian Liberals on the freedom of the Church and the school; and a struggle was engendered by the restrictive measures which were forced on the ministry. In this struggle the Bishop of Mentz, as the champion of religious liberty, became the most unpopular and calumniated person in the country. For him, and for the zealous men who stand with him in the focus of the conflict between the world and the Church, the immediate dangers and the present antagonism are of overwhelming interest. Looking about for the daily means of acting on opinion, in order to sustain an ardent fight against ignorance, violence, and hatred, they find them not in the remoter benefits of science, but in a close adhesion to the Holy See, and in the sympathy they are enabled to acquire in Germany by their writings, and still more by their influence in the annual Catholic assemblies. In this effort many persons have come by degrees to make their own opinions the test of fidelity to the Church they represent,[1] and to look with suspicion on the orthodoxy of those who are at variance with the views which in the midst of strife they themselves have been induced to proclaim. Their organ, the *Katholik*, has allowed itself, at various times, considerable licence in denouncing the chief scholars of Catholic Germany. The Jesuits and the disciples of the schools of Rome constitute the bulk of their adherents; but the views of the party have their most intense expression in the seminary of Mentz—partly because it is placed in the midst of the conflict, and partly because its isolation from the influences of a university deprives it of the natural stimulants to scientific research.

The most serious theological dispute of recent years in Catholic Germany is one in which the organ of the Mentz divines was engaged against the teaching of a still more influential school. Tübingen has possessed for nearly forty years a theological faculty of high repute among Catholics. The professors of this faculty have conducted with great ability the most valuable theological review which, so far as we know, exists in the Church, and have been, since the time of Möhler, strenuous promoters of the pat-

---

[1] The following passage, from the last volume of the *Katholik*, shows how boldly this identity is asserted: "Täusche man sich nicht, die Theologie der Orden und der Germaniker (the German college in Rome) ist, unbeschadet der von der Kirche unentschiedenen Controversen, auch die Theologie Rom's und der ganzen katholischen Welt . . . Der Theologie der Kirche gegenüber eine andere deutsche Wissenschaft statuiren wollen, ist nicht im Geiste der Kirche."

ristic theology. The most voluminous of their writers, Hefele, who is generally known as the author of a sophistical defence of the Inquisition in his life of Ximenes, has since the publication of that book obtained a purer fame by his learned history of the Councils. Another of them, Professor Kuhn, is a more definite and original thinker; and his great work on Dogmatic Theology, appearing at long intervals, kindled the controversy. His method is to trace the progress of each dogma through the assaults of heresy, the decisions of popes and councils, and the treatises of divines, and then to deal with it speculatively, in the light of modern philosophy. By thus adopting the theory of Development, and rejecting the scholastic philosophy, he is directly opposed to the prevailing schools. His theory, though not influenced by that of Dr Newman, with whose work he was not acquainted, is very similar to it. His application of it is made in such a way as to involve him in almost insurmountable difficulties, and to do nearly as much violence to patristic texts as they suffer from the advocates of mere tradition. He is further open to the imputation of having failed to understand the great defect of modern speculation, since he deserts the old systems not only on the ground of the advance of knowledge, or the impossibility of constructing theology *a priori*, but because of their ruling principle of submission to the authority of the Church. He not only insists on making philosophy independent of theology, without which they cannot aid each other, but he separates them entirely, saying that one has its source in revelation, and the other in reason. This theory of the freedom of science is as extreme in its way as the deliberate hostility which his adversaries display to the progress of knowledge beyond its ancient forms and limits; and a discussion on the subject, which has interested all Catholic Germany, has been carried on for several years between the Tübingen Quarterly and the *Katholik* of Mentz.

A more exaggerated view than that of Kuhn has been maintained by Dr Frohschammer of Munich, who emancipates philosophy entirely from the control of religion and revelation, and affirms that it cannot be compelled to revise its conclusions, even when they are manifestly at variance with articles of faith. These opinions are confined to a narrow circle of adherents. The philosophy of Günther, which penetrated far more widely, survives, since its condemnation, not as a system, but only as an influence leavening the thought of Germany. Its disciples are no longer distinguished by the special doctrines of the school—for these have in substance been unreservedly abandoned—but rather by an attachment to intellectual freedom, and an anxiety lest the failure of the only system that was adopted in great part of Austria and Germany should prejudice the formation of other philosophies, and lead to the stagnation of speculative activity. The Prussian universities of Breslau and of Bonn, the old home of Hermesianism, betray the influence of this solicitude, and retain some traces of the extinct philosophy. In all these factions, therefore, differing as they do on many questions of detail, the great problem of the day is the definition of the rights of reason and science among Catholics.

The internal dissensions of Catholic scholars not only cause the waste of much valuable power, but seriously injure the authority of the Church. For it is always of the gravest importance that the utterances of supreme authority should be anticipated and supported by a general understanding and agreement among the faithful, so that there may be no temptation to impugn their rightfulness, and error may be intercepted and refuted before it comes into collision with authority. It is the duty of ecclesiastical science to stand between the Church and her assailants, to justify her decrees, to prevent conflict, and to settle theological disputes before they involve danger to faith. In order that this may be accomplished, it is requisite not only that learning should be diligently cultivated, but also that it should mature some degree of unity and harmony of opinion; in other words, it is necessary that the best results of theological science should be generally known, and that there should not be too great an inequality between the proficiency of different schools. When the French clergy were the most learned in Europe, this unity and authority of theology was represented by the Sorbonne; and in times not far distant the same prerogative might become the portion of the divines of Germany, if the superiority of their training were not neutralized by their divisions. It is obvious that, where there is no uniform teaching or close organization, this better understanding and more intimate union can be obtained only by means of conferences, at which opposition may be allayed and misunderstandings removed, which may make the knowledge and the ways of each school familiar to all, and in which personal intercourse may make up for the absence of an enforced unity, and of the sameness that springs from intellectual lethargy.

The idea that an attempt might be successfully made to promote this important result had lately begun to gain strength. Some preliminary negotiations had taken place, we believe, between several divines of southern Germany; and the scheme had been warmly applauded at Vienna by the nuncio, Cardinal De Luca. At the beginning of the summer vacation, a letter signed by Dr Döllinger, Abbot Kunsburg, and the ecclesiastical historian Alzog of Freiburg, was sent round to the German divines and scholars, proposing the establishment of annual conferences, to be begun at Munich in September. The author of the paper takes the following ground: Unbelief is visibly advancing, and can be arrested only by positive science, which flourishes only in a Catholic soil, and which the Germans, who in their greatest errors have never lost a sincere love of truth, are called on to restore. This has not yet been done, because, in a period of transition like the present age, when many new ways are opened, differences necessarily arise; and the very earnestness of thought and depth of conviction tend to embitter them, so that the ardour of literary enterprise is depressed, and discredit is brought upon Catholics. An exclusive and suspicious censorship would be fatal to the progress of science, which cannot exist in the Church unless it breathes an atmosphere of freedom. Error on particular points is easily set right by the reaction of the general opinion, but intellectual stagnation is a more serious danger. For the conflict in which Catholics are engaged against the enemies of religion demands that all their resources should be combined for mutual support. By the introduction of periodical meetings men would be brought together from a distance. They would exchange their ideas and settle their disputes, or at least learn to carry them on in a spirit of conciliation and religion. Such meetings would afford an opportunity for deliberation on the pressing questions of the day, and the means of combining in great literary undertakings, and associating to give increased power to the Catholic press. The paper declared, in conclusion, that no personal objects should be allowed to assert themselves, but that a purely scientific tone should reign in the meetings; and the bishops were asked to support the scheme.

After the circular of the three divines had been issued an event occurred which made it doubtful whether it would have the intended effect. Time had been wanting to increase the number of subscribers. The document did not even proceed from the faculty of the university; but appeared to be virtually the work of only two professors. The condemnation and contumacy of a priest and professor of Munich, who had been sustained by the government and had obtained much sympathy among the clergy and in the university, had lately brought the place into ambiguous repute. It was at that very moment the scene of the greatest scandal of recent years, and the cradle of a theory, touching the liberty of speculative opinion, which was utterly in contradiction to orthodoxy. To discuss grave theological problems at Munich appeared to many, under the circumstances, like arguing the question of the temporal power at Turin. It was true that the dean of the theological faculty had originated the idea of the Congress, and that, in a series of lectures on the rights and limits of authority, he had publicly repudiated the theories of Frohschammer. But there were other reasons why even Döllinger's illustrious name would not avail to disarm that sort of suspicion which had now been awakened. The magnitude of his services and his capacity is not disputed; but the very qualities which are the secret of his eminence have had their drawbacks, and have been the indirect causes of a resistance to his influence in minds of several descriptions. His rigorous method and inexhaustible resources, and the spirit in which he applies them, are too entirely devoted to the service of truth to be adapted to compromise or dissimulation, or to the necessities of defective knowledge. The weapon so potent against the outward adversaries of the Church retains its force against defects within, and seems in its passage to smite insincerity or treason as well as open enmity. Any writer who uses a dishonest artifice, meets a difficulty with a hasty answer, or ekes out his ignorance with falsehood, would be sensible that he would do well to conceal his act from one whose knowledge of controversy is so extensive, who can never be made an accomplice, and who has a knack of turning all the untenable positions occupied by Catholics. Nor is it only his superior learning and honesty, or his resolution to tolerate no unsound link in the chain of his reasoning, which offends those who in these respects are not free from reproach. His published sentiments on the Roman question differ conspicuously from those of the majority of the episcopate; and his exposure of the defects of the Papal Government has seriously embarrassed its defenders. In a later work, where he related historical events which contradict the theological opinion that the Pope cannot fall into heresy, he has exhibited no solicitude to disguise the facts or to deprecate the consequences; whilst he has shown that certain things which have had an important bearing on the constitution of the Church have taken their origin in illusions or in fraud. Above all, his use of the theory of development innovates far more than that of its other professors on the ordinary teaching of divines. It takes less than this to isolate a priest who is a pioneer of learning, and who publishes many results which he is the first to discover, and many more to which those who accept them dare not give expression.

This antagonism between the overwhelming personal authority of Dr Döllinger and the reaction against it is a point of high importance, and the real key to the incidents of the Munich Congress. We are the more inclined to give it prominence because it would appear, from many indications, that he himself did not realize the fact when he gave the impulse to the meeting, or even when it was brought rudely home to him by several significant events. In sending forth the circular, he seemed to have forgotten the storm which had burst over his lectures and his book on the Temporal Power, the angry denunciations of which he had been the object, the motives imputed to him, and his breach with a portion of the episcopate. In inviting the sanction of the bishops to an assembly in which he undertook to unite and reconcile the theologians of his country, to moderate their councils, and to guide their resolutions, it was necessary to assume that the breach was healed, that the storm had subsided, and that confidence was reposed in the author of so good a work. And, in the deliberations that followed, Dr Döllinger insisted so warmly on the need and the possibility of concord, that he seemed to ignore the existence of other than superficial elements of division; he entered so frankly into explanations, and spoke with so much simplicity the matured and intimate convictions of his mind, that one would suppose he thought it possible to remove by arguments the difficulties that might be placed in his way, and reckoned on finding in others a fairness and sincerity equal to his own.

This was the source of a fallacy and unreality that showed itself in the proceedings. It was assumed that Catholics are separated by no broad chasm; that the causes of difference between them are not deeply seated; that charity, piety, and a common purpose in what is most essential would break down all barriers; and that something would actually be done if there was but the will to do it. If all who were there assembled had possessed the clear vision and profound learning of the president, a few brief conferences might have done something towards this end. But the forces that are warring within the Church are not so easily reconciled. The methods and principles of different periods and worlds of thought are contending; ancient and tenacious traditions are suffering transformation; and the truths which are claiming recognition, and the abuses which are struggling for existence, cannot escape the agonies of childbirth or of death. The strict orthodoxy of one body of Catholics is questioned, and the intellectual morality of the other; and when such accusations are exchanged, they cannot both be entirely unfounded. There are none of these elements of contradiction perhaps that will not be absorbed in the progress of knowledge and experience; but they will not depart without a struggle; and peace can only be the result of a decisive or an exhaustive war. The speediest remedy for the defects, the sorrows, and the scandals of our time will come not from an anxiety to avoid every manifestation of the opposing tendencies, but from a definite and unrelenting exposition and comparison of contending opinions, and from the resolute prosecution of ecclesiastical knowledge. When the Fathers of Trent met in council, under the guidance of the Holy Ghost, they did not quash their differences or silence objections, but let each opinion assert itself manfully, and even rudely, in what may be justly called a trial of strength. Some of the problems which the congress of the German divines will hereafter be invited to solve are even of a more delicate nature than those which were decided at Trent, and will require to be considered with less assistance from tradition or authority, because they belong to those questions in which no general consensus can be established until science leads the way. In the course of these inquiries, before the conclusions of the deepest thinkers become the accepted property of all, even in the select circles of German learning, they will have to do battle for their systems as was done of old, and on a greater occasion, by Canus and Laynez, by Danès and De Martyribus.

Under the influence of the feelings which were afterwards more publicly manifested, the nuncio at Munich, Monsignore Gonella, conveyed to Rome the apprehension which had been created by the unauthorized step of the three divines. He received a reply which he hastened to communicate to the bishops, expressing, it is said, the surprise of the Holy See at a proceeding so unwarranted and presumptuous, and desiring them to take precautions that no evil consequences might ensue. This was a very serious affair. By putting the adverse opinion of the Holy See into the balance, not, indeed, in the form of a command, but in the form of an unmistakeable wish, it was made extremely probable that the plan of the Congress might fail. If, on the other hand, it should take place, it had become very difficult to prevent the fact of its occurrence from appearing in the light of a repulse to the authority of Rome, since the nuncio had undertaken to measure his influence with that of the author of the invitation. Fortunately the influence which prevailed was sufficient, not only to overcome this obstacle, but to prevent it from converting the result into a protest or a party demonstration. The effect of the communication from the nuncio, however, is visible in the warnings of those bishops who greeted the scheme most warmly, as well as in the silence of many others. It acted further on the constitution and proceedings of the assembly, for it caused the absence of many whose presence would inevitably have occasioned dissension, and so far diminished the chances of discord while restricting the comprehensive character of the meeting. But the resolution to keep away was not universal among those who shared the uneasiness of the nuncio; and opposite counsels prevailed with some who were not attracted by the ideas of the circular. It was evident that if only those attended who disregarded the objections that had been urged, the danger, whatever it might be, of an injurious issue would be increased. If any ill was to be apprehended, it seemed the fairest course to face it with some counteracting force. Since it was clear that those who hoped well of the Congress would be in a majority over those who feared it, it was important that the minority should be represented, in order to check if they could not control, to denounce if they could not prevent, proceedings which were anticipated with a vague inarticulate alarm. It happened that the convention of the Catholic associations was held at Frankfort in the week preceding the date fixed for the Munich Congress. Several persons, whose ideas were not fully represented by the language of the circular, met and conferred on this occasion, and were confirmed in the resolution of testifying against the tendencies they opposed, at the critical moment which was approaching.

Since the fifteenth century Germany has never beheld so numerous an assembly of her ecclesiastical notables as that which, after hearing High Mass in the Basilica of St Boniface, on the morning of the 28th of September, adjourned to the neighbouring monastery. Several great schools of learning, however, were not represented. Kuhn, whose appearance might have been the signal for stormy debates, had lately been assailed by the leading periodical of Munich on account of his opposition to the scheme of founding a Catholic university in Germany; and he was in his tents, publishing a reply. His less obnoxious colleague, Hefele, was in Italy; and none of the brilliant Catholic school of Tübingen came. The Austrian Jesuits were also absent. It was not known at first who was there and who had stayed away, for several meetings had been held before a list could be made out. Many a man found himself on that day, for the first time, in the presence of writers whose works had deeply influenced his mind, or whose fame had long excited his curiosity, without knowing their features. It was an interesting moment, therefore, when the names were called over, and each man rose for a moment in answer to his own, in order that the meeting might know him again. About fifty of those who were present had written books which are known and valued by scholars beyond the limits of their country.

Nearly one-third of the members belonged to the diocese of Munich. Among these were several distinguished laymen. One was Ringseis, the most Catholic among the eminent physicians of Germany. Another was Professor Sepp, the sole disciple of the mighty Görres, who is publishing, in an improved form, the voluminous life of Christ which he composed many years ago in reply to Strauss. He is the most ardent and venturesome of the German laity, a brilliant parliamentary speaker, and a very imaginative historian, but rather hasty in council, and not much relied on in literature. He was not a prominent actor in the subsequent proceedings. A third layman, Dr Jörg, who began in literature as a historical inquirer of the school of Döllinger, but who for ten years has conducted with ability and vigour the *Historisch-*

politische Blätter, did not exercise on this occasion an influence commensurate with his just renown as a political writer, and appeared undecided as to the side on which his weight ought to be cast.

Frohschammer, to whom the meeting would have been a welcome arena for the defence of his theories, afterwards affirmed that he had been excluded by order of the archbishop. The fact of the exclusion, as well as of any interference on the part of the archbishop in the affairs of the Congress, had been denied on authority; but there were probably few who regretted that an additional source of discord was not supplied by the presence of a suspended priest, whose writings, in the estimation of nearly the whole assembly, are at variance with dogma. His views on the independence of philosophy were, however, represented by a layman, probably his equal in knowledge, and not so distasteful to his opponents. This was Professor Huber, who has written on the philosophy of the Fathers, and more deeply on Scotus Erigena, and who furnished that report of Döllinger's lectures on the Temporal Power which caused so much sensation three years ago. In his last book he has openly defied the Index; and he is one of those writers whose independence and catholicity of thought are the most visibly affected by the study of Protestant writings. But he spoke gracefully and with moderation; and, having declared that he belonged to the extreme Left of the assembly, he was probably not surprised to find himself on one occasion registering a solitary vote.

He was generally supported by Professor Mayr of Würzburg, a speaker of less prepossessing address, but a philosopher whose methodical precision of thought it was a pleasure to follow, although he did not seem familiar with the problems and motives that occupied the thoughts of his audience. The partisans of the utmost independence of science might have expected more efficient aid from Dr Schmid of Dillingen, a divine of rising reputation, whose recent volume on the scientific tendencies of Catholic Germany proves him more deeply versed than almost any other man in the several currents of thought that separate the schools. But although he is the only priest who contributes to Frohschammer's review, the *Athenäum*, and appears to occupy nearly the same ground as Kuhn, he observed an obstinate silence, and did nothing for the propagation of his views. Indeed, it is to be regretted that, among so many scholars of high repute, who would have secured a hearing, there were so few who claimed it. The discussion turned much on philosophy and on practical questions, attractive to those who were curious in the movements of parties; but it left untouched great departments of ecclesiastical science. Biblical scholars like Reischl who has translated the Bible into German, Thalhofer who has written on the Psalms, and Schegg of Freising, one of the most prolific and interesting of recent commentators, had no opportunity of using their special accomplishments. The professors of theology at Munich were for the most part inactive, either because they wished to dissociate their faculty from the responsibility of the meeting, or because they thought it sufficiently cared for by their colleagues who had taken the lead. Yet two of the Munich divines, Professor Rietter and Dr Oischinger, have written on St Thomas, and well understood the questions which were argued. As much might be said of Dr Sighart of Freising, the biographer of Albertus Magnus; but the merit of his recent history of art in Bavaria has eclipsed his reputation as a master of the mediaeval philosophy. The last of the silent metaphysicians is Dr Hayd of Munich, who has lately published an important work on Abelard.

Austria was represented by four of her most distinguished writers—Phillips, Schulte, Werner, and Brunner. The first of these, who is a convert, from the North of Germany, but of English descent, published valuable works on the early constitutional history of England in the time of George IV. Then, having been for many years a most successful lecturer and writer on German jurisprudence, one of the founders of the *Historisch-politische Blätter*, and the most conspicuous layman in the group of Catholic writers that surrounded Görres, and influenced so deeply the mind of Catholic Germany, he was involved in the proscription of the Ultramontane professors in the days of Lola Montez, and has since devoted himself, at Vienna and Salzburg, to the composition of the most elaborate treatise of canon law that the nineteenth century has produced. His name has been, for a quarter of a century, a household word among his Catholic countrymen; and, in spite of a certain deficiency of logic and condensation, and a ponderousness of learned detail that oppresses his ideas, he was, in point of literary reputation, nearly the first man in the assembly. Nevertheless, he seems to have spoken hardly more than once, for his name appears only among the after-dinner speeches. He submitted to the impulse of more ardent men, and figured at one important moment in their wake.

A younger canonist, Schulte of Prague, is a remarkable contrast to his more famous rival. Those who reproach him with writing too much and too hastily, admit that, of all modern works on canon law, his are of most practical utility, and contain the greatest abundance of original thought, though without the immense erudition of Phillips. He spoke often, and nearly always with force and clearness, and acquired far the greatest influence of all the laymen in the assembly. He was one of those who most efficiently supported the president in moderating extremes and keeping the assembly in the course which, by conceding nothing to the exclusive tendencies of particular sections, could alone assure its success in time to come.

A similar influence would probably have been exerted by the most learned of the Austrian priesthood, Professor Werner of St Pölten; but the death of his bishop summoned him away from Munich. It is probable that many who, on the first day, had seen a small, retiring man sitting awkwardly in a coat that did not seem his own, and apparently scared and humbled by all that surrounded him, were afterwards surprised to hear his honoured name. Unlike other disciples of Günther's sterile school, Dr Werner has been almost too productive. His moral theology is the most valued that has appeared in German; and his great work on St Thomas raised his reputation to a level which his book on Suarez and the first volumes of a history of apologetic literature have not sustained. But in the series of histories of the sciences in Germany which was set on foot by the King of Bavaria, and for which the most eminent writers have been chosen, the history of Catholic theology was, at Döllinger's recommendation, entrusted to Dr Werner. On the great questions of reason and faith, and of the value of the scholastic divinity, very few were so competent to speak. But, either from weakness or timidity, he could not make himself heard, though he put on paper several propositions, which were read from the chair and adopted in the protocol.

From the first, considerable interest had been exhibited in the project at Vienna, and it was supposed that some of the Viennese theologians, and among others the Jesuit Schrader, Passaglia's former colleague, would have been present. But Vienna is not a theological capital, and was perhaps more fitly represented by a vigorous and courageous journalist, Dr Brunner, the stalwart adversary of the demoralized rabble that have long predominated in the Austrian press. He contributed, however, rather sense and humour than deep learning to the Munich councils, and sometimes diverted with timely pleasantry the troubled minds of the assembly. In most respects he presented a singular contrast to other men who, like himself, are involved in the pressure and anxiety of popular discussion.

The University of Breslau was represented solely by Dr Reinkens, a Rhinelander by birth, whose recent investigations have diminished the lustre of the Jesuit schools in the seventeenth century, and who, in an unguarded passage of the work in which this was done, has exasperated the national, or rather the provincial, feelings of the Silesian clergy. An uncommon shrewdness of expression and a thoughtful manner would lead one to believe that he was not likely to write imprudently. A life of St Hilary by him was already announced, but he has not yet been a productive writer; and the suspicion of an attachment to the doctrines of Günther, which rests on one of the leading professors of the faculty to which he belongs, seems on this occasion to have somewhat impaired his influence. This at least might be gathered from the fate of a proposal which he submitted to the Assembly at the opening of its deliberations. It would be useful, he said, to establish, in addition to the reviews representing the different schools, a central organ which should impartially register the progress of learning, and in which various opinions should be allowed to meet, and, if possible, be reconciled. He proposed that a periodical of this kind should be founded, or that one of those already existing should be enabled to supply the want. The idea was encouraged by Dr Döllinger, on the ground that it was desirable to be informed of the mere advance of science through some medium coloured by no distinctive opinions, and that an arena open for the discussion of debatable questions might be a means of promoting concord. Nevertheless, all parties united in condemning the plan—some on the ground that the existing reviews were not sufficiently supported, others on the ground that an editor must not promote any views except those which he thinks are right, and others, again, on the ground that even the opposition of contending schools is not to be deprecated, provided they proceed scientifically. The proposition was summarily snuffed out without being put to the vote.

The very decided opponent of Dr Reinkens on this occasion, though generally, it would seem, but little divided from him, was Professor Floss of Bonn, a grave and wary man, and not easily committed to questionable or impractical schemes. He is one of the most indefatigable explorers of manuscript texts, a dry and colourless writer, but a sound critic and a man of facts, as it has been said a German should be. The only collected edition of the writings of Scotus Erigena is due to him. Many of his treatises on mediaeval history possess acknowledged value; and the only thing which hindered him from playing one of the first parts at the meeting was apparently a want of fluency in speaking.

Dr Hagemann of Hildesheim would have to be referred to the same group as these two historians, if his attainments may be estimated by a book which is not yet published, and his opinions by a single remark with which he took part in the last skirmish with the Mentz divines. He is the author of a history of the Church of Rome during the three first centuries, which was, we believe, already in print, and which is said to be the most valuable treatise on a subject on which many of the most learned Germans have been his rivals; but he exhibited throughout a disappointing taciturnity.

The ecclesiastical historians, animated by the spirit of the great master of Church history, constituted the centre, and were the ruling power in the Congress. The secretary, Father Gams, whose history of the Church in Spain has been noticed in our pages, must be included among them, as well as several other Munich scholars, such as Dr Pichler, who, after writing a volume on Polybius, has devoted himself to the history of the Eastern Schism, and Dr Friedrich, whose writings have been chiefly confined to the history of the fifteenth century. For these two men it was evident that the meeting possessed an almost painful interest. They are the junior members of the faculty of theology, and probably find it difficult to counteract the powerful attraction which the theories of Frohschammer exercise over the students. It was therefore important for them to obtain some declaration on the disputed questions, by which the liberty of thought might be so completely vindicated that nothing should remain to justify complaints against the exercise of ecclesiastical authority. Dr Reusch of Bonn, who in a recent volume of lectures on the cosmogony has walked in the footsteps of Cardinal Wiseman, and who has translated several of his writings, seemed to emulate the good sense and moderation of his colleague Floss. It was understood that he had undertaken the editorship of a theological encyclopaedia, which was one of the literary enterprises most warmly taken up by the assembly.

Without the ballast with which these men steadied the ship it would have been tossed about by the conflicting opinions of others. Dr Knoodt of Bonn, formerly a strenuous adherent of Günther, placed himself unequivocally on the side of authority, taking the ground that the Church, being infallible, cannot really injure the freedom of science, which is liable to err. This declaration fell very far short of that which the adversaries of freedom desired, and in fact avoided the real issue; but yet the attitude assumed by the speaker, who we believe was, with one exception, the only priest present whose works are on the Index, proved at least that the apprehensions for the rights of authority were groundless, and that whatever disputes might arise would be confined to the narrower ground of expedience and formality.

A heavy gray-haired man, deliberate in manner but of fluent speech, was perpetually on his legs, and was heard with much impatience. This was Dr Eberhard, now the parish priest of a village on the Danube, but many years ago a preacher who gained in the pulpit of the cathedral of Munich successes which remind one of those of the great orators of Notre Dame. He it was who carried among the burghers of the Bavarian capital that new spirit of Catholicism which the persecution of the Archbishop of Cologne had kindled in Germany; and devout people are still named who were among his converts in those days, and were brought by his sermons from indifference to the practice of their religion. In later years he has written on metaphysics, and has joined the *Katholik* in its crusade on behalf of the Index, but without sharing all the fervour or all the opinions of its conductors. In an evil hour he undertook to describe the several schools of thought in Catholic Germany; and the grave and passionless tone of the beginning gave promise at least of an equitable treatment. But the meeting shrank from this self-knowledge. Dr Heinrich, the editor of the *Katholik*, vehemently interrupted the speaker, whose rude touch threatened to destroy the harmony which had just been painfully established, or at least to dispel the illusion of its existence. The president pronounced this objection perfectly legitimate; and Dr Eberhard came down to his place with a smile at his own simplicity.

Dr Michelis, a priest who, in the solitude of a country parish, has risen of late years to great note and influence in Westphalia, was a still more frequent speaker. His distinctly marked opinions were expressed with an ardour that provoked contradiction; and he strode about like a gigantic athlete, interrupting the speeches of his opponents, and disturbing somewhat the decorum and order of the meeting. After writing the cleverest of the refutations of Günther, he published a very elaborate work on Plato, and has ever since been at war with his critics and with those who omitted to notice it. The review which he superintends, *Nature and Revelation*, gives the praiseworthy example of an effort carried on with great constancy to follow the progress of natural science, and to revise the solutions by which, at a less advanced stage of inquiry, it was brought into harmony with religion. Of all the Prussian priests he is the one most regarded and most trusted by that section of the Lutherans which is tending more or less consciously to union with the Church. But among Catholics he appears the most disputatious, and therefore unpopular, of men. He has broken a lance with many of those whom he met on this occasion, and is at open war with the school of Mentz, and with the friends of Günther. Others probably were sometimes annoyed by his vehemence, or angry with his passion for speaking his mind; but his honest and uncompromising spirit enabled him to do much for conciliation, for it was more easy to quarrel with his manner than to refute his opinions.

There was an uncouth person in the meeting, uncourtly and unadorned, little versed in ancient or modern languages, and weighed down as to his literary reputation by the defects of his earlier writings, who is yet the most perspicuous of the German philosophers, and in some respects the most profound. This was Dr Deutinger, who was dispossessed, like many other professors at Munich, in 1847, and has never been restored; but whose recent works on the history of modern philosophy and on the Gospel of St John are of the very first merit. His essays on the dispute between Kuhn and Clemens, Kuhn's assailant in the *Katholik*, and in the affair of Frohschammer, foreshadow the solution of the problem of authority and freedom, revelation and reason, to which German theology will inevitably tend. His speech on this subject is, next to the inaugural address, the most valuable thing in the report.

The school of Mentz was led by Canon Moufang, the most eloquent man in the Congress, and by Professor Heinrich, from whom the organ of the party receives its tone. A broad provincial accent disfigures the speaking of the latter; and it seemed more suited to his temper to interrupt or to rise to order than to deliver a set speech. He alone among the assembled divines has the neatness and unction of the French priesthood; and his delicate features and mild expression of countenance are not suggestive of the unyielding energy and bitterness which appear in his writings. He was supported with greater moderation by Professor Hergenröther of Würzburg, the special champion of Roman theology, and author of a vindication of the government of the Holy See, and by his colleague, Dr Hettinger, who has published a popular apology for the Christian faith, and who once, in the heat of discussion, tried to silence the voice of the laity.

It was to an assembly so composed that Dr Döllinger, having been elected president, delivered his inaugural address on the history, condition, and duties of Catholic theology. The leading ideas of this address were as follows:

Christian theology owes its origin to the union of Greek philosophy with Hebrew learning at Alexandria, where, contemporaneously with the appearance of the first Christian divines, the last original thinker of antiquity, Plotinus, made the last attempt to supply a pagan substitute for the discarded religion of the people. The child, as it issued from its mother's womb, was deeply tainted with the vices of the parent. The grave dogmatic errors of Origen, the father of Christian science and the founder of the earliest school of theology, served as a warning that the treasure is contained in earthen vessels, and that the intellectual study of religious truth needs the watchful supervision of the Church. A less speculative and more purely biblical school than that of Alexandria afterwards arose at Antioch. While theology remained the almost exclusive possession of these Eastern churches, the dogmatic struggle was chiefly confined to the doctrine of the Person of Christ, to theology, in that narrower sense in which the

term *theologus* was applied to St John and to St Gregory Nazi-
anzen. Even St Gregory of Nyssa, the most original of the Greek
fathers after Origen, scarcely passed the bounds of that circle of
ideas. The doctors of Latin Europe borrowed their views from
the Greeks, and did not go beyond them until St Augustine, who
stands alone among the Western divines, extended the limits
of theology, and became the teacher and master of the Latin
Church. The Greek theology in the period of its decline shone
once more in the works of St Maximus, and put forth its last great
divine in St John Damascene. During a thousand years since his
death it has made no progress, has done nothing for ethics or for
the dogmas of grace and redemption, and has been content with
the achievements of early times in Scripture and Church history.
Excepting the appearance of one divine, who wrote against
Proclus, and the deplorable transformation of the doctrine of the
Holy Ghost in the contest with the Western Church, it has ever
since been stationary.

For five centuries after the great migrations theological science
in the West lay in its winter sleep. The Church was busy with the
reconstruction of society; and the best writers, such as Paulinus
and Alcuin, were only equal to the task of preserving from extinction the knowledge which had come down to them. Controversy was revived for a moment in the ninth century, but died
speedily away: and the Neoplatonic philosophy of Scotus Erigena, which stood alone, awakened no interest and exerted no
influence.

Modern theology aims at understanding, connecting, and har-
monizing the whole system of doctrine, with a completeness and
comprehensiveness unknown in the eleven first centuries of the
Church. It began with St Anselm, and has continued ever since,
with increasing energy, to strive for the attainment of its end. As
theology had begun in the combination of the Platonic philosophy with the dogma at Alexandria, so now, down to the sixteenth century, it was governed by the philosophy of Aristotle.
But the scholastic divines were unable to remedy the vices of their
starting-point and their method. Their analytical process could
not construct a system corresponding to the harmony and wealth
of revealed truth; and without the elements of biblical criticism
and dogmatic history they possessed only one of the eyes of theology. The one enduring achievement of those times is the creation

of a system of ethical science by St Thomas, albeit on Aristotelian principles.

All the chief nations of Europe laboured together on the scholastic theology, with the same language and method, and without any national distinctions. In Germany a reaction began early in the fourteenth century, and the ablest divines were attracted by the unexplored treasures of speculative mysticism. The Areopagitical writings, not being fully understood, were supposed to be orthodox; and experience had not yet taught how easily mystic contemplation glides into theosophic pantheism. The works of Eckart, Tauler, and their school, will always retain their value, though none but minds well trained in philosophy and history will be competent to use them. In the fifteenth century Gerson undertook to reconcile and combine the mystic with the scholastic method; while Nicholas of Cusa anticipated many of the later discoveries of speculative and historical theology.

The scholastic theology had been generally abandoned, and a craving for a method more suited to the nature of Christianity and the wants of the human mind was strong in Germany when the Reformation broke out, caused not so much by the defects of theology as by the evils which its decay had helped to develop in ecclesiastical life. But the contest which followed had to be fought out on the domain of doctrine. Here the old scholastic armoury supplied no weapons capable of defending the Church against her new assailants; and she was compelled to have recourse to the biblical and historical studies which had commenced with the Revival. The rupture of the unity of Christendom, considered in its influence on religious science, proved highly beneficial; and the idea that Christianity is history, and that in order to be understood it must be studied in its development, began to effect a transformation of theology which has not yet attained even a temporary conclusion. These fruits of the Revival and of the Reformation did not ripen for Germany. France, Italy, and the Netherlands could boast of great divines. England gave birth to Stapleton, the most eminent of all the champions of the Church against the new doctrines. And throughout the sixteenth century theological science flourished above all in Spain. But the expulsion of the Protestant leaven brought on the relapse which shows itself in the uncritical eclecticism of the later scholastics; and a scientific divinity was finally extinguished by the Inquisition.

After the death of Baronius and Bellarmine the intellectual decline of Italy made itself felt in her theology; and her ablest men,
such as Sarpi, Galileo, and Campanella, earned their distinction
in other paths. The sceptre had passed to the clergy of France,
who became the creators of patristic theology and ecclesiastical
history, and to whom belongs the praise of having delivered religion from one of the worst evils of modern times—the immoral
and unscientific teaching of the casuists. The rest of Europe did
not profit as it might have done by this renovation of ecclesiastical
learning; for the French divines, after the example of Duperron,
had generally discarded the use of Latin, and by adapting their
own tongue to the uses of theology had given their writings rank
and influence in the classical literature of their country. The same
thing was done, though not so thoroughly, for the English, by
Hooker, Bramhall, Baxter, and others. But the Italians have
never raised their language to a level with the Latin; Spain has
been silent in both languages; and the German has but lately
acquired that flexibility and perfection to which it was already
rapidly approaching in the fourteenth century.

The introduction of modern languages into purely theological
literature was a new Babel for divines; and it would have hindered co-operation, and encouraged national individuality at the
expense of Catholicity, if the tendency of recent years had not
been to break down the barriers that divide the nations, and to
make the intellectual acquisitions of each the common property
of all. The actual result, however, gives a great advantage to the
Germans, who are more skilled than the Latin races to understand the languages and characters of foreign countries. Before
the middle of the eighteenth century the light of theology was
eclipsed in France; and the apologists of those days were not able
to command the literary popularity of their illustrious predecessors. The university which for six hundred years had been the
glory of the French Church perished in the Revolution; and since
that catastrophe there has never existed a centre of theology in
Christendom invested with the authority of acknowledged learning, nor has theology itself revived in any part of Latin Europe.
The works of Balmez exemplify its low condition in Spain, where
native history is the only study that appears to thrive. In the age
of Benedict XIV many eminent scholars had arisen in Italy, and
especially in Rome; but after his pontificate theology rapidly de-

clined. For centuries no important work on Scripture has been
written by any Italian divine; and the suppression of the Jesuits
deprived the other orders of a rivalry which had been a useful
stimulus to exertion. In our generation the three most gifted members of the Italian priesthood, Rosmini, Gioberti, and Ventura,
of whom Balbo prophesied twenty years ago that they would raise
the body whose ornaments they were to a high place in the opinion of the world, came into collision with Rome. Two of them
died in exile; and the divine who passed for the best of his country
has abandoned his former studies. No nation perhaps that experienced the troubles and commotions which have visited Italy
in our century could have escaped the same effects.

France has one great advantage in the possession of able and
zealous laymen who are efficient advocates of the Catholic cause;
and the names of Gerbet, Maret, Lacordaire, Gratry, Bautain,
Dupanloup, Ravignan, and Félix prove that there is a school of
men among the clergy who understand the wants of their people
and their age, and are able to present religion to them in an attractive form. But there are no real divines of the type of Petavius,
Bossuet, and Arnauld, because there are no institutions in which
theological science can be taught. The seminaries produce excellent priests, but no scholars; and if nothing is done to establish a
university, it is to be feared that the French clergy will lose all
influence over the male part of the population, and will fall into
a social seclusion. It is fortunate for the Germans that they have
preserved their universities, and that theology is represented in
them; for at length the time has come when the office of carrying
onward the torch of ecclesiastical learning has devolved on them.
The Greek and Italians, the Spaniards, the French, and the English, have gone before:

> *Illos primus equis Oriens afflavit anhelis,*
> *Nobis sera rubens accendit lumina Vesper.*

For the Germans the advancement of theology is not only a
grave religious duty, it is also a great national necessity. Not only
is the exhaustless power of research and love of labour their special
intellectual gift, but the curse of the great separation is upon
them, and is felt in every moment of their existence. The nation,
like Philoctetes, is wasting under this poisoned wound. No political remedies will avail until German theology comes, like the

spear of Telephus, to cure the evil it has caused. The unity of Germany is the union of the churches; and that will one day follow as surely as the nation is not decaying but full of life; as surely as the Church possesses the promise that the gates of hell shall not prevail against her.

The Catholic divines can accomplish this reunion upon three conditions. First, they must overcome, with all the means which the progress of the age supplies, all that is really anti-Catholic and an element of separation in the system of their adversaries. Next, they must present the Catholic doctrine in all its organic completeness, and in its connection with religious life, rigidly separating that which is permanent and essential from whatever is accidental, transitory, and foreign. This work is very far from being yet accomplished; and the explanation of the neglect would be a valuable contribution to our self-knowledge. Lastly, theology must give to the Church the property of the magnetic mountain in the fable, that drew to itself all the iron in the ship, so that the ship fell to pieces; it must sift from the admixture of error all the truths in doctrine, history, and society which the separated communities have brought to light, and then frankly accept and claim them as the legitimate though unrecognized property of the one true Church. Catholics cannot pretend that they really desire union until they prove that they desire the means of union, which are humility, charity, and self-denial, honest recognition of what is good and true wherever it is found, and a thorough insight into our own vices, scandals, and defects; and this points out to us the part which falls to theology in the great work of reconciliation. It is theology that gives life and force to the true healthy public opinion in ecclesiastical affairs before which all must bow, even the heads of the Church and those who wield her power. As among the Jews the schools of the prophets existed beside the regular priesthood, so in the Church there is beside the ordinary powers an extraordinary power, and that is public opinion. Through it theological science exercises its legitimate authority, which nothing can permanently resist. For the divine judges things in the Church according to the ideas that are in them, whilst the generality of men judge the idea by the fact which they behold. All reform consists in making every practice and every institution in the Church correspond with its idea.

Germany is henceforward the home of Catholic theology. No

nation has cultivated so successfully the sciences which are the eyes of theology, viz. history and philosophy; and no source of information, no criterion of scientific truth which they supply can be neglected. The day has gone by when a man could pass for a good dogmatic divine without a thorough knowledge of exegesis and ecclesiastical history, of the patristic writings, and of the history of philosophy. No German, for instance, could give the name of a theologian to one who was ignorant of Greek, and therefore unable to understand or to explain the Vulgate.

The question as to what constitutes a theologian must be answered according to the age, and its demands upon a scholar, and especially a divine. Though the modern weapons of science may be used for destruction, they cannot be set aside in the work of reconstruction; and the difficulty of theology has not diminished. Time has swept away many bulwarks behind which former generations thought themselves safe. A Protestant may overlook whole centuries, and content himself with a fragment of the Church; but Catholics must know her in the totality of her progress from the beginning to the present day, without any gap in the continuity of her development, or any fault in the harmony of her system; and this is the labour of a life. No effort, therefore, can dam up the current of theology, or force it back into a bed which it has long since overflowed.

It is the privilege of true theology to change all that it touches into gold, and, like the bee, to extract pure honey from poisonous flowers. Error has its salutary influence upon the Church; it is an incentive to progress, and becomes a peril only when theology fails to meet it with a true solution. Every truth that religion professes must at some period be purified and refined in the fire of contradiction. Therefore the test of a genuine theologian is to labour without ceasing, and not to flinch from conclusions that are opposed to favourite opinion and previous judgment. He will not take to flight if the process of reasoning threatens to demolish some truth which he had deemed unassailable, or imitate the savage who trembled during an eclipse for the fate of the sun. He is sure to gain one step in wisdom, if he does not let the occasion slip from him. The Holy Spirit, who teaches the Church, gives to the theologian that light of grace without which his eyes are blind to the things of God, and consumes the chaff of human error slowly but surely. Later generations often have to atone for the faults of short-sighted predecessors; and the example of the schoolmen who, in their disregard for history and their self-sufficient ignorance of the whole Anatolian tradition, powerfully contributed to the fatal breach with the Greek Church, is a warning to leave theology her freedom, and not to elevate her unsettled conclusions prematurely into articles of faith.

Our principle of tradition, the motto *quod semper, quod ubique, quod ab omnibus*, which is written on our banner, has been misunderstood by friends as well as by adversaries. A miser who buries a treasure in a hole, preserves it indeed, and it may remain for centuries without increase or loss; but in that case it will remain also without life or fruit. The doctrine cannot act on the minds and lives of men without undergoing the reaction of their influence. Its force is in its incessant growth. But in the dull and thoughtless hands of a theology that professes to be conservative it can shrink and wither like an old man's body, and in its impotence cease to generate life and light. For the definitions of the Church are only words, which, however accurately chosen, need to be impregnated with thought by the preacher and the divine; and while they may become bright gems in the hands of a true theologian, they may be converted into lustreless pebbles by the manipulations of a rude mechanical mind.

The freedom of the Catholic divine is linked to the authority of the Church, with which he feels himself in harmony even when it does not speak; for he knows that it will always save him from the tyranny of uncertainty and mere opinion, that its utterances will always be a guide to truth, that it can never mislead. Whilst he understands that the progress of knowledge must be for ever breaking down hypothesis and opinion, every difference between his conclusions and the dogma warns him of an error on his part, and not in the teaching of the universal Church. He assumes at once that there was a defect in his process of inquiry; and he at once conscientiously revises the operation, with the certainty that, with more or less exertion, he will discover the seat of his error.

In Germany there is no established theological school or schools; and it is well that it is so, for the ancient chain of theological tradition has been interrupted, the old forms are too decrepit to be repaired, and the moment of transition has arrived, when a new edifice must be reared in their place. Materials already abound, but the building itself is very far from complete; and many works recall those provisional wooden crosses in the churchyards with the inscription "Until the erection of a monument". The new theology must reverse the analytic method of the Middle Ages, and must carry out strictly and fully the principle of historical development. It must be vast enough to comprehend the whole of the past, and to leave room for the future, which will be not less active in the work of dogmatic evolution. It must be universal, like the Church, and like her embrace the past, the present, and the future. It must provide for the future, not by artificially covering and concealing the gaps that remain in the system, but by ascertaining and recognizing their presence, and by rejecting every hasty and arbitrary attempt to invest the opinions of a school with the authority of ecclesiastical doctrines, and to adopt them in the reconstruction of theology as materials similar in nature and equal in value to the universal dogma of the Church. In such matters it must protect the rights of freedom for the present, and refer to the future, when opinion has become permanent and certain, the duty of deciding.

The presence of different systems is not an evil, but an advantage, provided they maintain a scientific character, and each respects the freedom of the other. That freedom is as necessary to science as air to life, and it is a short-sighted and suicidal policy to deny it on the ground of danger to faith. A real dogmatic error against the clear and universal teaching of the Church must be pointed out and retracted; but a purely theological error must be assailed only with the resources of scientific discussion. It is no argument to say that all error is connected with dogmatic error. It would be possible to extract from the *Summa* of St Thomas a series of propositions which, in their logical consequences, would lead to the most fatal error. The faults of science must be met with the arms of science; for the Church cannot exist without a progressive theology. That in theology it is only through error that truth is attained, is a law which will be as valid in the future as it has been universal in the past.

It is impossible to read this address, which contains the most distinct and pregnant exposition its author has ever made of the spirit of his theology, without perceiving that it challenges discussion on a great variety of points, and controverts many opinions which are by no means universally abandoned. For ourselves, we cannot acquiesce in the justice of totally excluding England from the survey of the theology of the present day, or admit that we have no ecclesiastical writers of the rank of Bautain and Ventura, and no divines who deserve to be placed as models before the educated clergy of Germany. Those, however, are fortunate whose sensitiveness is wounded only by omissions; for the speaker appears to have touched with careful deliberation on all the characteristic faults of Catholics in our time.

Two years ago the author of this address, in his protest against the abuses of the Roman Government, and on behalf of civil rights and freedom, touched merely on the externals of ecclesiastical polity in its contact with the outer world. Now, he penetrates to the very heart of the defects that afflict the Church, to the causes of her injured influence and the source of great spiritual evils. He speaks not for administrative reform, but for the renovation of theology, and the advancement of that which gives religion power against error, for intellectual as well as political liberty. When we consider the position of the speaker, and the influence which the Congress he thus inaugurated will hereafter exercise, we cannot find that any thoughts which reach so far or penetrate so deep have been uttered in our time. Their effect in the Church would depend in great measure on the reception they met with from an audience which has in its hands the formation of theological opinion in great part of Catholic Germany. They were not spoken as a programme or manifesto representing the thoughts of the meeting, but rather as a topic for discussion and a test for the comparison of views. So far, therefore, the address invited comment; and it would unquestionably have provoked it in any assembly of divines. Those who had come with the design of watching and confronting the speaker, would have been clumsy tacticians if they had extracted from it no opportunity of delivering their protest. There was hardly a paragraph that could pass unquestioned from their point of view. In a paper which was drawn up by Dr Heinrich, and read on the following day by Canon Moufang, and which was signed by the Würzburg divines, by Phillips, and by three doctors of divinity, exception was taken to several passages.

The remarks on French and Italian learning would probably have been heard with pain by a native of France or Italy. For the former there was nobody to speak; but the criticism on Italian theology threatened to shake the authority of the Roman divines, on whom an important school relies. In order to rescue their reputation and influence, several names recently commemorated in an essay by Dr Hergenröther were cited, to prove the injustice of the estimate. On this point of literary criticism discussion of course was fruitless. A more serious matter was the vindication of the German clergy from the imputation of indifference to the use of the means by which the reconciliation of Protestants can be effected. This indifference was indignantly repudiated; but here again argument was vain. Dr Döllinger had defined his meaning to be, that a sincere desire for the accomplishment of an object must manifest itself in a readiness to adopt the necessary means; and it was very easy to show that the language and policy of many Catholics are more repulsive to those beyond the pale of the Church than any of her doctrines. He had said the same thing in *Kirche und Kirchen*; and everybody knows how many impediments obstruct the path of converts, from the ignorance, the imprudence, the want of candour, or the want of discrimination, which is sometimes shown by Catholics.

A graver controversy arose, however, on that passage which asserted the universal law, that the way to truth leads through error. The idea is found, indeed, in every theology since the days of St Augustine, and is exemplified in every age of the history of the Church. But being coupled in this case with an exhortation to tolerate and forbear, it was probably looked on as tending to invest theological science with functions which have been claimed for ecclesiastical power; and fears were entertained that if the frequency of appeals to the Congregation of the Index were thus checked, the effect of a favourite instrument in discussion might be weakened, and the exercise of the authority of Rome over literature circumscribed. The difficulty of assailing a statement which, as it stood, everybody knew to be true, without betraying the real motive of the objectors, vitiated their argument, and diminished the force of the attack.

Dr Döllinger, after a brief explanation of what had been misunderstood in his address, speedily took advantage of the false position into which his opponents had fallen; and they, one by one, in a short but sharp debate, in which he was supported by Schulte and Michelis, endeavoured to set themselves right. One admitted that he had in some degree mistaken the drift of the speech; another that he had not heard it, and had given his name on the strength of the report that had been made to him. No understanding was arrived at, however; and the assembly passed on to other matters. But Dr Döllinger seems to have been determined to expel from the minutes of the proceedings this documentary evidence of existing dissension, and at the last sitting he again brought the question forward. It was necessary to decide on the drawing up of the report, and he began by declaring that he would not permit his address to be published. The objectors, he said, would expect their protest to appear with it, and the effect would be to commemorate and proclaim an impeachment of his theological teaching. Dr Heinrich, the author of the paper, protested solemnly against this interpretation. He declared on his priestly word that he had intended no imputation on the dogmatic correctness of the president, whose fame he hoped would be handed down as a treasure to the latest ages of the Church in Germany. He had only wished to mark his dissent from certain opinions which either required qualification to be true, or explanation to save them from the danger of being misunderstood. This, however, did not satisfy some of his supporters; and, whilst they contradicted each other, the logic of their antagonist pressed them hard. At last they went out to deliberate; and presently agreed to suppress their protest, and to consent to the publication of the inaugural address in the Acts of the Congress. Then, with a cruel taunt at his discomfited assailants, Dr Döllinger declared himself satisfied, and explained that he had felt compelled, as a professor of theology, to vindicate his theological good name. At these words the whole assembly rose with one accord to bear testimony to him; and the memorable deliberations closed.

The question of the liberty of human thought, which was introduced by Dr Döllinger in his address, had from the beginning anxiously occupied the minds of the assembled scholars; and from different motives each party was very desirous that something should be done. The occasion was manifestly the best that could be devised, if not the only one that could be conceived, for a practical effort to reconcile the most momentous difference which subsists in the Catholic body. For where the individual is openly at issue with the supreme authority, or where the limits of power and of liberty are in question, no official decree, and no private argument, can settle the dispute. The voice of authority is not obeyed when its rights are challenged; and a private individual who sets about reforming the Church by the influence of his own word adds at once by his isolation to the force of the adverse opinion. But an assembly of the most learned members of the most learned clergy in Europe would, in approaching the rulers of the Church, be sustained by a prestige not easy to resist, while the men of science would feel its interests safe in their hands. Their appeal for freedom, instead of exciting insubordination and resistance to the decrees of the Holy See, would come as a constitutional remonstrance against dangerous restrictions; while those limits which the most profound scholars and original thinkers were ready to observe could not well be rejected by any who claimed to understand the hierarchy of literary merit.

The assembly was agreed upon a further point beyond the general expedience of some declaration. Whether they wished to preserve authority by restriction, or to promote religion by liberty, they agreed at least in believing that the Holy Spirit protects the Church from falling into dogmatic error, and that human science has no such assurance. If they united in proclaiming in some measure the misgivings that had arisen; and, whilst it was an indispensable preliminary to the future discussion of the rights of intellectual freedom, it would exclude from that discussion opinions which do not stand on the same basis. For men who profess to believe the Catholic teaching have put forward systems in which its indefectibility is virtually denied. It has been said that a proposition at variance with revelation may still be scientifically true; that the universal Church possesses no voice which is the organ of infallibility; that not only is the expression of dogma modified by the initiative of science, but that even its substance is altered in the progress of religious knowledge, and that ecclesiastical authority being liable to error and abuse, its bounds can never be assigned nor its interference admitted in literature. The genesis of these errors in minds more solicitous about the present than studious of the examples of the past is not very difficult to understand. It is conceivable how such conclusions present themselves to men who are conscious of the loss which religion suffers from the enforced stagnation and sterility of Catholic thought, who have watched the blunders in Church government, and seen how school opinions have been identified with the criteria of orthodoxy in an age in which many views once thought essential have become obsolete and ridiculous. If at one time false opinions have been held universally and under pain of censure, and if there is no fixed distinction between open and decided questions, and if an ill use has been sometimes made of the supreme authority in the Church, then, they argue, infallibility does not reside in her. One fallacy runs through all these arguments; but it is a fallacy far more universally prevailing than the conclusions which in this case it supports. It is the confusion between the Church and the authorities in the Church, between matters of faith and matters of opinion, and between development and change. A very slight exaggeration of the theory of Kuhn, that philosophy is as independent of revelation as other secular sciences, joined to that of his extreme opponents who strive to invest the Index with an authority universally binding on the conscience, must result in this attempt to subject even dogma to the authority of science.

On the morning of the second day of the Congress Dr Michelis demanded that the assembly should pronounce its judgment on the controverted question of the rights of intellectual freedom, or, as he put it, in favour of "the unqualified freedom of scientific investigation". Authority, he maintained, has nothing to fear, inasmuch as every Catholic thinker knows the criteria of certainty, and admits that his conclusions are not infallible, and does not therefore claim for them an acceptance derogatory to the Church. The proposal was received with general favour; but it was met by Dr Döllinger with a protest against abstract resolutions on questions of principle. It may be that he did not trust the elements that composed the assembly, or that he thought its future influence might be compromised if it should embark at the very beginning, before its authority was securely established, on questions of so much delicacy, or that the flame of opposition would be fanned by the licence which would be taken in debate. He induced Dr Michelis to drop two out of his three resolutions, and to refer to a separate committee of philosophers the one which remained, touching the relations of ecclesiastical authority with the freedom of science. The meeting took place that evening, and was attended, among others, by Michelis, Heinrich, Deutinger, Reinkens, Mayr, and Knoodt.

Late that night a report flew over Munich which produced an almost comical sensation. The philosophers, it was said, had adopted certain propositions unanimously, harmony had crowned their labours, and the great struggle between reason and faith was at an end. In a place where the minds of men were perplexed and excited by the theories of Frohschammer, and by the almost unexampled scandal they had caused, it was just possible to forget that the dispute was one of about seven hundred years' standing, and that a thesis on which a dozen professors speedily agreed was not likely to settle it. The sitting of the following morning opened amid much agitation; strangers congratulated each other; and the particulars of the evening discussion were listened to as curiously as the adventures of a jury that has been locked up all night. One gentleman immediately requested that the names of the philosophers should be communicated to the meeting, as he wished to know who were the men to whom he would entertain a life-long gratitude. They are printed accordingly in the report. The two propositions were to the following effect: "1. A close adhesion to revealed truth, as taught in the Catholic Church, is an important and indispensable condition of the progressive development of a true and comprehensive speculation generally, and in particular of victory over the errors that now prevail. 2. It is a matter of conscience for all who stand on the basis of the Catholic faith to submit, in all their scientific investigations, to the dogmatic utterances of the infallible authority of the Church. This submission to authority is not in contradiction to the freedom natural and necessary to science."

The debate which followed was often extremely brilliant. The two propositions were criticized, and were defended with great fairness and discrimination by Dr Deutinger, and with great earnestness by the Mentz divines, as the basis of a permanent understanding. Dr Friedrich was dissatisfied because they supplied no weapons against the school of Frohschammer, and Dr Huber, because they gave him no assistance in his struggle for the liberty of thought. Professor Mayr alone made a serious effort to have them modified; not so much, he said, because they unnecessarily repeat what is to be found in the Catechism, but because they are very vague and indefinite. "I wish," he said, in conclusion, "for propositions that show on the face of them that they are really the work of *men*." Dr Michelis instantly protested that these propositions showed that they were drawn up by honest fearless men. "On the face of them," cried Mayr, as he sat down—"I said, on the face of them." And people who saw things only on the outside thought his censure just. Not so those who understood the circumstances under which the Congress had assembled, and the peculiar significance of the occasion.

The terms of these propositions show that what had been apprehended was not the assertion of any legitimate freedom within the limits of faith, but an opposition not merely to the undue exercise of authority, but to fundamental doctrines. They were the very least that it was possible for a vigilant orthodoxy to demand. They were what the extremest advocate of intellectual liberty must needs hold if he holds the creed of Catholics. On this basis, therefore, the cause of freedom will henceforth be sustained without that suspicion which has fallen upon it from the faults of treacherous defenders; and its true friends have emphatically testified that it is compatible with the most entire and hearty submission to the doctrines of the Church. They have delivered it from the effects of a disastrous combination with tendencies essentially uncatholic—tendencies which have hitherto found strength in the confusion outwardly existing between the liberty to hold all truths and the liberty to subvert all dogmas. It is the first step which it was necessary to take in the path of intellectual freedom; and the way has been carefully kept open for further progress hereafter. It admits no obstruction from authorities not infallible, or from utterances not dogmatic; and the saving clause at the end of the second proposition renders it impossible to recede in that direction. Inasmuch as dogmatic utterances are very rare, and the authorities which generally intervene in matters of science have no part in infallibility, these propositions implicitly claim for science all the freedom which is demanded in Dr Döllinger's inaugural address. Both parties, therefore, might with reason be content. The president, who had been averse to any general resolutions, warmly supported them when he heard what they were. He saw the importance of bringing the Congress to so unequivocal an assertion of the rights of authority, and he evidently judged that this prudent measure would give them strength and confidence hereafter to establish more definitely the exact nature of the liberty which science ought to enjoy in the Church. This, he announced, would be the business of the next meeting, which is to be held at Würzburg in September; and the Report adds, that he wished this declaration to be inserted in the minutes. Dr

Huber alone voted against the propositions; and in the *Allge-meine Zeitung* Professor Frohschammer fiercely accused the Congress of having shrunk from the discharge of its duty.

The questions raised by the inaugural address and the discussion on the rights of science were the most important matters which occupied the attention of the Congress. It shows itself in its weakness in the report of a debate raised by a motion of Professor Alzog, that an association of learned men should be formed for the refutation of the current accusations against the Catholic Church. Here we find ourselves at once amid spongy conventionalities. This notion of refuting calumnies is an insidious fallacy, and has done the greatest harm to literature and religion. The worst things are not the calumnies, but the true charges—the scandals concealed, denied, and at last discovered, the abuses, the hypocrisy, the timidity, the uncharitableness and mendacity which, under pretence of a good cause, make men often unscrupulous, and at last almost unable to distinguish between right and wrong. The question how these are to be dealt with in literature would have been better fitted for the consideration of the Congress than those complaints of prejudice and slander which lead Catholics to believe that there is nothing for Protestants to criticize, and that all hostile criticism is insincere. Something might also have been said of the readiness of Catholics to believe evil of their adversaries, and of the example given by some of our apologists of collecting without discrimination all manner of scandals against them. The kind of literary spirit Dr Alzog's scheme would foster was apparent when Dr Brunner recommended that a series of histories should be written, treating the English Reformation after Cobbett, and the Spanish Inquisition after Hefele. It would be the destruction of all sound historical research; and, worse still, it would accustom men to look only for what is popular and acceptable in religion, and to lose sight of the consistency of all its truths, and of those awful depths in it from which worldly men recoil. It would make their religion as shallow as their science.

Two subjects were brought forward by the president which were not received with equal favour. One was a motion that the Congress should undertake to consider, at a future meeting, the means of improving the mode of catechetical instruction. Dr Döllinger affirmed that the manner in which religion is popularly taught in Germany is exceedingly defective, and that the inquiries and suggestions of experienced divines could not fail to be useful in aiding its reform. There was no question, he said, on which all were more completely agreed, and none of more general importance. This idea was opposed, on the ground that it involved an invasion of the province of the episcopate. It was said that the Congress would be taking the initiative, in a practical question, out of the hands of the bishops, and that it ought not to declare that the catechisms used in the several dioceses with the sanction of authority were in urgent need of improvement. The tendency of this opposition was, however, so obvious that it had no effect; and on a division it was supported by only three votes.

The last subject which Dr Döllinger introduced was the necessity of so extending and modifying the teaching of moral theology as to do justice to the problems of political and economical science. Unfortunately his discourse on this topic, which was greatly admired, is very imperfectly preserved; and it is not clear, from the discussion which followed, that he was entirely understood. He showed that the current theological systems have no solution for the numerous difficulties that arise in the progress of society, and that both in literature and in the cure of souls the clergy are confronted by problems which they have not learned to meet. And yet, both in the principles and in the practical treatment of poor relief, emigration, association, over-population, the Christian religion has its own system, and is able to guide and to assist the inquiries of science. Ignorance of political economy has frequently led to grievous mistakes on the side of the Church— for instance, in the matter of the interest of money; and it is impossible for the canon law to deal with questions of Church property, or the payment of the clergy, without reference to economical laws. Nor is it to be apprehended that the Church will suffer from the recognition of this new influence, or that there will be any inducement to reject or alter the legitimate and independent conclusions of the science. For political economy, at the point of development to which it has now reached, is a powerful aid in the apology of Christianity, and the best exponent of the services performed by the Church to the social progress of mankind. These ideas were carried out and illustrated with a knowledge of the subject, and a mastery of the theories of Malthus, of Hermann, and of Roscher, which showed how little the speaker contemplated that violence should be done to science, or that theology could supply its imperfections. It was therefore rather discouraging to hear a professor allege that it was very important for theology to settle the question of free trade, by which, he said, consciences are often disturbed on the Rhine. The debate on the use of political economy in theology and canon law promised, however, to lead to studies which will help to restore the direct social influence of religion in Germany; and of all the questions discussed in the Congress it was the one which elicited the most hearty and general agreement.

Before the meeting broke up Dr Döllinger addressed it in a farewell speech, not, he said, as its president, but as a professor speaking from the experience of a long career. He repeated with impressive earnestness his exhortation to maintain peace and goodwill among Catholics, and to observe in theological discussion the charity and gentleness of which St Augustine was a pattern in his dispute with St Jerome. Divinity, he declared, could not flourish if it was pursued with unscientific instruments; and the bitterness of personal attacks, and the habit of denouncing opponents, had already operated in a manner disastrous to Catholic literature in Germany. His last words to the assembly, therefore, were an appeal for unity and concord.

And now, to what is this movement likely to lead? What is the future that may be prognosticated for it from the signs amid which it was ushered into the world? Will the German divines be sustained by the Episcopate in their undertaking to establish that connubium between science and authority which was the parting aspiration of the Bishop of Augsburg? May it be hoped that the clash of hostile sections will be prevented by the authority of a moderator who does equal justice to the rights of the Church and the liberty of science, when Dr Döllinger's place shall be vacant? Is there no danger that a crisis may come, when the party that at Munich could muster only eight voices out of eighty will invoke the intervention of Rome against the renewal of conferences which may result in formidable demonstrations against their views? It cannot be denied that this uncertainty exists, and that there is safety only in the continuance of wise and impartial vigilance. The Congress must not be taxed beyond its strength. It must obtain confidence before it attempts reform.

This at least may be with certainty predicted, that the Congress will never swerve from the line which has been traced by the

transactions of the first assembly. It can never betray that submission to the dogma of the Church which was proclaimed in the
two resolutions; and it can never abandon that earnest care for
the rights and interests of science which was impressed upon it by
the example and the warnings of the president. These things are
its vital principle. By being faithful to this its origin it will have
power to infuse a new spirit into the Catholic body, and to create
a new and authoritative centre of learning, which shall prevent
hereafter the conflict between science and religion. It will enable
the Catholic writers of Germany to vindicate the Church from
the reproach that faith is inimical to freedom, that we are hampered in our investigations, that we acknowledge a power which
may prevent the publicity of truth, or impose untruths on our belief. Then indeed it will mark the dawn of a new era, and will
justify the words of the Bishop of Augsburg, that, in giving the
impulse to it, Dr Döllinger has set the crown on the splendid
series of his services to the Church.

V

MEDIAEVAL FABLES OF THE POPE[1]

IT was a saying of Hegel's that if all the dreams which men had dreamed during a particular period were written down, they would give an accurate notion of the spirit which prevailed at the time.[2] A collection of the fables accepted as true in different ages would be more seriously instructive; for imaginary facts exercise a real power over the thoughts and deeds of man. The recognised inventions, indeed, by which a party supports its views possess scarcely even a momentary importance; but those fictitious events which, by imperceptible degrees, have established themselves in unquestioned belief, actually control and modify, and sometimes even form, opinion both on matters of theory and practice. Among the different elements which go to make up the body of opinion in a given age, there is scarcely one which has been so little investigated as this belief in fables. The interests and passions of each age, its ruling ideas, the degree of its enlightenment, and the extent of its knowledge, have often been carefully studied by historians who have cast aside as unconnected with the investigation of truth, and as only likely to mislead; ideas which are proved to be absolute and unreasonable delusions.

There are at all times many false notions which are traceable to no facts at all, and many historical fancies which are of no practical significance. It would gratify merely an idle curiosity to know what the soldiers of Charlemagne, or the companions of St Francis, thought of the exploits of Alexander, or how they represented to themselves the court of Haroun. But men are influenced directly by traditions which they understand to be their own. A thoroughly fictitious idea of French history had much to do with the Revolution; and a living writer, justly arguing that the re-

---

[1] *Die Papstfabeln des Mittelalters, Ein Beitrag zur Kirchengeschichte,* von J. v. Döllinger, München, 1863, Literarisch-artistische Anstalt. (From *Home and Foreign Review,* No. 6, Oct. 1863, pp. 610–37.)

[2] Heine, *Französische Zustände,* ii, 194.

sults of Niebuhr's researches have not impaired the value of the legendary records of early Rome, because it behoves us to know not only the true course of events, but that impression of it which was a living force in the Roman mind, has rehearsed with erudite solemnity the poetic fables of Picus and Evander, of the she-wolf and of the grove of Egeria.

If this is a consequence of that continuity which unites past and future in the institutions of states, it is still more important in the Church. For here precedent is the sovereign argument, and the present is controlled by the past. A stubborn reliance on an imaginary fact or a spurious text may affect for centuries the course for theological speculations, and the administration of the canon law. The ignorance of history in an uncritical age is the most insidious channel by which error penetrates into the Church. Against false doctrines and erroneous interpretations she possesses an unfailing defence. But historical untruths, of which she has no sure criterion, may, in their practical consequences, infringe on the fundamental principles of her discipline and her law; and yet while she casts out error of doctrine, she sometimes cherishes error of fact. Her history, whether true or false, is constantly bearing fruit. It is perpetually adopted and introduced into her present life, either as canonical precedent or as devotional example. It is always fashioning habits and opinions; and any important discovery concerning it may lead to a very extensive revision of accepted views.

In the Church, therefore, fables are often serious realities. They may cause an imaginary person, or even a heretic, to be reverenced as a saint; they may find their way into acts of councils and bulls of Popes, into the Missal and Breviary; they may give currency to superstitions very difficult to eradicate; they may become the basis of laws, and the test of theological opinions; they may influence for a time the constitution of the Church, or permanently alter the destiny of nations. In the ecclesiastical sphere they possess a tenacious vitality which they nowhere else acquire. For that confidence and veneration which support the Church are weakened if men discover that they have been deceived. Heresy, they are told, sustains itself by inventing an imaginary past, and is known by the falseness of its instances and authorities. What if they should find that a fact asserted by the Church in her solemn utterances, mingled with her authorized devotions, introduced into the Mass, appealed to in controversy by her divines, trusted by the Popes as the origin and the proof of their rightful power, is the product of ignorance or fraud? They are told that to apply the mythical theory to the history of religion is a malignant artifice of those who would resolve all Christianity into a catalogue of fancies and inventions. If they should discover that some of the stories most universally received in the lives of the Popes and of the Saints have arisen in much the same way as the stories of Hercules or Romulus, they will be puzzled to know where this process is to stop, and what presumptive authority and what prescription amounts to a certain test of credibility, or possesses any claim on our assent. The progress of knowledge has exploded some narratives, which, four centuries ago, it was deemed heresy to question, and which it would have been impossible to contradict without open defiance of the ecclesiastical power. If we admitted that at one time it might be absurd to believe what at another it was sinful to doubt, should we not be saying that the supreme authority of the Church had used its anathemas to defend untruth, and that the facts on which it had raised up its system were doomed to vanish one by one before the increasing light of modern science? These considerations have hitherto made it no easy matter to profit by the discoveries of a better-informed age, in order to revise the mass of ecclesiastical fancies that were believed in credulous times; and even fables of no innocent or gratifying description have long been protected by the same dread of inquiry.

The difficulty consists not in any hesitation to accept the scientific results of research,[1] but in solicitude for the preservation of the legend. For the legend, like the parable, has a value of its own,

[1] Even this feeling, however, may be discerned in some writers. In the preface to his *Life of St Francis* (p. xiv) M. Chavin de Malan says: "La Réforme avait produit de telles calonnies que les savants catholiques crurent qu'il était nécéssaire de faire des concessions à l'opinion publique trompées; et une fois entrée dans cette rue perileuse, la verité s'obscurcit et s'altera. Les plus beaux monuments littéraires du siècle de Louis XIV sont incomplets, quand ils ne sont pas faux. On a défiguré les faits, travesti les meilleurs intentions, mutilé les textes des auteurs anciens, et l'antiquité chrétienne, si pure et si courageuse, se trouve avec stupeur complice des lâchetés du présent. Je ne veux pas citer les noms de Launcy, de Baillet et de tous ces écrivains douteux et presque schismatiques, aujourd'hui dédaignés avec une sorte de rancune, mais je prononcerai avec une respectueuse tristesse les noms de Fleury, de Tillemont, et de leur savante école."

which is independent of historic truth. A critical examination threatens to dissipate many edifying examples, and to introduce an unnatural and unreasonable comparison between legend and history.

The tone of a narrative must correspond with the character of the events described. A reasoning and reflecting age demands a rational and prosaic record, and an intelligent and intelligible explanation of the practical or interested motives of its actors. But the early life of nations, before the rise of civilization and method, before the distinction between custom and law, reason and faith, furnishes arguments for epics rather than materials suitable for history, and is naturally recorded in verse. For then nature and impulse predominate over the reflective powers and cultivated will of man; there is a want of intention in the sequence of events; the past survives by its impression on the imagination; and men look forward to the future without deliberate calculation, in a spirit of resignation or adventure. This romantic and poetical character belongs to certain classes of events even in a refined and civilized age, wherever there is the same uncertainty or improvidence, the same sense of subordination to the forces of nature, the same feeling of helplessness before the manifestations of the power or the anger of God. Legends and fables still spring up in the midst of our prosaic existence where there is war, or pestilence, or maritime adventure, or settlement in savage countries; and they group themselves round the early history of our mercantile colonies, round Polar voyages, and Indian campaigns.

Events which are preserved by oral tradition, and are put on paper long after the epoch to which they are attributed, live during the interval in the mouths of those classes which, in their ignorance and their imaginativeness regarding the things of public life, approach most nearly the simplicity of the romantic age. In early and barbarous times oral tradition is preserved by the most intelligent and cultivated part of society; in a more civilized age, when all important things are speedily put on record, it is exclusively left to the most ignorant. Now the memory of the people, though unfitted to retain facts, is very capable of developing legends. The lives of the saints particularly invite this sort of treatment. They defy the rational explanations which are suited to ordinary life, and founded on the known principles of human nature. A supernatural order of grace is revealed in them, governed by its own laws, and exhibiting a regularity and method unknown to common experience. It is this system of laws, and this mode of divine action on souls delivered from many of the curses of sin, that the legend illustrates. It furnishes instances— the application of which to a particular person is sometimes arbitrary, and sometimes an anachronism—of God's ways with His saints, of the inner life and of the suspension of natural laws; instances which may be as true to the nature of that existence as the story of *Lear* or *Hamlet* to the common nature of man, but with which actual historical truth has nothing to do. The regularity, harmony, and probability of the mystic life are entirely distinct from those of the common world; and when it is proved that a particular circumstance of one saint is told with better authority of others, the spiritual truth and fitness of the story— the only quality which makes it worth repeating—is confirmed, while the historic character is destroyed. But the men to whom these legends are repeated believe that they express what really happened; and this conviction forms part of their mental and moral resources. The most edifying and suggestive narrative leaves them cold, unless it is connected with some individual who is a reality in their eyes. An uneducated person can feel a special devotion and personal affection only for a limited number of saints; but the number of pious legends he is able to believe and to enjoy is boundless, and must be distributed among comparatively few individuals. There is consequently a species of competition in legendary renown among the saints of different countries; and a process of accumulation and redistribution, utterly inconsistent with truth and probability, is, in the nature of things, unavoidable. This is the reason why so many biographies of holy persons, written for the purpose of edification, are so colourless and monotonous and vague, so deficient in individuality, and so like one another.

Religious people will not willingly surrender legends which, in their particular connection, have become precious to them. To be told that what they have been used to believe of a saint whom they knew and loved was borrowed from the biography of some other person whose name they had never heard, or that their favourite legend was founded on a mistake or an imposture, would often be a grievous trial to them. Yet this must follow whenever a serious attempt is made to separate truth from false-

hood in hagiography, whenever, therefore, exertions are made
to authenticate a portion of the legends of the saints. For the laws
of evidence, by which true facts may be rescued from the suspicion which poetry often engenders, are fatal to the whole fruit
of that process of assimilation and selection which makes many
typical narratives the common property of many different saints.
Where there is the authority of contemporaries, or the sworn
testimony of eye-witnesses in the acts of canonization, it is generally of decisive value, and a safe test of subsequent narratives,
collected at second-hand, after the fame of the saint has occupied
the popular fancy. The effect of this kind of test is far greater
when it is applied to miraculous than when it is applied to profane history, which is less liable to be travestied and transformed
by repetition. Such a revision was executed long ago for the acts
of the early martyrs; but it has not yet been accomplished with
equal success for the lives of the mediaeval saints.

To educated Catholics it is a matter of spiritual necessity to
know the saints, and to obtain distinct notions of their personal
qualities. It would be intolerable to think that their idea of St
Francis of Sales is furnished forth with some traits borrowed from
St Charles Borromeo; or that, instead of studying the examples of
a real life, they are reading a work of imagination. In particular,
it is needful that we should know in accurate detail the character
of those canonized saints who have played a great part in history,
like St Gregory and St Anselm, St Bernard, St Thomas, and St
Lewis. Further, we are compelled to seek proofs against those
who may deny the sanctity or dispute the history of particular
saints, and to apply to the establishment of facts those resources
of criticism by which adversaries endeavour to demolish legends.
To these general causes the present age has added one which is
decisive. The manuscript texts in all the libraries of Europe have
been collated by the laborious authors of the new critical editions; interpolations have been discovered; the original form has
been restored; and many a popular and venerable anecdote has
been swept away. It would be well, indeed, if this revision could
be completed, and if we could obtain for the period of the Crusades what we already possess for the days of persecution. Every
advance of inquiry since Baronius' first essay has dissipated some
fable, exposed some fraud or corrected some error. Before long,
all the mediaeval records will be even more critically edited than

the works of the Fathers by the Maurine Congregation. Ample materials will then exist for the sifting of all the legends of the Middle Ages; and these materials will not be accessible to Catholics alone. They will be in the hands of men who are interested in the demolition of the Catholic legend, and who will be eager to avail themselves of the effective argument, *ab uno disce omnes*. They will spread confusion and perhaps anxiety among the faithful; and it is to be feared that the defenders of Catholicism will yield ungraciously, even if they resist the temptation to fight a battle as wicked as it is hopeless against the rules of evidence and the demonstration of science.

An investigation of this kind, while it clears away much that is ludicrous or unedifying, will be especially fatal to the most beautiful and touching legends; and, while it places authentic miracles on a firmer basis, will considerably alter our notions of religious biography. For instance, we possess three lives of the most wonderful of mediaeval saints, Francis of Assisi, all written within one generation of his death by persons who had been his contemporaries. From none of them does it appear that he wrought miracles during life, if we except the cure of sickness. But in the latest of these books, that by St Bonaventure, it is related that a man whose eyes had been put out recovered his sight by the intercession of the saint. This circumstance, however, was not recorded by St Bonaventure; but, as the Bollandists have shown, the passage in which it is mentioned was inserted in the work after his death. Malvenda has crowded his extraordinary life of St Dominic with an account of the miracles he performed. But the first biographer of the saint declares that the stories he had heard were so contradictory and so difficult to verify that he thought it better to omit them.[1] It is well known how abundant are the contemporary notices of the life of St Elizabeth of Hungary. But the writers during the first half-century after her death record no miracle as having been wrought in her lifetime. The beautiful legend of the roses first appears with the fifteenth century, and is in direct contradiction to the report of the Landgrave's conduct given by his chaplain in his recently published biography. The story that the birth of Elizabeth was predicted by the famous magician Klingsor of Hungary is repeated even

[1] "Constat eum fulsisse virtutibus, coruscasse miraculis, et ex iis plura audivimus, sed ob diversitatem narrantium scripto mandata non sunt."

by her latest and most critical biographer, Simon, a Lutheran clergyman; and Count de Montalembert, in telling the story, is solicitous to guard against the suspicion of believing in astrology. Yet Klingsor is a mythical personage, and it is perfectly certain that he never existed. Great part of the legend of St Elizabeth may be traced to Theodore of Apolda, who tells the ridiculous story of St Dominic, that he compelled the devil to hold his candle until it burned down to his fingers, and caused him horrible pain.[1]

If a natural and lawful regard for their devotional value has continued to protect the legends of the saints against discriminating researches, the fables that once clustered round the public history of the Church have obtained no such favour. The scholars of the seventeenth century, beginning with Baronius and ending with Tillemont, swept away an incredible mass of late traditions and deliberate fictions in the history of the early Popes. As the genesis of error is an important element in the study of dogmatic progress, the influence exercised by fictions likewise deserves to be investigated as a part of the constitutional history of the Church. An inquiry into the history of some of these fables has been published by Dr Döllinger, as a prelude, he tells us, to a comprehensive work on the history of the Papacy. Each of the essays which it comprises is complete in itself. In their isolation, and in the profusion of ecclesiastical learning which they display, it is easy to see that they are broken fragments of a larger work. Such universal and yet microscopic knowledge of mediaeval literature could never have been acquired in order to be deliberately wasted on episodes like these.

At the beginning of the chapter on Pope Joan, which is the first of the nine dissertations, a passage occurs which suggests some preliminary observations. The opinion of those who maintain that the fable of the maiden of Mentz who dishonoured the See of St Peter is a satire on the Rhenish origin of the spurious decretals is manifestly false, inasmuch as the fable arose at a time when the authenticity of the decretals was questioned by none. Dr Döllinger, having shown this, goes on to say that in those days there was no sense for satirical allegory; and he derides the contrary opinion of Gfrörer as utterly inconsistent with the character

[1] On which the celebrated Dominican Melchior Canus remarks: "Non autem decebat veras sanctorum res gestas falsis et commentariis fabulis contaminari."

of the thirteenth century. The point is of some interest, for it illustrates a fundamental difference in the interpretation of mediaeval historians; and it appears to us that, although one view is the exaggeration of a perverse ingenuity, the opposite theory, which is maintained by Dr Döllinger, is too absolute and inflexible.

The plain rule of historical criticism, which is simply the teaching of common sense, is, putting aside all those writers whose date or position deprives them of immediate knowledge and authority, to rely exclusively on those who were nearest to the time and scene of the events described, and to examine in all cases the source whence their information is derived. The application of this rule differs in dealing with different ages. In ancient history, where the sources are few and much has been lost, later authorities do not always lose their value. In consideration of the lost books he had read, Plutarch may be quoted by the side of Thucydides on the Peloponnesian war. In modern times, where enormous masses of materials are unpublished, a later writer who consults them often understands events far better than a contemporary; and we may fairly prefer Ranke to Thuanus, and join Guizot to Clarendon. But in the Middle Ages later writers neither consulted works which have subsequently perished, nor documents which were not previously known. A writer of the thirteenth century is on the same footing as a writer of the fifteenth century for the history of the eleventh. The value of testimony is of course further qualified by the intellectual stature, the motives, and the disposition of the writer. Gfrörer, the most brilliant and dexterous of the German historians, made this the basis of a critical method as revolutionary as that of Niebuhr, and equally surprising in its results.

In most mediaeval histories there is a lack of colour, and little beyond a dry record of facts. This poverty of art is due to two causes. Sometimes the writer did not comprehend the reason and connection of transactions; sometimes the fear of offending deterred him from explaining what he knew. A competent scholar, who is familiar with every source of information, and surveys the whole course of events, is able to supply this deficiency. He has to make that intelligible which has been left in obscurity; he must introduce harmony and connection where there is confusion; he must bring fragments together from distant quarters; and the whole result must be different from the parts. In many cases he must follow a hint, and interpret an allusion, where the author has been studiously reserved; and he may be sure that all such timorous reservation conceals some iniquity, and must be explained to the disadvantage of some leading character. The effect will be consequently very vivid, but very unfavourable as to the moral aspect of the times.

This theory, in which truth and error are dangerously mingled, is in substance rejected by Dr Döllinger. He refuses to add by his own combinations and conclusions to the texts of his authorities, and to allow his narrative to be composed of probabilities and certainties united. He sets aside later authorities, however plausible their statements, unless he can trace them to their sources; and he never reconciles conflicting statements by devising a third view which is different from both. His method is founded on the theory that the writers of the Middle Ages, however they may have been swayed by partiality or interest, express simply and directly their real thoughts. It was an age of much rudeness, ignorance and violence, but men were sincere in their speech: the motives for duplicity and the capacity for simulation were wanting, and history was seldom written to court popularity or to influence opinion. It is not, perhaps, unfair to attribute these canons of criticism to the theological training and to the special dogmatic training of the author. The monuments of tradition possess in the eyes of the Catholic divine a special sacredness. They are the immovable basis of the system of the Church, the standard by which she defines her doctrine, the guide of her progress, her bulwark against innovation. If they are exposed to the hazards of conjecture, there can be no certain knowledge of her teaching, her nature, or her spirit. Therefore Catholics attach an importance to the authentic record of the acts and decrees of the Church such as Protestants assign to the Bible alone. By reason of this supreme value and authority all historical information respecting them, if sure and authentic, is invaluable, and must be gathered with infinite care; but if only conjectural, and the result of plausible combinations, it is not only worthless but injurious. This is more particularly the view which a divine will naturally take who holds the theory of the development of doctrine. No temptation is more common among men of a different persuasion than the impulse to describe the theology of a particular age from the testimony of later writers. From this point of view it is fatal to an opinion that it cannot be shown to have been ancient or continuous; and to hold, for instance, that the Fathers before St Augustine erred in the doctrine of grace is to renounce the principle of tradition, while to prove it would be to overthrow tradition. It was an extreme caricature of this idea when Melanchthon said, that although there was no evidence in favour of the Lutheran doctrine during the Middle Ages, yet it was unquestionably held by men wiser than those whose opinions are recorded. This sort of reasoning is of necessity abhorrent to that theory of development which our author has worked out farther and more consistently than any other theologian. He is bound, therefore, to ascertain the belief of each period from its own monuments and records, and rigorously to exclude all inferences drawn from later times, and all forced and far-fetched interpretations. But ideas and customs are flexible materials, which tradition can more easily deface than the simplest record of deeds and events, and in respect to this rule of criticism theology and history are not strictly analogous.

The thirteenth century dealt largely in both satire and allegory. Poetry was often allegorical, and historians condescended to be satirists. When the indignant feelings that appear in Matthew Paris and in Dante, in Freidank and Ruteboeuf, penetrated among the people, they found expression in allegory. It was precisely in the thirteenth century that this censorious discontent began to be prevalent among all classes. The old popular allegories supplied a framework, and a satirical intention was infused into them which was foreign to their original nature. Thus it was with part of the great cycle of the legends of the Holy Grail, and with the ancient fable of the Beasts. *Reinecke Fuchs* and the *Roman de la Rose* grew into satirical allegories; and the first great poem in our language, the *Vision of Piers Plowman*, is animated by the same spirit.

Forty-four pages of Dr Döllinger's work are devoted to the fable of Pope Joan; a fable of which the ages of faith were quite as tenacious as of those which were honourable to the Holy See. Critics have been hitherto so unsuccessful in their attempts to explain its origin, that a recent writer has declared his belief that the enigma can never be solved. Baronius thought it was a satire on the weakness displayed by John VIII in that dispute with

Photius which was the beginning of the great Eastern schism. Others referred it to the period when Theodora and Marozia governed the rulers of Rome. Gfrörer connects it with the false Isidore. Some thought it was a calumny invented by the Greeks, though no Greek writer mentions it before the fourteenth century. Pagi attributed it to the Waldenses; but its chief promoters were not heretics or schismatics, but their most determined enemies, the mendicant orders. All these explanations fail because the fable arose at a time when the events of the ninth century were too little known to provoke legendary interpretations. There is no trace of it prior to the middle of the thirteenth century. This fact has been only recently ascertained, since the manuscripts of the mediaeval writers have been examined and compared. No mention of the fable can be discovered in any manuscript written before the year 1240. It found its way into the text in later times, as a marginal note, and was first inserted into some books by the editors in the sixteenth century. Its earliest appearance is in an unprinted work by Stephen of Bourbon, who died in 1261; but it obtained general credence only through the popularity of the chronicle of Martin of Poland, written towards the close of the century. Even there it was an interpolation; Martin did not speak of it himself. It is not found in the earlier MSS. of his works, but was added after his death, first on the margin, and then in the text. This must have happened almost immediately, for Martin died in 1279; and Ptolemy of Lucca, who terminated his ecclesiastical history in the year 1313, says that Martin introduces Johannes Anglus between Leo IV and Benedict III, but that no other chronicler knows of his existence. From this time the story was constantly repeated by the friars in the fourteenth century, at first as a mere report, but soon without reserve or hesitation.

In the first years of the fourteenth century, therefore, the story of Pope Joan is found only in MSS. of a single writer; almost immediately after it becomes universally credited, and the authors of its popularity are the Franciscans, and still more the Dominicans. Next to the origin of the legend, this is the most curious part of its history. It was of course considered a grievous scandal, and a lamentable disgrace to the Holy See. Now, from the end of the thirteenth century, the mendicant orders were bitterly hostile to Boniface VIII. They opposed his policy, reviled his name, and took a particular delight during many years in

crowding their chronicles with stories against the Popes. Under
these circumstances, nothing could be more welcome than the
fable of Pope Joan; and they multiplied copies of the books in
which it was contained. It soon ceased to be doubted. The bust
of Pope Joan was set up among those of other Pontiffs in the
cathedral of Siena, and remained unchallenged for two hundred
years. When, at the Council of Constance, John Hus defended
his thesis, that the Church could get on without a Pope, by point-
ing to the interval of two and a half years during which a woman
had occupied the See of St Peter, nobody disputed the fact.
Gerson himself had shortly before used the same instance for a
somewhat similar purpose. Even the great defender of the Papal
prerogative, Cardinal Turrecremata, treats it as a notorious fact,
and makes it support a theory. It was spread by the zeal of the
Dominicans against the Holy See, and for eighty years was incessantly repeated in books published in Rome, in books dedicated to Popes, and in the writings of the Popes themselves. But
its origin was free from any motives of hostility or malice. The
tale is told with many variations. The earliest authority, Stephen
of Bourbon, supposes the event to have occurred towards the
year 1100. How it came to be transferred to the year 855 is
explained most ingenuously by Dr Döllinger, as follows: first,
it is found in late MSS. of the biographies of the Popes that bear
the name of Anastasius. In that series the lives of Leo IV, and
of Benedict III, betray different hands. Consequently there must
have been copies which ended with Leo IV. Probably the fable
was afterwards added as a curiosity at the end of one of these,
and this was then supposed to be its right date. Secondly, Martin
the Pole, who gives a line to the events of each year in the
Chronicle of the Popes, had nothing to say for the last years of Leo
IV, and left a blank from 850 to the election of Benedict III, in
855. So the tale passed easily from the end of Anastasius to the
top of the page in Martin of Poland which embraces the second
half of the ninth century. Thirdly, Dr Döllinger uses an argument which pushes ingenuity almost too far. According to the
fable, Joan owes her elevation to her great proficiency in knowledge; therefore, he says, it was necessary to assign her a date
when learning was a ladder to the pontifical throne. Now, during
three centuries and a half, from John VI to Gregory VII, Martin
of Poland knows of no Pope conspicuous for learning except Leo

IV. About the time of his pontificate, therefore, learning was esteemed at Rome, and an accomplished adventuress was more likely to have succeeded then than at any other time. Still this would not be a reason for altering a date which was originally fixed immediately after Gregory VII—that is, in a very literary age.

Four things combined gave rise to the story: the use of a chair of uncommon form at the coronation of Popes, which was introduced about the year 1100, when Pope Joan first appears; an inscription and a statue, found close together, which it was assumed were respectively an epitaph and a female figure; and the custom of taking a circuit in processions in order to avoid a particular street, which was so narrow and incommodious that it was afterwards removed. The statue and inscription have disappeared. The former represented a pagan divinity, or a priest, together with the figure of a child. The inscription, put up by a priest of Mithra in commemoration of some solemn sacrifice, appears to have contained the following words: "Pap. Pater Patrum P.P.P." "Pater Patrum" was a title borne by the priests of Mithra, and the words stood for "Papirius Pater Patrum Propria Pecunia Posuit." Curiosity was awakened by the strange shape of the porphyry chair, and by the obscure inscription and nameless statue, and the practice of avoiding the street in which they were found. The popular imagination devised a solution which harmonized all the difficulties. It was said that a woman, who concealed her sex, had been chosen Pope for her great learning; that, whilst passing in procession through a street which was ever afterwards avoided in consequence of the scandal, she had given birth to a child; and that, dying there, she had been buried on the spot. A statue of her and her child was supposed to mark the place; and the event was thought to be commemorated by an inscription, of the several readings of which the most ingenuous is, "Papa Pater Patrum Peperit Papissa Papellum." Ever since then, the legend added, the sex of the new Pope must be ascertained on the day of his coronation. This was the only reason that could be discovered for the ceremony of seating the Pope, once only in his life, on one of these chairs, which had in reality belonged to the Roman baths, and were selected on account of the splendour of the material. This fabulous custom is first mentioned by Robert D'Usez, who died in 1291, and is therefore as old as the fable of Pope Joan. During many ages, until late in the seventeenth century, this stupid and degrading story continued to be repeated, and was not contradicted, though every prelate in Rome knew its falsehood, and the porphyry chair had been disused ever since the time of Leo X.

At first Pope Joan is described as "Johannes Anglus natione Moguntinus." She comes sometimes from Mentz, and sometimes from England. Her English origin may point to the quarrel between King John and Innocent III, when England was regarded at Rome as the most hostile of the Christian States. In like manner she came from Mentz because the legend was used as a satire on the Ghibelline Germans and Mentz was regarded as practically the capital of Germany: "Moguntia, ubi maxima vis regni esse noscitur," says Otho of Freysing. She studies at Athens because Athens was the old seat of learning until the *Studium* was transferred to Paris. The time of the transition was but vaguely conjectured; but one chronicle says: "Anno D. 830 Romanum studium, quod prius Athenis exstitit, est translatum Parisiis."

The most important thing in Dr Döllinger's volume is an investigation of the origin and history of the famous instrument by which it was once believed that Constantine had conferred temporal dominion and royal dignity upon the Popes. It is commonly supposed that the great domains which became the basis of the temporal power were partly the gift of Constantine; and the life of St Sylvester enumerates the grants of land which were attributed to him. Dr Döllinger, however, is disposed to question the accuracy of this belief, and to deny altogether that the emperor bestowed any landed property on the Holy See. There is no contemporary authority for it. In the year 370 it is probable, from the words of Ammianus, that the Church had no estates. The Life of St Sylvester, a late compilation, is little to be relied on; while it attributes so much land to the first Christian emperor, there is no mention of any other imperial donations until the time of Justinian. It appears, therefore, to Dr Döllinger that the compiler of that work simply referred to Constantine the origin of all the possessions which the Church of Rome owned at the time when he wrote—that is, in the time of the seventh or eighth century. No doubt it is true that the Life is full of fables; but there must have been some better reason than this would have been to determine the selections of those grants attributed to Constantine. In the Epistles of Gregory the Great we have a record of the Roman domains which includes estates not mentioned by the biographer of Sylvester in the seventh or eighth century. It is, therefore, hardly credible that he can have included the whole of the possessions of the Holy See in his time among the gifts of Constantine. If, on the other hand, there is no conclusive authority in favour of donations of land made by him to the Pope, it appears to us that there is no strong motive for doubt. The Roman Church possessed land, though without legal sanction, even under the pagan emperors; and after the confiscations under Diocletian, Constantine ordered it to be restored. By the edict of 321 he permitted the Church to receive bequests (*bona*); and this permission must have included land. At the beginning of the fourth century the Church of Rome had some landed property. In the sixth we know that it had a great deal. A Greek writer of that age, indeed, says that this was not the practice;[1] but his statement is a flagrant contradiction of the testimony of St Gregory; and we must suppose that at one period the estates that were bequeathed to the Popes were sold, in order to enable them to pursue the vast work of charity, of which we read, towards the faithful of other churches. In the year 370 a restriction was imposed on the accumulation of wealth by the clergy. It is scarcely probable that the wealth increased more rapidly afterwards than before; and if it is a mistake to suppose that the Popes owned no land in the middle of the fourth century, it is unreasonable to reject the report that Constantine, having opened the door to such bequests, having restored the confiscated lands, and having exhibited great generosity towards St Sylvester, included domain in the gifts which he bestowed. It is possible that Dr Döllinger may have it in his power to throw new light on the policy of Constantine towards the Holy See; but until he has more fully explained his view, we are inclined to receive it with much hesitation.

His subtle and powerful argument for the earliest of the three periods to which the origin of the edict of Donation may be plausibly referred will carry conviction to many minds. The answer to Baronius, Bianchi, Richter, and those who attribute the forgery to the Greeks is decisive. The document was not known to the Greeks for three centuries after it was current in the West. The

---

[1] See Bingham's *Antiquities*, ii, 63.

opinion of Morinus, that it was written in the tenth century, is thus met by Dr Döllinger: "His chief argument is that Otho III, in his deed of the year 999, designates a certain deacon John, who was nicknamed *Digitorum mutius* (mutilus), as the man who wrote the document in the name of Constantine with letters of gold. Morinus supposes that this Johannes Diaconus is the same whom Pope John XII first made use of as his instrument, and whose right hand he afterwards caused to be cut off in 964. But he is wrong; for a man who had lost his hand would not be called 'with mutilated fingers' " (p. 70). Dr Döllinger's own opinion is in favour of the eighth century. His argument is as follows: the Donation is mentioned by Hadrian I in 777, and was probably composed about the time when Pepin gave the Pentapolis to the Pope, in order to justify his territorial independence, and to show that it was no injury to the empire, as it had been already conceded by the first Christian emperor. The document cannot have been written after the year 774, when the establishment of the Frankish monarchy deprived the Holy See of the hope of political sovereignty. There is another document, of the time of Charlemagne, a symptom of the same tendency that produced the Donation, which purports to be Pepin's account of his negotiation with the Greeks and with the Pope, and represents him as bestowing the whole of Italy on St Peter. The edict is adopted by the author of the spurious decretals; but it cannot be his work, for it was written at Rome, and its sole object is to exalt the Holy See and the Roman clergy. Several of its articles point distinctly to the middle of the eighth century. The old senate had disappeared for more than a hundred years, when a new senate arose, which is first mentioned in the year 757, and consisted of the new nobility. Now the edict extends the senatorial honours to the clergy of Rome, and makes the priests rank with the patricii and the consuls, dignities which were also revived precisely at the same time. The statement which it puts into the mouth of Constantine, that it had given to the Church of Rome lands in the East and in the West, in order to keep up the lights which burn perpetually before the tombs of the Apostles—"quibus pro concinnatione luminarium possessiones contulimus"—exactly tallies with the words of Paul I, that Pepin made war on the Lombards in order to restore the lights of St Peter—"pro cujus restituendis luminariis decertatis". The Donation was therefore forged at Rome, between the years 754 and 774; was circulated by pseudo-Isidore from the year 840; and is mentioned vaguely under Nicholas I by Hincmar and Ado, and distinctly, in 868, by Aeneas, Bishop of Paris.

Of course, if Dr Döllinger is right in saying that Hadrian I mentions the document in the year 777, his case is proved. But the words of Hadrian are: "Potestatem in Hesperiae partibus largiri dignatus est." This is a very inadequate description of the contents of the Donation, and rather applies to the grants of land enumerated in the Life of St Sylvester, and to the consequent authority which many Popes, such as Celestine, Leo, and Gregory I and II, are known to have exercised: for he goes on to speak of "alia quae per diversos imperatores, patricios etiam et alios Deum timentes—in partibus Tusciae, Spoleto seu Benevento, atque Corsica . . . concessa sunt". These things are reckoned in continuation of the similar gifts of Constantine; but if the latter had been understood in the sense of the Donation, there would have been no occasion to add the rest, for all Italy was included in it. Hadrian would not have quoted a deed forged in his own lifetime, and only a few years before he wrote. If we put aside his testimony as irrelevant, the argument founded on a comparison of the terms of the Donation with the state of things at Rome towards the year 755 remains. But this conformity between the text and the circumstances of the Church is not quite confined to this particular period; and in insisting on the coincident revival of ancient Roman institutions, Dr Döllinger treats the fact that a period singularly poor in historical records is silent on the subject as equivalent to the proof of the actual suspension of those institutions. It is not likely that, at the very moment when the Church of Rome was receiving a large portion of the territory of Italy, she would set up a claim for the whole; or that this claim by which the merit of the gift was diminished should have been put forward under Charlemagne. The Roman clergy were still imperial subjects, and there had been a succession of Greek Popes. Such ignorance of the law and the nature of the empire as the author of the Donation betrays would at that time have been unnatural.

If the victory of Charlemagne in 774 deprived the Popes of the chance of recovering their rightful power, this would be a further argument against Dr Döllinger's interpretation of the words of

Hadrian. If it was useless to compose the Donation after that year, it was vain to quote it. But those hopes of dominion over Italy which were unsuited to the time when the foundations of the Carolingian empire were laid became more reasonable after its fall. In the tenth century the monarchy of Charlemagne had fallen asunder, and the partial sovereignty which the Holy See had enjoyed was at an end. At such a time the hope of recovering, and even increasing, the power which was lost might revive. The idea involved no menace to the empire, for the empire had long disappeared from Italy. When, therefore, the Popes conceived the design of calling in imperial aid for the restoration of their own authority, they might naturally deem it expedient to take the precaution of raising such a claim as should secure them from the danger of its control. The opinion that the Donation was fabricated in the tenth century has this advantage over every other hypothesis that it gives the name of the author on almost contemporary authority. Dr Döllinger's answer to the argument derived from the act of Otho III is founded on a mistake. It is not true, that John, the cardinal-deacon, lost his hand. Two of his fingers were cut off, and therefore the designation *Digitorum mutilus* was exactly appropriate. Liutprand, who is Dr Döllinger's authority, describes the punishment inflicted by John XII on his enemies, the cardinal-deacon and his protoscrinarius Azo: "quorum alterum manu dextera, alterum lingua digitis naribusque abscic, Johannes abdicatus defoedaverat." The order in which the names stand has misled many writers into the belief that John lost his hand, and Azo his fingers and nose. But this is an error. Benedict of Soracte, in his barbarous Latin, says: "Azzo protoscrinium manum abscidi precepit, cum quo brebe scribebat, et Johannes diaconus nasum ejus abscidi fecit."[1] The acts of the Council of Rheims confirm this version: "Octavianus (John XII) Roman redit, Leonem fugat, Johannem, diaconem naso, dextrisque digitis ac lingua mutilat."[2] Otho unquestionably believed and intended to say that the forger of the Donation was the Cardinal John, who, after having been an agent of Pope John XII, denounced him at the Synod of 963, and was afterwards punished by mutilation.

The terms in which the emperor accuses the Popes of having

[1] Apud Watterich, *Pontificum Romanorum Vitae*, i, 42.
[2] *Acta Conc. Rem.*, cap. 28.

squandered the property of the Church apply perfectly to the middle of the tenth century. The first thought of Octavian, when he was raised to the pontifical throne, was to recover the ancient rights and territories of his see. He declared himself the enemy of Berengarius of Ivca, who was recognized in the north as King of Italy; and he commenced an unsuccessful expedition against Benevento and Capua. Finding himself too weak to erect the Roman See into a great temporal sovereignty, and to obtain for himself and his clergy the political importance for which he longed, he betook himself to the King of the Germans. Since the decline of the Carolingian dynasty, its successor had ceased to be formidable to Italy or to the Church; and it was hoped that Otho would restore the Papal power in return for the imperial crown, and would not be eager to exercise rights which had long been dormant, and which he had shown no disposition to claim. In this conjuncture the edict of Constantine would be an invaluable safeguard. The agent of the Pope on this occasion was John the Deacon. He it was who brought the Germans once more to Rome, to renew the fallen empire of Charlemagne and who, before proceeding on that eventful mission, wrote in letters of gold a document which promised to protect the Holy See from the ambition of its new ally, and to give to the measures which were expected from him the character, not of concessions, which might demand an equivalent return, but simply of a restitution. We know that John XII was capable of entertaining and executing designs as nefarious as this; and the distinct statement of Otho III forbids us to doubt that the Pope's confederate really wrote a splendid copy of the Donation.

The action was less iniquitous than Otho imagined, for the document was already in existence. It was copied but not forged by Johannes Diaconus, and had already been mentioned a century before, though never previously quoted by a Pope. Though neither Hadrian I, nor Ado, nor Hinemar positively allude to it, we can hardly doubt that it was known to Aeneas. Not that this is so clear to us as it appears to Dr Döllinger, who certainly puts a forced construction on the words. "Maximam partem diversarum provinciarum ei subjecit" does not mean that he gave the Pope authority over a great number of different provinces, "eine grosse Anzahl verschiedener Provinzen" (p. 77); but "a very large part of different provinces". Consequently the words apply to the domains, which were numerous and extensive, and in many provinces, rather than to the sovereignty over all Italy, as it stands in the Donation. Other passages in the work of Aeneas are, however, more significant than those which Dr Döllinger relies on, and we have no difficulty in surrendering the point. For we have evidence, the most decisive that can be imagined, that the Donation was extant at the time when Aeneas wrote. It exists in a manuscript of the False Decretals which is as old as the Pontificate of Nicholas I.[1] This makes it certain that the Donation of Constantine is as old as 860, and makes it probable that it was a product of the same age that witnessed the stupendous forgery of the Decretals. The one occurred in France, the other in Rome; but their result was very speedily combined. This simultaneous and independent production of false texts tending to enhance the authority of the Holy See, and the readiness with which both were admitted even by men like Hinemar, a great master of Christian antiquities, and the first prelate against whom the new system was put into effect—all this proves how little the ideas that prevailed at that time were exaggerated by the authors of these documents.

The importance which the writer of the Donation attaches to pomp and dignities points to the same period, for Nicholas was the first Pope who assumed the crown. Whilst, therefore, we hold it on the evidence of manuscripts alone to be incontestable that the edict of Donation was in existence in the year 860, we cannot discover in Dr Döllinger's arguments any proofs of equal force in favour of an earlier date.

It is very curious to follow our author as he traces the subsequent repute and influence of the spurious document. It was never brought forward by any Pope until the year 1054, when Leo IV recited nearly the whole of it in a letter to Michael Cerularius, the Patriarch of Constantinople, "ne leviter suspicemini ineptis et anilibus fabulis sanctam Romanam sedem velle sibi inconcussum honorem vindicare". This is the only occasion, however, on which any Pontiff has openly challenged criticism by resting his claims on the text of the Donation. It was never cited by Gregory VII, although he ransacked the archives in

---

[1] Camus in *Notices et Extraits des MSS. de la Bibliothèque Nationale*, vi, 275, 288. As long as the fifty codices of the spurious decretals have not been examined for a critical edition, this question can probably never be settled.

order to obtain documentary evidence in support of his policy. But in 1091 it is used by Urban II to establish the rights of the Holy See over Corsica, although it would have been more simple to quote the authentic grant of that island by Charlemagne. The next step was to assume that all the islands of the West were included in the original Donation; and this was soon so firmly believed that it was deemed by Hadrian IV to justify the gift of Ireland to Henry II, although that island had never been subject to the empire, and was hardly known by name to the Romans in the days of Constantine.

Opposition to the prevailing view was not altogether silenced. In the year 1105 the monks of Farfa asserted that the jurisdiction of the Holy See was exclusively spiritual; and in 1152 the followers of Arnold of Brescia denounced the deed as a monstrous fiction. Meanwhile its tenor was gradually enlarged. Anselm of Lucca has it: "Constantinus Imperator Papae concessit coronam et omnem regiam dignitatem in urbe Romana, et Italia, et in partibus occidentalibus." Otho of Freising, in the middle of the twelfth century, says that the See of Rome consequently claimed tribute from all the states of the West, excepting France and Germany. It necessarily followed, however, from the sense in which the words were taken, that the empire itself came to be regarded as a gift of the Holy See. Not that the successors of Constantine were imagined to have received their crowns from the Popes, but the Popes, as the sovereigns of Rome, inherited and exercised the right, originally inherent in the Roman people, of conferring the imperial dignity. The kingdom of Italy belonged of right to the Popes since the days of Constantine, and, as the empire now went with it, they both indirectly proceeded from the same source. The prevalence of this view of the imperial power at Rome caused the storm of indignation that arose in Germany when Hadrian spoke of the crown as a *beneficium* which he had conferred on Frederick. At the end of the twelfth century the authority of the Donation was firmly established; and, as it found its way into the canon law, the jurists became its decided advocates. Innocent III believed in it; and in 1236 Gregory IX declared that the empire belonged to the Popes, who surrendered no part of their supreme jurisdiction when they invested each emperor with the power of the sword. Then, in the year 1245, Innocent IV, going beyond all his predecessors, affirmed that

Constantine had only restored or recognized that double authority which Christ gave from the beginning to Peter and his successors. Half a century later, the author of the two last books of the famous treatise *De Regimine Principum* describes the act of Constantine as an abdication in favour of the Popes, so that all temporal power is held by their gift. Aegidus Colonna, the Archbishop of Bourges, held the same opinion;[1] and Dr. Döllinger thinks that the extreme views which culminated in the writings of Augustinus Triumphus and Alvarez Pelayo were provoked by the desire of meeting objections to the Donation of Constantine, and especially of counteracting such ingenious theories as that of Marsilius of Padua, who argued that as the authority of the Pope is derived from Constantine it is of human origin, and therefore inferior to that imperial power from which it sprang.

We believe it might be shown, however, that the successive exaggerations of the theory of the political supremacy of the Popes followed each other by a kind of logical necessity; that they arose naturally, not from an original delusion, but in the course of the warfare with the feudal power; and that this process, substantially independent of the Donation, was so vigorous and so agreeable to the tendencies of the day that it disregarded the limits of the grant, arbitrarily altered its terms, and bore it along as an obedient and flexible instrument, rather than an initiating and controlling force, in the development of the hierarchical system.

When Hildebrand commenced the great reform of the eleventh century, he found the celibacy and the morality of the secular clergy grievously fallen, simony prevailing throughout the Church, and the civil power exercising an absolute control over the prelates by virtue of a mode of investiture which disguised the true source of spiritual jurisdiction. In his first efforts to restore ecclesiastical discipline, he was supported both in Germany and Italy by a portion of the laity, but he was opposed by the simoniacal and dependent priesthood. The fidelity owed by a vassal was too powerful a link to be broken at the summons of the Pope, or out of anxiety for the welfare of the Church. It was necessary to emancipate the Bishops from this thraldom, the effect of their

[1] "Omnia temporalia sunt sub dominio Ecclesiæ collocata, et si non de facto, quoniam multi forte huic juri rebellantur, de jure tamen et ex debito temporalia summo pontifici sunt subjecta."

exalted position in the state. Gregory could not destroy feudalism and shatter the existing framework of Christian society. He had no choice but to make the Bishops resign their fiefs, or to deprive the prince of the rights of feudal suzerainty. Long after his death the first of these alternatives was made a familiar idea to Catholics by the example of St Francis, and by the theory of some of his later disciples. But at the time when the reaction occurred, wealth had become not only a source of political dependence, but also of moral corruption; and the reaction itself was caused by the luxurious life of the clergy, which estranged them from the people, not by the evils of vassalage, which made them dependent on the state. Gregory could invoke no force sufficient for so vast a revolution; he recurred to the other alternative. He exerted himself to induce the kings of Europe to acknowledge St Peter as their feudal lord, to receive their crowns from his successor, and thus to invert the relations between the civil and the ecclesiastical power.

In Germany the position of affairs was different, for there the crown was elective. But the King of the Germans claimed to receive the crown of the Roman Empire from the Pope, and the empire included the protectorate of the Church. This office could not rightly be bestowed on an unsuitable person. It was monstrous that the Pope should be compelled to elevate to the dignity of his protector, and the arbiter of his election, a prince whose goodwill he had reason to distrust, or whose religion he suspected. For the emperor still enjoyed substantial rights at Rome, and Gregory himself had submitted to have his election confirmed by Henry IV. If, therefore, he showed symptoms of heresy, that is, if he questioned or defied the laws of the Church or the authority of her ruler, it was impossible that he should retain the imperial crown. It followed that the Pope, whose right and duty it was to apply this test, could refuse or withdraw the empire on the same principle as that on which he might eject even sovereigns from his communion, not wantonly, but on valid grounds. He could not modify or curtail the power which belonged to the empire, but he could give it or take it away.

This was the course of reasoning which the Roman divines pursued between Gregory VII and Gregory IX, guided rather by the nature of things than by any existing law, and as it appears to us, without regard to the Donation of Constantine, which was never appealed to in critical moments, which was known, for instance, to Nicholas III in its original modest form, and which was quite inadequate to support such a superstructure. The opponents of these opinions held doctrines quite as excessive; and of them it may be truly said that they were misled by their belief in the edict. Gervase of Tilbury says that the Popes received their power from Constantine; that the giver is greater than the receiver; and that the imperial power is from God, the Papal from the emperor.[1] Even the advocates of the Holy See, such as Leo IX and Bonizo of Sutri, imagine that the primacy was not recognized before Constantine.[2]

Whilst, therefore, the imperialists could argue very effectively on the inferences from the supposed Donation, and the curialists were obliged gradually to interpolate and to disregard its text, it is hardly just to attribute to its influence the exaggerations of the thirteenth and fourteenth centuries. They are due to the peculiar position of the empire in its struggle with the Church, and to the universal ignorance of Christian antiquities, which gave free scope to the speculations of the schools. These speculations constantly tended to work out to its uttermost consequences any principle which seemed honourable or advantageous to the Holy See. For in proportion as the scholastic literature increased and flourished, the study of ecclesiastical history decayed; and criticism deteriorated considerably after the end of the twelfth century. "If we reflect", says Dr Döllinger, "how well history was understood as early as the twelfth century, we shall be inclined to say that for three hundred years this sort of knowledge went backward rather than forward" (p. 95). Leibniz uses still stronger language: "I hold the thirteenth century, and that which succeeded it, to have been the most stupid since the Christian era. Good writers suddenly disappeared; jurisprudence and the subtleties of the schools became almost the sole object of study ... The fables which had hitherto penetrated only the legends and

[1] "Quis ergo major in terrenis, qui dat, an qui accipit? profecto qui dat autor est honoris, non qui accipit. Deus autor imperii: Imperator autor papalis triumphi" (Leibniz, *SS. Rer. Brunsvic.*, i, 882).

[2] "(Privilegium) contulit pontifici romano ... ut in toto orbe sacerdotes ita hunc caput habeant, sicut omnes judices regem" (*Leonis Ep.* 10). "Legem posui evangelicæ doctrinæ consonantem, ut omnes episcopi Romanum episcopum haberent caput, sicut omnes judices regem" (*Bonizo ad amicum. Oefelde Rer. Boic. SS.*, ii, 795).

the miraculous lives of saints rapidly inundated all literature."[1]

The Donation was of little practical service to the Popes. It directly influenced no important act except the grant of Ireland; and it gave rise, later in the Middle Ages, to the bitter attacks of men who believed it to be authentic. The rapid growth of the temporal riches of the clergy provoked an ardent and very general condemnation of a wealthy Church. The Waldenses and the Mendicants combined to spread the idea of the poverty of Christ, and to represent the gifts of Constantine in that gloomy light in which Dante speaks of them in one of the most famous passages of the *Inferno*. The fabled Donation came ultimately to be regarded as the origin of all the ills the Church was suffering; and a legend arose that on the day when it was made, the voice of an angel had been heard to proclaim that poison had been administered to her.

This was the point of view from which the fraud was for the first time unmasked. Doubts occurred about the same time to four celebrated men, who seem to have written independently of each other. Aeneas Sylvius and Nicholaus Cusanus speak with some hesitation, Reginald Pecock shows much less reserve. The first of all was Valla, who, writing in 1439, at a time when his patron the King of Naples refused to recognize the lawful Pope, maintained that the temporal power was the deplorable result of the fiction. It is true, as Dr Döllinger says, that he afterwards received an appointment at Rome from Nicholas V, and that no retraction was ever exacted. But in a letter written in the year 1445, soliciting admission into the Papal service, Valla asks forgiveness for what he had done; partly, he says, at the instigation of others, partly out of contentiousness and ambition. Eugene IV, however, rejected his petition, and Valla fled secretly from Rome. At that time there still were writers, whom our author enumerates, who held that it was heretical to deny the genuineness of the Donation; and it continued to find defenders until it was rejected by Baronius.

The story of the Donation was supported by that of the baptism of Constantine at Rome by Pope Sylvester, which was believed for eight hundred years. It was incredible to the mediaeval mind that Constantine should have surrendered Rome to the Pope, and loaded him with wealth and privileges, without being

[1] *SS. Rer. Brunsvic.*, i, Introductio, lxiii.

a Christian; or that, after watching the Arian controversy, and assisting at the first general council, he should have postponed his baptism to receive it on his deathbed from an Arian Bishop. Although this was the account unanimously given by the genuine authorities on the history of the fourth century, a version more consonant with antecedent probability appeared at Rome about the year 500, in the spurious acts of St Sylvester. Bede is the earliest author of eminence who adopted the legend, and his chronicle helped to circulate it; yet long after him, in books of the eleventh century, and even in a chronicle of the year 1175, the authority of Eusebius and St Jerome seemed to prevail. But the Popes themselves—Hadrian I, Nicholas I, and Leo IX—publicly expressed their belief that Constantine was baptized at Rome; and after the time of Gregory VII the story is commonly accepted by historians. The Greeks who venerated Constantine as a saint, and would not, therefore, admit that he had so long remained a Pagan, adopted the Roman legend much sooner than the Latins. Here, again, the first doubts were expressed by Pius II and by his friend Cardinal Cusanus; but the fable continued to be believed by Pole, Bellarmine, Baronius, and others, down to the middle of the seventeenth century, when the comparison of testimony was for the first time methodically pursued.

Till that time the legendary tradition overwhelmed all real evidence, and wrought its wayward will with the history of the Papacy, converting one Pope into a heretic, inventing another, and, most strange of all, raising up an Arian anti-Pope to the honours of the altars. This was Felix II, who was consecrated by the Arians in the place of Liberius—the Pope who wavered for a moment in the great Athanasian controversy, but who, as Dr Döllinger shows, never fell into actual heresy. The legend was severe on Liberius, and represented his opponent as a holy man. The latter was reverenced as a martyr on the 29th of July, from the eighth century to the sixteenth. Baronius, becoming suspicious, wrote a book to prove that Felix was neither a saint nor a legitimate Pope; and a congregation was appointed to investigate the question. Just then an inscription was found, bearing the words "Corpus S. Felicis Papae et Martyris", which soon disappeared again, but not until it had removed the scruples of Baronius, and obtained for Felix a place in the corrected Martyrology. The opinion of most learned men was against him; but even Benedict XIV affirmed, "de F. Felicis II sanctitate et martyrio nullam amplius superesse dubitationem". Since that day, however, Dr Döllinger can only find one writer who denies that Felix was an intruder.

In the middle of the twelfth century, when the bones of St Ursula's companions were dug up, near Cologne, it happened that several skeletons of men were found from time to time among them. The circumstance was calculated to throw suspicion on the legend of the British virgins, had not a number of epitaphs been brought to light, attributing these bones to a variety of priests and bishops, to an Archbishop of Ravenna, and to several Cardinals. A stone was at length discovered, which bore the name of Pope Cyriacus. The abbot began to suspect that these inscriptions might be forged, and, in order to make sure, he sent them to St Elizabeth of Schönau. She had already been occupied with the legend of St Ursula; and it was desired that she might determine through her visions the nature of what had been discovered. The result of the inquiry was the following legend. Pope Cyriacus had occupied the Roman See for more than a year, when he received a warning in his sleep that he was to accompany St Ursula and her companions, in order to share the martyrdom which awaited them. He obeyed, resigned his office, and departed; but the Romans were so displeased that they struck his name out of the list of Popes. In the following century it began to be suspected that he had not acted from the purest motives. But his martyrdom was unquestioned; and his name stood in the Breviary until the time of the Council of Trent. In the time of Boniface VIII, when the right of his predecessor Celestine V to resign his see was disputed, the example of St Cyriacus was one of the three examples quoted in his favour. These were all alike fictitious. Pope Cyriacus, whose supposed date is 238, was never heard of until the twelfth century. He held his ground in the collection of decretals down to 1553.

We have not space to follow Dr Döllinger in his account of the rise and progress of several similar legends, respecting Marcellinus, Honorius, and Gregory II. The most singular case he mentions is that of Pope Sylvester II, who, after having been universally revered by his contemporaries, was believed, a century after his death, to have been a magician, and to have been carried away by the devil. Cardinal Benno, the bitter enemy of Gregory

VII, is our first authority for this fable, about the close of the eleventh century. He says that Gerbert had introduced the black art at Rome, had founded a school of its professors, one of whom taught it to Hildebrand. But our author deems it probable that some rumour of the kind was already extant in Rome, where the wise and learned foreigner was an object of wonder and dismay.

Dr Döllinger's little volume is a masterpiece of critical art. From a psychological point of view it is a marvel. The author is renowned for his knowledge of mediaeval literature; and his powers of minute criticism were displayed in his work on Hippolytus. But there are two kinds of proficiency in historical science which have rarely or never been combined before in any high degree. Whilst the historian is sifting evidence and ascertaining his facts, he is obliged to put away from his mind all the influences of opinion, doctrine, and belief. He extracts the pure gold from the ore, without troubling himself as to whose image will be stamped upon it. In this preliminary operation no ulterior object can guide his hand without abating the value of his work, and he must be as free from all emotions as a surgeon when he is inflicting a salutary pain. But as soon as this is done, when the materials are to be used, and to receive their due place in history, when the lessons are to be drawn from them, and they are introduced into political, or literary, or religious discussions, a new rule of action interposes, different faculties come into play, and the facts are brought into contact with important interests and cherished opinions. The historian now converts his facts into arguments, fits them into the system of truths, and weighs attentively all the results they afford to previous inquiries. The union of these two things—the power of investigating facts, and the power of reasoning on theory—is extremely rare. It would have seemed barely possible for the same man to have equal familiarity with two such different states of mind—at one moment to be utterly regardless of the argumentative value of his materials, and at another to study them with the keen eye of a controversialist. If he mingles the two, he is either an unreliable critic or a feeble dialectician, and he either injures science or damages his cause.

Now the author of this book is a practised controversial writer, very dexterous in the management of historical evidence, and vigilant in detecting the value and the bearing of every fact that will tell in the defence of religion. If anywhere there is any document or any circumstance which may be plausibly used against some Catholic doctrine, or made to excite a prejudice against the Church, it is to his coming volumes on ecclesiastical history that men will look to find it reduced to its just place and proportion. It is there that he will draw the conclusions which the Christian annals supply to the apologist of Catholicism and its theology. That he should be able, with this mighty task before him, and under the sense of the general expectation that has been sustained so long, to pause in his work, and examine the origin and influence of fables that were long mingled with questions of government and discipline, without betraying for the moment the slightest bias, or seeming to remember that discussion is not yet over—this is a memorable example to men, of whatever religion they may be, who imagine that the position of a Catholic divine involves some surrender of intellectual freedom, or some compromise between truth and interest. It gives promise that the work of which the present volume is a preliminary fragment will be an inestimable treasure in the literature of Catholics.

VI

BOSSUET[1]

AMONG all the remarkable theologians of every age, Bossuet is one of the most remarkable. Everything in his mind was on the gigantic scale. Though far from being universal, and in fact though less versatile than other great minds are sometimes found to be, yet there have been few minds possessing so much largeness and power. Uniting, as he did, a learning quite extraordinary to a rare facility for exposition in the grand style, an acuteness in polemics to a never sleeping common sense, an unquestionable sincerity and simplicity of intention to an untiring energy and devotion to the cause he espoused; and lastly, so far as can be ascertained, possessing a certain charm of manner, which softened the pain of submission in those who were forced to yield to his somewhat despotic will—such a man was formed to rule in his generation, and to produce an impression upon his country not easily effaced. We may differ from his views on some or many points; we may criticize his personal character with more or less friendliness or severity. But we must still admit that few complimentary titles have ever been given with so much truth as that of the "Eagle of Meaux," which has been popularly assigned to Jacques Bénigne Bossuet.

It is perhaps hardly too much to say that no single prelate, either before or after his time, ever exercised a more powerful practical influence on the opinions and conduct of his contemporary fellow-Catholics. The times, no doubt, were suited to the man; and it would be most unjust to measure the capacity of any person by the precise amount of power which he has attained over his generation. The fact, nevertheless, is deserving of notice. Taking the four chief subjects with which the name of Bossuet, as a practical controversialist, is associated, we cannot call to mind any other theologian who has made his contemporaries and posterity so much to feel his power. Gallicanism, Quietism, Jansenism and Protestantism—these four words suggest reminiscences

[1] *The Rambler*, June 1858.

of an exercise of successful energy, which dwarf the accomplishments of most other men to a tolerably low standard. On Protestantism *proper* his influence was perhaps less than on the other subjects in which he was specially occupied. That it was very considerable, practically speaking, is certain; and that his anti-Protestant writings display an amount of erudition and force quite worthy of himself, is also true. But the greater number of Protestant objections to Catholicism being based on an admission of some of the fundamental principles of Catholicism, the controversy has usually assumed much of the nature of an *argumentum ad hominem*. Consequently Bossuet's anti-Protestant labours tell only against certain classes of Protestants, and are chiefly useful to those who wish to deal with objectors like those with whom he argued.

It was in the matter of what was termed "Gallicanism" that, to our mind, the endowments of Bossuet were displayed in their most striking colours, as it is undeniable that in this matter their practical influence was the most widely extended. To comprehend the significance of the course of action adopted by Bossuet in the conflicts between Louis XIV and the Papal See, we must recur to the ideas which the seventeenth century had inherited from the Middle Ages, as well as to the fundamental views on the natural relations of Christianity and the State in all ages. Towards the close of the seventeenth century these contradictory opinions come into direct struggle in the matter of the *régale*. At that period the system of feudalism still so far prevailed in France, that the temporal property of each ecclesiastical benefice, whether episcopal, parochial or otherwise, was regarded as a fief held under the crown. This was undoubtedly the case in earlier times. Bishops and the Superiors of monasteries held their possessions on precisely the same tenure as did the lay nobility and owners of land. All alike were bound to render military service to the sovereign in time of war, as the condition on which they possessed their estates. In the case of the clergy this service was of course usually rendered by deputies, who represented the churchmen disqualified by their character from taking the field. At the same time, it is likely that to the existence of this tenure of property must be partly attributed the readiness with which the Middle Ages acquiesced in the spectacle of warlike ecclesiastics, and were less shocked than their descendants would be at the sight of fighting Bishops, and Abbots armed in coats-of-mail.

As, then, in ordinary secular fiefs the property held by any family reverted to the crown in case of failure of heirs, or in case of non-fulfilment of feudal duties, so, according to the view of one party, in ecclesiastical fiefs the natural possession of the property reverted to the Crown while the benefice was vacant; in other words, while there was no heir. In secular fiefs descending by hereditary descent, there was of course no single instant during which the property had no owner, so long as legal heirs survived. But in Church fiefs, every time the holder of a Church benefice died or vacated it, an interval elapsed during which period, on the principles of the very tenure itself, it was maintained that the revenues belonged to the sovereign.

In opposition to this view was that termed the Ultramontane, espoused by many of the Popes and generally by the Italian clergy, as the other theory was usually held by temporal princes and by many of the clergy in France and Germany, as also in England before the Reformation. The anti-Gallican principle maintained that the Church, as a spiritual corporation, is the real holder of all ecclesiastical property of every kind. It disallowed alike the details of feudalism and the political economy of modern times. Property, it held, once consigned to the Church, ceases to be subject to those claims on the part of the State to which it was subject so long as it remained the private possession of individuals; the act of consecration destroying all previous rights on the part of the secular power, whether exercised by government or private persons. Accordingly, with perfect consistency it was urged that a spiritual benefice is never vacant. The temporary and inferior holder may die or go elsewhere; but the real holder, which is the Church, never dies, and therefore never vacates. By indefeasible rights it is she who originally nominates the individual who fills the post to which the benefice is attached; and when this nomination is made by the secular power, it is only because the Church confers the privilege upon it. Consequently the king has no more right to the revenues of a vacant benefice than to those of the Papal See itself.

Concordats at various periods endeavoured to smooth over the difficulties which necessarily grew out of the practical action of these contending opinions. As in all matters, however, which are of the nature of a compromise, the parties to these agreements frequently felt that their interests still practically clashed. In France the right to the *régale* was conceded for certain benefices specially designated; but the temporal power was always on the watch to extend its influence farther and farther. A monarch like Louis XIV, who had subjugated prince, noble and peasant alike in temporal affairs, was not likely to relax in his efforts at subjugating the spiritual power in a similar way. In 1673 he took the decisive step of publishing an edict extending the rights of the *régale* to all benefices, with certain exceptions; and the French Bishops were called upon to take an oath of fidelity to this edict. Two only refused to acquiesce . . .

Innocent in the meantime had begun to remonstrate with Louis . . . denouncing the motives of the king's chief advisers. In December 1679 the Pope issued a third brief to the king, in which he threatened him with excommunication if he did not respect the rights of the Gallican Church, which concluded its work in 1682, and which was unquestionably one of the most momentous demonstrations of ecclesiastical opinion which modern times have witnessed. The French episcopate and the Holy See were about to be drawn up face to face; and no mortal eye could foresee the issue of a conflict which, the longer it lasted, seemed to make all hope of agreement more and more improbable. Powerfully as the actual consequences told upon the practical unity of France with the Holy See, there can be little doubt that but for the genius, the acquirements and the energy of one man, the results to Catholicism might have been of a more formidable description. The *deus ex machina* was Bossuet, the newly-made Bishop of Meaux . . .

His object was to avoid pronouncing a dogmatic decision; to yield to the king in the majority of individual cases, inducing him to make a few decent concessions by way of balancing accounts; and to win the court of Rome to acquiescence by urging upon it the mischiefs that must follow upon an unconciliating maintenance of abstract rights. With his views, there was perhaps no other policy to be adopted. The king, of course, was satisfied when he got the pudding, though without all the plums; the episcopal instinct of the Bishops was lulled by the abstaining from any dogmatic treatment of principles; and the Pope—so it was calculated—would accept the solution as the best possible under the circumstances, from his dread of driving Louis into open schism, and converting him into another Henry VIII of England.

But Innocent was too acute to be led into what he held to be a snare to induce him to betray the rights of the Holy See; and he retorted upon the Bishops, when they wrote at once to hope for his acquiescence in their proposal, with what we should familiarly term a rap on the knuckles . . . telling them that he had read with horror that portion of their letter in which they said that they abandoned their rights and transferred them to the king, as if they were the masters and not the guardians of the churches entrusted to their charge, he ended by annulling all they had done with respect to the *régale* and commanding all who had taken part in it instantly to retract.

When the brief reached the assembly, instantaneous differences of opinion were displayed as to the mode in which it was to be received. Some were for siding with the king *à l'outrance*; others shrank from breaking with the Holy See; irritation against the Pope alone seemed capable of uniting all minds in one common action. It is perhaps one of the most striking proofs of the power of a mind like Bossuet's over inferior intelligences that he succeeded in calming the storm to such an extent as to lead the assembly to do nothing at all . . . The assembly simply received the letter without protest. Whatever the reader may think on the questions involved, he will probably agree with us, that the cowardice of the French episcopate was on a par with their ingenuity in attempting to bribe the king, and to flatter the Pope, into a comfortable compromise.

However, in the meantime, ignorant of the lesson that Innocent was preparing to read them, they had been continuing their discussions, and had drawn up the four famous articles known by the name of the "Declaration of the clergy of France on the ecclesiastical power." Whether or not it was Bossuet's personal wish that anything should be formally put forward on so delicate a subject, may be a matter of doubt. In fact, however, he considered that the thing must be done; and he himself drew up the propositions as requested by the assembly . . .

"1. St Peter and his successors, Vicars of Jesus Christ, and the whole Church herself, have received power from God alone in spiritual things and those which concern salvation, and not in temporal and civil things; Jesus Christ Himself teaching us that

'His Kingdom is not of this world'; and in another place that 'we must render to Caesar the things which are Caesar's and to God the things which are God's'; and that thus the precept of the Apostle St Paul cannot be changed or overthrown—'That every person should be subject to the higher powers; for that there is no power which is not from God, and that it is He who ordains those which are on earth. He, therefore, who opposes the powers, resists the ordinance of God'; we declare accordingly, that kings and sovereigns are not subjected to any ecclesiastical power by the ordinance of God in temporal things; that they cannot be deposed, directly or indirectly, by the authority of the chiefs of the Church; that their subjects cannot be dispensed from the submission and obedience which they owe them, nor absolved from their oath of fidelity; and that this doctrine, necessary for public tranquillity, and not less advantageous to the Church than to the State, ought to be invariably followed, as conformable to the Word of God, to the tradition of the holy Fathers, and to the example of the Saints.

"2. The plenitude of power which the Holy Apostolic See and the successors of St Peter, Vicars of Jesus Christ, possess over spiritual things, is such, that nevertheless the decrees of the Holy Oecumenical Council of Constance, contained in its fourth and fifth sessions, approved by the Holy Apostolic See, confirmed by the practice of all the Church and of the Roman Pontiffs, and religiously observed at all times by the Gallican Church, remain in their force and efficacy; and the Church of France does not approve the opinion of those who attack these decrees, or who weaken them by saying that their authority is not well established, that they are not approved, or that they only regard schismatic times.

"3. Thus the use of the apostolic power is to be regulated by following the canons made by the Spirit of God, and consecrated by the general respect of all the world; the rules of manners and the constitutions received in the kingdom and in the Gallican Church ought to retain their force and efficacy; and the usages of our fathers ought to remain unshaken; and it even tends to the greatness of the Holy Apostolic See that the laws and customs established by the consent of this venerable (respectable) See and of the Churches should possess the force which they ought to possess.

"4. Although the Pope has principal part in questions of faith and his decrees regard all the Churches and each Church in particular his judgement nevertheless is not otherwise than subject to correction at least so far as the consent of the Church has not confirmed it."

The day after the adoption of this declaration, it was presented to Louis at St Germains, with a prayer that he would promulgate it as the law of the Church, which he did. The edict of Louis was registered by the parliament; and it rendered signature to the four articles obligatory.

Judging these events by the light of subsequent history, it appears astonishing that a man with the practical acuteness and knowledge of mankind possessed by Bossuet could have flattered himself that the promulgation of such propositions as these famous four should have lulled the disputes between Louis and Innocent. That prelates who were prepared to follow the king to any extent should rejoice in their publication was natural enough; but the fact that a mind like Bossuet's, earnestly desirous of promoting the peace of the Church, should have anticipated anything approaching to a *bona fide* settlement with the Pope, serves only to show what a marvellous difference there is between that judgement which decides after action and that which decides before it.

Of course the storm instantly raged more fiercely than ever. Bossuet wrote his well-known "Defence of the Declaration of the Clergy", and many theologians most vehemently attacked it. The sounds of the controversy echoed from the Sorbonne in Paris to the archiepiscopal palace of Gran in Hungary ... Louvain and Douai became fresh centres of agitation of opinion; and Bossuet began to tremble seriously for the consequences of the daring movement in which he was the half-unwilling commander of a belligerent host ...

Notwithstanding Bossuet's anticipations, the policy adopted by the court of Rome proved somewhat different from that which he was dreading. His conciliatory schemes were a total failure; but Innocent, for whatever reason, did not strike the Four Articles with the same force with which he had smitten the preliminary declaration on the subject of the *régale*. He appointed a special congregation to examine the articles, but he never published the condemnation which they drew up. He contented himself with marking with a personal stigma the priests who had assisted in the assembly of 1682, whenever they were nominated Bishops by Louis refusing the bulls for their consecration. Louis then, for the future, by some device, got the names of any of these obnoxious persons whom he wished to appoint included in the bulls for other Bishops. And so affairs remained during Innocent's lifetime.

If we should wish to account for Bossuet's mistakes of judgement in all these struggles, we may perhaps find a clue in two special causes. He was by nature, as well as principle, a man given to seek union among opposing parties by what he thought the methods distinctly adapted to their personal characters. It was a portion of his essentially *governing* capacity. No man was ever less of a theoretical controversialist, or was more inclined to overlook the facts of the moment as the elements from which to construct the temple of peace which he sought to build ... "I do not comprehend how a man of ability has the patience to make a book for the sole pleasure of writing." In conjunction with many acts of his life, this saying helps to show us the practical statesman of his own time, as distinguished from the lawgiver, and from the philosopher so passionately enamoured of truth as to long to pour forth his convictions as a relief to his overburdened mind. Hence his aversion to push anything to a needless extreme; his desire to diplomatize between Pope and king; and his occasional adoption of a policy which in a man of another temperament might be condemned as inconsistent and cowardly. Hence his expectations as to the probable conduct of Innocent. It is a tendency of honest and ardent minds always to overrate the probability that other people will act as they would themselves in any emergency. Bossuet judged Innocent by himself; the court of Rome by his own personal notions of ecclesiastical statesmanship. Hence too, in some degree, his idolizing of the royal power as embodied in Louis XIV, and his inability to devise any more profound or liberal philosophy of politics. We need hardly say that his worship of the king as a king, and his subservience to a man like Louis, are in our eyes simply abominable, viewed in themselves. But in Bossuet himself we cannot but think that they should be viewed in connection with the general cast of his character. In the world of politics and government, the autocratic king of France was to him the greatest fact in existence. His practical temperament led him to kneel before the royal foot-stool, shutting his eyes to the material of which his idol was composed, and to offer to him that incense of veneration which in the nostrils of a constitutionalist of today exhales an odour the reverse of sweet. And thus it was, that while he showed no tendencies to adopt the extreme Ultramontane views with respect to the Popes as autocratic monarchs of the Church, he never shrank from attributing to the French sovereign, in things temporal, the absolute power which he refused to the Pontiff in things spiritual. The first principles of social order, in his view, logically led to the autocracy of kings; but he never argued by similar reasoning that the first principles of social order in religious matters led logically to the autocracy of Popes. On the contrary, he treated the theories of Bellarmine—not a little similar in the philosophy of governing to his own—with undisguised contempt. Had he rejected this style of argument in both cases, there would have been no inconsistency; but how was it that the man who would not worship the pious Innocent could worship the "most Christian king" Louis XIV?

We imagine that the explanation must be sought in the tendency of intellects of the intensely practical class to estimate "facts" by their personal proximity to themselves. Some men see truths dissociated from almost all admixture of time, place and individual ... One man feels the importance of a great truth with scarcely any vividness till it is embodied in a practical case before him. Another looks not only before him, but all around; and his eye, with the prophetic perception of unerring logic, foresees the operation of truths whose very enunciation is a puzzle to his contemporaries. With this latter class argumentative inconsistency is a source of positive pain. The former feel only annoyance when the world about them cannot be brought to the best practical solution of difficulties which circumstances allow. Every truth comes to them represented by some living person with whom they personally converse, or on whose conduct their own daily habits and prosperity depend. With them the near is the real, and the farther off a man lives the less important is his position as a member of the vast world of humanity.

Had Bossuet been a Roman, living and brought up in Rome, with the Pope as frequently before his eyes as Louis was in France, we have little doubt that he would have been as vigorous an

Ultramontane as he was vigorously Royalist. His learning might
have been as great, his character might have been the same; but
the great fact before his eyes would have been as prominent in his
view at Rome as the political world was to him in France.
"Order" would still have been the keystone to his practical philosophy, with this sole difference—that the king and the Pope
would have simply changed places in the structure . . .

How little the servility of the episcopate towards Louis was
accompanied by a consideration for the political rights of
Frenchmen in general, and how very easy it was for men to dis-
dain a Papal, while they maintained a Gallican infallibility, a
very few years sufficed to show.

Louis, on looking over his dominions, beheld a large multitude
of men, who, while they refused to obey the Pope, had the un-
heard-of temerity also to refuse to obey the king . . . Notwithstanding all his blandishments, and all his efforts at effecting
their conversion, by the utmost stretch of legal severity, such as
the law then was, the French Protestants obstinately adhered to
their opinions, and presented the one single ugly fact which contradicted the king's celebrated assertion, that he himself *was* the
State of France.

To have simply revoked, on secular grounds, the law by which
Protestantism was tolerated in France would have been entirely
out of harmony with the usual policy of the French king. . . . Why
should a king, blest with the most obedient of clergy, lose so
favourable an opportunity of renewing the brightness of his reputation as a faithful follower of Jesus Christ, and an enemy
of anything verging on heresy? A hierarchy that would bite at a
Pope, would swallow a whole legion of Huguenots at a mouthful.
A second edition of St Bartholomew, even with all "legal"
sanction, would have been too absurd.

Accordingly, a measure which, by finally treading under foot
the last remains of the principle that kings are not the divinely
appointed judges of religious doctrine, cleared the way for the
national atheism of a hundred years after, was introduced in
reply to the request of an assembly of the French clergy, professing nothing but zeal for the Catholic religion. Whatever may be
our opinion on the subject of religious persecution, or on the
political wisdom of the revocation of the Edict of Nantes, we
ought never to overlook the impulse which the politico-spiritual

tyranny of Louis XIV communicated to the atheism even then rapidly advancing throughout Europe. Once constitute the secular power into an inspired authority on the subject of divine revelation, and the human mind speedily revolts against the very idea of God Himself, far more universally and eagerly than when rebelling against polytheism, superstition, and fanaticism. In our eyes, the mind of France did but run its natural course, when, just a century after the revocation of the Edict of Nantes, it threw off all obedience whether to the laws of God or of man.

In 1685 the Assembly of the Clergy formally called upon Louis to extirpate Protestantism from France. Harlai, the Archbishop of Paris, one of the king's most subservient creatures, presented the request in the month of August, and in October the royal mandate went forth, and was followed by a crowd of additional decrees, by which the Protestants were stripped of all their civil rights secured them at Nantes; half of the property of refugees was given to informers; the children of Protestants, between the ages of five and sixteen, were taken from their parents and handed over to Catholic relations or hospitals; widows were forbidden to dispose of their property; and such as had given tokens of incipient conversion, and yet refused the sacraments when seriously ill, were consigned to the galleys on their recovery.

In the assembly which called on the king to revoke the famous edict Bossuet took no part; and it is not unlikely that he personally contributed to soften the rigour of the terrible persecution which followed. He distinctly, however, approved of the act of revocation . . . He maintained a strenuous controversy with the Bishops of Languedoc against the utility of the measures they adopted to force the Protestants actually to come to Mass; asserting that it was injurious to the holy mysteries to compel people to attend them who disbelieved in their validity. At the same time he wrote to Basville: "I agree without difficulty to the right of sovereigns to force their erring subjects to the true worship under certain penalties." So that he held that kings have a right to compel people to that which is in itself insulting to God. Such are the inconsistencies of those who once admit the power of the State to judge in religion.

In his own diocese Bossuet ever leant to the more mild and rational method; and while the atrocious *dragonnades* made certain nominal Catholics, he undoubtedly effected many conscientious conversions. The Protestant minister Du Bourdieu bears a striking testimony to the conspicuous gentleness of Bossuet's methods in these matters . . .

Long before these disputes and their practical consequences had died away, the materials for a fresh conflict, this time within the Church, were speedily gathering together. Fresh combinations were about to take place, and the places of the actors in the former scenes were to be partially modified, but only to display the personal influence and energy of Bossuet in a more striking light than ever. To the last the antagonism between the Jesuits and Bossuet remained intense. Their union with him in the matter of the Gallican articles and in the revocation of the Edict of Nantes never softened the asperity with which he from time to time expressed himself with regard to their morals. But now, in the matter of Fénelon and the Quietist controversy, they were to be placed in practical opposition. Not that the Jesuits generally supported the Quietist extravagances, but that personally Fénelon was held in high esteem by many Jesuits, while between Bossuet and Fénelon, to use a common saying, there seems to have been little love lost at any time . . .

That Bossuet's antagonism to Fénelon served in no way to diminish his anxiety to crush what he held to be his errors, can hardly be doubted. There is no doubt that . . . he was a thoroughly "good hater". However, Fénelon's Quietist ideas were precisely of that absurdly unpractical kind which were peculiarly odious to a mind like that of Bossuet . . . In the theory of the Quietists, action went for nothing. Man, according to this whim, was made to think and rest, simply contemplating God, without regard to outward and corporeal acts, which in their nature are wholly indifferent. The circumstance that religious minds should have ever been insensible to the necessary deductions from this theory is but one proof out of many of the lengths to which mere piety uncontrolled by common sense will run. Unbiassed common sense, apart from profound philosophy, would have seen in an instant that Quietism leads logically to Antinomianism; that if external acts may be indifferent, there is an end of all distinction between right and wrong in actual conduct. It is a proof of eminent sanctity and pure love to God, said the Quietists, to be indifferent to one's salvation; not perceiving that if it is lawful to be indifferent to salvation, it is also lawful to be indifferent to the things on which salvation depends; in other words, to be indifferent altogether to the Will of God. So that, under the pretence of glorifying the Will of God, this preposterous theory tended to dishonour and disregard that Will to the utmost possible extent . . .

The chief modern defender of Quietism, up to the period before us, was Molinos. He had many followers, including men of high ecclesiastical position, and people of undoubted piety. In Italy Quietism had numerous adherents, especially in religious houses, where of course would be found many more people likely to embrace it than in the busy active world without. In France one of its most distinguished supporters was a Barnabite, the Père de la Combe, among whose disciples was a lady (Madame Guyon) who enjoys the unenviable reputation of having led astray the amiable Archbishop of Cambrai . . .

The king was persuaded to constitute a commission to inquire into the new doctrines. The commission consisted of Bossuet, Noailles (the Bishop of Chalons), and Tronson, the superior of St Sulpice . . . The reconciliation which followed between the chiefs of the opposite parties soon proved to be perfectly hollow. St Simon declares that Bossuet was duped by the *tendresses* of Fénelon. At any rate, the antagonism rapidly grew more decided than ever. Fénelon cultivated still closer friendship with the Jesuits about the king, and Madame Guyon vigorously propagated her theories. Bossuet, following the natural instincts of his character, wrote a book, and produced one of his most masterly performances, the *Instruction sur les États d'Oraison*. Fénelon, however, was determined not to be behindhand, and forestalled its publication by issuing his own equally famous *Maximes des Saints sur la Vie Intérieure* . . .

The moment Bossuet's book was out, Fénelon felt the force of the blow. The king called on him to submit his book to a new commission, all of whom were either his declared adversaries or mere court bishops . . . The favour of the Jesuits was not enough to support Fénelon . . . He next appealed to the Pope, sent him his book, and wanted to go to Rome himself; but Louis, being despot over men's bodies, as he wished to be over their souls, would not let him; and the poor Archbishop had to content himself with a dry acknowledgement from His Holiness, while Bossuet's book was warmly welcomed . . .

At last the condemnation came. Twenty-three propositions from the *Maximes des Saints* were pronounced as rash, dangerous and erroneous. Fénelon was just mounting his pulpit when the letter reached him. He proceeded immediately to declare his submission . . .

The king sent the brief to all the metropolitans, with an order to them to assemble their suffragans, and to pronounce on the Papal condemnation of Fénelon's book. Thus the final authority was apparently transferred to the local Bishops, who absurdly enough did not see that in fact they were conceding their jurisdiction to the king. They were content, however, to accept one autocracy in place of the other; and having given their consent to the Papal judgement, they sent their reports to the French court; and the parliament, having thus won *its* battle, readily registered the original mandate. The Pope felt very much like a chess player who is stalemated; but he took no further steps, and Louis XIV once more reigned supreme.

What may have been the personal feeling which remained in the breasts of the two chief theological combatants in the strife, it is not easy to say. It is the bane of historians and biographers, that they insist upon interpreting every man's actions according to their own personal likes and dislikes. And the system of interpretation has been strenuously carried out in the case of Bossuet and Fénelon, though with but slender foundation in facts. That Fénelon should have been infinitely more irritated against Bossuet than Bossuet against Fénelon was but natural. In the first place, Bossuet won the day; and it is easier for the victor to shake hands with the vanquished, than for the vanquished to do the same with the victor. Then, again, the characters of the two men were totally different. Bossuet's natural character was intensely proud; Fénelon's infirmity was probably rather in the way of vanity; and a proud man can forgive more easily than a vain man. Moreover, looking at the whole affair in connection with the ecclesiastical politics of the day, it is evident that the triumph must have been peculiarly soothing to Bossuet, and peculiarly galling to Fénelon. What could a vigorous Gallican more enjoy than to employ the Papal authority to crush *the* Utramontane French prelate, and finally to see the supreme Papal authority, as such, quietly set aside by the device adopted by Louis before the brief received parliamentary registration? Add to this, Fénelon *must* have felt that he had been made a fool of by a woman of more brilliance than solidity, and more fascination than piety— not a soothing thought; so that if Fénelon to the end of his days had no particular fondness for his victor, he only felt what almost every man in his circumstances must have felt . . .

The Jansenist controversy served once more to display the peculiar cast of Bossuet's mind, and brought him again into direct contest with Rome. That he himself held the Port-Royalist doctrine on the subject of divine grace is incontestable. He considered himself, rightly or wrongly, a thorough Augustinian. Moreover, he absolutely detested the casuistry popularly attributed to the Jesuits, and was thrown into repeated controversy with them. With Arnauld, Nicole, and the other learned Port-Royalists, he maintained relations of affection and friendship. But when the condemnation of the celebrated "five propositions" was issued by Rome, Bossuet found himself in a position not precisely the same with that of the leading Port-Royalists, or Jansenists . . .

The French clergy, almost universally, held that though the Church is infallible in matters of doctrine, she is not so in matters of fact, whether those facts are historically connected with the preservation of doctrine or no. Facts, they said, are not matters of revelation at all. We know them by the ordinary human means of knowledge. The Church, on the other hand, is the appointed guardian of those supernatural truths which reason cannot learn by herself, and in those, and those alone, she is free from possibility of error. The opposite school, represented at this time in France by Fénelon and the Jesuits, maintained that the Church is infallible in matters of fact also.

When, then, the Jansenists refused to admit that Jansenius' book actually contained the five obnoxious dogmas, simply because the Pontifical decision declared that such was the fact, a fresh bull, the *Vineam domini*, was issued, which did not, however, absolutely compel those who denied the infallibility in facts to renounce their opinions. Fénelon and others drew a distinction between "Dogmatic facts" and other facts, by way of simplifying the questions involved; but the *real* subject was left untouched.

Bossuet's embarrassment with respect to his Port-Royalist friends arose from the circumstance that he, personally, did consider that Jansenius' book actually contained the Calvinistic propositions condemned. As the condemnation included no distinct statement on the limits of infallibility he had therefore no difficulty whatever himself in giving his signature. His practical advice to the Jansenists was characteristic. He wished them to sign the formulary, as an act of obedience and humility to the Supreme Pontiff, not as an act of faith in the Church as the divine viceregent exerting its dogmatic rights. They were quite willing to go so far as to preserve silence on the subject, out of deference to authority; but he wished them to go a step further, and to say to the Pope: "As you say so, and you are the supreme magistrate in the Church, it would ill become us, inferior persons, and men of no authority, to differ from you in opinion." It is well known that the leading Jansenists did not adopt Bossuet's device.

But Bossuet's time was drawing to a close. On April 12, 1704, the struggles, powers and pains of the great controversialist were ended ... Little as we shall be expected to agree with some of his views, and fatal as we consider was the influence of his support of despotic power, we cannot but admit that time has done less to dwarf his reputation than it does in the case of ordinary celebrities; and that as a practical controversialist, his equal, of whatever school has not appeared since he left this world.

NICHOLAS OF CUSA[1]

URING the first half of the fifteenth century the spirit of Europe was deeply moved. The Church was suffering and sick—a state which, though not originally produced, had been brought into relief and exacerbated, by the long schism. The profound and universal feeling of the need of a reformation which should not destroy, but heal and build up, had enlarged the spiritual horizon of men. It had shown them the necessity of passing over from the narrow sphere of scholasticism to the field of ecclesiastical life, and of reviving and creating such institutions as might serve as bulwark against arbitrary despotism or the malversation of ecclesiastical influences through love of greed. This situation of things, and the aims which grew out of it, produced in France such men as the Chancellor Gerson, Cardinal d'Ailly and Clamenges; while in Germany Nicholas of Cusa stands fitly by their side. He was for his country what Gerson had been for France. Unequal, perhaps, to the Chancellor in clearness and practical insight into the needs of the Church, he was far superior to any of the three Frenchmen as a philosopher and metaphysical thinker. No other German of the fifteenth century combined such comprehensive knowledge, depth of speculation, and earnestness of religious life. It is true, as Ranke says, that the ideas which change the world always announce themselves at first in a few prominent minds, and Cusa was in the truest sense of the words a prophet and precursor of the Reformation. The causes which most naturally account for that event are most clearly displayed in the history of his mind and life. When development is obstructed or paralysed, revolution is the natural result. The first sixty or seventy years of the fifteenth century were a period of universal commotion, a period of sharp contrasts, from the strongest assertion of independence and freedom to the strictest centralization and absolutism. Every thinking man was more or less conscious of a feeling that the old state had

[1] *The Chronicle*, Sept. 7, 1867, pp. 565–7.

become impossible and that some new thing was to be brought about. Among those who gave expression to their thoughts and made proposals of reform, Nicholas of Cusa was the most profound and the most able. His views included both Church and State, and had reference to the whole Empire of Germany. A fatal disease, he said, had attacked the whole Empire, and death would assuredly follow, unless an effective cure could be found. His mournful forebodings found expression in prophetic words. The Empire, he predicted, shall be sought and shall not be found; strangers shall take our land, and dwell among us; and we shall become the subjects of another people. He lamented that the two supreme powers, the Papacy and the Empire, had been shaken, and that laws and canons had lost their authority. All public spirit, he said, had vanished, and every man looked out for his own immediate gain. The hierarchy seemed to him in even a more hopeless condition than the Empire, while he thought that the latter alone would restore the fallen fortunes of the Church. He was ready, therefore, to concede to the Emperor an authority in ecclesiastical affairs inconsistent with the freedom of the Church, and only to be explained by the view that the power of the Church was sunk too low to justify confidence in it without the support of the State. He conceded to the Emperor, as protector of the faith, the right to convene a general council without the authority of the Pope, but held it rather to be the highest of the Emperor's privileges that he was, according to St Paul, "a servant of God" and at the same time, "the vicar of Christ". The fact that the Emperor was anointed and crowned by the Pope did not prove to his mind that the election was subject to the Papal confirmation or rejection. He was also the first who disputed, if somewhat waveringly, yet with great learning and acumen, the genuineness of the Donation of Constantine.

In questions of faith he recognized no deciding authority except that of a general council; for, he says, if these definitions were only to be established by the Pope, the inspiration of the Holy Spirit would be in the power of the Pope and the Church would be placed in serious danger. He also declared himself opposed to compulsion in matters of religion. The nature of Christianity, he says, excludes all compulsion.[1] Not less bold and beyond his time were his views with regard to the temporal pos-

[1] *Concordantia Catholica*, ii, 34.

sessions of the churches. He believed that, owing to the fault of the prelates, the temporal possessions of the Church had become prejudicial to her. "Of what good", he explains, "are the temporal possessions of the Church to the common weal, or to the State, or to the people? Certainly little or none. That was not the object of the Emperors. They did not intend that the earthly things which they gave the Church, to promote heavenly things, should swallow up the latter."[1] In no case, he says further, should Popes and Bishops either control the temporal business of their principalities, or allow it to be administered by the clergy, but by laymen, for it is contrary to the canons of the first centuries of Christianity. He appeals to Hugo of St Victor, his countryman, who was also of opinion that Bishops should employ none but laymen in the administration of their temporal dominions.

Herr Stumpf, in his recent work on Cusa's political ideas, observes with truth that the notion of popular consent is the soul of the Cardinal's proposals for the reforms of the Empire. The swelling stream, he thought, could not be kept back, nor the dangers of the advancing flood averted, by the Pope and the Emperor alone, nor by the violent suppression of liberal opinions, nor by a scornful rejection of territorial and national movements in Church and State, but only by a reconstruction of the existing constitution on the principles of a constitutional aristocracy, with annual diets and councils. But the elements which made up these assemblies were so little competent to restore unity upon the old basis, that they rather tended to promote and at length to complete the process of dissolution. Cusa certainly saw farther than most men of his time; but he still clung to the mediaeval notion of a Holy Roman Empire and could not understand the vastness of the coming change.

He was so far, however, from having the courage to go to this extreme, that he shrank from the means which he had himself recommended as soon as he saw their working. We quite agree with Herr Stumpf, that it was not ambition alone, as Voigt and others hold, which induced him to desert the Basel party and go over to the side of Pope Eugene IV. "No one in Germany", says Herr Stumpf, "would have held Nicholas to be an apostate had he merely withdrawn from the Council and retired to his cloister. It would have been easy for him to justify his conduct to his

[1] *Concordantia Catholica*, iii, 29.

countrymen by holding once more before their eyes the ideal picture of the Church which he cherished in his heart. His talents seemed to exalt the reform movement in Germany above all selfish considerations. But Nicholas chose otherwise. He went over to Eugene and thus decided the course of his life. It is hard to say what can have moved him into this step." It is not likely that he expected to gain over the Roman theologians to his ideas of an aristocratic constitution. But we are inclined to suspect that he lived in hopes of bringing over to his own views (which did not seem inconsistent with scripture and the practice of the early Church) the Pope himself, in the interest of a union with the Eastern Church, upon which it was quite impossible to force the developed Papal system, and which recognized a general council as the only supreme ecclesiastical authority. As Nicholas had no idea of dispensing with the primacy, he could give his assent to the Florentine decree. He did not at all mean in doing so to give up his principle of the supremacy of the Council over the Pope, and in fact he afterwards maintained this in his celebrated letter of May 20, 1442, addressed from Frankfurt to the ambassador of the King of Castile. "No episcopal see", he says in it, "is bound more strongly than that of the Pope to hold inviolate the canons of the Fathers. Were the Pope to undertake anything contrary to the canons, he would be exceeding the limits of his power, and the Church might withdraw from him." There has been much dispute among the Germans as to whether in this letter he retracted the ideas which he maintained in the *Concordantia Catholica* (1443). Dux and Voigt have held that he did, Scharpf, and recently Pichler, that he did not. Stumpf thinks that both his views are in a sense justified, but that in principle the letter is as complete a retraction as possible. We cannot agree with him. Cusa retracted absolutely nothing. He supplemented in the letter the previously one-sided and partial exposition of his views. Practically, it is true that after he had been made a Cardinal (1448) and Bishop of Brixen, he ruled absolutely, as has often happened both in political and ecclesiastical history. It is only necessary to allude to his dispute with Sigismund of Austria, in which he repeatedly proved untrue to his principles, and set a bad example to the whole of Germany. The champion of liberty and independence became by his own conduct the open violator and arbitrary over-ruler of canonical regulations. He not only applied ecclesiastical penalties, such as suspensions, forfeiture of benefices, interdict, and excommunication, but he tried every temporal means of compulsion which the influence of a Pope and Cardinal could set in motion; he appealed to the Emperor to sequestrate the lands of Sigismund by force of arms, and strove to impoverish and starve out his adversary. The Emperor decided against him; and the Cardinal died, on August 11, 1464. Herr Stumpf's verdict is a just one: "We cannot but disapprove the violent and defiant conduct of the temporal princes; but we leave the consideration of these events, not with a feeling that a Martyr suffered for ecclesiastical liberty, but with lively regret that a remarkable intellect should have wasted itself in striving after impossible ends, by false ways, in opposition to the man's better self."

After the Council of Constance, its chronicler Dacher said: "The Council has been dissolved and no reformation has been effected, such as the Emperor wished and desired. Up to the present day both clergy and laity shrink from such a reformation." Things had not yet become much worse. The reforming party had wasted itself away at Basel, uncertain and indefinite in its aims, owing to the want of religious earnestness among its representatives. Cusa, the ablest of them, had been driven away by their excesses. The victory of the court party was thus secured; and had their triumph been wisely made use of, by acceding to the just demands of national interests, the failure of the Liberal party might have led to a restoration of Papal power. Since the schism, no such favourable opportunity had presented itself. But it was not used—at least, not used for self-reformation and self-examination, but only to reassert old pretensions for which there had long been no historical ground. The consequence was a thorough restoration of the absolutist system, which found a scientific supporter in Cardinal Torquemada. But the triumph was of short duration; and its fruit was the reformation of the sixteenth century.

VIII

FRA PAOLO SARPI[1]

FATHER Paul Sarpi, of Venice, was not only the most powerful writer of his age, but the truest exponent of the character of his native commonwealth. His life is full both of
thought and action. No man, perhaps, has ever shown so little
vacillation of opinion, and such entire consistency of conduct,
during a long and arduous conflict. His career has been the subject of books in many languages; yet much that is uncertain remains to be decided and much that is mysterious to be explained.
The attempted assassination, which is the best-known incident
in his life, has never been cleared up beyond an obscure suspicion
. . . The origin of his ecclesiastical opinions, the exact nature of
his religious opinions are still open to controversy . . .

His books against Rome have diverted attention from his
writings on the art of government, which supply the key to his
character, and give him a high place in political literature. The
Tract on the Venetian Republic, written with Aristotelian sobriety
and observation, expounds the natural properties of oligarchies
as ably as *The Prince* of Macchiavelli reveals the theory of petty
despotisms. Macchiavelli's pre-eminence in fame as well as in
infamy is a usurpation, and has caused men to overlook until
lately doctrines more startling than his own. For Macchiavelli
was nursed in the pagan revivals, and lived in a society notorious
for religious indifference, and for a refined immorality. The
state of Italy at the time was so desperate that necessity seemed
to excuse the most immoral acts, and the example of contemporary princes more than fulfilled his most deadly precepts. He
sinned grievously in the means which he proposed; but he sinned
for the sake of exalted ends, for he meant the independence, the
power, and the unity of his country. He was before his age in his
objects, and not below it in his ethics. But Sarpi lived in the
midst of the Catholic Revival, at a time when religious fervour
had been renewed throughout Europe. He was reverenced by

---

[1] *The Chronicle*, March 30, 1867, pp. 14–17.

his brethren in religion, consulted by the government in the affairs of the Church, admired and trusted by the zealous chiefs of Calvinism. He said Mass regularly, and bore himself in all outward respects like a pious monk. Yet he composed a treatise as coldly wicked as *The Prince*, and unredeemed by any higher or remoter purpose than the increase of an authority already quite despotic. Sarpi advises the government of Venice to control the press, to oppress the colonies, to confiscate the privileges of the subject cities, to reduce their inhabitants to poverty, and to destroy men of dangerous influence, either by aid of corrupt judges or by the safe agency of poison. This must always be borne in mind in judging the motive and intention of his ecclesiastical writings. The fame which they have earned for him depends on the assumption that he rejected arbitrary power in the Church because it is immoral and demoralizing, and that he defended a principle of freedom. But as a supporter of arbitrary power in the State he was naturally averse to the authority and the immunities of the hierarchy, because they were a limit to the civil power, and a real, though feeble, element of liberty. His opposition to the Roman claims cannot be due to motives which his secular writings prove to have been totally absent from his mind. In his lifetime it was believed by many that he was a Protestant at heart. He found it useful occasionally to encourage this belief; and it has often been adopted by Catholic writers since his death. He corresponded with many conspicuous Protestants; and they came to visit him from France, and Switzerland and Holland. Diodati, the Italian translator of the Bible, went to Venice to concert with him the introduction of Protestantism. It was reported that 14,000 Venetians were ready to abandon their Church, and that the priests of Sarpi's party encouraged their penitents to take the step. Bedell, who was English chaplain at Venice before obtaining his Irish See, affirmed that Sarpi was accustomed to omit the words of consecration in saying Mass. His greatest work was revised and published by De Dominis, who had renounced the archbishopric of Spalatre for a prebend under King James. The letters of Duplessis-Mornay show what sanguine expectations he had raised. But these hopes were given up before he died, and the publication of his *History* made the Protestants less anxious to claim him.

A far greater weight of authority is arrayed on the side of those who argue that he was a sincere Catholic, the wisest and most enlightened of his time. The antagonism of learned Protestants had begun to be mitigated by the new study of Christian antiquity. The example of the Lutheran Calixtus, the Calvinist Casaubon, the Anglican Andrewes and the Armenian Grotius show that the change proceeded from general causes of sectarian theology. All these men were attracted to Catholicism by its agreement with patristic ideas; and they were repelled by acts of modern Popes for which they saw no warrant in the Fathers. The same comparison of the present with the past produced a corresponding effect among Catholics. Eminent prelates and divines acknowledged the defects of the existing system, and attributed them to the abuse of the papal power, and the exaggeration of papal claims. The arguments of men who accepted nearly all the Catholic dogmas, but were shocked by the dispensing power and the deposing power, by the claim to judge sovereigns and to control governments, by the Bull *Unam Sanctam* and the Bull *In Coena Domini*, would make little impression on believers in the papal infallibility; but men who had not that belief concluded that the wrong notion of the Church, among Protestants, was caused by a wrong notion of the papacy, among Catholics, and so were brought to the conviction that the most urgent matter for the reform and the defence of their Church was to abate the pretensions of Rome. Those pretensions had passed triumphantly through the ordeal of the Council of Trent, the last and chief occasion on which the Church herself had an opportunity of regulating and reducing them. The only remaining force by which they could be permanently curbed was the State. From this point of view it was natural to hold that the Council of Trent had failed miserably by reason of the intrigues of Rome; to sustain to the uttermost the civil power; and to wage a war of extermination against the Jesuits, who were the extreme advocates of ecclesiastical power. These were the principal cares of Sarpi's life. Many of his opinions were widely shared by Catholics. Others have been established by modern legislation, recognized by Concordats, carried into operation by Innocent XI and Benedict XIV, by Clement XIV, and Pius VII. His reforming zeal was as legitimate as that of Dante, of Erasmus, or of Gioberti. The things with which he reproached the Popes have been urged by the most illustrious Cardinals—by Morone and Seripando before him, by Sacchetti and Passionei afterwards. The habit of judging the present by the norm of the past—of assuming that whatever differs from the primitive discipline is a human innovation on the divine institution—was more honest than the expedient of twisting texts, and pretending that things which rested on no written testimony floated upon oral traditions. Therefore, it is maintained, Sarpi must be esteemed not a traitor or an enemy to his Church, but a wise and bold reformer, who opposed the abuse, but not the rights, of authority, and defended the ecclesiastical law against arbitrary change; who rejected nothing but that which was doomed to pass away; who resumed the interrupted task of the Catholic reformers, and laboured to complete the work of Trent. It is in this character that his name is held in honour, like that of another Savonarola, by his Venetian countrymen, and that his testimony is prized by Protestants. Johnson employed himself much in studying the *History of the Council*; and a note is to be seen in Lord Macaulay's copy, stating that he had twice read it through and was each time impressed with its extraordinary merit.

This way of reading Sarpi's works and character is contradicted by both internal and external evidence. It raises him very high indeed, as a man of genius and as a religious hero. If it is true, he enjoyed, intellectually and morally, an immunity from the prejudices of his age which was denied to men who were equal to him in ability and far superior in knowledge, such as Arnauld and Bossuet. It is not conceivable that a man so superior to accidental influences, so far from the corrupting sophistry of party conflict, whose judgement was so objective, and whose zeal was uncontaminated by passion, should have preached perfidy and murder. A philosopher says: "Le fanatisme, dans la religion, est l'alliance des passions qu'elle condamne avec les dogmes qu'elle professe." This certainly does not apply to the character of Sarpi, according to either hypothesis. The exalted notion of his admirers is inconsistent with his political system. The theory of assassination could only be defended by an ardent enthusiast or by a disbeliever in Christianity. When Aerssens, the ablest diplomatist of the House of Orange, was at Venice, Sarpi assured him that they agreed in thinking that the Pope is Antichrist. This was a new article of faith, lately adopted by the Calvinists, as Vossius declared, in order to counteract the retrograde movement which was setting in from Geneva towards Rome. Some years earlier, before he had written against the Holy See, it had begun to be whispered that he was, in fact, a free-thinker, like his contemporaries, Bruno and Cremonini. On March 20, 1606, a French agent wrote to Paris: "Ils ont choisy un grand personnage, et fort estimé par l'Italie, mais il y a plus d'un an j'ai appris qu'il tenois plus du philosophe et du libertine que du moine." These words are true. Sarpi's own diaries and notebooks, containing the record of his inmost thoughts, and the secret of his religious views, are still preserved. The views are singularly striking and original. But they are not Christian. Sarpi admits neither the divine origin of the Church, nor the divine character of Revelation. Judaism and Christianity, Catholicism and Protestantism, are forms of speculation which he tries to explain by human causes, valuing them not as influences, and studying them as phenomena with less interest than Schelling or Comte —without passion, but without approbation or any degree of assent. These fragments deserve to be admitted in a complete and critical edition of his works, if his countrymen resolve to do for him what Alberi has done for Galileo and what Villari is doing for Savonarola. They exhibit his opinions and the nature of his faculties better than his books or letters. They will overturn the image which Venice preserves of him, and will put an end to that controversial use which has given so much vitality to his fame. But they make his character consistent. It was known that he defended despotism and murder. It is now certain he despised the doctrines which he taught, and scoffed at the mysteries which it was his office to celebrate. Therefore, his writings must have been composed in order to injure, not to improve, the religion he professed to serve. And if any lesson is to be drawn from his example, the advocates of the Papal theory have a better right to claim its testimony than their opponents; for they can point to the most consummate tactician in modern polemics, a sceptic and an absolutist at heart, who sought to compass his evil ends in Church and State alike by assailing the authority of the Holy See.

The controversy which Sarpi's writings made so famous was not provoked by him. Venice had been faithful to the Papal cause at Trent, and had immediately accepted the decrees. Later, in the same century, in the height of the struggle with

Protestant princes, the Pope adopted a system of interference in affairs of state for the protection of ecclesiastical interests, which called forth even in Catholic countries an opposition which was strong enough to seat the King of Navarre on the throne of France, and which obtained supremacy in Venetian councils in 1606, when Donato was elected Doge. The Papacy had just been conferred on Borghese, the last Pope who seriously and earnestly believed that the theories of Pius V and Sixtus V could yet be more than theories. The conflict which ensued has much analogy with that which ranged at the same time between Rome and England, in consequence of the Gunpowder Plot and the oath of allegiance. While Barclay and Preston were denying the deposing power, their comrades in Venice were combating the immunities of the clergy and the jurisdiction of Rome in civil affairs. When Paul V laid the State under an interdict, the theological advisers of the government were specially excommunicated. The quarrel between the Holy See and the Republic was settled by the mediation of France. But a difficulty remained after the settlement, which sheds more light than any other occurrence on the character of that epoch of transition. Hundreds of tracts had been published on both sides; and those of the Venetians contained things which, in Rome, were deemed heretical. Several of the writers belonged to religious orders whose privilege it was that the heresies of their members should be judged by their immediate superiors. Paul V abolished this practice and summoned all the offenders before his own tribunal. Two of them fell into his hands. The writings of both were condemned. One of the writers was absolved and obtained a pension; the other was put to death. He was the last noted and remembered heretic who was publicly executed in Rome. The Spanish Inquisition has made the Roman appear so insignificant that it has been possible for bold men to say, and for honest men to repeat, that the odium of having shed blood for religious error does not rest with the modern Popes. De Maistre invented the statement when it was his object to prove that the victims of the Spanish Inquisition were condemned for reasons of State, and that the responsibility lay with the secular arm. Perrone affirms that few or no heretics suffered under the Roman Inquisition; and Balmez accepted the statement of de Maistre. Döllinger appears to imagine that there were no victims after Giordano

Bruno, who died in the last year of the sixteenth century. In reality, these executions can be traced nearly to the end of the pontificate of Urban VIII, after which they are no more heard of. The Roman tribunal seems to have laid aside its vigour when Protestantism lost the spell which had given it aggressive power, and acquiesced in the limits which had been won in the wars of religion.

The monk who was put to death was an underling. The soul of the Venetian party was Father Paul; and Rome required that he should be delivered up. His letters were intercepted, and were sent to Paris, in order to satisfy Henry IV of his formal heresy, that he might advise the Venetians to comply with the Pope's desire. Cardinal Borghese, however, did not think the evidence sufficient, and suggested that the Nuncio should not press the matter until he had a stronger case. The Nuncio represented to the king that the Inquisition, though contemptible and odious to Frenchmen, was held in awe and reverence (*sacrosanto e riverito*) by the Italians; and reminded him of the example of the Grand Duke Cosmo, who had surrendered his secretary to the Pope, adding that he would have given up his son with the same alacrity. Henry replied that they had better take care lest, in upholding the Inquisition, they should pull down the Church. He would not interfere; and the Republic rejected the demand. The refusal of the Venetians put the Inquisition in a great embarrassment. It was universally known that Sarpi had published the opinions for which he was arraigned. They were opinions which involved imprisonment for life. His contumacy was equally notorious; and heretics who persisted in error were punished with death. If the Venetian government, in the moment of reconciliation, protected an heretical friar, who ought to be tortured and put to death, it was plain that they had mocked the Holy See with a simulated submission; and this defiance of the Inquisition would be more injurious to the authority and the reputation of the Pope than the original matter in dispute. There was no doubt of Sarpi's guilt; no doubt as to the penalty due to it. No defence was possible; he stood convicted without need of further process. According to the theory of the Holy Office he was an outlaw. Therefore, when he was stabbed in a dark street of Venice, he uttered the well-known words: "Cognosco stilum curiae Romanae." The murderers fled into the States of the

Church. They occupied two carriages, in which were heavy boxes, full of money; and a priest was in their company. They were armed to the teeth, and never laid aside their loaded weapons, even at meals, saying that they had licence to go armed throughout the Pope's dominions. In this way they went south along the coast road from Rimini, through Pesaro, Fano, Simigaglia to Ancona. Wherever they stopped they boasted that they had killed Father Paul. The proclamation of the Venetian Government was one day's journey behind them; and those who had let them pass pleaded afterwards that they would have killed them if they had seen it in time. Travelling by easy stages, and spending some days at Ancona, the murderers appeared in Rome on October 29, 1707. The news of the attempt and of its failure had preceded them, and caused dismay. Paul V said to the French ambassador: "I regret what has happened; not that I do not wish harm to Sarpi, but because that will be imputed to me which was at best an act of indiscreet and foolish zeal." The fear was justified. The Venetian government endeavoured to fix the guilt upon the Pope; but the accusation could not be supported by the slightest positive evidence. His nephew wrote to Bentivoglio that several men had offered their services to the Pope to carry Sarpi off, or to kill him; but they had been summarily dismissed. Nevertheless it was the common opinion in Rome that the Pope could not refuse a safe-conduct to men who had attempted the life of a heretic. It is true that his heresy had not been formally declared; but it was considered certain in Rome, and that was enough to justify his assassination. This view was defended by a bishop in the palace of the Secretary of State, and startled nobody. Sarpi himself had recommended secret murder for reasons of State, and whilst most of his books were on the Index, the one which contained this proposition was spared. A writer who undertook to answer his political treatise, in behalf of the Church, entertained, on this particular point, the same ideas. A circumstance related by Cantù in his *History of the Italians* shows how seriously the habits engendered by the religious conflict had weakened respect for the sacredness of human life and had made consciences familiar with schemes of murder. Certain natives of Lucca went into foreign countries and became Protestants. A law was made by which any citizen of the Republic who should kill one of the refugees was to be rewarded with a free pardon for all former crimes; and if the indemnity was of no use to him, he might transfer it to any friend who happened to need it; so that the murder of a heretic was not only an innocent but a meritorious action—so meritorious that it was held to compensate and to redeem the guilt of any quantity of other murders. Cantù says that this enactment was applauded by the Archbishop of Milan and by the Pope, that is to say, by St Charles Borromeo and St Pius V. The murderers of Sarpi remained for some time in Rome unmolested. Ultimately the Viceroy of Naples was requested to give them a pension and to keep them out of the way.

Sarpi took ten years to prepare his vengeance. Then he published the *History of the Council of Trent*. The prodigious reputation and the influence of the book will not survive the opening of the archives. It has resisted the assault of Pallavicini, partly by reason of its astonishing ability and vigour, but especially from the fact that Pallavicini, who had almost unexampled opportunities in knowing truth, was unable to prove it, because he could not produce his authorities. He consulted the MSS of the Vatican, of the Jesuits, of the Dominicans, and of Cardinal Barberini; but nobody was allowed to test his references. To this day the opinions of the divines and the correspondence of the Legates, that is, the dogmatic and political history of the Council, remain unknown. There is a saying among the Jesuits that their only Cardinal of whom they can be proud is Bellarmine; and the suppression of the Tridentine papers looks like a suspicion of the good faith of Pallavicini. Some of his documents have been printed, and the MSS of others are in this country. They are not in all respects favourable to his honesty; but they support him generally in his controversy with Sarpi. The concealment of others makes his triumph impossible, and secures an unfair advantage to his adversary. Many of the Venetian documents from which Sarpi compiled his book have perished. His statements will not be definitely verified or his bad faith demonstrated, until Rome reveals her secrets. When that day comes, many of the men whom she has honoured will no doubt forfeit part of their reputation; but no name is likely to suffer more decisively than that of the best informed, the most artful, and the most feared of her accusers.

IX

THE CATHOLIC PRESS[1]

IN the course of last year we twice took occasion to consider our present duties and position as Catholics in England; and gave utterance to some thoughts, which we believe had occurred to many besides ourselves, on questions which nobody can with propriety overlook, and which nobody can hope to set at rest. An obstacle in the way of all who wish for agreement on the subject is that whilst every judgement which we form on our present condition is determined in great measure by the views we entertain relative to past history, we are no more agreed about the past than about the present. Where our knowledge of events is not obscured by time, it is often quite as much distorted by partiality. We should peradventure be obliged to go back to the time of the schism and the spoliation of the Church, to get clear of the debatable land, and obtain firm footing on ground that affords no matter for Catholics to contest about. Those who look only to the external apparent effect may consider that such practical discord is a strange unkindly fruit of the unity of faith, and may argue that an excessive licence *in dubiis* shows a deficiency either of faith or unity *in necessariis*. But our differences, however deplorable in their consequences, may readily be explained and excused, if we consider the causes which produce them. While the Protestant is obliged to cling to a mendacious tradition on matters of fact to make up for the extreme divergence of opinions on matters of faith—because such secondary things, which are of no great consequence to us, are to him of more vital concern than questions of doctrine—the Catholic is not interested in maintaining a particular view of the details of history or of natural science. His religion is no more affected by the detection of a scandal in the Church than by the discovery of a fossil man, or of an African tribe whose heads do grow beneath their shoulders. It is not for him that vindications of Catholic times and personages are written. He has no difficulty in admitting the virtues

[1] *The Rambler*, vol. xi, Feb. 1859, p. 73.

of his adversaries—the humility of Calvin, the temperance of Luther—when they are proved ("quamquam id non meritorium vitae aeternae"); on the contrary, the sin of heresy is so enormous, that a Catholic may be easily indulgent on smaller things. When a man has been guilty of treason and murder it seems both superfluous and spiteful to reproach him with breaking the Sabbath, or cheating his washerwoman. Whilst, therefore, we are content to rely on the laws of historical evidence applied with the utmost rigour, the Protestant must make them bend to the exigencies of his case. His facts must be as false as his theory; he is obliged to be consistent in his perversion of truth.

No true Protestant can surrender the historical assumption on which the Reformation rests—the corruption of the Church in doctrine and discipline during the Middle Ages. If the Popes were justified in condemning heretics, and resisting the temporal power, the Reformation has nothing to stand upon. This is the foundation of all specifically Protestant views of history, and must be held to as firmly as the history of the Apostles. As a real Protestant, he can no more give up one than, as a Christian, the other; so long as his Christianity believes the history of St Peter, his Protestantism cannot do justice to that of St Peter's successors.

The really valid excuse for the existing variety of views on our past—from which a similar variety of views on our present must needs follow—is, that our history is very imperfectly known. If it were more thoroughly cleared up—the earlier period from the mists of ignorance, the later from the mists of prejudice—it would then be possible to appeal with effect to the experience of English Catholics as a lesson for their present guidance. The man would render us an incalculable service who displayed the energy, the zeal, and, above all, the courage to bring to light the whole truth concerning both the noble and consoling history of the persecutions, and the less edifying story of our gradual emancipation. It is to illustrate the former that our labours have, by a sort of instinct, been chiefly directed. It would be less easy indeed, but more instructive, to show clearly how, whilst the penal laws were being slowly relaxed, the Catholics dwindled to an insignificant body in the State, weak in numbers, in knowledge, and in zeal; and how, after Milner had seen the dawn of a brighter day, we obtained political consequence through Ireland, and intellectual importance from another source. This would help us to judge the last scene of all—to understand what advantages have been derived from emancipation, especially from the admission of English Catholics into Parliament, and how we have turned to account in literature and education the vast accession of strength which the Oxford Movement sent us; how the old elements have amalgamated with the new, and what has proceeded from their harmonious action.

This last point brings us to a question which has become of serious importance, and for the discussion of which the time seems to have arrived—the condition and prospects of our literature, and of our periodical press in England. Not that we are about to exercise our function of criticism on the writers of books, or to disturb the peaceful enjoyment of their popularity or their dusty repose; our business is with our periodicals; but we may introduce it with one or two general remarks.

If we except certain very elaborate essays in the *Atlantis* there is hardly anything serious or durable in the productions of the Catholic literature of the day. Entertaining books abound; we have history made edifying, science religious, and religion exceedingly attractive—in short, plenty of most unobjectionable reading. But a popular literature cannot stand alone; it must be fed by the overflowings of more serious books. It is incapable of progress or improvement; and, if cultivated to the exclusion of more substantial things, must inevitably degenerate. By itself it is injurious: it encourages people to forget that something else is wanted, and promotes a superficial self-contented way of looking at all things, of despising difficulties, and overlooking the force of objections. It nourishes the delusion that we have only to communicate truths, not to discover them; that our knowledge needs no increase except in the number of those who participate in it. This indifference to real learning is so great that the very meritorious project of a library of translations, which certainly did not begin with books of a very profound character, met with no support. The consequence is, that we have not half a dozen books which will bear critical examination, or which we are not ashamed of before Protestants and foreigners; and we contribute nothing to the literature of the Church. Lingard's *History of England* has been of more use to us than anything that has since been written; it was so far superior to the books that preceded it—to Hume, who could not be trusted, and to Henry, whom nobody could read—

that all educated men were obliged to use it, and thus became accustomed to the Catholic statement of the subject. It is to this day a tower of strength to us. Its deficiencies are so notorious, that it is quite the fashion to complain of them; and yet nobody has shown himself able to correct them. A single serious treatise of theology or philosophy or history, if merely as a proof that we have somebody who understands such things, would be of more value than almost all the flimsy publications of Catholic book-sellers for the last ten years. Now, though our writers are capable of better things, and though this mode of writing is sanctioned by great examples, and almost imposed on us by circumstances, yet it is our interest and duty to let nothing prevent us from endeavouring to supply its deficiencies.

The great object of our literary efforts ought to be to break down that Protestant tradition which pervades all the literature, serious as well as popular, and enchains all the intellect, of the country; which meets us at every turn, and often forces us into an antagonistic extreme. For, in the absence of a solid literature of our own, we are generally compelled to meet objections by simple negation and contradiction, and by arguing against each particular error on the assumption that the contrary is true. Where there is nothing to fall back upon, no basis of operations, no Catholic literature and traditions of equal weight and standing and consistency to refer to in argument, it is a natural consequence that we should blindly run into extremes, adopt any view and any argument that helps to refute the proposition we are opposing, and have recourse to hasty statements and solutions, which seem safe because they sound well to pious ears, but which really lead to greater difficulties, and expose Catholics to very unpleasant rejoinders. We have a noteworthy example of this in a neighbouring country, where a party of Catholic apologists are for ever answering the falsehoods of an infidel press with statements almost as startling and equally unscrupulous. Perhaps the worst sign of our own imperfection is the want of sensibility to the lessons this spectacle should teach us. We have a Helot perpetually drunk before our eyes, and are hardly moved to a suitable disgust at the hideous sight. Unfortunately there are others upon whom it is not lost, and who know how to avail themselves of it with lamentable effect.

Nothing can be better adapted to raise the character of our

literature than the Reviews; and, considering the state of things we have described, it is to them we must chiefly look for improvement: it is for them to point out deficiencies, and to indicate and to promote the remedy.

Last summer *The Tablet* published a letter, in which the Catholic body was informed that our chief Review could not continue to appear in the state to which it was reduced; and that the editor proposed to resign his charge into other hands, if a successor could be found fitted for the task. This announcement scarcely excited either surprise or regret: it was no secret that the means were wanting for keeping up the character of the Review in the manner desired by its conductors and its readers, and by very many Catholics besides. Not long after, the *Weekly Register* told us that no change had taken place in the management; it is therefore certain that the recent numbers have been prepared under the same auspices which presided over the better days of the Review, when it held among Catholics and Protestants a high and honourable position. Whilst the conductors are still the same, whose competency has been so clearly proved, the public from whom they might expect support has greatly increased, and the addition to the number of writers whose contributions would be extremely valuable has been in proportion still greater. The expectations of the public and the means of satisfying them have risen, yet the Review has declined. Though there is now amongst us an amount of literary ability sufficient, if concentrated, to constitute a first-rate journal, and an educated public quite large enough to support it, yet the writers as well as the readers of the only Catholic Quarterly have fallen off to such an extent that it cannot maintain itself without showing signals of distress. How comes it that, together with such a growth of resources and of legitimate claims, there should be such a diminution of performance? The problem is the more curious, that the deplorable state of things is the consequence of no controversy, of no competition —at least, within the limits of the Catholic body. Whilst the Review has been permitted to censure and attack with impunity, nobody has attacked or desired to injure it; and, what is most remarkable, nobody has profited by its decline. This is the really significant circumstance, that there has been no compensation; it is a dead loss to the Catholics in England. That infidel publication which is the most ably conducted Quarterly in the country, after swallowing up large sums of money for many years, is still unable to subsist without considerable subsidies, and has no difficulty in obtaining them; but an appeal to English Catholics for such assistance as was given to their Review at its commencement seems to have been unsuccessful. Is this apathy to be explained by the hypothesis that Catholics prefer the ability of Protestant organs to the orthodoxy of their own, and are content to read nothing more edifying than the *Edinburgh* or *Westminster*? The true explanation, we rather think, will be found in the history of the Review itself.

If we compare our days with the period when it was started, more than twenty years ago, it is obvious that times are so much altered as necessarily to affect the character and aim of a publication which should attempt to be now what it was then, the organ of the English and Irish Catholics. A consciousness of this, by the way, has been shown in the circumstance that a series of articles has appeared with the acknowledged object of modifying and correcting the views of Lingard, one of the early patrons of the Review. But, in reality, it has not adapted itself to the progress of things. Times have changed, and it has not changed with them.

It is, if we mistake not, to that very increase among Catholics, which ought to have enriched the Review, that its decline is to be ascribed. The narrow ground which it was forced to occupy at a time when our literature was in its infancy afforded no space for an increase of range. New ideas and wants arose, which had not been thought of at first, which, as it never enlarged its horizon, it never succeeded in satisfying. Instead of leading, it has fallen behind the march of Catholic thought in England, and has given little aid in keeping pace with it abroad. Not only did many eminent men continue unattached to it, and deprived of encouragement and of an opening for their studies, but it did not always succeed in competing with Protestant periodicals for the services of Catholic writers. Judged by the interests of the Review, this was a serious defect; for the Catholics generally it was a real calamity. This exclusiveness obliged other organs of the Catholic press to occupy the positions which were neglected; and forced them, where opposition was not intended and competition impossible, into a sort of involuntary antagonism. The ideas which were excluded—we will not say proscribed—by the Quarterly, whose voice was too weak to cause an echo, had to obtain a hearing in other places, where a different tone prevailed. It was of more importance to supply its deficiencies than to promote its influence; and the attempt to make up for its exclusive character almost inevitably assumed the appearance of an exclusiveness of another kind.

Thus, in restricting its own sphere, the *Dublin Review* soon looked with an increasing jealousy upon all who did not accept the same limitations; and the elements which were not yet brought into perfect harmony amongst us assumed, in the periodical press, the semblance of discord. This was the more to be regretted, that it was not seriously the case. Differences such as subsist amongst us, founded upon questions of personal influence, and nourished by immaturity of thought and knowledge, though they may have the venom, have neither the permanence nor even the dignity of disputes on principle. But no great question of principle has in our day divided the English Catholics.

Parallel with this increasing deficiency with regard to ourselves, another soon grew up in respect of the Protestant world. The attention of the *Dublin Review* was from the first concentrated upon the Oxford Movement. The party of which the *British Critic* was the mouthpiece was intellectually the most important in the Established Church, and the one with which controversy was most called for and most likely to avail. But since that day great changes have ensued. New schools have risen into importance, already strong in numbers, and far more formidable in point of talent; and all the learning of misbelieving foreigners is made to contribute to their support. The ablest English Quarterly derives its inspiration from Germany, the ablest Weekly from France; and the American Unitarians have a visible influence upon a portion of the Press. With these new adversaries, armed with new and unexpected weapons, the Review has hardly attempted to wage what would certainly be an unequal war. It has not kept pace with the intellectual movement of the country. It has been hampered by its own traditions. It has neglected to draw the attention of its readers to the things which it is most important for them to know, and to inform them of the real secret of the enemy's strength. This omission has led to one most pernicious result. It has encouraged the insane delusion that scientific infidelity is not, like heresy, an antagonist that it behoves Catholics to encounter; that misbelievers and disbelievers must be allowed to fight it out between them, and the dead left to bury their dead; that no danger threatens the Church from that party, and that Catholics have no special duty towards it. People are permitted to imagine that this is no new enemy, that calls for new efforts of polemics or irenics to controvert or to reconcile, and are suffered to indulge the indolent propensity of subsisting on the capital accumulated by their fathers. Why should we be disquieted by the attacks of presumptuous infidels? Is not all this answered in our books? Is not St Thomas good enough for them, or Bellarmine, or Bossuet, or Butler? What need they more? Did not the Crusaders, with bow and battle-axe, conquer Jerusalem? Wherefore waste gunpowder on miserable Hindoos? Thus an Irishman who has taken a bath in the dogdays considers himself provided with cleanness to last him all the year round. With this supine self-confidence, we have neglected to make the vast advance of European learning available to us; and we consequently find ourselves opposed at a far greater disadvantage to our infidel antagonists now than to the Tractarians eighteen or twenty years ago.

The Catholic public has felt convinced that the most important topics would not be found discussed in its chief literary journal, and that hardly any topics would be found discussed in it by the most competent men. We have enlarged upon these circumstances, not by way of disparagement, but for the purpose of explaining a deficiency which nobody disputes. Before a remedy can be applied the cause of the disease must be ascertained; on the other hand, it is a sign neither of good policy nor of self-respect to betray the wants of one's own party without showing at the same time the prospect and the means of relieving them. In this case, the object of our wishes will not be questioned, we apprehend, by any of our readers.

All Catholics would be proud of a Review worthy to uphold their cause and to command the respect and attention of Protestants. We are impatient of that reproach of inferiority which we know to be unjust, but which we must bear so long as a large proportion of the literary power which is amongst us has no opportunity of being employed. We wish the knowledge and ideas of the best men in the Catholic body to be the common property of the whole. We want an organ, which shall speak with the authority both of talent and position, to assist us in our self-improvement and in the perpetual contest with the enemies of the Church. In the knowledge and performance of our social duties it cannot assist us; but in politics and literature it is our only resource. It should keep us informed not only of the progress of Catholic learning, but of the position of the Church in other countries, in order that we might learn by the experience of others, and compare it with our own. A Review has space both to state the facts and to point the moral; and we require its protection against the ignorance, the malignity, and the mendacity of the Protestant press. The spectacle of the comparative prosperity of religion in different countries is full of political instruction as well as religious interest. It shows the Catholics of France paying for an unsafe prosperity a price which goes far to deprive them of all influence and public esteem; in Russia it exhibits the hostility of an inflexible system baffling the apparent benevolence of the imperial family towards the Church; and in Naples it displays despotism producing abuses in religion such as we hardly dare allude to, and such as would scarcely be believed if told even of the Muscovite clergy. Nor do democracies afford a more consoling aspect than absolute governments. In Switzerland the tyranny of a radical majority weighs heavily upon the Church; whilst in the United States, exposed to the caprice of a half-civilized population, she is beset with dangers unknown to the Old World. Again, we should observe how in Catholic countries mean governments, by the confiscation of ecclesiastical property, have strengthened religion by diminishing temptation, but have injured the State itself by a revolutionary measure; how, since the Belgian revolution, the Dutch Catholics have obtained a freedom they hardly know how to use, whilst in Belgium they are losing the advantages of their victory, and have escaped a Protestant domination only to become the victims of their liberal allies. Most satisfactory of all perhaps we should find the condition of the Church in Prussia, where, in a position nearly resembling our own, the Catholics possess far greater power; and in Austria, where, in laborious conflict with long-cherished customs and with her own traditions, she is acquiring an independence which will transform the empire. With all these things it would be well if we were more familiar, and were more able to follow and sympathize with the contests which are everywhere waging for the freedom and the progress of religion.

If we had been led by the contemplation of the Church in other countries, as well as other times, to draw the inferences to which it irresistibly leads; to understand that democracy is no friend to religion, and that despotism either oppresses or corrupts it; that representative institutions are the protection of the Church in Protestant States, and in Catholic States too frequently her scourge; and that she has more to fear from political than from religious systems—we should possess some criterion of our own by which to judge political affairs, and should have obtained some basis of political principles. If this had not been unfortunately neglected, a sound tone might have been created; we might have learnt to consider more than interests, and a regard might have been kept alive for higher ideas, which is easily lost in the midst of continual strife.

Formerly the Catholics of England were accustomed and content to suffer, when their principles exposed them to terrible penalties. Their resolution was not shaken by the prospect of petty relief; only when a great change approached, and hopes of total emancipation came to be entertained, they accommodated their conduct to circumstances, and sided, contrary to every tradition, with the party which, for no principle, but for purposes of its own, temporarily supported their claims. Hope had more power over us than fear. Since then we have lived from hand to mouth, contemptuous of the morrow. But though the season has arrived when the system of adaptation and the alliance, which would have been ignoble but for the imperiousness of O'Connell, is no longer necessary or excusable, we have yet to learn the wisdom and confidence of a new position. Vices may take the place of virtues in critical moments. There is some general truth in Royer-Collard's panegyric of a famous statesman: "He was ignorant and brutal. These two virtues were the saving of France." But the day comes when these qualities are exhibited with less propriety, and when it is a relief to submit to the habits and precepts of ordinary times. We are, politically, still in a state of transition. If we no longer borrow our doctrines from the system of a party, we are hardly yet conscious of any of our own. Our querulous murmurs, petty skirmishing, and vexatious grievance-hunting, are supported by no consistent plan, by no higher purpose. We have quitted our old ranks, but have not set up a banner of our own, and incur some of the risks of those who have no colour to show.

We have our hierarchy, in spite of the law of the land; we ought to acknowledge our principles, in defiance of its prejudices. English Catholics have, indeed, few opportunities of political action, and little occasion of educating themselves for it. But this is precisely the want which it beseems the gravity of a Quarterly Review to supply.

We believe we can discern in that instinctive jealousy with which many Catholics regard the efforts of government to promote education—a jealousy for which we, at least, should be unwilling to admit no deeper cause than that to which it is generally referred—some reason to hope that they will be among the first to understand and to resist the encroachments with which we are threatened in other departments of the State. We alone have something which cannot be sacrificed to its purposes, in which we cannot suffer control. We trust that the principle of resistance to the increasing power of the State over the nation, which is the secret of true liberty, will find amongst Catholics, in political as well as religious matters, its most determined adherents. But it requires more political sagacity and experience than are common in a country where such dangers are new, to detect in the measures of government all the consequences of the principle on which they are based. For the heathen and revolutionary system of compulsion for the public good, of the greatest happiness of the greatest number, by which the whole is distinct from the several parts, and is preferred to them, and by which an abstraction reigns supreme over each individual, has already taken root amongst us. But this is a point on which we shall not learn wisdom from our Protestant contemporaries, and on which it would be well to have a teacher of our own.

Still more do we need a guide, an example, and an authority in literature; and this would be the great purpose which a Review could accomplish. The literary inferiority of Catholics is due to the absence of the will, not of the power to excel. Where they are inferior it is because they do not feel the value and the dignity of the pursuit. The contempt and indifference with which knowledge is often regarded, soon engender aversion and dread. The studies which Catholics neglect are cultivated by others; and if not made to serve the Church, are inevitably used to injure her. Our inferiority is the penalty of our indolence. At the Revolution, as at the Reformation, the literature and science of the day had completely severed themselves from religion. At both periods learning had suddenly advanced, and important discoveries had been made, in which Catholics had had no part. They were almost completely excluded from the intellectual movement of the age; and the hostility of religion and learning, which one party was interested in proclaiming, was foolishly acquiesced in by the other. In the nineteenth century, as in the sixteenth, the lost ground was recovered by the same means—by claiming for the Church the principle of scientific investigation which seemed to threaten her, and binding to her service the force with which she was attacked. This was the great idea expressed by Copernicus in his dedication to Paul III. He knew well, he said, the contempt with which his discoveries would be received by those who play among philosophers the part of drones amongst bees; and if he considered his own comfort, he would communicate them privately, like Pythagoras, to his disciples. But he confidently commits them to the protection of the Pope himself, whose cause they cannot but serve, in spite of the clamour they may at first excite. This was the answer of a great ecclesiastic to the *Epistolae Obscurorum Virorum*, and to the popular scoffs of an illiterate clergy. In the same way, and in the same proud spirit of confidence in the virtue of real science as an auxiliary of true religion, the revival of the nineteenth century has been accomplished. Yet the tradition of those hundred years of the intellectual as well as political degradation of religion, from the time of Fénelon and Noris to Schlegel and de Maistre, has not yet lost all its power. There are many venerable people who still refuse to travel by steam; and there are many who cannot reconcile themselves to the alliance of the Church with that secular science which they have accustomed themselves to consider her foe. The confidence with which the men of science have asserted that religion is opposed to it, has promoted an awe of falsehood and a distrust of the power of truth. The phantom of the eighteenth century pursues many Catholics, and makes them look with suspicion upon the policy which has proved itself the best safeguard of religion.

The necessity of waging this double contest, at once with those who are of little faith and with those who have none at all—with those who for the sake of religion fear science, and with the followers of science who despise religion—is the fruitful cause of so much scandal and vexation in the Church. The devil must be equally gratified with the zeal of either party; for they equally serve his purpose, by confirming the fatal notion of the incompatibility of faith and reason. In reality this pretence of antagonism is on neither side sincere. Solicitude for religion is merely a pretext for opposition to the free course of scientific research, which threatens, not the authority of the Church, but the precarious influence of individuals. The growth of knowledge cannot in the long run be detrimental to religion; but it renders impossible the usurpation of authority by teachers who defend their own false opinions under pretence of defending the faith which they dishonour by their artifices. Such men by their narrow-minded indolence are the advocates of mental lethargy and repression, whether maintained by an inquisition such as ruined the intellectual service of religion in Spain, or by a well-organized police such as has silenced it with the significant applause of a Catholic party in France: and when they find that their influence is lessened because all men are not their dupes, instead of acknowledging that the old conflict of doctrine must be decided by the sword of science, and that the urgency of the case requires them to mend their slovenly ways, they content themselves with denouncing those who, by refusing to share in their dishonest practice, make it the more conspicuous and the more unavailing. They impute to others the evils they themselves have caused, and do not see that the progress of error and unbelief is their own work. Partly afraid of the truth, and partly ashamed of it, they want to shelter their own ignorance by preserving that of others. But religion is not served by denying facts, or by denouncing those who proclaim them. A fire is not put out by a policeman's whistle, nor a thief taken by the cry of "Stop thief!" Truth is not the exclusive possession of the ignorant; the sun does not shine only for the blind. Authority can only condemn error; its vitality is not destroyed until it is refuted.

One of the fruits of this system is mendacity. Ignorance can only be defended by falsehood; every artifice is deemed lawful; a little fraud becomes a necessary ingredient in controversy. Hence means which only the most worthless of her adversaries have the baseness still to use are sometimes pressed into the service of the Church by those who have not the candour or the courage to adopt that method of defence by which alone success is ultimately infallible.

The one thing needful at the present day, when science has made such progress, and has so much perfected its methods as to be far more powerful, whether for friendship or enmity, than ever before in the history of the Church, is to accept it as her necessary and trusty ally. It became hostile to Catholicism only when they had rejected it. Nothing else can save religion from the twin dangers of unbelief and superstition. "Nihil veritas erubescit nisi solummodo abscondi."[1] ("Truth is only ashamed of concealment.") The common reluctance on the part of Catholics to consent to the results of science indicates as much a defect of faith as of knowledge. We are bound to see that the laws of true reasoning and of historical criticism are not tampered with; it is by them only we can know in their reasonableness and their integrity the doctrines which have been revealed and developed in the process of history—"juxta ordinatissimam dispositionem temporum", says the (IV) Council of Lateran. We have to apply to this inquiry only the methods which are developed in the pursuit of other sciences: hence there is something in the progress of all learning with which it is almost sacrilegious, or at least suicidal, to interfere in the name of religion. Nothing can be more insane or more pernicious than to insist on immediate practical advantages, on the premature harmony and conciliation of science and faith. How often has the eagerness and presumption which has based the defence of religion on proofs which later discoveries have exploded covered her with the appearance of ridicule! Those who are too impatient to wait till their wine is fermented are rewarded with a particularly nasty draught. Every branch of learning pursued for the sake of its own conclusions will result in the vindication of religion, and in the discomfiture of those who believe in their antagonism. The progress of knowledge is often more beneficial to the cause of religious truth than any professed apology. The controversial interest which formerly prevailed occupies now a very subordinate place in our literature. The old contrasts are no longer so distinctly marked. Whilst Protestantism has lost much of its dogmatic character, rationalism and infidelity have diverted the attention of disputants, and diminished their asperity. Catholics have sometimes been joined by Protest-

[1] Tertullian, *Adversus Valent.*, 3.

ants in the defence of their common points of belief; sometimes they have found the arguments of infidels a powerful auxiliary against heresy.

When the prevailing mood of infidelity arose, it encountered no visible adversary; neither Kant or Goethe nor Hegel found Catholicism or Protestantism either able to resist or ready to protest. The new schools of philosophy had no occasion for animosity against the Christianity which seemed already gone. Here lies the essential practical difference between the infidelity of the eighteenth century and that of the nineteenth. Voltaire and his school resolved to extirpate religion; and all their writings aimed at this single end; they lied, scoffed and blasphemed; against such adversaries there was nothing to be done, and nothing was done. They were not vulnerable by any weapon of controversy; their spirit was one that can only be exorcized by prayer and fasting. But the modern infidels generally look upon Christianity with the serenity of victors; and their indifference to its claims makes them often willing to recognize its merits. Their position towards it was not that of the pagans, who were still attached to the old mythology; but rather that of the Neoplatonists, such as Porphyry. Those philosophers did not deny that Christianity taught truths, but that it possessed the whole truth; they did not attack its doctrine because it was false, but because it claimed to be divine. In detail they were often full of admiration for it. So there are many amongst our contemporaries who will admit almost anything except the divine character of the Church, and object to nothing in Christianity excepting Christ. Having no religion, and recognizing in history only its human aspect, they highly appreciate all that has been achieved by natural means in the pursuit of a supernatural end. In place of religious zeal, the motive of their life is the desire of scientific truth. Men of this stamp can be answered with no subterfuge; they must be beaten with their own weapons. In encountering them we have a great advantage, which fails us in conflict with Protestant theology. They assail us in the name of science; but they submit to the authority to which they appeal. They are, at least the best of them, sincere in their arguments, without the malice or the guilt of apostasy. Their objections are frequently a sign of their real love of truth; for there are many points on which they are very imperfectly answered by that system of Catholic polemics which has grown up since the Reformation in conflicts with another description of opponent. A fortress proof against battering-ram and catapult needs new defences against Lancaster guns. It has been the great benefit of the rise of the new learned infidelity that it has greatly raised the character and increased the influence of Catholic learning.

The strongest recommendation of true science is the effect it has had in the hands of infidels themselves. When Lingard's *History* appeared, a much better case had been established for the mediaeval Church, and her character and influence had been spoken of abroad by learned men who were not Catholics with more favour than he thought he could manifest, or his readers would accept. It is in history, the branch of learning which has most suffered from the perversions of Protestants, that the principle of impartial inquiry has achieved the greatest results. In the hands of strangers, if not of enemies, it has fought our battles better than we have ever fought them ourselves. If there were no Catholics to use it, the progress of learning would result in the justification of the temporal human part of the history of the Church. All the lies of the Protestants of the sixteenth century are being rapidly refuted by their descendants of the nineteenth. If Catholics only furnish materials for the defence of the Church, there are others who will be sure to use them. A really scientifically learned work, written without any religious interest, helps the truth in spite of its author; whilst a superficial apology will do little or no good, and probably some harm, in spite of the zeal and good intention with which it is written. We have no right to be jealous of an instrument which in the hands of our enemies has turned against them, and forced them like Balaam to bear witness to the truth. The impartiality of scientific research is our surest ally if we adopt it, and if we reject it is sure to cover us with confusion. Its first fruits, the first sign that it has prevailed, will be an intelligent tolerance of error, combined with a consciousness of the limits of our knowledge. We must have confidence in the power of argument and reason to give victory to truth. An error, like a disease, must be brought to a crisis; it must be developed by argument, not smothered. With every undeveloped error, some truth is lost. In order that it may do its part of good in the world, and aid in promoting truth, it must be helped on to its logical results, and made to show itself in all its deformity.

The mere statement of the claims of science, and of its present character, is enough to indicate how far we are from really accepting it, and how great are the services that might now be performed by a Review that kept aloof from none of the intellectual or social problems which occupy the world. In insisting on a high standard of learning and criticism as the great object of a Catholic Quarterly, we have had also our own interest in view; for though our movements are in a more humble sphere, yet we are sensible that so long as this desideratum is not supplied, our efforts must be very imperfect, if not fruitless. We recognize and act upon a principle which is not within the province of a journal such as ours to bring to supremacy. We have no space or opportunity to set up a theory of all that Catholic politics and literature ought to be, or to give sufficient examples of it. This is the privilege of others. We can only give conclusions which we have not always room to prove, and which ought to require no proof, and proceed upon a system which we cannot for ever be explaining and recommending. We are therefore necessarily exposed to perpetual misinterpretation. Nobody will judge us by the criterion which alone we admit, and which we wish to apply to others. In proportion as the *Dublin Review* has fallen short of the position we desire to assign it, our own position has become unnatural and difficult to maintain. When a Review is established answering in some measure to our ideal description, it will be a great benefit to the Catholics in general, but more especially a boon to us; for it will enable us fairly to pursue our proper ends, and occupy our legitimate place: and therefore we need scarcely say how glad we are to hear that a new arrangement is on the point of taking place, and that an infusion of young blood is likely to give new vitality to our old and respected Review. Without any feelings of envy, and renouncing the idea of competition, we shall cordially hail the appearance of a worthy representative of our intellectual culture, and shall anxiously look for the announcement of wider views and an enlarged plan. The great question has hitherto been, not *what* principle shall prevail, but whether principles shall prevail at all. We are not alive to censure in particulars where we know that our fundamental ideas are not admitted. Our premises are denied, it is idle to defend our conclusions. The discussion of a point of learning is superfluous and hopeless where no respect for the freedom and authority of learning exists; all such controversies have generally a very subordinate and contemptible character. In this respect, therefore, we have nothing to modify. But we wish it to be distinctly understood that the *Rambler* is not a theological Review, and that we do not design to treat questions of theology, or to transgress that line which separates secular from religious knowledge. The principle of independent inquiry, within the bounds, and for the promotion, of the Catholic faith, it is our pride and our duty to maintain; the more because the obloquy we thereby incur shows how urgently such advocacy is needed. Speaking for no party ourselves we naturally excite the dislike of all partisans. Doubtless we shall incense many soothing prejudices and contradict many cherished opinions, and shall continue objects of aversion to all who are more attached to persons than to principles, to habits than to ideas. Whoever defies an idol must be prepared for the clamour of its worshippers; nobody who assails folly and error is surprised at being answered by a falsehood or an insult. These, as we well know, besides personal imputations and calumnies which it is infamy to utter, are the fit and natural weapons of many adversaries of the ideas which we defend. But though every human enterprise in which there is no proportion between the trouble and the chance of success is wisely abandoned, it is not so with the higher service to which our efforts are devoted. They are supported by a more powerful encouragement than the immediate prospect of success. Under all circumstances we shall keep in mind the example of forbearance set us by a great and holy man on a very memorable occasion. In that remarkable autobiography, which seems to have been the great obstacle to his canonization, Cardinal Bellarmine relates how he returned good for evil to the Pope, who, after highly applauding his learning, had ended by putting his best work on the Index.[1] The edition of the Vulgate which Sixtus V had prepared,

[1] "Anno 1591, cum Gregorjus XIV cogitaret quid agendum esset de Bibliis a Sixto V editis, in quibus erant permulta perperam mutata, non deerant viri graves qui censerent ea Biblia esse publice prohibenda; sed N. (Bellarminus) coram pontifice demonstravit Biblia illa non esse prohibenda, sed esse ita corrigenda, ut salvo honore Sixti V Pontificis Biblia illa emendata proderentur, quod fieret si quam celerrime tollerentur quae male mutata erant, et Biblia recuderentur sub nomine ejusdem, Sixti, et addita praefatione, qua significaretur, in prima editione Sixti prae festinatione irrepsisse aliqua errata vel typographorum, vel aliorum; et sic N. (Bellarminus) reddidit Sixto Pontifici bona pro malis. Sixtus enim propter illam propositionem de dominio Papae directo in totum orbem posuit controversias

was found after his death to be so full of faults that some were for prohibiting it altogether. But, in order to save his memory from this indignity, Bellarmine undertook to correct it himself; showing how little he was moved by the intemperate attack of which he had been the object, and exhibiting an instance of generosity and forgiveness of injury which deserves to be remembered.

---

ejus in Indice librorum prohibitorum donec corrigerentur: sed ipso mortuo sacra Ritum Congregatio jussit deleri libro indicis nomen illius. Placuit consilium N. (Bellarmini) Gregorio Pontifici" (*Vita Ven. Card. Rob. Bellarmini, S. J., quam ipsemet scripsit*, p. 22).

X

THE CATHOLIC ACADEMY[1]

THE appearance of this polished and eloquent discourse claims our attention on account both of the distinguished personage whose views on a very important question are expressed in it, and of the occasion and the purpose for which it has been written. From the beginning of the century a Society has existed in Rome, to which for more than thirty years the Cardinal has belonged, and whose labours are dedicated to the illustration and defence of the Catholic and Christian faith. Founded at a period which witnessed the almost unexampled combination of persecution with the prostration of religion, and in which weakness and coldness of faith united with the most bitter animosity to afflict the Church, the Catholic Academy has been one of the instruments of the revival of a better spirit, and has enjoyed the countenance and support of many of the most eminent persons in Rome. The object of its members has been to promote the reconciliation of religion with the advancement of learning, and at the same time to initiate in these studies the educated youth of the city. If we may draw an inference from what we hear and from what we do not hear, it would appear that the last of these objects has been more successfully attained than the former. The good that has been done seems to be principally confined to the society of the capital, and the printed acts of the Academy have not become widely known. So many reasons for this are at once suggested by the circumstances of place and time that have surrounded the institution, that it by no means follows either that the plan is radically defective, or that it would not achieve greater success and wider utility in another sphere.

Dwellers on the outer frontier of Catholicity, surrounded by an atmosphere of unbelief and hatred, and exposed to dangers both of attack and temptation against which the Church has always

[1] His Excellency Cardinal Wiseman, *Inaugural Discourse Pronounced at the First Meeting of the Academy of the Christian Religion*, June 29, 1861; Burns & Lambert. [From *The Rambler*, vol. v, Sept. 1861.]

endeavoured to protect those who live in the centre of the fold, we might be justified in envying our brethren in the Eternal City an institution which, as a safeguard, we require more than they do, and which we have, in some respects, greater means of using as a weapon for the intellectual support of religion. In no country would there be a better field for its action, or more ample conditions of success, than in England.

The object of the Academy is not controversy; it does not address itself to those who are out of the Church, but seeks to digest and assimilate the results of scientific inquiry, and to maintain the harmony of sacred and secular science. The Catholic body amongst us has especial need of a work of this kind, and possesses the materials for it; and it is one of the greatest misfortunes that no such combination for a definite purpose subsists among its members. It is a consequence of the very advantages of our position, though it detracts from them, that the elements which are united in the Catholic Church in England are of such various derivation that we do not possess even common prejudices, the very lowest symbol of unity; and the bonds of faith and charity are not always powerful enough to secure either the necessary agreement, or the freedom of discussion, or the tolerance of differences enjoined by the well-known Protestant maxim which Catholics have consecrated by attributing it to St Augustine. The cultivation of literature in a spirit inseparable from Catholicism, and on a basis which no Catholic refuses to acknowledge, is perhaps at the present time the only way that could be devised of reconciling, in a higher harmony, divergencies which proceed partly from the contrast of early education and partly from an imperfect and unequal conception of the present position of the world and its works in relation to the Church. It is an enterprise, which, in the beginning, contradicts no opinions, and in the end must reconcile them. When, therefore, Cardinal Wiseman undertook to establish in England a branch of the Roman Academia, he planted it in a soil prepared to receive it, where it has a vast opportunity of doing good, and in which, if it is only understood, it ought surely to thrive.

The Inaugural Address consists of two parts. The topic of the first portion is the idea that the Church has encouraged and adopted all that was most admirable in the secular movements of different ages, and has enriched herself with the best treasures of the outer world. Unchanged herself, she received and retained the impression of all that touched her. "Such has been the Church in every age. Whatever is good, whatever virtuous, whatever useful in the world, at every time, she has allowed to leave its seal upon her outward form."[1] There are some considerations suggested by this passage which it is important that the Society to whom it was addressed should not overlook.

In speaking of the temporal action of the Church, or of her success in spiritual things, it behoves us to define and to distinguish, and to eschew generalities which disguise a truism or conceal a fallacy. The divine purpose, which is her essential mission, she can never fail to fulfil; and in pursuing it, she has accomplished innumerable secondary and collateral ends, and, while teaching the transitoriness of all earthly things, has conferred immeasurable temporal benefits on mankind. But it is not this that constitutes her proper vocation, and it is not just to dwell on this in supporting her claims to the reverence and gratitude of those who do not believe in her. In comparison with the higher duty she discharges for the world, the encouragement at one time or another of literature or agriculture, of art or of commerce—merits which are primary subject of consideration in discussing polytheism or Islamism—are altogether insignificant and imperceptible. Nor, if this human point of view is put prominently forward, would it be fair to say that men are under obligation to her for all the things which constitute terrestrial advantages, or that in every thing in which religion can affect civilization, Christianity surpasses every other system in a degree at all proportionate to her intrinsic superiority. In these matters her influence has not been always alike, nor her policy consistent or always in harmony with her nature. It belongs both to her character and her interest to require the development of literature and science for the performance of her own great intellectual work, and to promote political liberty because it is the condition of her social action. There were times when she did both these things, and then a time came when that part of her influence was abandoned to those who were not of her. Then the two great forces, freedom and knowledge, were converted into weapons of assault; they seemed to justify while they avenged the neglect, and, in spite of Protestantism, they prospered better among Protestants than among Catholics. In

[1] p. 20.

England the spirit of political liberty, in Germany the spirit of scientific research, overcame the barriers of religious antagonism, and as it were spontaneously did homage to the Church, and protested against their estrangement from her. Human learning has often been an instrument, but not a source, of hostility to religious truth. It has served it in spite of great outward difficulties, of a long separation, and of a heavy bribe, and it has acted as a corrosive to all false religions ever since the time when the gods of Greece began to wane before the rising brightness of her philosophy. And this is a character of the present age which we are hardly accustomed to consider, and which we have not used as we might for the advantage of our cause, that learning has acquired an authority before which even religious rancour must give way, and is an ally to the Church that would be more powerful if it was more trusted. So long as its alliance is not claimed by the truth, it is certain to be used against it.

Cain.   I never
         As yet have bowed unto my father's God; . . .
         Why should I bow to thee? . . .
Lucifer.   He who bows not to Him has bowed to me.
Cain.   But I will bend to neither.
Lucifer.   Nevertheless,
         Thou art my worshipper; not worshipping
         Him makes thee mine the same.

The great error of the day, in reference to the position of the Church between science and policy, is that Catholics, men of science, and politicians are inclined to recognize only one authority. In the domain of learning, as well as in civil society, there is an authority distinct from that of the Church, and not derived from it, and we are bound in each sphere to render to Caesar the things that are Caesar's. There can be no conflict of duties or of allegiance between them, except inasmuch as one of them abandons its true purpose, the realization of right in the civil order, and the discovery of truth in the intellectual. Political wrong and scientific error are the only sources of hostility in either department to the Church, and this is met by the restoration of right or of truth, that is, by the advancement of learning or of politics. If we neglect this, we are ourselves responsible for disputes and conflicts in which the right may not be on our side, and we shall have no criterion to apply but which we believe to be the interest of religion; forgetful that a true principle is more sacred than the most precious interest, and that the consideration of interests is suspended where the obligation of principles is acknowledged. The danger comes from those who consider only one thing, and take their stand either exclusively on the secular or on the ecclesiastical ground. All that we demand is that science should be true to its own method, and the State to its own principle, and beyond this the interests of religion require no protection.

From the second part of the discourse we learn that this and no other is the spirit in which the English branch of the Academy has been instituted. The Cardinal exhorts its members to follow "without anxiety, but with an unflinching eye, the progress of science". The perversion of learning alone must be resisted and exposed, but the spirit of investigation is to be humbly, joyfully and gratefully accepted; and the day will hereafter come when men will look back with admiration upon its works, and upon the important part it has had in promoting the progress of religion. The rise of this new and mighty power, due in great measure to the lull of religious controversy at a time when Protestantism had lost its vigour, and the Church seemed to be absorbed in her internal troubles, is justly compared to the revival of ancient learning in the fifteenth century. That, too, was a new and powerful element in civilization which might and did accomplish both great evil and great good, and which was viewed by some with confidence, by others with alarm, and by many with satisfaction as a welcome auxiliary against the Church. Then as now, in presence of a somewhat similar phenomenon, the Catholic world resolved itself into three sections. There was a large party, who knew that all the resources of criticism and learning belong to the armoury of the Church, and who greeted in the new discoveries accession to her strength. This was the feeling that for a hundred years uniformly prevailed in Rome; it was shared by the most illustrious prelates of that age, by Ximenes, by Lindanus, by John Dalberg, by Gioberti, and by the two great Cardinals of the House of Borromeo; and the author of this discourse, whose name is in the foremost rank of those who have combined elegant literature with severer learning, naturally ranges himself on their side. Then there was a party in which it would be unjust to place Erasmus, because his satire of the clergy that so readily accepted the doctrines and precepts of the Reformation was at least redeemed by his dogmatical opposition to Luther, who, seeing nothing but paganism in antiquity, followed it instead of Christianity, and beheld in the clergy a set of ignorant and selfish conspirators against knowledge. Such were the authors of the *Epistolae Obscurorum Virorum*, who, although the publication of the first volume preceded by two years the outbreak at Wittenberg, became Protestants for the most part, and whose ridicule of the priesthood was in intention and in reality an insult to the Church. Lastly, there were those whose conduct justified the attacks it drew down on them, who feared and deprecated the introduction of the new studies. But few men of note in the Church shared these views, and it is not probable that they will find favour in the Academy, if the traditions of its inauguration and the spirit of its founder survive in it. Much may be expected from the pursuit of literature by a body of earnest Catholics, who are impressed with the conviction that the harmony of religion with profane learning cannot be made, but may be found; who regard scientific investigation as a suspension rather than an occasion of controversy; and who understand that an important preliminary towards encountering with success the anti-Catholic prejudices of scientific men is the suppression of an unscientific tendency among Catholics. For knowledge, says Thomas à Kempis, has no enemy but the ignorant. "Truth," says John of Salisbury, "becomes obscured as often by the negligence of those who profess it as by the assaults of error."

When Frederick Schlegel concludes his *Philosophy of History* with a chapter on the general restoration as the predominant sign of the age, he touches upon the great point of resemblance between the present time and the period of the Renaissance. For the development of the scientific spirit has proceeded from a revival of forgotten knowledge as comprehensive as that of the fifteenth century, and by the resurrection of a buried world whose influence is as profound and as important for civilization as that of the ancients. The antiquity that was brought to light was partly Christian and partly pagan, but it was a period of civilization deformed by corruption, and of Christianity beset with heresy. The influence of the revival corresponded to this character. It was in the first place aesthetical rather than practical. We still associate with the word *Renaissance* above all the notion of art. The Humanism of Italy was a study of beauty, of enjoyment, of refinement; what was beautiful was placed before what was true. The bearing of these pursuits on actual life was generally injurious. We need not point for proofs of this to the erotic literature of the fifteenth century, or to the demoralization of the courts; they are most visible in the ideas of politics and of government which were derived from the ancients. The example which the history of their states supplies is only a lesson of false republicanism, generating in its corruption an unlimited despotism. Even the increased insight into the early period of the Church, though it modified and enriched the scholastic teaching, promoted only an archaeological and fragmentary, not a complete, historical study of Christianity. The connection with the immediate past was interrupted, and the continuity of institutions, the genesis and succession of ideas, were completely lost sight of. A time came when the ancients were the only authorities, antiquity the only study, and when the thousand years that separated its restoration from its fall were as little understood as the classic world had been during the supremacy of the barbarians who destroyed it.

The spirit of investigation was rapidly absorbed by the passion of formal elegance. At one moment it appeared as though it would be otherwise, but the first efforts of criticism, eminently characteristic of the times, were not followed up. In the middle of the fifteenth century, Valla wrote a treatise to prove that the Donation of Constantine could not be genuine, and in this he easily succeeded, though it was reserved for our time to ascertain the origin of the forgery which gave Ireland to England, and the Indies to Spain. The result of Valla's skill was merely negative. Finding in the period whose records he had studied no authority for existence of the pontifical state, and certain of the spuriousness of its most famous title-deed, he conceived that the whole fabric of the temporal power was a usurpation, and insisted that it ought to be surrendered. "Men say", he writes, "that the Church is at war with Bologna or Perugia. It is not the Church but the Pope, of his own ambition, that is at war with the towns." But the pope was not alarmed by the Humanists, and Valla obtained promotion at Rome; but here a serious charge was brought against him, and he was denounced to the ecclesiastical authorities for that, puffed up with pride, and abandoning himself to an unseemly and hazardous temerity of statement, he taught that Tarquin the Proud was not the son of Tarquin the First. This was in the early period of the movement. It was not by criticism, but by frivolity and free-thinking, that the classical scholars did harm to religion; their researches were dangerous neither to faith nor to credulity. It was in anticipation of such a change, which did not, however, actually ensue for centuries, that Pius II uttered a cautious saying, which is not in the tone of mediaeval Catholicism: "Christianam fidem, si miraculis non esset approbata, honestate sua recipi debuisse."

That anticipated innovation, which the classic revival failed to introduce, constitutes the essence of the corresponding revival of the nineteenth century. The most comprehensive and penetrating influence, which marks our age, as the Renaissance the age of Medici, and which is the strongest current that counteracts that which set in before the Revolution, is the Restoration of mediaeval learning. Its tendency is in almost every respect exactly contrary to the other revival. The ignorance of the Middle Ages, during the period between the Reformation and the Revolution, amounted to physical blindness. The remains of mediaeval art were not even curiosities. An intelligent traveller could visit Cologne, describe several of the smaller churches, and declare that there was nothing else worth seeing in the place, though the Cathedral towered above the city with that irregular and striking outline which all remember who saw it before the works were commenced for its completion. The great Gothic churches, it has been truly said, had to be discovered again, like Pompeii, after lying hid for ages. The mediaeval world was a palimpsest that had yet to be deciphered. Its history formed no part of education, and it was the great business of governments to obliterate all the traces it had left upon the State. Even in theology those who must faithfully preserve its forms were not likely to study its history. Its languages were extinct among the learned, and no man knew that they possessed a vast treasure of poetry, epic poets who could compare with Dante, and ballads such as in the hands of Percy and of Scott introduced a new era in the literature of England. The poetry of the romantic school, the art of the foreign pre-Raphaelites and of the Goths, are the most familiar outward tokens of a revolution immeasurably more profound and more extensive. The mediaeval revival involves a return to continuity in social institutions, to tradition in ideas, and to history in science. The presiding impulse in this pursuit is the opposite of that which guided the Humanists. It is not the charm of beauty or of eloquence, for that is the privilege of antiquity, nor a delight in idle enjoyment, or even the cultivation of the mind; for in these things the Middle Ages have incomparably less to offer. We go back to the Middle Ages in order to know the realities of the past. The poverty of forms, the repulsiveness of style, restrict the inquiry to that which is alone of actual value, the facts of medieval life. For the civilization of that age, its ideas, habits, and institutions, possess a direct importance for us who are its descendants and its heirs. Our society is the development of that of the medieval chivalry; our civilization is founded on theirs. Our national instincts and character were moulded by them. Our modern history has been occupied in destroying or modifying what they have left us; it is filled with the contest between medieval facts which were no longer understood, and ancient ideas which have no basis in real life. The classical revival was the conquest of an unknown world. The medieval revival is a pilgrimage to the homes of our fathers, to the graves of

> The dead but sceptred sovereigns, who still rule
> Our spirits from their urns.

The heroes of the revival of letters went forth in the spirit of adventure, and are of the same type as the men who discovered a new world in the age that had revived the old. Ours is a spirit of reverence and piety, as of men returning after a long migration to places hallowed by the recollections and the traditions of their race.

The aim, then, of these studies is not beauty or pleasure, but truth and instruction. Their method therefore is critical, and their form is historical: for it is less the works of individuals that attract us than the general ideas and deeds of those days. A classical scholar has such a rich literary world before him that he may be anything but a historian. But it is only for the historian that the bulk of medieval literature has any attractions. Not only, therefore, does the study of the Middle Ages promote the historical art, and a stricter critical method than the classics, but it has given rise to a totally new feature in the moral sciences, the supremacy of the means over the end. Many problems about which men have disputed and fought naturally resolve themselves when considered as history. Numberless systems and opinions lose their absolute character, and appear in their conditional relative truth when the mode of their formation and the modifying influences of time and place are understood. Ecclesiastical history is filled with conflicts which a knowledge of the history of development would have made superfluous, and in all other branches of learning history is a peacemaker and a destroyer of idols. Until the Middle Ages were reinstated in their proper position, the scientific study of history was in its infancy; for the omission of a large and essential portion of the subject gave the rest a merely antiquarian interest, as a curiosity, not as part of a single and consecutive process to which the present belongs.

Religion has been served by this phase of literature in two ways. The least important is the rehabilitation of the ages of faith by its enthusiastic admirers, like Count de Montalembert and Mr Digby. What is of far greater consequence is the establishment of those fixed rules, and of that disinterested spirit of investigation, which rigidly exclude the influence of prejudice, interest or passion, pursue not the application of truth so much as its discovery, and apply to moral science something of the patient self-denial and closeness of observation which belong to natural philosophy. If these qualities have been rare till lately in modern times, they were not unknown to an earlier age. Bishop Adelbold of Utrecht begins his life of St Henry with the following definition of the duties of a historian: "Scriptor veritatem tenere nequit nisi haec quatuor aut potenter devitaverit, aut aliquatenus a mente deposuerit: odium et carnalem dilectationem, invidiam et infernalem adulationem. Odium enim et invidia bene gesta aut omnino tacent, aut dicendo transcurrunt, aut calumniose transmutant. E contra male gesta dicunt, dilatant et amplificant. Carnalis autem affectio et infernalis adulatio, quae male gesta sunt, scientes ignorant et ignorantiam simulantes, veritatem occultant; bene gesta autem, placere quaerentes, spaciose dicunt, et plus justo magnificant. Sic per haec quatuor, aut in bene gestis aut in male gestis veritas evanescit, falsitas superducto colore nitescit. Spiritualis autem dilectio veritatis amica, nec male gesta celat, nec bene gesta pompose dilatat; sciens quia et male gesta saepe prosunt ad correctionem, et bene gesta frequenter obsunt, dum ducuntur in elationem."

We gather from the names that have reached us of the members of the Academy that the moral sciences will be chiefly cultivated, for in the others few of course are really competent, and the interference of amateurs can only lead to a demoralizing shallowness. It will be well if this is so, for those branches of learning are of more vital importance than physical science. They touch religion and morals more directly, and influence more powerfully men of cultivated minds, whilst illiterate persons are more easily struck with the facts and influences of the material world. It is, we presume, only for the facility of illustration, and perhaps from old reminiscences, that so many of the Cardinal's instances are drawn from geology and the physical creation. These sciences are of subordinate utility to religion, even when cultivated in a religious spirit; and when directed against religion, have not the same force as the sciences which are connected with her origin, her history and her doctrine.

Much will depend on the regulations which are to guide the Academy, and on the changes which will become necessary in order to adapt the original rule to new wants. As learning does not flourish even with protection so well as with freedom, no institution without some degree of self-government can retain an enduring vitality. The less it resembles a manufacture, and the more it obtains the character of an organism, the better it will fare. In the constitution of the French Consulate, the majority of the senate was originally appointed by the government, and it then completed its numbers by election. We know not whether this is the plan adopted by the Academy, but we have no doubt that the original list has been drawn up in conformity with the rule which was followed on that occasion. "We put aside", said the Third Consul, "all personal affection in our choice, and considered nothing but the merit, the reputation, and the services of the candidates."

The Academy of the *Lincei*, which is alluded to in the discourse, may supply some useful hints to the new association. Their historian, the Duke of Cezi, tells us that they were different from the philosophers of our day; for they considered religion not only the first of all sciences, but as the only safe basis, the principle and true source of all knowledge—an idea which is better expressed by a writer already quoted: "Quia tam sensus quam ratio humana frequenter errat ad intelligentiam veritatis primum fundamentum locavit in fide."[1] Amongst their rules we applaud the following: "Non minus sedulo et hoc observent ne Lynce-orum quemquam aut voce aut calamo perstringant, quorum tamen opiniones, ut amplectantur, non ob id adstringantur, cum cuilibet proprii genii, et ingenii modulo in hujuscemodi discip-linis philosophari, et ad veritatem quam proxime collimare libere linquatur." It is easy to see that the *Lincei* were not the party who were disposed to give up religion and theology for the sake of an elegant Latinity.

The purpose of an Academy has been defined to be to advance learning, whilst the mission of a university is to communicate it. This distinction, founded on the necessity of a fixed and finished matter for the instruction of youth, and of a direct religious con-trol which the growth of science will not bear, did not originally subsist. The first Academy was also the first university, and the name of the spot where Plato lectured on the banks of Cephisus has survived in both. We should think little of a university which did nothing for the enrichment of literature, and produced men, and not books. But it has been usual for academies to addict them-selves more exclusively to their own special function of acquiring, not of distributing knowledge; and it is not one of the least meri-torious points in the Society of which we are speaking, that it returns in some manner to the old plan, and proposes to extend to younger men the advantage of witnessing its proceeding and gathering something of its spirit. The majority of the academies which sprung up in every part of Italy, in consequence of the num-ber of universities and the deficiency of public employment, can supply no useful example for the serious and practical design which the Cardinal is endeavouring to realize amongst us. The scheme of Leibniz for the Academy of Berlin, the purpose of which was to advance at the same time the public good, learning and religion ("un point des plus importants serait aussi la pro-pagation de la foi par les sciences"), is the only one with which we are acquainted that combines such exalted ends.

[1] *Metalog.*, iv, 41.

XI

POLITICAL CAUSES OF THE
AMERICAN REVOLUTION[1]

A T the time of the utmost degradation of the Athenian
democracy, when the commanders at Arginusae were
condemned by an unconstitutional decree, and Socrates
alone upheld the sanctity of the law, the people, says Xenophon,
cried out that it was monstrous to prevent them from doing whatever they pleased.[2] A few years later the archonship of Euclides
witnessed the restoration of the old constitution, by which the
liberty, though not the power, of Athens was revived and prolonged for ages; and the palladium of the new settlement was the
provision that no decree of the council or of the people should be
permitted to overrule any existing law.[3]

The fate of every democracy, of every government based on
the sovereignty of the people, depends on the choice it makes
between these opposite principles, absolute power on the one
hand, and on the other the restraints of legality and the authority
of tradition. It must stand or fall according to its choice, whether
to give the supremacy to the law or to the will of the people;
whether to constitute a moral association maintained by duty, or
a physical one kept together by force. Republics offer, in this respect, a strict analogy with monarchies which are also either absolute or organic, either governed by law, and therefore constitutional, or by a will which, being the source, cannot be the object
of laws, and is therefore despotic. But in their mode of growth, in
the direction in which they gravitate, they are directly contrary
to each other. Democracy tends naturally to realize its principle,
the sovereignty of the people, and to remove all limits and conditions of its exercise; whilst monarchy tends to surround itself with

[1] *The Rambler*, vol. v, May 1861, pp. 17–61.

[2] τὸ δὲ πλῆθος ἐβόα δεινὸν εἶναι εἰ μή τις ἐάσει τὸν δῆμον πράττειν ὃ ἂν βούληται. *Hellen*,
i, 7, 12.

[3] ψήφισμα δὲ μηδὲν μήτε βουλῆς μήτε δήμου νόμου κυριώτερον εἶναι. Andocides, *de Myst.*
(*Or. Att.*, ed. Dobson, i, 259.)

such conditions. In one instance force yields to right; in the other might prevails over law. The resistance of the king is gradually overcome by those who resist and seek to share his power; in a democracy the power is already in the hands of those who seek to subvert and to abolish the law. The process of subversion is consequently irresistible, and far more rapid.

They differ, therefore, not only in the direction, but in the principle of their development. The organization of a constitutional monarchy is the work of opposing powers, interests, and opinions, by which the monarch is deprived of his exclusive authority, and the throne is surrounded with, and guarded by, political institutions. In a purely popular government this antagonism of forces does not exist, for all power is united in the same sovereign; subject and citizen are one, and there is no external power that can enforce the surrender of a part of the supreme authority, or establish a security against its abuse. The elements of organization are wanting. If not obtained at starting they will not naturally spring up. They have no germs in the system. Hence monarchy grows more free, in obedience to the laws of its existence, whilst democracy becomes more arbitrary. The people is induced less easily than the king to abdicate the plenitude of its power, because it has not only the right of might on its side, but that which comes from possession, and the absence of a prior claimant. The only antagonism that can arise is that of contending parties and interests in the sovereign community, the condition of whose existence is that it should be homogeneous. These separate interests can protect themselves only by setting bounds to the power of the majority; and to this the majority cannot be compelled, or consistently persuaded, to consent. It would be a surrender of the direct authority of the people, and of the principle that in every political community authority must be commensurate with power.

Infirma minoris
Vox cedat numeri, parvaque in parte quiescat.

"La pluralité", says Pascal, "est la meilleure voie, parcequ'elle est visible, et qu'elle a la force pour se faire obéir; cependant c'est l'avis des moins habiles." The minority can have no permanent security against the oppression of preponderating numbers, or against the government which these numbers control, and the moment will inevitably come when separation will be preferred to submission. When the classes which compose the majority and the minority are not defined with local distinctness, but are mingled together throughout the country, the remedy is found in emigration; and it was thus that many of the ancient Mediterranean states, and some of the chief American colonies, took their rise. But when the opposite interests are grouped together, so as to be separated not only politically, but geographically, there will ensue a territorial disruption of the state, developed with a rapidity and certainty proportioned to the degree of local corporate organization that exists in the community. It cannot, in the long run, be prevented by the majority, which is made up of many future, contingent minorities, all secretly sympathizing with the seceders, and unwilling to compel them to remain, because they dread to perpetuate the tyranny of majorities. The strict principle of popular sovereignty must therefore lead to the destruction of the state that adopts it, unless it sacrifices itself by concession.

The greatest of all modern republics has given the most complete example of the truth of this law. The dispute between absolute and limited power, between centralization and self-government, has been, like that between privilege and prerogative in England, the substance of the constitutional history of the United States. This is the argument which confers on the whole period that intervenes between the convention of 1787 and the election of Mr Davis in 1861 an almost epic unity. It is this problem that has supplied the impulse to the political progress of the United States, that underlies all the great questions that have agitated the Union, and bestows on them all their constitutional importance. It has recurred in many forms, but on each occasion the solution has failed, and the decision has been avoided. Hence the American government is justly termed a system of compromises, that is to say, an inconsistent system. It is not founded, like the old governments of Europe, on tradition, nor on principles, like those which have followed the French Revolution; but on a series of mutual concessions, and momentary suspensions of war between opposite principles, neither of which could prevail. Necessarily, as the country grew more populous, and the population more extended, as the various interests grew in importance, and the various parties in internal strength, as new regions contrasting with each other in all things in which the influence of nature and the condition of society bear upon political life were formed into states, the conflict grew into vaster proportions and greater intensity, each opinion became more stubborn and unyielding, compromise was more difficult, and the peril to the Union increased.

Viewed in the light of recent events, the history of the American Republic is intelligible and singularly instructive. For the dissolution of the Union is no accidental or hasty or violent proceeding, but the normal and inevitable result of a long course of events, which trace their origin to the constitution itself. There we find the germs of the disunion that have taken seventy years to ripen, the beginning of an antagonism which constantly asserted itself and could never be reconciled, until the differences widened into a breach.

The convention which sat at Philadelphia in 1787, for the purpose of substituting a permanent constitution in the place of the confederacy, which had been formed to resist the arms of England, but which had broken down in the first years of peace, was not a very numerous body, but it included the most eminent men of America. It is astounding to observe the political wisdom, and still more the political foresight, which their deliberations exhibit. Franklin, indeed, appears to have been the only very foolish man among them, and his colleagues seem to have been aware of it. Washington presided, but he exercised very little influence upon the assembly, in which there were men who far exceeded him in intellectual power. Adams and Jefferson were in Europe, and the absence of the latter is conspicuous in the debates and in the remarkable work which issued from them. For it is a most striking thing that the views of pure democracy, which we are accustomed to associate with American politics, were almost entirely unrepresented in that convention. Far from being the product of a democratic revolution, and of an opposition to English institutions, the constitution of the United States was the result of a powerful reaction against democracy, and in favour of the traditions of the mother country. On this point nearly all the leading statesmen were agreed, and no contradiction was given to such speeches as the following. Madison said: "In all cases where a majority are united by a common interest or passion, the rights of the minority are in danger.

What motives are to restrain them? A prudent regard to the maxim, that honesty is the best policy, is found by experience to be as little regarded by bodies of men as by individuals. Respect for character is always diminished in proportion to the number among whom the blame or praise is to be divided. Conscience, the only remaining tie, is known to be inadequate in individuals; in large numbers little is to be expected from it."[1]

Mr Sherman opposed the election by the people, "insisting that it ought to be by the State legislatures. The people immediately should have as little to do as may be about the government."

Mr Gerry said: "The evils we experience flow from the excess of democracy. The people do not want virtue, but are the dupes of pretended patriots . . . He had been too republican heretofore; he was still, however, republican, but had been taught by experience the danger of the levelling spirit." Mr Mason "admitted that we had been too democratic, but was afraid we should incautiously run into the opposite extreme". Mr Randolph observed "that the general object was to provide a cure for the evils under which the United States laboured; that, in tracing these evils to their origin, every man had found it in the turbulence and follies of democracy: that some check, therefore, was to be sought for against this tendency of our government."[2]

Mr Wilson, speaking in 1787, as if with the experience of the seventy years that followed, said: "Despotism comes on mankind in different shapes; sometimes in an executive, sometimes in a military one. Is there no danger of a legislative despotism? Theory and practice both proclaim it. If the legislative authority be not restrained, there can be neither liberty nor stability."[3] "However the legislative power may be formed", said Gouverneur Morris, the most conservative man in the convention, "it will, if disposed, be able to ruin the country."[4]

Still stronger was the language of Alexander Hamilton: "If government is in the hands of the few, they will tyrannize over the many; if in the hands of the many, they will tyrannize over the few. It ought to be in the hands of both, and they should be separated. This separation must be permanent. Representation alone will not do; demagogues will generally prevail; and, if separated, they will need a mutual check. This check is a mon-

[1] Madison's *Reports*, 162.   [2] ibid., 135, 138.   [3] ibid., 196.
[4] ibid., 433.

arch . . . The Monarch must have proportional strength. He ought to be hereditary, and to have so much power that it will not be his interest to risk much to acquire more . . . Those who mean to form a solid republican government ought to proceed to the confines of another government . . . But if we incline too much to democracy, we shall soon shoot into a monarchy."[1] "He acknowledged himself not to think favourably of republican government, but addressed his remarks to those who did think favourably of it, in order to prevail on them to tone their government as high as possible."[2] Soon after, in the New York convention for the adoption of the constitution, he said: "It has been observed that a pure democracy, if it were practicable, would be the most perfect government. Experience has proved that no position in politics is more false than this. The ancient democracies, in which the people themselves deliberated, never possessed one feature of good government. Their very character was tyranny."[3]

Hamilton's opinions were in favour of monarchy, though he despaired of introducing it into America. He constantly held up the British constitution as the only guide and model; and Jefferson has recorded his conversations, which show how strong his convictions were. Adams had said that the English government might, if reformed, be made excellent; Hamilton paused and said: "Purge it of its corruption, and give to its popular branch equality of representation, and it would become an impracticable government; as it stands at present, with all its supposed defects, it is the most perfect government which ever existed." And on another occasion he declared to Jefferson: "I own it is my own opinion . . . that the present government is not that which will answer the ends of society, by giving stability and protection to its rights; and that it will probably be found expedient to go into the British form."[4]

In his great speech on the constitution, he spoke with equal decision: "He had no scruple in declaring, supported as he was by the opinion of so many of the wise and good, that the British government was the best in the world, and that he doubted much whether anything short of it would do in America . . . As to the executive, it seemed to be admitted that no good one

[1] Hamilton's *Works*, ii, 413-417.   [2] Madison's *Reports*, 244.
[3] Hamilton's *Works*, ii, 440.   [4] Rayner's *Life of Jefferson*, 268.

could be established on republican principles. Was not this giving up the merits of the question? For can there be a good government without a good executive? The English model was the only good one on this subject . . . We ought to go as far, in order to attain stability and permanency, as republican principles will admit."[1]

Mr Dickinson "wished the Senate to consist of the most distinguished characters—distinguished for their rank in life and their weight of property, and bearing as strong a likeness to the British House of Lords as possible."[2]

Mr Pickney, of South Carolina, said: "Much has been said of the constitution of Great Britain. I will confess that I believe it to be the best constitution in existence; but, at the same time, I am confident that it is one that will not or cannot be introduced into this country for many centuries."[3]

The question on which the founders of the constitution really differed, and which has ever since divided, and at last dissolved the Union, was to determine how far the rights of the States were merged in the federal power, and how far they retained their independence. The problem arose chiefly upon the mode in which the central Congress was to be elected. If the people voted by numbers or by electoral districts, the less populous States must entirely disappear. If the States, and not the population, were represented, the necessary unity could never be obtained, and all the evils of the old confederation would be perpetuated. "The knot", wrote Madison in 1831, "felt as the Gordian one, was the question between the larger and the smaller States, on the rule of voting."

There was a general apprehension on the part of the smaller States that they would be reduced to subjection by the rest. Not that any great specific differences separated the different States; for though the question of the regulation of commerce and of slavery afterwards renewed the dispute, yet interests were so different from what they have since become, and so differently distributed, that there is little analogy, excepting in principle, with later contests; what was then a dispute on a general principle has since been envenomed by the great interests and great passions which have become involved in it. South Carolina, which at that time looked forward to a rapid increase by immi-

[1] Madison's *Reports*, 202.   [2] ibid., 166.   [3] ibid., 234.

gration, took part with the larger States on behalf of the central power; and Charles Pickney presented a plan of a constitution which nearly resembled that which was ultimately adopted. The chief subject of discussion was the Virginia plan, presented by Edmund Randolph, in opposition to which the small State of New Jersey introduced another plan founded on the centrifugal or State-rights principle. The object of this party was to confirm the sovereignty of the several States, and to surrender as little as possible to the federal government. This feeling was expressed by Mr Bedford: "Is there no difference of interests, no rivalship of commerce, of manufacturers? Will not these large States crush the small ones, whenever they stand in the way of their ambitions or interested views?"[1]

"The State legislatures," said Colonel Mason, "ought to have some means of defending themselves against encroachments of the national government. In every other department we have studiously endeavoured to provide for its self-defence. Shall we leave the States alone unprovided with means for this purpose."[2]

These speakers may have been good or bad politicians, they were certainly good prophets. They were nearly balanced in numbers, and surpassed in ability, by the centralizing party. Madison, at that time under the powerful influence of Hamilton, and a federalist, but who afterwards was carried by Jefferson into the democratic camp, occupied an uncertain intermediate position. A note preserved in Washington's handwriting records: "Mr Madison thinks an individual independence of the States utterly irreconcilable with their aggregate sovereignty, and that a consolidation of the whole into a simple republic would be as inexpedient as it is unattainable."[3]

In convention he said: "Any government for the United States formed on the supposed practicability of using force against the unconstitutional proceedings of the States would prove as visionary and fallacious as the government of Congress."[4]

The consistent Federalists went farther: "Too much attachment", said Mr Read, "is betrayed to the State governments. We

---

[1] Madison's *Reports*, 173.   [2] ibid., 170.
[3] William's *Statesman's Manual*, 268.   [4] *Reports*, 171.

must look beyond their continuance; a national government must soon, of necessity, swallow them all up."[1]

Two years before the meeting of the convention, in 1785, Jay, the very type of a Federalist, wrote: "It is my first wish to see the United States assume and merit the character of one great nation, whose territory is divided into different States merely for more convenient government."

Alexander Hamilton went farther than all his colleagues. He had taken no part in the early debates, when he brought forward an elaborate plan of his own; the most characteristic features of which are, that the State governments are to be altogether superseded; their governors to be appointed by the general government, with a veto on all State laws, and the president is to hold office on good behaviour. An executive, elected for life, but personally responsible, made the nearest possible approach to an elective monarchy; and it was with a view to this all but monarchical constitution that he designed to destroy the independence of the States. This scheme was not adopted as the basis of discussion. "He has been praised," said Mr Johnson, "by all, but supported by none." Hamilton's speech is very imperfectly reported, but his own sketch, the notes from which he spoke, are preserved, and outweigh, in depth and in originality of thought, all that we have ever heard or read of American oratory. He left Philadelphia shortly after, and continued absent many weeks; but there can be no doubt that the spirit of his speech greatly influenced the subsequent deliberations. "He was convinced," he said, "that no amendment of the confederation, leaving the States in possession of their sovereignty, could answer the purpose ... The general power, whatever be its form, if it preserves itself, must swallow up the State powers ... They are not necessary for any of the great purposes of commerce, revenue or agriculture. Subordinate authorities, he was aware, would be necessary. There must be distinct tribunals; corporations for local purposes ... By an abolition of the States, he meant that no boundary could be drawn between the national and State legislatures; that the former must therefore have indefinite authority. If it were limited at all, the rivalship of the States would gradually subvert it ... As States, he thought they ought to be abolished.

[1] Madison's *Reports*, 163.

But he admitted the necessity of leaving in them subordinate jurisdictions."[1]

This policy could be justified only on the presumption that when all State authorities should disappear before a great central power, the democratic principles, against which the founders of the constitution were contending, would be entirely overcome. But in this Hamilton's hopes were not fulfilled. The democratic principles acquired new force, the spirit of the convention did not long survive, and then a strong federal authority became the greatest of all dangers to the opinions and institutions which he advocated. It became the institute of the popular will instead of its barrier; the organ of arbitrary power instead of a security against it. There was a fundamental error and contradiction in Hamilton's system. The end at which he aimed was the best, but he sought it by means radically wrong, and necessarily ruinous to the cause they were meant to serve. In order to give to the Union the best government it could enjoy, it was necessary to destroy, or rather to ignore, the existing authorities. The people was compelled to return to a political state of nature, irrespective of the government it already possessed, and to assume to itself powers of which there were constitutional administrators. No adaptation of existing facts to the ideal was possible. They required to be entirely sacrificed to the new design. All political rights, authorities and powers must be restored to the masses, before such a scheme could be carried into effect. For the most conservative and anti-democratic government the most revolutionary basis was sought. These objections were urged against all plans inconsistent with the independence of the several States by Luther Martin, Attorney General for Maryland.

"He conceived," he said, "that the people of the States, having already vested their powers in their respective legislatures, could not resume them without a dissolution of their governments . . . To resort to the citizens at large for their sanction to a new government will be throwing them back into a state of nature; the dissolution of the State governments is involved in the nature of the process; the people have no right to do this without the consent of those to whom they have delegated their power for State purposes."[2] And in his report to the convention of Maryland of the proceedings out of which the constitution arose, he said:

[1] Madison's *Reports*, 201, 212.   [2] ibid., 218, 248.

"If we, contrary to the purpose for which we were intrusted, considering ourselves as master-builders, too proud to amend our original government, should demolish it entirely, and erect a new system of our own, a short time might show the new system as defective as the old, perhaps more so. Should a convention be found necessary again, if the members thereof, acting upon the same principles, instead of amending and correcting its defects, should demolish that entirely, and bring forward a third system, that also might soon be found no better than either of the former; and thus we might always remain young in government, and always suffering the inconveniences of an incorrect imperfect system."[1]

It is very remarkable that, while the Federalists, headed by Hamilton and Madison, advocated, for the soundest and wisest object, opinions which have since been fatal to the Union, by furnishing the democratic party with an irresistible instrument and consequently an irresistible temptation, Martin supported a policy in reality far more conservative, although his opinions were more revolutionary, and although he quoted as political authorities writers such as Price and Priestley. The controversy, although identical in substance with that which has at last destroyed the Union, was so different in form, and consequently in its bearings, that the position of the contending parties became inverted as their interests or their principles predominated. The result of this great constitutional debate was that the States were represented as units in the Senate, and the people according to numbers in the House. This was the first of the three great compromises. The others were the laws by which the regulation of commerce was made over to the central power, and the slave-trade was tolerated for only twenty years. On these two questions, the regulation of commerce and the extension of slavery, the interests afterwards grew more divided, and it is by them that the preservation of the Union has been constantly called in question. This was not felt at first, when Jay wrote that "Providence has been pleased to give this one connected country to one united people; a people descended from the same ancestors, speaking the same language, professing the same religion, attached to the same principles of government, very similar in their manners and customs."[2] The weakening of all these bonds

[1] Elliot's *Debates*, i, 350.   [2] *Federalist*, 2.

of union gradually brought on the calamities which are described by Madison in another number of the same publication:
"A landed interest, a manufacturing interest, a mercantile interest, a moneyed interest with many lesser interests, grow up of
necessity in civilized nations, and divide them into different
classes, actuated by different sentiments and views. The regulation of these varying and interfering interests forms the principal task of modern legislation, and involves the spirit of party
and faction in the necessary and ordinary operations of the government . . . When a majority is included in a faction, the form
of popular government enables it to sacrifice to its ruling passion
or interest both the public good and the rights of other citizens
. . . It is of great importance in a republic not only to guard the
society against the oppression of its rulers, but to guard one part
of the society against the injustice of the other part. Different
interests necessarily exist in different classes of citizens. If a
majority be united by common interests, the rights of the minority will be insecure. There are but two methods of providing
against this evil: the one by creating a will in the community
independent of the majority, that is, of the society itself; the
other, by comprehending in the society so many separate descriptions of citizens as will render one unjust combination of a
majority of the whole very improbable, if not impracticable . . .
In a free government, the security for civil rights must be the
same as that for religious rights. It consists, in the one case, in
the multiplicity of interests, and in the other in the multiplicity
of sects."[1] That Madison should have given so absurd a reason
for security in the new constitution can be explained only by
the fact that he was writing to recommend it as it was, and had
to make the best of his case. It had been Hamilton's earnest endeavour to establish that security for right which Madison considers peculiar to monarchy, an authority which should not be
the organ of the majority. "'Tis essential there should be a permanent will in a community . . . The principle chiefly to be established is this, that there must be a permanent will . . . There
ought to be a principle in government capable of resisting the
popular current."[2]

This is precisely what Judge Story means when he says: "I
would say in a republican government the fundamental truth is,

that the minority have indisputable and inalienable rights; that the majority are not every thing, and the minority nothing; that the people may not do what they please."

Webster thought the same, but he took a sanguine view of actual facts when he said: "It is another principle, equally true and certain, and, according to my judgment of things, equally important, that the people often limit themselves. They set bounds to their own power. They have chosen to secure the institutions which they establish against the sudden impulses of mere majorities."[1]

Channing was nearer the truth when he wrote: "The doctrine that the majority ought to govern passes with the multitude as an intuition, and they have never thought how far it is to be modified in practice, and how far the application of it ought to be controlled by other principles."[2]

In reality, the total absence of a provision of this kind, which should raise up a law above the arbitrary will of the people, and prevent it from being sovereign, led the greatest of the statesmen who sat in the convention to despair of the success and permanence of their work. Jefferson informs us that it was so with Washington: "Washington had not a firm confidence in the durability of our government. Washington was influenced by the belief that we must at length end in something like a British constitution."

Hamilton, who by his writing contributed more than any other man to the adoption of the constitution, declared in the convention that "no man's ideas were more remote from the plan than his own," and he explained what he thought of the kind of security that had been obtained: "Gentlemen say that we need to be rescued from the democracy. But what the means proposed? A democratic Assembly is to be checked by a democratic Senate, and both these by a democratic chief magistrate."[3]

"A large and well organized republic", he said, "can scarcely lose its liberty from any other cause than that of anarchy, to which a contempt of the laws is the high-road . . . A sacred respect for the constitutional law is the vital principle, the sustaining energy of a free government . . . The instruments by which it must act are either the authority of the laws, or force. If the first be destroyed, the last must be substituted; and when this becomes

[1] *Works*, vi, 225.   [2] *Memoir*, 417.   [3] *Works*, ii, 415.

the ordinary instrument of government, there is an end to liberty."[1]

His anticipations may be gathered from the following passages: "A good administration will conciliate the confidence and affection of the people, and perhaps enable the government to acquire more consistency than the proposed constitution seems to promise for so great a country. It may then triumph altogether over the State governments, and reduce them to an entire subordination, dividing the larger States into smaller districts . . . If this should not be the case, in the course of a few years it is probable that the contests about the boundaries of power between the particular governments and the general government, and the momentum of the larger States in such contests, will produce a dissolution of the Union. This, after all, seems to be the most likely result . . . The probable evil is, that the general government will be too dependent on the State legislatures, too much governed by their prejudices, and too obsequious to their humours; that the States, with every power in their hands, will make encroachments on the national authority, till the Union is weakened and dissolved."[2]

The result has justified the fears of Hamilton, and the course of events has been that which he predicted. Democratic opinions, which he had so earnestly combated, gained ground rapidly during the French revolutionary period. Jefferson, who, even at the time of the Declaration of Independence, which was his work, entertained views resembling those of Rousseau and Paine, and sought the source of freedom in the abstract rights of man, returned from France with his mind full of the doctrines of equality and popular sovereignty. By the defeat of Adams in the contest for the presidency, he carried these principles to power, and altered the nature of the American government. As the Federalists interpreted and administered the constitution, under Washington and Adams, the executive was, what Hamilton intended it to be, supreme in great measure over the popular will. Against this predominance the State legislatures were the only counterpoise, and accordingly the democratic party, which was the creature of Jefferson, vehemently defended their rights as a means of giving power to the people. In apparent contradiction, but in real accordance with this, and upon the same theory

[1] *Works*, vii, 164.   [2] ibid., ii, 421, 450.

of the direct sovereignty of the people, Jefferson, when he was elected, denied the right of the States to control the action of the executive. Regarding the President as the representative of a power wholly arbitrary, he admitted no limits to its exercise. He held himself bound to obey the popular will even against his own opinions, and to allow of no resistance to it. He acted as the helpless tool of the majority, and the absolute ruler of the minority, as endowed with despotic power, but without free will.

It is of this principle of the revolution that Tocqueville says: "Les gouvernements qu'elle a fondées sont plus fragiles, il est vrai, mais cent fois plus puissants qu'aucun de ceux qu'elle a renversés; fragiles et puissants par les mêmes causes."[1]

Hence Jefferson's determined aversion to every authority which could oppose or restrain the will of the sovereign people, especially to the State legislatures and to the judiciary. Speaking of an occasion in which the judges had acted with independence, Hildreth says: "Jefferson was not a little vexed at this proceeding, which served, indeed, to confirm his strong prejudices against judges and courts. To him, indeed, they were doubly objects of hatred, as instruments of tyranny in the hands of the Federalists, and as obstacles to himself in exercises of power."[2]

His views of government are contained in a paper which is printed in Rayner's life[3] of him. "Governments are republican only in proportion as they embody the will of their people, and execute it . . . Each generation is as independent of the one preceding as that was of all which had gone before. It has, then, like them, a right to choose for itself the form of government it believes most promotive of its own happiness . . . it is for the peace and good of mankind, that a solemn opportunity of doing this, every nineteen or twenty years, should be provided by the constitution . . . The dead have no rights . . . This corporeal globe and everything upon it belongs to its present corporeal inhabitants during their generation . . . That majority, then, has a right to depute representatives to a convention, and to make the constitution which they think will be best for themselves . . . Independence can be trusted nowhere but with the people in mass." With these doctrines Jefferson subverted the republicanism of America, and consequently the Republic itself.

---

[1] *L'ancien Régime et la Révolution*, p. 13.   [2] *History of the U.S.*, vi, 70.
[3] l.c., 378.

Hildreth describes as follows the contest between the two systems, at the time of the accession of Jefferson to power, in 1801: "From the first moment that party lines had been distinctly drawn, the opposition has possessed a numerical majority, against which nothing but the superior energy, intelligence and practical skill of the Federalists, backed by the great and venerable name and towering influence of Washington, had enabled them to maintain for eight years past an arduous and doubtful struggle. The Federal party, with Washington and Hamilton at its head, represented the experience, the prudence, the practical wisdom, the discipline, the conservative reason and instincts of the country. The opposition, headed by Jefferson, expressed its hopes, wishes, theories, many of them enthusiastic and impracticable, more especially its passions, its sympathies and antipathies, its impatience of restraint. The Federalists had their strength in those narrow districts where a concentrated population had produced and contributed to maintain that complexity of institutions, and that reverence for social order, which, in proportion as men are brought into contiguity, become more absolutely necessaries of existence. The ultra-democratical ideas of the opposition prevailed in all that more extensive region in which the dispersion of population, and the despotic authority vested in individuals over families of slaves, kept society in a state of immaturity."[1]

Upon the principle that the majority have no duties, and the minority no rights, that it is lawful to do whatever it is possible to do, measures were to be expected which would oppress most tyrannically the rights and interests of portions of the Union, for whom there was no security and no redress. The apprehension was so great among the Federalists that Hamilton wrote in 1804: "The ill opinion of Jefferson, and jealousy of the ambition of Virginia, is no inconsiderable prop of good principles in that country (New England). But these causes are leading to an opinion that the dismemberment of the Union is expedient."[2]

Jefferson had given the example of such threats, and owed his election to them during his contest for the presidency with Colonel Burr. He wrote to Monroe, February 15, 1801: "If they could have been permitted to pass a law for putting the government into the hands of an officer, they would certainly have pre-

[1] *History of the U.S.*, v, 414.   [2] *Works*, vii, 852.

vented the election. But we thought it best to declare openly and firmly, one and all, that the day such an act passed the middle States would, and that no such usurpation, even for a single day, should be submitted to."

Shortly afterwards a conjunction arose in which Jefferson put his principles into practice in such a way as greatly to increase the alarm of the North-Eastern States. In consequence of Napoleon's Berlin decree and of the British orders in council, he determined to lay an embargo on all American vessels. He sent a pressing message to Congress, and the Senate passed the measure after a four-hours' debate with closed doors. In the House the debate was also secret, but it lasted several days, and was often prolonged far into the night, in the hope of obtaining a division. The Bill was passed December 22, 1807. The public had no voice in the matter; those whom the measure touched most nearly were taken by surprise, and a conspicuous example was given of secrecy and promptitude in a species of government which is not commonly remarkable for these qualities.

The embargo was a heavy blow to the ship-owning States of New England. The others were less affected by it. "The natural situation of this country", says Hamilton, "seems to divide its interests into different classes. There are navigating and non-navigating States. The Northern are properly the navigating States; the Southern appear to possess neither the means nor the spirit of navigation. This difference in situation naturally produces a dissimilarity of interests and views respecting foreign commerce."[1]

Accordingly the law was received in those States with a storm of indignation. Quincey, of Massachusetts, declared in the House: "It would be as unreasonable to undertake to stop the rivers from running into the sea, as to keep the people of New England from the ocean. They did not believe in the constitutionality of any such law. He might be told that the courts had already settled that question. But it was one thing to decide a question before a court of law, and another to decide it before the people."[2]

Even in a juridical point of view the right to make such a law was very doubtful. Story, who first took part in public affairs on this occasion, says: "I have ever considered the embargo a

[1] *Works*, ii, 433.   [2] Hildreth, *History of the U.S.*, vi, 100.

measure which went to the extreme limit of constructive power under the constitution. It stands upon the supreme verge of the constitution."[1]

The doctrine of State-rights, or nullification, which afterwards became so prominent in the hands of the Southern party, was distinctly enunciated on behalf of the North on this occasion. Governor Trumbull, of Connecticut, summoned the legislature to meet, and in his opening address to them he took the ground that, in great emergencies, when the national legislature had been led to overstep its constitutional power, it became the right and duty of the State legislatures "to interpose their protecting shield between the rights and liberties of the people, and the assumed power of the general government".[2]

They went farther and prepared to secede from the Union, and thus gave the example which has been followed, on exactly analogous grounds, by the opposite party. Randolph warned the administration that they were treading fast in the fatal footsteps of Lord North.[3]

John Quincy Adams declared in Congress that there was a determination to secede. "He urged that a continuance of the embargo much longer would certainly be met by forcible resistance, supported by the legislature, and probably by the judiciary of the State . . . Their object was, and had been for several years, a dissolution of the Union, and the establishment of a separate confederation." Twenty years later, when Adams was President, the truth of this statement was impugned. At that time the tables had been turned, and the South was denying the right of Congress to legislate for the exclusive benefit of the North-Eastern States, whilst these were vigorously and profitably supporting the Federal authorities. It was important that they should not be convicted out of their own mouths, and that the doctrine they were opposing should not be shown to have been inaugurated by themselves. Adams therefore published a statement, October 21, 1828, reiterating his original declaration: "The people were constantly instigated to forcible resistance against it, and juries after juries acquitted the violators of it, upon the ground that it was unconstitutional, assumed in the face of a solemn decision of the district court of the United States. A Separation of the Union was openly stimulated in the public

[1] *Life*, i, 185.   [2] *History of the U.S.*, vi, 120.   [3] ibid., vi, 117.

prints, and a convention of delegates of the New England States, to meet at New Haven, was intended and proposed." That this was true is proved by the letters of Story, written at the time: "I was well satisfied," he says, "that such a course would not and could not be borne by New England, and would bring on a direct rebellion . . . The stories here of rebellion in Massachusetts are continually circulating. My own impressions are, that the Junto would awaken it, if they dared; but it will not do . . . A division of the States has been meditated, but I suspect that the public pulse was not sufficiently inflamed . . . I am sorry to perceive the spirit of disaffection in Massachusetts increasing to so high a degree; and I fear that it is stimulated by a desire in a very few ambitious men to dissolve the Union . . . I have my fears when I perceive that the public prints openly advocate a resort to arms to sweep away the present embarrassments of commerce."[1]

It was chiefly due to the influence of Story that the embargo was at length removed, with great reluctance and disgust on the part of the President. "I ascribe all this," he says, "to one pseudo-republican Story."[2] On which Story, who was justly proud of his achievement, remarks, "Pseudo-republican of course I must be, as every one was, in Mr Jefferson's opinion, who dared to venture upon a doubt of his infallibility."[3] In reality Jefferson meant that a man was not a republican who made the interests of the minority prevail against the wish of the majority. His enthusiastic admirer, Professor Tucker, describes very justly and openly his policy in this affair. "If his perseverance in the embargo policy so long, against the wishes and interests of New England, and the mercantile community generally, may seem to afford some contradiction to the self-denying merit here claimed, the answer is, that he therein fulfilled the wishes of a large majority of the people . . . A portion of the community here suffered an evil necessarily incident to the great merit of a republican government, that the will of the majority must prevail."[4]

We have seen that in the case of the embargo, as soon as this democratic theory was acted upon, it called up a corresponding claim of the right of the minority to secede, and that the democratic principle was forced to yield. But secession was not a

[1] *Life*, i, 187. [2] *Correspondence*, iv, 148. [3] *Life*, i, 185.
[4] *Life of Jefferson*, 322.

theory of the constitution, but a remedy against a vicious theory of the constitution. A sounder theory would have avoided the absolutism of the democrats and the necessity for secession. The next great controversy was fought upon this ground. It exhibits an attempt to set up a law against the arbitrary will of the government, and to escape the tyranny of the majority, and the remedy, which was worse than the disease. An ideal of this kind had already been sketched by Hamilton. "This balance between the national and state governments ought to be dwelt on with peculiar attention, as it is of the utmost importance. It forms a double security to the people. If one encroaches on their rights, they will find a powerful protection in the other. Indeed, they will both be prevented from overpassing their constitutional limits, by a certain rivalship which will ever subsist between them."[1] This was also what Mr Dickinson looked forward to when he said in the Convention of 1787: "One source of stability is the double branch of the legislature. The division of the country into distinct States forms the other principal source of stability."[2]

The war with England, and the long suspension of commerce which preceded it, laid the foundations of a manufacturing interest in the United States. Manufactories began to spring up in Pennsylvania, and more slowly in New England. In 1816 a tariff was introduced, bearing a slightly protective character, as it was necessary to accommodate the war prohibitions to peaceful times. It was rather intended to facilitate the period of transition than to protect the new industry; and that interest was still so feeble, and so little affected by the tariff, that Webster, who was already a representative of Massachusetts in Congress, voted against it. It was carried by the coalition of Clay with the South Carolina statesmen, Lowndes and Calhoun, against whom this vote was afterwards a favourite weapon of attack. In the following years the increasing importance of the cultivation of cotton, and the growth of manufactures, placed the Northern and Southern interests in a new position of great divergency. Hamilton had said long before: "The difference of property is already great amongst us. Commerce and industry will still increase the disparity. Your government must meet this state of things, or combinations will, in process of time, undermine your system."[3]

The New England manufacturers were awakened to the ad-

[1] Works, ii, 444.   [2] Madison's Debates, 148.   [3] Elliot's Debates, i, 450.

vantage of protection for their wares. In the memorial of the merchants of Salem, written by Story in 1820, he says: "Nothing can be more obvious than that many of the manufacturers and their friends are attempting, by fallacious statements, founded on an interested policy, or a misguided zeal, or very short-sighted views, to uproot some of the fundamental principles of our revenue policy ... If we are unwilling to receive foreign manufactures, we cannot reasonably suppose that foreign nations will receive our raw materials ... We cannot force them to become buyers when they are not sellers, or to consume our cotton when they cannot pay the price in their own fabrics. We may compel them to use the cotton of the West Indies, or of the Brazils, or of the East Indies." About the same time, May 20, 1820, he writes to Lord Stowell on the same subject: "We are beginning also to become a manufacturing nation; but I am not so much pleased, I am free to confess, with the efforts made to give an artificial stimulus to those establishments in our country ... The example of your great manufacturing cities, apparently the seats of great vices, and great political fermentations, affords no very agreeable contemplation to the statesman or the patriot, or the friend of liberty."[1]

The manufacturers obtained a new tariff in 1824, another was carried by great majorities in 1828, and another in 1832 by a majority of two to one. It is the measure of 1828, which raised the duties on an average to nearly fifty per cent on the value of the imports, that possesses the greatest importance in a constitutional point of view. "To it," says the biographer of Mr Calhoun, "may be traced almost every important incident in our political history since that time, as far as our internal affairs are concerned."[2]

At this time the interests of North and South were perfectly distinct. The South was teeming with agricultural produce, for which there was a great European demand; whilst the industry of the North, unable to compete with European manufacturers, tried to secure the monopoly of the home market. Unlike the course of the same controversy in England, the agriculturists (at least the cotton-growers) desired free trade, because they were exporters; the manufacturers protection, because they could not meet competition. "The question", said Calhoun, "is in reality

[1] *Life*, i, 385.　　[2] *Life of Calhoun*, p. 34.

one between the exporting and non-exporting interests of the country." The exporting interest required the utmost freedom of imports, in order not to barter at a disadvantage. "He must be ignorant of the first principles of commerce, and the policy of Europe, particularly England, who does not see that it is impossible to carry on a trade of such vast extent on any other basis than barter; and that if it were not so carried on, it would not long be tolerated . . . The last remains of our great and once flourishing agriculture must be annihilated in the conflict. In the first place, we will be thrown on the home market, which cannot consume a fourth of our products; and instead of supplying the world, as we would with a free trade, we should be compelled to abandon the cultivation of three-fourths of what we now raise, and receive for the residue whatever the manufacturers—who would then have their policy consummated by the entire possession of our market—might choose to give."[1] It seemed a fulfilment of the prophecy of Mr Lowndes, who, in resisting the adoption of the constitution in South Carolina forty years before, declared that "when this new constitution should be adopted, the sun of the Southern States would set, never to rise again . . . The interest of the Northern States would so predominate as to divest us of any pretensions to the title of a republic."[2] Cobbett, who knew America better than any Englishman of that day, described in his *Political Register* for 1833 the position of these hostile interests in a way which is very much to the point. "All these Southern and Western States are, commercially speaking, closely connected with Birmingham, Sheffield, Manchester, and Leeds . . . they have no such connection with the Northern States, and there is no tie whatsoever to bind them together, except that which is of a mere political nature . . . Here is a natural division of interests, and of interests so powerful, too, as not to be counteracted by any thing that man can do. The heavy duties imposed by the Congress upon British manufactured goods is neither more nor less than so many millions a year taken from the Southern and Western States, and given to the Northern States."[3]

Whilst in England protection benefited one class of the population at the expense of another, in America it was for the advan-

---

[1] Calhoun's *Works*, vi, 12.   [2] Elliot's *Debates*, iv, 272.
[3] *Political Works*, vi, 662.

tage of one part of the country at the expense of another. "Government", said Calhoun, "is to descend from its high appointed duty, and become the agent of a portion of the community to extort, under the guise of protection, tribute from the rest of the community."[1]

Where such a controversy is carried on between opposite classes in the same State, the violence of factions may endanger the government, but they cannot divide the State. But the violence is much greater, the wrong is more keenly felt, the means of resistance are more legitimate and constitutional, where the oppressed party is a sovereign State.

The South had every reason to resist to the utmost a measure which would be so injurious to them. It was opposed to their political as well as to their financial interests. For the tariff, while it impoverished them, enriched the government, and filled the treasury with superfluous gold. Now the Southern statesmen were always opposed to the predominance of the central authority, especially since it lent itself to a policy by which they suffered. They had practical and theoretical objections to it. The increase of the revenue beyond the ordinary wants of the government placed in its hands a tempting and dangerous instrument of influence. Means must be devised for the disposal of these sums, and the means adopted by the advocates of restriction was the execution of public works, by which the people of the different States were bribed to favour the central power. A protective tariff therefore, and international improvement, were the chief points in the policy of the party, which, headed by Henry Clay, sought to strengthen the Union at the expense of the States, and which the South opposed, as both hostile to their interests and as unconstitutional. "It would be in vain to attempt to conceal", wrote Calhoun of the tariff in 1831, "that it has divided the country into two great geographical divisions, and arrayed them against each other, in opinion at least, if not interests also, on some of the most vital of political subjects—on its finance, its commerce, and its industry . . . Nor has the effect of this dangerous conflict ended here. It has not only divided the two sections on the important point already stated, but on the deeper and more dangerous questions, the constitutionality of a protective tariff, and the general principles and theory of the constitution

[1] *Works*, iv, 181.

itself: the stronger, in order to maintain their superiority, giving a construction to the instrument which the other believes would convert the general government, with the total destruction of liberty."[1] "On the great and vital point—the industry of the country, which comprehends almost every interest—the interest of the two great sections is opposed. We want free trade, they restrictions; we want moderate taxes, frugality in the government, economy, accountability, and a rigid application of the public money to the payment of the debt, and to the objects authorized by the constitution. In all these particulars, if we may judge by experience, their views of their interest are precisely the opposite."[2] In 1828 he said of the protective system: "No system can be more efficient to rear up a moneyed aristocracy"; wherein he is again supported by Cobbett, in the well-known saying, uttered five years later, concerning the United States: "It is there the aristocracy of money, the most damned of all aristocracies." South Carolina took the lead in resisting the introduction of the protective system, and being defeated by many votes on the question itself, took its stand on the constitutional right of each sovereign State to arrest by its veto any general legislation of a kind which would be injurious to its particular interests. "The country", said Calhoun, "is now more divided than in 1824, and then more than in 1816. The majority may have increased, but the opposite sides are, beyond dispute, more determined and excited than at any preceding period. Formerly the system was resisted mainly as inexpedient, but now as unconstitutional, unequal, unjust, and oppressive. Then relief was sought exclusively from the general government; but now many, driven to despair, are raising their eyes to the reserved sovereignty of the States as the only refuge."[3] Calhoun was at that time Vice-President of the United States, and without a seat in Congress. The defence of the theory of the constitution devolved therefore upon the senator from South Carolina, General Hayne; and a debate ensued between Hayne and Webster, in January 1830, which is reckoned by Americans the most memorable in the parliamentary history of their country. Hayne declared that he did not contend for the mere right of revolution, but for the right of constitutional resistance; and in reply to Webster's defence of the supreme power, he said: "This I know is a popular

[1] *Works*, vi, 77, 78.   [2] ibid., vi, 31.   [3] ibid., vi, 80.

notion, and it is founded on the idea that as all the States are represented here, nothing can prevail which is not in conformity with the will of the majority; and it is supposed to be a republican maxim, 'that the majority must govern' ... If the will of a majority of Congress is to be the supreme law of the land, it is clear that the constitution is a dead letter, and has utterly failed of the very object for which it was designed—the protection of the rights of the minority ... The whole difference between us consists in this —the gentlemen would make force the only arbiter in all cases of collision between the States and the federal government; I would resort to a peaceful remedy."[1]

Two years later Mr Calhoun succeeded Hayne as senator for South Carolina, and the contest was renewed. After the tariff of 1828 Virginia, Georgia, and North Carolina joined in the recognition of the principle of nullification. When the tariff of 1832 was carried, South Carolina announced that the levying of dues would be resisted in the State. Calhoun defended the nullifying ordinance in the Senate, and in speeches and writings, with arguments which are the very perfection of political truth, and which combine with the realities of modern democracy the theory and the securities of medieval freedom. "The essence of liberty", he said, "comprehends the idea of comprehensible power—that those who make and execute the laws should be controlled by those on whom they operate—that the governed should govern ... No government based on the naked principle that the majority ought to govern, however true the maxim in its proper sense, and under proper restrictions, can preserve its liberty even for a single generation. The history of all has been the same—violence, injustice, and anarchy, succeeded by the government of one, or a few, under which the people seek refuge from the more oppressive despotism of the many ... Stripped of all its covering the naked question is, whether ours is a federal or a consolidated government; a constitutional or absolute one; a government resting ultimately on the solid basis of the sovereignty of the States, or on the unrestrained will of a majority; a form of government, as in all other unlimited ones, in which injustice and violence and force must finally prevail. Let it never be forgotten that, when the majority rules without restriction, the minority is the subject ... Nor is the right of suffrage more

[1] Elliot's *Debates*, iv, 498.

indispensable to enforce the responsibility of the rulers to the ruled, than a federal organization to compel the parts to respect the rights of each other. It requires the united action of both to prevent the abuse of power and oppression, and to constitute really and truly a constitutional government. To supersede either is to convert it in fact, whatever may be its theory, into an absolute government."[1]

In his disquisition on government Calhoun has expounded his theory of a constitution in a manner so profound and so extremely applicable to the politics of the present day, that we regret we can only give a very feeble notion of the argument by the few extracts for which we can make room.

"The powers which it is necessary for government to possess, in order to repress violence and preserve order, cannot execute themselves. They must be administered by men in whom, like others, the individual are stronger than the social feelings. And hence the powers vested in them to prevent injustice, and oppression on the part of others, will, if left unguarded, be by them converted into instruments to oppress the rest of the community. That by which this is prevented, by whatever name called, is what is meant by constitution, in its most comprehensive sense, when applied to government. Having its origin in the same principle of our nature, constitution stands to government as government stands to society; as the end for which government is ordained would be defeated without government, so that for which government is ordained would, in a great measure, be defeated without constitution . . . Constitution is the contrivance of man, while government is of divine ordination . . . Power can only be resisted by power, and tendency by tendency . . . I call the right of suffrage the indispensable and primary principle; for it would be a great and dangerous mistake to suppose, as many do, that it is of itself sufficient to form constitutional governments. To this erroneous opinion may be traced one of the causes why so few attempts to form constitutional governments have succeeded; and why, of the few which have, so small a number had durable existence . . . So far from being of itself sufficient—however well guarded it might be, and however enlightened the people—it would, unaided by other provisions, leave the government as absolute as it would be in the hands of irresponsible rulers, and

[1] *Works*, vi, 32.

with a tendency at least as strong towards oppression and abuse of its powers ... The process may be slow, and much time may be required before a compact, organized majority can be formed; but formed it will be in time, even without preconcert or design, by the sure workings of that principle or constitution of our nature in which government itself originates ... The dominant majority, for the time, would have the same tendency to oppression and abuse of power which, without the right of suffrage, irresponsible rulers would have. No reason, indeed, can be assigned why the latter would abuse their power, which would not apply with equal force to the former ... The minority, for the time, will be as much the governed or subject portion as are the people in an aristocracy, or the subject in a monarchy ... The duration or uncertainty of the tenure by which power is held cannot of itself counteract the tendency inherent in government to oppression and abuse of power. On the contrary, the very uncertainty of the tenure, combined with the violent party warfare which must ever precede a change of parties under such governments, would rather tend to increase than diminish the tendency to oppression ... It is manifest that this provision must be of character calculated to prevent any one interest, or combination of interests, from using the powers of government to aggrandize itself at the expense of others ... This too can be accomplished in only one way, and that is, by such an organism of the government—and, if necessary for the purpose, of the community also—as will, by dividing and distributing the powers of government, give to each division or interest, through its appropriate organ, either a concurrent voice in making and executing the laws, or a veto on their execution ... Such an organism as this, combined with the right of suffrage, constitutes, in fact, the elements of constitutional government. The one, by rendering those who make and execute the laws responsible to those on whom they operate, prevents the rulers from oppressing the ruled, and the other, by making it impossible for any one interest or combination of interests, or class, or order, or portion of the community, to obtain exclusive control, prevents any one of them from oppressing the other ... It is this negative power—the power of preventing or arresting the action of the government—be it called by what term it may, veto, interposition, nullification, check, or balance of power—which in fact forms the constitution

... It is indeed the negative power which makes the constitution, and the positive which makes the government ... It follows necessarily that where the numerical majority has the sole control of the government, there can be no constitution; as constitution imimplies limitation or restriction; ... and hence, the numerical, unmixed with the concurrent majority, necessarily forms in all cases absolute government ... Constitutional governments, of whatever form, are, indeed, much more similar to each other in their structure and character than they are, respectively, to the absolute governments even of their own class; ... and hence the great and broad distinction between governments is—not that of the one, the few, the many—but of the constitutional and the absolute ... Among the other advantages which governments of the concurrent have over those of the numerical majority—and which strongly illustrates their more popular character—is that they admit, with safety, a much greater extension of the right of suffrage. It may be safely extended in such governments to universal suffrage, that is, to every male citizen of mature age, with few ordinary exceptions; but it cannot be so far extended in those of the numerical majority, without placing them ultimately under the control of the more ignorant and dependent portions of the community. For, as the community becomes populous, wealthy, refined, and highly civilized, the difference between the rich and the poor will become more strongly marked, and the number of the ignorant and dependent greater in proportion to the rest of the community ... The tendency of the concurrent government is to unite the community, let its interests be ever so diversified or opposed; while that of the numerical is to divide it into two conflicting portions, let its interest be naturally ever so united and identified ... The numerical majority, by regarding the community as a unit, and having as such the same interests throughout all its parts, must, by its necessary operation, divide it into two hostile parts, waging, under the forms of law, incessant hostility against each other ... To make equality of condition essential to liberty, would be to destroy liberty and progress. The reason is both that inequality of condition, while it is a necessary consequence of liberty, is at the same time indispensable to progress ... It is, indeed, this inequality of condition between the front and rear ranks, in the march of progress, which gives so strong an impulse to the former to maintain their position, and to the latter to press forward into their files ... This gives to progress its greatest impulse ... These great and dangerous errors have their origin in the prevalent opinion, that all men are born free and equal, than which nothing can be more unfounded and false ... In an absolute democracy party conflicts between the majority and the minority ... can hardly ever terminate in compromise. The object of the opposing minority is to expel the majority from power, and of the majority to maintain their hold upon it. It is on both sides a struggle for the whole; a struggle that must determine which shall be the governing and which the subject party ... Hence, among other reasons, aristocracies and monarchies more readily assume the constitutional form than absolute popular government."[1]

This was written in the last years of Calhoun's life, and published after his death; but the ideas, though he matured them in the subsequent contest on slavery, guided him in the earlier stage of the dispute which developed nullification into secession, during the tariff controversy of the years 1828 to 1833. Many of those who differed from him most widely deemed that his resistance was justified by the selfish and unscrupulous policy of the North. Legaré, the most accomplished scholar among American statesmen, afterwards Attorney General, made a Fourth-of-July oration in South Carolina, during the height of the excitement of 1831, in which he said: "The authors of this policy are indirectly responsible for this deplorable state of things, and for all the consequences that may grow out of it. They have been guilty of an inexpiable offence against the country. They found us a united, they have made us a distracted people. They found the union of these States an object of fervent love and religious veneration; they have made even its utility a subject of controversy among very enlightened men ... I do not wonder at the indignation which the imposition of such a burden of taxation has excited in our people, in the present unprosperous state of their affairs ... Great nations cannot be held together under a united government by any thing short of despotic power, if any one part of the country is to be arrayed against another in a perpetual scramble for privilege and protection, under any system of protection."[2]

Brownson, at that time the most influential journalist of America, and a strong partisan of Calhoun, advocated in 1844 his

[1] *Works*, i, 7-83.   [2] *Writings of Legaré*, i, 272.

claims to the Presidency, and would, we believe, have held office in his cabinet if he had been elected. In one of his earliest numbers of his well-known *Review* he wrote: "Even Mr Calhoun's theory, though unquestionably the true theory of the federal constitution, is yet insufficient . . . It does not, as a matter of fact, arrest the unequal, unjust and oppressive measures of the federal government. South Carolina in 1833 forced a compromise; but in 1842 the obnoxious policy was revived, is pursued now successfully, and there is no State to attempt again the virtue of State interposition . . . The State, if she judged proper, had the sovereign right to set aside this obnoxious tariff enactment in her own dominions, and prohibit her subjects or citizens from obeying it . . . The parties to the compact being equal, and there being no common umpire, each, as a matter of course, is its own judge of the infraction of the compact, and of the mode and measure of redress."[1]

The President, General Jackson, had a strong aversion for the theory and for the person of Calhoun. He swore that he would have him impeached for treason, and that he should hang on a gallows higher than Haman's. One of the nullifying declarations of his Vice-President reached him late at night; in a fit of exultation he had the law officers of the government called out of their beds to say whether at last here was not hanging matter. He issued a manifesto condemning the doctrine of nullification and the acts of South Carolina, which was very ably drawn up by Livingston, the Secretary for State, famous in the history of legislation as the author of the Louisiana code. Webster, the first orator of the day, though not a supporter of the administration, undertook to answer Calhoun in the Senate, and he was fetched from his lodging, when the time came, in the President's carriage. His speech, considered the greatest he ever delivered, was regarded by the friends of the Union as conclusive against State-rights. Madison, who was approaching the term of his long career, wrote to congratulate the speaker in words which ought to have been a warning: "It crushes nullification, and must hasten an abandonment of secession. But this dodges the blow by confounding the claim to secede at will with the right of seceding from intolerable oppression."

Secession is but the alternative of interposition. The defeat of

[1] *Quarterly Review*, ii, 522.

the latter doctrine on the ground of the constitution, deprived the South of the only possible protection from the increasing tyranny of the majority, for the defeat of nullification coincided in time with the final triumph of the pure democratic views; and at the same time that it was resolved that the rights of the minority had no security, it was established that the power of the majority had no bounds. Calhoun's elaborate theory was an earnest attempt to save the Union from the defects of its constitution. It is useless to inquire whether it is legally right, according to the letter of the constitution, for it is certain that it is in contradiction with its spirit as it has grown up since Jefferson. Webster may have been the truest interpreter of the law; Calhoun was the real defender of the Union. Even the Unionists made the dangerous admission, that there were cases in which, as there was no redress known to the law, secession was fully justified. Livingston gave the opinion that "if the act be one of the few which, in its operation, cannot be submitted to the Supreme Court, and be one that will, in the opinion of the State, justify the risk of a withdrawal from the Union, this last extremity may at once be resorted to."[1]

The intimate connection between nullification and secession is shown by the biographer of Clay, though he fails to see that one is not the consequence, but the surrogate, of the other: "The first idea of nullification was doubtless limited to the action of a State in making null and void a federal law or laws within the circle of its own jurisdiction, without contemplating the absolute independence of a secession. Seeing, however, that nullification, in its practical operation, could hardly stop short of secession, the propounders of the doctrine in its first and limited signification afterwards came boldly up to the claim of the right of secession."[2]

Practically, South Carolina triumphed, though her claims were repudiated. The tariff was withdrawn, and a measure of compromise was introduced by Clay, the leading protectionist, which was felt so great a concession that Calhoun accepted, whilst Webster opposed it, and it was carried. But the evil day, the final crisis, was only postponed. The spirit of the country had taken a course in which it could not be permanently checked; and it was certain that new opportunities would be made to assert the omnipotence of the popular will, and to exhibit the

[1] Elliot's *Debates*, iv, 519.   [2] Colton's *Life of Clay*, v, 392.

total subservience of the executive to it.[1] Already a new controversy had begun, which has since overshadowed that which
shook the Union from 1828 to 1833. The commercial question
was not settled; the economical antagonism, and the determination on the part of the North to extend its advantages, did not
slumber from Clay's Compromise Act to the Morill Tariff in
1861; and in his farewell address, in 1837, Jackson drew a gloomy
and desponding picture of the period which is filled with his
name. "Many powerful interests are continually at work to
procure heavy duties on commerce, and to swell the revenue beyond the real necessities of the public service; and the country
has already felt the injurious effects of their combined influence.
They succeeded in obtaining a tariff of duties bearing most op-
pressively on the agricultural and labouring classes of society,
and producing a revenue that could not be usefully employed
within the range of the powers conferred upon Congress; and in
order to fasten upon the people this unjust and unequal system of
taxation, extravagant schemes of internal improvement were got
up in various quarters to squander the money and to purchase
support . . . Rely upon it, the design to collect an extravagant
revenue, and to burden you with taxes beyond the economical
wants of the government, is not yet abandoned. The various interests which have combined together to impose a heavy tariff
and to produce an overflowing treasury, are too strong, and have
too much at stake, to surrender the contest. The corporations
and wealthy individuals who are engaged in large manufacturing establishments desire a high tariff to increase their gains.
Designing politicians will support it to conciliate their favour,
and to obtain the means of profuse expenditure, for the purpose
of purchasing influence in other quarters . . . It is from within,
among yourselves—from cupidity, from corruption, from disappointed ambition, and inordinate thirst for power—that factions will be formed and liberty endangered."[2]

Jackson was himself answerable for much of what was most
deplorable in the political state of the country. The democratic
tendency, which began under Jefferson, attained in Jackson's

---

[1] ὁ γὰρ δῆμος οὐ βούλεται εὐνομουμένης τῆς πόλεως αὐτὸς δουλεύειν, ἀλλ' ἐλεύθερος εἶναι
καὶ ἄρχειν, τῆς δὲ κακονομίας αὐτῷ ὀλίγον μέλει· ὃ γὰρ σὺ νομίζεις οὐκ εὐνομεῖσθαι, αὐτὸς ἀπὸ
τούτου ἰσχύει ὁ δῆμος καὶ ἐλεύθερός ἐστιν. Xenophon, *Athen. Republ.*, i, 8.

[2] *Statesman's Manual*, 953-960.

presidency its culminating point. The immense change in this respect may be shown in a single example. Pure democracy demands quick rotation of office; as all men have an equal claim to official power and profit, and must be supposed nearly equally qualified for it, and require no long experience (so that at Athens offices were distributed by lot), the greatest possible number of citizens should successively take part in the administration. It diminishes the distinction between the rulers and the ruled, between the State and the community, and increases the dependence of the first upon the last. At first such changes are not comtemplated. Washington dismissed only nine officials in eight years, Adams removed only ten, Madison five, Monroe nine, John Quincy Adams only two, both on specific disqualifying grounds. Jefferson was naturally in favour of rotation in office, and caused a storm of anger when he displaced thirty-nine official men in order to supply vacancies for supporters. Jackson, on succeeding the younger Adams, instantly made 176 alterations, and in the course of the first year 491 postmasters lost their places. Mr Everett says very truly: "It may be stated as the general characteristic of the political tendencies of this period that there was a decided weakening of respect for constitutional restraint. Vague ideas of executive discretion prevailed on the one hand in the interpretation of the constitution, and of popular sovereignty on the other, as represented by a President elevated to office on overwhelming majorities of the people."[1]

This was the period of Tocqueville's visit to America, when he passed the following judgment: "When a ma , or a party, suffers an injustice in the United States, to whom ca 1 he have recourse? To public opinion? It is that which forms the majority. To the legislative body? It represents the majority, and obeys it blindly. To the executive power? It is appointed by the majority, and serves as its passive instrument. To public force? It is nothing but the majority under arms. To the jury? It is the majority invested with the right of finding verdicts. The judges themselves, in some States, are elected by the majority. However iniquitous, therefore, or unreasonable the measure from which you suffer, you must submit."[2] Very eminent Americans[3] quite agreed with

---

[1] *Memoir of Webster*, p. 101.   [2] vol. ii, cap. vii.
[3] There is a remarkable passage in Story's letters on Tocqueville's celebrated book: "The work of De Tocqueville has had great reputation abroad, partly

him in his censure of the course things had taken, and which had been seen long beforehand. In 1818 Story writes: "A new race of men is springing up to govern the nation; they are the hunters after popularity; men ambitious, not of the honour so much as of the profits of office—the demagogues whose principles hang laxly upon them, and who follow not so much what is right as what leads to a temporary vulgar applause. There is great, very great, danger that these men will usurp so much of popular favour that they will rule the nation; and if so, we may yet live to see many of our best institutions crumble in the dust."[1]

The following passages are from the conclusion of his *Commentary on the Constitution*: "The influence of the disturbing causes, which more than once in the convention were on the point of breaking up the Union, have since immeasurably increased in concentration and vigour . . . If, under these circumstances, the Union should once be broken up, it is impossible that a new constitution should ever be formed, embracing the whole territory. We shall be divided into several nations or confederacies, rivals in power and interest, too proud to brook injury, and too close to make retaliation distant or ineffectual." On February 18, 1834, he writes of Jackson's administration: "I feel humiliated at the truth, which cannot be disguised, that though we live under a republic, we are in fact under the absolute rule of a single man." And a few years later, November 3, 1837, he tells Miss Martineau that she has judged too favourably of his country: "You have overlooked the terrible influence of a corrupting patronage, and the system of exclusiveness in official appointments, which have already wrought such extensive mischiefs among us, and threaten to destroy all the safeguards of our civil liberties . . . You would have learned, I think, that there may be a despotism exercised in a republic, as irresistible and as ruinous as in any form of monarchy."

The foremost of the Southern statesmen thought exactly like the New England judge. "I care not," said Calhoun, "what the form of the government is; it is nothing, if the government be

---

founded on their ignorance that he has borrowed the greater part of his reflections from American work, and little from his own observation. The main body of his materials will be found in the *Federalist*, and in Story's *Commentaries*" (*Life of Story*, ii, 330).

[1] *Life*, i, 311.

despotic, whether it be in the hands of one, or of a few, or of many men, without limitation . . . While these measures were destroying the equilibrium between the two sections, the action of the government was leading to a radical change in its character, by concentrating all the power of the system in itself . . . What was once a constitutional federal republic is now converted, in reality, into one as absolute as that of the autocrat of Russia, and as despotic in its tendency as any absolute government that ever existed . . . The increasing power of this government, and of the control of the Northern section over all its departments, furnished the cause. It was this which made an impression on the minds of many, that there was little or no restraint to prevent the government from doing whatever it might choose to do."[1] At the same period, though reverting to a much earlier date, Cobbett wrote: "I lived eight years under the republican government of Pennsylvania; and I believe that to have been the most corrupt and tyrannical government that the world ever knew . . . I have seen enough of republican government to convince me that the mere name is not worth a straw."[2] Channing touches on a very important point, the influence of European liberalism on the republicanism of America: "Ever since our revolution we have had a number of men who have wanted faith in our free institutions, and have seen in our almost unlimited extension of the elective franchise the germ of convulsion and ruin. When the demagogues succeed in influencing the ignorant multitude, and get office and power, this anti-popular party increases; in better times it declines. It has been built up in a measure by the errors and crimes of the liberals of Europe . . . I have endeavoured on all occasions to disprove the notion that the labouring classes are unfit depositaries of political power. I owe it, however, to truth to say that I believe that the elective franchise is extended too far in this country."[3]

In 1841 he described very accurately the perils which have since proved fatal: "The great danger to our institutions, which alarms our conservatives most, has not perhaps entered Mr Smith's mind. It is the danger of a party organization, so subtle and strong as to make the government the monopoly of a few leaders and to insure the transmission of the executive power

[1] *Works*, iv, 351, 550, 553.   [2] *Works*, vi, 683.
[3] *Memoir of Channing*, 418, 419.

from hand to hand almost as regularly as in a monarchy ... That this danger is real cannot be doubted. So that we have to watch against despotism as well as, or more than, anarchy."[1] On this topic it is impossible to speak more strongly, and nobody could speak with greater authority than Dr Brownson: "Our own government, in its origin and constitutional form, is not a democracy, but, if we may use the expression, a limited elective aristocracy ... But practically the government framed by our fathers no longer exists, save in name. Its original character has disappeared or is rapidly disappearing. The constitution is a dead letter, except in so far as it serves to prescribe the modes of election, the rule of the majority, the distribution and tenure of offices, and the union and separation of the functions of government. Since 1828 it has been becoming in practice, and is now substantially, a pure democracy, with no effective constitution but the will of the majority for the time being . . . The constitution is practically abolished, and our government is virtually, to all intents and purposes, as we have said, a pure democracy, with nothing to prevent it from obeying the interest or interests which for the time being can succeed in commanding it."[2] Shortly before his conversion he wrote: "Looking at what we were in the beginning, and what we now are, it may well be doubted whether another country in Christendom has so rapidly declined as we have, in the stern and rigid virtues, in the high-toned and manly principles of conduct essential to the stability and wise administration of popular government ... The established political order in this country is not the democratic; and every attempt to apply the democratic theory as the principle of its interpretation is an attempt at revolution, and to be resisted. By a democracy I understand a political order—if that may be called order which is none—in which the people, primarily and without reference to any authority constituting them a body politic, are held to be the source of all the legitimate power in the state."[3]

The partisans of democratic absolutism who opposed State-rights in the affair of the tariff, and led to the unhappy consequences and lamentations we have seen, were already supplied with another topic to test the power of their principle. The question of abolition, subordinate at first, though auxiliary to the

---

[1] *Memoir of Channing*, 421.
[2] Brownson's *Quarterly Review*, 1844, ii, 515, 523.   [3] ibid., i, 84, 19.

question of protection, came into the front when the other had lost its interest, and had been suspended for a season by the Compromise Act. It served to enlist higher sympathies on the side of revolution than could be won by considerations of mere profit. It adorned cupidity with the appearance of philanthropy, but the two motives were not quite distinct, and one is something of a pretext, and serves to disguise the other. They were equally available as means of establishing the supremacy of the absolute democracy, only one was its own reward; the other was not so clearly a matter of pecuniary interest, but of not inferior political advantage. A power which is questioned, however real it may be, must assert and manifest itself if it is to last. When the right of the States to resist the Union was rejected, although the question which occasioned the dispute was amicably arranged, it was certain to be succeeded by another, in order that so doubtful a victory might be commemorated by a trophy.

The question of slavery first exhibited itself as a constitutional difficulty about 1820, in the dispute which was settled by the Missouri compromise. Even at this early period the whole gravity of its consequences was understood by discerning men. Jefferson wrote: "This momentous question, like a fire-ball in the night, awakened and filled me with terror. I considered it at once as the knell of the Union. It is hushed, indeed, for the moment. But this is a reprieve only, not a final sentence."

In 1828, when South Carolina was proclaiming the right of veto, and was followed by several of the Southern States, abolition was taken up in the North as a means of coercion against them, by way of reprisal, and as a very powerful instrument of party warfare. Channing writes to Webster, May 14, 1828: "A little while ago, Mr Lundy of Baltimore, the editor of a paper called *The Genius of Universal Emancipation*, visited this part of the country, to stir us up to the work of abolishing slavery in the South; and the intention is to organize societies for this purpose ... My fear in regard to our efforts against slavery is, that we shall make the case worse by rousing sectional pride and passion for its support, and that we shall only break the country into two great parties, which may shake the foundations of government."

In the heat of the great controversies of Jackson's administration, on the Bank question and the Veto question, slavery was not brought prominently forward; but when the democratic central power had triumphed, when the Bank question was settled, and there was no longer an immediate occasion for discussing State-rights, the party whose opinion had prevailed in the constitution resolved to make use of their predominance for its extinction. Thenceforward, from about the year 1835, it became the leading question, and the form in which the antagonism between the principles of arbitrary power and self-government displayed itself. At every acquisition of territory, at the formation of new States, the same question caused a crisis; then in the Fugitive-Slave Act, and finally in the formation of the republican party, and its triumph in 1860. The first effect of making abolition a political party question, and embodying in it the great constitutional quarrel which had already threatened the existence of the Union in the question of taxation, was to verify the prophecy of Channing. Webster, who had been the foremost antagonist of nullification in the affair of the tariff, lived to acknowledge that even secession was being provoked by the insane aggression of the North. In one of his latest speeches, in that which is known as his speech for the Union, March 7, 1850, he denounced the policy of the abolitionists: "I do not mean to impute gross motives even to the leaders of these societies, but I am not blind to the consequences of their proceedings. I cannot but see what mischief their interference with the South has produced. And is it not plain to every man? Let any gentleman who entertains doubts on this point recur to the debates in the Virginia House of Delegates in 1832, and he will see with what freedom a proposition made by Mr J. Randolph for the gradual abolition of slavery was discussed in that body . . . Public opinion, which in Virginia had begun to be exhibited against slavery, and was opening out for the discussion of the question, drew back and shut itself up in its castle . . . We all know the fact, and we all know the cause; and everything that these agitating people have done has been not to enlarge, but to restrain, not to set free, but to bind faster, the slave-population of the South."[1]

Howe, the Virginian historian, in principle though not in policy an abolitionist, says: "That a question so vitally important would have been renewed with more success at an early subsequent period, seems more than probable, if the current opinions of the day can be relied on; but there were obvious causes in

[1] *Works*, v, 357.

operation which paralysed the friends of abolition, and have had the effects of silencing all agitation on the subject. The abolitionists in the Northern and Eastern States, gradually increasing their strength as a party, became louder in their denunciation of slavery, and more and more reckless in the means adopted for assailing the constitutional rights in the South."[1]

Story writes, January 19, 1839: "The question of slavery is becoming more and more an absorbing one, and will, if it continues to extend its influence, lead to a dissolution of the Union. At least there are many of our soundest statesmen who look to this as a highly probable event."[2]

At that time the abolitionist party was yet in its infancy, and had not succeeded in combining together in a single party all the interests that were hostile to the slave States. Lord Carlisle, describing a conversation he had in 1841 with the present Secretary of State, Mr Seward, says: "I find that I noted at the time that he was the first person I had met who did not speak slightingly of the abolitionists; he thought they were gradually gaining ground."[3]

But in the following year the abolitionist policy rapidly grew up into a great danger to the Union, which the great rivals, Webster and Calhoun, united to resist at the close of their lives. Commercially speaking, it is not certain that the North would gain by the abolition of slavery. It would increase the Southern market by encouraging white emigration from the North; but the commerce of New England depends largely on the cotton crop, and the New England merchants are not for abolition. Calhoun did not attribute the movement to a desire of gain: "The crusade against our domestic institution does not originate in hostility of interests . . . The rabid fanatics regard slavery as a sin, and thus regarding it deem it their highest duty to destroy it, even should it involve the destruction of the constitution and the Union."[4]

In this view he is fully supported by Webster: "Under the cry of universal freedom, and that other cry that there is a rule for the government of public men and private men which is of superior obligation to the constitution of the country, several of the States have enacted laws to hinder, obstruct, and defeat the enactments in this act of Congress to the utmost of their power . . . I suspect all

---

[1] *Historical Collections of Virginia*, 128.   [2] *Life*, ii, 307.
[3] *Lectures on America*, p. 27.   [4] *Works*, iv, 386.

this to be the effect of that wandering and vagrant philanthropy which disturbs and annoys all that is present, in time or place, by heating the imagination on subjects distant, remote, and uncertain."[1]

Webster justly considered that the real enemies of the constitution were the abolitionists, not the slave-owners, who threatened to secede. To appeal from the constitution to a higher law, to denounce as sinful and contrary to natural right an institution expressly recognized by it, is manifestly an assault upon the Union itself. The South have the letter and the spirit of the law in their favour. The consistent abolitionists must be ready to sacrifice the Union to their theory. If the objection to slavery is on moral grounds, paramount to all political rights and interests, abolition is a peremptory duty, to which the Union itself, whose law is opposed to compulsory abolition, must succumb. It was therefore perfectly just to remind Mr Seward that in attacking slavery, and denying that it could be tolerated, he was assailing the law to which he owed his seat in Congress. "No man", said Webster, "is at liberty to set up, or affect to set up, his own conscience as above the law, in a matter which respects the rights of others, and the obligations, civil, social and political, due to others from him."[2]

Dr Brownson says with great truth, as only a Catholic can: "No civil government can exist, none is conceivable even, where every individual is free to disobey its orders, whenever they do not happen to square with his private convictions of what is the law of God ... To appeal from the government to private judgment, is to place private judgment above public authority, the individual above the state."[3]

Calhoun was entirely justified in saying that, in the presence of these tendencies, "the conservative power is in the slave-holding States. They are the conservative portion of the country."[4]

His own political doctrines, as we have described them, fully bear out this view. But the conservative anti-revolutionary character of the South depended on other causes than the influence of its master mind. Slavery is itself in contradiction with the equal rights of man, as they are laid down in the Declaration of Independence. Slave-owners are incapacitated from interpreting

---

[1] *Works*, vi, 556, 561.   [2] ibid., vi, 578.
[3] *Essays and Reviews*, pp. 357, 359.   [4] *Works*, iv, 360.

that instrument with literal consistency, for it would contradict both their interests and their daily experience. But as there are advanced democrats at the South as well as at the North, and as, indeed, they have succeeded in resisting so long the Northern politicians, by using the jealousy of the Northern people against the wealthy capitalists, and the appearance of aristocracy, they find means of escaping from this dilemma. This is supplied by the theory of the original inferiority of the African race to the rest of mankind, for which the authority of the greatest naturalist in America is quoted. "The result of my researches", says Agassiz, "is, that Negroes are intellectually children; physically one of the lowest races; inclining with the other blacks, especially the South Sea Negroes, most of all to the monkey type, though with a tendency, even in the extremes, towards the real human form. This opinion I have repeatedly expressed, without drawing from it any objectionable consequence, unless, perhaps, that no coloured race, least of all the Negroes, can have a common origin with ourselves." If this theory were not the property of the infidel science of Europe, one would suppose it must have been invented for the Americans, whom it suits so well.

Webster spoke with great power against the projects of the North: "There is kept up a general cry of one party against the other, that its rights are invaded, its honour insulted, its character assailed, and its just participation in political power denied. Sagacious men cannot but suspect from all this, that more is intended than is avowed; and that there lies at the bottom a purpose of the separation of the States, for reasons avowed or disavowed, or for grievances redressed or unredressed.

"In the South, the separation of the States is openly professed, discussed, and recommended, absolutely or conditionally, in legislative halls, and in conventions called together by the authority of the law.

"In the North, the State governments have not run into such excess, and the purpose of overturning the government shows itself more clearly in resolutions agreed to in voluntary assemblies of individuals, denouncing the laws of the land, and declaring a fixed intent to disobey them ... It is evident that, if this spirit be not checked, it will endanger the government; if it spread far and wide, it will overthrow the government."[1]

[1] *Works*, vi, 567, 582.

The language of Calhoun about the same period is almost identical with Webster's: "The danger is of a character—whether we regard our safety or the preservation of the Union—which cannot be safely tampered with. If not met promptly and decidedly, the two portions of the Union will become thoroughly alienated, when no alternative will be left to us, as the weaker of the two, but to sever all political ties, or sink down into abject submission."[1]

His last great speech, delivered March 4, 1850, a few days before his death, opened with the words: "I have believed from the first that the agitation of the subject of slavery would, if not prevented by some timely and effective measure, end in disunion." And he went on to say: "If something is not done to avert it, the South will be forced to choose between abolition and secession. Indeed, as events are now moving, it will not require the South to secede in order to dissolve the Union."[2]

The calamity which these eminent men agreed in apprehending and in endeavouring to avert, was brought on after their death by the rise of the republican party—a party in its aims and principles quite revolutionary, and not only inconsistent with the existence of the Union, but ready from the first to give it up. "I do not see," said the New England philosopher Emerson, "how a barbarous community and a civilized community can constitute one State." In order to estimate the extravagance of this party declaration, we will only quote two unexceptionable witnesses, who visited the South at an interval of about forty years from each other; one a Boston divine, the other an eager abolitionist. "How different from our Northern manners! There, avarice and ceremony, at the age of twenty, graft the coldness and unfeelingness of age on the disinterested ardour of youth. I blush for my own people when I compare the selfish prudence of the Yankee with the generous confidence of a Virginian. Here I find great vices, but greater virtues than I left behind me. There is one single trait which attaches me to the people I live with more than all the virtues of New England—they love money less than we do."[3] Lord Carlisle says, in the lecture already referred to: "It would be uncandid to deny that the planter in the Southern States has much more in his manner and mode of intercourse that

---

[1] *Works*, iv, 395.   [2] ibid., 542, 556.   [3] *Memoir of Channing*, p. 43.

resembles the English country gentleman than any other class of his countrymen."[1]

Emerson's saying is a sign of the extent to which rabid abolitionists were ready to go. Declaring that the Federal Government was devoted to Southern interests, against Northern doctrines, they openly defied it. Disunion societies started up at the North for the purpose of bringing about separation. Several States passed laws against the South and against the constitution, and there were loud demands for separation. This was the disposition of the North at the presidential election of a successor to Pierce. The North threatened to part company, and if it carried its candidate, it threatened the Southern institutions. The South proclaimed the intention of seceding if Fremont should be elected, and threatened to march upon Washington and burn the archives of the Union. Buchanan's election pacified the South; but it was evident from the growing strength of the republican party, that it was their last victory. They accordingly made use of their friends in office to take advantage of the time that remained to them to be in readiness when the next election came. Secession was resolved upon and prepared from the time when the strength of the republicans was exhibited in 1856. In spite of all the horrors of American slavery, it is impossible for us to have any sympathy with the party of which Mr Seward is the chief. His politics are not only revolutionary, but aggressive; he is not only for absolutism but for annexation. In a speech on January 26, 1853, he spoke as follows: "The tendency of commercial and political events invites the United States to assume and exercise a paramount influence in the affairs of the nations situated in this hemisphere; that is, to become and remain a great Western continental power, balancing itself against the possible combinations of Europe. The advance of the country towards that position constitutes what, in the language of many, is called 'progress' and the position itself is what, by the same class, is called 'manifest destiny'."[2]

When Cass moved a resolution affirming the Monroe doctrine with regard to Cuba, Seward supported it, together with another resolution perfectly consistent with it, of which he said: "It is not well expressed but it implies the same policy in regard to Canada

[1] l.c., 35.   [2] *Works*, iii, 609.

which the main resolutions assert concerning Cuba."[1] Nor is this the limit of his ambition. "You are already", he says to his countrymen, "the great continental power of America. But does that content you? I trust it does not. You want the commerce of the world, which is the empire of the world."[2]

When Kossuth was received in the Senate, he was introduced by Mr Seward, whose European policy is as definite and about as respectable as his American. Speaking of Hungary, he writes, in December 1851: "I trust that some measure may be adopted by the government which, while it will not at all hazard the peace and the prosperity of the country, may serve to promote a cause that appeals so strongly to our interests and our sympathies, viz. the establishment of republicanism, in the countries prepared for it, in Europe."[3] And again, two days later: "Every nation may, and every nation ought to make its position distinctly known in every case of conflict between despots and States struggling for the inalienable and indefeasible rights of independence and self-government, that when despots combine, free States may lawfully unite."

It is as impossible to sympathize on religious grounds with the categorical prohibition of slavery as, on political grounds, with the opinions of the abolitionists. In this, as in all other things, they exhibit the same abstract, ideal absolutism, which is equally hostile with the Catholic and with the English spirit. Their democratic system poisons everything it touches. All constitutional questions are referred to the one fundamental principle of popular sovereignty, without consideration of policy or expediency. In the Massachusetts convention of 1853, it was argued by one of the most famous Americans, that the election of the judiciary could not be discussed on the grounds of its influence on the administration of justice, as it was clearly consonant with the constitutional theory. "What greater right", says the *North American Review*,[4] "has government to deprive people of their representation in the executive and judicial, than in the legislative department?" In claiming absolute freedom, they have created absolute power, whilst we have inherited from the middle ages the notion that both liberty and authority must be subject to limits and conditions. The same intolerance of restraints and obligations, the

---

[1] *Works*, 609.   [2] ibid., 618.   [3] ibid., 505.
[4] vol. lxxxvi, 477.

same aversion to recognize the existence of popular duty, and of the divine right which is its correlative, disturb their notions of government and of freedom. The influence of these habits of abstract reasoning, to which we owe the revolution in Europe, is to make all things questions of principle and of abstract law. A principle is always appealed to in all cases, either of interest or necessity, and the consequence is that a false and arbitrary political system produces a false and arbitrary code of ethics, and the theory of abolition is as erroneous as the theory of freedom.

Very different is the mode in which the Church labours to reform mankind by assimilating realities with ideals, and accommodating herself to times and circumstances. Her system of Christian liberty is essentially incompatible with slavery and the power of masters over their slaves was one of the bulwarks of corruption and vice which most seriously impeded her progress. Yet the Apostles never condemned slavery even within the Christian fold. The sort of civil liberty which came with Christianity into the world, and was one of her postulates, did not require the abolition of slavery. If men were being free by virtue of their being formed after the image of God, the proportion in which they realized that image would be the measure of their freedom. Accordingly, St Paul prescribed to the Christian slave to remain content with his condition.[1]

We have gone at inordinate length into the causes and peculiarities of the revolution in the United States, because of the constant analogy they present to the theories and the events which are at the same time disturbing Europe. It is too late to touch upon more than one further point, which is extremely suggestive. The Secession movement was not provoked merely by the alarm of the slave-owners for their property, when the election of Lincoln sent down the price of slaves from 25 to 50 per cent, but by the political danger of Northern preponderance; and the mean whites of the Southern States are just as eager for separation as those who have property in slaves. For they fear lest the republicans, in carrying emancipation, should abolish the barriers which separate the negroes from their own caste. At the same time, the slaves show no disposition to help the republicans, and

---

[1] 1 Cor. vii, 21. The opposite interpretation, common among Protestant commentators, is inconsistent with verses 20 and 24, and with the tradition of the Greek Fathers.

be raised to the level of the whites. There is a just reason for this fear, which lies in the simple fact that the United States are a republic. The population of a republic must be homogeneous. Civil equality must be founded on social equality, and on national and physiological unity. This has been the strength of the American republic. Pure democracy is that form of government in which the community is sovereign, in which, therefore, the State is most nearly identified with society. But society exists for the protection of interests; the State for the realization of right— "concilia coetusque hominum *jure* sociati, quae civitates appellantur."[1] The State sets up a moral, objective law, and pursues a common object distinct from the ends and purposes of society. This is essentially repugnant to democracy, which recognizes only the interests and rights of the community, and is therefore inconsistent with the consolidation of authority which is implied in the notion of the State. It resists the development of the social into the moral community. If, therefore, a democracy includes persons with separate interests or an inferior nature, it tyrannizes over them. There is no mediator between the part and the whole; there is no room, therefore, for differences of class, of wealth, of race; equality is necessary to the liberty which is sought by a pure democracy.

Where society is constituted without equality of condition or unity of race, where there are different classes and national varieties, they require a protector in a form of government which shall be distinct from, and superior to, every class, and not the instrument of one of them, in an authority representing the State, not any portion of society. This can be supplied only by monarchy; and in this sense it is fair to say that constitutional government, that is, the authority of law as distinguished from interest, can exist only under a king. This is also the reason why even absolute monarchies have been better governors of dependencies than popular governments. In one case they are governed for the benefit of a ruling class; in the other, there is no ruling class, and they are governed in the name of the State. Rome under the Republic and under the Empire is the most striking instance of this contrast. But the tyranny of republics is greatest when differences of races are combined with distinctions of class. Hence South America was a prospering and flourishing country so long as the

[1] Cicero, *Somnium Scipionis*, 3.

Spanish Crown served as moderator between the various races, and is still prosperous where monarchy has been retained; whilst the establishment of republics in countries with classes divided by blood has led to hopeless misery and disorder, and constant recourse to dictatorships as a refuge from anarchy and tyranny. Democracy inevitably takes the tone of the lower portions of society, and, if there are great diversities, degrades the higher. Slavery is the only protection that has ever been known against this tendency, and it is so far true that slavery is essential to democracy. For where there are great incongruities in the constitution of society, if the Americans were to admit the Indians, the Chinese, the Negroes, to the rights to which they are justly jealous of admitting European emigrants, the country would be thrown into disorder, and if not, would be degraded to the level of the barbarous races. Accordingly, the Know-nothings rose up as the reaction of the democratic principle against the influx of an alien population. The Red Indian is gradually retreating before the pioneer, and will perish before many generations, or dwindle away in the desert. The Chinese in California inspire great alarm for the same reason, and plans have been proposed of shipping them all off again. This is a good argument too, in the interest of all parties, against the emancipation of the blacks.

This necessity for social equality and national unity has been felt in all democracies where the mass as a unit governs itself. Above all it is felt as a necessity in France, since the downfall of the old society, and the recognition, under republic, charter, and despotism, of the sovereignty of the people. Those principles with which France revolutionizes Europe are perfectly right in her own case. They are detestable in other countries where they cause revolutions, but they are a true and just consequence of the French Revolution. Men easily lose sight of the substance in the form, and suppose that because France is not a republic she is not a democracy, and that her principles therefore will apply elsewhere. This is the reason of the power of the national principle in Europe. It is essential as a consequence of equality to the notion of the people as the source of power. Where there is an aristocracy it has generally more sympathy and connection with foreign aristocracies than with the rest of the nation. The bonds of class are stronger than those of nationality. A democracy, in abolishing classes, renders national unity imperative.

These are some of the political lessons we have learned from the consideration of the vast process of which we are witnessing the consummation. We may consult the history of the American Union to understand the true history of republicanism, and the danger of mistaking it. It is simply the spurious democracy of the French Revolution that has destroyed the Union, by disintegrating the remnants of English traditions and institutions. All the great controversies—on the embargo, restriction, internal improvement, the Bank-Charter Act, the formation of new States, the acquisition of new territory, abolition—are phases of this mighty change, steps in the passage from a constitution framed on an English model to a system imitating that of France. The secession of the Southern States—pregnant with infinite consequences to the African race, by altering the condition of slavery, to America by awakening an intenser thirst for conquest, to Europe by its reaction on European democracy, to England, above all, by threatening for a moment one of the pillars of her social existence, but still more by the enormous augmentation of her power, on which the United States were always a most formidable restraint—is chiefly important in a political light as a protest and reaction against revolutionary doctrines, and as a move in the opposite direction to that which prevails in Europe.

XII

NOTES ON THE PRESENT STATE
OF AUSTRIA[1]

IT is idle to hope that Austria can remain as she is. There are events in history which are not the act of man's will, but the products of a natural process, which *grow* but are not *done*; for which, therefore, no particular person is responsible, and to which the ideas of right and wrong, though easily applicable in words, will never be found to apply in fact. In the life of mankind, there are active forces which are not moral; there is a physical necessity which goes its way, regardless of ethical considerations. Nations and families, subjects and rulers, live by physical laws, and are prone to disease, madness, exhaustion, decline, extinction, as well as to progressive increase and improvement. Under the pressure of these physical necessities, it is lost labour to declaim about law; and those who cannot or will not understand, and distinguish when the matter before them is natural, and when moral, only exhibit a weakness and folly such as they are willing to deride in the Legitimists of France. Neither can these natural tendencies be arrested by the expedients of state-craft. Justice is not so easily satisfied. Providence allows the evil to continue till the measure is full, and then exacts the penalty. It only makes the lesson more solemn if the doomed representative of the iniquitous system should be the best of his race, should be really willing to repair the unrighteousness of his forefathers; for when the guilt is not individual, but collective and traditional, poisoning the state from generation to generation, the destruction of a few guilty individuals would be but a poor lesson; the hard necessity of the unchangeable Nemesis is best exhibited for the warning of all tyrants who have any regard for their posterity, when it seizes the innocent victim, and, in its stern reprisals, crushes his bones for the crimes of his fathers.

I fear that these hard sayings may be found applicable to

[1] *The Rambler*, vol. iv, Jan. 1861, p. 193.

Austria. Its government, though called paternal, was for generations a revolutionary despotism; and the just resistance of
Brabant to the laws of Joseph II was only an example of what
would have been equally justifiable in the other provinces. The
old system was hatefully oppressive, and the immorality of its
officials and their contempt for religion have survived its alteration. Thus, for the 54,000 Protestants who served in the Austrian
Army there was last year but a single chaplain. Though the suppression of religious orders and the oppression of the Church are
things of the past, the results continue. The evil examples of the
nobility are as scandalous as ever. The Archduke Charles was
epileptic; but so was Cæsar. The Emperor Joseph was a well-
meaning and active tyrant; Francis I was a slow, repressive, suspicious despot, fearful of progress, of improvement, of intellect,
and of change, cold-hearted and narrow-minded, though not
stupid; the ex-Emperor Ferdinand is half an idiot and one or
two of his brothers are no better; and Francis Joseph himself has
exhibited no superiority. These things lead, by a kind of physiological necessity, to changes, whether in the way of punishment
or in the way of remedy, but either of them equally disastrous to
existing interests.

Since the outbursts of 1848, Francis Joseph has had ten years
to try if haply he might be allowed to heal the wounds of the
empire. It was, of course, a hazardous experiment. Every great
change in the political life of nations has led to a change of
dynasty, or the Stuarts and the Bourbons might still be seated
on their ancestral thrones. The half-aristocratic rule of the
Rurics lasted in Russia until absolutism and servitude were
established; and we have yet to see whether the despotism of the
Romanoffs can survive the radical changes of Alexander II.
But in Austria the danger is still greater. It is not a nation, but an
assemblage of nations, brought together by no internal or external necessity, but by the accidental results of imperial marriages
and dynastic wars; it is the work of the dynasty, and its existence
is scarcely conceivable apart from the family of the Habsburgs.

Since 1848, the internal perils of Austria are generally to be
attributed to unconstitutional parties, who aim, not at the reformation, but at the destruction, of the State, and who therefore become more powerful and more dangerous by every concession. For, as Fiévée says, it is only a strong power that can be

conciliatory without endangering itself, or can consider objections without seeming to give up its principles as doubtful. The parties are (1) the Hungarian Separatists; (2) the advanced Liberals, consisting chiefly of Jews, who are not more anxious for the advance of their opinions and the advantage of their interests than for a vengeance that shall recompense them for their long disabilities, even at the price of a national collapse; (3) the Italian party, who desire a united and independent Italy; (4) the Panslavist Party, strong in Bohemia and Galicia, who wish for one great Slavonic empire or confederation. It is clear that the Austrian Government, in order to maintain its own existence, must wage unconditional war with all these separatists, and must consider any understanding with them to be unattainable. This was the idea of Bach, who was the soul of the Austrian policy since 1848. He aimed at the entire unity of the monarchy, and made no concessions either to the various separatist parties, or to the aristocratic Tories who desired the restoration of things to their state before 1848. But the real errors of Bach's policy raised up against him elements of opposition, which, uniting with these separatists, soon brought him to a stand-still.

Bach's plan was to make the empire one in every sense. It was to be administered by the same laws throughout, and all its resources were to be developed to the utmost, and brought as much as possible within the sphere of the State's action. The uniform legislation was to be backed up and strengthened by a system of public instruction, high enough, but uniform for provinces five hundred years apart from each other in civilization and progress, and by the favour of the Church, which he proposed to purchase by the restoration of her freedom. The development of national resources was to be attained by free trade, abolition of the feudal system, and of mercantile restrictions, and by a grand system of railways. The defects of this intelligent plan were, that it was founded neither on the old traditions, nor on the concessions of 1848. It confirmed the abolition of all old privileges, all mediaeval reminiscences, while it destroyed the great objects of the revolution, provincial independence and provincial parliaments. The system, therefore, could only enlist a narrow circle of adherents, attracted by the desire of power for the State, of wealth for the nation, and of liberty for the Church. The rest were offended by its sacrifice of the very notion of legitimacy and historical continuance, in not professing either to uphold the new institutions of 1848 or to reform the old. It had no national historical basis; its instruments, therefore, were not traditions or habits or aspirations, but only a well-organized bureaucracy. Popularity could not be expected till time had developed the benefits of the legislation; but the building of railways and the execution of the Concordat was an affair of years. The progress has been enormous in the development of the commercial resources of the country; vast sums have been embarked in speculation; the funded capital of the nation has increased; and the amount raised by taxation has nearly doubled. But these benefits have been obscured by the dishonesty and financial incapacity of the minister Bruck. If he contributed to enrich the nation, he also brought the currency into a state of confusion, from which there seems to be no escape. The charges of corruption which led to his fall are insignificant in comparison to what might have been brought against his former doings. In the affair of the sale of the Austrian railways to a foreign company, he agreed for a consideration, that all the iron should be furnished by foreign contractors—an arrangement by which his country lost 5,000,000 *l.* The judges who investigated the conduct of suspected persons after the crash traced many a thread to the finance minister, who resisted their claims to examine him, till his dismissal from his post enabled them to require his attendance. His credit had been lost by his raising the national loan for 50,000,000 *l.*, which he made more compulsory than voluntary, to 11,000,000 *l.* more than the sum authorized. When this was discovered, in the autumn of 1859, after the war, a new loan became necessary, and Bruck went into the market for 20,000,000 *l.*, but only got 7,000,000 *l.*, so greatly was the public credit shaken. After Bruck became minister, he did not cease his connection with the Trieste houses, with whom he had been in business. When the great Vienna bankers Arnstein and Eskeles, ruined by the war, asked him for help, he gave them hopes, and delayed their fall for two days, during which he telegraphed to his Trieste friends to secure their deposits; when this was done, he told the Vienna bankers that he could do nothing for them. The impossibility of confidence and security under the rule of such a minister occasioned the failure of the attempts to raise the material condition of Austria.

The same causes have made the Concordat, so far, a failure.

It was originally a purely political measure. Felix Schwarzenberg, who, in October, 1848, a time of great political stress, undertook the formation of a new ministry, and exacted from all his colleagues their agreement to the introduction of the Concordat, was notoriously the most dissolute man among Austrian officers and diplomatists, and lived more like a Turk than a Christian. His religious sentiments certainly had no part in the resolution. It was one of his methods for enforcing unity. But the Concordat was sure to cause more divisions than it healed if it dissatisfied the masses of Josephine Catholics and Protestants; these would only be satisfied by being allowed the same amount of liberty as was granted to the Church. But this would completely annihilate the benefits expected from the Concordat, one of which was to be the destruction of the independent influence of the Hungarian clergy; for another independent body of Protestant clergy would be set up in place of the Catholics. Thus the original sin of the measure, and the insincerity of its first authors, has avenged itself on them. It has been a source of divisions, it has confirmed the Hungarian Protestant opposition, and has hitherto done little good to religion. Not that I question the sincerity of the Emperor; all that has been in his power, the appointment of Bishops, has been most admirably performed; and if this is the only lasting result of the first twelve years of his reign, the Church will have gained not a little by him. But our sympathy with him as the giver of the Concordat must be modified by the patent fact that he was deficient either in intelligence, or in will, or in power, to carry out the system of which it ought to have been only a part. But now, while he recognized the right of the Church to define her own doctrines, the statute which he gave the Protestants made the conservation of *their* doctrines an affair of state. No doubt Protestants in other Catholic countries admit the sovereign to be head of the Church; no doubt also the reservations of Francis Joseph are good for the preservation of what Protestants still retain of sound doctrine. But is it rational that a prince who claims to be arbiter of doctrine should also talk of religious liberty? Is it consistent that, while he lets the Catholics rule themselves by their own institutions, he should impose an external authority on the Protestants? Though this external authority appeared so natural, that most of the Lutherans accepted it, and the German conservative Protestants were in raptures at the check which they hoped it would give to rationalism; though the measure was generous and greatly to the benefit of the Protestant religion—it was quite inconsistent with the principle of the Concordat, which is self-government. Farther, when once a deep and prolific principle is admitted, it cannot be confined in an arbitrary manner; when once its claim is allowed in the instance of a religious body, not only other religious bodies will prefer their claims, but it will demand an application on purely secular matters. The principle of self-government implies decentralization, and the localization of government; but for this Bach did nothing, whatever were the reasons that prevented him. For ten years nothing was done; and when at last a commencement was made it was useless, because it ought from the first to have run parallel with efforts at concentration; but the latter principle had won so long odds, that the struggles of the other tendency appeared only irregularities and exceptions. Perhaps, however, it was not in the Emperor's design to carry out the principle of self-government; and if it was, men's public life is weighed by what they do, not by what they wish to do. I have always hoped that the Concordat was the declaration of a great principle, and not merely an insulated act; even if it is carried out, it is worthless, because it is only a manifestation of feeling, of religious attachment, of mere interest, and not of principle; and therefore stands alone, unsupported, insecure, untrustworthy. We see in France the insecurity of institutions when their liberty depends on arbitrary will. Sometimes Louis Napoleon performs an act to gain the clergy; then he does something to gain the republicans. Now he coaxes the Catholics, and now he oppresses them to make friends in another quarter. If religion gains by this, no thanks to him. In the same way, the very reasons which led to the Austrian Concordat, when modified by a change of policy or any other external causes, might naturally and logically upset it. There is no safety unless the Concordat is part of a system, founded on principle, and standing or falling with other liberties. Alone it cannot help to save the State.

Though Francis Joseph restored self-government to the Church, he never seemed to have any conception of the political application of the idea; he never thoroughly understood the significance of representative institutions, and the incompatibility of anything else, in the long run, with a civilized and progressive people. *In the long run*, I say, because though such institutions are not always necessary, they are the test and token of freedom. The free classes can only hold their own by self-government; that is, by some kind of participation in the general government. In early times only certain classes were free, and then the kings surrounded themselves with a council of those classes, the nobles and the clergy. But as history advanced and freedom developed, other classes rose by degrees, first to social freedom, then to political liberty, and so to political power. This produced in various places three, and sometimes four, estates, according to the general law which guides the adaptation of the state to society through the social organism itself. Now, however, we often see it happen, that though society is an organism, the state is a mere machine; not fitted on to society like a glove, but rather compressing it like a thumbscrew; not growing out of society like its skin, but put upon it from without like a mould, into which society is forced to pour itself. But clearly the state could never grow out of society as its expression and fruit, unless society were organized and distributed into distinct classes and corporations, each enjoying social power in its own sphere; where the distribution is wanting, and the social mass comprehends no moral persons, but only physical units, society is atomic; and the state cannot be an organism, an expression or organ of society, but is supreme and absolute, whatever its forms and constitutional pretences may be. Under these circumstances representative institutions are a delusion and a snare, as they were in France from 1815 to 1848. In this manner the capacity for real representative government is a test of the maturity and health of society. Austria may be expected to have that capacity, for her social state is not in the least atomic; she has everywhere a great noblesse and in Hungary a wealthy clergy.

The late ministry, of which Goluchowsky was a member, was one of concessions made by fear to strength, not by reason to right. It gradually gave up all the policy of Schwarzenberg and Bach, and restored the critical independence of Hungary in such a way as to give Hungary a vast preponderance in the empire. In the first place, the Hungarians got everything by clamour; the Germans, who were tolerably silent, obtained much less. Their provinces did not receive a collective representative government, but each territory was to have its separate provincial estates. Thus the Hungarian Diet represented a far greater power than any of the others; it was as if, while Ireland had a collective parliament at Dublin, England were to have a separate parliament for each State of the Heptarchy. Collectively England would be the stronger nation; but each provincial English parliament would be feebler than the Irish. This was the first great error in the constitutions. The next was that—to judge from the constitution of Tyrol, the only one I yet know in detail —the number of representatives in the estates is too small. They will have no independent authority, will inspire no confidence, will be managed by two or three men, and will be open to corruption. This was the very disease that destroyed the old system of estates in Germany. Few people care to be present, so that the power subsided into the hands of the few, who were easily managed by the ministers; and thus the whole institution lost its vitality. The Tyrolese are anything but grateful for what has been given them; the measure does not compensate for the debased state of the currency. Their language is often perfectly ferocious against the government, and they curse their "folly" in 1809 in resisting their union with Bavaria.

But neither is Hungary at all reconciled by the great concessions made to it. In fact, the dissatisfaction and disaffection is rather increased than diminished, because the concessions are only interpreted to be a proof of fear. Concessions made at the last moment, and extorted by threats, never yet got any thanks. There is, so to say, no government party in Hungary. The great nobility, or magnates, lost most of their influence by the abolition of the feudal rights; and yet it was chiefly in favour of this declining body that the new system was contrived. The lesser nobles, who are enormously numerous, and the middle class, are for separation, and for the most part would prefer to belong to Russia. We may read in Georgei's memoirs how the plan was entertained in 1849, and how the Russians tried to make friends in the country by treating all who surrendered to them with signal courtesy. In spite of Nicholas' conservatism, they would never have put down the insurrection of 1849, except on account of their fears for Poland, excited by Kossuth, who surrounded himself with Bem, Bembinsky and other Polish refugees, and tried to extend the revolutionary movement into that country.

But now the action of the Hungarian emigrants, Kossuth, Klap-
ka, and company, counts for next to nothing in Hungary, and
Russia is not likely to be drawn in to assist Austria again, except
compelled to do so in self-defence. The opposition comes from
the middle class and lower noblesse, men full of distrust of
Austria and of crude political notions, burning with just hatred
for the equally crude ideas and for the hard proceedings of
German *employés*; and proud of their old constitution, which is
as bad as it is old—a mediaeval ruin transplanted into a modern
city-square. In 1848–49, Hungary was in arms for the Magyar
interests; but the Croatian, Slavonic, and Roumanic popula-
tions were on the Austrian side. But now they are all as discontented as the Magyars. The centralizing system, which was
formerly exercised for the advantage of the Hungarian government, has of late been in the hands of the Austrians, and the
sufferers have transferred their hatred to their new oppressors.
On a late occasion, when there was a famine in Croatia, the
Hungarians with wise generosity sent large supplies, and gained
the people's heart. And now the great movements which are
taking place in the Danubian provinces are against Turkey and
Austria, and afford to the Hungarians an opportunity of forming
a powerful eastern monarchy, if they separate from Austria.
This may be the providential purpose of the grievous troubles of
Austria on that side. The late ecclesiastical movement of the
Bulgarians shows the importance of a strong power not hostile
to Catholics having the command of the Lower Danube.

Another capital fault of Goluchowsky's measures was, that
they provided a new system without looking for new men to
carry it out. The statute overthrew the intelligent but pedantic
bureaucrats of Bach, who had succeeded the stupid bureaucrats
of Metternich's time, and who were omnipotent and very unpopular. Yet they were to carry out the new system. Their
cause was conquered, and yet by their instrumentality their
employer expected to construct his new system. Those men whose
moral influence in the temporary Reichsrath carried these concessions in spite of the resistance of ministers, though placed in
offices of more or less importance, were not entrusted with the
carrying out of the new system, which was left in the hands of
the old opponents of all change. As might be expected from such
unintelligent persons, they doled out their measures only as they

were forced; while Hungary contemptuously carried off almost everything, the Germans squeezed out mere driblets, unwillingly conceded, and not a whole system—a great statesmanlike measure to be carried out consistently. It was not a policy, nor the idea of a statesman, but only the surrender of as little as might be of popular demands to popular clamour. All that self-government gained, bureaucracy was to lose; but it by no means intended to lose anything at all in substance.

The substitution of Schmerling for Goluchowsky was a partial remedy for this capital fault. The new minister, who has played no public part for the last ten years, was Minister of the Interior in the National Assembly at Frankfurt, and was the first parliamentary and administrative genius there. He predominated so completely in that great parliamentary assembly, that he is certainly able to understand, appreciate, and manage representative institutions. He is the right man for a new policy.

The external dangers of Austria lie partly on the side of Italy, partly on that of Prussia. As for Venetia, unless the war in the spring ends in a great victory, that province will be the source of infinite danger to the monarchy. Provision is being made for a desperate struggle: the fortifications that are being erected on the Adige and the Adriatic are described as terrible, and the whole force of the empire will be poured into Italy and Croatia. The Confederation has waived its claim to the services of the Austrian contingent, amounting to 130,000 men, in case of war on the Rhine; this is the whole aid that is to be expected from Prussia; but though it is a great assistance to Austria, it argues not much generosity on the part of her rival. For if there is war on the Rhine, while Napoleon has 200,000 men in Italy, his fleet fully manned, and his fortresses on the Rhine and the Flemish frontier garrisoned, the Germans can make a very good fight without Austrian assistance, and Prussia will have the undisputed lead of the army of the Confederation. As Russia is opposed to the proceedings in Italy, it will not threaten the rear of the Austrians, and may even protect them against revolutionary movements; and the whole military force of the empire can be concentrated on the Drave and the Adige. Already the army in Italy and about the head of the Adriatic amounts to nearly 300,000 men; there is no disaffection in the Hungarian regiments, and the popularity of Benedik is immense. But the military system of Austria is wretched. The science of the officers is not to be compared to that of the Piedmontese; there is no good staff, nor any well-organized body of engineers; many of the officers are incapable, and others unable to speak the language of their soldiers. And there is among some of them a feeling that they are about to fight for what they are persuaded is a hopeless cause. If this was a common persuasion, no anticipations could be too gloomy for the future of Austria.

Whilst in Austria everything smacks of decline and fall, the Prussians are full of lofty aspirations. The government is secure, and, in spite of the late police scandals, on the whole well administered and popular. There is some injustice, but no known corruption. The danger which menaces Germany on the Rhine, and the dismal condition of Austria, both play into the hands of Prussia; for the Germans, indignant at their helplessness, can only look to her to save them. A like result follows from the corruptions of several of the lesser states, and the consequent discontent of their subjects; from the democratic tendencies which remain from 1848, and from the Prussian intrigues. Any day a movement may break out in Central Germany, encouraged by the party of Gotha, justified in many minds by the imminence of the French danger, pioneered by the example of Italy, and half invited by the Prussian ministry to condemn what is going on there. German unity, moreover, is an older ideal than the unity of Italy; only the former is historical. Italy from the sea to the Alps never at any time formed one State, and its possibility is all speculation and aspiration. But Germany was once one from the Somme to the Drave, and from Lyons to Königsberg, and the reminiscences are preserved in many traditional institutions and phrases. Every German knows that the misfortunes of his country, and its weakness in Europe, arose from the dismemberment of the Empire, the feebleness of the central power, and the rise of the great nobles to territorial independence. The unity of Germany is an aspiration that has once been realized; that is the aim of all patriots, and that has never been quite lost sight of as a hope or a regret. It was through the tendency to unity that in 1806 and in 1815 such numbers of independent sovereigns were swept away; that from more than 365 they have been reduced to 34. The notion of continuing in the same course is not a purely revolutionary idea, but an historical development of the reaction against the process of separation which went on during the fourteenth, fifteenth, and sixteenth centuries.

In case of a movement in favour of this idea taking place, Prussia, with its finances flourishing and its army in the best order, and supported by the patriotism of all Germany, is ready to intervene as the restorer of order, and to assume, quite naturally, the command over all the German troops. It will everywhere find many friends: almost all the Protestants, all the advanced liberals who are not yet democrats—to make sure of whom Prussia is meditating a reaction against Catholics, and a withdrawal of some of the concessions, in imitation of the measures which the Prussian government has persuaded the Baden ministry to adopt, and in deference to the non-Popery agitation which has been lately commenced by the leading Prussian reviews against Catholic immunities as exaggerated and dangerous. All the left bank of the Rhine, in fear of becoming French, and unable to help itself, looks to Prussia. Even in Bavaria, the largest, most Catholic, and most Austrian of the lesser states, there is a powerful Prussian party, not only in Nuremberg and the Protestant towns, but at court, among the friends of the king, who has already been opposed to Austrian influence, partly because he studied at Berlin, and has a Prussian wife, partly because he dislikes the clerical system as he supposes it to exist in Austria, and partly because he is so overshadowed by his great neighbour. It is in the more distant states, which are in no danger of annexation, that Austria is most popular; as with the old King of Württemberg, the Duke of Nassau, and the Grand Duke of Darmstadt, whose brother is one of the most popular commanders in the Austrian service. Among the Prussian influences we must not forget the newspapers in that interest that are largely paid by that government throughout Southern Germany, and the intrigues at the courts against the princes, for which incredible means are adopted, money being given to women to swear away the characters of Francis Joseph and of the King of Saxony. In Hesse Cassel, the worst governed State of Germany, a perpetual constitutional controversy is maintained: the Radical Constitution of 1831, being found incompatible with order, was abrogated in 1848, and another issued; and there is an endless agitation in favour of the restoration of the former, which is fed by Prussia, in hopes of finding an occasion of intervention. In

Baden, the rejection of the Concordat was a Prussian manoeuvre aimed against the throne of the Grand Duke; and this breach of faith has quite alienated the Catholic population from him.

The Liberals now in power at Berlin are thus indifferent to all law, civil or international. The bulk of the literary men in Prussia, and in great part of Germany, as well as most of the Protestant interest, belongs to them. Their head is the Princess of Prussia, the Regent's wife, one of the most able and ambitious of living women. She prompted the king to accept the imperial crown, when it was offered to him in 1848. She has made great efforts to conciliate the Catholics of Western Prussia, where she used to frequent the convents, and sometimes to shut herself up in one for a week, and, as was to be expected, found the Catholics good-natured enough to be duped by her demonstrations. Auerswald is her instrument in the ministry; and her policy, which carries away Schleinitz and Bethmann-Holweg, is the union of Germany under the Prussian sceptre. The policy of Radowitz, the great Catholic statesman from 1848 to 1850, was not very different. As for the Regent, he is a man of honour and good feeling, and desirous to act even chivalrously by Austria; but he is carried away by the party in power.

The Prussian Catholics, who are mostly Silesians and Rhinelanders, and so only Prussians since 1745 and 1815, do not desire the increase of Prussia, as they dread the Berlin system and its prevalence in Germany. But the most remarkable of its opponents are the strict Protestant party of the Kreuzzeitung, that was in power under the late king, but is now powerless;—aristocratic and conservative, like Burke, but more advanced than he; —when in power, not always just, especially to Catholics, and making use of corruption somewhat after the manner of Guizot; —high Protestants, like the advanced Tractarians, singularly fond of the mediaeval Church, with its monks, partly because of its analogy to their form of Christianity, partly because they consider Catholicism to be a great and beneficial social power;— haters of the revolution, but not always so strongly opposed to revolutionary measures from above as to those from below, and therefore inclining to Russia rather than to France, which they abhor;—full of admiration for an ideal England, and of comtempt for the present government;—Prussians of the old stock, and therefore preferring a powerful Prussia within its own limits to a Prussified Germany, in which their nationality would be destroyed, and liberalism would be triumphant. Hence these men are the most ardent defenders of the Pope's rights, of the King of Naples, and of the Austrians in Italy. This feeling is so strong among them, that their ablest representative, Leo, a month or two ago, had some meetings with certain Catholics at Erfurt to discuss the combinations that seemed possible; but when the report got about that he and his friends were about to become Catholics, they withdrew. This party, however, is much too weak to be of any real service to Austria.

Such is the present seething condition of a people numbering more than 60,000, of rare gifts, both of intellect and character, and destined apparently to play a remarkable part in the future history of Europe. Among the many openings for speculation is the effect of the Pope's possible, if not probable sojourn at Wurtzburg, on the frontierland of the Protestants and Catholics, and in the presence of an influential body of religionists like those of which Leo is the representative. The action which such an event might have on the population in Germany, and its reaction on the Italianism of the Papal Court, would probably be immense; but it is too large a subject for me to pretend to discuss at the end of an Article.

XIII

CONFESSIONS OF FREDERICK THE GREAT[1]

THE political testaments of monarchs and statesmen often explain not only their own conduct, but also the policy of the successors whom they aspired to guide. The men who have impressed their own characters most deeply upon the State, who have been the creators or leaders of new systems of government, or who have altered the course of their country, have naturally desired to turn their example into precepts, and in vindicating their own acts to insure those of their successors. And those successors, in their turn, have found that authority is easily preserved by the same arts by which it was obtained, and have been willing to accept their policy from the hands from which they received their power. These testamentary bequests have occasionally been given to the world. Sometimes they have been preserved among the *arcana imperii* until the vicissitudes of war or revolution brought them to the light; and the secret has then been divulged long after it had lost its efficacy. To the historian these are the most valuable, because they are the most sincere. Public statements of policy may be intended to influence opinion: secret directions are meant to control action.

From the time when Augustus bequeathed to the Senate the narrative of his reign, to be graven on tablets of bronze at the entrance to his tomb, many among the greatest of rulers of men have left behind them an exposition of their art. "Abiturus e vita", says Richelieu, in the unpublished dedication of his *Testament Politique*, "loquor veritatem eo momento quo nemo mentitur . . . Ostendi orbi praeterire aetatem Hispaniae, et redire seculum galliae." Louis XIV wrote directions for his grandson on the government of Spain, as well as reflections on the profession of a king, in which Voltaire considers that he is too severe to himself. In the present century his memoirs have been collected

[1] *Home and Foreign Review*, No. 3, Jan. 1863, pp. 152–71.

and published, and they exhibit his most intimate ideas; but, as Chateaubriand truly says, they betray nothing ignoble, and reveal none of those shameful secrets which the human heart too frequently covers. The policy of the Russian emperors is traced out for them in the political Testament of Peter the Great. And Washington's Farewell Address, conceived in the spirit and almost in the words of Hamilton, recommended to the United States, as the condition of their existence, those principles of federalism on which their constitution as well as their independence was founded.

Neither the system of the French, nor that of the Russian, monarchy is as worthy of study as the philosophic absolutism of the second half of the eighteenth century. Burke has thrown the mantle of his incomparable eloquence over the governments of those days; and thousands whom his rhetoric has dazzled have taken its figures for historical realities. Others are tempted to conclude, from the prodigious violence of the uprising against it, that the old *régime* was a system of unmitigated oppression. But whilst the apostles of enlightenment were contriving the subversion of the State in France, their principles were adopted and put in practice by the governments themselves in Austria and Russia, in Spain and Portugal, in Naples and Parma. Modern liberalism, like the philosophy of the eighteenth century, has taken the princes of that age under its protection. If they were stern upholders of the dignity of the crown, at least they were enemies of the priesthood. They were despotic; but they used their power against the aristocracy, not for the oppression of the people. They were intolerant of resistance or popular control; but they believed in the greatest-happiness principle, and their strength was founded on material resources, not on that reverence for authority which is an inheritance of feudal and religious ages. Their greatest enemies were those which the Revolution attacked; their chief strength was in principles which the Revolution proclaimed. The substitution of democratic for feudal monarchy was in progress before the democracy took it in hand, and the revolutionists could fraternize with kings who understood sovereignty so differently from the believers in Divine right. According to the profound observation of Donoso Cortés, monarchy is the revolution conquered, while the empire is the revolution crowned; and the monarchies of the eighteenth century, under the influence of the public opinion of the day, were rapidly putting off the traditional and conservative, and assuming the imperial character. The change is important in history, because, although it led to great and beneficial improvements, it prepared the way for the success of the Revolution and of Napoleon, by concentrating and isolating the power of the State, and by destroying everywhere the elements of social resistance.

We want an authentic record of the motives and sentiments of European monarchy in the generation which preceded its fall. No Macchiavelli has been inspired by sympathy, or by hatred, or by envy, to gather together the lessons which it has left us. No Richelieu of that age consented to publish to mankind the ideas by which European absolutism was impelled and guided in its latest, its most intelligent, and its most vigorous phase. There has hitherto been no authoritative interpretation of its acts and its designs. The man most competent to speak of it would be Frederick the Great. He was not the instrument or the mouthpiece of other men. He did not take his notions of government out of a book, as Joseph II borrowed his ideas from the *Monarque Accompli*, and Ferdinand of Parma from the *Cours d' Études* of Condillac. His originality of ideas was equal to his energy in action. He covered a decrepit society with the splendour of his genius; disguised by his vigour the weakness of his state; gained the applause of the revolutionary philosophers by his scoffs at religion; sheltered the Jesuits when they were expelled from Catholic states; and in his day was foremost in intellect and strongest of will in all the dynasties of hereditary kings.

Frederick wrote much about himself and his times; but he wrote for publication. He wrote history, and with an eye to the future. He wrote on political morality; but it was before the theories had stood the test of experience and temptation. He uttered many precepts; but he did not illustrate them by his own example. It would have been madness to publish his inmost thoughts, or to reveal to his enemies the key to his policy and the secret of his astonishing success. For he owed that success in a great degree to his own ingenious arts; and he had reduced kingcraft to a system as settled and complete as his theory of war.

But he did not intend that his successor should be left in ignorance, like the rest of the world. He believed that nothing but fidelity to his own example would avail to preserve the state which he had constructed. It was necessary that those who were to continue his work should not be deceived as to his character and his policy. His kingdom was a thing of violent and artificial growth, surrounded by obstacles, beset by irreconcilable enemies; and ruin would assuredly fall on his successors if they should be deluded into an inadequate idea of the talents, or into an exaggerated idea of the virtues, of him who was the author of their greatness. It was essential that they at least should know the whole truth, both regarding the political calculations which guided him and the moral considerations which he deemed it necessary to set aside. He accordingly provided this information for them.

Late in his career, when the tumult of his reign was over, and he was peacefully hoarding the harvest of his exertions, he wrote instructions in the art of reigning, for the use of the nephew who was to be his heir. The authentic text of this important work has at length appeared.[1] It contains the most portentous exposition of the state of waning royalty in Europe a century ago, when it had lost its chivalrous and religious character, and had not submitted to the control of religion and law. It is the code of the absolutism of a cultivated and unbelieving age; when religion had lost its authority with the masses; when the nobles were corrupt and the administration centralized; when the power of the press was exerted by the propagation of certain theories, rather than by the publicity of authentic information, and consequently lay at the disposal of intriguers; and when the magistracy was the only influence that retained any vestige of independence. To this age and this system it is what the *Principe* was to the tyrannies of the fifteenth century, and the *Discorso* of Sarpi to a patrician oligarchy. It is even more. For it is not only the work of a philosophical observer, but of one who himself perfected and exercised the art he teaches, and whose purpose and character gave him the strongest inducements to reveal even his most secret thoughts. The political lessons which it teaches are not always of general application; but its historical authority is greater than that of any similar work. It will not diminish the estimate which the admirers of Frederick entertain of his abilities, nor reverse the judgement which his enemies have passed on his character.

[1] *Les Matinées Royales, ou l'Art de Régner*, opuscule inédit de Frederic II, dit le Grand, Roi de Prusse; Londres: Williams et Norgate.

Frederick's art of reigning, or *Matinées Royales*, is divided into four principal subjects. It begins with a description of his kingdom, then examines the policy of the State towards the two powers which may curb the royal authority, viz., religion and law, and concludes with the general theory of government. The very first precept marks the tone and character of the whole: "Ne vous avisez plus de faire l'enfant, et sachez pour toujours qu'en fait de royaume, on prend quand on peut, et qu'on n'a jamais tort quand on n'est pas obligé de rendre." Frederick most assuredly cannot claim to be the author of this maxim. Others have believed it and have acted upon it before. But till his time no man could act openly on such a principle with impunity. Iniquitous and violent acts had been committed without number; but in the then state of opinion in Europe it was impossible to neglect the pretence of justifying them. There was not less violence, but there was more sophistry, and wrong was particular in assuming the guise of justice, and vice in paying tribute to virtue. The Partition of Poland was the first great public event in which this solicitude for appearances was openly discarded. Even the seizure of Silesia was defended by legal arguments. Poland was the first victim to bare expediency; and the author of the Partition very appropriately lays down with ingenuous simplicity the principle on which it was accomplished.

The precepts regarding religion which are given in the book are remarkable. Frederick was an infidel; but he understood the power of religious belief, both as a limit and as a protection to authority. He considered that the morality of Christianity acted as a check on the people, and need not be feared by the rulers, because it was simply a restraint, not an incitement. But men might be enthusiastic for a dogmatic system; and their attachment to a visible religious body or authority might counteract their allegiance to the State. He therefore wished to obliterate the distinctive characters of the different denominations, and to effect a general union of Catholics, Lutherans and Calvinists, on a much more comprehensive basis than that which was introduced among the Protestants in Prussia thirty years after his death. The scheme had been originally devised by his father. The conquest of Silesia, by adding considerably to the number of his Catholic subjects, gave it greater importance and larger proportions; and it was warmly taken up by the French philosophers, nearly all the most eminent of whom were to have a share in the work.

From the description which Frederick gives of the two projects, his father's and his own, it appears that the first was conceived merely in the spirit of Rationalism, out of a sort of disgust and impatience at the continuance of dogmatic disputes in an enlightened age and under a monarch so arbitrary as Frederick William; while the second was founded on deeper motives of policy. At first, Lutheranism was taken as the basis of the new system; but the Lutherans were expected to give up whatever repelled other men. The mysteries of religion were to be surrendered, because "there must be good sense in all things, and we must not stick to words." Public communion was to be abolished, as an expedient to conciliate the Calvinists. The use of images and the invocation of the saints were accepted as useful for the lower orders; but the Catholics were to be isolated from Rome, as they afterwards were in Austria under the Emperor Joseph, and the celibacy of the clergy was to be given up.

These ideas were considerably developed by Frederick himself. He was resolved to put an end to all that could divide men amongst themselves, in order that their duty as subjects might take precedence of everything else, "en leur inculquant la nécessité absolue de vivre et mourir en paix, et de faire leur unique bonheur des vertus sociales". For this end he sought to undermine religious zeal, or, as he says, prejudices, on every side: "I cause to be disseminated in every thing that is written in my kingdom a contempt for the reformers; and I lose no opportunity of exposing the ambition of Rome, and of both priests and ministers." But this negative action was not enough. He undertook to provide a definite system of faith and worship, and to induce his people to adopt it: "As a form of worship is required, I shall, if I live, cause some man to arise and preach one. At first I shall pretend to persecute him; but by degrees I shall declare myself his protector, and warmly embrace his system." That system was completely ready. The preamble, in which the hopeless uncertainty was demonstrated by the impossibility of agreement, and each of the existing religions was ridiculed with great dexterity and apparent good faith, was composed by Voltaire. The constructive part of the system was drawn up by D'Alembert and Maupertuis; and their argument was so elaborate, that it seemed, says Frederick, as if they had begun by convincing themselves, before they demonstrated the truth to others. They laboured to prove the sacred history a fable, "and had compiled at least thirty reflections on each passage of the Bible". Rousseau was engaged in preparing the refutation of all conceivable objections; and Voltaire and d'Argens had arranged a plan for a council, to be presided over by the king, at which each of the three recognized religions was to be represented by one of its ministers, and every province of the kingdom by two deputies of the nobility and as many of the third estate. "Our ancestors became Lutherans in the sixteenth century, in order to take the property of the Church; and Calvinists in the seventeenth, in order to gain the Dutch in the cause of the succession of Cleves. We may well become indifferent to all religion, in order to preserve tranquillity in our dominions."

Frederick cannot help admiring the skill of his ancestors, who were so highly favoured by circumstances that they could "make a reform which gave them the air of apostles, while it filled their purses. This is unquestionably the most reasonable change of the kind that ever occurred; but as there is nothing to gain, and as it would be dangerous just now to walk in their footsteps, we must hold fast to toleration." He was probably the first sovereign in Europe who was tolerant purely from motives of policy. He could not understand the stern intolerance of Protestantism, but he shared the fanatical hatred of Rome which was general among the French infidels; and the example of many Catholic countries in his day might have urged him to persecute. He calls the Catholics the most fierce and atrocious fanatics; their clergy, he says, are wild beasts, and wield a despotic authority, and the Pope still lords it over kings. Yet, with all this fear and hatred in his soul, he insists that every man must worship in his own way, and that to neglect this maxim would be the ruin of the State. The prince, by keeping aloof from religious controversy, extinguishes it in his dominions, "car les parties ne se forment que sur la faiblesse des princes . . . Le meilleur moyen d'écarter le fanatisme de ses états, c'est d'être de la plus froide indifférence sur la religion." A wise sovereign, moreover, will not persecute, because he will not be under the influence of religion himself: "Je ne dis pas pourtant qu'il faille afficher l'impiété et l'athéisme, mais—il faut penser selon le rang que l'on occupe . . . La vraie religion d'un prince veut l'intérêt des hommes et sa propre

gloire. Il doit être dispensé par état d'en connaître d'autre . . .
Ce serait le comble de la folie, si un prince s'attachait à des petites
misères qui ne sont faites que pour le peuple . . . Si nous nous
souvenons que nous sommes chrétiens, tout est perdu, nous serons
toujours dupé.'' The people, therefore, are to be under the authority of morality, but not of doctrine; whilst the sovereign must be
free from even the last restraint upon his will. The public good
and his own glory are the supreme law. If he is subject to scruples
of conscience he will be the victim of a less scrupulous and less
superstitious enemy, and where he makes an unjust war he will
see an army of devils arrayed against him. In this part of his
argument Frederick falls into a vulgar cynicism.

We recognize his political acuteness again in the chapter on
the administration of justice. It is of the utmost consequence, he
maintains, that the law should be justly and impartially administered among the subjects. The prince who attends to this will be
adored by them. But the king is not subject to the law: "Il ne
doit y avoir aucune égalité entre le droit du monarque et le droit
du sujet ou de l'esclave." Justice is an altogether arbitrary notion.
It is not understood alike in any two countries. Every one, therefore, must interpret it in his own way and to his own advantage.
Old laws and customs possess a time-honoured authority which
may be inconvenient to the king, whilst a code of laws which is
his own work and subsists by his own sanction cannot be a limit
to the exercise of his power. "Je suis né trop ambitieux pour souf-
frir qu'il y ait quelque chose dans mes états qui me gêne, et très
certainement qui m'a obligé à faire un nouveau code." Frederick,
by this remarkable admission, proves the case of Savigny and the
historic school of jurisprudence in their resistance to codification.
There is a close parallel between his views on law and on religion;
and the formula with which he overthrows the idea of right is
borrowed from his argument against Christianity: "Why is it
extraordinary if a man chooses to be just in his own way?" The
negative toleration which is founded on indifference allows no
religious basis, and therefore no moral sanction for laws. On the
other hand, jurisprudence is founded on ethics, and morality on
dogma. An original unity of belief, or, in other words, intolerance,
is therefore implied in the common law of every nation that retains its own.

As the supremacy of law is the most grievous impediment to

the enjoyment of sovereign power, an independent body of jurists is the most formidable enemy of absolutism. Frederick's reflections on this topic are more profound than anything in the rest of his work: "That which caused me most concern was the sure and constant course of the law, that spirit of liberty inseparable from its principles, and the dexterity with which jurists press their advantages and crush their opponents under the appearance of the severest equity . . . For these reasons I determined to sap the foundations of this mighty power; and by simplifying the law as much as I could, I reduced it to the point which I desired. You will be surprised, perhaps, my dear nephew, that men who never speak of the sacred person of the king but with respect, should be alone capable of giving him the law. It is for this very reason that it is easy for them to set bounds to our power."

He had seriously weighed the merits and disadvantages of constitutional government:

"I have often meditated on the advantage which a kingdom derives from a body that represents the nation, and is the guardian of the laws. I think a king is more secure on his throne when he is placed or retained upon it by such an assembly. But he must be an honest man to allow his actions to be examined daily. If you are ambitious, you must abandon the idea." There is a comparison between the position of a despot and that of a constitutional sovereign, which concludes by recommending a despotism for a great man, for the singular reason that his courtiers dare not deceive him, while a limited monarch is misled by adulation. But Frederick admits that it is a misfortune for the people to live even under an enlightened despotism. This is, perhaps, the only passage in which he presents a favourable contrast to Louis XIV. Frederick sees clearly, and is not blinded by pride or a narrow-minded hypocrisy. He has a more honest mind than Louis and less of that awe and superstition, with which the latter was filled by the contemplation of his own greatness. He explains, as follows, one of the beneficial fruits of despotism: "My monarchy is despotic; therefore I alone bear the responsibility. If I did not travel through the provinces, the governors would put themselves in my place, and would gradually divest themselves of the principle of submission, to adopt those of independence. As my commands are necessarily haughty and absolute, those who represent me would assume the same tyrannical tone; whereas by occasionally visiting the different parts of my kingdom, I become aware of every abuse of the powers I have committed to others, and bring back to their duty those who have transgressed it."

On the balance of power Frederick speaks with the knowledge and penetration we should expect in the man who overthrew it: "There are bad politicians who imagine that a state which has grown to a certain point must not think of increasing, because the system of the balance of power assigns its corner to each ... The 'balance of power' is a word which has subjugated the whole world, because people believed that it secured permanent possession; but in reality, it is nothing but a word ... When Prussia has accomplished her fortune, she may give herself an air of good faith and moderation, which only suits great states and very small ones."

That day was still remote, and Frederick was conscious that his actual resources were not equal to supporting the position he had gained. "The first means of success is to possess real power and resources; the second is to employ well what one has. We are not in the first position."

He employed two methods to deceive the world as to the extent of his power. One was to make men believe that the Potsdam drill and manoeuvring had some real value and efficacy. This was important, not so much because of the fear with which it inspired his enemies, as on account of the confidence with which it animated his own troops: "All the world believed themselves lost if they could not move their arms, their feet, and their heads *à la prussienne*. All my soldiers thought themselves worth twice as much when they saw that they were imitated everywhere." He tried to gain their attachment by a trick which was adopted afterwards by Napoleon. Before a review, he learnt by heart the names of some of the officers and sergeants, and spoke to them by name as he passed through the ranks: "Cela me donne un air singulier de mémoire et de réflexion." His other artifice was the employment of men of letters to publish his praises. He knew the value of their aid; but he despised them heartily: "Between ourselves, they are a cursed race; they are insupportably vain, proud, full of contempt for the great and of thirst for greatness, tyrannical in their opposition, implacable enemies and inconstant friends, hard to deal with, and often flatterers and satirists in the same day ... But they are necessary to a prince who means to reign despotically, and who is fond of glory ... In the midst of my greatest misfortunes, I took care that the pensions of the men of letters should be paid." He explains his treatment of Voltaire as follows: "In reality, I feared him; for I was not sure of treating him always equally well, and I knew perfectly well that one crown less would bring two blows."

In fact, his whole life, down to the smallest details, was carefully studied, for the purpose of deceiving and astonishing the world. "When I arrive at a place, I always look fatigued, and show myself in public in a very bad coat, and with my wig uncombed: *ce sont des riens qui produisent souvent une impression singulière.*" He was fond of good living, but obtained a reputation of great sobriety. When he dined in public, his German cook prepared the dinner, and he drank beer. But when he was alone, his French cook found it hard to satisfy him. "You would hardly believe", he says, "how important it is for a king or a state to quit the beaten track. It is only by the marvellous that one imposes, and makes oneself a name." Finally he sums up his whole system in these words: "Voulez-vous passer pour un heros? Approchez hardiment du crime. Voulez-vous passer pour un sage? Contrefaites-vous avec art."

It is easy to see how far these confidential explanations modify, and how far they confirm, the common opinion about Frederick the Great, such as Macaulay represents, or the admiration of those who think, with Mr Carlyle, "that in his way he is Reality; that he always means what he speaks; grounds his actions, too, on what he recognizes for the truth". They show him as completely destitute of moral principle as Macchiavelli's Prince, but less liable to sacrifice great aims to petty weaknesses than any conspicuous character of modern times. No biographer has ever done justice to his profoundly calculating intellect, to his power of dissimulation, to his cynical candour, or to his knowledge of the men of his time. But there is no pretext left for those who have made him their idol to attribute to him either moral respectability, honour, or public spirit. Yet the *Matinées* have not remained entirely unknown to this day. Several editions are enumerated in Barbier's *Dictionnaire des Ouvrages Anonymes*, s.v. *Matinées*, and in the Berlin edition of Frederick's writings, *Table Chronologique générale*, p. 159. A most corrupt and often unintelligible text was published only three years ago in the *Correspondence inédite de Buffon*, ii, 423, from a copy given to the son of Buffon, at Sans Souci, by Frederick himself, in 1782, as the editor imagines, for the first time—"Ce manuscrit ne fut jamais publié" (p. 421). The text now published is taken from a different and more reliable source.

In the year 1806, when Napoleon was at Berlin, his private secretary, the Baron de Méneval, found the manuscript of the *Matinées* at Sans Souci. Judging it to be in the handwriting of the king, with which he must have been acquainted, he took a copy, which forms the basis of the present edition. There are many characteristic signs that he had the original autograph before him. It is written incorrectly, in a rapid, uneven style, and is not unfrequently obscure. A very superficial comparison with Buffon's copy will be enough to prove the higher authority of that of Méneval. In the former we read: "Notre maison a eu, ainsi que toutes les autres, ses architectes, ses Cicérons, ses Nestors, ses Nérons, ses imbéciles," etc. This passage in the new edition is as follows: "Notre maison a eu ses Achilles, ses Cicérons, ses Nestors, ses imbéciles," etc. To put "Architectes" for "Achilles" might be only the blunder of a copyist; but the introduction of Nero shows that the writer of the copy did not understand the original. Three successive Margraves of Brandenburg were surnamed respectively Achilles, Cicero, and Nestor. Nero is mere amplification. Nearly all the most significant passages are entirely omitted in Buffon's text—amongst others, that in which Frederick expresses his opinions of the Catholics; that in which he declares that justice must be done only when no interests of the State are involved; that in which he asserts the superiority of despotic government; and all the bitterest remarks on the men of letters. Many little touches which would not sound well in the ears of a French philosopher are carefully expunged, and almost every alteration is evidently suggested by the desire of appearing to advantage. Each of the two copies bears the most ample and satisfactory testimony to the authenticity of the other; but it is unquestionable that the real intimate ideas of Frederick are to be found in the text of M. de Méneval.

The great Berlin edition of the works of Frederick, which was completed in 1857, three years before the correspondence of Buffon was published, does not contain the *Matinées*. The exclusion is accounted for in the following note: "Matinées Royales, ou Entretiens sur l'Art de Régner (sans lieu d'impression), 1766, 60 pages in-8. Les éditions et les manuscrits de cette mauvaise satire contre Frédéric qui datent d'avant 1770 ne renferment que cinq matinées . . . Plus tard les éditeurs ont ajouté les deux matinées *Du Militaire* et *De la Finance*, et intitulé l'ouvrage: *Les Matinées du Roi de Prusse; adressées à son neveu*. Les archives de la maison royale conservent trois manuscrits de l'ouvrage en question, dont deux portent des notes de la main de M. de Catt, lecteur de Frédéric. On lit sur l'un, composé de cinq matinées: 'Envoi de Mr Grimm de Paris pour en rendre compte au Roi'; et sur l'autre, de sept matinées: 'Envoi de Mr Grimm pour montrer au Roi ou lui en faire part.' M. P. R. Angouis a reproduit six matinées sous le titre de *Les Conseils du Trône donnés par Frédéric II, dit le Grand, aux Rois et aux Peuples de L'Europe*, Paris. 1823. M. Techener parle de l'ouvrage qui nous occupe dans sons *Bulletin du Bibliophile*, Paris 1843, in-8, p. 172, 173. Voici ce qu'il en dit: 'Ces *Matinées Royales* n'ont pu être composées que par un des ennemis de Frédéric. Il ne faut pour en convaincre que lire dans la quatrième matinée, au paragraphe sur les Plaisirs, la manière dont on lui fait faire l'aveu de la plus avilissante faiblesse.' Thiébault, dans ses *Souvenirs*, quatrième édition, tome iv, pp. 181–183, attribue les *Matinées* à un officier français qu'il ne nomme pas (il s'appelait Bonneville), mais qu'il désigne comme ayant accompagné le maréchal de Saxe en qualité d'aide de-camp; il ajoute que cet officier, s'étant hasardé à reparaître dans les états de Frédéric après avoir paraître en Hollande cet ouvrage apocryphe, fut arrêté et conduit à Spandau, où il fut enfermé pour le reste de ses jours et où il mourut en effet. Ce fait prouve que ce n'est ni à Voltaire, comme l'a prétendu M. Jouyneau des Loges, ni au baron Patano, ainsi que l'a avancé l'abbé Denina, que l'on doit imputer les *Matinées Royales*. On peut enfin consulter Barbier, *Dictionnaire des Anonymes*, t. ii, pp. 335 et 336, article Matinées, et la notice littéraire que nous avons inserée dans la *Staatszeitung*, Berlin, 1845, 26 juin, no. 175, p. 852, lorsque le Constitutionnel avait reproduit les *Matinées Royales*, qui ont aussi paru sous le titre de *Entretiens sur l'Art de Régner, divisés en cinq soirées* (sans lieu d'impression), 1766, 24 pages in-8."

This is all that the editors tell us about the *Matinées*. If it was intended as an argument against the genuineness of the work, there would be a manifest *petitio principii;* for it begins by assuming that it is a worthless satire. Two of the MS. copies in the royal archives are accounted for, and the third is passed over with a silence which would be very significant if the notice pretended to critical accuracy. If it is a copy of the printed work, it would not be so carefully preserved; certainly it would not be deposited in the archives without note or comment; and if it bore any sign or mark by which it could be proved to be no original, so important a testimony against the hypothesis that it is the work of Frederick would not have been omitted by the editors. The admission that this third manuscript copy exists in the archives is of some consequence, as it is without doubt the one which M. de Méneval transcribed. We can either believe that he would have taken the trouble to copy manuscripts which had been sent from Paris by Grimm, or that, having access to the papers of Frederick, he was ignorant of his handwriting. But though the editors throw no light on the subject, they refer us to the authority of M. Techener for the internal criticism of the piece, and to the narrative of Thiébault for its material history; and they appear to suppose that the words of these writers possess some actual value.

Thiébault was one of those Frenchmen with whom Frederick delighted to surround himself. He spent twenty years at Berlin, and wrote a collection of anecdotes in honour of his patron, which acquired no little popularity, and contributed to establish the ordinary view of the character of the king. The evidence he gives concerning the matter in question is to the following effect: "The marshal of Saxony came to visit the king, doubtless in order to concert the plan of the next campaign. A French officer, who was still young, though he had already served in America, accompanied the marshal as his aide-de-camp. This officer was a man of parts, but neither prudent nor delicate. It is said that he obtained of the copyist of Frederick the *Matinées du Roi de Prusse*, or discussions between that monarch and the eldest of his brothers and his heir, for twenty-four hours only; and that, as a natural return for this indiscretion, he lent at the same time to the copyist the manuscript *Rêveries* of the marshal; that, in spite of the most solemn promise to read the works without transcribing them, they both sat up all night secretly copying them; and that, in this way, the public had on the one hand, the first edition of the *Rêveries*, and on the other the Dutch edition of

the *Matinées*. There must be some error in this story. It is quite
certain that Frederick never composed these pretended *Matinées*,
although it is possible, and even likely enough, that he may have
said in different conversations some of the things which they
contain. Perhaps his secretary had gathered up some of these
real or supposed utterances; and perhaps this collection came
into the hands of the French officer, and was converted into the
Matinées. I offer this suggestion, because it is true that the latter,
having quitted the marshal and gone to Holland, there published
these apocryphal *Matinées*, and was fool enough to imagine that
his secret was known to nobody; that afterwards, being in search
of employment, he flattered himself, on the strength of some
vague promises, that he could obtain a commission in the Prussian service; and that, having ventured to appear in the dominion
of Frederick, he was arrested, carried to Spandau, where he was
imprisoned for the rest of his days, and where he died many years
ago."

Thiébault evidently knew nothing about it. The marshal of
Saxony was at Berlin in 1749, and died in 1750. The *Matinées*,
whoever may be their author, were written after the end of the
Seven Years' War in 1763. They are addressed to Prince Frederick William, who was born in 1745. The writer is not a Frenchman, for the style is full of Germanisms. Yet it may very well
be that the French officer Bonneville, who died at Spandau,
came by some unknown means into the possession of the manuscript, and caused it to be printed. It appeared first in 1766, and
was sent by Grimm to the king's private secretary, de Catt. The
hypothesis that Bonneville was the author stands altogether unsupported. Dr Preuss, the royal Prussian historiographer, informs us[1] that, as soon as the book reached Berlin, on March 4,
1766, the king caused an article to be inserted in the Hamburg
and Altona newspapers, by his resident at Hamburg, Colonel
Quintus Icilius. Its purport was as follows: "A certain book has
been lately printed under the title of *Les Matinées du Roi de
Prusse*. It is astonishing that people can be so impudent and so
malicious as to write such false, unfounded, and nonsensical
things, and use the name of a great monarch. If neither the dishonour, nor the impropriety, nor the insolence of such conduct
restrained the author and the printer from outraging polite

[1] In an article in the *Magazin für die Literatur des Auslands*, of April 10, 1861.

society in such a way, they ought to have been prevented by the danger to which they exposed themselves of meeting one day with the punishment they have deserved."

We learn nothing from this article. Frederick must necessarily have been angry at the publication, whether the book was genuine or fabricated. He could not avoid expressing, in either case, his protest and his displeasure. It appears, therefore, that the publisher must have known that he could not visit Prussia in safety. If he had forged the book, and had drawn out of his own heart the lineaments of the infamous character of the king, it is incredible that one who was so familiar with the depth of human selfishness should have trusted himself, with the consciousness of his guilt upon him, within the grasp of the man he had so grievously libelled. The fate of Bonneville does not offer the same inexplicable mystery, if we abandon the hypothesis of Thiébault and Preuss. He had obtained a copy of the original manuscript in some way which in all probability could not be justified, and he had published it. He had committed a great act of indiscretion, perhaps a breach of confidence. But his crime against the king was incomparably less than the deliberate composition of such a work under his name. That he should, under the circumstances, have put himself in the power of Frederick, was another act of imprudence, but an act less inconsistent with this interpretation of his character than with the villainy which, on the other alternative, we must attribute to him.

The only hypothesis which has been devised by those who deny the authenticity of the *Matinées* has nothing in the external facts of the case to support it. Neither Thiébault nor Dr Preuss produces a single argument against the opinion that the real author was Frederick. So far, therefore, that opinion is not conclusively established; but no other person can be found whose claims possess the slightest force. The only argument derived from the tenor of the text itself is conveyed, by the editors, in the form of a quotation of the French bibliographer M. Techener. It is, he says, impossible that any man could have confessed his own degrading vices. In fact, this is the only logical argument which the editors have ever brought forward to justify the omission of the *Matinées* from their collection of Frederick's writings.

Dr Preuss is a gentleman of such extraordinary credulity where the honour of Frederick is at stake that he may be sincere in considering the argument decisive. He has read all the works of the king, including his letters to Voltaire, d'Argens, and Prince Henry, and nevertheless he is able to affirm that "Frederick never spoke of the Christian religion otherwise than with the most suitable reverence."[1] It does not matter, however, whether we assume that the editor is destitute of the critical faculty, or that his private conviction was overruled by a different motive. In neither case could the *Matinées* have been included in an official edition, printed by the king's printer and superintended by the historiographer royal. The fame of the great king is a tower of strength to his descendants. The belief in his patriotic policy and character is partly the cause of the sympathy which the House of Hohenzollern enjoys in Germany. The official recognition and adoption of the confidential statement of his system would be an ungenerous and destructive blow at the foreign policy of the country. In another point of view it would be even more than impolitic. The *Matinées* contain a description of the Prussian people scornful and insulting in the highest degree, and yet not so unfair as to be without a sting. To publish this as the estimate formed of the character of his subjects by the greatest king of the race, in an edition of his writings published officially, with the sanction of government, would be an outrage which no sovereign possessing the least sense of honour or of his own dignity would think of committing, and which no sovereign could commit with impunity. We are inclined to think that it is owing as much to this feeling of the utter impossibility of involving the royal family in the responsibility of the *Matinées*, as to a reluctance to alter the popular belief in the virtues of Frederick, that the editors, in excluding them from their edition, have taken so little pains to justify the omission.

For the passage to which M. Techener alludes is in perfect harmony with the cynical tone of the whole work. The same spirit animates every part. Everywhere we find the same unwavering egotism, the same heartless sneer at every moral virtue—redeemed only by the candour and self-knowledge with which it is put forth, and by the sagacity with which it is applied, for good as well as for evil, to the art of government. Other men have been as selfish in their objects, and as vicious in their acts. But very few have been so distinctly conscious of the nature of their

[1] Preuss, *Friedrich der Grosse*, iii, 175.

motives; and few intellects have been so highly sharpened by
interest to discern some of the highest truths of policy. The
Matinées are in this respect a masterpiece, such as no writer could
have conceived or executed who had not the model before him.
The author must have sat for his own portrait; he must have
possessed the wonderful character and intellect which he describes.

Frederick is perfectly aware of the immorality of his precepts;
but he does not believe in morality. He knows that he is not
raising himself in the eyes of his nephew; but he tells him to put
off the simplicity of childhood, and to understand the qualities
which make not a good man, but a great king. He exposes his own
moral faults without pride or humiliation, but in order that his
successor may learn, at his expense, the secret by which power
is increased. Accordingly, he disguises nothing which may contribute to that end. His purpose is clear, and the book corres-
ponds accurately with it. There are many traits in his correspondence, as it is included in the late edition of his works, which confirm the statements of the *Matinées*.

The same considerations which have caused their exclusion
have determined the choice of his letters. The edition is not complete. An official edition probably could not be complete. Although it is distinctly affirmed that all Frederick's writings are
included, there is only one letter to Catherine II. It is dated April
22, 1871,[1] and congratulates the Empress on having dictated the
Peace of Teschen, by which Russia acquired the right of interfering in the concerns of Germany, which had, since the year 1648,
been enjoyed by France. Now Frederick was in intimate alliance
with Catherine for twenty years, during which time several
matters of a very delicate nature were negotiated between them.
Amongst these were the Partition of Poland, and the marriage of
the Grand-Duke Paul with a Princess of Hesse Darmstadt, which
was arranged by Frederick. Is it credible that during all this
time he never wrote to her except in the one single letter which
is contained in the *Œuvres*? Dohm, who was not an enemy of
Frederick, tells us that the flattery with which he kept his ally in
good humour was not always worthy of him; but that he was
preserved from greater degradation by the admiration which
Catherine had always entertained for him.[2] He adds that he can

---

[1] *Œuvres*, xxvii, 3, 323.   [2] *Denkwürdigkeiten*, iv, 259.

say this with confidence, because he had seen several of Frederick's letters to her which were still unpublished. Judging from the tone of the published letter, it is probable that the others were not creditable to the writer's sense of dignity; and it is fair to conclude that this was the motive of their exclusion. We can hardly suppose that both originals and copies are lost. At any rate, we might expect that the editors would have given some explanation which might remove our suspicions, and that the all but total omission of this important part of the correspondence of Frederick would have been accounted for.

We admit that the reasons for the exclusion of the *Matinées* were overwhelming, although there is absolutely no argument against their authenticity. At the same time, when the edition of the *Œuvres* was completed in 1857, the proofs of Frederick's authorship did not amount to a certainty. It may be that the third manuscript copy in the Prussian archives is not in the handwriting of the king; and the former editions, which attribute the work to him, do not prove it. They contained different texts, and no text coincided with that of the Berlin manuscript. The internal evidence, moreover, could never be conclusive against the voice of Prussian patriotism and a cherished tradition. That is a sort of uncritical resistance which could only be overcome when every link in the chain of external evidence was complete. This is now the case; and the authorship is brought home by the following note of the editor of Buffon's correspondence, M. M. H. Nadault de Buffon. The son of the great naturalist visited Berlin in the summer of the year 1782, and was received with great distinction by the king:

"À son retour d'Allemagne, le Comte de Buffon remit a son père un manuscrit que lui avait confié le Grand Frédéric, et qui a pour titre: *Les Matinées de Frédéric II. À son neveu Frédéric Guillaume, son successeur à la couronne.* Ce manuscrit que Buffon fit voir à ses amis et dont les *Mémoirs* de Bachaumont font mention, ne fut jamais publié. M. Humbert-Bazile, son secrétaire, fut chargé par lui d'en faire plusieurs copies, dont l'une lui est restée. Mme Beaudesson, sa fille, a bien voulu m'en donner communication. En publiant aujourd'hui le manuscrit du roi de Prusse, je dois dire cependant qu'en 1844 M. Humbert-Bazile ayant remis ses papiers à M. Isidore-Geoffroy St Hilaire, ce savant fit paraître en feuilleton quelques extraits de cette pâte des mémoirs du Grand

Frédéric. Cette publication, incomplète du reste, n'enlevera rien à l'intérêt avec lequel sera lu ce fragment vraiment curieux. Il trouve d'ailleurs naturellement sa place ici.

"Un passage des mémoires inédits laissé par M. Humbert-Bazile en détermine l'authenticité:

" 'Plus tard, est-il-dit à la page 328, t.i. du manuscrit: M. de Buffon me valut un désagrément sérieux auquel je n'avais cependant point lieu de m'attendre. M. le Comte était aller passer la journée a St Ouen; durant son absence, son fils vient me prendre, pour aller rendre visite au célèbre peintre Julien de Parme, qui habitait alors la rue de l'Estrapade. À mon retour le portier de l'hôtel me prévient que pendant mon absence M. le Comte est rentré, et qu'il a témoigné un vif mécontentement en apprenant que j'étais sorti. Je cours à son appartement; M. de Buffon me reçoit froidement, et me témoigne son mécontente-ment. M. Necker, me dit-il, est venu avec moi à Paris pour voir les présents de l'impératrice et prendre lecture de ses lettres, et en même temps *du manuscrit du roi de Prusse* que je vous ai donné à copier: qu'en avez-vous fait? Je répondis avec respect: J'ai soigneusement renfermé les lettres de l'impératrice et le manu-scrit du roi de Prusse dans le meuble où je range ceux de vos ouvrages que vous voulez revoir; en voici la clef. Je ne pensais que M. le Comte fut de retour a l'hôtel avant moi; au reste, je ne sors que rarement, et je mets le plus d'exactitude possible à executer vos ordres; mais cette fois M. votre fils m'a pressé de l'accompagner, et dans la crainte de le désobliger, je suis sorti avec lui. C'est bien, dit il, tout en se promenant dans son cabinet, c'est fini; mais ne recommencez plus."

The testimony of the editor and of the secretary of Buffon is incontrovertible. Dr Preuss has attempted to meet it in an article we have already referred to. He quotes the words in which Buffon relates to Mme Necker that his son had been presented to the king, and adds: "Here is nothing about the king having given to the young officer for his father this satire as his own work." The omission of any notice of a fact is very rarely a decisive proof that it has not happened. Buffon, on July 12, 1782, writes a long letter to Mme Necker; at the end he adds a postscript: "Encore une petite gazette, puisqu'il reste de la place." Then he fills up the space with a short account of his son's interview with Freder-ick, in which there is nothing about the *Matinées*. It may be that he had not room for it, for he ends with an "&c". Or it may be that he did not think of it. Or his son may not have told him at the time; for the audience took place on May 18. Or he may have thought it unnecessary or unwise to write to Mme Necker about it. Certainly he did not yet know of the contents of the book, as his son did not return for many months. There are many reasons why Buffon may not have mentioned the *Matinées* in the letter on which Dr Preuss comments, but it is impossible to find a motive on the part of M. Humbert-Bazile, or of M. H. Nadault de Buffon, for the falsehood of which he accuses them.

He supports the imputation with another argument: "In the letter to d'Alembert, of the 18th May 1782, the day on which young Buffon and the Abbé Raynal were presented at Potsdam, Frederick the Great speaks circumstantially of the latter, but says nothing of the former." This might be an argument to prove that young Buffon never was presented; but it does not bear in any way upon the question as to what passed at the interview. It is, however, a very good instance to show the absurdity of supposing that there is anything unlikely in the omission of the story of the manuscript in the letter of the younger Buffon to his father, or in the letter of the father to Mme Necker. It is in fact very improbable that Dr Preuss made these objections from any other motive than that of official propriety. If the positive evidence did not conclusively establish the authenticity of the *Matinées Royales*, the question would be settled by the total absence of any argument against it on the part of those who are strongly interested in the cause.

(*See Note on p. 473.*)

XIV

NOTICES OF BOOKS

DÖLLINGER'S HISTORY OF CHRISTIANITY[1]

THERE is a witty saying of Jean Paul, suggested by the political and literary aspect of Europe at the beginning of the century, that the dominion over the earth belongs to the French, the sea to the English, and the air to the Germans. "Ideas", says the best historian of German poetry, "are our sword, and literature our field of battle." For ages past the Germans, who for a thousand years after the fall of Rome were the foremost power in the world, have been a people of thought more than action; their influence has been intellectual rather than political, and their speculative activity has been sometimes a consolation and sometimes a source of public disasters and humiliations to the people. Those realms of thought in which they are most thoroughly at home have neither geographical boundaries nor national character, and that universality which is the special quality of their literature forms, in the absence of a jealous and exclusive patriotism, their chief political defect.

> What is it but a vain and curious skill
> If sapient Germany must lie deprest
> Beneath the brutal sword? Her haughty schools
> Shall blush; and may not we with sorrow say,
> A few strong instincts and a few plain rules,
> Among the herdsmen of the Alps, have wrought
> More for mankind at this unhappy day
> Than all the pride of intellect and thought?

The whole range of human knowledge is embraced in their studies; every science is equally cultivated, and the history of other countries and of other times is pursued almost as zealously as their own. Yet this very universality raises a barrier between

[1] *Christianity and the Church*, Ratisbon, 1860. [From *The Rambler*, vol. iv, Jan. 1861, p. 145.]

them and other nations, and provokes that feeling of repulsion for the works of the Germans which is as common in England as in France and Italy. There is a want of human interest about the things they write; they do not seem to be actuated in literature by the same motives as ourselves, or to feel the same aspirations and passions, but live and write in a region we can hardly understand, and pursue objects for which we do not care. Their vast labours are carried on apparently without any definite purpose, without aiming at any particular result. With us Oriental learning is kept alive by our Eastern empire; ecclesiastical history is studied for the sake of controversy, English history for political reasons. If we had no Asiatic possessions, no political parties and no religious sects, all these departments of literature would probably fall into comparative neglect. But in Germany external accidental considerations of this kind have very little weight. The increase of knowledge has been one of the necessities of the German mind since it was awakened by Lessing, and the practical applications, the moral and social consequences, however serious they may be, and however eagerly they may be discussed in popular regions, are not the primary motives of inquiry. For instance, the great critic who did most to establish the text of the *Iliad,* and that of the *Nibelungenlied,* Lachmann, also published the best text of the New Testament which appeared before Tischendorf. The same critical skill and interest which he exhibited in examining the composition of the Greek and German epics also set him to work upon the Bible. Now this is widely remote from the practical spirit in which learning is pursued in this country. We have but little experience of that abstract love of knowledge for its own sake, of that self-denying and disinterested indifference to consequences, and of that faith in the consistency and harmony of all truths, which inspire the energy of the laborious German. We are always tempted when we meet with a new fact, and before we take the trouble to make a note of it, or to recognize its existence, to ask what it proves and where it will lead to, rather than to inquire how it is proved and what it is the result of; and we can hardly appreciate the pleasure with which men who have perfected to the utmost the instruments and the method of scientific research employ their lives in applying them indefinitely to every conceivable object.

As a natural consequence, there are two principal objections which are generally made to the historical and theological books of the Germans—that the former are defective in form and arrangement, and the latter incurably fanciful and unsound. As it is commonly understood, this implies much more than if it were said, what is notoriously true, that many famous scholars are bad writers, and that many of the German divines are rationalists, and much of their philosophy is pantheism. Nor is it enough to say in explanation of the first complaint that the language, rich and pliable beyond others, is less cultivated and refined than some. As a literary language, it has not existed in reality much more than a century. Leibniz was obliged to use French and Latin, and Frederick the Great could not write German correctly. Even now it is not an instrument which every educated man is competent to handle, or that can be managed without an effort; and many writers have neither time nor inclination to take the requisite trouble. But that the defect so far is in the men, not in the language, the works of Schiller are alone enough to prove.

The chief object of a scholar in writing a book lies in the new matter he can bring to light, in the novelty either of his facts or of his conclusions. But new discoveries cannot be dug up, and hewn, and polished into shape all at once. The new matter must pass often through many hands before its right place and proportion are assigned to it, and before it is permanently absorbed and admitted into the department to which it belongs. A writer who rests his aim and his fame in the advancement of learning may be satisfied with the performance of part of this labour. Other considerations make a book popular, but if it adds to the sphere of human knowledge and ideas, it is remembered for that alone. The progress of learning is so rapid that every book must soon become in some measure antiquated and superseded, and then the only merit that will be regarded is that of having contributed to the progress by which it has been left behind. This is the fruit of competition. Each writer knows that his book, in order to be read, must surpass those of his competitors in some substantial points, and that it must appear as soon as is consistent with excellence, otherwise the place it aimed at will be occupied, and the gap it was destined to fill will disappear. In order to obtain the success he seeks, eloquence is not required, and, besides, there is no time for it. In short, literature is so constituted in Germany, that an eminent author does not find it worth his while to write for those readers who are attracted by the beauties of style.

The charge of dullness is in reality nearly allied to the charge of a general obliquity of views, which is of more importance and of more general justice, but which is likewise founded on that method of scientific research which to the uninitiated is so distasteful and so strange. Our writers endeavour to please their readers by making their style as agreeable, or striking, or insinuating, as possible, and by presenting their ideas in the most acceptable light. Inasmuch as they aim at popularity, they are conscious that they are addressing an incompetent audience, that they will be read chiefly by persons who are not always prepared for the truth in its nakedness; and they therefore imitate Solon, and give not the best they have, but the best that will go down. They think more of the ignorant who are to be persuaded and more of the public that requires to be taught, than of the truth which requires to be proclaimed. There is a sort of bargain between the author and his readers, in which some concessions must be made to their ignorance, their weakness, or their prejudices. A national, political, or sectarian partiality taints almost the whole of our literature; that is, an author considers not only what he believes to be true, but what the party he addresses will be disposed to believe; and the first test that will be applied to his book will be to inquire whether it says what has been said before, whether it is within the range of ideas and of knowledge of the persons who judge it. Now a book that extends knowledge, a book of original thought and original research, has the very opposite character. Its effect will be to dissatisfy partisans, and to break down the exclusiveness of parties; to compel men to make room for the new facts, and to revise their opinions in conformity with them. Nowhere, except in Germany, are the dignity, the freedom and the authority of learning acknowledged in this manner; and it is this which alienates us from their writings far more than the impieties of Feuerbach or Strauss. It is not so much the offensiveness of particular conclusions that repels us as the spirit in which all their inquiries are conducted. In this respect the Catholic and Protestant literatures of Germany are alike, and their effects upon Catholics and Protestants in other countries are the same; for, although the action of science has been more conspicuous in Protestant Germany, where the best and soundest of their divines and historians, who went out to curse the Church of God, have been compelled, in defiance of the traditions and even of the principles of their party, to utter blessings, and to bear an unwilling testimony to her, yet the same principle of conscientious inquiry, the same reverence for the authority of science, has established itself during the last thirty years among the Catholics as well. They have abandoned the tone and the character of advocates, and have ceased to treat Catholicism as a party question, in which the object is to put forward the best side of things, to deny or conceal by the artifices of rhetoric whatever may be less to the advantage of their cause, and to make the best use of the *argumentum ad hominem*.

They have regarded the ends of controversy as in no way distinct from the ends of learning, and have deemed the advancement of the one equivalent to the advancement of the other. For that which was said of the Popes by de Maistre is true, in a higher sense, of the Church—that she has need of truth, and nothing else. For to her, who is the depositary and the protector of truth, truth alone is natural and congenial; and inasmuch as ignorance and error cannot permanently be kept asunder, inasmuch as truth belongs to the nature of God, and religion is allied with all truths and contradicted by all errors, the Church is not only the enemy of falsehood, but indirectly, though necessarily, the promoter of all knowledge. She not only does not fear its increase, but requires it. Every other religion not only fears truth, but requires that it should be concealed or disguised. That which upholds the one destroys the other; consequently the adoption of the same principle of scientific inquiry by the writers of both parties has done as much for the disorganization of Protestantism as for the support and corroboration of Catholicism; but on either side it has effected a great internal revolution. For whilst the old traditions and opinions which were the foundation and the pillar of Protestantism have been shaken in the eyes of the Protestants themselves, many traditions and habits which were the bane and the weakness of Catholic controversialists were struck by the same blow. In adopting the new mode and instruments of warfare, Catholic writers have necessarily taken up a position very remote from those extremes, and from those resources of argument, to which, in the conflicts with Protestants, Jansenists, Gallicans, with the scoffers of the eighteenth century, and the scientific incredulity of the nineteenth, their predecessors have so often had recourse. For it is not too much to say—and we cannot say it without shame for ourselves and grief for thousands of souls that have suffered by it—that calumny has been hardly a more popular weapon among our adversaries than mendacity with ourselves; and this has been, not the error of blindness or of ignorance, but in many cases the result of consistent and elaborate design. Whilst the doctrines of the Reformation have been maintained by means of conventional fictions, which no believing Protestant ventures to assail, men have been found amongst us also whose faith was equally weak, and whose conscience at least equally elastic. It has therefore been seen, at every great stride, made by profane or ecclesiastical learning, that its progress was resisted on grounds of religion even by Catholics themselves. It was so with the study of nature in the time of Galileo, and it was so likewise when the critical study of history was created by Tillemont and Mabillon, Papebroch and Noris.[1] And in our own time, if there is not the same resistance and the same antagonism, yet the chasm which separates the leaders of the new school of learning from the followers of the old is scarcely less extensive or less deplorable.

In one respect we English Catholics are at a great disadvantage. One of the chief means by which the spirit of learning has been developed in the Church in Germany is here totally wanting. Not that we are destitute of the example and guidance of writers of the first order, but that they are destitute of opponents who are worthy of them. It is in the nature of things that a man should be influenced almost as much by the character of the adversary with whom he carries on a prolonged contest, as by that of the friend with whom he lives. For he is compelled to adapt himself in some degree to the sort of hostility he encounters; he imitates the arts of his adversary, sometimes his artifices, often his faults. Where this cannot be, the fighting is all on one side; and thus Voltaire had it all his own way. He could not drag his adversaries down to his own level. Ferocity, marauding, neg-

---

[1] Attempts were made to obtain the prohibition of the works of each of these eminent men, because, said one of their most learned contemporaries, they were in contradiction with certain opinions on matters not of faith but of fact. See Fontanani's memorial to Clement XI, in defence of the annals of Tillemont (CC. *Venetorum ad Magliabechium*, i, 267).

ligence are things learnt in war from an enemy, as well as discipline and vigilance. Now English Protestantism stands much higher morally than the Protestantism of Germany, but much lower intellectually. It is a much more conservative system, but it is much less addicted to, and less dependent upon, science and learning. The qualities in which it shines the Catholics possess, for the most part, in a still higher degree. In those things in which we most require instruction, it has little that will avail us. Precisely because Protestantism is more respectable here than abroad, it is more unprofitable to contend with it. In England a man shrinks from pursuing his opinions to their logical consequences, or from uttering them if they lead to consequences he is afraid of. Mr Mill, Mr Grote, and Mr Buckle are as far removed from every positive form of Protestantism as Proudhon from every form of Christianity, but their tone is generally decorous. Mr Darwin refrains from publishing the opinion which it is not denied that he holds, that men grew out of apes; and in the debate on the Census in the House of Commons, it was urged that it would be a great hardship and injustice to compel free-thinkers to declare that they believed in God. We may applaud this reserve; yet it signifies that the English people, who tolerate every opinion, are not ripe for the recognition of that principle of free inquiry which, while it leads Protestants to unbelief on the one hand, carries them also to the Catholic Church. That is another reason why it cannot make its way. Dislike of Popery is as strong an element of Anglican theology as dislike of unbelief. A moderate amount of sincere investigation would scatter to the winds most of the stories on which that part of the popular belief is founded; consequently a species of artificial terrorism keeps down a movement which would certainly be fatal to Protestantism, and as certainly would be favourable to Catholicism. Speaking of his own country, Möhler writes: "As long as the doctrines of Luther and Calvin were really believed, the Protestant Church possessed no poetry, no history, no philosophy. It is certain that whilst the Protestant community was Lutheran it had no philosophy, and when it obtained a philosophy it was no longer Lutheran. Thus their faith repels philosophy and their philosophy repels faith. When their common faith was set aside, and there was no longer a link connecting them with each other, then came the meridian of their literature . . . And it was needful that it should attain that high perfection, that the nature of Protestantism was brought to light. That nature is now in all respects abundantly ascertained, and can be concealed from nobody. The literature of Protestantism is a great fact in the history of mankind, but a dark spot in the history of Christianity. In the Catholic Church art and learning were always Christian; and when they could not exhibit that character, preferred to be silent altogether. Nothing is more certain than that the more the principle of individualism is carried out in Protestantism, the more brilliant its products will be; and, on the contrary, the more perfect the unity of the Catholic community, the more arts and sciences flourish within it."[1]

HEFELE'S LIFE OF XIMENES[2]

PROFESSOR HEFELE of Tübingen has acquired by his excellent History of the Councils a very great name in the ecclesiastical history of our time. His *Life of Ximenes*, though a clever and successful work, is not distinguished by the same profound research, and it does not possess the advantage of manuscript information, which gives a real value to all the writings of Prescott. Though it is unquestionably the best history of the great Cardinal, the popularity it has acquired is probably chiefly due to the critique of Llorente's History of the Inquisition. Even on this subject, however, it brings to light no new matter, and repeats with great point and fullness, but little addition, much that has been often urged before. The author has not entirely escaped the partial and argumentative tone of apology and advocacy which was during the last generation so common among Catholic historians, and which sanctioned and almost justified the method of the Protestant and infidel writers, whose conclusions they questioned, and not unfrequently disproved. This may perhaps be attributed partly to the insidious influence which biography exercises over those who write it. For that most entertaining branch of literature is also the most apt to distort the facts and

---

[1] *Gesammelte Schriften*, p. 261.

[2] Dr von Hefele, *The Life of Cardinal Ximenes;* translated from the German by the Rev. Canon Dalton, Catholic Publishing Company, 1860. [From *The Rambler*, vol. iii, July 1860, p. 158.]

proportions of history, by the interest with which the hero inspires his biographer. For a person is more attractive than a principle, and an impartial biography is far more rare than an impartial history. In proportion as a cause is bad in itself, it becomes necessary to exalt those who are its representatives. This is one great reason of that unfairness of Protestant writers which is often unjustly attributed to hatred of the Catholic Church. A reforming party cannot admit that those who instituted the reformation were not really better than those who rejected it. It is unreasonable to expect of a zealous Protestant that he will give up the character of his leaders, or recognize the superiority of Catholic heroes. Infidels and rationalists are not so bound. They do not look for authorities. They depend on themselves, and make their own subjective consciousness the supreme test of truth. Their case does not stand upon the merits of any set of men, and they may be perfectly disinterested in all disputes regarding persons. Indeed, their attention is more particularly directed to the impersonal forces in history, and it is in this way that they have erected the philosophy of history into a scientific system of laws. For this reason also they are so often astonishingly fair and favourable in their judgement upon men whom it has been a Protestant tradition to denounce. In many particulars their views approach very nearly to those of Catholics, and their method of investigation is more Catholic than their results often are. They have made the progress of learning independent of the interests of parties, and by this means have rendered the greatest service to the Church. Unfortunately we ourselves have not escaped the influence of Protestant examples. We too often think that the cause of our religion is at stake in the vindication of some great character, and degrade what is divine to the level of human weakness. We do not keep sufficiently distinct the purposes of edification and of scientific research; consequently our interests are often safer in the keeping of others than in our own.

At any rate, Canon Dalton deserves our thanks for bringing this work within reach of English readers. He has been assisted by a German gentleman, who will be able to be of great use in introducing us to the Catholic literature of his country, when he has succeeded in acquiring greater correctness and facility of language. Canon Dalton has brought to bear upon the undertaking a great love for the subject, knowledge of foreign literature, zeal for the cause of religion, some acquaintance with several Spanish books that were not known to Hefele, and some gleanings of the literary gossip of Valladolid. His greatest merit is a perfectly disinterested and good-humoured love of truth—at all times a rare possession. It frequently appears in the Introduction, and in the notes he has appended to the work. When, for instance, Hefele says that when the Council of Toledo decreed the expulsion of the Jews, in consequence of their having conspired against the State, it was intended only to banish those who had actually joined in the treason, his translator gives an extract in a note to show that in fact all were banished. It is equally characteristic of his notions of historical science, that he attempts to control Hefele's statement by quoting in Spanish the text of a council of the seventh century; or that he concludes that the older Spanish writers "had better means of appreciating the character" of Torquemada than Mr Prescott *because* "they speak of him with the highest respect." But in spite of such defects as these, the simplicity and sincerity of his remarks oblige us to overlook the claims of strict criticism in admiration of the great scenes he has brought once more before us.

In the Introduction Canon Dalton endeavours to modify Hefele's view of the political origin and purpose of the Inquisition. We will not say that he proves his case; but at the same time this portion of the original is so very defective that we will join the translator in his attempt to improve and correct it. Any discussion of the subject must, however, be considered premature, whilst a work which has long been in preparation by a laborious Frenchman, Mr Du Boys, who has occasionally contributed some fragments to the Catholic Reviews, remains unpublished.

It is really an idle inquiry whether the most powerful and characteristic of the national institutions of Spain owed its establishment to political or religious considerations, for at that time they were nearly identical in Spain. The existence from the first of a political element is manifest from the fact that the old Inquisition still subsisted in Aragon at the time when the new one was introduced, and had frequently taken cognisance of those religious transgressions against which the new tribunal was particularly directed. If, therefore, religious motives had alone prevailed, it would have been enough to extend the Inquisition of Aragon to the kingdom of Castile. This was not done, simply because a purely ecclesiastical tribunal would not have served the purpose of the Catholic kings. The new Inquisition was in fact more particularly wanted against the *Maranos* of Aragon. But it was first introduced in Castile because it was thought that the liberties of the Aragonese would put some obstacle in the way. There is no doubt, however, that Hefele, following the lead of de Maistre, a more seductive but unsafe guide in matters of history, has exaggerated the extent to which purely political motives influenced the Spanish sovereigns. The character of the tribunal became afterwards chiefly secular; and the royal power, not the Church, derived the chief profit from its existence. But that advantage was obtained in an almost equal degree during the earlier period, when its whole constitution and action were entirely ecclesiastical. For there is no greater auxiliary of absolute power than the presence in the State of an oppressed religious body; and no government is more powerful than one in whom the people behold its vigilant guardian against an enemy of its religion. Tyrants, says Herrera, always cover themselves with the mantle of religion. It was in their capacity of defenders of the faith, by virtue, therefore, of the tribunal by which they fulfilled that duty, that the kings of Spain, even at the time of their worst misgovernment, retained the obedience and the love of their subjects. Thus, in 1770, Burke, instituting a comparison between the revenue of George III, which, including a civil list of £800,000, he estimated at more than a million, and the ostensible expenses of the court, affirmed that the greater portion of it served to increase, by means of corruption, the unconstitutional power of the crown. But a larger sum than that which at the close of the eighteenth century seemed dangerous to the liberties of the nation was drawn at the beginning of the seventeenth century, by our most despotic king, from the Catholic ransom. It would not be difficult to show that the rise of the system of penal laws coincided with the excessive growth of the monarchical power in the sixteenth and seventeenth centuries, and its decline with the progress of political freedom in the eighteenth and the nineteenth, when the strongest resistance to Catholic emancipation was offered by the crown. In Spain, in like manner, the king owed his great power to his zeal for religion; and the provision for defending the one inevitably promoted the other. The existence of the State had depended for centuries upon its resistance to hostile religions; and the vigour with which the Inquisition pursued heretics, infidels, and Jews had its origin in the danger which at different times the State encountered from all three. The Spanish monarchy was first securely established by the victory of Catholicism over Arianism. The victory over the Moors of Granada was the commencement of its unparalleled ascendency in the affairs of Europe. After waging almost incessantly for 700 years a holy war for their hearths and homes, the Spaniards commenced in the fifteenth century a crusade against the Reformation. They grew accustomed to consider national interests identical with religious, and never understood that their religious wars were exhausting the country, or that the absolutism of the crown, which was their pride, was degrading the Church at home. Their zeal for the faith made them blind for the ruin of the State, and their patriotism concealed from them the disastrous condition of the Church. The time came when the danger of heresy had passed away, and the Inquisition, as a religious tribunal, had done its work. Then the political element which had lurked in it from the beginning survived alone, and absorbed the whole activity of the tribunal. Its constitution was not altered, and it served the State in the same way that it had seemed to serve the Church. In the eyes of a Spaniard of true blood there was no difference in principle between the crime of the relapsed Jew who was burned by Torquemada, and that of the smuggler who was denounced to the Holy Office under the Bourbons.

The religious intolerance of which the Inquisition is the most striking expression holds a conspicuous place in the history of Spain, from the time of its conquests by the Arian Visigoths. There, as well as in Italy and in Southern Gaul, the Gothic kings found that their dominion was uncertain and precarious so long as a barrier of religious animosity separated the conquerors from the natives. The national hostility of the Roman people would have been overcome in time by intermarriage, and by the superiority of the government of the Goths to that of the emperor, who was hardly less an alien than they. This superiority was so strongly felt that the conquest seemed to many a deliverance—"ut inveniantur quidam Romani qui malint inter barbaros pauperem libertatem quam inter Romanos tributariam solicitudinem sustinere."[1] But whilst Arianism was the religion of the Gothic state,

[1] Orosius, vii, 38.

and Catholicism that of the Roman nation, a durable union was impossible. The religious question determined the existence of all the new kingdoms. The immediate conversion of the Franks from the worship of Odin to the religion of the people at once rendered the monarchy of the Merovingians the most stable and the most powerful of all the Teutonic conquests. The fate of the Goths in Italy was equally significant. Though founded and governed by the wisest and ablest chief who appeared in the age of the great migrations, their monarchy never took root among the people in consequence of their Arianism, and was completely and speedily destroyed. Theodoric sought to avoid every occasion of discontent. He gave the Romans their own laws and liberties, and sought to destroy neither the religion nor the institutions of imperial Italy. This very tolerance was fatal to his throne. His people remained strangers in the land. They formed a separate state, governed by its own laws, and supported by its own power, without the help or the sympathy of the Italians; and they were compelled to meet the armies of Justinian in the midst of the ill-will of the people they had delivered.

The lesson of contemporary history was not lost upon the Gothic kings in Spain, where there was every sign that the same causes would produce like results. It became the first maxim of their policy that their power could be consolidated only through the union in the same religion of the dominant and the subject races. Naturally they strove to impose their own belief upon the people. For all the Goths clung with a strange tenacity to the form in which they had first known Christianity. For this the Ostrogoths were exterminated; and the Visigoths did not yield until it had cost them Aquitaine, and threatened to ruin their power in the Peninsula. The adoption of Arianism by the Spanish people would confirm the supremacy of the ruling race, and would break off for ever the connection between their subjects and the Catholic empire. Unity and independence seemed alike to call for the predominance of the Arian faith; accordingly Lewigild set about converting the Catholic Spaniards. First he tried conciliation. An Arian synod at Toledo abolished the practice of re-baptizing the Catholics who joined the Arian communion. When it was found that this concession was ineffectual, severer means were adopted, and a persecution commenced which led to a partial apostasy, but ended in a civil war. Warned by his example, his son and successor Recared sought the same political results in another policy. Whilst his father had provoked an armed resistance in attempting to force Arianism upon the Spaniards, Recared found that there was no resistance and no difficulty in converting all the Arians to Catholicism. The danger of religious differences had nowhere been more keenly felt, and was nowhere more deeply feared, than in Spain; and the preservation of religious unity became a political principle, to which in almost every age the most stupendous sacrifices continued to be made, and were made in vain.

The Jews form the connecting link between the intolerance of the Goths and that of the later Inquisition, and they contributed more than any other religious party to its introduction. Their persecutions had begun at the conversion of Recared, when the principle of religious unity was first made a law of the State. At that time they were already numerous, and began to consider Spain as a new land of promise, and the scene of their future greatness. Under the Moors, these hopes were partly realized. Cordova, Granada, Toledo, says the greatest of their modern historians, sound like home and household names to a Jewish ear, as much as Jerusalem or Tiberias. They asserted that they had been settled in the country ever since the days of Solomon, in order to prove that they had no part in the death of Christ. Previous to the Teutonic invasion they were not molested. The Theodosian code only forbids them to possess Christian slaves, or to build new synagogues, and to hold judicial or military offices. Under the Arian Goths they retained their own laws. At Naples they exhibited their gratitude by defending the city against Belisarius. At Rome the people plundered their houses and burnt their synagogue, in order to spite their protector Theodoric.

In Spain the Jews and the Christians lived on the best terms together. They frequently intermarried; and one of the first Spanish Councils had occasion to forbid the faithful to allow their crops to be blessed by Jews. Christian slaves were common in Jewish houses. It is remarkable how little abhorrence of the Jews was manifested by the Christians in the age which immediately followed their crime, and when the remembrance of the terrible expiation under Titus and Hadrian was fresh in all men's minds. The germs of an altered feeling were laid under the Arian ascendency. The Goths protected and preferred the Jews. They were more highly civilized, more adapted to civil offices than the Goths themselves, and they were not by their religion, like the Catholics, natural allies of the Emperor. Whilst the Goths and the Spaniards were governed by their separate laws, the Jews were often admitted to authority over the Spaniards, but never over the Goths. The restrictions imposed upon them by the Roman law were no longer enforced; consequently the evils which those restrictions had been designed to prevent began to spread, and at the conversion of the Goths a reaction ensued which aimed at first only at the restoration of the Theodosian law. The Council of Toledo, under Recared, at once decreed that they should not hold civil offices, "per quae eis occasio tribuatur poenam Christianis inferre." They were not to have Christian wives, and the children of mixed marriages were to be baptized. The most important point was that they were forbidden to have Christian slaves. Under the empire the law obliged them to purchase heathen slaves wherever they could be got, and it sometimes happened that a slave, to escape from a Jewish master, professed to have been a Christian. As the Goths did not enforce the Theodosian decree, it became more and more common for Christians to be made the slaves of Jews. Now it was particularly offensive to a Jew to have in his house persons who did not obey his ceremonial law; and the Talmud ordained that the slaves should either be circumcised or sold again. This was a great danger and injury to religion, and it is due to the intolerance of the Jews themselves that the first oppressive measures were adopted against them. It has never been their practice to modify their regulations so as to make them more palatable to the Christians. Not many years ago, when the removal of their civil disabilities was being debated in several European Parliaments, one of their most eminent writers urged in vain the abrogation of that precept by which it is made lawful to cheat a Christian. So it was in Spain in the seventh century. It was morally impossible for a Jew to permit his Christian slaves to profess their own religion. It was materially impossible for him to exist without slaves. Heathens could no longer be got. So long as the Jews were Jews, it seemed that the Catholic faith would be constantly exposed to a great profanation and injury. Something required to be done. Then, in the first moment of the victory over Arianism, in the midst of the strong political reaction towards religious unity, a measure was resolved upon which has thrown a gloom over the whole history of Spain, which proved in its results injurious to the Church, pernicious to the State, and which was the real cause of the establishment of the Inquisition, and of the consequences which ensued. King Sisebut, in the year 612, decreed that all the Jews who did not consent to be baptized should leave the country before a certain date. Many preferred exile to apostasy. A large number remained and were baptized. It is evident that the government imagined that Judaism could be as easily renounced as Arianism, and that they had no conception of its vitality, or of the vigour of the Jewish belief. St Isidore censured the act of the king: "aemulationem quidem Dei habuit sed non secundum scientiam"; but it was supposed that even if those who had been converted by violence should never become sincere Christians their errors would not be inherited by their children. "Nec hoc inutiliter facimus, si pro levandis pensionum oneribus eos ad Christi gratiam perducamus, quia etsi ipsi minus fideliter veniunt, hi tamen qui de eis nati fuerint jam fidelius baptizantur."[1] The great evil of the measure lay in the success which partly attended it.

A few years later the law of Sisebut was repealed, the exiles returned, and the converts relapsed. In the year 633, at a Council at Toledo, in which Isidore of Seville was the leading mind, it was determined that the Jews were not to be converted by force or by threats, but that those who had once been baptized could not be permitted to return to their old errors. Those who persisted were to be reduced to slavery. Henceforward they continued to be regarded as heretics and apostates, and no relaxation of the severities against the Jews brought any relief to them. The government could not escape from the terrible consequences of the first compulsory conversion, by which an element of unbelief and hypocrisy was introduced into the Church, which she could neither crush nor cast out. The establishment of the Spanish Inquisition was a last desperate effort to remedy the consequences of that fatal measure. It was the last practical development of the system inaugurated by the Councils of Toledo against a danger from which the Church of Spain had never ceased to suffer, and which she never ceased to combat. A learned Jewish historian says: "The real necessity and possibility of such a tribunal lay simply in the dread of the gigantic influence of the converted Jews in society

---

[1] Gregory the Great, *Epist.*, v, 8.

and in religion. However we may curse the names of those on whom lie the tears and the blood of thousands of innocent men, one thing excuses them—that what they desired to extirpate had struck such deep root that it could be removed only by the greatest energy and exemplary severity." At first the Jews themselves felt no evil consequences from the Inquisition. Six years after its introduction Abarbanel was holding high financial office; and in his introduction to his commentary on the Book of Kings, he describes the condition of his people in no way worse than before- There was so little fanaticism in the popular mind against them, that when Philip the Fair died, his death was attributed to the part he had taken in their expulsion. But the presence of the Jews was incompatible with the real conversion of the *conversos*. It was only by isolation that these could be made to surrender their practices, and that the influence of their religion could be neutralized. The Inquisition had a hopeless task with the relapsed, so long as the real Jews were tolerated. Therefore, as soon as the Moors were expelled from Granada, Ferdinand resolved that the Jews should either follow them or receive baptism. As the first persecution had followed immediately on the defeat of Arianism, the prospect of perfect unity opened by the fall of Granada led to a new attempt to coerce them. Accordingly it was decreed that all who refused baptism should leave Spain, and that they should take no coined money with them. The menace of confiscation added to that of exile would, it was expected, prove irresistible; and people were so little prepared for the great emigration that ensued, that alarm was expressed, not at the loss which the country would suffer by the execution of the decree, but at the danger to the purity of the Spanish blood from intermarriage with so many converted Jews. "No agrado a algunos este mandato de los reyes, por lo que ellos sospechavan, y especialmente por la mucha mezela que a la nobleza d'España avian de causar con sus casamientos."[1] Nevertheless, 300,000 Jews went into poverty and exile. In all matters relating to the Jews Hefele is very unsatisfactory, as he has neglected to make use of Jewish authorities. But there is no country in which they played a more important part than Spain, and nowhere is so much information to be obtained for national history from their writings. It is, however, a source that has been little explored by Christian writers.

[1] Garibay, *Compendio Historial*, lib. xix, cap. 1.

Another most important part of the history of the Inquisition into which he has failed to inquire, is its position in the Church. It was the great barrier to the exercise of the Papal authority in Spain, and practically secured to the crown all the power which in France was aimed at by the Gallican system. The manner in which the rights of the Holy See were appropriated by means of it, and the contests between the court of Rome and the Spanish government on questions of jurisdiction[1] may be found in the works of the Spanish canonists. It appears to us that this is the portion of the history of the Inquisition by which most light may yet be thrown upon its character, and its influence on the destinies of Spain; all the information given on this topic by our author consists in an extract from Ranke's *Spain in the Sixteenth and Seventeenth Century*.

It will be found that it was most injurious to the Church, whom it was its mission to protect. No other ecclesiastical institution was ever so completely exempt from the Papal jurisdiction; none formed so great an anomaly in the hierarchical system. It interposed between the Holy See and the Bishops, and between the Bishops and their flocks. It interrupted the connection between the religious orders and their generals in Rome, so that they degenerated, and came in the eighteenth century to be less respected than the secular clergy. In the sphere of doctrine its action was not more beneficial than in the domain of government. It has long been usual to palliate its many defects by saying that at least it saved Spain from heresy, and from the calamities of religious war. This is not true, and it is doubtful praise if it were true. If there had been any Protestant tendencies in Spain, there would have been some symptoms of opposition and resistance to the tribunal which was particularly vigilant against heresy. But instead of that, it was always a popular institution. Moreover, the control exercised over theological and historical literature would have made it impossible to meet Protestantism in open combat and controversy. But there never was any serious danger from Protestantism, which would have been encountered with as much success if there had been no Inquisition. The recent history of Spain, as of Italy, makes it doubtful whether it is greatly for the

---

[1] Louville, who was in Spain at the time of the accession of the Bourbons, speaks of the Inquisition as "toujours en guerre, au dehors avec le pape au dedans avec les sujets" (*Memoirs secrets*, 1818, i, 69).

advantage of a Catholic nation that it escaped the ordeal of the Reformation; whether to prevent a crisis is not to make the action of the poison more prolonged and more insidious, to convert an acute into a chronic disease, and make it impossible to overcome and cast out the danger. The means taken to resist Protestantism opened the way for infidelity. The Inquisition tried to prevent a conflict, not to prepare for it; and this policy, which was successful as long as a conflict could be avoided, made resistance almost impossible when it became necessary. The postponement of the religious controversy in Spain from the Protestant to the infidel period rendered it in every way more difficult and more dangerous. That is not due to the Inquisition alone; but the Inquisition is responsible for the means which were employed for the purpose.

Of these the most efficacious and the most injurious was the system of intellectual repression. Not only was the Spanish Index far more comprehensive than the Roman, but it was conducted on a different principle. The Roman practice was to point out the danger, and to caution men against it. The denunciation presupposed the intellectual confutation of the error, and was based upon it. It was understood that there was a class of learned men whose business it was to take cognisance, in the interest of orthodoxy, of the literary movement of the age, and to profit alike by its good and bad elements, whilst the generality of the faithful were excluded from this arena. Thus it was imagined that religion would have all the advantages both of security and of controversial exercise. But in Spain the dread of error was so great that it led to a fear of all mental activity. Literature was sacrificed to religion. Because faith might be imperilled by science, science was proscribed; and a system of stagnation was introduced, by which the Church was deprived of the aid which literature affords to her. The greatest severity was exercised over every branch of ecclesiastical learning. The Spanish intellect, it is true, is not remarkable for versatility or comprehensiveness. There are departments for which Spaniards never have exhibited the smallest aptitude. When we speak of Spanish literature, we think generally of great poets like Cervantes and Calderon, or of great divines like those who did so much of the work of the Council of Trent. But at the revival of letters it had seemed for a moment that Spain was to rival Italy on a far wider field. Of the Oriental studies of Alcala we hear something in the *Life of Ximenes*. Ancient learning had brilliant representatives in Vives and Augustinus. Throughout the sixteenth century there were great scholastic divines, and great mystical writers; and the Spanish historians, from Zurita to Mariana, rivalled the Florentines. But all this splendid promise faded away; and when in Italy, France, and England, learning began to be more sound and literature more rich, in Spain they were already nearly extinct. After the beginning of the seventeenth century no great works appeared on ecclesiastical or pagan antiquities, on metaphysics or natural science. Even those branches of divinity which had most flourished in Spain, flourished but a short time. No history was cultivated but their own. In philosophy, antiquities, and natural science, Spain has the lowest place among the great nations of Europe. All this destruction the Inquisition wrought in a very short space. For the first half-century it had little to do with literature and literature accordingly flourished. Its attention began to be given to it when the Reformation called for some measures of resistance. Between the middle of the sixteenth century and the beginning of the seventeenth, during the reigns of Philip II and Philip III, the whole intellectual movement of Spain was entirely crushed. Each branch of letters suffered in proportion as it was most nearly allied with religion, and most capable of serving it. Nothing survived intact but poetry and romance.

This is the great injury that the Inquisition inflicted on religion. It deprived her of the intellectual and literary service of the Spanish people; yet in the face of the most obvious and conspicuous fact of modern history, writers are still found who deny that the Inquisition was injurious to literature. Because there were many great writers after its establishment, it is argued that it cannot have been hostile to the intellect. Hefele has written upon this point a sentence marvellously foolish: "Llorente, it is true, enumerates 118 learned men who were prosecuted by the Inquisition, but omits adding that they escaped without personal injury" (p.365). By this we are to understand that a scholar is not interrupted in his studies until he is burnt at an *auto da fé*. The *post hoc ergo propter hoc* argument which is used to defend the literary merits of the Inquisition may be applied just as well to the political career of the Habsburgs in Spain. They no sooner ascended the throne, in the person of the Emperor Charles V, than the monarchy became the most powerful in the world, and retained its supremacy for near a hundred years. It is therefore idle to say that the Habsburg dynasty can have had any part in the decline of Spain during the last century of its rule.

In the attempt to glorify the Inquisition in departments in which it was an unmitigated evil, its really great merit has been generally overlooked. It was a true and effective guardian of the morality of the people. Acting as a sort of religious police, it succeeded in eradicating certain vices and certain crimes. The medieval wars had developed among the Spaniards of the fifteenth century a barbarous ferocity, and all the evil effects of continued warfare. The Inquisition was the instrument by which greater humanity, morality, and subordination were restored. It was the only disguise in which the Spaniards would submit to the interference of a state police.

This, again, leads us to the second great mischief of the Inquisition next to the repression of religious thought. It was the religious mask, by means of which absolutism was imperceptibly introduced; for crimes against the State were subject to its jurisdiction as much as crimes against religion. Those, for instance, who exported horses to France in time of war came before its tribunals. It defended the authority of the crown against the nobility and against the Church with as much energy as the purity of faith and morals. But it is due to the Inquisition to admit that, if it was instrumental in establishing despotism in Spain, it likewise saved the people from being degraded by it, and greatly mitigated its oppressiveness. The severity of its procedure, the 20,000 criminals who suffered death during the 300 years of its activity, are the picturesque details which strike the imagination of men, excite their passions, and conceal from them the serious feature of its character, and the real part it has performed in history. It did more than any other thing for the ruin of Church and State in Spain, by promoting political despotism and intellectual stagnation.

PROFESSOR DROYSEN AND THE PRUSSIAN HISTORIANS[1]

PROFESSOR DROYSEN is known as the head of that section of German historians which assign to Prussia the providential mission of establishing German unity, by reducing the smaller States under her own dominion, and separating Austria from the rest of the nation. He traces this mission back to the Mark of Brandenburg, and conceives the whole history of the Brandenburg Princes, and afterwards of the Kings of Prussia, to be nothing else but its gradual fulfilment. It was to establish this view that he many years ago undertook his *Geschichte der Preussischen Politik* of which two new volumes have just appeared. These volumes embrace the period from 1713 to 1740, and form an independent work, under the title of *Frederick William I, King of Prussia*. In reality, however, they only deal with the King's foreign policy, and this was the weakest side of a government which in other respects may justly claim to constitute an epoch. "It was at this time", says the author, "that Prussia first took that sharp hard stamp which has remained characteristic of her: the army, the administration, and the finances then received a shape and organization the outlines of which have endured to the present day." But instead of showing the real grounds and methods of this process, the two volumes merely exhibit a series of political transactions. These the author gives from his researches in the Berlin Archives, following every turn of diplomacy with minuteness, but failing in lucidity and condensation. His habit of considering questions from an exclusively Prussian point of view leads him into many errors in dealing with German affairs, the interest of which at that time did not centre in Berlin; and the same defect is still more striking in his treatment of matters belonging to the general politics of Europe, in which Prussia then bore no considerable part. He often represents events as though the whole politics of the day had been revolving round Berlin; and in one place he says that the new era of Europe was inaugurated in Prussia. In the same tone of exaggeration, speaking of the Treaty of Schwedt, which Prussia concluded with Russia in 1713, and by which she gained a portion of what was then Swedish Pomerania, he declares that since then the centre of gravity for

[1] Book review in the *North British Review*, Jan. 1870, p. 556.

the Baltic countries has lain in Prussia. The truth is rather that the preponderance of Russia on the Baltic dates from that time, and that Prussia instead of hindering has promoted it. Later on, the author does not deny this, he recognizes the threatening position Russia has occupied from that time, but attributes the fault to the other States of Europe rather than to Prussia. The fact, however, remains that Prussia, to further her schemes of aggrandizement, allied herself persistently with Russia; and Herr Droysen relates how repeatedly and how vainly England and Austria endeavoured to bring the King to an anti-Russian policy. The two powers no doubt were actuated only by self-interest and not by great ideas or by any sense of moral obligation. But this was according to the genius of the eighteenth century; and the motives of the Prussian policy were not of higher order. Frederick William was chiefly bent on the acquisition of new territory, so that right scarcely entered into the question. Conquest seemed to him the best of rights. When Russia proposed to him an alliance against Poland, with the prospect of gaining what is now called West Prussia, he wrote on the draft with his own hand: "Paratissimus sum." On another occasion he showed an equal readiness to seize Silesia, provided he received assistance, and was guaranteed in the possession of the province, for he did not love to run great risks. Nevertheless, he had a sort of soldier-like honourableness, to which the byways of diplomacy were strange and distasteful. Hence he was often baffled by political intrigues; and if he afterwards became conscious of having been misled, he gave vent to violent fits of anger, which often in their turn drove him into false positions.

As Prussia at that time played a small part amongst the powers of Europe, her relations with the Empire and the Emperor were the main subject of Prussian politics. The chief point was the claim of succession to the Duchy of Juliers. It was in the nature of things that the Emperor should be unfavourable to the growing power of Prussia, which was a danger for Austria, while it threatened the constitution of the Empire. The young kingdom has possessions scattered over Northern Germany, and an army of the disproportionate strength of 80,000 men to a population of only 2,500,000. It thus presented the aspect of a military State bent on conquest and became an object of suspicion and offence to most other North German States, especially to Saxony and

Hanover, whose interests were at that time connected with the policy of England. It is not surprising that all these States should have been more disposed to hinder than to promote the aggrandizement of a dangerous neighbour. But it was an evil day when the Emperor attempted to play a double game, and, while he formally recognized the King's claim to the inheritance, at the same time promised it to another house. The King, betrayed by the Emperor, was thrown into the arms of France and concluded an agreement with that power in 1739, upon the subject of his inheritance. Then the Silesian war of Frederick the Great may be said to have been already prepared. The King himself had designated the Crown Prince as his avenger. A little before his death he explained to him that the root ideas of his policy had been "the honour and advancement of his house, and the prosperity of his provinces". There is no mention of rights, but only of interests. Nothing is said of the German Empire or the German nation which was only regarded as material for the aggrandizement of the House of Hohenzollern. It is a falsification of history to see in this anything but a self-seeking dynastic policy, differing from that of the Emperor or the other German Princes only by its greater energy. By the aid of a considerable army, to which all the resources of the country were devoted, this policy naturally succeeded; and Prussia accordingly rose, while other German States sunk in proportion. The German nation became no greater by the change; but it had to bear the burden of the wars which the Prussian policy of aggrandizement brought forth.

T. E. MAY: "CONSTITUTIONAL HISTORY OF ENGLAND"[1]

THE second volume of Mr May's *Constitutional History* concludes a work which is the most valuable in our literature as a guide to the system and spirit of the English government. In abundance and accuracy of facts it surpasses all our histories; and questions of principle are decided in it with rare wisdom and equity, and with the practical sense of a man averse to political speculation. Of the two great questions which occupy

[1] *Home and Foreign Review*, July 1863, p. 715.

this volume it is but justice to say that one, that of the Catholic claims, has never been treated in so complete and satisfactory a manner. The unjustifiable use of the term "a sect of Catholics" (p. 345) to denote the Cisalpine party, was not, we believe, deliberately used; and Mr May is no doubt aware that it involves a contradiction. But the progress of emancipation, the influence of Ireland and of the Dissenters, and the manner in which religious liberty was taken up, sometimes from interest and sometimes as a principle, are traced with admirable ability. Mr May justly says that "toleration to the Catholics formed no part of the traditional creed of the Whig party" (p. 335). But he is not always so free from a certain bias in discussing the leading question with which this volume opens—the theory and nature of our political parties.

In Mr May's opinion, party is not only inseparable from free government, but its very condition. "We find that government without party is absolutism, that rulers without opposition may be despots ... We feel that party is essential to free institutions ... Who can fail to recognize in party the very life-blood of freedom?" (p. 93). This is so far from being true that parties have been the ruin of constitutional life in France, in Belgium, in Prussia, and in Switzerland. The Continental States do not possess the means of neutralizing its ill-effects. The dangers of invasion and revolution producing vast standing armies, a system of militia, and an organized political police, the disappearance of an hereditary aristocracy based on primogeniture, or, which is equally pernicious, the absorption of the lesser aristocracy, corresponding to the English gentry, by the higher, and the subordination of the Church to the civil power, which, though more complete in Protestant than in Catholic States, is nearly complete in both—these things, resulting not from any theory, but from the whole course of modern history, have broken down the elements of self-government, and established centralization in constitutional and despotic countries alike. The agents of this centralized system, animated by no principle but fidelity to the governing power, make it irresistible, and are equally at the disposal of any party that obtains office, for the suppression of its adversaries and the promotion of its interests. The State, moreover, possesses in many countries a great resource of influence in the public works, in the concession of commercial privileges, and in the dependence of the school and its teachers upon the government; and it is absolute in almost all, in Belgium and Switzerland as much as in Russia or France. But the internal evils of absolutism are greater where authority changes hands than where it is fixed; and the omnipotence of the foreign State converted into an instrument of party-offence is a more serious thing than Mr May considered when he wrote in such unqualified terms. Burke, whom he quotes, does not admire, as he supposes, the balance and conflict of parties, but the concentration of the constitutional idea in a single party whose function it is to preserve the national institutions, just as it is the office of the judges to preserve the law. "When bad men combine, the good must associate; else they will fall one by one an unpitied sacrifice in a contemptible struggle."[1]

In a country where freedom is not of recent growth there can be but one constitutional party. The constitution may be assailed on different sides: only that party which faces all attacks is constitutional. A party that defends only one breach, and resists only one form of encroachment or change, has its centre of gravity beyond the limits of the constitution. Those who look with exclusive or excessive favour either on tradition or on progress, alike renounce one essential principle. Our political system is founded on definite principles, not on compact or compromise. Every compromise marks an imperfect realization of principle—a surrender of right to interest or force. The constitution stands by its own strength, not by the equal strain of opposite forces. Mr May asserts the contrary in his opening passage: "The parties in which Englishmen have associated have represented cardinal principles of government—authority on the one side, popular rights and privileges on the other. The former principle, pressed to extremes, would tend to absolutism—the latter to a republic; but, controlled within proper limits, they are both necessary for the safe working of a balanced constitution." In all this an antagonism is assumed which does not exist. There is no antagonism, or even antipathy, between absolutism and a republic. There is no antagonism, on the contrary there is a necessary and inseparable union, between authority and liberty. When either is dissociated from the other, it loses its nature and changes its name. Authority is essentially an ethical term, but when separated from liberty it is nothing but force. Liberty is essentially a conditional term, and cannot be independent of law. This idea of harmony proceeding

[1] *Present Discontents.*

from discord—of a balance between contending elements—is derived from a mechanical notion of the State, which refuses to regard it as a physiological organism, founded on distinct principles and regulated by its own laws. But Mr May, in spite of this theory, describes Toryism in terms which, though perfectly just, show it to be utterly inconsistent with our constitution; and, on the other hand, attributes to the Whig party perfections which he does not admit in the Whig doctrine. Even after the secession of Burke, the Whigs appear to him an immaculate and almost infallible group of statesmen. His sympathies are entirely with Mr Fox. Yet Fox was not, like Pitt, a reformer on principle. He took up the idea of reform as a momentary instrument, and as a means of acquiring power. He wrote in 1796: "Parliament should first be reformed, and then restored to its just influence. You will observe that I state this opinion as being mine *now*, in contradistinction to those times when the Whig party was only beaten, but not dispersed, and when I certainly was of a different opinion. At present I think we ought to go further towards agreeing with the democratic or popular party than at any former period ... *We*, as a party, I fear, can do nothing." The fallacy that lurks throughout Mr May's account of the Whigs is his reluctance to recognize in the origin of the party a strong democratic ingredient. He fails to point out that two contrary principles at one time united in adopting the same name, and that if all the Whigs were united against the king's friends, there was a time when they would not all have combined against the regicides. As a party they by no means deserve the eulogy he bestows on them; and it is to be regretted that the failure to define closely the positive nature of their principles forms a serious blemish in an otherwise invaluable book.

E. A. FREEMAN: "HISTORY OF FEDERAL GOVERNMENT"[1]

THE wisdom of the ancients obtains but little authority in the political thought of our time. Our best writers and statesmen have hardly thought it worth their while to profit by the experience and speculation of antiquity. In former

[1] *Home and Foreign Review*, April 1863, p. 587.

times, when theological and juridical controversy was the ruling occupation of literature, and before the great revolutions of the seventeenth and eighteenth centuries had given the theory of government its great attractiveness to the minds of educated men, classical recollections and authorities overwhelmed those who wrote on politics. Lipsius and even Grotius could hardly move beneath the weight of their quotations; and there are Dutch and German books of that day in which the ideas of the author are actually concealed by uncritical and undigested extracts from the ancients. At present, most men are brought to the study of politics by the events of their own time, or by those which most nearly and directly influenced it; and they are tempted to confine their studies to that which immediately prompted them. Some men of real political insight and experience, such as Niebuhr and Mr Grote, have borrowed ideas from the actual history of ancient States. But the political thought and observation of the ancient writers is commonly rejected. Even industrious Germany has produced no commentary on the *Politics*. Great political thinkers, like Guizot and Tocqueville, have benefited but superficially by this source of wisdom. Macaulay, who was not acquainted with Aristotle, thought that the political judgements of Thucydides were puerile, that Xenophon had no knowledge of government, and that Polybius had no merit but that of a careful narrator of facts. There are probably few men living who have formed their political ideas in that unrivalled school, or who even know that Plato is one of the wisest of all political writers, and has traced with a masterly hand the principles of the constitutional system.

Mr Maine first taught English readers that the solution of political problems is to be obtained by historical analysis and comparison. To Mr Freeman belongs the praise of having first opened out that mine of political wisdom; and his *History of Federal Government* promises, by the first volume, to be one of the most able and profound histories in the language. He has undertaken to write the history of the four great confederacies, that of Achaia, and those of Switzerland, the Netherlands, and North America. The first volume, containing the introduction and the history of the Achaian League, possesses the rare merit of giving the real history of the League, while using it perpetually in illustration of the idea of federalism. The materials are circumscribed, and the facts tolerably free from doubt. In the later European portion of his work, great difficulties of historical investigation will beset the writer; and we shall be agreeably surprised if he succeeds as well with the Swiss and the Dutch as with the period in which he is guided, both in facts and in speculation, by so profound a politician as Polybius. We should be disposed to object that he has defined his subject too narrowly by taking only the instances in which federations have endured for some time. The federal idea is continually arising in certain junctures of national life, and either fails or disappears after doing transitory duty in the passage from one form of social existence to another. The principle is illustrated as much by its failures as by the rare instances in which it has obtained a qualified success. Federation is indeed one of the chief modes in which states take their rise. For they are generally formed either by the union of several nearly equal communities, or by the subjection of one to another. In the beginning of many States we find a sort of municipal league which disappears by degrees, or survives only in distinction of tribes or classes in the nation that grows out of their union. These instances are innumerable, and the laws of their existence seems to be uniform; whilst in states founded on conquest—states which in the nomenclature of the Middle Ages, are termed feudal—the regular process is towards the diminution of the supreme power, by the successive establishment of popular privileges. In federal States the central power gradually encroaches on the original independence, and accomplishes that which was the absorbing aspiration of the life of Hamilton, the combination of federation into unity.

Unless Mr Freeman enlarges his design, its narrowness will be in his way in the next volume, when he approaches the subject of the Swiss confederation, For during the later centuries of mediaeval history, that tendency towards federal leagues which led to the independence of Switzerland manifests itself in many other instances. The chief agents in this movement were the towns, which necessarily sought to emancipate themselves from the yoke of feudalism, to which their nature was abhorrent. The neighbouring feudal lord, familiar with the rule of country population, knew no cunning by which the very different interest of a town could be governed; and the imperial government existed in reality no farther than where the emperor himself was the

immediate lord. Between the absence of authority on the one
hand, and the proximity of a vexatious power on the other, the
towns sought to combine for their own protection and self-government. The most remarkable of these leagues was that of the
Swabian towns, in the fourteenth century, which, after having
been admirably treated in the classical history of Württemberg,
has now been described by Professor Vischer, whose excellent
treatises on Greek history, about the time of the Peloponnesian
war, are probably known to Mr Freeman. His choice of instances
is not, however, the only cause which makes us fear that the next
volume will hardly equal the first in value. The judgements on
parts of mediaeval history that sometimes occur in his account of
the Achaian League do not betray such familiarity with the history of those ages as he unquestionably possesses with that on
which he has written. Judging him, however, only by what he
has actually done, we must say, that among our best writers of
history, between Mr Grote, Dr Thirlwall, Mr Merivale, Dr
Milman, Mr Finlay, and Mr Froude, the author of this work
deserves a very high place.

J. G. PHILLIMORE: "HISTORY OF ENGLAND DURING THE REIGN OF GEORGE III"[1]

IT is certainly most desirable that something should be written
that would abate the conceit and self-satisfaction with which
we Englishmen contemplate ourselves. Many of the qualities
we prize most highly in theory are those which least visibly appear
in our history. No Christian annals are so sanguinary as ours. No
royal inheritance has been more fatal than the crowns of this
island. No other nation has borne so patiently a tyranny as brutal
as that of the second Tudor. Rarely has any foreign nobility
thronged a court more degraded by vice than that of nearly one
half of our modern kings. If there is humiliation, there is some
cause for pride in the recollection of these things; for the magnitude of the evils which have beset the nation is the measure of the
force of the national character, and of the virtue of the national
institutions which slowly triumphed over them. These two things
cannot be separated. The remedy for our national faults lay in

[1] *Home and Foreign Review*, July 1863, p. 713.

that system of laws which was common, in the germ, to all the States that were raised out of the chaos of the great migration by the influence of the mediaeval Church. The nation had no instinct and no productive power that emancipated it from the customs of its forefathers. Every appeal against oppression was to the hereditary rights; the only protection which the Englishman knew was in the traditional laws of his country. By means of this perpetual recurrence to old principles, and of the gradual contrivance of new forms in which to secure their action, the English people conquered their freedom. The intensity of their conservatism was an impulse as well as a guide of their progress. When this was neglected, and scope was given to a new faith, or new ideas derived from foreign examples, the result was the establishment of tyranny, the tyranny of Strafford or of Cromwell. The one thing that saved England from the fate of other countries was not her insular position, nor the independent spirit nor the magnanimity of her people—for we have been proud of the despotism we obeyed under the Tudors, and not ashamed of the tyranny we exercised in our dependencies—but only the consistent, uninventive, stupid fidelity to that political system which originally belonged to all the nations that traversed the ordeal of feudalism.

Mr Phillimore has the will, but neither the insight nor the temper, to moderate our illusions. His history of George III is a catalogue of iniquities and crimes, in which the blame alternates between the court and the people, and visits chiefly the basis of the constitution: "The people of England, obtuse and corrupted as they were, saw with scorn and disgust the gross disregard of all the courtesies and decencies of life, which the enslaved inhabitants of the little States of Germany submitted to, as they still do, with helpless servility . . . So positively servile, in spite of all that laws and institutions can do, is the Teutonic genius. That such a woman (as Catherine II) should have been praised by men of letters and philosophers, is one of the most frightful proofs of the tone of moral feeling in Europe during the eighteenth century, and of the condition to which the Gothic governments had brought mankind." Nevertheless, "no nation ever owed so much to their form of government as the English." The fact that Mr Phillimore should be so perfectly unable to comprehend the true source and spirit of that government is connected with the essentially formal, classical, rhetorical culture of his mind. History is but a branch of art in his eyes: of science he has no conception, or he knows only just enough to be sure that he will have none of it. He denounces its possessors as pedants, but with a ruder and vainer pedantry. The Spanish historians are in his judgement the best, because Spain possessed no historian but Zurita who had any merit more rare than eloquence. Opinions of this kind are freely scattered through his book. He gives us his views on Nie-buhr's theory, on the Neapolitan historians, and on many points on which nobody is concerned to know them. He even intimates by implication, in a note, as if every stray hint of his thoughts on things in general deserved to be treasured up, that Shakespeare is not the author of *Hamlet*. And with this petulant impertinence he shows no power of research, and no knowledge of the way in which a historian must approach his facts before he can deal with them.

These defects neutralize some very great qualifications which Mr Phillimore has brought to his task. He is sincere, courageously outspoken, superior in many respects to the slavery of party tradi-tions, full of scorn for hypocrisy and littleness, and full of indigna-tion for wrong. He writes very incorrectly, but with much anima-tion, and sometimes with a sort of artificial felicity. Thus he con-cludes his sketch of Lord Temple: "regular in his habits, munifi-cent in his gifts, pedantic and even brutal in his manners, fond of petty intrigue, and strangely eager for the trappings of a master whom he delighted to insult". He speaks of the riots at Birmingham "when Priestley's house was burnt over his head, because he was erroneously supposed to be a philosopher"; of "the harshness of Calvin's appalling creed (more immoral than any with which paganism can be reproached)", which he calls "the hideous doc-trine of that virulent inquisitor". On the intolerance of the Pro-testant establishment he says: "To exercise the right of private judgement so far as to quit the Church of Rome, which had gov-erned Christendom for centuries, was the duty of every Chris-tian; but to exercise it so far as to differ with the article put out one hundred years before by a church that did not pretend to be infallible, and teachers that laid no claim to inspiration, was a crime to be punished, in some instances, by the stake." His great merit is that he sees, better than almost any of our historians, the extent to which absolute power revived under the House of Hanover, when the Jacobite alarm was over, and how impotent were the laws made under William III to protect freedom against the Whig oligarchy, the Tories, and the dominant Church.

MR GOLDWYN SMITH ON THE POLITICAL HISTORY OF ENGLAND[1]

M R GOLDWYN SMITH's *Three English Statesmen* are well selected to exhibit his various powers as a panegyrist, an advocate, and an accuser. He portrays Pym without a shade, justifies Cromwell in his most arbitrary act—even in his Irish campaign; and reviles Pitt for his incompetence and his apostasy. His fondness for sweeping and positive assertions, the glaring illustrations of his striking and often lofty rhetoric, are not favourable to the display of exactness in the investigation of facts. To excuse Cromwell's alliance with France, and unfounded jealousy of Spain, he affirms that the decline of Spain was scarcely yet visible, even to the keenest eye. Now, the hollowness of the Spanish power was perfectly understood by Henry IV and Raleigh, and had since become manifest to the dullest observer by the revolt of her provinces, the loss of vast dependencies, and the defeat of her once invincible armies. To enhance the merit of Cromwell's intolerance of Catholics he declares that they were burning Protestants wherever they had the power. He can hardly be ignorant that nobody was burnt for religion's sake in those days except in Spain and Portugal, and even there we decidedly doubt whether he has heard of any Protestant executed at the time in question. What he means is that the Catholics got better treatment than they gave—a statement which would be unimpressive in comparison with the splendid enormity substituted for it. The same inaccuracy of fact and judgement in regard to foreign countries shows itself even in matters with which everybody is familiar. His estimate of Napoleon is scarcely different from that which makes the early numbers of the *Quarterly Review* such comic reading. He thinks the French Revolution the greatest disaster which ever befell the cause of human progress, and can discern no deeper current in it than the sterile philosophy

[1] *The Chronicle*, Aug. 31, 1867, p. 543.

of Robespierre. His real business is with politics, not with history. The great events and characters of English history serve to bring out a political system on which he has bestowed more care than on the investigation of events, and which he expounds with a vigour and earnestness that command attention.

The object of his strongest aversion is aristocracy. He supposes that it is connected in some way with the delusion of hereditary virtue, that it is founded on conquest, and subsists by an unnatural system of land tenure; and he rejects it as a foreign substance that preys on confiscated rights and properties. The sneer at hereditary virtue, if applicable at all, would apply only where the aristocratic character depends on purity of blood, not to a country where it depends on primogeniture. To connect aristocracy with the accidents of feudalism and military conquest is a confused generalization. Aristocracy is the product of inequality, as inequality is the product of liberty. The security for the continuity of law and the stability of political institutions is the permanence of influential families. Influence can only be made permanent by property, and property by primogeniture. This consecration of inequality creates the only force capable of resisting the impulse of the moment, and of protecting institutions from wanton change and perpetual reactions. Laws which express the will of the people for the time being are written on water. The people as well as the King requires a check in the exercise of sovereign power, lest it become despotic. The check on monarchy is representation. The check on democracy is primogeniture. It is the condition of unpaid self-government. Mr Goldwyn Smith is not only hostile to an obstructive House of Lords. His chief political merit is his eloquent denunciation of parliamentary omnipotence: "The tyranny of the crown is past: it is the tyranny of the House of Commons against which we have now to guard" (p. 263). He describes the defects of the parliamentary constitution principally to two causes, its power over dependencies, and the system of government by party. "The effect of incorporating a vast despotism like India with a free nation perhaps remains yet to be seen. There is a poison which is imbibed daily, though it is not perceived" (p. 208). The danger which he foresees, of men coming home politically demoralized and incapacitated for a career in a free country by the habits of absolutism in the East, appears to us less serious. India has been, in fact, a better school of statesmanship than England. But it is scarcely conceivable that an assembly exercising at the same time an unlimited and a limited authority should always separate the two; or that it should govern one people according to law, and another according to its will, without losing some respect for the sacredness of law, and confounding the means that prevent rebellion with the arts which overcome opposition. The House of Commons, with the practical tact of an illogical people, has met the difficulty by preferring dinner to an Indian debate. Mr Goldwyn Smith's strongest reproach to our system, and his reason for adjuring other nations to abstain from all imitations of it, is that it is governed by party. Party, he says, is an accident; it degenerates into faction whenever there are no real differences of opinion; it has proved a failure in many ways, and more particularly by the ascendancy it has given to Mr Disraeli, and generally to men who can speak over men who can govern. Although he returns to the subject at least four times, yet, with all his strength of language, Mr Goldwyn Smith has understated the case against a system which teaches men of honour to assert that which they know to be false, and to promote by word and deed what they believe to be wrong, and which produces effects among the elected not less immoral and disgraceful than among the electors. His remedy for the disease which is the scourge of the English State is the abolition of party. He desires to see a united and determined nation converting parliament into an instrument to execute its will, crushing all resistance, silencing all opposition, and combining all resources, until the State operates like an army. Such a system could exist only in moments of intense excitement, or in countries profoundly ignorant. Government is a complex art, founded on a knowledge of many sciences, which are neither stationary, nor popular, nor easy. Those who have mastered them are not always agreed among themselves, still less with those who have not their knowledge. The one broad distinction between those who understand and those who understand not must always subsist, and whenever principles are involved, the differences settle naturally into permanent divisions. The possessors of better knowledge will always have to contend against the ignorant masses of mankind. The conflict of ideas will outlast the varying antagonism of interest. Mr Goldwyn Smith's wish for the extinction of party is akin to his wish for the abolition of dogma. He imagines that a political view may be so comprehensive or so indefinite as to baffle opposition, as he imagines a Church so generous as to embrace all the varieties of opinion in the nation.

His quarrel being with aristocracy, not with monarchy, his language is not explicit when he approaches the throne. His horror of the Jacobins, his indignation at the execution of Charles I, and Louis XVI, would lead to the conclusion that he regards kings as above law. He intimates the belief that when the Horse Guards is brought under constitutional control, nothing will be left but the name and state of a king. In fact, he would scarcely leave so much as that. He would strip the throne of all its props. He would pull down the aristocracy and the Church, and he would get rid of the dependencies, without which it is hard to say what motive would remain for monarchy in England. A homogeneous people, educated and free, becomes a republic as naturally as a republic acquiring dependencies becomes a monarchy. Whether Mr Goldwyn Smith would retain or abolish the Crown is a delicate, and happily a superfluous, inquiry; he would certainly intend it to obey, and not to resist, the national will. Irresistible power wielded by a united people, and equality, as far as it can be obtained by a law of property short of actual confiscation, appears to constitute his political ideal. It is not easy to see in what essential point it differs from the Jacobins, whom he is never tired of abusing. The limit to his doctrine on the democratic side is set by political economy. But he seems unconscious of the fact. He is a zealous admirer of Adam Smith, and calls him the apostle of democracy. He was the adversary of aristocratic privileges, which is a very different thing. That which disturbs the equal mind of Mr Lowe—fear of the advent of classes whose political economy is not that of Adam Smith—is not a phantom. It is precisely in meeting the needs and growth of poverty that the teaching of the great economist and his school has proved inadequate. The economists who have pleaded for labour, and served its cause, have either attacked the basis of his system or passed immeasurably beyond its limits. The progress of political economy on the democratic side has been made in defiance and disparagement of his authority. Mr Goldwyn Smith's financial views are a case in point. He is hostile to the income-tax—the ideal tax of democracies—the tax which presses least on the mass of the population. When he prefers the succession duty—that is, revenue extracted out of capital—to revenue levied upon income, he no doubt enjoys the protection of a great name, but it must be remembered that Mr Gladstone's Budget Speech of 1853 was more statesmanlike than scientific.

Mr Goldwyn Smith gives utterance to one opinion which is still more widely at variance with the sincere and often spiritual tone of his liberality. He looks with favour upon the disabilities of the Catholics. "To restrain them from doing hurt was unhappily in those days part of a statesman's duty. They were liegemen and soldiers of that successor of the Apostles whose confederates were Philip II and Charles IX, and who struck a medal in honour of the Massacre of St Bartholomew" (p. 35). Strictly interpreted this sentence would involve many chronological difficulties. But Mr Goldwyn Smith means to say that the Catholics had no claim to full toleration because the canonical legislation of their Church made it apparent that they would extirpate the heretics if they had the power, that they were peaceful neighbours only through fear, and that their peace was a truce which they would break whenever they had the power. Therefore, he argues, the Protestants could trust them only in so far as they were made harmless. But the real motive of the penal laws in the seventeenth century was not the remote fear of retaliation. It was believed that the Catholics would hold themselves free from their allegiance and from the obligation to obey the laws, if the Pope so ordained it. For two centuries after the Gunpowder Plot the history of English Catholics turns on the tests by which the Government sought to secure itself against these opinions. Mr Goldwyn Smith is, in fact, less tolerant than Salisbury or Laud, for he does not discriminate between those who held the obnoxious tenets and those who rejected them. He does not say how or when the repeal of the penal laws became just and safe. Not when the Catholics ceased to be formidable; for it was by being formidable, and threatening Civil War, that they won their Emancipation. Not because their opinions changed; for they have not changed. The Catholics were divided upon these questions in the seventeenth century; and they are divided now.

"THREE LECTURES ON THE ANCIEN RÉGIME"
BY C. KINGSLEY[1]

PROFESSOR KINGSLEY's *Lectures on the Ancien Régime* are a good instance of his merits and defects. They are full of suggestive thoughts, and lighted up here and there with happy flashes of description. It cannot be said that they are altogether unhistorical, for the writer has drawn largely and discriminatingly from Tocqueville. But the ethical side of Mr Kingsley's mind so entirely dwarfs and overpowers the scientific that his inferences and illustrations have only the value of a homily on a text from one or other chapter in the Evangel of Carlyle. One first principle seems to be that physical force is the symbol of spiritual strength, and that the Teutons who broke up the Roman Empire showed themselves therein better men than the Latinized races whom they subdued. Now, without pausing to inquire into those spiritual gifts which the great conquerors of the world, Attila, Tamburlaine, or the first leaders of the Danes or Magyars, represented, we protest against the supposition that the capacity to conquer and enslave has any connection with inherent superiority. If there be one thing manifest in the history of the world, it is that the eminently warlike races, which pushed to the front rank in the great struggle for existence centuries ago, are being supplanted by the commercial. Roman, Norseman, Pole, Spaniard, and Magyar, the knights errant of old military ages, have shrunk back within the limits of their first dominion, and are either subject or second to the races on whose backs—to quote Mr Kingsley and Mr Carlyle—they once leaped. In some instances we can say with tolerable certainty that the weaker cause is the purer. The Covenanters, whom the troops of Charles II reduced; the Poles, whose gallant rallies for liberty have been fruitless of all but blood during three generations; the Camisards of the Cevennes fighting for freedom of faith against Louis XIV are obvious instances that Providence gives victory to the strong, as certainly as wealth to the prudent, or heaven to the good. And if it be false to say that an aristocracy in its commencements is of necessity morally better than those it governs, it is equally unphilosophical to connect the immediate circumstances of its fall with its moral degeneracy. The nobles of Castile were pious, hon-

[1] *The Chronicle*, July 13, 1867, p. 379.

ourable and brave men, during the century when Spain fell, by violating all laws of State policy, from the first place amongst nations. The nobles of the twenty years that preceded the French Revolution were undoubtedly better men than any of their ancestors since the generation among whom Corneille lived. If Choiseul, Lafayette, and La Roche-Jaquelein—if the framers and politicians of the Provincial Assemblies—will not bear comparison with Jacobin and Girondin, or with their greatest English contemporaries, there is an end to all standards of comparative excellence. Mr Kingsley speaks of the eighteenth century as dreaming, in its better moments, of shepherds and shepherdesses, while it "loved Gil Blas, and said: 'The problem of humanity is solved at last'." But, in fact, the taste for pastorals was a reminiscence of Italian poetry and French romances nearly two centuries before; while Gil Blas is modelled on the picaresque romances of Spain, that date from a minister of Charles V, and is delineated with such surpassing fidelity that Spanish patriots have claimed it as a national work. Where the eighteenth century really sinned was in a fondness for trashy sentiment. The impulse derived from *Clarissa Harlowe* was transmitted in the *New Heloise* and as late as 1785, M. de Fontanes, writing to Joubert, expressed his horror and surprise that the English preferred Fielding to Richardson. Mr Kingsley finds the cause of the French Revolution in the fact that "not merely institutions required to be reformed, but men and women." In a certain sense, this may be said of every generation. But it is difficult not to think that the French Revolution broke out because the higher morality and sounder intellect of Frenchmen generally, nobles as much as bourgeois, were at war with the rotten order of old traditions and laws. Men had died like dogs in the wars of Louis XIV, or in years of famine under his grandson; France had been dishonoured and oppressed; and there had been no movement because there was no life. Under Louis XVI, the nation had freed America and had forced an inglorious peace upon England; it was modelling its legislation anew as might suit a well-meaning king, and the hollow fabric of its society crushed suddenly in. But if we are to judge the men by the event, we must regard it as a supreme mercy, as God's crown upon honourable lives, that they were permitted to perish by the guillotine, or in La Vendée, instead of outliving their better selves in the aimless pettiness of ideas without result. Surely, Mr Kingsley's ethics are as imperfect as his philosophy. If the lightning always struck the perjurer and assassin, positive crime would be cast out by fear, but the love of good would go with it. The voluptuary transmits a tainted blood; the corrupt society bequeaths a heritage of ruin; and the suffering falls upon those who have not sinned. Constituted as the French nobility was, only two issues were perhaps possible for it —an impure decadence like that of the Roman Empire, or a baptism in blood into a new life. Seeing good clearly, it must either embrace it suddenly and to its ruin, or renounce it with more disastrous events in the future. Carried away by a splendid enthusiasm, it was prepared to renounce its privileges, and believed that it could conquer happiness for its country by the mere surrender of rank and prerogative. When it found that the sacrifice was fruitless, having learned to think and feel, it had the courage to die greatly; and though in human weakness it might have shrunk from the *noyades* of Nantes and the September massacres, if it could have foreseen them, it passed away with as much nobleness as has marked the ruin of any human institution, as fearless in failure as it had been honest in reform.

"DIE PREUSSISCHE POLITIK DES FREDERIZIANISMUS NACH FRIEDRICH II" VON ONNO KLOPP[1]

HERR ONNO KLOPP occupies a somewhat singular and isolated position among the German historians. The Prussian school predominates at the universities; but he has a numerous audience among those who are not worshippers of success, and who are disgusted at the art which selects, arranges and even alters the events of the past to justify contemporary acts and claims. Before the deposition of King George he was archivist at Hanover, busy on a work of national importance— the publication of the manuscripts of Leibniz. He has been driven into exile as a vengeance upon him for writings in which he exposed the partisan idolatry of Frederick II, and the political traditions which spring from him. When Germany had been

[1] *The Chronicle*, Oct. 5, 1867, p. 668.

overwhelmed by the policy whose origin and character he had traced, a new interest was awakened in his courageous and prophetic book. He published it again with the help of new materials, and added a supplement on the events of last year, which has appeared separately. It is a recapitulation of the lessons of the book to which it is appended, and shows in addition how faithfully the precepts and examples of Frederick have been followed by the inheritors of his power. The projects of aggrandizement were kept persistently in view, and the intervals of place and public confidence were employed to prepare new difficulties for Austria, and to acquire new influence for the Hohenzollern. For this purpose the middle states were kept in a temper of permanent jealousy of Austria, while Prussia was made to appear identical with Germany, and the only bulwark of the Protestant religion. The patriotism of the Prussians was shown in vilifying the Austrian rival and in mocking the old imperial ideas which survived under the federal system. The imperfect development of that system was still imputed to Austria, while Prussia took care to impair its vitality in order to be able one day to merge all Germany in the centralized absolutism which, in defiance of the parliamentary Constitution, was erected at Berlin. We have seen the result. It is the merit of Herr Klopp's book that he shows what led to it, and how long and consistently it was prepared. The parallel instances in which he compares the action of Frederick with that of his imitators are often striking. But, as the impulse to expand in Germany has increased, the immorality of the means has become more flagrant, and the liberties of the Prussians themselves have been sacrificed to the one overruling cause. The servile Parliament, which admits that the interest of the State is supreme over the rights of others, cannot vindicate its own. Herr Klopp, though he dwells on all this with invidious partiality, is not blind to the fact that the power of assimilation which dwells in the Prussian system is very great, and that the constant direction of forces towards the purposes of aggression has endowed the machinery of State with an almost unexampled elasticity and rapidity of motion. He is not prepared to say that it will break down under its own irremediable defects before it has accomplished the suppression of an independent Germany.

"GOTTFRIED WILHELM LEIBNIZ" BY
E. PFEIDERER[1]

JUST as Shakespeare was ignored or neglected for half a century in England, so in Germany during the epoch of Kantian and Hegelian supremacy Leibniz was scarcely known except by name. It is only since the elucubration of new systems, which so long engrossed the German mind, has given way to a study of the History of Philosophy that he has resumed his place in public estimation. The more deeply he has been studied the greater he has been found. It is like a new discovery. He had before been regarded exclusively as a deep thinker and a man of varied learning; but it has now come to be recognized that he was still more a great patriot and statesman, and that this practical tendency was the very essence of his character, and forms the only explanation of his life and works, considered as a whole. This new conception of his character was first established by the careful and learned writings of Guhrauer; and now a copious and very instructive work by Dr Pfeiderer follows the same direction, and treats exclusively the practical side of his career.

Later German philosophers have been almost without exception Professors, and, as such, have constructed formal systems, in accordance with the exigencies of their office; and to this fact no doubt is due the abstract scholastic character and difficult form of German philosophy. Leibniz, on the contrary, never occupied a professorial chair, but developed his philosophy amidst the occupations of real life. Born in Leipzig, he studied in his native town, and early acquired an extraordinary knowledge, especially in jurisprudence. At the early age of twenty-one he entered the service of the once famous Baron von Boyneburg, minister to the Archbishop Elector of Mentz, who, according to the old constitution of the Empire, was Arch-Chancellor of Germany. Thus he at once found himself at the focus of German affairs, which again were complicated with the general affairs of Europe; and this circumstance permanently influenced the direction of his life. At that time Germany lay prostrate after the sufferings and devastations of the Thirty Years' War, and seemed threatened with complete dissolution. France was in the ascendant, and was pushing those schemes of aggrandizement chiefly at the ex-

[1] *North British Review*, Jan. 1870, p. 255.

pense of Germany, which were the chief influence in European politics down to the peace of Utrecht. Leibniz lived through the whole of this period; and he took the keenest interest in all public questions till his death in 1716. From 1670 he was in constant communication with German princes and statesmen, and with the Imperial Council of Vienna.

His own part in these correspondences has not yet been fully brought to light. Even what was printed at the time is still incompletely known; for all his political writings were published anonymously, and many of them had been forgotten altogether. A great number have been brought to light by recent researches. In the Tübingen library Dr Pfeiderer has himself discovered twelve, which in all probability belong to the collection, and which were previously unknown. Many more may lie hidden in other libraries; but those which are already known show that Leibniz was one of the most fertile of German publicists. The diversity of their style and form is surprising; and so is the inexhaustible fund of their author's resources. To attract the attention of the general public, he sometimes assumed the garb of a courtier or diplomatist, sometimes of a pamphleteer and agitator. His deep learning, the acuteness of his logic, his eloquence, his wit, his satire, all serve him by turns. He enlists even poetry in his service, and according to circumstances propagates his political ideas in the form of German, French or Latin verses. That his nature was not devoid even of a martial vein, is shown by the lines:

> *Fasst einen Heldenmuth, ihr kühnen Reichssoldaten,*
> *Sezt gegen Eisen Stahl, schlagt auf den Franzmann zu!*

He wrote on the improvement of the military organization of Germany, and in 1692, when the French fleet had been destroyed at La Hogue, he planned a campaign for the allies, in which he proposed a landing in Biscay, with the view of operating against France from that quarter. So deeply was his mind engaged in practical politics, down to the very end of his life, that after the peace of Utrecht he wrote one of his most spirited works, *La Paix d'Utrecht Inexcusable*, in which he specially attacks the naval powers for their breach of faith. Dr Pfeiderer gives interesting extracts from all these works.

To the same connection belongs the Egyptian project, which

Leibniz hoped would divert the attention of France from Germany, by the suggestion of conquests in the east. In 1672 he sent a memoir on this subject to Paris, whereupon he was himself invited thither, and lived there for about four years, during which time he paid a visit to London. The *Consilium Aegyptiacum* which he wrote in Paris at this period was first re-discovered in 1798, when the enterprise which he had thus counselled to Louis XIV was undertaken by Napoleon. Even of the canal of Suez he had spoken at the same time. So ideas work on, and ultimately attain their realization, just as Leibniz himself expresses it in one of his main axioms: "No force perishes. It may be dispersed, but it reunites. Not only men's souls, but also their actions live for ever."

In 1676 Leibniz entered the service of the Duke of Hanover (Hanover only obtained the Electoral dignity in 1692) and thenceforth lived in the city of Hanover. Having been invited to write the history of the Guelphs, he went for a short time to Vienna and Rome to collect the necessary materials. A result of these researches was his *Codex Diplomaticus* and his *Scriptores rerum Brunsvicensium*, followed by the *Annales*, which are of great value for early German history. This last work actually remained unprinted for 127 years, and was recently, for the first time, published by Dr Pertz.

Leibniz's residence in Hanover was not without influence on his efforts to unite the Catholic and Evangelical Churches. For the Duke, having become Catholic while the whole country remained Lutheran, was of course deeply interested in the possibility of reconciliation. Leibniz was a man to whose mind such an idea was exactly fitted. He was earnestly religious, and at the same time free from all sectarian prejudice, tolerant in disposition, and always bent on reconciling and accommodating differences; and as a German patriot he had daily before his eyes the evil results of confessional antagonisms. His efforts in this direction lasted for several years, and were the occasion of his *Systema theologicum* and his correspondence with Pelissa and Bossuet, but remained without any decisive results.

Nor did a better success attend his labours for the union of the Lutheran and Reformed confessions through negotiations between the courts of Hanover and Berlin; they brought him, however, into close relations with the latter court, where the accomplished electoral Princess (Prussia became a kingdom only in 1701) gave him every possible assistance. At Berlin, the Academy of Sciences, of which he was the first president, remains as a scientific monument of him. His desire was that the Academy should not simply minister to the vanity of scholars (although this happened to it later, as it happens to all academies) but should, above all things, aim at making the sciences practically useful, and that no less in the domain of material life than in the highest spheres of the spirit, so that it might aid in the advancement of Christianity. For the glory of God he regarded as the highest aim of all science. He had various relations with missionaries who sent him scientific reports of their labours; and his correspondence of this kind extended as far as China. He was also personally acquainted with Peter the Great, and promoted the formation of an academy at St Petersburg. It was not established till after the Czar's death, when Leibniz's plan was carried out.

But all this did not by any means exhaust his activity. His energies were employed, as Dr Pfeiderer shows, on every question of Society and the State—the improvement of justice, education, political economy, the technical accessories of agriculture, mining handicrafts, and trade. So comprehensive was his mind that, compared even with such a man as Humboldt, he appears like a giant beside a dwarf. For Humboldt, in the main, embraced mathematics and physics only; Leibniz added to them the moral, political and historical sciences, in addition to that ecclesiastical sphere which was altogether strange to Humboldt. Moreover he was constantly engaged in practical politics. They were indeed his favourite pursuit, and prompted his remark: "Those who know me only by my published works, do not know me at all." And, in fact, it is only of late that the world has begun to know him. Dr Pfeiderer's work is a valuable contribution to this end, though its plan is sometimes confused and not always worked out with due care. The Horatian canon of delay applies with special force to any work on Leibniz.

TOCQUEVILLE'S "SOUVENIRS" [1]

TOCQUEVILLE'S recollections of the years 1848 and 1849 contain little that is absolutely new to history, and yet they are a revelation and a surprise. They disclose, for the first time, the real Tocqueville, and show how assiduously, in his writings, and even in his well-considered correspondence, he restrained the manifestation of personal opinion and temper. The love for sententious moralizing is the same, and words of wisdom flow complacently, and almost too easily, whilst he is writing without a thought of the future public. His saying that the cheapest bargain is that which is negotiated with the vanity of mankind, because it procures something in exchange for nothing, betrays a secret which was already some centuries old. But there are passages of higher quality. Much of the historian's craft is hidden in the remark that posterity remembers crimes better than vices. Tocqueville says of himself that the spark of truth is so precious to him, that he fears to agitate it lest it should go out. Of Louis Philippe: his enemies no longer cared to calumniate, or even to hate him—"injure, sinon plus grande, au moins plus rare de la fortune".

In two or three places he exhibits his own belief, or rather his doctrinal negation. He is persuaded that the infirmities of old societies are beyond recovery; the symptoms may change but not the disease, and the ancient powers will be transformed or perish. He is inclined to think that what we call necessary institutions are nothing but those we are accustomed to, and that in the constitution of society the margin of possible variations is almost infinite. In other words, political principles are little better than optical illusions—an instantaneous glimpse of the perpetual motion of life. This dogma of continuous change, which never rose to a distinct belief in development, progress or divine government, and was closely akin to pessimism, released Tocqueville from attachment to party; and it was thus that one who may reasonably be called the ablest Frenchman of his generation achieved so little in public life.

He displays his impartiality in the disposition to condemn all round. He thinks ill of his countrymen both in the present and

[1] *Souvenirs de Alexis de Tocqueville*, Paris, 1893. [From *Nineteenth Century*, vol. xxxiii, May 1893, p. 883.]

the past. The thoughtless impatience, the disregard for law, the facile yielding to example, the temerity in peril are inherited defects; but the passionate desire to live on public money is a recent growth of middle-class institutions.

On the party leaders of his time he delivers this judgement—that all were about equally unworthy to govern, some by the want of superior merit, more by the absence of all merit of any kind. As to military men he has observed that they are the first to lose their heads in a crisis.

EXTRACTS

THE (French) Revolution transferred to the order of right and politics what was true in the order of religion. Because a prophet has denounced vengeance upon a wicked king, subjects are not justified in rising against their prince. It is not theirs to judge and to punish his sins. Because all men are brethren in the eyes of the Church, that is no argument in favour of democracy. In the same way, Catholic divines, Suarez, for instance, and Mariana, have been made responsible for the crimes of regicides. Ravaillac had as much right to appeal to the teaching of the Jesuits, as the followers of Cromwell to justify their acts by the examples of the Old Testament. Gregory the Great says: "Mos medicinae est aliquando similia similibus, aliquando contraria contrariis curet"[1]; yet we have never heard the priority of the discovery of homoeopathy claimed for him.

The Rambler, vol. ii, 1859, p. 105.

THE WRITING OF HISTORY

What chiefly distinguishes the modern historical art from that of the ancients is, that the history of ideas is now understood in its bearing on the history of events. Formerly, it is true, the connection was less visible; the movement of mind was less rapid, ideas were not so easily interchanged, their consequences were not so quickly developed as now. In the Middle Ages, especially, the same stock of ideas continued to furnish several generations with their motives of action: whole centuries are occupied with the same problems, and the progress is slow. The number of

[1] *Moral.*, lib. xxiv, cap. 2.

writers and the number of books were far less than before or since. Even then there were moments when controversy was carried on briskly, and when long discussions were concentrated into a few years. The pontificate of Gregory VII is the earliest instance of this ... To exhibit the course of ideas and the course of events in their parallel progress, and their action on each other, is a principal function of the modern historian. Still it is rather a desideratum than an achievement of our time. Much has been done, especially by French writers, to illustrate the history of a period from its writings. Something too has been done, particularly in England, to make history interesting and distinct by descriptions of the state of society; and a strong materialistic tendency pervades a very popular portion of our literature. But what is really wanted, and what we ought to claim of our historians is the reverse of this. If history is to be understood as an intellectual, and not as a natural, process, it must be studied as the history of mind. The accidents will disappear, what seems episodical and isolated will be absorbed and ranged in the harmonious course of history, in proportion as we understand the ideas which have influenced each separate country and each successive age.

Literary history is commonly treated on too confined a scale to be of a very great service in this respect. It approaches the history of art more than the history of events. That species of thought which most directly and consciously influences action, is the least to be distinguished in that which is called national literature. The immediate historical importance of a work resides in its practical, not in its aesthetical, character; and books of a purely practical kind are excluded from the common definition of literary history, which deals only with those which possess aesthetical, artistic merit. Writings of an ephemeral kind, in the eyes of the literary historian, possess a value and a durability of another description in the events which they have influenced. The chief sources of historical knowledge are in few cases contained in works which have great literary fame. Our knowledge of modern history is derived from a very different style of histories from those which record the Peloponnesian or the Punic war. There is, then, a vast portion of writing which has no value in the estimation of literary historians, and is therefore generally forgotten; but which is of the utmost value to history. Those books which have most influenced men—the polemical writings of divines, and the political speculations of philosophers and statesmen—rarely possess that sort of merit which secures renown. But to the historian they are more important than works of great genius. He is more interested in *The New Atlantis* than in *The Advancement of Learning*, in the *Areopagitica* than in *Paradise Lost*.

Profane historians have yet a lesson to learn from the method of ecclesiastical history. There the history of doctrine is the soul and centre of events; and the thoughts of St Augustine or St Cyril are as much the real subject-matter as the deeds of Constantine or Charlemagne. The analogy between the influence of political and social theories upon profane history, and that of religious doctrines on the history of the Church, is closer than has been generally understood. There is a near resemblance, and even some connection, between the progress of some opinion and the revolution of political ideas. There have been times when political thoughts have influenced the Church as much as, at other times, theological controversy has influenced the outer world. In the Middle Ages the Church passed through a peculiarly social and a peculiarly political phase of existence. From the time of Gregory I, or even Leo I, she had to deal with the new ideas of society introduced with the barbarians. After the age of Gregory VII, she was engaged in perpetual conflict with a new political system. The theory of the sovereignty of the people has played as great a part in history as the doctrine of justification by faith only. The revolution which it inspired was quite as important an event as the Reformation. Both events were primarily the result of certain speculative ideas; neither would have been so successful but for external temporal circumstances. But they cannot be explained by these alone. Deeds as well as words are the signs of thoughts; and if we consider only external events, without following the course of ideas of which they are the expression and the result, and which they influence in their turn, we shall have but a lame notion of history, and shall overlook an alternate link in the chain of human progress. The taking of the Bastille, for instance, was a great sign; the appearance of Sieyès' pamphlet, *What is the Third Estate?* was a greater fact.

AUTHORITY AND LIBERTY

There is a wide divergence, an irreconcilable disagreement, between the political notions of the modern world and that which is essentially the system of the Catholic Church. It manifests itself particularly in their contradictory views of liberty, and of the functions of the civil power. The Catholic notion, defining liberty not as the power of doing what we like, but the right of being able to do what we ought, denies that general interests can supersede individual rights. It condemns therefore, the theory of the ancient as well as of the modern State. It is founded on the divine origin and nature of authority. According to the prevailing doctrine, which derives power from the people, and deposits it ultimately in their hands, the State is omnipotent over the individual, whose only remnant of freedom is then the participation in the exercise of supreme power; while the general will is binding on him. Nearly the earliest and clearest exponent of this doctrine is Spinoza, who says: "It is utterly inconceivable that each subject should be allowed by the constitution of the State to live according to his own choice." Christian liberty is lost where this system prevails: whether in the form of the utmost diffusion of power, as in America, or of the utmost concentration of power, as in France; whether, that is to say, it is exercised by the majority, or by the delegates of the majority—it is always a delusive freedom, founded on a servitude more or less disguised. In one form and under one pretext or another, the State has been absolute on the Continent of Europe for the last three hundred years. In the sixteenth century absolutism was founded on religious zeal, and was expressed in the formula *cujus regio, illius religio*. In the seventeenth century it assumed the garb of legitimacy and divine right, and the king was believed when he said: "*L'état c'est moi*." In the eighteenth century arbitrary government found a new and stronger basis in the theory of the public good, of the greatest happiness of the greatest number, and justified every act of tyranny by the maxim, "The king is the first servant of the State." All these principles of despotism are incompatible with the Catholic ideas, and with the system by which the Pope, on pain of being in contradiction with himself, and with the spirit and practice of the Church, is compelled to govern. They are condemned by the traditions, and by the moral obligations, of the Court of Rome, whose system is one of charity and of liberty, and which knows no public consideration which is superior to the salvation of souls.

The Rambler, vol. ii, 1860, p. 146.

ABSOLUTE GOVERNMENT

Absolute government must be either despotic or paternal. It is despotic if . . . it is used for public and external ends; it is paternal if . . . it confines itself to private concerns.

The Rambler, vol. ii, 1860, p. 147.

THE STATE

In our conviction the true view of the origin and nature of the State . . . is that which recognizes in the State the same divine origin and the same ends as in the Church, which holds that it belongs as much to the primitive essence of a nation as its language, and that it unites men together by a moral, not, like family and society, by a natural and sensible, bond.

The Rambler, vol. ii, 1860, p. 397.

STATE ABSOLUTISM

State absolutism . . . is the modern danger against which neither representative government nor democracy can defend us . . . If we do not bear this in mind, we shall be led constantly astray by forms to overlook the substance, to confound freedom of speech with freedom of action, to think that right is safer against majorities than against tyrants.

The Rambler, vol. ii, 1860, p. 397.

MARIA THERESA

Few periods of modern history have been so little studied as the reign of Maria Theresa. The absence of great intellects or eminent characters in the Austrian State at that time has generally deterred historians, while patriotic Austrians have had no encouragement to celebrate a period of great national disasters and considerable internal oppression . . . Maria Theresa introduced a new system of government, which is little remembered, because it was subverted by her son, but which is a remarkable instance of the absolutism of the eighteenth century, aggravated rather than tempered by the sovereign's regard for morality, and, as in most cases where absolutism is not intensified by centralization, neither oppressive nor unpopular in the more remote dependencies.

The Rambler, vol. ii, 1860, p. 397.

ON A WRITER OF HISTORY

He writes not judicially but polemically; and though he seeks to dispel error, he uses those arts of advocacy which are the very instrument by which it has been spread. He desires the advancemen of historical science, but he promotes it in the spirit of a partisan. Now it is better for science that men should acquire the methods of impartial learning than that they should defend the most respectable thesis by that sort of unfair dealing which conceals one side of the question. For where this controversial spirit prevails the goodness of the cause enhances its danger, and the partisan will multiply his artifices and manoeuvres in proportion to the zeal which the merits of his cause inspire. Such a policy is sure to stimulate the bitterness and the ingenuity of adversaries.

Home and Foreign Review, Oct. 1863, p. 713.

RANKE

Ranke has never shown his talent for extracting new and minute information on a familiar subject more remarkably than in the fourth volume of his *English History*, which extends from the death of Cromwell to the year 1674. It is a model of the art of using authorities; and the author has obtained so much new matter at Paris and Oxford, in the British Museum, and the Record Office, that he is entirely free from conventional influences, and presents many new points of view. There could not be a more instructive lesson in historital investigation than carefully to compare the methods used in this volume with those of Macaulay in the following reign. And yet the work has been coldly received among the writer's countrymen, and has not sustained his reputation. His strength does not lie in the history of free communities. He is the historian of courts and statesmen, incomparable at unravelling the web of an intrigue, and divining the hidden, changing schemes of the most expert politician; and he understands the force of convictions, the influence of literature, and the progress of theories; but he is happier when he has to deal with personal than with public opinions, with individuals than with masses. His miniature-painting preserves with a fidelity amounting to genius the features of royal and illustrious persons; but he has not the breadth of touch requisite to do justice to great popular and national movements, and to dramas in which the actors are whole classes and provinces of men. Therefore we feel that there is something inadequate, narrow, and unsympathizing in his treatment of the constitutional struggles and of the great political and religious parties, while his intimate knowledge of all the contemporary history of Europe is a merit not suited to his insular readers. But in all that relates to politics, as in the Triple Alliance and the character of Clarendon, the hand of a real master is not to be mistaken.

Home and Foreign Review, April 1864, p. 715.

TIBERIUS

The career of Tiberius exhibits the spectacle of a continuous and terrible declension. At the age of thirty he was perhaps a better man than Augustus at the same age; but while the nature of Augustus grew greater and grander with his years—was solemnized, and in some sense purified, by his ever-growing sense of the greatness of his mission—the nature of Tiberius hardened, shrank, and, one might say *mortified* under the same pressure. Do not the lives of these two great men present a commentary on the celebrated saying of William Humboldt, that the true object of each man's life is "the highest and most harmonious development of all his powers to a complete and consistent whole"? For a very few men—for the intellectual salt of the earth—the dictum looks as if it were true. Men with poised and symmetrical natures, and of great intellectual activity—men like Augustus or Goethe, or even like the Humboldts or David Hume—seem, as one reads their history, to have been independent of external aid, to have stood in need of no supernatural influences; they developed their faculties evenly and harmoniously because of the original happy tempering of their mental constitution. But a large proportion of mankind are onesided from the first; their personal standard of truth, beauty, and goodness deviates fatally from the true standard; and "development" only increases this deviation, as lines that diverge from each other, however small may be the angle, increase their distance the farther they are produced. Tiberius was by nature mistrustful of his fellow men; this mistrust led him, unlike Augustus, to refuse thorough confidence to able coadjutors, and endeavour to overlook the whole complex imperial system with his own eyes, using inferior men as mere agents. These inferior men, as was natural, often proved treacherous or incapable; whence the original mistrust in the emperor's mind gradually deepened into an incurable suspicion and ill opinion of mankind. From these feelings naturally arose a haunting fear lest treason and revolution should drive him from the throne; and suspicion and fear led as naturally to cruelty. But the exercise of cruelty drives a nature not intrinsically ignoble to despair; and this, as we know from his own lips, was the normal state of Tiberius' mind in his latter years. "Quod scribam vobis . . . Dii me Deaeque pejus perdant *quam perire me quotidie sentio*, si scio."[1] But an absolute monarch, with despair consuming his heart, and no effectual external aid to look to, is but too likely to seek a temporary relief in sensuality. To the symmetrical natures religion is indeed a crown of glory; nevertheless, so far as this world is concerned, they can grow and prosper without it. But to the unsymmetrical minds religion is a necessary condition of successful work even in this world; the weakness which they feel, and the mistakes which they commit, can only be supplemented and certified by recourse being had to an infinite fund of goodness and justice—eternal, invisible, yet ever present. The miserable Tiberius, had he known Humboldt's dictum, could not have profited by it; for harmonious development, by his own efforts, of ill-sorted and unequal powers was not possible for him. He consulted astrologers and soothsayers, who of course made matters worse. Only the religion of which his procurator, Pontius Pilatus, imagined himself to be trampling out the nascent spark on the hill of Calvary, would have enabled him to discharge with passable success the task which his mightier predecessor had bequeathed to him.

Home and Foreign Review, Jan. 1864, p. 280.

WHIGGISM

The essence of Whiggism is the acknowledgement of the supremacy of the divine will, or as we should say, if the term had not been degraded, of divine right over the will of man, whether represented by the sovereign, or by the people, in the institutions

[1] Tacitus, *Annales*, vi, 6.

of the past, or in speculative theories. It is the absolute exclusion from politics of that arbitrary element which asserts itself in Toryism by denying the claims of principle, and in Radicalism by rejecting the authority of fact. It upholds the laws of the country; but it clings to their spirit, not to the temporary forms by which that spirit is expressed or secured. In this way Selden shared in the Great Rebellion, Somers justified the Revolution, and Burke defended the constitutional idea in the American and the Revolutionary wars. But Locke derives civil society from a voluntary contract, and thus introduces a principle as arbitrary in its nature, and as dangerous to right in its consequences, as the maxim that kings are above the law.

Home and Foreign Review, Jan. 1863, p. 253.

FALSEHOOD IN THE SERVICE OF TRUTH

It is melancholy to think what would become of our knowledge of the past, but for the passions, interests, and prejudices which are the means of preserving the history they distort. The annals of happy nations are vacant; and annalists if they were wiser would probably be less industrious. It requires an impartial man to make a good historian; but it is the partial and onesided who hunt out the materials. If all writers were disinterested and sincere, history would not be filled with lies. But there is falsehood enough to keep up the investigation of truth, and plenty of men, patient, laborious, and passionate, to provide materials.

Home and Foreign Review, Jan. 1864, p. 236.

BIOGRAPHIES

Nothing causes more error and unfairness in men's views of history than the interest which is inspired by individual characters. The most absolute devotion to certain ideas and opinions is less dangerous, for they may be perfectly true, while no character is perfectly good; and the allegiance which is paid to doctrine is less blind and less unreasoning than that in which loyalty or friendship usurps the place of reason and duty. The schools of error live on the reputation of their founders and heroes, by proclaiming whose virtues they exalt themselves. They rely as much on the influence of personal authority and of human example as on the attractive force of theories. Their followers, instead of divesting themselves of prejudices, and of personal inclinations and affections, to prepare for the contemplation of truth itself, unmixed with falseness and unaccommodated to weakness, convert all the natural obstacles of knowledge into supports for their opinions. An indiscriminate admiration and jealousy of criticism marks the feelings of a sect and a party towards its leaders. Now this is a disposition strengthened in early life by the manner in which history is generally learnt. The interest of biography awakens a thirst for knowledge, long before history can be understood; and we have our minds crowded with objects of hero-worship before we can understand the intricacies of character, and before we can appreciate the sanctity of a cause. In this way the imagination may be aroused and the memory stored; but the judgement is warped instead of being formed, and the historical faculty and habit, which is the most valuable fruit of historical study, and may survive even historical knowledge, is spoiled. Something is wanted to counteract this effect, and to educate minds to take an interest in impersonal history, in events so great as to conceal the actors, and in a process more regular and more instructive than the vicissitudes of fortune and adventure. Otherwise history loses its moral and providential character, and appears an arbitrary and accidental series of figures and occurrences. And this is the reason why so few people understand that the criterion by which the acts of individuals are judged is distinct from that which tests the policy of states, so that in history the notions of error, fault, and crime are substituted for those of vice and sin.

Home and Foreign Review, Jan. 1863, p. 219.

RUSSIA

Russia has existed a thousand years; it is the most populous of the European nations, the most united and the vastest state in the world. And yet it has accomplished nothing for mankind, and has not produced a monument or an idea that men will be unwilling to forget. The Russians have created nothing; but they have not assimilated the foreign elements which their rulers have introduced. They have preserved the national character unchanged, in spite of the elaborate efforts of the government; and under an incessant despotism they have retained the art of providing for themselves. They do not resist the interference of the State; but they do not require it.

Home and Foreign Review, Jan. 1863, p. 285.

THE ROMAN EMPIRE

In the history of the empire during the first three centuries of our era, two centres of moral action may be distinguished as the foci whence the great leavening forces of society were developed —the imperial government, and Christianity realizing itself through the Church. And there is no *third* focus; there is, for instance, no independent development of science, such as we see in modern times, working out its own problems, and progressively improving the external relations of man, without necessary dependence either on government or on religion. Why this was so, is a question which every student of history must have asked himself, and to which various answers have been given. Besides other explanations more or less partial, M. Comte's famous theory of the three stages—the theological, the metaphysical and the positive—through which, by some supposed physical necessity, human society is obliged to pass on its way to enlightenment, may be plausibly applied to this as to other epochs, to account for the absence of the triumphs of positivism. But the Christian answer seems to be that the progress of science, so far as it relates to the external world, presupposes the thorough reception of the idea of the unity of nature, and again, in what belongs to the moral world, of the idea of the unity of man; and that these ideas, in order to be firmly grasped, required the previous indoctrination of the human mind in a yet higher idea—that of the unity of God. This indoctrination was to be, and was, in point of fact, effected by the spread of Christianity. Apart, then, from the diffusion of Christianity, the history of the empire resolves itself pretty much into a series of biographies of the emperors. When an emperor was weak, the empire became a chaos; and the inorganic is no subject for the historian. When an emperor was strong, the empire rested in peaceful servitude; and one cannot write the history of slaves ... The reduction of the laws of the empire to a uniform and consistent code, involving the constant reference to general principles, was the work, not of heathen, but of Christian, emperors. For the great gift of the civil law of Rome, modern Europe has not to thank Trajan or Antonine but Theodosius and Justinian. The production of codes professedly grounded upon bases independent of Christianity has taught men to admit, at least in theory, the doctrine of their universal brotherhood.

Home and Foreign Review, April 1863, p. 590.

THE SCHOOL OF GIBBON

Gibbon, though often unfair, is always self-consistent; his philosophy led him to take a low view of ordinary human nature, and especially to disbelieve in evangelical or monastic virtues; but his views are definite, and the reader does not look for an appreciation which he knows beforehand he will not find. The position of Gieseler and other rationalist historians is similar to that of Gibbon. As they start with the assumption that the supernatural element which appears to crop out in Church history exists only in imagination, they know exactly how to deal with their materials—how much to assign to fraud, and how much to superstition—what part to allot to enthusiasm or to ambition, and what to the convenient principle of legendary accretion. Holding themselves aloof from modern Christianity in all its forms, they can afford to have precise and clear views in dealing with Christianity in the past; they put everything in its right place except the divine fire at the centre, about which they know and care nothing. Again, a Catholic historian like Fleury or Bossuet is still more truly at home in such a field; for him the present of the Church explains her past, and her history in the third century is the same in all its main features with her history in the nineteenth. He finds the same struggle going on, the same enemies, the same dangers within and without, the same authority and the same ideals. But it is difficult to understand how a sincere Protestant could treat satisfactorily a period in which the growth of the Church was one of the most prominent movements. Either he would slide into the critical habit of the rationalists, and explain away, or treat as mythical, whatever in that movement appears to have a supernatural impress; or he would adventure upon the desperate undertaking of separating the progress of what he might deem to be religious truth from the intertwining growth of what his position obliged him to regard as error. In either case a mistiness of treatment, a hesitation of touch, would ensue, which would mar much of the effect of his work. The development of the primitive Church is the movement of one organic whole. As soon as study has made clear its main features and relations, the Protestant student finds himself compelled either to bless it or to curse it. If the former, he is far on the road to becoming a Catholic; if the latter, he is in the way of ceasing to be a Christian. For a knowledge that is more than superficial reveals the terrible resemblance of the primitive Church to an institution of our own day. *Apparent dirae facies.* "If", says a great thinker, after passing under review all the passages from contemporary writers which enable us to form a conception of the manner in which the world around it regarded the Church of the first centuries, "there is a form of Christianity now in the world which is accused of gross superstition, of borrowing its rites and practices from the heathen, and ascribing to forms and ceremonies an occult virtue; a religion which is considered to burden and enslave the mind by its requisitions, to address itself to the weak-minded and ignorant, to be supported by sophistry and imposture, and to contradict reason and exalt mere irrational faith; a religion which impresses on the serious mind very distressing views of the guilt and consequences of sin, sets upon the minute acts of the day, one by one, their definite value for praise or blame, and thus casts a grave shadow over the future; a religion which men hate as proselytizing, anti-social, revolutionary, as dividing families, separating chief friends, corrupting the maxims of government, making a mock of law, dissolving the empire, the enemy of human nature, and a conspirator against its rights and privileges . . . a religion the very name of which they cast out as evil, and use simply as a bad epithet, and which from the impulse of self-preservation they would persecute if they could; if there be such a religion now in the world, it is not unlike Christianity as the same world viewed it, when it first came forth from its divine Author."[1]

Home and Foreign Review, April 1863, p. 592.

LORD MACAULAY

Lord Macaulay's political career is attractive, not as that of a statesman who achieved great things, or pursued a great policy, but as the brilliant expression of the political ideas of one of the clearest, most consistent, and most accomplished thinkers of

[1] Newman, *Essay on Development*, p. 240.

modern times. The interest resides not in action but in ideas . . . Macaulay was by the character of his mind averse to the niceties of political speculation. No theoretic system enslaved him, or made him deaf to the dictates of a manly and sincere good sense. Whilst, therefore, his judgement was very rarely misled, his reasoning was very seldom profound, and he shrank from the depths of disputation with the horror of a practical statesman. Accordingly, his own views on all public questions were free from the exaggerations of absolute Liberalism; but he was unable to discern the speculative origin of those errors, or to ascertain the necessary applications of first principles. The nearest, simplest reason appeared to him the best; and he did not care that his argument should strike its roots into a very deep philosophy. Hence he is not always just in describing the doctrines of different parties, nor always consistent in his own relations towards them. For the party to which he belonged had a double pedigree, and traces its descent on the one hand through Fox, Sidney and Milton to the Roundheads, and on the other through Burke, Somers, and Selden to the old English lawyers. Between these two families there was more matter for civil war than between Cromwell and King Charles. The divergency between any two systems that result in arbitrary power cannot be so great as that between either of them and a system which subjects the sovereign to law; and there were more principles held in common by Falkland and Selden, when one was secretary of state and the other the colleague of Pym, than by Fox and Burke when they were in office together.

According to one theory, the king as well as the people was subject to the law, and both were bound to prevent or to avenge the breach of the constitution by the other. The laws of the land were not merely a privilege which the people had a right to defend, but the object of the highest moral sanction, which it was their duty to vindicate. The people could not be justified if they neglected this duty, and they would be guilty of a great crime if they defied or resisted the sovereign except in the case of a violation of the fundamental laws. This was well understood by the old constitutional lawyers:

"Our princes are tied up to the law as well as we, and upon an especial account obliged to keep it up in its full force; because, if they destroyed the law, they destroyed at the same time themselves, by overthrowing the very foundation of their kingly grandeur and regal power. So that our government not being arbitrary but legal, not absolute but political, our princes can never become arbitrary, absolute or tyrants, without forfeiting at the same time their royal character, by the breach of the essential conditions of their regal power, which are, to act according to the ancient customs and standing laws of the nation . . ."[1]

The men of the other school maintained the contrary principle of the right of every people to choose, and therefore to change, its own rulers. Not only a revolutionary but also an upopular act on the part of the king might forfeit his crown. The legitimacy of resistance was to be tested not by the laws of the land, but by the consent of the people; and the cause which justified rebellion was not the arbitrary violation of established or unquestioned rights, but opposition to an arbitrary caprice . . . The Whiggism that prevailed at that time in the society to which Macaulay was soon introduced was the Whiggism of Holland House—the Foxite school of Lord Grey and Lord Russell. This is the school which he always acknowledged as his own . . . "In their view (Milton and Locke) the end for which all governments had been instituted was the happiness of society."[2] Again and again the utilitarian notion of government recurs in his writings, and the writer seems as sincere a believer in the sovereignty of the people as Sidney, or Paine, or Lord Russell. "The Whig theory of government", he says, "is that kings exist for the people, and not the people for kings, that the right of a king is divine in no other sense than that in which the right of a member of parliament is divine, of a judge, of a juryman, of a mayor or a headborough is divine."[3] It is evident that he never mastered the real point at issue between the Whigs and all other parties; for in all these passages he overlooks the fundamental distinction between sovereignty and authority, and between rights in the sense of power and rights which imply duties. He was not acquainted with the political writings of Plato and Aristotle, in which he would have found more of the Whig doctrine than in the men he delights to quote. But he was guided throughout, and preserved from many errors to which his superficial treatment of principles would have exposed him, by an unswerving admiration for the writings of

[1] Somers, *Tracts*, x, 263.   [2] *History*, v, 75.   [3] ibid., iv, 2.

Burke. It is astonishing that he should never have understood, from the example of his friend Mackintosh, the extent of the chasm which parted the two schools he had not learned to distinguish. Mackintosh, after having made himself famous as the ablest antagonist of Burke, declared in 1804 that Burke was in every respect the wisest and ablest of human beings, and regretted deeply what he had written against him.

Home and Foreign Review, Jan. 1863, p. 258.

BOLINGBROKE AND TORYISM

The author of the peace of Utrecht is memorable in history for the greater achievement of having elevated Toryism for a moment to the dignity of a political theory. No other man has ever attempted this; and the loss of those great orations in which Secretary St John flung the mantle of philosophy over the October Club, and cajoled the stout defenders of the interests of their class into the exciting belief that they could understand and sustain a principle, deserved to be lamented by Mr Pitt, who led the Tories without dreaming of inspiring their minds with an idea. For it was in the nature and definition of Toryism that it lived on class interests or on religious opinions, and borrowed the elements of its vitality from a different order of ideas. At times it subsisted by the deliberate suppression of political thought; made the denial of principle pass for a principle, and the repudiation of obligations for a duty; and carried, under pretence of expediency, measures which it declared to be wrong. It raised some extraneous object above the consideration of public right, the very existence of which it was ready to question, if it appeared in antagonism with any cherished interest of some portion of society. The cry that the Church was in danger, or the landlord threatened, did duty instead of a political idea, and acted far more powerfully than any thing based on reasoning could have acted on uneducated minds. Therefore the most illustrious chiefs of the party either were not reared in its arms, or deserted it in the maturity of their powers; and they are all reckoned by their party either converts or apostates. A rational system could be created for it only by one who did not share its superstitions. Bolingbroke, a man free from very definite family traditions, of a philosophical turn of mind that impelled him to look for principles, and with a love of enterprise that was not curbed by the heavy responsibilities of wealth, at the same time a profligate and an unbeliever, was predestined to be the theorist of Toryism.

Home and Foreign Review, April 1863, p. 635.

PHYSICAL FORCE AND MORAL AUTHORITY

It is the distinction and separation of these that secures a really free submission. It is as necessary that society, when it is at issue with the State on account of its breaches of the law, should have force sufficient to protect its rights, as it is that the State should, under ordinary circumstances, be strong enough to enforce the law against the members of society. The maintenance of the civil and criminal code is the work of the State: the vindication of the public constitutional law is more particularly the duty of the nation. Therefore a State in which the law is powerless to punish a thief, or in which society is unable to restrict the action of the government, are equally opposed to the notion of polity. Anarchy follows in one case, and despotism in the other.

Home and Foreign Review, April 1863, p. 646.

ANSELM VON FEUERBACH

Anselm von Feuerbach was the principal reformer of the criminal law in Germany by his writings, and as the author of the Bavarian code, which was published in 1813, and has since been adopted by many states both in and out of Germany. Compared with the legislation of Frederick the Great, of Napoleon, of Livingstone, and of Macaulay, his code has a great superiority in point of precision and of philosophic system and symmetry, whilst in clearness and elegance of expression he is not surpassed by the eloquent author of the Indian code. It is the peculiar character of his juridical views that gives so singular an interest to his collection of remarkable trials. The prevention of crime is, according to Feuerbach, the end of punishment. The physical force exercised by the police is insufficient for that purpose, and must be supplemented therefore by psychological compulsion. The impulse to a wrong act resides in the expectation of pleasure which it will afford. This must be counteracted by the certainty of an amount of pain which will follow its performance more than equal to the pain of renunciation. It follows that the penalty should increase in proportion, not to the crime, but to the temptation, and that the punishment should be most severe when the real internal guilt is least. Punishment, indeed, could never be excessive, according to this theory of prevention, which allowed no discretion to the judge, but made the penalty certain, by binding the sentence closely to the letter of the law. At the same time Feuerbach accomplished the suppression of torture in Bavaria, in spite of the resistance of the king, who believed that the change would open the door to all manner of crimes. He was also ardently opposed to trial by jury. His philosophy was profoundly irreligious, and his philanthropy was of that sickly kind which revolts at one sort of severity and protects itself against the results of a superficial leniency by a new species of cruelty which the sanctions of age and religion, or the abuses arising from it, have not yet made hateful to systematic reformers.

Home and Foreign Review, April 1863, p. 647.

M. GUIZOT

It was never the character of M. Guizot's intellect to be either very original or profound. He has not, like Tocqueville, that art of acute observation which dissects the phenomena of public life, and discovers its laws with the exactness of natural history; and he has not the marvellous gift of Fiévée, in whom the genius of politics had become almost a sense, such as the arts sometimes develop in their greatest masters. It has not been given to him to bring down a practical philosophy from the very principles of ethics, as Plato, and in our own day Trendelenburg, have done. But in experience, and in the extent of his historical view, he infinitely surpasses all French writers; and he shows everywhere an unfailing judgement applied to an unequal knowledge of the art of government.

Home and Foreign Review, April 1863, p. 650.

LAWFUL GOVERNMENT

Although the lawfulness of a government does not depend on the part the people have in it, yet it depends on the part the law has in it; and whilst a government in which the people have no power is to be gradually modified, a State in which the law has no authority is not merely defective but criminal. There is all the difference between the two that there is between a school and a prison.

Home and Foreign Review, April 1863, p. 656.

S. R. GARDINER

Mr Gardiner chooses the period between 1603 and 1616 for his history of England, because it was the time during which, he says, the Constitution put on that Stuartine development of the supremacy of the prerogative, with power to suspend the sittings of parliament, and to remove judges at will, which was combated by the Rebellion and the Revolution of 1688 ... In its general scope his history is not a narrative written to show the triumph of right, or what he conceives to be so, and viewing all events from the moral elevation of a strong antecedent bias; but neither is it a passionless exposition of the series of events in their mechanical and metaphysical relation of cause and effect. He belongs to Mr Carlyle's school—a school which seeks to unite the moral interest of the first kind of history with the veracity of the second, by making itself the partisan of the fact, by subjecting the right to the test of success and by assuming that the conquering cause was the favourite of the gods. A historian of this school will select any great power that exists or has existed in the world, and trace the steps by which it came to be. In the history of this individual power, every man who contributed to consolidate it is set forth as a hero, and every one who opposed it, and was crushed by it, as an idiot. Whether the power is the English Constitution, or the Reformation, or the Napoleonic Empire, or the Prussian Kingdom, or the English Commonwealth, or the great war that ended with Waterloo, its central figure is always the hero of its history, and his might measures right, while opposition to him is the universal form of evil. Every reader of Hegel can recognize the pantheistic principle which lurks in his treatment of history as a war of forces, in which the greatest force is the more ample manifestation of the Universal Mind. However successful such a school may be in particular histories, it is clear that it is powerless to construct a universal history. For it has no one principle but to accept success as the justification of a policy; and since nearly all principles had their successes, nearly all are justified by it. But the school is well able to write monographs and particular histories. For as it makes success the final test of right, there is no previous idea which the facts are forced to illustrate; and as in the eyes of the historian the event proves the balance of right to be on the winning side, he can afford to allow for minor mistakes and lesser wrongs, which may diminish the final total, but do not alter its design. Thus Mr Gardiner says: "Some, either real or apparent, Antinomian sentences in Luther's polemical opinions cannot for a moment weigh against the hearty morality of his life, and the general tendency of his doctrines."

It is therefore in the general views of his preliminary chapters that Mr Gardiner shows the weakness of his school—warping the great principles of universal history to illustrate his particular issue, the growth of the British Constitution, and the failure of the Stuarts to impress their stamp permanently upon it. In general, this part of the book is an echo of the current prejudices of Englishmen, not corrected by any original investigation, as in the later chapters, but seasoned with a show of liberality and candour which can afford to praise every institution while it had vitality —that is, while it was victorious.

Home and Foreign Review, July 1863, p. 296.

SLAVERY

The abolition of slavery is one of those instances in which it is necessary to distinguish between the actual precepts of Christianity and the influence of the Church in her organization, between the direct and the indirect action of religion, or, in other words, between theology and ecclesiastical law. For the New Testament, according to the interpretation both of the Greek Fathers and the mediaeval divines, positively sanctioned slavery; and in the general sense of the early Church there was nothing immoral in it. In a spiritual point of view, it was even described as possessing peculiar advantages. It is probably in consequence of this marked tolerance of slavery that it came to be supposed that the Church was indifferent to freedom, and deemed even absolutism legitimate. The confusion arose from a false definition of the terms. Slavery is the condition in which certain definite rights are lost by the slave. Absolutism is the state in which no rights are assured to the subject. One is a danger, but the other is a wrong. An absolute government actually suspends or contradicts the divine law, and substitutes for it the rule of a more or less benevolent or enlightened human will. The people may be prosperous and contented, yet the system they obey is sinful in itself. A slave may be exposed to great pains and great dangers; but if his position is so regulated by law that nothing actually immoral, such as the refusal of education or the severance of the marriage-tie, is permitted, he still, in a certain sphere, enjoys a restricted freedom. Religion assents to gradations and limitations of freedom, but not to the rejection of law. A power which asserts itself superior to law is dishonourable to God, who is the author of law; but a power which the law allows to be very great is a constant part of the divine economy. The same theory of Christian right which calls upon the subject to reform or to subvert an arbitrary government may require that the slave shall obey his master. It is not, however, only the enemies of the Church who have overlooked this distinction; and we have partisans of an abstract abolitionism, as well as advocates of absolute power.

In the Middle Ages the Church regulated and mitigated servitude, but she never encouraged wholesale emancipation. As early as the seventh century, she required that the property of the serf should be treated as rightfully his own. In the ninth century, after she had been content for a time to forbid the re-marriage of a slave who had been separated from his wife, she established the indissolubility of the marriage of slaves; but it was not till three centuries later that she could obtain the recognition of marriages contracted by them without the consent of their masters. All this tended to soften servitude, but not to abrogate it. But while the Church formed the individual for that inner freedom which made even slavery an occasion of virtue, she educated the nations for that public freedom which penetrates and proclaims itself in every region of civil society. The same influence which disciplined the individual into submission to qualifications of liberty, promoted in the State the outward manifestation of this real internal freedom. The readiness of obedience anticipated and superseded the action of authority. In a Christian community, the spiritual emancipation of the subject involved his political liberation; and it followed that the State must recognize and exhibit the process of conversion which had been accomplished in the particular souls. That law of spiritual freedom which is indifferent to external restraint, which St Paul preached in a pagan empire, became in Christian society a law of political freedom; and the Church, which tolerated slavery and practised equality, helped by this apparent inconsistency to liberate the slave. In this sense we see some truth in the words of the most malignant and assiduous enemy that religion possesses in the literature of the present age: "Malgré l'Eglise, l'égalité religieuse devait conduire à l'égalité civile."[1] But this influence exerted by the Church less as a doctrine than as an institution belonged to her as a great independent authority in the State; and thus it came to pass that Protestantism, while preaching more absolutely the emancipation of the individual, nevertheless contributed ... to increase the horrors of servitude over a great portion of the Continent.

Home and Foreign Review, Oct. 1863, p. 719.

LEGITIMACY

The theory of legitimacy is of two kinds. On the one hand it affirms that the rights of authority depend merely on its origin; on the other, that they depend on the observance of kindred and equal rights. The former is the old doctrine of the Tories; the latter of the Whigs.

Home and Foreign Review, Oct. 1863, p. 719.

THE PESSIMISTS

Neither paganism nor Christianity ever produced a profound political historian whose mind was not turned to gloom by the contemplation of the affairs of men. It is almost a test to distinguish the great narrators from the great thinkers—Herodotus, Livy, Froissart, Schiller, Macaulay, Thiers, from Thucydides, Polybius, Tacitus, Macchiavelli, Raleigh, Gibbon, Guizot, Niebuhr.

Home and Foreign Review, Oct. 1863, p. 719.

ST BERNARD

St Bernard's position in the Christian Church presents many striking analogies to that of Samuel, whom Dr Stanley calls "the last representative of the ancient mediaeval Church of Judaism". Both were dedicated from their earliest infancy to the service of God, and prepared, not by any sudden conversion, but by a youth marvellously cogitative, and a continuous growth in holiness, for their future influence; for though St Bernard often spoke of his entering the monastery of Citeaux as a "conversion", it was not a conversion from sin, scarcely from worldliness. Both lived in a transition period, and were reared under a theocracy soon to pass away; for what the rise of the Hebrew monarchy was to the

[1] Laurent, *La Féodalité et l'Église*.

theocratic rule which had preceded it, the growing power of civil government and national sentiment was to the autocracy of the mediaeval popes, which had culminated under Hildebrand, and of which St Bernard already marked and almost prophesied the approaching decline, though it did not actually commence till a century later. Both exercised a deep and wide influence over their generation, not official but moral. Samuel was neither priest nor king, but he was through life the universal referee of ruler and ruled alike in every grave emergency; he established the monarchy and anointed the two first sovereigns; he was the great intercessor for his people; he shaped their policy, controlled their armies, and reconciled their dissensions. St Bernard was neither bishop nor pope, but for upwards of a quarter of a century he was the real ruler of Christendom; he guided the councils of five successive popes, of whom one was practically his nominee, and another had been his disciple at Clairvaux; the kings of France and England yield him homage; two councils are content to register his decisions; by his sole influence he healed a formidable schism, suppressed several powerful heresies, and organized an unpopular crusade. From Samuel date the "schools of the prophets"; and "the beginnings of scholasticism were contemporary with" Bernard, who was also himself, if not the founder of a new order, in one sense the founder of a new power in mediaeval monachism, from the new energy and character which he bequeathed to it. And lastly, not to multiply points of comparison, he recalls the memory of the great Hebrew prophet in his noble independence and fearlessness of temper, careless of popular favour, professional interests, or personal danger. He rebukes kings, prelates and popes with an outspoken freedom that sounds almost incredible to our ears; he comes forward alone with righteous indignation to rescue the persecuted Jews of Mentz from the miscreant, monk though he be, who is hounding on the murderers with the whole city to back him; he does not scruple to tell one pope that he has "blemished the honour of the Church", and another that the voice of the whole Church lays the blame of its abuses on the Court of Rome; while he presents to a third the confession of his belief with the statement that, whatever be His Holiness's opinion, he is "determined to alter nothing whatever".

The marvel of that irresistible power before which popes, kings, bishops, peoples, heresiarchs quailed is that it should have been wielded by a simple monk, with no jurisdiction except over his own abbey; who had superiors among his contemporaries in subtlety if not in grasp of intellect; who, though for thirty years the idol of his age and the almost absolute ruler of the Church, was scarcely conscious of his greatness, and certainly did not desire it; whose passionate complaints at being so often waked from the quiet of the humble monastery which he had entered as a youth, with the sole aim of dedicating his life to prayer, solitude and toil, into the turmoil of a world he thought to have renounced for ever, it is impossible not to believe sincere. Only in a state of society like that of the Middle Ages, rude and barbarous in some respects, but deeply penetrated with moral and religious conviction, is such ascendancy of a single mind conceivable, and only then perhaps could the man arise to exert it. The most remarkable thing about St Bernard is the union of almost ceaseless energy with profound humility and perfect internal peace. He was never more himself than when engaged in action, yet he never left, or wished to leave, the gates of his monastery without some imperious call to duty or obedience. His letters, ranging over every subject, from the gravest question of ecclesiastical policy, or the highest raptures of devotion, to complaints about stealing pigs, are the measure of the width and individuality of his sympathies. Nothing is too important for him to be consulted about, nothing too insignificant for him to attend to, if only the temporal or spiritual welfare of another be involved. His very faults are the exaggeration of his virtues, and belong rather to his age than to himself. The harshness which made him turn his married sister from the abbey gates, and insist on his elder brother leaving wife and children to enter the religious life, was an excess of the same stern, almost puritan, severity which he exercised chiefly towards himself, and which, in its more legitimate expression, moulded the great monastic reform of the twelfth century. The vehemence he exhibited about the disputed election to the See of Langres, and which certainly betrayed him into grave injustice, though Pope, Cardinals, and Bishops were constrained to yield to his will, sprang from the same spirit of burning zeal which never feared to rebuke spiritual wickedness in high places; which, by a few words, could annul a simoniacal contract, subdue a schismatical or adulterous prince, and pour the whole cavalry of Europe on the shores of Palestine.

Amid the endless varieties of an eventful life, two events seem to stand out with exceptional prominence—his conflict with Abelard, and his preaching the second crusade ... Their meeting was not that of two rival theologians; it was the meeting of the man of action and the man of speculation—the earnest believer and subtle disputant. It is obvious that St Bernard did not regard his opponent so much in the light of an heresiarch as of a sophist, whose teaching, whether or not it was technically orthodox, was undermining the practical belief of his age. And he was right. Abelard chose to be a preacher and a propagandist, and the inevitable effect of his preaching was to perplex the faith of his hearers. Such teaching in the twelfth century was more likely to be put down by authority than by argument; it was put down by the influence of Bernard and the sentence of the Council of Sens. For us, it is impossible to look back on Abelard's chequered career without a mingled feeling of pity and respect. The letters sent to the Pope by Peter the Venerable, in whose Abbey of Cluny the wearied man, monk, philosopher and heretic, found his latest earthly home, and who effected his reconciliation with St Bernard, is the one green spot in the bitterness of the long controversy. That controversy, though he often was involved in it, was most uncongenial to Bernard's energetic, loving spirit. He was more in his element at Vézelay, the spot famous just twenty years later as the scene of Becket's excommunication of the adherents of Henry II. Here, "pale and attenuated to a degree that seemed almost supernatural", he appeared at the bidding of Eugenius III to preach the second most disastrous crusade; and when the light from that thin calm face fell upon them, when the voice flew from those thin lips, and words of love, aspiration and sublime self-sacrifice reached their ears, they were no longer masters of themselves or their feelings ... But it is not in external conflicts or public triumphs that Bernard's real life is revealed to us. Perhaps there is nothing more characteristic of the man and of his age than the funeral sermon preached over his brother Gerard ... It affords convincing evidence that at the age of forty-seven neither ascetic rigour nor the multiplicity of incessant engagements had in any degree chilled the warmth of his heart, or blunted the keen edge of natural affection. His letters to his dying friend, the great Abbot Suger, written at sixty-two, the year before his own death, breathe the same spirit of intense yearning affection. It is clear that to kill human feeling was no part of Bernard's ascetic ideal.

Home and Foreign Review, April 1863, p. 608.

FATHER MATHEW

Father Mathew was prepared for his public mission by five and twenty years of zealous and unobtrusive labour as a priest in Cork. He was a Franciscan friar and attached to that "little friary" which was once the home of Arthur O'Leary. Both these men were faithful ministers of the Catholic Church, lovers of Ireland, haters of turbulence, and strenuous champions of religious toleration. They both died in disappointment, and both, strange to say, in receipt of a pension from the English Government. But these points of resemblance are outward merely. O'Leary was a man of powerful intellect, a well-read theologian and a scholar of large attainments. He was the first Catholic priest who, under the penal laws, had dared to make his voice heard upon public questions; and he spoke with such strength of reasoning, such breadth of view, and such soundness of judgement, that he soon made all Ireland his audience. He was elected by acclamation a member of the fraternity of the Monks of St Patrick, of which Curran and Barry Yelverton were the presiding spirits, and which, amid the freedom and jollity peculiar to the time, represented much of the best aspirations of Ireland at that day. To the "illustrious Fathers and reverend brethren" of that order he inscribed the dedication of his Essay—a dedication full of natural pride in the great prospects then dawning on his country, and in the contrast presented by the short-lived union of all her sects to the scenes of violence and persecution which in that year (1780) disgraced England and Scotland. We can still read with pleasure his answer to Wesley, whose defence of the Protestant Association, conceived as it is in a spirit of the most vulgar bigotry, made him morally an accomplice in the scenes of June. O'Leary's plea for tolerance is a masterly refutation of the sophism which pretends to confine toleration to truth and deny it to errors. His style was logical, trenchant, caustic. To all these qualities Theobald Mathew had no pretension. His understanding was certainly not above the average either in strength or breadth. In theological learning, or, indeed, learning of any kind, he was deficient, although he had the literary tastes of a

cultivated man. The root of his character was a thorough goodness of heart and a sweetness of disposition . . . Nature gave him
in a degree beyond most men a delight in conferring pleasure,
and an extreme reluctance to causing pain; and he had a prompt
and delicate discernment of and sympathy with the feelings of
others, which taught him at once how to administer that oil and
balm which he rejoiced to bestow. These gifts were cultivated
and matured by the habits of a Christian priest. He bore his
kindliness of heart in his face and voice; and such was the training
he gave himself, that the good which his presence promised was
sure to be fulfilled in deed. Qualities like these speedily endeared
him to all classes. He was very hospitable, and took especially a
gratification in giving feasts to children and young people. With
a disposition and manners suited to charm any society, he chose
by predilection and without a shadow of ostentation to devote
himself to the poor. He rose daily at five o'clock; and the great
portion of his day was spent either in hearing the confessions of
the poor, who flocked to him not only from the city but from all
the quarters round it, or in ministering to their wants—for he
was lavish in his charities.

He thus became the idol of Cork; and his power over the poor
was unbounded. He strove unremittingly to repress among them
the vice of drunkenness, then the disgrace of Ireland; but it was
long before he could be brought to adopt the views of the tee-
totallers. An elderly Quaker, William Martin, who was devoted
to the cause of total abstinence, has the honour of having first
enlisted him in the cause. He impressed upon him that with a
people like the Irish nothing short of a radical cure would be
effective. He at length yielded to the persuasions of his friend,
and began to preach total abstinence and to administer the tee-
total pledge. Then commenced one of those strange phenomena
of moral electricity which are manifested from time to time
amongst nations, and of which the Irish nature is peculiarly susceptible. There lay, no doubt, deep in the breasts of the people a
consciousness of the extent to which habits of drink had contributed to their degradation, and an unconscious aspiration to a
conquest over the evil, mixed with a despair of ever attaining to
that conquest. As soon, then, as the tidings began to spread that
by saying a few words to one of their own priests, the darling of

the poor, and by receiving his blessing, the drunkard was at once transformed into a sober and self-respecting man, that, as it were, the hopeless struggle and effort against the tyranny of recurring habit was rendered unnecessary, and that the change was as easy and rapid as it was immense, a perfect mania for self-regeneration seized upon the people. They flocked to Father Mathew in tens of thousands, so that the hours of the day did not suffice for the work. From Cork the flames spread to Limerick, to Waterford, all over the South of Ireland, then to the midland districts, to the metropolis, and to the north and west. Everywhere the people prostrated themselves before the apostle of temperance, believing profoundly in the virtue of the pledge taken at his hands, and attributing to him not merely the moral miracles which he truly wrought, but, in spite of his earnest disclaimer, the power of working physical miracles also. It was a manifestation which, taken for all in all, forms one of the brightest spots in Irish history, and the effects of which have been permanently beneficial . . .

It happened to Father Mathew, as to other men, that the hour of his glory and success brought the destruction of his happiness. He became deeply involved in debt, and that spectre pursued him to his grave. He was lavish by nature; and even in his early days what money reached him went at once in charity: but when he became the centre and director of a great movement, the organization and management of which required considerable outlay, his expenditure exceeded by thousands what he received. He was arrested in the middle of Dublin for a debt due to a manufacturer of temperance medals—the bailiff pretending to kneel and take the pledge when he gave him the writ, and Father Mathew aiding the pretence that he might save the life of the bailiff, who otherwise would have been torn to pieces by the people. Added to this, came the inevitable shafts of calumny. He was accused at this time of making a fortune by the temperance medals which he was unable to pay for. He felt it all keenly, but it could not succeed in souring his disposition. He remained as hospitable and gentle, but hardly so bright and joyous, as before. Then came the famine, during which his efforts and suggestions for the relief of the people were unceasing. In 1850 he was cheered and excited by a visit to the United States, where he received marked honour from both Houses of Congress, but was involved most reluctantly in the slavery controversy. His health, which had been previously impaired, broke down soon after his return; and he died tranquilly at Cove in the autumn of 1856...

Home and Foreign Review, Jan. 1864, p. 305.

DR MANNING

Dr Manning has recently published a volume of sermons on ecclesiastical subjects of which three were delivered in Rome, one in Paris and the rest in England. Criticism has no light word to say upon discourses the object of which is to promote the eternal interests of man; and if we are compelled to express our regret at some things which appear in this volume it is only because the writer has not always remained above on the firm ground of religious didactics, but has descended into the dark and troubled field of human politics and the interpretation of history. There are three points particularly insisted upon in various parts of the book. The first is that ever since the schism in the sixteenth century, every thing connected with the religious life in this country has been going from bad to worse; that England has been continually multiplying her misbeliefs, and is now falling fast into unbelief. The second is, that on account of the part which her government has taken on the question of the temporal power of the Pope, England deserves to be held forth as the chief and most malignant enemy of the Holy See and of Catholicism in the world. The third—which does not seem very consistent with the second—is, that it is piously probable that the return of England to Catholic unity may burst upon us "like a beautiful vision" much sooner than most of us expect.

We cannot follow Dr Manning through his historical sketch of the religious deterioration of England. Too much of it, of course, is sadly true. But is there nothing to be said on the other side? Is it well to dilate on the developments of rationalism, and represent England as increasingly hostile to Catholicism and Christianity, and yet not at the same time thank an overruling Providence that, in times of such difficulty and trial, faith in God and in a moral government of the world still stands up so firmly amongst us, and that the leading and educated classes in England have still so strong a hold on at least some form or view of Christianity?

Without concealing the dark side of the picture, might not Dr Manning have permitted some indication to appear of the existence of a brighter one?

No new light is thrown in this volume on the momentous question of the future relations of Italy to the temporal power of the Papacy. But the author's apparent inability to distinguish between the things of Caesar and the things of God in relation to this question, his attempt to protect the weak and earthly element by lifting it into the sphere of the spiritual and eternal, leads him to give a distorted picture of the state of opinion prevalent in this country. The majority of moderate and religious English Protestants are hostile to the Papal government, because they believe it to be a bad and oppressive government, not because the Holy Father is the head of the Catholic Church. They may be wrong as to their data; but, as they sincerely believe themselves to be right, they cannot justly be charged with hostility to Catholicism, merely because they build upon those data what seems to them the logical conclusion. After all, the temper of the country is not so utterly changed since the time, not sixty years ago, when England stubbornly vindicated the temporal sovereignty of the Holy Father against the assaults of its enemies. Religion was not the motive for the protection then, nor is it for the hostility now. Dr Manning should try, before condemning them, to place himself in the position of those who, standing outside the Catholic Church, cannot be expected to see, as Catholics see, how extremely important it is to the interests of religion to maintain the Holy See in a status of external independence, and upon whom, therefore, the obvious liberal reasonings in favour of Italian unity operate with their full force.

It seems ungracious to quarrel with speculations which anticipate a consummation longed for alike by all Catholics—the restoration of England to the unity of the Church. And when—as in many passages of this book—Dr Manning recognizes the true grounds of hope in the peaceful but partial triumph of faith —here a little and there a little—in the erection of new altars, the multiplication of religions, the increase of the Christian priesthood, secure in its orders and mission, and wielding, in the Sacraments, mighty and incommunicable powers—we are carried along with him completely. But it is idle or worse than idle to raise the faintest presumption, or build the slightest argument, in favour of the sudden and collective return of England to Catholic unity, upon the effects produced in the Roman world by the conversion of Constantine, when a moment's reflection would show that the entire set of circumstances in the two cases is different. In the first place, the "slow accretion of individuals" *had* preceded, and was, humanly speaking, a necessary pre-condition of, the official conversion of the Roman Empire. Secondly, no other form of Christianity at the beginning of the fourth century had a twentieth part of the intrinsic force and mass, relatively to Catholicism, which the Protestantism of Europe has at the present day. Thirdly, the power of an English sovereign over the religious convictions of the nation is inconceivably and infinitesimally small, compared to that which the divine Caesar exercised over his servile and degenerate subjects.

The introductory sketch of the "Relations of England to Christianity" may perhaps have some theoretical value; viewed as criticism, it is unimportant. It abounds in that kind of hasty and unsound generalization which the historical student of the present day has grown weary of, and rejects . . . But though we are compelled to dissent from some of Dr Manning's political reasonings, and to doubt his guidance in history, it is impossible to be blind to the excellence which he attains in a certain department of preaching, in which the faith, the sorrows and the sufferings of the past are turned to account, in order to purify and ennoble the religious life of the present . . .

Home and Foreign Review, Jan. 1864, p. 310.

DE MAISTRE

Of all the writers who defended society against the Revolution, he did most for the revival of Catholic ideas. He was the only French Catholic of his time who felt and urged the necessity of an alliance between the Church and modern learning. In this respect he indicated more than he achieved. His reading was desultory, and he has too much of the levity and unscrupulousness of statement which distinguish his infidel adversaries. For this reason, and because Lamennais appropriated and distorted some of his ideas, his influence has not been altogether beneficial, and there is an essential difference between de Maistre and those who are ostensibly his disciples.

The Rambler, May 1855, p. 74.

MR GLADSTONE

Mr Gladstone is equally remarkable for the highest moral integrity and rectitude and for the utmost intellectual duplicity. He is at the same time the most honest and the most deceitful of public men. His excessive earnestness of conviction is the great secret of the persuasiveness of his eloquence; but that earnestness is founded on an incredible power of persuading himself. Unfortunately he can convince himself as well as others of what he wishes to believe, or to be believed. He cannot see the flaw in his own case, though in an adversary's nothing escapes him. Hence that fatal instability of purpose which is, rather than inconsistency of opinion, the bane of his career.

The Rambler, Sept. 1860, p. 291.

ARISTOCRACY

An aristocracy ceases to be an aristocracy if it fails to take the lead in the movement of the age. In Sparta certain trades were forbidden, because they would have raised up a new nobility; and it is for a similar reason that in the Middle Ages there was so close a union between the nobles and the Church. The democratic character of the Catholic clergy was the safety of the nobles, because it gave an opening and a career to all the talents in the lower orders. In the same way, by the free competition which throws open all the chances of success to ambition, an aristocracy is still preserved in its integrity and its strength by allowing itself to be revived by the same means by which it was originally created. Nobility is properly an element of progress, for it subsists only on condition of moving in the front rank. Where it feels unable to keep the lead, it tries to maintain itself by impeding the general advance. Aristocracy, says Chateaubriand, has three successive ages: the age of superiority, the age of privileges, the age of vanities; proceeding from the first, it degenerates in the second, and expires in the third.

The Rambler, Sept. 1860, p. 293.

VOLUNTEER AND STANDING ARMIES

Jealousy of a standing army has been one of the chief securities of our institutions. Liberty can never be secure in the presence of a large force of mercenaries. The disappearance of the unbought armies of the feudal age, and the introduction of troops who served for pay, led to the establishment of absolute monarchy in Europe. It rendered the sovereign wholly independent of the nation, and separated the people from the State. It would be a dreadful thing, said Burke, if there were any power in this country of strength enough to oppose with effect the general wishes of the people. This is just what an army receiving the pay of the State is intended to do. The time has now arrived when we shall be always obliged to keep a considerable armed force at home. Who can say what circumstances may not hereafter arise which may make its presence dangerous here, as it has been everywhere else? Who can believe for an instant that Reform or Emancipation would ever have been carried if the government had had a force at hand proportioned to the armies of other States? We must have lost the instinctive foresight which has made us great in politics, if we had not provided, together with the means of defence against the enemy, a security against their abuse. By our volunteer army we have doubled our military force, and have doubled also our constitutional safeguards.

We have provided at the same time the most effectual security against insurrection. The Volunteers are no protection to the State against the people, but to property against spoliation, and to society against socialism. They have armed the upper and middle classes, and will arm as many of the lower classes as are ready to join the others. They will make revolution as impossible as invasion, and will be as effective a barrier against ochlocracy as against tyranny. They will verify the prophecy made by a great writer nearly a century ago that "nothing is more certain than that in a hundred years a national militia will be everywhere the chief element of defence, and will form a new security for freedom and property, which if our present mode of government continues, must otherwise be destroyed."

Other countries have sought for protection against a standing army in the establishment of a national guard. With this the Volunteers bear no analogy whatever; they are the creation of a totally different state of society. When the mass of the nation is in opposition to the sovereign power, it requires an armed force in order to be able to hold its own. Originally the creation of the national guard was an act of defiance and a proof of suspicion against the crown. In later times it has been the army of the *bourgeoisie* against the mob, the bulwark of property, independently of the authority of the State, and even in spite of it. The national guard is therefore in its nature revolutionary. It serves neither the State nor the nation, but a single interest and a single class of society. Where the sovereignty is in the hands of the nation, and there is no jealousy consequently, either of the State or of the masses, that is to say in all democracies, army and national guard are one and the same . . .

The Rambler, Sept. 1860, p. 294.

THE EVIL OF CONSCRIPTION

A people that relies on a permanent system of compulsory military service resembles the statesman who declared himself ready to sacrifice not only a part, but the whole of the constitution, in order to preserve the remainder. It is a system by which one great liberty is surrendered and all are imperilled, and it is a surrender not of rights only, but also of power.

The Rambler, Sept. 1860, p. 295.

REGULAR ARMIES

Standing armies alone have not preserved any European country from a successful invasion. In 1805 Napoleon crossed the Rhine, the 25th of September, and dictated the peace of Pressburg, the 26th of December. In 1806 he entered Berlin a fortnight after the first encounter with the Prussians. In 1814 the allies took only three months to march from the Rhine to Paris. Centralization increases the power of attack, but diminishes that of defence. In 1809 Tyrol held out longer than Austria in 1805, or France in 1814. It is, however, a question of civilization even more than of centralization. A highly civilized people possesses great resources for offensive purposes; a barbarous people is powerful in defence. It is impossible to concentrate in a regular army all the moral, or even the material, resources of a nation. They can act only spontaneously, and are not to be had to order. They can be reckoned upon only in a free country. An absolute monarch either will not venture to call the nation to arms, or if he does, it must lead to great internal changes, if not to revolution. But in a free country it is the natural mode of defence. There a large standing army is not tolerated, and every class is identified with the Government. All the State can do is, therefore, to assist and to sustain, as far as art can do it, the resistance of the whole people.

The Rambler, Sept. 1860, p. 296.

NAPOLEON III

The worst that can be said of him is that he absolutely ignores all moral considerations in pursuing the policy which is dictated by the instinct of self-preservation. He obtained his crown by immoral means; it is idle to complain that he preserves it in the same manner. He is strong and popular in France; it is absurd to separate him from the people as the object of special indignation. Nothing can be less inscrutable or more easy to calculate than his policy; nothing more certain than that some day a war with England will suit his interests, and that when that time comes he will not hesitate to declare it.

The Rambler, Sept. 1860, p. 300.

THE CHURCH AND EDUCATION

The Church is necessarily at all times an educational institution. The school is as necessary to her as the pulpit, and the Protestant Churches can no more do without it than the Catholic. Even the Peace of Westphalia calls it *annexum exercitii religionis*. and long after the Peace of Westphalia the school remained under ecclesiastical supervision in Protestant and in Catholic countries alike. For centuries it was never discovered that education was a function of the State, and the State never attempted to educate. But when modern absolutism arose, it laid claim to everything on behalf of the sovereign power. Commerce, industry, literature, religion were all declared to be matters of State, and were appropriated and controlled accordingly. In the same way as all these things education belongs to the civil power, and on the same grounds with the rest it claims exemption. When the revolutionary theory of Government began to prevail, and Church and State found that they were educating for opposite ends and in a contradictory spirit, it became necessary for the State to remove the children entirely from the influence of religion.

The Rambler, Sept. 1860, p. 419.

BURKE, THE HISTORIAN

Lappenberg, speaking of Burke's most remarkable literary production, *The Abridgement of English History*, says, that if Burke had devoted himself continuously to historical pursuits, England might have possessed a history worthy to rank with the master-pieces of the Attic and Tuscan historians. If we may believe the story that Burke desisted from the undertaking because Hume had taken up the same subject, it must ever be regretted that the reverse did not occur, and that the philosopher did not give way to the politician. We should certainly have had a much better History of England; for there is very little doubt that as Burke was our greatest statesman, so he would have been the first of our historians. In that part of the work which he completed, he speaks of mediaeval institutions with an intelligence and apprecia-tion which in his time were almost equally rare among Catholics, Protestants and infidels. The great ecclesiastical writers of the preceding age, such as Bossuet and Fleury, had about as little sympathy with the Middle Ages as Mosheim or Voltaire. Leibniz alone had written about them in a tone which would not now be contemptible. The vast compilations of great scholars, of Du-cange, Mabillon and Muratori, had not yet borne fruit on the Continent; and in England the rise of a better school of historians was still remote. Several generations of men were still to follow, who were to derive their knowledge of the Middle Ages from the Introduction to Robertson's *Charles V*, to study ecclesiastical history in the pages of Gibbon, and to admire Hume as the prince of historians. At the age of thirty, Burke proved himself superior to that system of prejudice and ignorance which was then univer-sal, and which is not yet completely dissipated ...

It is remarkable that so many of our public men should have written history. Our historians are more often great historical actors than great historical writers. Their works are generally remarkable for every quality except learning. It is character-istic of the English mind that we should so long have been with-out regular learned histories. In the most essential qualities, our historians cannot compete with those of other countries; and we have nobody who will bear a comparison with Niebuhr, or Hurter, or Ranke, any more than with Thucydides or Tacitus. Gibbon, Lingard, Grote are not equal to the moderns in learn-ing; Hume and Macaulay are inferior in art to the ancients. In the Middle Ages great deeds were performed by men who could not write. They were recorded by men who had not seen and could not understand them. Many of the greatest historians of the present day write from the seclusion of their libraries concerning events of which they have no experience. But the prevailing character of the English historians has been neither that of the monastic chronicler nor of the German professor. The catalogue is crowded with names distinguished in another sphere—Bacon, Raleigh, Milton, Clarendon, Burnet, Swift, Fox and Mackintosh. This connection between historical studies and political life has been more beneficial in developing the qualities of the statesman than of the historian. Our historical literature was long in emancipating itself from the traditional falsehoods which are so dear to the popular mind, and consequently such studies have not yet exercised that powerful influence for good which is so conspicuous abroad. But Burke was free both from vulgar prejudice and from pedantry; and no other man was so well fitted to adorn history with the attainments of a great scholar, and the reality and vigour derived from personal experience of public affairs . . .

The Rambler, April 1858, p. 270.

THE INDEPENDENCE OF GREECE

The Greeks neither deserved their independence nor acquired it themselves. The real significance of the event lies not in their character or achievement, but in the motives and the consequences of the European intervention. It was the first practical refutation of the legitimist doctrine, the first breach opened in the system of the Holy Alliance. Whilst the Austrians were suppressing the Revolution in Italy, and the French in Spain, the cause of the Greeks inspired a sympathy which even Metternich could not withstand; and the principle that the badness of a government is no reason for upsetting it had to be abandoned first in the case of the Turks. The precedent was afterwards successfully invoked by the Belgians; and when the Poles appealed to it, they enjoyed the secret but ardent good wishes of the Austrian statesmen. The conservative principle of the rightfulness of the *status quo*, in its absolute and revolutionary form, in the moment of its triumph at Verona and Cadiz, was destroyed for ever by the Greeks. But it fell, not to make way for a truer notion of right and wrong, but to be supplanted by a new error, which has since proved equally powerful and equally hostile to right and freedom. It was a victory gained not by the right of resistance, or by toleration, or by law against an arbitrary despotism, but by the principle of nationality. Beginning with the rebellion of Ali Pascha in the Adriatic provinces of Turkey, who cared neither for Moslem, Catholic, or Greek, it was carried to its successful end by the western powers, under the belief that the people of Hellas and Morea were the descendants of those to whom European civilization owes so much. Greece had fallen before the Turks, because the hatred of the Latins was stronger than the love of national independence, and she recovered her freedom when religious differences were hidden in the plea of nationality. Whilst the western powers pursued their chimera, the influence of Russia was founded on the firm basis of dogmatic agreement, and prevailed in consequence of the reluctance of the other powers, whose classical sympathies were bounded by Thessaly, to give to the new kingdom the means of real independence.

The Rambler, March 1862, p. 406.

THE PUNJAB

The history of the organization and administration of the Punjab is a practical lesson upon the duties of the English Government to its Oriental possessions. We have to accomplish a change both in the State and in society; to supersede the traditional government and the traditional civilization. Indian culture, though it was developed by the same Aryan race to which our own civilization is indebted, has been arrested in its progress. Its law has been identified with its religion, and therefore religion has tied down the people to the social usages and opinions which were current when the laws were first reduced to a code. The religion and manners of the Orientals mutually support each other; neither can one be changed without the other. Hence the pioneer of civilization has to get rid of the religion of India to enable him to introduce a better culture, and the pioneer of Christianity has to get rid of the Indian culture before he can establish his religion. Thus the future progress both of Christianity and of civilization demands that the Oriental career of England should not stop short at the point of contact with Eastern kingdoms and governments, but should go on to deal with Eastern society.

The transformation is difficult; but the ancient world has witnessed a similar one. The early law of the Italians was very like that of the Indians ... The Roman legists never thought to introduce violent changes into their law; their ideal law of nature was not an independent legal Utopia, but a system which their laws were supposed to express, however imperfectly; hence it was the expression, not the intention, of their laws, which they sought to improve. The intention was supposed to remain the same, the legal forms were preserved; and the ideal "law of nature" to which they ever tried to bring their law into greater conformity, was not a system imported from without, as Plato's "laws" might have been, but it was supposed to be the original intention and meaning of their law, at first clumsily expressed but gradually cleared and enucleated. The perfect legislation of Rome grew naturally out of just such a system as prevails in India; not by violent changes but by judicious developments. Just so is our work in India to be accomplished; and administrators like Lord Dalhousie, Sir Charles Napier, and the Lawrences, either by nature or by art, have been led to adopt the Roman method. They have imported no new laws or institutions; they have violently suppressed nothing by their extrinsic and arbitrary power. But they have systematically selected those elements of Indian legislation and custom which were capable of developments in the right direction; and by fostering the growth of these elements, they have already managed to choke all life out of some others which were most opposed to the new civilization ... The change is being brought about not by violent suppression, nor by forcible introduction of unknown usages, but by the careful development of elements already existing among the Indians. If the English Government could do the same for the rest of India, it would soon be on the way to give a satisfactory answer to the common question of Continental critics: "What evidence of its empire does England expect to leave behind it in India?" If our empire lasts a century longer, we may leave behind us a society freed from the fetters of superstitions which have checked its growth for ages; and ready, perhaps, to accept the teaching of a race more faithful than ours, who will then be able to make Indians Catholics, without incurring the suspicion of too great complaisance for Indian superstitions. As it is at present constituted, the social system of India cannot be made Christian, though individual Indians may become very sincere and good converts.

The Rambler, May 1862, p. 534.

THE CRUSADES

The Crusades were extremely unfavourable to historical literature, which degenerated from the close of the eleventh century, and came to be disfigured by an extravagant credulity and imaginativeness, and by all the licence which travellers immemorially assume. Modern writers are confounded by the mixture of practical designs with enthusiasm and very few can distinguish and appreciate the two. From the beginning a poetic and legendary tradition sprang up, which totally distorted the facts and proportions of history, and which soon supplanted the authority of more exact and sober narratives of contemporaries. The most popular myth is that which represents Peter the Hermit as the real author of the movement. This story arose among the lower orders, who formed the army which he led to Anatolia, and invests him with all the merit, to the exclusion of the Pope, and especially of the nobles; and this view took root in Constantinople, for in the narrative of Anna Comnena the Pope disappears altogether. It found its way into later works, and men still write that Peter had a vision in the Church of the Holy Sepulchre, and came to Europe to rouse the Pope and the nations for its deliverance. The original authorities know nothing of all this. The writers of his own country do not raise him above the level of many other popular preachers, and the contemporary writers of England, Germany and Italy scarcely mention his name.

The extravagance of such writers partly justifies the contempt with which the Crusades have so commonly been regarded, as a product of unthinking fanaticism, and has long concealed their real character and the profound design which inspired them. Before Jerusalem was taken by the Turks, and before the Greeks had applied for aid, the first outline of the prodigious scheme was traced by Gregory VII, almost immediately after his elevation. It was the Eastern counterpart of the policy by which he was seeking to raise the hierarchy above the states of the West. That policy would be strengthened by the rise in the lost regions of Asia of states where the Church would enjoy political sovereignty, and where the position of the feudal princes would resemble that which it was his object to establish in Europe. It was for this reason that Gregory wished to go himself, that Urban appointed a legate, that the clergy opposed the election of a king of Jerusalem, and that the patriarch was speedily involved in serious quarrels with him. The schism of the East was the second reason which suggested to the Pope the idea of a great expedition. "The Church of Constantinople", he says, "abandoned by the Holy Spirit, has turned away from us and requires to be united with the Apostolic See, whilst great part of the Armenians have abandoned the Catholic faith, and most of the Christians of the East await for St Peter to decide their disputes." The Grecian emperors had cut off the nations of the West from all intercourse with Asia, and had thus made Constantinople the emporium of all the commerce of the East. The schism made this exclusion a calamity for the Church as well as for the people, and the war with the infidel would necessarily break it down, and the hostility of the Greeks would be silenced by an enterprise which they could but approve. Hence there was as much fear of the sovereignty of the Holy See as mere political ambition in the eagerness with which Alexius exacted homage from the Latin chiefs. It was in accordance with the profoundly practical and statesmanlike genius of Gregory VII that he regarded the conquest of Jerusalem as the reward, not the object, of the expedition. When the Latin arms had established their power on the Bosphorus and in Armenia, Palestine would be securely theirs. Without such a basis, the kingdom of Jerusalem could not stand. Accordingly, the wisest princes of the first Crusade abandoned the army on its march, and set up States for themselves at Antioch and Edessa; and later on, St Louis reverted to the idea of St Gregory, and sought to found Frankish States in Africa as bulwarks of the Holy Land. But so lofty a design as that which is sketched in the letters of the great pontiff could not be intelligible to the narrow minds of the people, and his summons produced no effect. Urban II had recourse to a more powerful instrument of popular influence. He invoked the religious fervour, the chivalrous enthusiasm of mankind, and with this he succeeded. But the substance of the scheme of Gregory was sacrificed to obtain this support; for no idea can be popular without some alloy of error to recommend it to the vulgar mind, and this sacrifice was fatal.

The Church could not either guide or restrain the enthusiasm she had awakened. St Bernard discouraged at first the project of the second Crusade. It is better, he told the king of France, to combat our own vices than to fight the Turks; and it was only when Louis was resolute that the saint roused the empire to assist him and achieved in the Cathedral of Speyer that marvellous success which surpasses all that the imaginations of men had attributed to the eloquence of Peter the Hermit. But as there was at first more enthusiasm than policy in the Crusaders, so afterwards there was more selfishness than religion; and the Popes who had been unable to control the first impulse were helpless before the reaction. When the Crusades began, the feudal nobility had attained the summit of their power, and it was chiefly through them that the Papacy wrought out its ends. They were its auxiliaries against the tyranny of the kings, and its instrument for deliverance of the East. The Crusaders are the spontaneous external action of the Church during the period when her influence was exercised over a military aristocracy. They ended when the political authority of the Church, and the chivalrous society on which it stood, declined before the rise of absolute monarchy and of commercial republicanism. The decay of the great families by impoverishment, the prolonged absence and the loss of life which the Crusades involved, developed the power of the kings; and the destruction of the Templars marks at once the victory of the crown over the nobles, and the extinction of the crusading spirit. The rise of the Levantine commerce hastened the growth of the towns; and Venice and Philip the Fair instance the two tendencies to which it is due that the Holy See lost so much of its power, and Christendom the places which had been made holy by its Founder.

There is abundant evidence of the close connection between the Crusades and the predominance of the Church in its contest with the State, and of the identity of the spirit which animated the Crusader and the Guelf. The most comprehensive of the mediaeval chronicles was finished in a first edition by Abbot Ekkehard in the year 1099. The war between the priesthood and the empire was at its height, and the abbot was an imperialist. Seven years later he rewrote his work. In the interval he had been to the Holy Land, he had seen the handiwork of the Popes and he had become an ardent advocate of their cause. The testimony of the legend is not less significant. Godfrey, like Ekkehard, was originally a partisan of the emperor before he became the champion of the Church; and the poets who chose the first king of Jerusalem as their hero have heightened the contrast between the two portions of his career. They represent him as the foremost of the soldiers of the empire; in the battle between Henry and Rodolph he carries the imperial banner and slays with his own hand the emperor who had the support of the clergy. Then he followed his master to the siege of Rome, and was the first to enter the place. But the sacrilege was punished by an attack of the Roman fever so well known to the soldiers of the empire, which never left him till he made a vow to take the cross; and then, when he had performed his penance, and his work was over, God sent the fever once more, which carried him away in the first year of his reign. These fables, recorded by William of Malmesbury, show that the general belief agreed with the idea of St Bernard: "Ita qui corruerat contra pontificiam militans, major excitatus est." The same change is repeated on a much greater scale in the life of Frederick I. Whilst the beginning of the movement exactly coincides with that exalted position of the Church which was created for her by Hildebrand, they declined together, and the Pope stood alone for many generations, appealing in vain to the princes for a new Crusade. It was precisely at the close of that period of ecclesiastical supremacy that the news of the fall of Ptolemais and the total loss of the Holy Land reached Europe. The Pope wrote to France; but the prelates and nobles replied that to preach the cross was useless so long as the Greeks, the Sicilians and the Aragonese disturbed the peace of Europe. This allusion to the interests of France in Naples proves how completely, in the generation which had seen St Louis, attachment to the State prevailed over attachment to the Church, and the dynasty over the old *noblesse*. The Crusades had checked the ardour of the contest with the monarchy by enlisting all men in an enterprise with which every Catholic sympathized, but which necessarily placed him in a position of subordination to the Holy See, which Ghibelline feelings could not survive. Yet it is a singular fact that the idea of rescuing the holy sepulchre, which had derived all its vitality and power from the influence of the Holy See, should have outlived that influence, and have sought to recommend itself at the expense of the papal interests. A Frenchman of the reign of Boniface VIII, a disciple of St Thomas, submitted to the king of France a plan for the restoration of the Frankish dominion in the East, the first condition of which was the establishment of peace in Christendom. This, he says, would be obtained if Philip would convey the states of the Church into the hands of one of his sons, with the title of Senator of Rome, giving the Pope, by way of compensation, a yearly pension. His power, having the authority of the Holy See at its disposal, would then be supreme and the kings of the earth would be ready to follow him to Palestine.

The Rambler, Sept. 1861, p. 403.

GERMAN UNIVERSITIES

If Germany had possessed universities in the fourteenth century, the Teutonic jurisprudence would have had strength to resist the irruption of the Roman code, which ended in the ruin both of the liberties and of the laws of the nation. Afterwards the universities did harm by their number. The whole country could not provide so many professors, and the petty principalities had not resources to keep up their vitality. By the Reformation they were multiplied and degraded. Each Protestant state required that its clergy should be educated in the official divinity; and the theological faculty of the local university was the instrument by which the civil power controlled the religion of the people. That religion could be altered by laws and proclamations; the removal of a few professors and the appointment of new ones soon made the change a reality. The universities became schools of Roman law or of illiterate orthodoxy; in either case they were bulwarks of territorial absolutism. The liberal arts were contracted to the exigencies of the public service. Classical scholarship, the most healthy and incorruptible of all studies, fell into such decay that during two whole centuries Germany did nothing for the ancient writers. The liberality of the House of Hanover introduced a more free and tolerant spirit at Gottingen, and began the emancipation of the Germany universities and the era of their prosperity. Halle flourished as the seat of dogmatic Lutheranism, Jena as a school of speculative Rationalism . . . The institutions which Kant and Wolf made illustrious differed from those of other countries and of other ages in degree of excellence and in many qualities of detail; but though they betrayed the different influences of place and time, yet they were forms of the same idea and products of an old tradition. Their function was to prepare candidates for public employment and to teach things necessary to be known in order to obtain a salary under government or in the Church, as a doctor or a schoolmaster. They existed to promote certain public objects of society, not to promote the independent ends of literature and science. They suffer alike from the want of liberty and the want of discipline. They are subject to the patronage of the State and they exert no effective restraint over the lives of the students. The very theory to which they owe their fame and influence has done harm, by the utter sacrifice of educational to scientific purposes; for it supplies a more perfect machinery for the production of good books than of good men.

The Chronicle, 13 April 1867, p. 57.

THE CATHOLIC CHURCH AND LEARNING

When the Council of Trent required that the clergy should be educated in the seminary of each diocese and thereby unavoidably depressed the level of theological attainments, the object was not to advance learning or form really great divines but to maintain orthodoxy and authority. But conservation is not the only duty of the Catholic Church or the only consideration that guides her literary policy . . . Error in philosophy, in natural science, in history and criticism protects and perpetuates religious error. The Catholic Church would renounce her nature if she were content with a given aggregate of ideas, or an existing body of believers. She cannot desist from the effort to expand her bounds and to perfect her system. She requires to defend her doctrines and in defending to explain and to develop them . . . At all times and on every side she is bound to give account of her faith and to vindicate her decisions before those who deny her authority and reject her books. All the resources of human research are wanted in the incessant study and definition of her teaching, to withstand her adversaries and to convert the world. The most frequent impulse to advance in the settlement of truth and the most efficient proofs in its defence come to her from without. She has no institution of her own whose special function it is to fulfil that task of progress. The processes by which Scripture and tradition are investigated and made more clear are not hers exclusively, but are cultivated by those who are without her fold with a zeal which is equal to her own. She can forgo no means that can promote the knowledge of truth or contribute to the exposure of error. She can decline no combat. She can refuse no aid. Her schools and her congregations can no more dispense with the labours of Ewald and Tischendorf than with those of St Jerome and Baronius. Therefore the institutions devoted to the advancement of learning are her needful auxiliaries; and it is as essential to her cause that they should succeed in their objects as that her own people should learn to profit by them.

The Chronicle, 13 April 1867, p. 58.

THE PURPOSES OF PHILOSOPHY

There are few Englishmen who have the opportunity and fewer still who have the interest in philosophical research necessary for attaining a satisfactory knowledge of Hegelianism. England did indeed succeed in producing one philosopher worthy of the name—a philosopher who repudiated the claims of philosophy, but who based his repudiation on arguments so penetrating and original, that his writings form the turning point in modern metaphysics and led to a reconstruction similar to that which arose out of the scepticism of the Sophists. Kant himself attributes to Hume the impulse from which the critical philosophy sprang. But since that time philosophy in England has had little real connection with the progress of speculation in Germany. It is of course possible to question the serious nature of the loss which England has sustained by such a separation. It is easy to make merry over the unhesitating faith which has been accorded in Germany to one system after another; to point out how Fichte replaced Kant, and Schelling Fichte, and Hegel Schelling; how the Hegelians themselves split up into opposing camps, till at last even German patience was exhausted in the war of words and philosophy disappeared before the materialism it had despised. And if philosophy is regarded as a collation of positive truths, which possess, or ought to possess, the same sort of validity as those of physical science, time no doubt may be spent better than in threading one's way through a labyrinth which leads nowhere. Those on the other hand, who believe that the world is governed ultimately by ideas, and that some analysis of these ideas is necessary if we are to think at all, are neither surprised nor disturbed by the fact that no philosophy is able to establish itself as a final solution of the difficulties involved in the existing world. To them it is no condemnation of a philosophy that it makes way for another or is followed by a temporary lull in philosophical interest. The test by which they would judge a philosophical thinker is not whether his conclusions are accepted at the present hour, but whether he gave any real impulse to thought, whether his influence proved an abiding one, whether his ideas, changed it may be in form and modified by further knowledge, have passed into the ordinary thoughts and language of men. And it is because they regard this as the true criterion, because they refuse to believe that any great philosophy, however much its conclusions may be modified, can really pass away, that they regard the isolation which has characterized English philosophy during the eighteenth century as a subject of regret.

The Chronicle, 30 Nov. 1867, p. 858.

FOREIGN POLICY

Next to the management of dependencies the regulation of foreign policy is the most distressing and incongruous function of a popular Government. A nation can neither understand problems of law not its own, nor judge impartially and at once a series of distant and disputed facts. It would no doubt be desirable that some broad and easy principle should be discovered which should save the British public the trouble of thinking, or at least guide it with some consistency through the complications of foreign politics. We have indeed the constitutional theory, which promotes institutions like our own, and supports them against Imperialism in one quarter, and against Democracy in another, but which almost invariably fails in practice by confounding forms with substance. Then there is the commercial theory, founded on the example of the host who exhorts his customers not to cut each other's throats; and the bureaucratic theory that foreign affairs should be left by the nation to the care of experts. Lastly, there is the simple and economical view, that every people must settle its own affairs, and must be deemed right in its decisions because it is a waste of force to expend it in sustaining unpopular governments.

The Chronicle, vol. ii, 1868, p. 31.

MR GRANT DUFF

He is not a very passionate votary of political freedom. It would seem that he has at heart other objects more easy of attainment, it may be, under an enlightened and active despotism than in a self-governing community and that if he had to choose between the sceptre of an unprejudiced despot and a nation of Philistines free to err and prone to blunder, slow to learn and slower to forget, he would cast his lot with the former—with the Chinese model rather than with the British reality.

The Chronicle, vol. ii, 1868, p. 32.

FEDERALISM

The essential characteristic of the federal system of government is by dividing and distributing sovereignty to supply the most perfect check on the excess of power, and the most efficient of all known securities of freedom.

The Chronicle, vol. ii, 1868, p. 31.

CHURCH AND STATE

Real liberty depends not on the separation but on the distinct and appropriate, but continuous, action and reaction of Church and State. The defined and regulated influence of the Church in the State protects a special sphere and germ of political freedom, and supplies a separate and powerful sanction for law. On the other hand, the restricted and defined action of the State in ecclesiastical affairs gives security to the canon law, and prevents wanton innovation and the arbitrary confiscation of rights.

The Chronicle, vol. i, 1867, p. 746.

MR CARLYLE'S "FREDERICK THE GREAT"

It is a history made up of eccentricities. This is the way that Mr Dickens writes novels; for whom the spectacles of an elderly gentleman, a pair of mulberry-coloured hose, or a wandering American pig have greater attractions than any psychological problem.

The Rambler, Dec. 1868, p. 429.

ENGLISH INSTITUTIONS

Our institutions are part and parcel of the nation itself, not a garment that can be imitated by a skilful workman. What they

can teach foreign statesmen is to cling in every political change
to the traditions and character of their own people, and to distinguish between the institutions which are accidental and tran-
sient and those which are national and unchangeable.

The Rambler, Dec. 1868, p. 424.

MORIVILLIER, COUNCILLOR TO CHARLES IX

Jean de Morivillier, Bishop of Orleans, had a literary reputation among his contemporaries, and as he was known to be well
informed, he was urged to write a history of his time. "Je suis
trop serviteur de nos rois", he answered, "pour écrire leur histoire." The remark is at once a confession and a condemnation—
a condemnation of the kings and also of their councillor. A man
who does not venture to speak the truth of kings when they are
dead incurs a strong suspicion of not having spoken it to them
when they were alive.

North British Review, July 1870, p. 539.

LEIBNIZ'S THEOLOGY

There have been men whose religious insight was deeper than
that of Leibniz, and some, though very few, whose theological
knowledge was greater; but not one among the moderns has
equalled him in the amount of general scientific learning with
which he approached questions of divinity, or in comprehensiveness of genius, or in that keenness and elevation of judgement
which made him see so clearly the defects of the Churches while
recognizing all the value of ecclesiastical institutions. So much
impartiality in religious controversy has rarely been united with
so much earnestness, or so free from the reproach of indifference.
Not even Grotius or Fénelon is so instructive for the attitude of
his mind towards the claims of the Church . . . It was not his way
to compose systematically. He never at any time was thoroughly
master of all his thoughts. The fertility of his mind was such that
the harvest could never be completely gathered. New ideas came
crowding upon him when he sat down to write. The progress
was as incessant as the production. The sluggish pen refused to
register the working of that exhaustless brain. The wealth of
matter made his style confused. He was never satisfied with what
he had written, and came back to the same point, seeking the

exact expression to clothe and define his thought, and seeking it in vain. He was happier in writing letters than in writing books. His letters are not eloquent or brilliant but they are too short to suffer from the want of method and revision; and no other correspondence is so instructive. The greater part of the theology of Leibniz is found in them.

North British Review, July 1870, p. 551.

THE ABBÉ DE ST PIERRE

The Abbé was a man of restless imagination, and fertile inventions, of which many were in his own time regarded as utopias, and have only been realized after being re-invented a century later. Derided even during his life as a "projector", he bore the imputation with unfailing patience. "For twenty-five years", he wrote at the close of his life, "I have worked in the interest of the public but without credit, and consequently have been of little service to the present generation. Nevertheless my projects will survive; and many of them will be gradually accepted by the young minds who will rise to take part in the government; and thus they will become of great value to future generations. This anticipation of the future has always been an ample recompense to me for my mortifications in the present." The better to inculcate his ideas he adopted a method useful in conversation, but intolerable in writing: he incessantly repeated himself. Somebody once said to him: "There are excellent things in your writing, but they are repeated too often." He asked to be shown some instances which was easily done. "You see", he rejoined, "that you have remembered them; if I had only said them once, you would have forgotten them." It is for his work *Le Projet de Paix Perpétuelle*, the first volumes of which were published in 1713, that his name will be chiefly remembered. The scheme was summed up in five articles. Actual possession and the execution of the latest treaties were taken as the starting point; and all Christian sovereigns were invited to join the alliance. Each ally was to contribute in proportion to his revenues to a common fund, to be administered by plenipotentiaries at the place of their perpetual assembly. The allies were to pledge themselves severally not to use force for the settlement of their mutual differences, but to submit in all such cases to the mediation of the remainder of their body. If any member transgressed the laws of the alliance, the remainder were to arm against him and act on the offensive till he yielded and made proper reparation. The plenipotentiaries were to regulate the ordinary affairs of the alliance by the decision of simple majorities, but the fundamental articles were not to be changed except by the unanimous consent of the allies. These articles substantially anticipate the idea of a European confederation with an arbitrating tribunal which is now so widely spread.

North British Review, July 1870, p. 557.

MASSIMO D'AZEGLIO

It is easy to see why Azeglio, with a character which raised him far above Cavour as a man, had to yield to him as a politician. He was a pioneer, who organized the impulse to Italian unity, purified it from many of its extreme elements, and prepared it as the action of a strong statesman. This he probably could not have effected without the high scale of morality which he demanded in politics, and which made him so desponding when he examined the materials he had to work upon. "To have a good dinner", he says in allusion to this subject, "it is not enough to have the best cook in the world if you only provide him with dead cats as *materia prima*; and above all, if you refuse him a single grain of salt." His conception of the radical nature of the reforms required helped him to escape superficiality in the measures he proposed. At the same time his opinion of the treachery and imbecility of public men prevented his taking the requisite trouble to make them act as he wished. It is not that he was too pure-souled for a politician, or too conscientious about his means; that would be impossible. But he was too fastidious about the character of those he had to act with, and made too great requisitions on their manner and tone.

North British Review, Oct. 1870, p. 285.

LORD PALMERSTON

Lord Palmerston's career as Foreign Secretary first under Lord Grey and then under Lord Melbourne is described by Sir Henry Bulwer as "constituting the foundation of that reputation which he still enjoys among foreign nations". Perhaps it would be more accurate to call it foundation and superstructure too; for though he held the same office from 1846 to 1851, it was under circumstances far less favourable to his fame. The questions which presented themselves during this latter period involved political principles; those with which he had to deal from 1830 to 1841 involved only national interests. It was only as the "Minister of England" that Lord Palmerston had any title to the character of a statesman. His later foreign policy was too often a mere careless adoption of liberal commonplaces which, as he used them, had not even the merit of being truisms. But when he was resisting the designs of France upon Belgium or upon Egypt, his energy and boldness were seen to the best advantage.

North British Review, Jan. 1871, p. 588.

SIR WALTER SCOTT

Scott was greatly aided by the peculiar character of English history in which the present is closely linked with the distant past. In other countries the want of such a continuous development makes it hard for a poet to transplant himself into earlier times, and often gives the efforts a laboured and unnatural appearance, as in the case of the German romance-writers. Scott treated history as a poet, but at the same time with such simplicity and truthfulness that his influence was felt on the writings of history. He taught the nineteenth century the vividness of historical conception.

North British Review, Jan. 1871, p. 606.

CHARLES BAUDELAIRE

His opinions—convictions he had none—were merely the contradiction of what others were thinking; and the paradoxes of his conversation offended listeners whom the tone of his writings did not conciliate. His life, like his opinions, was an evolution by antagonism. Respectability drove him into Bohemia; among Bohemians he was an exquisite. But behind the vagaries of an exaggerated self-consciousness his friends recognized an artist who in his devotion to art was never influenced by love or gain, a kindly humourist who would present the children of the poorer streets with toys in order to enjoy their innocent amazement . . . The artistic side of Baudelaire's nature was indeed the most influential and the most apparent to the world . . . His affectation for Satanic wickedness appears to have been little more than a reminiscence of Byron. He slandered himself and was never so grieved and surprised as when he was taken for that which he was at such pains to appear to be.

North British Review, Jan. 1870, p. 578.

ABSOLUTISM AND THE CHURCH

There was once a time when it was the common belief, both of churchmen and statesmen, that the Church had great need of the State, and that her prosperity was proportioned to the favours she received from it. She was regarded as a useful ornament about the throne of absolute sovereigns; and the pious protection extended to her by Catholic monarchs, such as Philip IV or Louis XV, was deemed a prodigious security for religion. A prince who expelled the Protestants from his dominions was permitted to beard the Pope. A prince who chiefly proved his orthodoxy by an occasional auto-da-fé was *par excellence* the Catholic king. In the eyes of most men the fatness of benefices was the measure of the prosperity of the Church. Consequently religion was strong only in the strength of the State; the decline of the monarchy deprived the Church of her chief support and, when the Revolution came, she was its first and easiest victim. The result of that old *régime* was that the king of France was beheaded and the Pope died in a French prison. In those days people wondered, for it was the first time such things had been. But in the midst of that memorable ruin a lesson was learnt which has borne imperishable fruit. In the times which have succeeded the Church has taken her stand on her own everlasting foundation— on the words of Christ, not on the gifts of Constantine. More than once since then, in different places, she has been stripped of that terrestrial splendour which had proved such a fatal possession; but she has stood her ground in the wreck of those political institutions on which she no longer relied, and alone has saved society. The old position of things has been reversed; and it has been found that it is the State which stands in need of the Church, and that the strength of the Church is her independence . . . A free Church implies a free nation. The absolutism of the State recovers all its oppressiveness where the vast domains of religions

are not protected from its control by a Church in which there is
no room and no excuse for arbitrary power. He, therefore, that
deems he can advocate the cause of religion without advocating
at the same time the cause of freedom, is no better than a hypo-
crite and a traitor.

The Rambler, Dec. 1868, p. 421.

NOTE ON "CONFESSIONS OF FREDERICK THE GREAT"

(see pages 353-373)

ACTON's publication of the *Matinées Royales* caused a good deal of
excitement, especially in Germany. From Berlin the Princess
Royal wrote to Queen Victoria, on January 13th, 1863:

> Sir John Acton has published a Book called *Matinées Royales*,
> an infamous libel against Frederick the Great, well known here
> as such, ever since Frederick the Great's own time; and now
> Sir John Acton publishes it as a composition of Frederick the
> Great's. I can not tell you what indignation it has caused here
> in all circles—and to have the First of our Kings so blackened,
> at a time when the whole of Europe is laughing at our sad,
> crippled conditions, is bitterly felt. The newspapers have taken
> it up very warmly and the King and Queen feel very much hurt
> at Sir J. Acton's having brought out the Book as he was treated
> with so much kindness here by everybody last year at the
> Coronation. If the book had not been well known as a fabrica-
> tion (not authentic) less might have been said about it, but
> even Carlyle in his work pronounces it spurious, and it is no-
> thing else than a really shocking Libel. I live in dread of this
> being the cause of another quarrel like the Macdonald Affair.

The Queen, very perturbed, passed the letter on to Lord Granville who wrote to Acton reporting their conversation.

> I have told the Queen that you will be sorry to know that the
> Princess Royal is annoyed and that your wish will be to meet
> the Queen's desires but that if you continue to believe in the

authenticity of the writings, it is difficult to know what you can do. That the great point in your controversy with the Cardinal is that truth in history must be sought, and when ascertained be published without reference to its appearing to favour or not the cause one has at heart. That I doubt whether you will accept Carlyle's authority as conclusive, but if you could be convinced that you had been deceived by a spurious document, I was sure you would be anxious to make a public acknowledgement of the mistake.—Have you any doubts?

Acton's reply is missing, but the Princess Royal on January 26th wrote to the Queen:

Many thanks for the copy of Sir J. Acton's letter to Ld. Granville, also for the original 2nd letter to Ld. G. Both confirm what I was perfectly sure of and what I said to every one here, which is that his interest in the thing is purely literary and that he is not actuated by any other motives. I defended him both to the King and Queen and to all the infuriated historians here, and I hope you will tell Ld. Granville this. To my mind it is as clear as sunlight that these *Matinées* are not by Frederick the Great, as since I have been here I have had so much opportunity of becoming fully acquainted with his sentiments, character, habits and peculiarities. Many of the sentiments are no doubt his, though just as many are not—but the way of expressing them—and the style and the arguments are most certainly not his. In England he is not sufficiently known for people to be able to distinguish between his real and his popular character but here—every child knows all about him, and those that knew him are still alive; I know two people who knew him.

The verdict of Frederick the Great's latest biographer, Dr G. P. Gooch, was expressed in a private letter in which he wrote:

Frederick only wrote the two *Testaments* described in my book. The *Matinées* are ignored by biographers because they are a fake—one of many such concoctions in the 18th and early 19th centuries. When Acton says that there were many omissions in the Preuss edition of the Correspondence, we must remember that he was writing before the vast (and still unfinished) *Politische Korrespondenz* began to appear.

INDEX

Dates following entries are *regnal* dates in the case of kings, emperors and Popes; otherwise, dates of birth and death.